CW00536250

THE
TORPEDOMEN

THE
TORPEDOMEN

HMS Vernon's
story 1872-1986

Rear Admiral
E N Poland CB CBE

ACKNOWLEDGEMENTS

The photographs used in this book have been reproduced by kind permission of Mr P Bathurst, Commander JR Blake, Captain RS Browning, HMS Dryad Archives, Fleet Air Arm Museum Yeovilton, Commander G Gutteridge, Imperial War Museum, Captain HL Lloyd, National Maritime Museum, Rolex Watch Co Ltd, Royal Naval Museum Portsmouth and Vosper Thornycroft (UK) Ltd.

© Rear Admiral E N Poland CB CBE

Printed in Great Britain

British Library Cataloguing-inPublication Data
A catalogue record for this book is available from the British Library
ISBN 0-85937-396-7

My time as Commanding Officer of the Minehunter H.M.S. BRONINGTON gave me something of an insight into the work of HMS VERNON and her ship's company. For over one hundred years, officers and men of the Torpedo Branch have not only looked after torpedoes but, at one time or another, held responsibility for such varied matters as electric power in ships, fire control, wireless, mine countermeasures, demolitions, diving, chemical warfare and anti-submarine warfare. A strong esprit de corps, early responsibility, and love of innovation and invention have been characteristics of torpedomen since their inception and these attributes have been nurtured in H.M.S. VERNON, at Portsmouth. Indeed, I have the impression that VERNON became more of an alma mater than a school to generations who trained and served there.

This book tells their story and the author, a torpedo and anti-submarine specialist, who has held a number of important positions including that of Director of Undersea Warfare, is well qualified to tell it.

However, times change. There have been immense advances in weapons techniques and many changes in the organisation culminating in the closure of HMS VERNON. Notwithstanding the many developments that have taken place over the years, the spirit of those torpedomen lives on, and this book should ensure that their great contribution to the Navy and to the country will not be lost to future generations.

Charles

CONTENTS

Introduction

It was droll if apt that it should have been a Gunnery Officer who drew attention in 1982 to the tide of events sweeping away the last vestiges of the old navy to make way for the press button era of sensors, gas turbines and 'intelligent' weapons. Captain Stephen Roskill had written an impassioned letter to *The Times* criticising the government's decision to close the two most famous establishments, *HMS Excellent* and *Vernon* at Portsmouth.

Both schools had ceased to function as gunnery and torpedo anti-submarine alma maters but Roskill's concern shortly before he died was that with their closure all links with the past would be lost, and the achievements of the Torpedo, Mine Clearance and Diving Branches would disappear. On August 4, 1983 *Vernon's* Captain J D W Husband called a meeting to discuss the production of a *Revised history of HMS Vernon*, starting with the limited ambition of updating Sayer's *History of HMS Vernon 1872-1930* and Webb's *HMS Vernon 1930-1955*. With me at the meeting were Captain J D W Husband, Commander W Burroughs, Commander J C Mearns, Lieutenant Commander G J McGeown and Lieutenant Commander R S C Robinson.

I found myself both potential author of a history book and organiser of what at first seemed to be a fairly simple project. I was grateful for the financial and editorial support of everyone at *Vernon*, both serving and retired. It soon became apparent that what Roskill had in mind was more than just a history of the *Vernon* establishment. What was needed was a record of the achievements of their people and the impact upon maritime warfare of the weapons and equipment for which they were responsible. This would require a dedicated team to research and commit to paper. Done properly it would be an expensive business and we had only £800.

The immediate need was to call upon as many serving and retired offices and men and scientists as possible to send us their memoirs, anecdotes, comments and opinions. With the help of Lieutenant Commander G J McGeown, the naval staff author (ASW) at *Vernon* and *Dryad*, and Gus Britton, the archivist at the RN Submarine Museum, a request for help was widely circulated. I am grateful to the editors of the *Naval Review*, *Navy News* and *Portsmouth News* for the publicity they gave to the project.

By 1984 I was beginning to realise that my knowledge of *Vernon's* history was far less than I had thought. Fortunately a strong team was becoming involved in the research which was to continue for another six years. The diversity of information meant that a great deal of travelling was required and we needed recorders, a word processor, or preferably a computer, and a printer for the storage of data, far beyond our meagre means. Response to our request for help was generous, and we are most grateful, to BP Exploration Co Ltd, British Aerospace Plc, Britoil Plc, Holman and Sons Ltd, Imperial Chemical Industries Plc, J & S Marine Ltd, Marconi Underwater Systems Ltd, Mobil North Sea Ltd, Occidental Oil Inc, Plessey Naval Systems Ltd, Racal Electronics Plc, The Rolex Watch Co Ltd, Shell UK Exploration and Production, UEC Projects (Pty) Ltd S. Africa & Vosper Thorneycroft UK Ltd.

We were fully financed until April 1986 when the project was given a grant by the Leverhulme Trust and placed under the Imperial War Museum's supervision. We are indebted to Sir Rex Richards, director of the Leverhulme

Trust and to Mr D A Thompson, the financial secretary for their forbearance and advice. I am confident that the fruits of our labours will provide a valuable source of information for future generations. We also owe a debt of gratitude to Dr Christopher Dowling at the Imperial War Museum for his advice in organising our finances.

The members of the project committee came together gradually. Captains W D S White and H L Lloyd and Lieutenant Commander D D MacFarlan were the first. Being all of one generation we needed a broader base and recruited Rear Admiral Sir Morgan Morgan-Giles, Captain R C Lewis, Rear Admiral G F Liardet and Commander A J W Wilson. Mr J A Lee, of King's College, Taunton was our literary adviser who kept the grammar within bounds and gave us a layman's view of the script. Each member played an important part in the project for which no words are sufficient to express my thanks. Towards the end we were joined by Eric Grove to help edit the original manuscript. I am indebted to Captain A B Sainsbury RNR who joined the committee and brought us down to earth with a bang, eliminating the clutch of cliches of which I had been guilty from the first draft.

In the bibliography I pay tribute to specialists in various areas of undersea warfare but I must express my thanks here to Commander G Gutteridge and Lieutenant Commander W B Filer for providing such a complete coverage of mine clearance and diving. Gordon Gutteridge carried out the painstaking investigation into the Crabb affair: further speculation about this sad event should no longer be necessary. We must thank Marion Stewart, the archivist at Churchill College, Cambridge, and Commander David Brown, Mike McAloon, Alan Francis, Dave Ashby, Philip Wilton and Fred Lake of the Naval Historical Branch, Ministry of Defence, for helping us to unearth a great deal of valuable information. That we reached the point when publication became possible was entirely due to the hard work of Alastair Wilson and the practical support of Morgan Morgan-Giles and Captain Ashe Lincoln.

It remains only for me to say that this long haul has renewed old friendships and made new ones, with the good humour and comradeship which have always been present when servicemen are gathered together, but I like to think that in the underwater weapons and equipment branches there is something extra and rather special which we share with submariners.

E N Poland
Wilton, January 1993

ALTHOUGH *VERNON* NO LONGER EXISTS as a Naval establishment, and the name is not at present carried by one of the Queen's ships, it is still and always will be synonymous with underwater weapons and much that is associated with them. At first afloat in the hulks of venerable ships, then ashore on the old Gunwharf at Portsmouth, there were men who created a spirit of service and dedication which is now part of our naval history and which is still an inspiration to their successors. This book records the development of the establishment and its ethos, chronicles the major themes and some of the major incidents in that saga and suggests a few lessons.

HMS *Vernon* seemed the best ship available in 1872 to be converted into a 'torpedo ship' for training and experimental work. Aptly, for a vessel that was to become synonymous with with a new form of naval warfare, *Vernon* had been herself a revolutionary and controversial ship. She had been designed by Captain William Symonds, an amateur naval architect, who persuaded the Admiralty that his new frigate had better manoeuverability, seakeeping qualities and ammunition supply arrangements than any existing design. Symonds was a good intuitive but unscientific designer who erroneously tried to expand a successful yacht design into one for a general purpose warship. His concept, which gave speed and good handling suitable for small craft, also gave pronounced and unpredictable motion. Indeed, ships built on

The frigate Vernon showing her great beam

his lines were very bad gun platforms in anything of a sea and, therefore, poor fighting ships. Symonds' enthusiasm extended to the construction of the ship and he hastened her building at Woolwich to such an extent that she was decked too early; she thus suffered from dry rot throughout her career, but this did not detract from an important improvement in ship design, her enlarged beam, which allowed increased headroom between decks, which had hitherto seldom exceeded six feet; seven foot deckhead height was an unheard of luxury, making this new frigate ostensibly the most comfortable ship afloat in the Royal Navy - and an excellent hulk in later life.

She was launched on 1 May 1832, and named not for the famous eighteenth century Admiral, Edward Vernon (Old Grog) but after his descendant - and friend of Sir William Symonds - the Hon G Vernon, who had put up a substantial bond to guarantee the performance of one of Symonds' earlier designs. Although the great Admiral's name has become associated with the ship and with the specialist branches of the service for whom she was home, the figurehead, which stood for many years in the grounds of the *Vernon* shore establishment, is clearly not a likeness of 'Old Grog'. The rather crude carving resembled a younger man dressed in the fashion of the early nineteenth century and seems to have been intended to be the Hon. G. Vernon. The only connection with the Admiral was the family motto that adorning the frigate's stern, 'Vernon semper viret'.

Vernon served in the blockade of Dutch ports during the Belgian crisis in 1832 and then on the North America and West Indies Station and in the Mediterranean before being paid off in 1837. She was recommissioned in 1840, seeing service first in the Mediterranean, then on the south east coast of South America and finally in the East Indies. She paid off in 1848 having made as many friends by her good sailing qualities as she had made enemies by her wet and uneasy habits in heavy seas. She remained at Chatham for nineteen years, laid up in a remote corner of the dockyard. In 1867 she became a floating coaling jetty at Portland. Her broad beam and generous headroom between decks had a higher purpose, however, and were noted when the Admiralty was looking for a home for torpedo instruction and development. In 1872 she was towed to Portsmouth Dockyard for conversion to the *Vernon* (Torpedo Ship) and, on completion, she was moved to Fountain Lake to be moored astern of HMS *Excellent* and HMS *Calcutta*, which housed the Gunnery School.

This had been founded in 1830, using the hulk of the old three decker, Collingwood's *Excellent*, who gave her name to the whole establishment. *Excellent* had two main functions, training and what would now be called 'research and development'. *Excellent's* work on new weapons became associated not only with guns but also with underwater weapons of all types. For most of the nineteenth century, all the latter went under the generic term 'Torpedo', derived from an electric ray fish named from the Latin 'torpere', to 'render numb'. 'Torpedo' was applied from the start to any form of underwater explosive weapon- in the early days, what we would now call 'mines'.

Explosive charges to attack ships were developed at the end of the eighteenth century by two Americans, David Bushnell and Robert Fulton. They developed floating mines and bombs for delivery by primitive submarines; both sometimes called their weapons 'torpedoes'. In August 1801

Fulton used his alternative delivery platform, a pinnace propelled by cranks, to swing a 20 pound 'submarine bomb' into a 40 foot sloop which was destroyed, the first ship ever to be sunk by an underwater explosive device. The British got wind of Fulton's experiments and posted extra lookouts on their ships off Brest: they also rowed guard around their ships. This prevented Fulton, who had decided to concentrate on the submarine, from mounting a successful operational attack (despite several attempts) and official support was withdrawn. By this time Fulton was thinking of a campaign using moored 'torpedoes' to close English ports, the first time this kind of mining campaign had ever been proposed.

Fulton was then persuaded to come to London where, with the patronage of Pitt the Prime Minister, he persuaded the Government to adopt his clockwork time-fused, partially submerged torpedoes called 'coffers', 'casks' or 'catamarans'. Connected by a coupling line, they were carried in among the enemy in cutters and dropped overboard to drift down on to the enemy, wrapping themselves around anchor cables and automatically laying themselves alongside the ships. An attack was made on French ships at Boulogne on 2 October 1804 and although only a small one was sunk French morale was somewhat shaken. Another attack, with two 'catamarans' in September 1805, had less effect. Only one gunboat was caught and the torpedoes exploded harmlessly. The only casualties were four men killed trying to beach the other device the following morning: perhaps the first mine disposal casualties in naval history. Fulton now altered the design of his torpedoes, suspending them from cork filled boxes to allow them to explode close under the target's hull and this did the trick. Less than a week before Trafalgar, two small boats laid torpedoes next to the Danish brig *Dorothea* procured by Fulton for the test. The ship was broken in two but the difficulties of repeating this operationally, together with the strategic common sense that the British had little to gain from forcing the pace of technological change, combined to produce a British reluctance to go any further. As St. Vincent observed, 'Pitt was the greatest fool that ever existed, to encourage a mode of war which they who had command of the seas did not want and which, if successful, would deprive them of it'.

A twice frustrated Fulton returned to the U.S.A. in 1806 but failed to interest Presidents Jefferson and Madison and the U.S. Navy in drifting torpedoes, harpoon torpedoes (suspended from a harpoon fired into the side of an enemy ship), spar torpedoes (carried on a long swivelling spar on the bows of a small boat) and stationary buoyant submarine mines exploded by contact levers. He left his mark with his suggestion of moored 'mines' and his popularisation of the word 'torpedo' in his book 'Torpedo War and Submarine Explosions' (1810). A cultural prejudice against 'infernal machines' played its part in Fulton's failure but technology was still hardly up to the task of producing reliable and effective underwater weapons.

A major step forward in producing practical devices was Samuel Colt's development in the USA of an electrically fired torpedo, which by 1844 succeeded in destroying a moving ship. This connection of electricity with underwater explosions was to have a decisive impact both on HMS *Vernon* and the structure and role of the Torpedo Branch in the Royal Navy.

The latter faced Russian 'infernals' in the Crimean War (1854-56) but they did not prove very effective. One only caused serious concussion to Admiral Seymour when it exploded while he prodded at it on the quarterdeck of his flagship! It was the American Civil War which marked a decisive step forward in the awareness of the potential of 'torpedoes' of all kinds. The Confederates used a wide variety of moored and drifting devices both in rivers and to defend their major ports. On 12 December 1862, the ironclad USS *Cairo* was destroyed in the River Yazoo by a mine detonated from the bank. This was the first combat success of a controlled mine and a fully submerged explosive device. Buoyant moored static torpedoes with sensitive cap exploders were also dangerous opponents. In August 1864 Union Admiral Farragut uttered the memorable words 'Full speed ahead and damn the torpedoes' as he sailed into Mobile Bay. His large monitor *Tecumseh* had just been lost with heavy loss of life. The mines could be heard making contact with the hulls of his ships but happily for the daring admiral making 'torpedoes' explode reliably was still a problem. Both Union and Confederate navies scored successes that year with spar torpedoes carried by, respectively, a small launch and a semi-submersible, but both sinkings caused the loss of the attacker as well as the attacked. In all, however, the Confederates managed to sink thirty Union vessels and damage another eleven with 'torpedoes' of various kinds.

Underwater weapons could no longer be ignored, especially by the better trained officers now passing out from *Excellent*. Interest in underwater weapons grew rapidly in the mid-1860s but the situation was complicated by torpedoes, like all ordnance matters, being the responsibility of the War Office. Prompted by both Professor Frederick Abel FRS of the War Office's laboratory at Woolwich and the Director of Naval Ordnance, Rear Admiral Astley Cooper Key, the War Office suggested that naval personnel, including a gunnery lieutenant, be sent to Woolwich and a recently qualified officer, HC Kane, was appointed. Key, however, already seems to have decided, with Captain AWA Hood who had succeeded him in command at *Excellent*, that torpedo instruction should be established as soon as possible at *Excellent* and the Devonport Gunnery School, founded in 1838 and transferred to *Cambridge* in 1856. This would ensure full naval control of this vital new weapons technology. When Kane went to Woolwich he was also appointed to *Excellent*, and, on completing the course, was given the task of setting up a torpedo section and initiating a course on mining, counter mining and torpedoes. Although torpedo courses were being started at both *Excellent* and *Cambridge*, officers continued to be sent to Woolwich until October 1867 and Key successfully fought off the War Office suggestions that all torpedo instruction be given in future by the Royal Engineers at Chatham. A member of the last course of RN officers at Woolwich was a young gunnery lieutenant from *Excellent* called John Arbuthnot Fisher, the the most remarkable naval officer of his generation, and one of the most important and extraordinary - and certainly one of the most controversial - in the history of the Service.

Fisher went to *Excellent* in 1862, to qualify as a gunnery lieutenant: in those days there was no 'long course' and he joined the staff; in 1863 he was appointed to the pioneer ironclad *Warrior* in which he qualified as a 'gunnery lieutenant' in November 1863. After a year in *Warrior* he returned to *Excellent*, appointed in command of the gunboat *Stork*, one of the tenders in which gunnery classes underwent sea training, and to work for a first class gunnery certificate which he was awarded in 1866. Fisher then joined the main establishment where he made the acquaintance of one of the lieutenants qualifying in gunnery, Arthur Knyvet Wilson; they were to have a profound effect on the emergence of torpedo warfare as a potent force in naval operations.

Fisher may already have interested himself in torpedoes at *Excellent* before going to Woolwich but there he was able rapidly to provide himself with real expertise in the subject. It is likely that Kane was given among his other tasks the preparation of an electricity and torpedo manual. In fact Fisher completed the project before either his colleague or Professor Abel who, together with his assistant ED Brown, had been preparing a comprehensive 'Manual of Electric Torpedo Service'. By January 1868, Fisher had produced, 'A Short Treatise on Electricity and the Management of Electric Torpedoes'. It was privately printed by Annett of Bridport, but Key, who had been kept fully informed, recommended that it should be published, and issued not only to *Excellent* but to the Fleet.

Abel took his upstaging by Fisher well as he had a high regard for the dynamic, if imperious, young officer. He described the 'Treatise' in generous terms:

The first part of the book (Chapters 1-10) is a concise, clear and for the most part very correct account of some of the most important fundamental principles of electric science, compiled as Mr. Fisher states from Works on Electricity; and is well adapted to aid those going through a course of instruction in the employment of electrical Torpedoes. The remainder of the book, exclusive of the Appendix and of a short account of the experiments with outrigger torpedoes conducted at Portsmouth, consists in substance of the notes of my course of instruction in electric torpedo service and gives a clear outline of the more important points connected with the system of constructing, firing and testing Torpedoes which has been worked out in this Department, and which are described in full detail in the Report of the Committee on Floating Obstructions, very shortly to be submitted to the Secretary of State for War.

Fisher's Treatise provided not only an instructional manual for the new Torpedo Section at *Excellent* but also the mould for the shape of the Torpedo Branch, linking the study of underwater weapons with the new study of electricity. This seemingly incongruous relationship was to endure for nearly eighty years at the Torpedo Schools, in the personnel structure of the Royal Navy and in the organisation of its ships.

It is doubtful whether the crude underwater weapons of 1867 would have justified the establishment of an independent school, even when associated with the rapid increase in the use of electricity. The most practical available device was 'Harvey's Sea Torpedo', designed by Commander Frederick Harvey, attached to *Excellent* to instruct in torpedoes in April 1870, and his brother Captain John Harvey. This weapon worked like a paravane on the deflected tow principle; the torpedoes had an exterior case of seasoned elm, iron bound with watertight packing, containing an interior case made of copper holding 33 lbs. of gunpowder or, in later versions, 58 lbs. of com-

A nineteenth century sales pitch by the Harvey brothers

pressed gun cotton or 66 lbs. of gunpowder. The charge was fired by explosive bolt operating through a lanyard and a series of levers until electrical firing was devised. The whole device was complicated and difficult to operate but it was adopted into service in 1870. Great hopes were pinned on it. A contemporary lithograph showed graphically the fate of 'an iron-clad fleet surprised at sea by a squadron of torpedo craft armed with Harvey's Sea Torpedo'. It continued in service for twenty years, and at the time was far less impractical than some of the other notions on offer. The Admiralty was beseiged by inventors anxious to sell their dubious wares but few caught the imagination of a justly sceptical Board which preferred to place its faith in the devils it knew rather than in the uncertain future of such devices as rocket powered self propelled torpedoes. A more practical 'locomotive torpedo' was, however, well on the way to development. Its inventor was Robert Whitehead.

Whitehead was born in Bolton, Lancashire in January 1823 and inherited from his parents an inventive genius acquired by an engineering heritage on both sides of the family. At the age of sixteen he was apprenticed as a draughtsman and then went abroad to work at the La Seyne shipbuilding and engineering yard at Marseilles. With his newly acquired marine engineering knowledge, Whitehead decided two years later to go into business on his own account. He moved to Milan where he set himself up as a consulting engineer, and then to Trieste where he attained a remarkable reputation as an outstanding designer of marine engines. In 1856 he accepted an attractive offer of employment from the company Stabilimento Technico Fiumano which in the early 1860s was awarded the contract for the design and construction of the engines for the new Austrian ironclads. This contract led Whitehead to make useful contacts with officers of the Austrian Navy.

The Austrians were well aware of their fleet's inferiority to that of the newly unified Italians, and sought a means of redressing the balance. Amongst many devices considered was a development of the fireship, a small vessel powered by a clockwork engine and remotely controlled from the shore by tiller ropes. The original design was improved by a retired officer, Fregattenkapitan Giovanni de Luppis, who modified it to carry an explosive charge detonated by a contact percussion pistol fitted to the bows. De Luppis's design, which he christened Der Kustenbrander (the Coastal Fireship), was submitted to the naval authorities in Vienna. They were interested but doubtful about the practicability of the project. De Luppis was, however, encouraged to develop the idea, particularly as regards the means of propulsion and guidance, and in 1864 resolved to seek the Englishman's advice. The two inventors joined forces to build a prototype. It was not a success; its range was too short, its engine unreliable and its tangle of tiller ropes made the whole concept impractical. Whitehead had, however, become fascinated by the idea of producing a locomotive torpedo and set about redesigning the engine and the guidance system. But he soon came to realise that the concept of a surface craft in this role was too vulnerable to countermeasures and his thoughts turned to design of a submerged locomotive design: soon he could think of little else.

Whitehead was quick to recognise the enormous potential of such a weapon upon naval warfare and the financial rewards which would benefit his company. His enthusiasm knew no bounds; he translated his ideas into designs, and his designs into hardware, helped by the outbreak of war in 1866 between Italy and Austria. The Battle of Lissa demonstrated both the effectiveness of underwater damage - inflicted in this case by the ram - and the success of his engines in the new Austrian ironclads established Whitehead as an engineer and inventor to be taken seriously. Tegethoff, the Austrian commander, ascribed his victory to Whitehead's first class engines.

The Austrian Navy began trials with Whitehead locomotive torpedoes before the end of 1866. They were not entirely successful but Whitehead persevered and news of his work reached the British Mediterranean Fleet. In September 1868, the Commander in Chief, Vice Admiral Lord Clarence Paget was sufficiently impressed by the implications of these stories to request a visit to Fiume to inspect the invention. Lord Paget was but one of a number of visitors for whom Whitehead prepared a series of demonstrations. Paget's report was farsighted and of great significance; he wrote:

Another very formidable engine is in process of development which bids fair to surpass even the ram - the torpedo. The importance of the invention may be assumed from the fact that the Austrian Government is said to have awarded £20,000 to Mr. Whitehead, the inventor. The French also sent an official to negotiate and I have advised the British Government to do likewise.

Their Lordships were not in a hurry. They were aware that the US Navy disagreed with the Austrian government and did not considered Whitehead's invention worth the £20,000 price tag. The French and the

Prussians had taken note of Whitehead's torpedo but showed no sense of urgency in acquiring it. Nearly a year after Paget's submission reached the Admiralty, the Commander in Chief Mediterranean was authorised to send a committee of gunnery officers to Fiume to carry out a more thorough investigation. They returned from Fiume deeply impressed by what they had seen; their report was enough to persuade the Admiralty that Whitehead should be invited to carry out trials of his torpedoes in England with a view to purchase of his 'Secret'.

The 'Secret' was the means by which the locomotive torpedoes kept their depth. Whitehead's prototypes had performed erratically: they had some problems holding their course but a more serious difficulty was a tendency to veer from the set depth. By the time that the Mediterranean Fleet Committee arrived at Fiume Whitehead had solved this problem by designing a hydrostat-pendulum combination. The hydrostat was set to the pressure of a given depth and was connected to the torpedo elevators via a pendulum that damped the movement of the elevators according to torpedo pitch angle. This reduced depth errors from plus/minus 40 feet to plus/minus 6 inches and became a commonplace of torpedo design as the balance chamber. In 1869, however, it was the 'Secret', surrounded by mystery and locked doors. A 'need to know' was strictly applied by Whitehead. It was his most saleable commodity and he was determined to extract from it the greatest possible financial return. Almost thirty years later, in 1896, in in his treatise on 'Torpedoes and Torpedo Vessels', Lieutenant GE Armstrong wrote:

This part of the torpedo's anatomy was always kept a profound secret until four or five years ago, except to those officers who went through the special course of Whitehead instruction. The pains taken to preserve this secret were as elaborate as they were futile. The room where the great mystery was unravelled was closed with locked doors, with sentries on guard outside, and every porthole and window carefully screened or closed. The secret, however, was too commercially and strategically valuable to be kept for long, and a few years ago the authorities having discovered that it was known to every civilized power in Europe, impressed upon Mr Whitehead the futility of any further mystery.

In deciding to proceed with the trials of the Whitehead torpedoes the Admiralty took into account a document which seemed to confirm the recommendations of the Mediterranean Fleet Committee. Fisher had consolidated his position as the Navy's leading 'torpedo' expert, but his current major preoccupation was the development of controlled minefields. His objections regarding the use of mechanically detonated mines were to prove a hindrance to the development of British mines for many years to come. Fisher was convinced that moored mechanical mines do not possess the power of selection and consequently are as dangerous to friend as to foe. Fisher's flawed genius confused the argument between the relative merits of electrical and mechanical detonation with that between independent and controlled minefields. Whatever his intention, it was not until after the Russo-Japanese War of 1905 that his judgement was seriously challenged and even then he was to declare that the submarine possessed the power of selection thus rendering the mine obsolete. Fisher was not alone in his hostility to independent mines, which were later to prove amongst the most effective weapons in the naval armoury. Many of his contemporaries agreed with his condemnation of contact mines and with his reluctance to accept Whitehead's torpedoes as a practical proposition.

It was ironic, therefore, that when he was sent to Germany in the summer of 1869, Commander Fisher, as he had just become, included, without comment and as an appendix to his report on static mining and searchlights, a copy of a statement by the Austrian Torpedo Commission which commented favourably on Whitehead's invention. This was noted at the Admiralty, where by now there were two strong recommendations in favour of Whitehead's 'Secret'. Admiral Sir Sydney Dacre, the First Sea Lord, was impressed by the reports but Captain Hood, now the Director of Naval Ordnance, urged caution. He, like Fisher, favoured static defences using electrically detonated mines. The concept of the locomotive torpedo was still a matter of secondary consideration, particularly as it was considered to be rather unreliable. Hood was, however, sufficiently open minded to agree to extensive trials of Whitehead's torpedo and he commented that if these trials were successful the use of fast, manoeuverable types of vessel to deliver this torpedo 'would be most formidable in action with ironclads'. Whitehead was invited to bring to England two torpedoes and a submerged tube for the purpose of carrying out exhaustive trials and experiments.

There followed a delay of several months whilst the Admiralty tried unsuccessfully to persuade the War Office that the Army should be charged with the expenses of the Whitehead torpedo trials. On 17 January 1870, the Treasury, now convinced of the importance of the trials, earmarked a sum of £2,000. Six months later, Whitehead arrived in England; accompanied by the Admiralty representative, a Mr. Crossland, he travelled to Sheerness where a number of Admiralty vessels were available from which he could select one suitable for his experiments and the trials which were to follow. *Oberon*, an iron paddle-wheel sloop, met his requirements. Before returning to Fiume he prepared drawings needed by the dockyard at Chatham for the fitting of the bow tube. The first of many thousands of British torpedo trials was scheduled for 31 August 1870.

Whitehead, accompanied by his son-in-law Count Georg Hoyos, a veteran of the Battle of Lissa, escorted the two crated torpedoes across France where, for a while, the authorities detained them demanding to know what the boxes contained. Only the timely intervention of the British ambassador prevented the French from discovering what was afoot. The two torpedoes were of different dimensions:

Specification	Length	Max Diam	Charge	
Large Torpedo	14ft 0in	16in	67lbs	*Guncotton*
Small Torpedo	13ft 10in	14in	18lbs	*Glyoxilin*

On 12 May 1870 a committee made up of Captains W Arthur and Morgan Singer and Lieutenant A K Wilson had been appointed to supervise the trials. This was a formidable team, William Arthur was to become the first Captain of the newly independent command, HMS *Vernon*, in 1876, with Arthur Wilson as his Commander. Morgan Singer, as Chairman of a number of

committees was to have a great influence on torpedo procurement and design. All three were to reach Flag Rank. They were intelligent officers but were nevertheless suspicious of all new inventions, especially those for which extravagant claims had been made. They were irritated by the secrecy demanded by Whitehead who insisted that the committee was not allowed 'to examine the working parts of the machine'. They would be a hard team to convince and Whitehead had a battle on his hands. He was clearly self-interested and the British officers knew it.

Although the two torpedoes to undergo trials were different in size the engines were identical, each having two oscillating cylinders set at right angles with a constant speed being maintained by an automatic device regulating the cut off valve. The energy source was compressed air charged to a pressure of approximately 700 lbs per square inch. The air chamber, constructed of ordinary boiler plate, could sustain little more than that. Some of the eccentricity of earlier models had been eliminated by the addition of vertical fins running the length of the torpedo, but the tendency to veer off line occasioned by the single screw was not entirely overcome by this device.

On 31 August 1870, *Oberon* was ready for trials. The paddle sloop had been fitted with the submerged bow tube from which the torpedoes were to be discharged by a rod driven by compressed air. Others were to be dropped from a frame mounted on a small boat. Whitehead, Hoyos and the torpedoes were embarked at Sheerness, where they were joined by the members of the committee. A net, one hundred feet long and fifteen feet deep, designed to contain the torpedoes at the end of each trial run, was suspended from a lighter positioned on the Kent Sands, two miles east of the Nore Lightship. The committee considered that discharging the torpedoes from a submerged tube would not meet all the requirements of the trial and insisted that half the runs should be made with the torpedo put into the water down a ramp frame mounted on the stern of a launch.

The trials started disastrously for Whitehead. The 14-inch torpedo was swept away by the outgoing tide. Whitehead and Hoyos, used to trials in the tideless Adriatic, had made no allowance for the tidal conditions; an elementary mistake. The air pressure to the engine was increased, which overcame the tidal effect and the second run was successful. The trials continued until 20 September by which time Whitehead was becoming anxious about the ability of his torpedoes to withstand the wear and tear imposed by the fifty three runs already completed. The committee conceded that as the torpedo is only intended to be used once on active service, there would be no object gained by giving it sufficient strength to stand continued running. All fifty three runs had been carried out using the smaller torpedo, but trials now continued with the larger model until over one hundred runs had been successfully completed at an average speed of 8.5 knots for 200 yards and 7.5 knots for 600 yards. The committee reported that a stationary vessel might be struck with a high degree of probability broadside on at ranges up to to 400 yards. End on this maximum effective range was halved, as it was if the target was moving at moderate speed.

It was now only left only to prove that a lethal charge could be carried to the target and exploded by Whitehead's torpedo. For this final trial the coal hulk *Aigle* (a former 38 gun frigate of the Napoleonic wars hulked in 1853) was towed to Sheerness and moored in the Medway in 20 feet of water, to act as a target for the armed torpedoes. So that nothing should be left to chance Professor Abel was asked to prepare the charges. Lieutenant Abney, Royal Engineers, was present to photograph the expected impact and explosion. The larger torpedo was fired at 136 yards but insufficient allowance had been made for the tide with the result that the torpedo struck only 18 feet from the sternpost at a depth of 10 feet. The 67 lbs guncotton charge exploded with spectacular effect, throwing up a cloud of dense smoke and water and tearing a hole 20 feet by 10 feet in the frigate's hull: *Aigle* settled in the mud. The smaller torpedo was then fired at what was left of the target. No further damage was caused. The 18 lb charge exploded on contact with the edge of the 80 foot net which had been suspended from the spars with the intention of protecting the target. The Committee duly reported 'that it was unanimously of the opinion that any maritime nation failing to provide itself with submarine launched torpedoes would be neglecting a great source of power both for offence and defence'.

The Whitehead torpedo was adopted by the Admiralty. Arrangements were made to purchase torpedoes from Fiume where the 14-inch (minus longitudinal fins) went into production in 1871 as the 'Fiume Small' and the 16-inch as the 'Fiume Standard'. Britain also purchased 'The Secret' and the right to manufacture its own version of the larger weapon at Woolwich Arsenal, under the control of the Superintendent of the Royal Laboratory which gave its 'RL' initials to the torpedoes built there. The British weapon introduced contra-rotating propellers which gave increased power and helped overcome the torque whereby the torpedo veered off line; the longitudinal fins were, however retained. Higher air pressure also contributed to a maximum speed of 12 knots, almost twice Whitehead's figure. The two bladed propellers were place abaft the rudders, the opposite to the arrangement in Fiume built weapons. The propeller shield was also dispensed with. The improved British torpedo entered service as the 16-inch MkI* RL in 1872, and Britain became the first country outside Austria to adopt Whitehead's torpedo, improving it into the best device of its time in the world.

Although the Whitehead would eventually monopolise the word 'torpedo', in 1870 it was only one of an increasingly bewildering array of underwater explosive devices of which technologically trained naval officers had to be aware. In December 1871 Hood wrote to the Controller, urging him to give greater priority to torpedoes and asserting that the increasing responsibility for torpedo instruction at *Excellent* should be removed from the senior staff officer, who was inevitably preoccupied with gunnery. He recommended that a chief instructor in torpedoes should be appointed, responsible directly to the Captain of the establishment, to be assisted by a staff officer, a gunner and some seamen gunners. The Chief Torpedo Instructor would have entire charge of all aspects of instruction, trials and experiments in torpedoes and should be closely identified with the Chief Instructor at the School of Military Engineering at Chatham. The appointment was to carry the rank of Commander and be for three years. Hood's memorandum continued:

The point of primary importance to ensure success is the selection of the officer to fill the position of Chief Instructor; he must be thoroughly conversant with the subject

Recovering an early Whitehead locomotive torpedo

in all branches, and should possess great zeal and ability. Commander Fisher, now serving in Ocean and who will probably arrive in England about the end of March, is without doubt the officer best fitted in every way for this appointment; he has thorough knowledge of the subject, has paid great attention to it during his absence from England, and possesses considerable ability and zeal.

A minute by the First Sea Lord, Admiral Sir Sydney Dacres, gave only limited support for the proposal but he added:

I am prepared to approve of the substance of the plan, namely to appoint an official instructor for torpedoes in EXCELLENT.

Fisher, promoted Commander in 1869 at the early age of 28, had sailed for the China Station in *Donegal* (later to form part of *Vernon*) at the end of the year. He had obtained Admiralty permission to publish a new edition of his torpedo 'Treatise' which he completed on passage. It was published by Griffin of Portsmouth under the title 'Treatise on Electricity and the Control and Management of Electrical and Mechanical Torpedoes', but was out of date before it appeared as it contained no reference to Whitehead's torpedo. Fisher transferred to the ironclad *Ocean* as her Executive Officer in May 1870. From correspondence whilst on the China Station it is apparent that he was not kept informed of the Whitehead torpedo trials. He continued to direct a great deal of his attention to the development of static 'electric torpedoes' which he used to remove the upper deck of the wreck of the *Dunmail* which had struck a rock off the anchorage at Hong Kong. Lloyds' agents reported that 'the exertions of Commander Fisher and the divers' had allowed the salvage of much cargo.

Inspired by this success, Fisher offered to write further submissions on subjects connected with the management of torpedoes. Their Lordships did not reply but they acknowledged Fisher's good work. He now decided to put into practice his ideas about using electricity to fire guns. *Ocean* became the first British warship to be fitted with electric firing, a success that refuelled Fisher's restlessness. He sublimated his isolation from *Excellent* and the experimentation with new weapons and equipment which was going on in England by continuing his own lines of investigation into towed torpedoes and electricity. Relief came with the appointment dated 16 July 1872 as Chief Torpedo Instructor at *Excellent*. Now he could look forward to a task which would fully occupy his restless mind. His appointment read:

Commander Fisher to EXCELLENT *additional for service in Torpedo Instruction with provision and lodging allowance. Appointment to be for not more than three years. Captain of* EXCELLENT *to select a Gunnery Lieutenant to assist Commander Fisher. Appointment to be for one year. Mr F May Gunner appointed to* EXCELLENT *as an assistant in Torpedo Instruction. Appointment to be for five years. Seaman Gunners to be selected from* EXCELLENT *.*

On 23 September Lieutenant GJ Parker was appointed to assist Fisher. *Ocean* returned to Plymouth on 5 June 1872 and paid off there on 22 July. Fisher was impatient to get started but was to be on half pay until 19 September. Bored and irascible, he wrote to Rear Admiral Geoffrey Hornby, on the 'lamentable' condition of *Excellent*, asserting that this was due to the 'absence of real talent from top to bottom of the staff of the ship'. It was fortunate for the future of *Vernon* and the Torpedo Branch that Captain Boys had not been informed of the contents of Fisher's letter when he joined *Excellent* in the last week of September 1872. He started at the double and did not relax his pace for nearly four years.

When Fisher joined, the *Vernon* hulk was in Portsmouth Dockyard being converted to a Torpedo Instruction Ship. Understandably, the dock-yard officials were more concerned with refitting and repairing ships of the active fleet and progress with *Vernon* was painfully slow. Fisher appealed to the Admiralty for improved priority but Their Lordships were adamant; the active fleet must come first. It was not, therefore, until the spring of 1873 that *Vernon* was towed to Fountain Lake where she was moored astern of *Calcutta* and attached as a tender to *Excellent*. With *Vernon* as his new base, Fisher struggled to assert his authority; at one stage he threatened to resign 'if I find that I am not independent'. He found himself at odds with many of his colleagues but this he expected; he was reported to have said in lectures to the early torpedomen, 'If you are a gunnery man, you must believe and teach that the world must be saved by gunnery, and can only be saved by gunnery. If you are a torpedo man you must believe and teach the same thing about torpedoes....The man who doubts or is half-hearted never does anything for himself or his country. You are missionaries; show the earnestness, if need be, the fanaticism of missionaries'. And for the benefit of his students he prefaced his 'Treatise' on electricity and torpedoes with this Shakespearean quotation:

Hamlet . . . *it shall go hard but I will delve one yard below their mines and blow them at the moon.*

During Fisher's time in charge of the Torpedo School he completed the 'Addenda to the Second Edition of the Treatise on Electricity and Torpedoes'- which included details of the Whitehead torpedo for which he had become a recent and typically enthusiastic convert. Another concern was the Admiralty's Torpedo Committee. Fisher had recommended the creation of such a body in 1869 but the actual decision to set it up had more to do with the interest of the Board itself, notably Sir Alexander Milne, First Sea Lord, and Captain Hood who, as Director of Naval Ordnance, was its main adviser on the subject. The 'Committee on Torpedoes' met at the Royal Naval College, Portsmouth in May 1873 under the Chairmanship of Captain Morgan Singer and with Captain Boys of *Excellent* as a member. Fisher as 'Head of the Naval Torpedo School' was 'to give his assistance to the Committee, when he is not employed in his instructional duties'. The committee was to investigate:

1. *The most efficient manner of protecting vessels, both at sea and at anchor, from the attacks of offensive torpedoes of the various natures known; viz., the Whitehead, the locomotive torpedo invented by Lay, and von Scheliha, the Harvey torpedo and the Outrigger torpedo.*
2. *The best means to be adopted for operating efficiently against an enemy's vessel, under various conditions, with the various offensive torpedoes known.*
3. *The best mechanical or practical system of arranging impromptu means for naval torpedo attack or defence.*
4. *The most efficient manner of clearing a passage through the torpedo defences of an enemy, and of destroying booms and other submarine and floating obstructions.*

The committee's Preliminary Report of October 1873 called for effective British contact mines :

A good mechanical mine is very essential for Naval Torpedo Operations. Among the more important uses of this mine may be mentioned the great facility it would give

a Fleet, possessing a number of them, of sealing up a port, either partially or wholly, so as to make it dangerous of egress or ingress by enemy's vessels. With a view, therefore, of obtaining reliable data on this point, the Committee propose to make experiments with the following:
1. Abel's primers.
2. Singer's improved Mechanical Torpedo.
3. The instantaneous fuse.
This series of experiments will probably enable the Committee to report definitely whether any and what Mechanical Torpedo is suitable for general service, or admissable on board ship . . .

Another mine detonation mechanism was, however, soon on offer. In April 1874 Hood made a positive response to a proposal that Dr Albert Hertz, the electro-technologist at the Torpedo School of the newly unified German Empire should be allowed to visit *Vernon* as part of a reciprocal information exchange. In return for Hertz's visit the Germans intimated that 'a British naval officer of experience would be allowed to visit and obtain every information from the torpedo establishments at Wilhelmshaven and Kiel, proceeding there at the most favourable time for witnessing experiments. Everything they said, 'should be laid open for inspection' by their British visitor.

Dr Hertz, accompanied by the German naval attache, spent two days at *Vernon* early in April 1874. Fisher concentrated on telling the Germans all about his 'extempore torpedoes', electrically detonated charges that could be made on board ship. Hertz, at his own request, 'witnessed the whole process from beginning to end of preparing and laying out an extempore mine and circuit closer, and went through the testing and then saw the mine exploded by the Steam Pinnace making contact with the circuit closer. He afterwards asked to see the arrangements for clearing a channel through hostile torpedoes, and at his request a countermine was prepared and laid out.' Fisher went on to report that Hertz had informed him of the German's work on a new electro-contact mine using the acid filled 'Hertz horn'. When struck by a ship the acid created an electrolyte that actuated the mine's electrical firing mechanism. Fisher was not especially interested as he did not approve of contact mines and he certainly did not put his weight behind this highly effective mechanism.

From *Vernon*, Hertz went to London for discussions with the Director of Naval Ordnance. Hood recognised in the Hertz horn a development of some significance, and he sent samples of 'a portion of the circuit closer adopted in Germany and of their platinum and wire fuses' to Portsmouth for examination by the Torpedo Committee. Hood commented, 'the plan is simple, very much cheaper than is the plan at present adopted for supplying electro-contact mines in this country, and is stated to work in a very efficient manner'.

Fisher made his return visit to Germany in 1874, followed later that year by Colonel Stotherd of the Royal Engineers. Both reported favourably on the Hertz horn but it remained only one of a number of detonation mechanisms on offer. The Torpedo Committee's eventual report, issued in July 1876, was preoccupied with the enormous impact of torpedoes and mines of a multitude of kinds. The outlook was none too good. 'Offensive Torpedoes' like the Whitehead were correctly identified as being 'specially inimical to the manoeuvring of large squadrons, and as having a tendency to reduce to one common level the Naval Power of the greatest and the most insignificant nations.' As for the Royal Navy's vital blockading potential, the Committee 'had no hesitation in expressing their opinion that none of our large vessels could remain for any length of time during war off an enemy's port without the imminent risk of destruction by offensive torpedoes'. There might however be potential in the new weapons that could be turned to advantage. 'In the event of war with any great maritime power,' the committee argued, 'the first consideration in naval strategy would be, as hitherto, to confine the enemy's ships to his own ports. A well considered system of mechanical mines, which could be readily laid down before the chief military ports of the enemy, would materially supplement the efforts of the Blockading Squadron and admit of a reduction in its size. The Committee would, therefore, urge the consideration of the most convenient mode of effecting this, so that it may be ready for adoption when required.'

The committee's recommendations on mechanical mines were not followed up. Electrically detonated mines, both of the observation and contact variety were acquired for coastal and harbour defence. The former were large 500 lb devices fired electrically from the shore. The latter were smaller, with 76lb charges energised from the shore and exploded by an inertia weight or displacement of mercury when hit by a target ship. The War Office deployed these for home defence and the Navy had similar weapons to defend temporary bases. But neither of these devices could be laid other than from a friendly shore. Yet Britain effectively refused to develop the classic horned mine for more than forty years after it became available.

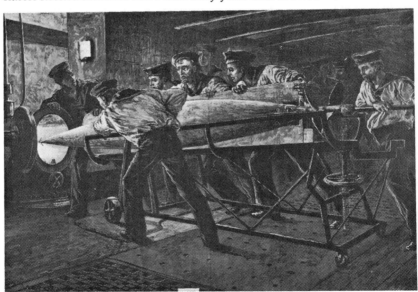

Torpedo discharge 1875 style. HMS Thunderer

Fisher's lack of interest and anti-mine prejudices had much to do with this failure. But if he was unsound on contact mines he was not alone in his prejudices, and in many other ways Fisher's thrusting personality whilst at *Vernon* led to rapid advances in efficiency and weapons. Submerged broadside torpedo tubes were developed; the problem of deflection by the ship's motion was largely overcome. Trials in the new turret ship *Glatton* showed that torpedoes could be fired successfully at 20 knots with only 3 degrees deflection. Fisher next turned his attention to upper deck discharge. After experiments with pushing a 16 inch torpedo off a mess table lashed against a gun port, a frame apparatus was developed and adopted; a hydraulic ram system pushed the torpedo out through a port. Hoyos wrote to the Admiralty objecting to Whitehead's delicate machinery being treated in so cavalier a fashion but was ignored.

1876 was the year in which *Vernon* became an independent command. Fisher's ambitions, both personal and professional, led him to campaign for a torpedo establishment separate from and independent of *Excellent*. His efforts were based on a firm and growing grasp of the technical developments and their implications. He later characteristically claimed all the credit:

I originated the Vernon, *the Torpedo School of the Navy. There was terrible obstruction! The First Sea Lord's argument was impregnable! There were no torpedoes when he came to sea and he didn't see why there should be any now!*

This allegation was the opposite of the truth. The two successive First Sea Lords of this period, Admirals Sir Sydney Dacre and Sir Alexander Milne, were advocates of the Whitehead torpedo, and their support led to its adoption. There is no trace of any opposition from Milne to the concept of a separate and independent Torpedo School. Fisher no doubt exerted 'behind the scenes ... influence' on successive Captains of *Excellent*, Henry Boys and Thomas Brandreth, as well as on the Second Sea Lord, Vice Admiral Sir Geoffrey Hornby, to set up a separate Torpedo School, but one of Fisher's most reliable biographers concludes that in the end 'it was the Admiralty that took the initiative over separating the *Vernon* from the *Excellent*'.

Fisher's official initiatives had been concerned with size rather then subordination. In November 1873, he had asked Captain Boys for an increased complement for the Torpedo School to allow experimental work to be carried out continuously as well as teaching. Boys, supported by Hood at the Admiralty, remained unconvinced that *Vernon* should spend so much time on research better, and more economically, carried out by the War Office at Woolwich and Chatham, but allowed Fisher some more personnel. In August 1875 Fisher, promoted Captain the previous year, sent Captain Brandreth a request for a further increase in complement, including a Commander to act as second in command. This was supported by *Excellent* and by C-in-C Portsmouth, Admiral Elliott. The Second Sea Lord was also supportive and went further. Possibly primed verbally by Fisher, he wrote in approval of the latter's request for a Commander, 'And in view of the increasing importance and magnitude of the subject of Torpedo Management I think it quite true that the *Vernon* should be separated from the *Excellent* and kept as separate establishment under the DNO, Lieuts being allowed to take up Torpedo instruction separately from gunnery'. Milne, the First Sea Lord, agreed on 2 October. Thus it was that on 26 April 1876 *Vernon* was commissioned as a separate command.

Perhaps oddly, Fisher was not her first commanding officer. He had expressed a desire to go to sea and remained only a few months at *Vernon* in an advisory capacity before joining the ironclad *Pallas* in the Mediterranean in December 1876. His continued presence prompted the appointment of a more senior Captain and William Arthur, formerly of the 1870 Whitehead Committee, was chosen. The Executive Officer was another Committee member, a friend of Fisher and the original choice as his replacement, Commander Arthur K Wilson. Fisher left them a tradition of dedication and determination. On leaving *Vernon* he said, 'It is with the deepest regret that I terminate my connection with the torpedo school. I have done my utmost to develop it, from a conviction that the issue of the next naval war will chiefly depend upon the use that is made of the torpedo, not only in ocean war, but for purpose of blockade'.

It was now time for *Vernon* to make its mark as an independent command and for the Torpedo Branch to take its proper place in the order of naval affairs. To provide more accommodation for the independent establishment *Vernon* was joined at Fountain Lake in 1876 by an extra 'living ship', the former 26 gun steam frigate *Ariadne* launched at Deptford in 1859. She was moored ahead of *Vernon* which became the instructional hulk, and between them was *Florence Nightingale*, a small lighter, originally built during the Russian War to carry wounded from the hospital ships at Spithead to a temporary hospital on the Gunwharf called the Balaclava Shed. She had arrived in 1872 to act as a running stage for torpedoes and was placed so she could fire them up the adjacent creek. She later became an extra floating workshop.

In 1874 the Torpedo School had also been allocated a Whitehead Experimental Tender, *Vesuvius*, a most interesting vessel. She was the the Royal Navy's first specialised torpedo craft and was built to make silent, unseen attacks with a bow mounted 16 inch submerged tube. Of 245 tons, she was fitted with specially silenced 350 hp engines. Originally designed with side vents for her coke fired smokeless boilers, she was fitted with a tall funnel while fitting out to make it easier to raise steam. Her low speed of just under ten knots made her unfashionable in an era of fast but unseaworthy small torpedo boats, and she was felt to be more suitable for duties with *Vernon* where she was sent in the year of her completion. She remained until January 1923, and was the ship for which the so-called Whitehead Commanders drew their command pay. Within the walls of these heterogeneous ships *Vernon* was created. Some called it 'Fisher's Empire', but Arthur and Wilson accepted it with gratitude. The new Torpedo School was indeed a fitting tribute not only to Fisher but also to an enlightened Admiralty and to many dedicated and unnamed men who had worked so hard to create it.

AFTER EMANCIPATION IN 1876 the torpedomen at *Vernon* developed a new spirit, no less professional than, but very different from, that inculcated in *Excellent*. The Gunnery School was concerned with more than the latest gunnery techniques; it also trained men in the use of rifles and cutlasses, skills that were much in demand in the late Nineteenth Century. *Excellent* cultivated military precision, which had a functional purpose besides giving the Royal Navy an unmistakeable panache. Torpedomen were required to carry out a great deal of work in boats, and to become involved in practical work and a thoughtful approach to technical innovation. It needed a less formal and more relaxed mental attitude. Surgeon Rear Admiral TT Jeans, who served in *Vernon* during these early years, commented upon the differences he found. Torpedo and gunnery officers, he wrote:

looked on progress in their own particular realms from entirely different points of view. The torpedo officer seemed only too anxious to utilise any mechanical, scientific or metallurgical advances which would help to make his erratic torpedo into a weapon of precision, a torpedo which would keep its depth, run fast, and above all run straight; the gunnery officer seemed to acquiesce grudgingly in improvement in ordnance design. In fact, the one school always tried to take the initiative and the other to resist it.

Jeans is being more than a little unfair to the gunners, some of whom were about to develop their own advanced instruments and techniques and revolutionise naval warfare with them, but the very process of naval gunnery, the use of men as the cogs in loading and aiming machines, emphasised a mind well drilled into automatic precision - and would continue to do so throughout the first half of the Twentieth Century.

Jeans, as a young doctor, found the *Vernon* atmosphere much to his taste with new ideas, even 'radical political doctrines' being debated without 'excessive rancour'. Torpedo officers pointed humorously to 'the new pattern seamen's gaiter, lately evolved by the Gunnery School' as the gunners' idea of progress. The Gunnery Branch, not to be outdone, looked scathingly upon the more relaxed atmosphere in *Vernon*; before long they concocted the infamous and unofficial motto of *Vernon*, 'Swing it 'til Monday'.

Fountain Lake is in the north east corner of Portsmouth Harbour. *Vernon* and *Ariadne* lay close by the Duke of Wellington's steps from which access by boat could usually be obtained. The Torpedo School was housed in *Vernon* whilst a gangway from her bows connected her to the living quarters in *Ariadne*. Jeans liked *Ariadne*:

a beautifully modelled ship, but not the most comfortable. My tiny cabin, on the orlop deck, had a port-hole scuttle at the end of a sloping pipe through her thick wooden side, and it could only be opened or closed by means of a long prong-shaped bar. It rose but a few inches above the sea level, so even the splashes from the wash of a passing steamboat found their way into my bunk, and it had, therefore, to be kept closed, almost always, and while closed, the only change of air - one could not call it ventiliation -came from the musty hold spaces below. In the daytime, the light coming down this pipe was just sufficient to read a newspaper; after dark, even in this Torpedo School, with all its germinating electrical devices, a single candle, swinging in its navy-pattern brass holder, gave the only source of light, and that so dimmed by a thick opaque shade, that reading by it was out of the question. However, it was my first cabin and I did not despise it.

Actaeon 26 gun sixth-rate - Vernon's practical workshop

A third hulk was added to *Vernon* in October 1879, *Actaeon*, another former 26 gun sixth-rate, launched in 1831 and used latterly as a survey ship; she became *Vernon's* 'practical work ship'. A major reorganisation occurred when the former two deck ship of the line *Donegal* arrived in January 1886. She assumed the original *Vernon's* role as a more spacious torpedo school ship. *Donegal* became *Vernon* and the original frigate *Vernon* replaced *Actaeon* as practical work ship and took her name; the original *Actaeon* was scrapped.

Aptly, it was only a year after *Vernon* obtained its independence that torpedoes were used operationally for the first time. The two frigates first fitted with hydraulically activated torpedo carriage launchers were the sisters *Inconstant* and *Shah*, two of the fastst ships of their day. The latter commissioned in 1876 as flagship of the Pacific Station. On 25 May 1877, *Shah* sighted the rebel Peruvian ironclad *Huascar*. Admiral de Horsey, the C-in-C, had already decided to treat that ship, which had stopped and searched British merchantmen, as a pirate and now he decided to attack her. *Shah* could easily outmanoeuvre *Huascar*, but she was completely unarmoured and would have been easy meat for the heavy guns of the Peruvian ironclad if they had been capable of accurate fire. *Huascar* attempted to escape, but was soon overhauled and a shot across her bows brought her to. The Admiral sent Lieutenant Rainier to demand that she should haul down her colours at once and deliver herself up peacefully. Rainier returned with the message: 'The President of Peru is on board. *Huascar* had committed no illegal acts and her colours should not be hauled down.' Action was joined in mid afternoon and

Shah opens fire on Huascar before launching the first locomotive torpedo in an action

continued for two hours. *Huascar's* gunnery was poor but *Shah* hit her repeatedly only to discover that her pounding was ineffective against the turret ship's armour. In the fading light, *Huascar* turned towards *Shah* with the evident intent of ramming. At fourteen minutes past five on 25 May 1877, the order was given to launch a torpedo. *Shah* seems to have been equipped with purchased Fiume Standards rather than the improved 16-inch RLs, and although the weapon ran straight *Huascar* turned tail and outstripped the 7-knot torpedo, a disappointing end to a historic event and proof enough of the limited operational potential of the first generation Whitehead.

A further torpedo attack upon *Huascar* was planned for the night of 31 May in the port of Ilo but she had vanished, to surrender later to the Peruvian Fleet. The night attack had been carefully planned. The expedition, under the command of the gunnery officer, Lieutenant Lindsay, consisted of a steam pinnace with two spar torpedoes, a cutter carrying both a Gatling gun and a Fiume Standard torpedo on a davit, and a whaler to manage the Whitehead in the water. An extract from the orders for the operation indicates clearly the perils and pitfalls of early close range torpedo operations.

in an expedition of this sort, much must be left to the discretion of the officer in command, but as a general idea, after discovering the whereabouts of the HUASCAR, you should lower the Whitehead torpedo from the cutter and take it in tow of the whaler and proceed to approach the HUASCAR by the route that seems least likely to attract attention, probably from inshore of her. The steam pinnace, with the cutter near, and both concealed as much as possible, should be prepared to attack on the opposite side to which you propose to fire the torpedo, but not to disclose themselves unless firing is heard from the ship, or they have good reason to suppose that you have failed. In either of these cases, the pinnace should be directed to steam straight for the HUASCAR and endeavour to blow her up with the outrigger torpedoes, meanwhile the cutter with the Gatling gun, pulling and taking up such a position as will best enable her to clear the Huascar's upper deck of riflemen etc., but with positive orders not to fire unless fire is opened on the pinnace. Bearing in mind the dangerous character of the Whitehead torpedo and the disastrous calamity that could ensue if from careless aim or otherwise, its course should be directed so that it might strike another vessel instead of the HUASCAR, you are to most positively ordered not to project it unless certain that it will hit the HUASCAR direct, and at not more than 80 yards distance. The torpedo is to be fitted to run not more than 200 yards and then to sink. If, from the position in which the Huascar is lying or other causes, it seems impossible to fulfil these conditions, you should consider the advisability of abandoning the idea of using the Whitehead and attempt the service with the pinnace.

It is not surprising that one of *Vernon's* main preoccupations was the further improvement of torpedoes into fully practical devices.

Although Captain William Arthur was in command from 1876 to 1879, another, and more striking personality, was the executive officer, the enigmatic Commander Arthur Knyvet Wilson. Born on 4 March 1842, at Swaffham in Norfolk, he was the son of Rear Admiral George Knyvet Wilson and never had any doubt that what he wanted to do in life was to follow his father's footsteps. He was soon to see action as a midshipman during the Russian war, followed by service on the China Station where he was shipwrecked in *Raleigh* before taking part in the capture of Canton in December 1857 and in the destruction of the Peiho Forts in May 1858. In 1866, Wilson attended a course in *Excellent* where one of the lecturers was John Arbuthnot Fisher. His brilliant style greatly attracted Wilson and the two of them soon became friends. No two men could have been more different; Fisher was dynamic and volatile, whilst Wilson was the perfect example of the reticent Victorian gentleman. A classic entry in his diary was 'Docked ship. Received VC'. These two officers, who were to have such a profound effect upon the shape and size of the Royal Navy, kept in close touch during the remainder of their long and distinguished careers.

As Commander, and later Captain, of *Vernon* Wilson became well known to the lower deck as 'Old 'ard 'eart' but they respected the uncomprising honesty and fairness of this formidable and rather frightening man. He was tough, uncompromising and at times too impatient with the harmless foibles of less robust temperaments. Wilson was also a man of supreme obstinacy and at times he lacked the necessary vision that ought to have accompanied his undoubted technical accomplishments. He was a complex character, full of paradoxes.

Wilson's first appointment to the staff of *Vernon* ended in 1880 on his promotion to the rank of Captain. For a short time he was employed bringing the torpedo manual up to date but the long list of officers of his rank waiting for employment enforced a period on half pay before he was appointed to the command of *Hecla*, the new torpedo depot ship attached to the Mediterranean Fleet. *Hecla* had been laid down as a merchant ship the *British Crown*, and was taken over while under construction. She carried a large outfit of mines, cables and torpedoes, and six second class torpedo boats and machinery for executing small repairs. Wilson was determined that his command should be seen as an important unit of the fleet. He wrote to Sir Astley Cooper Key, who was

Captain Arthur Knyvet Wilson and officers of Vernon 1889

First Sea Lord at the time, expressing his opinion of the uses to which his new and novel fleet unit should be put:

I consider that the Hecla is first of all a specimen of an armed merchant ship, a pattern by which any number can be turned out in case of war. It should be our business to find out in every possible way how far merchant ships can be made to do the duties of men of war, and how they can be most efficiently converted. For this purpose when attached to a squadron she should take much the same place in proportion to the number of men as any other unarmoured ship, such as the IRIS, *joining in all evolutions etc. as far as her means will allow. Secondly, she is a torpedo store ship to enable a squadron to carry out any operations of attack or defence at the shortest possible notice.*

On arrival in the Mediterranean, Wilson and his ship became involved in the operations at Alexandria to quell the rebellion of the Egyptian Army under Arabi Pasha against the Anglo-French Condominium. Fisher was also present at Alexandria in command of *Inflexible*, the first ship in the Navy to be fitted with electric light. The bombardment of the forts at Alexandria succeeded in making Arabi withdraw from the city but he was soon threatening to destroy the Suez Canal, and this led to the formation of the Naval Brigade under the command of Fisher. Fisher and Wilson, who was also appointed to the Naval Brigade, were soon in action together. They proposed that an ironclad armoured train should be created, armed with Gatling guns. This suggestion was welcomed by Major General Sir Archibald Allison, who commanded the troops. Fisher became ill and had to return to *Inflexible*, but Wilson stayed with the Army as it advanced into the Sudan in 1883. He was at the Battle of El-Teb, initially as a spectator, but was drawn into the action and performed with such nonchalant gallantry that he was awarded the Victoria Cross.

Wilson described the incident in a letter to *Vernon's* captain from 1883 to 1886, Albert Hastings Markham, who would later achieve flag rank and be involved in the tragic *Victoria/Camperdown* collision:

Dear Markham,
Thank you very much for your kind note, and will you also thank Durnford for his congratulations and the good wishes he sent me from the gunners and others of the VERNON. *The papers have only arrived today, and I see they have been telling wonderful sensational stories about me. What really happened was this: When we got within thirty yards or so of the battery where the Krupp guns were, about a dozen of the 65th, evidently thinking the place was deserted, rushed forward out of the ranks, but they no sooner looked over the edge of the parapet than back they came with twenty or thirty Arabs after them. I stopped two or three of the soldiers, and made them turn round and face the Arabs, the greater part of whom were shot before they got to close quarters. One fellow got in close to me and made a dig with his spear at the soldier on my left. He failed to reach him, and left his whole side exposed, so that I had a cool prod at him. He seemed to be beastly hard, and my sword broke against his ribs. The man on my right was a plucky fellow, and collared him round the neck and tried to throw him. The Arab still held on to his spear, so I hacked him in a futile kind of way with the stump of my sword, and while I was doing so a second Arab came up and hit me over the head with a sword. My pith helmet took the greater part of the blow, so it only just cut the scalp, and I hardly felt it. Both Arabs were shot and bayoneted on the ground almost instantly. If I could only have got a basin of water and washed my face I should have escaped notoriety, but I only had a little cold tea in my water bottle, and until we got to the well there was no water to be got, so the blood ran all over my face, and the Correspondents spotted me. General Buller, who was close behind, congratulated me in his cheery way, and he has since recommended me for the VC . It had been a wonderful piece of luck, as I only walked out in the morning*

as a loafer just to see the fight. The Admiral has, however, since put me down as accompanying him. Nothing was further from my thoughts than going in for distinction of any kind, but as I happened to stumble into a hot corner I could not possibly have done anything but what I did, unless I took to my heels ... I have given you a long yarn about myself. I hope you will show it to anybody you think it will interest.
Believe me,
Yours very truly, A K Wilson

Markham wrote to Wilson on behalf of *Vernon's* officers offering him a new sword in token of their appreciation of his gallantry. Wilson replied thus:

Dear Markham,
I hope you will give my very best thanks to the officers of the torpedo school who have so kindly offered to present me with a sword. My previous letter will have told you there was nothing in my share of the fight at El Teb to call for any special notice, but I should, nevertheless, have been proud to accept this gift as a sign of the interest felt by the torpedo school and all those who have belonged to it, were it not that the Queen's regulations so distinctly forbids officers to allow themselves to be complimented in this matter. I can assure you that I feel deeply grieved at the necessity for this refusal, as I know it will give pain to those who have only wished to testify their goodwill towards me, and to foster the esprit de corps that already exists among torpedo officers, but I think if you read the instructions on this point you will see yourself that I could not accept this present without a breach of the regulations, which I am sure the officers of the torpedo school would be the last to wish me to commit. I am sorry for the delay in answering your letter, but it only reached me on my arrival here, and I have taken a few days to consider my reply.
Believe me, yours truly,
A.K. Wilson.

The affair of the sword was soon resolved - Markham obtained special permission from the Admiralty to present it. The same thought had occurred to wives of brother officers at Malta and in the end Wilson arrived back home at Swaffham with two presentation swords. He was greeted by the crowds as a national hero with streets decorated with flags, the shops closed, the local volunteers with a band and local pensioners, wearing their medals, assembled in the station yard.

Wilson was next appointed to the frigate *Raleigh*, a sister of *Shah*, as Flag Captain to the Commander-in-Chief, Cape of Good Hope Station. This was a happy and care free commision and Wilson had mixed feelings when he received a letter offering him the newly created post of Director of Torpedoes at the Admiralty. In 1886, the crucial decision was made to transfer the charge of Naval Armaments and Ordnance from the War Office to the Admiralty. This greatly increased the responsibilities of the Director of Naval Ordnance, now Fisher, who had expressly requested that Wilson should be appointed as Director of Torpedoes, but when he arrived at the Admiralty in early 1887 he found his new job to be not quite what he expected:

I understand I am to be called Assistant Director of Torpedoes, Captain Fisher being called Director of Naval Ordnance and Torpedoes instead of only Director of Naval Ordnance. I made a slight protest but was told it was all settled and could not be altered. It is rather as if they had offered me a situation as cook and then made me scullery maid. They are going to be very liberal in the matter of pay, however, as they propose to give me £950 a year, and I was rather glad to see that in explaining the matter to get the money out of the Treasury the Admiralty were obliged to say that, although I was called Assistant Director, I should have the greater part of the work of the Director.

Wilson's duties ranged far beyond the Whitehead torpedo. He was involved in electrical developments, principally concerning lighting and gun firing circuits. But the most immediate problem facing him was to find the best way of launching torpedoes, a problem which was giving a great deal of concern to the Torpedo Discharge Committee. The best solution seemed to be the torpedo tube but so great were the differences of opinion regarding the relative merits of above water or submerged tubes that the committee could not reach agreement on a sensible programme of trials. Wilson's drive and initiative succeeded in setting up these trials in the new cruiser *Mersey*, but the results were disappointing, many torpedoes being damaged on discharge. A new method of retaining the torpedo within the tube was required and Wilson himself devised new hook brackets to replace the T-piece used previously. A number of other minor adjustments were made and the trials were concluded successfully. The Committee was able to recommend adoption of the new torpedo tubes and its report also reflected the Assistant Director's strongly held opinion that when torpedoes were carried in major war vessels they should, as a precaution against detonation by enemy gunfire, only be discharged submerged. Britain developed torpedo tubes for both above water and submerged application.

Wilson's undoubted technical flair was marred by a certain narrowness of view and his strength of character degenerated into obstinacy over the years. Nevertheless his qualities still dominated his shortcomings when he returned to *Vernon* as Captain on 1 June 1889. Under his guidance the establishment prospered. It became a regular port of call for distinguished men and Members of Parliament anxious to see for themselves the development of novel instruments and weapons. The Queen paid a visit, sending a message desiring Wilson's presence, which reached him at a moment when he was deeply engaged in completing the connection of some vital electric circuits. Wilson, ignoring the etiquette usually observed on these occasions, sent back word that he would come as soon as he could. Her Majesty, though unaccustomed to such a reply, made no comment, but after the exhibition she personally conveyed to him her pleasure at what she had seen.

Wilson, straightforward, firm and no personal stickler for outward show, imposed no petty restraints on the liberties of officers and men. There grew up a spirit of cheerful co-operation between the staff and students, between departments and between the wardroom and the lower deck. *Vernon* from the outset was a happy ship, and so it remained for over a century. Whether ashore or afloat it contained a unique blend of tolerance and professionalism. To Wilson 'materiel' was everything: anything which detracted from its study was useless diversion. This clear assessment of the establishment's priorities imprinted itself upon the image and activities of *Vernon* to such an effect that it became the quintessence and ethos of the Torpedo Branch and its successors.

Vernon became the Royal Navy's centre for training in all things electrical and Torpedo Officers were the Service's electrical specialists. Given the importance of electricity in early mine (i.e. 'torpedo') warfare this was a natural association, although it was also a connection that soon seemed increasingly curious as torpedoes became an important branch of development in their own right and the uses of electricity proliferated far beyond 'torpedoes' of various kinds. Fisher and Wilson were as much concerned with

Vernon 1889 – 'No difficulty baffles great zeal'

electricity as they were with torpedoes. As one sailor put it: 'Electricity is a suttle and himpondrous fluid invented by Captain Fisher and perfected by Captain Wilson.' This was about as good as more sophisticated formulations in these early days. Fisher in his 1873 Addenda to his Treatise quoted ME Edlund thus: '... electric phenomena, static as well as dynamic, can be explained with the aid of a single fluid, which in all probability is no other than the aether, we assume the existence of a subtle, and in the highest degree elastic, substance diffused throughout the universe, not only in empty space, but also in the parts occupied by ponderable matter... The electric aether most closely resembles an ordinary gas.' By 1887 the Torpedo Manual no longer sought to explain the nature of electricity, and men under training had to be content with the simple explanation that: 'Electricity is intimately connected in some way with the force of cohesion, so that when particles of any substance are torn away by friction, some portion of the attractive power appears to come with the particles removed; positive electricity appears to be pulled away with the particles and negative to be left behind.'

The accounts of service in *Vernon* during the last quarter of the nineteenth century contain few references to instruction in electricity. Rear Admiral Sir Sydney Eardley-Wilmot, a senior lieutenant in the early years, remarked only that in mines and other matters 'electricity played an important part and had to be imparted to officers and men who went through a course'. He does not mention that in January 1883 he wrote a memorandum entitled:'Our Present Position as Regards Electric Lights for Search and Internal Lighting in HM Ships'. It is a comprehenssive review of the situation in which he reveals the reason for the adoption of direct current dynamos for use in British warships. When referring to the increase in candle power obtained from searchlights he wrote:

The increase in candle power is due not only to the greater quantity of electricity generated, but also to the method of its production. In the Wilde machine an alternating current is obtained in which each carbon is alternatively positive and negative, so both are consumed in a similar manner. In the Gramme a direct current is produced by which one carbon is always positive and the other negative. The action of the positive current is to form a hollow or crater in the extremity of the carbon, while the end of the negative carbon remains pointed. As the most powerful light rays proceed from the crater, it is found advantageous to incline the carbons so as to allow these rays to impinge upon the reflector ... With the alternating current, each carbon being alternately positive or negative, the crater cannot be formed, and hence a less powerful light is the result. A direct or continuous current machine is, therefore, now considered essential.

The 'Wilde machine' was the first electric dynamo system used in the Royal Navy. Henry Wilde was an astute business man who was in touch with influential contacts at the Admiralty. He was aware of the existence of the Torpedo Committee of 1873, part of whose remit was the consideration of defence aginst attacks by torpedo boats, with special reference to the detection of darkened craft at night. Wilde made certain that the committee's attention was directed towards the use of the electric searchlight, which in its primitive form comprised of a hand fed arc-lamp positioned in a cylindrical barrel at the approximate focus of a lens system. The members of the Committee were impressed but they imposed a condition that the target must be illuminated at a range beyond that of contemporary locomotive torpedoes, which in the case of the Whitehead was 400 yards. Trials were carried out in the gunboat *Comet*, which was fitted for the purpose with a Wilde alternator driven by a six horsepower steam engine. The 22-inch diameter searchlight developed 18,000 candlepower which illuminated a pale coloured target at a distance of one mile and a black one at half a mile.

By the early 1880s, twenty ships, beginning with the broadside ironclad *Minotaur*, had been fitted with Wilde dynamos, but improved machinery was soon available. Both German Siemens and Belgian Gramme dynamos were tried, of which the Gramme proved the more satisfactory. It was procured in two types, the 'D' and 'CT'. 'D' Gramme machines were used to power the searchlights of the turret ironclad *Inflexible* which was also fitted with a separate internal lighting system. This was a British high voltage alternating current system using arc lamps.

The system was successful but resulted in the first death by electric shock in the Royal Navy's history. Leading Stoker Suddaby had been supervising the cleaning of paintwork in the *Inflexible's* port foremost stokehold when the ship gave a lurch as it ploughed into a head sea. Suddaby reached out to steady himself, grasping the first solid object which came to hand which was the uninsulated part of a Brush lamp. Poor Suddaby, with his feet firmly placed upon the iron deck, became a high resistance shunt with a potential of 200 volts between his feet and the upper part of his body. It was a fatal shock. An enquiry decided that the cause of the accident was 'a leak to earth somewhere in the field magnet's circuit'.

This accident led to more reliance being placed upon steam and hydraulic powered auxiliary machinery. The decision was also made to adopt as standard a 60 volt DC complete wire circuit for both searchlights and internal lighting by incandescent filament lamps. The first ship fitted with such a system powered by these Gramme dynamos was the new turret ship *Colossus* in 1886. Soon, however, a new and even more deadly peril appeared. The cables were rubber insulated and cotton taped or braided, coated with preservative varnish, and run in teak casings embedded in putty. Sea water constantly soaked the wood casings and attacked the dynamos causing short circuits and fires.

British dynamo design had been fundamentally improved in the 1880s when Mather and Platt of Manchester, who had purchased Edison's manufacturing rights, introduced a generator capable of delivering more than twice the power of the original American dynamo. A new sea water and sailor proof dynamo was next designed by a Mr Lane in Portsmouth Dockyard. The first of these generators, together with improved, lead sheathed rubber cable, was fitted in the ironclad ram *Rupert* when she was reconstructed in 1891-3. About this time, in order to combat the unreliability of the pre-Portsmouth dynamos, a spare generator, the 'peace' or day-time dynamo was usually sited on the upper deck.

In addition to the Portsmouth dynamo, the Dockyard designed a switchboard, the entire new system being fitted in 1892 in the new battleship *Centurion*. Gradually the demand for electricity grew until by 1895 the capacity in the latest 'Majestic' class of battleships, then under construction, had increased to 160 kilowatts. Yet the Royal Navy remained reluctant to over-commit itself to electric power. For good reasons of reliability it continued to use hydraulic power in its heavy gun mountings, and whilst in foreign navies electric deck machinery was generally adopted steam still billowed from the auxiliary machinery on the decks of British warships. In the words of Admiral Hezlet: 'Whereas electric lighting, bells and remote firing circuits contributed to the efficiency of warships in action, the spread of electric power in such vessels cannot be claimed as very significant. Opinion varied widely as to whether it was better than hydraulic or steam power which were certainly complete substitutes.'

Vernon classes were taught that 'Electricity owes its introduction to the naval service, as well as its application to general purposes, mainly in its giving power of practically annihilating time and space', but its use was approached with caution. Students were instructed that 'Electricity should never be introduced unless making every allowance for the effect of wear and tear, damage by shot and shell, and unskilled handling.' Mechanical or hydraulic devices were more reliable 'not because the laws of electricity are less certain than those on which mechanical contrivances depend, but because the causes of failure are less obvious to untrained men'. The limited application of electricity in the Royal Navy that followed from this logic had the effect of making electricity remain the responsibility of the seamen of the torpedo branch rather than of specialist electrical engineers until the inevitable creation of an electrical branch in 1946.

The torpedo schools therefore had to double as electrical training centres, and *Vernon* alone could not handle the training requirements of the entire fleet. Torpedo training was also given in *Perseus* a tender to *Cambridge* in Devonport. At the end of 1884, an independent torpedo school was set up there along the lines of *Vernon*. It used the hulk of *Defiance*, one of the last of the wooden steam ships of the line which had been launched in 1861. She was moored in the St Germans river with the *Perseus* hulk, and with the gunboat *Scourge* as tender. *Defiance*, like *Vernon*, had facilities for both theoretical and practical torpedo and electrical training and for research and development, but *Vernon* retained pre-eminence as the principal home of torpedo warfare in the Royal Navy and all the multifarious activities of the Torpedo Branch.

Torpedo trials with officers and ratings cavorting in the water alongside their charges made only too clear the capricious behaviour of these early devices. Eardley-Wilmot remembered an incident in 1877 when a torpedo discharged into the harbour ran wild:

the stopping gear failed and it ran into a yacht off Gosport, causing alarm to the inmates. For exercise they had wooden heads the weight of the explosive, but the sharp nose made a hole in the yacht. One of our games was to swim with it, and then depressing the head with one hand to pull back the air lever with the other which sent it on its course. At first we often used to lose torpedoes at exercise owing to inability to see them after coming to the surface, especially in rough water. Hearing of this when on a visit to Portsmouth, Mr. Joseph Holmes hit on an excellent device in fixing to the nose a small tin of calcium which when brought in contact with water emitted flame and smoke observable by day and after dark. This saved many torpedoes and made recovery easy.

A picket boat detonating a spar torpedo in Portsmouth harbour circa 1880

Vernon concentrated its work on the Whitehead and outrigger (ie.spar) torpedoes. The establishment also kept a weather eye on foreign torpedo developments. The Whitehead, in the words of the Annual Report for 1888, remained the 'only recognised locomotive torpedo in use on the continent' but *Vernon* was clearly impressed by the flywheel powered Howell torpedo developed in the United States and procured in quantity by the US Navy. At that time, France was experimenting with the Howell and was 'obtaining some very striking results from it. A weapon which while its weight is only one half of that of a Whitehead can be made to travel at an equal speed and to carry an even heavier charge, and which, moreover always runs straight, is by no means to be despised'. In the end it was limited development potential that killed this weapon as Whitehead's 1890's models totally out-classed it.

Another less practical American designed device was the Lay, a huge 25 feet long contraption guided by electrical cable. The charge was fired by remote control which also released unpowered 'slave' torpedoes towed behind the main appliance and even raised and lowered marker flags to show the torpedo's position. One was used in action by *Huascar* against the Chileans in August 1879. It reversed course and narrowly missed the firing ship, which was saved only by the bravery of an officer diving overboard and diverting the torpedo's course. The Lay torpedo behaved no better at *Vernon*, where it was rejected. Almost ten years late a similar weapon, the Patrick, was evaluated by *Vernon*. In a fair appraisal, it was assessed as being 'formidable' because of its heavy charge and long range. 'The fatal objection to it for use aboard ships' was, however, 'its size. A weapon as long as an ordinary ship's launch, and which weighs upwards of three tons is heavily handicapped in any competition for a place among Naval torpedoes.'

A third torpedo, adopted for British service in the 1880s - but not by the Admiralty - merits attention. This was the Brennan, invented by an Australian and powered by a steam engine ashore via wires that were also used for guidance. It had a range of 3,000 yards at 20 knots and was purchased by the Royal Engineers for harbour defence based at a number of stations. The stable winch platform which was required precluded the Brennan's use at sea and it proved incapable of further development, though it remained in service for over twenty years, by which time Whitehead torpedoes were beginning to catch up with its performance and it is still remembered as the prototype guided missile.

The Admiralty is often accused of conservatism but it was always conscious of the danger of falling astern in the naval technological race. It was bombarded with rival claims and new ideas that often reflected vested interests both financial and political. Happily for those in Whitehall a calm and thoughtful atmosphere prevailed at *Vernon*. Fisher, Arthur and Wilson created a tradition of careful and painstaking analysis of trials results which allowed no room for fantasy: a weapon had to be of proven reliability and to reach specified operational requirements. During the closing years of the nineteenth century it became increasingly harder for the inventors to peddle their wares. Only the Whitehead torpedo measured up to *Vernon's* stringent standards.

The Royal Navy felt obliged to observe a strict code of secrecy in accordance with their agreement with Whitehead. The original committee report in October 1870 had observed that:

By the Admiralty letter 3/5688/6101 of the 3rd August 1870, the Committee were informed that, as Mr Whitehead had not patented his invention, he was desirous that everything connected therewith should be kept as secret as possible, and, consequently, they could not be permitted to examine the working parts of the machine;

The Royal Navy had then purchased Whitehead's 'Secret' but the inventor still refused to patent his modifications and improvements, thus exposing himself to wholesale exploitation and industrial espionage. In 1875, the Berlin engineer, Louis Schwartzkopff, pirated the design - which he probably stole- and offered for sale an almost identical torpedo to Whitehead's. Indeed, by using phosphor bronze in the construction of their torpedo, the Germans improved upon the reliability and maintenance requirements of the original version. As phosphor bronze did not rust, the constant need to strip and clean after every immersion was avoided. This made the the Schwartzkopff design especially attractive to new navies like the Japanese.

The competition provided by Schwartzkopff did Whitehead no harm. The German Navy stuck with him and in response to its stipulation of a minimum performance of 550 yards at 16 knots he adopted the three cylinder radial engine produced by Peter Brotherhood of Peterborough. The new 14-inch Fiume model also benefitted from work carried out at the Royal Laboratory, Woolwich where manufacture of the 16-inch RL Mk I* torpedo was proceeding. Whitehead's 14-inch Fiume Mk I incorporated the contra-rotating propellers of the British weapon, which also had an air operated servo motor between the depth gear and the rudders to improve response. Whitehead moved the depth chamber to a position abaft the air vessel thus avoiding having to fit the latter with a central tube for the accommodation of the rudder rod. The Fiume 14-inch Mk I weighed 530 lbs., carried 26.5 lbs. of wet guncotton, was 14.5 feet long and was charged with air at 1,000 lbs per square inch. With a range of 600 yards at 17.5 knots it was the first really successful torpedo.

Impressed by Whitehead's new torpedo, the Royal Navy ordered 225 Fiume 14-inch Mk I weapons from the Austrian factory, and in 1877, discontinued manufacture of the 16-inch model at Woolwich in favour of the 14-inch RL Mk I. This was similar to Whitehead's new torpedo, but with the rudders mounted as in the previous 16-inch RL torpedo, ahead of the propellors rather than abaft of them. The three cylinder engine used in both torpedoes was the Brotherhood B3. It admitted air by cam-operated valves, originally of the piston type. Exhaust air escaped through ports in the cylinder walls which were uncovered towards the end of the power stroke, and thereafter through a slot in the piston. From the crankcase the exhaust air passed through the hollow propeller shaft to the sea.

Before the intoduction of gyroscopically controlled steering, a number of passing runs had to be carried out on the proving ranges to achieve straight running. Each torpedo was carefully adjusted to run straight by means of small vertical rudders set on the horizontal fins. The first torpedo range was in a canal at Woolwich and was 300 yards long and 11 feet deep. This was replaced in 1884 by improved facilities in a fitting out basin in Chatham Dockyard; the new range was 450 yards long and 25 feet deep. From 1883 each Royal Navy torpedo had its own log book that recorded all its trial runs. This attention to detail obtained the best results from these flawed early weapons but it was a time and labour intensive process and a sign of the immaturity of torpedo techniogy.

The demand for torpedoes, in spite of the drawbacks, grew steadily throughout the 1880s until, by the middle of the decade, it outstripped supply. The Royal Laboratory at Woolwich steadily improved its 14-inch RL, the Mk IV of 1883 having new nose contours and a warhead of 60 lb, almost twice the weight of its predecessors. This followed a series of trials conducted by Dr RE Froude at the Admiralty Experimental Works at Torquay. The new shape improved hydrodynamic performance but it also led to a dramatic increase in the explosive effect of the torpedo. As the Royal Navy's requirements could not be satisfied by Woolwich Arsenal's production the Admiralty approved the placing of an order for one hundred Mk IVs with the Leeds engineering firm of Greenwood and Batley Ltd. These were originally tested in a nearby fresh water lake at Lindley Wood. The Royal Navy also found it necessary to purchase 470 14-inch torpedoes from abroad, 50 Schwartzkopff, 220 Fiume Mk IVs and 200 Fiume Mk Vs. Also acquired were 10 of the experimental Fiume 'Baby' 12-inch torpedoes for use from boats.

The 1880s saw automobile torpedoes score their first successes. On 23rd April 1881, during the Chilean Revolutionary War, the British built torpedo gunboats *Almirante Condell* and *Almirante Lynch* fired six 14-inch Fiume torpedoes at the ironclad *Blanco Encalada*. One of the salvoes, fired at 100 yards by *Lynch*, hit and *Encalada*, water tight doors still open, quickly sank with heavy loss of life. Then in 1894, during the Brazilian Revolutionary War, another British built torpedo gunboat, *Gustavo Sempaio*, forced the turret ironclad *Aquidaban* to beach herself after scoring a hit with a 16-inch torpedo fired at 150 yards. Finally in 1895 in two attacks Schwartzkopff torpedoes fired by the Japanese torpedo boat flotilla sank two Chinese turret ironclads, an armoured cruiser and a sloop at Wei-Hai-Wei. The Royal Navy's faith in the Whitehead torpedo, the establishment of an independent torpedo school, and the creation of a specialist torpedo branch had been completely justified.

From 1890 onwards, the Royal Gun Factory at Woolwich took over the design of torpedoes. The first RGF torpedoes were the 14-inch Short designed for boat use and larger 18-inch RGF Mk I. The latter was based upon the 18-inch Fiume Mk I and was a great leap forward in performance but Wilson, whose obstinacy was beginning to get the better of him, opposed its introduction. In September 1890, he was informed that his successor as Assistant Director of Torpedoes, Captain EF Jeffreys, had supported the purchase of 150 torpedoes of a new and larger pattern from the Whitehead factory. Wilson, who was chairman of the Torpedo Design Committee, was infuriated by the fact that he had not been consulted in what he considered to be a very important new departure. He was adamant that there were many disadvantages, particularly that these torpedoes had not been tested in the United Kingdom. His absence on the summer manoeuvres had meant that he had not been kept in the picture, but Captain Gallwey, commanding *Hecla* in the Mediterranean and an acknowledged expert in torpedo work, had reported very favourably on the performance of the new Whitehead 18-inch torpedo. With many new ships authorised by the Naval Defence Act of 1889 a rapid decision had been essential. Robert Whitehead was prepared to give the British Government the first refusal regarding the supply of these new torpedoes, but he set very firm dates for a decision. Jeffreys had therefore energetically supported the proposal to adopt these weapons and he had the full backing of the Director of Naval Ordnance and the Controller.

The new torpedo had an increased range, 800 rather than 600 yards; it was also faster and carried a charge of 200 lbs. of guncotton instead of 60 lbs. Wilson, however, considered that these improvements did not justify the resulting duplication of patterns of weapons, mountings, tools and fittings. Furthermore, he believed that this larger torpedo was too heavy for use from boats, and that the Navy had no experience whatever as to its behaviour when discharged from submerged tubes. He was over-ruled and it was decided to arm the new battleships, cruisers and torpedo gunboats with this 18-inch torpedo. Only one concession was made to Wilson's opinions; he was instructed to carry out a long series of trials from submerged tubes fitted in *Vulcan*, the new 6,600 ton torpedo-boat-carrying cruiser. Perhaps to Wilson's chagrin the new torpedo performed excellently and the purchase of the weapon was considered to have been amply justified. The 18-inch torpedo bore little resemblance to earlier models and had a distinctly modern appearance. The 18-inch RGF underwent rapid development with Mks II, III and IV produced in quick succession. The Mk V of 1898, however, introduced an entirely new feature that would have a dramatic effect upon the future success of the torpedo; gyro control of steering.

Robert Whitehead and his son John had for some time considered that a gyroscopic device might be fitted to the steering mechanism of the torpedo to overcome its inherent inaccuracy. The Russian engineer, Petrovitch, had produced a crudely designed gyroscope which Whitehead and his son used in their early experiments. Failure was due more to the inherent design faults of the gyroscope than to the lack of viability of the idea. Captain John Howell of the United States Navy had also used the gyro for stabilisation in his fly-wheel torpedo. But it was Ludwig Obry, formerly in the Austrian Navy, who provided Whitehead with a practical and well designed gyroscopic apparatus. Obry's gyroscope consisted of a 1.75 lb wheel of 3-inch diameter supported in gimbals with its axis along that of the torpedo. The apparatus weighed 8.5 lbs. The gyro was spun to a speed of 2,400 revolutions per minute by means of a pre-tensioned spring, triggered as air was admitted to the engine, thus ensuring that the gyroscope was in control of the directional stability of the torpedo by the time it entered the water. Steering control was applied by a rotary valve mounted in the frame of the gyroscope.

The Royal Navy, having 4,000 torpedoes in service, each with its log book, felt at first that there was little advantage in fitting the gyroscope to all torpedoes in an expensive modification programme. In 1897, in spite of these objections, a number of Obry's gyroscopes were fitted for trials in the Channel and the Mediterranean Fleets. A year later the apparatus was adopted and manufacture commenced in Britain on payment of royalty of £25 per set to Whitehead. It was also fitted into earlier torpedoes, a process that took only two years. Four bladed propellers also appeared in the late 1890s on the 14-

inch RGF Mks IX and X, but the range of torpedoes at the end of the century remained only 800 yards at thirty knots.

There was much uncertainty over the best kind of platform for these short-ranged weapons. *Vesuvius*, built in 1874, was stealthy and seaworthy, but slow. Thornycroft thought he had a better answer with the 32• ton, 19 knot, torpedo boat *Lightning* which, like *Vesuvius*, was used as a tender by *Vernon*.

Vesuvius – Whitehead experimental tender 1874

Eleven more slightly smaller boats appeared in 1878-9. Other builders supplied similar vessels; all were in the 28-33 ton bracket and none was very long lived (*Lightning* was broken up in 1896). Even smaller were the 10-15 second class torpedo boats built from 1878. More substantial was the controversial 'torpedo ram' *Polyphemus*. An attempt to provide a practical sea going torpedo vessel, she combined a heavy armament of five 14-inch submerged torpedo tubes with a ram and for those days relatively high speed of 18 knots. The wonder of her age (she appears in HG Wells' War of the Worlds), she was of novel design being a submerged cigar with hull built up on top. Sadly, both her tubes and engines gave trouble and she was soon made obsolete by the development of quick firing guns able to penetrate her 3-inch armour.

The demand was still to find the right compromise between high speed and full seagoing potential. When war threatened with Russia and her torpedo flotillas in the 1880s, the demand was for both 125 feet long first class torpedo boats and larger seagoing vessels. Two 'torpedo cruisers' were laid down in 1884, *Fearless* and *Scout*. Their task was to provide a defensive screen against torpedo boats, but they turned out to be an unsatisfactory compromise, being both too slow and insufficiently seaworthy. A more successful attempt at a 'torpedo boat catcher' was *Rattlesnake*, launched by Lairds in 1886, designed with a speed of 19 knots and a displacement of 450 tons. She was officially classified as a 'torpedo gunboat'. By 1887, therefore, the fleet possessed a motley collection of torpedo craft and in that year trials were carried out by *Vernon* to assess the efficiency of the various classes.

The 'Experimental Cruise' of 1887, which had such far reaching results, was the first time so large a number of torpedo boats had operated as a single unit. The ships of this combined force commissioned at their respective bases and assembled at Portland, with *Rattlesnake* as flagship and *Seahorse* as depot ship, for an experimental cruise of fourteen days. The squadron consisted of 24 first class torpedo boats, 16 of Thorneycroft's, 4 of Yarrow's and 3 of White's boats of 125 feet in length, plus No 81 built by White of 150 feet in length as leader. The aim of the cruise was described as 'to give officers and men thorough practice in handling the boats under various conditions, performing manoeuvres at different rates of speed, to test the efficiency of the several types of vessels, and to work out the following points, as far as circumstances would permit'. The most important objectives proved to be:

(a)   *The determination of the highest speed that could be maintained under various circumstances of sea and weather, whilst keeping station.*
(b)   *The measurement of sea-going qualities, habitability, and actual coal endurance at cruising speed.*
(c)   *The comparison of loss of speed in a moderate seaway with relative behaviour of different patterns of boats.*

During this fortnight the boats were constantly exercised, night and day, in manoeuvering in large and small groups at different speeds, attacking *Rattlesnake* and ships at Portland under different conditions, running full speed trials and exercising the firing of guns and torpedoes. The results of the 'Experimental Cruise' shed new light upon the capabilities and limitations of torpedo boats and torpedo gunboats, and it marked a turning point in the tactical appreciation of their value and employment. The object of previous torpedo boat trials conducted by *Vernon* had been very limited, being carried out to find out how closely torpedo launches could approach a man-of-war under cover of night without being seen or heard. These earlier trials had been concerned with the tactics employed by the torpedo launches carried in major warships but they were applied generally to all classes of torpedo carrying small craft and had no relevance to attacks by torpedo boats on the fleet at sea. The 'Experimental Cruise' held many lessons and Captain S Long of *Vernon* left no room for doubt in his report that in open waters the torpedo boats were of very limited use except in comparatively moderate sea conditions when their speed advantage over the *Rattlesnake*, and all existing torpedo gunboats, made them very effective against such slow moving armoured ships. It was clear from the results of the trials that in attack and in defence the Royal Navy lacked the correct balance of forces needed to ensure the continuation of British supremacy at sea in time of war. The torpedo gunboats and torpedo cruisers were too slow to catch torpedo boats, and the latter's poor sea keeping qualities confined them to coastal operations. *Rattlesnake* performed well as a sea boat but her fragile construction provided a poor gun platform for the five-inch armament. Nevertheless it was too late to stop completion of three more of the class in 1888, *Grasshopper*, *Sandfly* and *Spider*, and trials with these vessels continued during the manoeuvres of that year.

Torpedo Boats prior to the 'Experimental Cruise' of 1887

Such activities were a drain on the limited resources of shore establishments like *Vernon*. Wilson, in his first annual report as Captain of the Torpedo School, found it necessary to point out to the Admiralty that the year 1888, 'like its predecessor, has only afforded nine months for instruction in the Torpedo Schools, *Vernon* and *Defiance*, as three months were occupied in the mobilisation and subsequent operations.' One distinguished torpedoman affected by this was Lieutenant Harry Jones, appointed for the Torpedo Course. In the Summer of 1888 he had to join other officers and men, from the Reserve Fleet and other training establishments, for the purpose of commissioning ships of the Reserve Fleet for the annual Manoeuvres.

Jones was typical of the many gifted officers who qualified as Torpedo Officers during the last two decades of the nineteenth century. He had joined the *Britannia* in 1877, passing out top of his class two years later. He served in the frigate *Inconstant* in the Mediterranean in which the Sub Lieutenant of the Gunroom was JR Jellicoe, and in which was also serving a Lieutenant Battenberg. Jones went on to obtain first class passes in all his Lieutenant's examinations, followed by the award of a special prize of £100 for the officer obtaining the highest marks in the Gunnery and Torpedo Officers qualifying courses. In 1891, during his time in the new battleship *Anson* in the Mediterranean, he was decorated by the King of Italy for saving life in the *Utopia* disaster. Jones again distinguished himself during the war in South Africa when, as Commander of the old ironclad *Monarch*, he was detached as a qualified Torpedo Officer to mine the Orange River against raids by de Wet's commandos. This very able Torpedo Officer seemed set for Flag Rank when he was struck down by a kidney disease from which he died in April 1914. Of the events in his distinguished career one of enduring interest was his brief period in command of *HMTB 58* during the Summer Manoeuvres of 1888. He had just completed the academic session of the Torpedo Officers' qualifying course at the Royal Naval College, Greenwich when he was ordered to Plymouth with instructions to commission Torpedo Boat 58, a small second class torpedo boat, 66 feet in length, capable of 19 knots and built by Thornycroft.

At Plymouth Rear Admiral Sir George Tryon was in command of the Reserve Fleet and Commander-in-Chief of the 'enemy' forces during the forthcoming exercises. These were days when the Press kept a constant vigil, monitoring the activities of the Navy. At these manoeuvres they were present in force, encouraged by the Admiralty to give full coverage to this trial of the defences of the British Isles against an attack by the forces of the old enemy, France.

Tryon's headquarters were at Berehaven, in Bantry Bay on the south west coast of Ireland. Here in his flagship, the 8,000 ton ironclad *Hercules*, he exercised command over the 'enemy' fleet of five ironclads, several cruisers and supporting light forces. At Lough Swilly, 250 miles to the north east, he commanded another squadron of battleships, corvettes and torpedo boats. The blockading British fleet, consisting of thirteen ironclads and a large force of cruisers and torpedo craft, was under the command of Vice Admiral JKE Baird. Its task was to keep an effective blockade upon the 'enemy' forces at Berehaven and Lough Swilly, which Tryon christened the 'Achill Fleet', after the island of that name halfway between his bases. Some very senior officers considered this to be pretentious and publicity seeking but Tryon was unmoved, his purpose being to impart a sense of unity to his command.

'War' was officially declared on 24 July 1888, by which time the British cruisers, under the command of Rear-Admiral AH Markham, had established inshore patrols off Berehaven and Lough Swilly. But the blockading forces were in for an uncomfortable and boring patrol in choppy seas, whilst in the placid waters of Berehaven and Lough Swilly the 'Achill Fleet' lay peacefully at anchor, Tryon having stated that he would 'lie comfortably in harbour, take his own time, create false alarms, worry and harass without serious intent, and, finally, when the blockaders were worn out and sick of the cry, Wolf! Wolf!, his forces would attempt to break the blockade.' The scene was set and naval correspondents of the British and foreign Press were there in force; it was a golden moment for any officer who was seized with ambition, a moment which the imposing, intimidating and non-conformist Tryon was determined to exploit to the very best of his ability. The opposition, in the form of Baird and Markham, were officers of a different sort; able, honest, hard working and conformist. The tactics which they employed differed little from the concepts of the Napoleonic Wars, in which Markham's ancestor had been a Naval Lord as a Captain with St Vincent and Troubridge in 1801, before becoming First Naval Lord himself in 1806. An inner ring of frigates and smaller vessels kept close watch on the enemy's bases, ready to signal back to the battle fleet should the enemy venture forth. It was Baird's ironclads which waited for the signal from Markham's cruisers to crush the 'Achill Fleet' should it leave Berehaven or Lough Swilly. Tryon knew that Baird and Markham would not venture far from accepted rules and he was determined to keep them worried and guessing by launching his torpedo boats against their squadrons, causing confusion and allowing his ships to break the blockade under cover of darkness.

Lieutenant Jones, commanding *HMTB 58*, was on night patrol from the start of hostilities on 24 July, but apart from a gun fight with enemy torpedo boats on the 27th he patrolled uneventfully until 2 August. That afternoon Jones, accompanied by the commanding officer of the brand new torpedo gunboat *Spider* (450 tons, 19 knots), obeyed a summons to report to Tryon. Their instructions were to accompany the corvette *Calypso* whilst she attempted to run the blockade. *Spider* in company with *HMTBs 51 and 58* proceeded up Lough Swilly, the three units reporting to *Calypso* at 2130 and passing Dunaff Head at 2145 in a heavy swell and choppy sea the force proceeded eastward, being abreast Inistrahull at 2250, when the torpedo boats parted company from *Spider* and *Calypso* and headed back towards Lough Swilly. *Calypso* proceeded eastwards, completely avoiding the blockading forces. At 12.30 the torpedo boats sighted a green light on the port bow; each boat selected a target and proceeded to attack with torpedoes (fitted with practice heads). Jones reported that *HMTB 58* passed 150 yards from *Inconstant* and discharged a Whitehead torpedo which struck the 5,672 ton cruiser on the starboard side abreast the funnels. The torpedo was recovered with its copper head crushed in by the contact. Torpedo Boat 51 attacked the ironclad *Neptune* but was unable to confirm a hit, the torpedo having been lost. Jones' log recorded that after torpedoeing *Inconstant* he: 'Opened fire with rifles. Hoisted bow and steam lights. Out dinghy. Brought torpedo alongside and took it in tow shaped course for Lough Swilly.'

Tryon showed his gratitude to Harry Jones of *HMTB 58* by presenting him with a silver cup inscribed at the bottom '*HMTB 58*' and round the rim 'Presented to Lieutenant and Commander Harry Jones by Rear Admiral Sir George Tryon'. Tryon and Markham, who was Captain of *Vernon* from 1883 to 1886, were to meet again as Commander in Chief and Second in Command of Her Majesty's Ships in the Mediterranean, a relationship which led to the disaster when *Victoria* collided with *Camperdown*.

Tryon's 'Achill Fleet' succeeded in breaking the blockade. His ships caused havoc around the coast of the British Isles and dismay at the Admiralty, where his tactics were often described as unfair and contrary to the rules laid down for the exercise. Tryon's reply was that there would be no such rules in a real war. Whatever opinions were held at Admiralty, important lessons had been learned, capital ships had proved to be vulnerable to attack by torpedo boats, and the need had been established for highly mobile, fast and powerful torpedo boat destroyers.

The '*Sharpshooter*' and '*Alarm*' classes of torpedo gunboats were designed, intended to be faster, heavier and better armed; but they suffered from chronic trouble with their locomotive-type boilers and failed to reach their designed speed. Fisher, a Rear Admiral by this time, then reappeared on the scene when he succeeded Vice Admiral John Hopkins as Controller of the Navy and Third Sea Lord in February 1892. One of his first acts was to appoint a committee to examine the problems created by the failure of the '*Sharpshooter*' class. He knew exactly what he wanted the committee's finding to be be, since as Director of Naval Ordnance he had already recommended the building of a class of ship of about 300 tons displacement, sufficiently larger than the existing torpedo boats to give it superior sea keeping qualities, and faster than anything built hitherto. His recommendations were endorsed by the committee and became the guidelines for the construction of the first class of true torpedo boat destroyers, two of which were ordered from Thornycroft, Yarrow and Laird. All six boats were designed for a top speed of 27 knots which was achieved with ease.

The first of the class to enter service was *Havock*, built by Yarrow. She was of 240 tons displacement, 180 feet in length, two locomotive boilers, one 12 pounder gun, three 18-inch torpedo tubes and a complement of 46. After extensive trials during which *Havock* was matched against torpedo boats and the torpedo gunboat *Speedy* (whose special boilers made her the only '*Alarm*' class to make her designed speed). The Captains of *Excellent* and *Vernon* reported that *Havock* could catch within three hours any torpedo boat sighted, but that she might be vulnerable to cruisers in rough weather. *Havock's* commanding officer commented on the new vessel's poor sea-keeping qualities. The ship's behaviour and accommodation were such that nobody got undisturbed rest at sea even in fine weather, while in bad weather, no one got any rest at all. The boat was hot and damp and the wretched stokers had to wash on deck.

There was clearly no ideal solution to the problem of designing the optimum defensive and offensive torpedo craft but *Havock* proved the beginning of a line that lasted. The warship classification, Torpedo Boat Destroyer, was formally adopted in an Admiralty memorandum dated 8 August 1892 but the prefix Torpedo Boat was soon dropped and, by common

HMS Bat. Destroyer 1896

usage, this type became known simply as Destroyers. Initially they were not universally popular. Some of the older officers and ratings had not seen a shot fired in anger and had become used to the peacetime standards of spit and polish, the solid reliability of wooden decks holystoned to a dazzling whiteness, and yard arms braced dead square. These new ships were ugly and insubstantial. But the younger generations welcomed the new, exciting and more tolerant atmosphere which was nurtured by the rugged and uncomfortable conditions in these thin steel craft.

Wilson, promoted to Rear Admiral, found himself in 1895 conducting a series of exercises to prove the new torpedo boat destroyers. He flew his flag in the cruiser *Hermione* and had under his command her sister ship *Fox*, twelve destroyers, twelve torpedo boats and four auxiliary ships to act as depot ships to the small craft. Communications between the conning towers and the engine rooms of the smaller boats were completely inadequate, and the bridges were enveloped in spray and smoke so that signals could not be read even if seen. Wilson realised how difficult station keeping could be. Considering it to be almost impossible, he sent the torpedo boats ahead and despatched the destroyers to chase them. After a week of gun and torpedo practice he divided his force into two squadrons, one which he called the English, consisting of the *Hermione*, *Fox* and the twelve destroyers and the other, the Irish, comprising two of the auxiliary ships and the twelve torpedo boats. The Irish force was distributed at certain ports on the Irish coast with instructions that they were to find and attack the English cruisers patrolling in the Irish Sea, screened by two destroyers. It soon became apparent that the torpedo boats were no match for the destroyers. Wilson's analysis of the results of the exercise was regarded as a masterpiece, but the lessons had been learnt the hard way. He reported:

My destroyers have been watching the torpedo boats outside the Irish harbours for two nights in very bad weather, to prevent them getting out if they can, there has been any amount of chasing, the torpedo boats generally getting the worst of it. I have just had all the Captains on board to find out what everybody did, as most of the work took place in the darkness. They are a very haggard and worn looking lot after their two nights out of bed, and I think they will all sleep well tonight. We have had a great deal of bad weather, but that was just what was wanted to try the vessels. I have finished the manoeuvres now, and the next three days will be principally taken up with inspections, and then comes the worse part of it all which is drawing up the report.

The destroyer concept had been vindicated by these exercises, which it will be noted had concentrated on blockading enemy torpedo craft in their ports rather than screening the fleet. Even as the exercises were being held work was beginning on eight new, slightly larger '30-knot' destroyers. Wilson's report helped confirm orders for over forty more such boats under the 1895-6 and 1896-7 estimates.

Destroyers were not the only answer to the menace of the torpedo. Thoughts had soon turned to torpedo nets and to their construction and handling. Captain Arthur had become so absorbed in this problem that he was reported as having been observed sitting cross legged on the upper deck of *Vernon* 'enmeshed in wire grommets and impenetrable secrecy'. The Admiralty considered that anti-torpedo nets were such a sensitive subject that there should be the least possible reference to them in correspondence or printed reports. *Vernon* designed its first torpedo net in April 1878 but the interlaced design was difficult to manufacture and a simpler design connected by iron rings and produced by the Warrington Wire Ropes Works Company was adopted for service. The Admiralty got itself and the Warrington concern into legal tangles with the rival Bullivant Company as a result of using the latter as a producer of its prototype nets. Bullivant felt that their contribution to the development of the torpedo net entitled them to patent rights, and the Admiralty eventually had to award the firm a sum of £2,500 in 1891 as 'full compensation for the future use by the Admiralty, their agents, contractors, and others, for the service of the Crown of all or any of the aforesaid patents and suggestions'. This did not solve the problem. Bullivant continued a legal process that it eventually lost, as it did any further Admiralty net contracts.

Development of nets at *Vernon* continued. Between 1897 and 1900 three Admiralty secret patents were obtained making significant improvements in net design and reintroducing the interlacing principle to achieve improved pliability. Even so torpedo nets were only of much use with the ship stopped. After much experimentation a method was evolved of lowering the booms close to the water which allowed a ship proceeding very slowly to keep its nets down; this was not of much use in action. Nets, however, had other uses. They were a wonderful substitute for rigging as a test of the

'Out nets' took the place of rigging drills

alertness of ships' companies at 'General Drills'. The order 'Out Nets' meant that nets were dropped and swung out into position on their 30 foot booms in ten seconds and refurled on to the shelves in one minute. The record times were even less. Thus highly competitive captains had an alternative to sail drill as the paramount index of a ship's efficiency.

Although the War Office retained control of the defence of ports, the development of torpedo nets at *Vernon* included consideration of their use in conjunction with boom defences. Matters were brought to a head by the success of torpedo boats in the summer manoeuvres of 1889 when Tryon's fleet was successfully attacked by a torpedo boat flotilla based at Alderney. The incident confirmed the need for providing protection and security to a fleet at anchor. The proposed method of effecting this was to enclose certain harbours, of which Portland was one, with a continuous boom moored outside the anchorages. A plan of such a boom was designed and it was decided to test its efficiency. A section was made consisting of a strong wire hawser and large baulks of timber, 12-inches square, armed with powerful steel spikes. This was moored in Portsmouth harbour and *Vernon* was ordered to test it. Wilson sent a torpedo boat, commanded by Lieutenant Sturdee, one of the attackers of the 1889 manoeuvres, to attempt to penetrate the boom at full speed. The boom failed entirely in its object, the torpedo boat cutting easily through it without suffering any damage.

A new design, called the 'ladder boom', was submitted by a committee sitting in the Mediterranean. It consisted of baulks of timber placed transversely across four wire hawsers, and shod with a steel point and a double row of strong steel spikes or spurs. Four feet above the baulks was stretched another 6-inch wire hawser to sweep the deck of any craft that tried to break it. It was common knowledge that almost any boom could be breached by a vessel heavy enough to sweep it aside, but the purpose of these trials was to show that light craft could not penetrate such a barrier. Wilson again selected Sturdee to test the 'ladder boom'. For this dangerous task *HMTB 76* was fitted with a stout wooden 'horse' from stem to stern, which formed a fore and aft bridge structure with sloping ends, duplicated against the funnel which was hinged so that it could fall towards the stern allowing the boom's 6-inch hawser to slide over it. Sturdee raced his command at full speed into the boom, the bow rode high up unchecked by the 6-inch hawser, but the torpedo boat was brought to a shuddering stop by the steel spurs, and began to sink. *HMTB 76*, going full stern, slid backwards off the boom and sank before she could be beached. Torpedo nets were fixed to the booms thus making ships in anchorages comparatively safe from attack by torpedo carrying light craft.

Wilson had much to occupy him during his command of *Vernon* from 1889 to 1892. He inherited a significant shortfall in the numbers of torpedo specialists.

Torpedo Lieutenants	25%
Torpedo Gunners	9%
Instructors	38%
Torpedo Coxswains	86 trained - no stated numbers.
Artificers	13%
Leading Torpedomen	30%

Wilson urged the Admiralty to increase the training capacity at Devonport, where the Torpedo School was beginning to produce results and to be a popular appointment for officers and men. The former were, perhaps, influenced by the duty free wines and spirits which were available in the wardroom. *Defiance* had been the living ship for the 'fleet in ordinary' and as such qualified for duty free privileges for the wardroom and warrant officers' messes. Meanwhile the underwater activities of the fleet in all quarters of the world brought daily into *Vernon* a flood of reports requiring analysis and assessment, which had to be correlated with results of trials being carried out at *Vernon* and *Defiance,* and recommendations sent to the Admiralty.

Amongst these reports demolition and salvage operations began to feature prominently and to have a significant effect upon the design and use of underwater explosives. Enthusiastic torpedomen blew up whatever was to hand. Wrecks were popular targets. In 1888, *Mariner* carried out operations at Grand Port, Mauritius, to obtain relics of the British ships *Sirius* and *Magicienne,* lost in 1810. The same year *Bellerophon* destroyed the hazardous wreck of the small brigantine *Arab* at Halifax, Nova Scotia.

Explosive devices, demolitions, salvage, torpedo boat trials, torpedo tubes, torpedo nets, mining;- these were but a few of the multitude of 'other things' for which *Vernon* became responsible. As electricity became more widely used it brought many 'other things' in its wake. Telephones (Bell himself demonstrated the telephone at *Vernon*), searchlights, portable electric light systems, batteries for special purposes, improvements to dynamos, dissipation of heat in dynamo rooms, automatic search lamps, continuous burning hand lamps, electric motor trials, incandescent lamp trials, electric semaphore, electric circuit trials, lead sheathed cables, gunnery firing circuits, switches for turret circuits and so on, an almost endless list taken from a single *Vernon* annual report, that for 1888.

One more device, one that would have an impact on naval warfare as great as any technological development was to make its appearance before the end of the century. This was radio and a very distinguished torpedoman played a major role in its development. This was Henry Bradwine Jackson, later, like Wilson, to become First Sea Lord. He came from the farmlands of Yorkshire, entering the Royal Navy in December 1868 at the age of thirteen. From the outset Jackson was attracted to the more scientific aspects of life in the Service. He was a silent and reticent man but possessed one of the most brilliant and technically innovative brains ever to belong to a Naval officer. In 1881, he joined *Vernon* as a Lieutenant and served for three and a half years. It was during this appointment that Jackson began to consider ways and means of improving tactical communications, at first aimed at identifying friendly torpedo boats.

In 1891, Jackson first considered the use of 'Hertzian' (ie. radio) waves for signalling from torpedo craft. Appointment to the command of *Defiance* at the beginning of 1895 (he was promoted Captain in June 1896) allowed him carry out experiments. Hertz, Lodge and Crooks had shown that sudden disturbance in the equilibrium of one simple circuit was capable of producing a momentary flow of electricity in another similar circuit in close proximity. Jackson produced a spark transmitter and a simple receiver both using the 'coherer' developed by the Indian scientist Professor Jagadis Chunder Bose. This was a glass tube with two plugs of silver a fraction of an inch apart with the intervening space partially filled with nickel and silver filings. Bose had found that in their normal state of disarray the nickel and silver filings were a poor electrical conductor, but directly there was an electrical disturbance the filings 'cohered' in metallic contact. The coherer in the receiver could be activated by the transmitter circuit some distance away. By accident Jackson found that it was better to connect the receiver circuit to separate long conductors. By mid-August 1896 transmitting and receiving circuits were set up in *Defiance* separated by the length of the ship, ie. about 250 feet from each other. Jackson was able to transmit intelligible morse signals through the intervening bulkheads.

It was only a few days after the successful *Defiance* experiments, on 25 August 1896 that Jackson first met Guglielmo Marconi. This was at a War Office meeting which Captain Jackson had been directed to attend. Although the work of these two pioneers was of a very similar nature they had differing objectives. Jackson's aim was to improve the efficiency of communications in the fleet, whereas Marconi was concerned with commercial long distance wireless communication. Both were at roughly the same stage of development. Jackson continued to improve his equipment and obtained ranges of 300 yards. He took advantage of Marconi's ideas on electro magnetic induction using aerials. Using the masts of *Defiance* as supports for 70 foot wires he obtained ranges of 1200 yards and by the time Jackson left at the end of 1897, to take up appointment as Naval Attache in Paris, the range of his equipment was measured in miles.

In 1899, Jackson was temporarily appointed to *Vernon* to supervise the purchase and installation of the first 12 wireless sets in HM ships. He developed a tuner that was the subject of a secret Admiralty patent: this was further developed when Jackson was appointed to the Mediterranean Fleet's torpedo boat carrier *Vulcan*. Again Jackson's work paralleled that of Marconi and it is to Jackson's credit that he never showed any animosity towards his more famous co-inventor, who had been able to concentrate on the development of wireless without all the distractions of a busy Torpedo Officer's life. Indeed Jackson encouraged the placing of a contract with the Marconi Company for the supply of wireless sets to the Royal Navy. In 1901 Jackson's work was recognised by his election as a Fellow of the Royal Society to which, a year later, he contributed an important paper 'On Some Phenomena Affecting the Transmission of Electric Waves Over The Surface Of The Sea'. Fisher, who returned to the Admiralty that year from the Mediterranean as Second Sea Lord, made Jackson, together with another torpedo Captain, RH Bacon, one of the team of 'seven brains' that he used as an unofficial staff of experts. A naval revolution was in the making with the technologies and skills developed and fostered at *Vernon* at its heart.

The first quarter of a century of *Vernon's* existence as an independent command had seen the rapid and wholehearted adoption of the torpedo by the navies of the world, with the Royal Navy at the forefront of development. Production of torpedoes in Britain was, by 1900, undertaken at the Royal Gun Factory at Woolwich Arsenal, at the Leeds factory of Greenwood and Batley Limited and at the new factory opened by Whitehead's at Weymouth in 1891. The main range was at Horsea Island, Portsmouth, 750 yards long and opened in 1886. It was used by the Portsmouth Torpedo Depot, also opened that year, the Woolwich staff and Greenwood and Batley. Whitehead's had their own range at Portland. The Portsmouth Torpedo Depot, at the Unicorn Gate, replaced a smaller pioneer facility opened in 1878. It was under the direction of *Vernon* and was the principal depot where all torpedo records were kept; it was also the receiving and distribution depot for all torpedo stores and the supervising establishment for torpedo modifications, and the Sub Depots at Devonport, opened in 1887, Chatham, opened in 1888, and similar establishments set up on foreign stations.

The new Torpedo Branch was well established and was attracting new and exciting responsibilities. It had survived a great deal of scepticism during the years of torpedo mania but by the turn of the century Gunnery and Torpedo specialists stood shoulder to shoulder as a new breed of seamen, with a healthy rivalry and an esprit de corps born of pride in an essential job well done. With the beginning of the new century *Vernon's* fledgling years were over.

CHAPTER THREE
THE APPROACH TO WAR

By the end of the Nineteenth Century, Britain's maritime supremacy was being challenged by her old adversaries, France, Russia and America, and by other new, and perhaps even more dangerous potential opponents, Germany and Japan. America was appeased in the Western Hemisphere; an alliance signed with Japan; and an Entente concluded, first with France and then with a Russia whose Navy had just suffered a catastrophic defeat at the hands of Japan. The Royal Navy was also increasing greatly in size but as money became short, as it did in the early twentieth century years, it had increasingly to look to technological quality as well as sheer quantity to keep ahead, putting a strain on the training establishments, which were expanded to take more students and to teach more subjects. Development work also became more intense as Britain's need to keep ahead put her at the forefront of the major revolution in naval warfare that is symbolised by the word 'Dreadnought', but which covered all aspects of naval warfare on , below and even above the sea.

On 23 April 1895, the three hulks that made up *Vernon* had moved to a new home in Porchester Creek. More acommodation was required by the growing size of courses and another old ship of the line hulk was obtained, that of the old three decker *Marlborough*, replacing *Ariadne*. She became *Vernon II* and was connected by bridges to *Actaeon* and the old *Donegal*, which became *Vernon I* moored at the northern head of the line.This arrangement did not last long. In 1904 the pioneer ironclad *Warrior* arrived as a floating workshop, power plant and wireless telegraphy instructional ship. She was connected in the middle bows on to *Vernon I* on the northern side and and stern on to *Vernon II* on the southern. In order to release her name for a new armoured cruiser, tho old ironclad hulk became *Vernon III* and a white line was painted along her gunports to conform with her wooden companions. *Actaeon*, the former *Vernon*, still acting as practical work ship, was moved out of line and moored on the eastern side of Porchester Creek abreast of *Vernon II*. She soon re-acquired her old name as *Vernon IV*; *Ariadne* had not been dismantled but had been sent to Sheerness in 1904 to become the nucleus of a new torpedo school at that port and was renamed *Actaeon* in the following year. By this time almost everyone was completely confused by the frequent changes of ships' names!

Excellent had moved ashore to Whale Island in 1891 but the different atmosphere between the two establishments remained marked, as one young officer officer found:

'From Whale Island we went to the Torpedo School,..No two training establishements could have differed more in their methods than Whale Island and the *Vernon* did.... Whale Island men prided themselves on their smart appearance; *Vernon* cared nothing for appearance and usually dressed in old sweaters and seaboots. The *Vernon* men never paraded for drill; they spent most of their time in boats, handling torpedoes and mines and becoming covered with mud and oil in the process. They claimed they were the best seamen in the Navy and referred to Whale Island as the Gas and Gaiters establishment. After the rigorous discipline of the Gunnery School we all thought the *Vernon* course great fun. We fired and picked up torpedoes, laid minefields, learnt some shiphandling in small boats, and a little about the electrical instruments which were daily increasing in importance.'

Upwards of three hundred men were accommodated each night in *Vernon*, classes under instruction being embarked daily from the Duke of Wellington's steps. In the early years of the twentieth century ratings were beginning to find conditions in the old hulks a little harsh. On the messdecks the subdued light and the monotonous rows of messdeck tables provided little comfort to men who accepted some hardship as a natural part of a seaman's life. The monotonous food - beef, lard, bread and potatoes, indifferently prepared, began to pall as the working man's dietary expectations became more varied. Neverthless, duty in *Vernon* did have its compensations, notably access to the shore and the excitement provided by the shops, pubs and street life of Portsmouth.

The sanitation, in particular, began to fall behind the improving standards ashore. Edward West, a steward serving aboard *Vernon* in the hulks' final days remembered that the 'sit down toilets consisted of galvanised troughs with the necessary holes cut in, there were no partitions or doors'. The troughs were flushed out by salt water when the external valves were opened to allow the contents to be sluiced into the harbour, supposedly to be taken out of the harbour by the receding tide. There was always a long queue at the turn of the tide of desperate men anxious to use the 'heads'. Those who remained too long perched upon the horrible troughs could sometimes be hurried along by floating a burning newspaper upon the rushing salt water as it flushed the troughs into the sea. When the fleet returned to home ports, and its major units were moored in the centre of the harbour, pollution reached a peak, with sewage floating everywhere, much of it finishing up in the creeks and inlets at Tipner, the Gunwharf, Whale Island and Haslar. Eventually, amidst an uproar of disapproval, the Admiralty agreed to place steel lighters alongside *Vernon* for the collection of sewage. The lighters were unloaded at sea to the indignation of the fishing fleet, but, as Edward West pointed out, mackerel became more plentiful in the fishmarket at Old Portsmouth!

Wash rooms, or 'lavatories', were equipped with small troughs rigged along the ship's side, the galvanised tops being cut to accommodate pivoted enamel bowls. Hot water was provided from a tank heated by steam from a coal fired donkey boiler, which had also to provide hot water for tea making, washing clothes and shaving. Seamen, denied the use of baths or showers, had to be content with 'wash downs' from buckets which they had to provide from their own meagre resources. These privately owned buckets were tolerated by officers provided that they were kept brightly polished and stowed out of sight during Admiral's inspections. As general standards of hygiene rose the sailors were forced to keep up by dashing for 'real baths' at the Royal Sailors Rest or the Salvation Army Hostel.

Hammocks were kept, as was the normal custom, in nettings during daylight hours, and slung at night on the messdecks. Decks, tables and stools were scrubbed daily between 8 and 9 a.m. A variety of steel and wooden lockers, always kept padlocked, were supplied for the storage of ready use kit and personal belongings. The remainder of a rating's possessions were left in kit bags stowed in a compartment set aside for the purpose. Each man owned a ditty box kept with those of his mates in racks in each mess. The boxes were scrubbed and locked, with the metal tallies brightly burnished. Space heating was supplied by coal fired 'Beeston' stoves, their T-shaped funnels protruding on to the upper deck where they spewed soot upon the Commander's clean decks and paintwork. Each stove was attended by one man, who was the only person allowed to refuel it or to open the flap door. Burning of refuse of any kind was strictly forbidden.

The daily routine remained virtually unchanged for the first forty years of the *Vernon's* independent existence

AM

2.00	Rounds Correct
4.00	Rounds Correct
6.00	Turned hands up
7.00	Breakfast
7.45	Hands clean decks
9.00	Divisions and prayers
9.15	Hands employed about torpedo work generally.
	Hands preparing for torpedo experiments.
	Divers away searching for lost torpedo.
	Senior classes to instructions.
	Pumped out VERNON.
	Up Coal.
	Stowed Hold and spirit room Etc.
12.00	Dinner

PM

1.00	Hands employed as requisite
4.00	Landed liberty men
4.35	Evening Quarters
	Fire stations
9.00	Rounds of messdecks
11.35	Rounds

The 24 hour clock was not used in those days

The constant fire risk of these hulks was understood and the number of men stationed at each of the four main pumps was carefully recorded at Evening Quarters. Fire hoses were flaked down, their highly polished nozzles fitted and ready for use. Stand by hoses were kept on reels and the salt water tanks which provided emergency water for the hoses were kept filled.

The work done on board *Vernon* contrasted greatly with the primitive living conditions on board. Advanced scientific and engineering experiments contrasted oddly with such an old fashioned environment. *Vernon's* staff, particularly the Whitehead section, were hard pressed to meet the demands

The Armourers' workshop Vernon circa 1905

placed upon them by the many and important innovations which came to them for assessment. Particularly important was the increase in the range of torpedoes with the adoption of 'heater' engines. The gunners had been forced by the torpedo threat to exploit more fully the range potential of their latest long barrelled breech loading weapons fired with slow burning propellants. As the gunners adopted new techniques of 'fire control' to shoot accurately at ranges measured in thousands of yards the torpedomen were put on their mettle to make their weapons acquire comparable accurate ranges.

At the beginning of the twentieth century, most torpedoes could only be fired at long range at speeds that made effective hitting near impossible; the Japanese for example liked to set their weapons to run at over 3,000 yards at 15 knots. Under combat conditions against the Russians in 1904-5 they soon found that hits were only possible if the speed was increased to 25 knots and the range correspondingly reduced to just over 1000 yards. The latest torpedoes using higher air pressures and modified engines could double this performance. The 1905 18-inch Fiume Mk III had a claimed range of over 1,000 yards at 39 knots, and over 2,000 yards at 29 knots, and the new RGF Mk VI had similar potential. With gunnery ranges now at 5,000 yards however this was not enough. Help was on the way for the outranged torpedomen. In 1904, Armstrong, Whitworth and Company patented a device called the Elswick heater, named from the site of the Newcastle works. This was designed to pre-heat the contents of the torpedo's air vessel using a spray of liquid fuel injected by compressed air and ignited by the firing of a cartridge. This added energy and, hence, speed and/or range.

Both British and Japanese officers attended the 1905 trials of the Elswick heater carried out at Weymouth using a modified 18-inch Fiume Mk III torpedo. Over the 1,000 yard run the the heater gave an increase in speed of 9 knots. In America, the Bliss company developed a similar system but these 'dry heaters' were unsatisfactory in various ways; they suffered from uneven heating, deposited soot inside the air vessels and were subject to heat losses between air vessel and engine. The Whitehead Company therefore developed a superior 'wet heater' system in which fuel was sprayed into a combustion chamber through which the air passed before entering the engine. To reduce the temperature in the combustion chamber to acceptable levels water was also injected which created steam, adding further to the energy availble to drive the engine. With this improved 'wet heater' system a Fiume Mk IIIH 18-inch heater torpedo could travel just under 2,200 yards at 34 knots and 4,370 yards at 29 knots. The Royal Navy, while happy with the principle of the wet heater, was not satisfied with the complexity of the Fiume design. A simplified wet heater was designed by one of its own engineering officers, Lieutenant S.U. Hardcastle, and it became became known as the RGF heater. It was combined with a new four cylinder engine better able to cope with the high temperatures in the 18- inch Mk VII of 1908; this had a range of 7,000 yards at 29 knots or 5,500 yards at 35. From 1909 heaters were also fitted to older Mk VIs to produce the 18-inch RGF Mk VIH torpedo, whose maximum range was 3,500 yards at 45 knots and 6,000 yards at 35 knots.

In order to improve striking power the Germans adopted a 19.7 inch torpedo in 1906. This had double the charge of an 18-inch weapon and Britain replied with a 21-inch torpedo in 1908, the RGF Mk I which was replaced by the Mk II in 1910. The 21-inch RGF Mk II had a 400 lb head compared to the 200 lb charge of the 18-inch Mk VII. It could travel 5,000 yards at 35 knots or 8,000 at 29 knots. 21-inch torpedo tubes were adopted in British destroyers from the 'Beagle' Class, launched in 1909-10, onwards, in the 13.5 inch gun super-dreadnought capital ships and in light cruisers starting with the 'Weymouth' Class of 1910.

In 1912, manufacture of torpedoes ceased at Woolwich and a new Royal Naval Torpedo Factory was opened at Greenock. The first new torpedo to bear the RNTF name was the 18-inch Mk VIII specially designed for submarines which retained tubes of that calibre. Whiteheads built torpedoes of RGF design for the Admiralty as well as some torpedoes of their own 'Fiume' and 'Weymouth' models, a few of which were purchased by the Royal Navy. Theirs became the only private torpedo factory in the United Kingdom when Greenwood and Batley ceased production in 1909.

Higher torpedo performance needed longer torpedo testing ranges. In 1905 the Horsea Range was lengthened to 1,000 yards. Whitehead's range was also lengthened to 1,500 yards, the original length of a separate Admiralty range set up in Portland Harbour in 1902; the latter was later doubled in length. Another 1,500 yard range was established at Devonport where a new Torpedo Sub-Depot was established in 1909. In 1912 a long 7,000 yard range was established at Loch Long to support the new Greenock factory. RGF heaters were considered too secret to be fitted at Whitehead's works and torpedoes made there were sent up to Greenock to receive their heaters and then to Loch Long for proving trials.

Heater torpedoes gave considerably greater power to all forms of torpedo craft. They forced capital ships to fight at even longer ranges so providing a major stimulus to the rapid deployment of long range gunnery techniques mainly associated with the 'Dreadnought' revolution. They also gave extra power to the submarine, a weapons platform that, contrary to popular belief, the Royal Navy adopted with remarkable enthusiasm once its practicality had been demonstrated by the American inventor JP Holland. Despite the opposition of Wilson, who was by then Controller, the first five British submarines were built by Vickers at Barrow and were in service by 1903. Reginald Bacon, a torpedoman and the first Inspecting Captain of Submarines, was well aware of the offensive promise of submarines but, in view of their fragile construction and limited range, he considered that they were especially suited to the role of anti-invasion patrols in the vicinity of harbours. In a report dated 31 May 1903 he suggested that submarine patrols should replace defensive minefields. Fisher, who, unlike Wilson, was fascinated by the 'submarine boats', was quick to give his support to Bacon's recommendations. By 1905 defensive minefields at British ports were beginning to be withdrawn and by the outbreak of war in 1914 the Royal Navy had a large force of submarines, mainly small coast defence boats.

This was a mixed blessing for the submariners who had relatively few longer range sea going vessels. It was also another milestone in the wretched story of the pre-1914 development of British mines. In 1895 the decision had been made not to use contact mines for blockade purposes as they would stop the enemy's fleet coming out to be defeated in battle; experiments at *Vernon* therefore stopped. An independent electro-mechanical mine had been under development for the previous decade based on the existing 76 lb electro-contact mine but with a battery mounted in the mine rather than ashore. The mine was activated by a mercury circuit-closer and proved far too prone to premature explosions. In 1900 Fisher pressed *Vernon* to begin work on contact mines again but this stopped in 1903 when the War Office abandoned its defensive mining organisation. The Admiralty retained some mining equipment in store but British mining was in deep hibernation.

Then in 1904-5 the Russo-Japanese war suddenly showed the potential impact of mine warfare. Several battleships were sunk or badly damaged and an Admiralty committee was set up to consider 'The number of automatic submarine mines required to be held in readiness by the Navy.' Captain Charles Ottley was appointed as Chairman. He had been responsible for *Vernon's* outstanding contribution to mine development so far, i.e. the automatic sinker designed to allow mines to be laid at pre-determined depths.

The *Vernon* Annual Reports of 1905 and 1906 indicate clearly that neglect of mine development was a serious mistake and that in a future war a navy unprepared for mine warfare might suffer crippling losses. There was an urgent need to develop a new type of mine which would be easy to manufacture in large numbers and which could be used in either the defensive or the offensive roles. The Ottley Committee recommended the provision of ten thousand new contact mines. Development work was put in hand immediately and the result was the British Spherical or Naval Service mine.

The most fully tested and successful method of detonating a moored mine was still the German Hertz horn, but Britain's mine experts doubted the ability of British manufacturers to produce mines up to the high standards of watertightness required. First mechanical pistols based on the inertia or pendulum principle were tried in the mines Marks I and II: these were unsuccessful as they tended to fire prematurely in severe sea conditions. The Mk III mine was actuated by a horizontal firing arm pivoted on the top of the mine case. When the arm was struck a spring loaded pin struck the detonator which fired the primer and the main charge. Conversion of mines to Mk III standard began in 1912, but the work was incomplete when two years later war broke out.

Various types of free floating mine were considered for laying in large quantities in the shallow waters off the enemy's harbours. Fisher also suggested that such mines could be dropped in the path of an advancing enemy fleet. However, it was very soon apparent that such uncontrolled devices drifting at random might be as much of a menace to the mine layers as to the enemy forces and all British mines were designed to be laid on sinkers in defined fields. The Ottley Committee's plan in case of war with Germany was to lay three thousand mines in the North Sea, about 10 miles off the mouths of the Elbe, the Weser and the Jade rivers. These plans did not find favour with the Admiralty and there were no firm plans for minelaying by the outbreak of war in 1914. Defensive fields were investigated, but mining enemy waters was not seriously contemplated. By then there were about 4,000 Service Mines available and although *Vernon* was happy with the latest modification this confidence was to be sadly misplaced.

To lay these mines seven minelayers were made available, old 20 knot second class cruisers of the '*Apollo*' class laid down under the Naval Defence Act of 1889 and converted in 1907-10; *Apollo, Andromache, Intrepid, Iphigenia, Latona, Naiad* and *Thetis*. Each 3,400 ton ship could carry 100 mines each. In 1907 *Vernon* also recommended that minesweeping be adopted rather than the countermining preferred hitherto. Twelve torpedo gunboats of the '*Jason*' class were so equipped and a trawler reserve earmarked; hand books and courses in the subject were prepared. It was a start , although it would turn out to be hardly adequate when the test of war came.

The lack of an effective British mine warfare capability was a most serious oversight. To some extent it reflected Britain's inability to manufacture equipment up to the highest world standards and a natural tendency to try to make one's own design work even when better foreign alternatives were available. But there was a more fundamental problem, the Royal Navy's lack of an institutional brain, ie a proper staff. Fisher eventually became First Sea Lord in 1904 but his style only emphasised the undisciplined way in which policy was made in the Admiralty. The positive side of this was that a battleship of revolutionary design, *Dreadnought*, could be built in a year and a day. The negative side was that weapons which did not reflect the official enthusiasm of the moment were neglected. Moreover, money was short and had to be concentrated on the developing Anglo-German naval race in capital ships and the maintenance of the two power standard. There was no coherent strategic doctrine to provide a basis for overall weapons development. There was always in the background the debilitating prejudice that mine warfare was of little interest to a dominant naval power like Britain. The Ottley Committee made a serious effort to integrate mines into British naval strategy but even then there was insufficient contact between the users and the designers to produce effective results.

Vernon might call for more attention to be paid to mine warfare in general terms but neither it, with all its other manifold preoccupations, nor the contemporary Admiralty was capable of responding in an effective manner. To *Vernon's* credit it had been able to detect the serious problems with the Mks I and II mines but it still thought the mechanical pistol was the best solution and would defend this decision well into the war. Perhaps the establishment's attention was at this time becoming spread over too wide an area and it was unable to concentrate sufficiently on underwater warfare. It was responsible for assessing the value of virtually any new device or technical development which seemed likely to be of benefit to the Service. More good people thinking about mines and fully committed to mine warfare might have detected the problems with lever-detonated mines more clearly. The very success of the torpedomen in becoming the Navy's reservoir of technological talent was diverting attention from the Branch's major responsibilities.

What was more important to *Vernon* was the modernisation of the electrical equipment of the new capital ships. Ships constructed at the turn of the century were equipped with a two wire parallel system in which the dynamos were connected to one or more switchboards. The supplies to the various services were distributed by a tree system. Hand switches enabled any dynamo to feed all or part of a system, thus reducing the risk of disabling damage. There were two systems, high power which varied from 80 volts DC to 100 volts DC and low power, of 24 volts DC. This simple direct current system was sufficient for the comparatively light loads of the period, but in 1904 it became apparent to CH Wordingham, head of the Admiralty Electrical Engineering Department, that the growing demand for power in warships would require a new ring main system of distribution. It was estimated that a considerably increased high power supply voltage, 220 volts DC, would be required to meet all the demands. This was agreed in spite of the opposition of senior electrical engineers who considered this voltage to be dangerously high. The first ships to be fitted with ring mains were the 14,600 ton armoured cruiser *Defence*, and the revolutionary 17,350 ton battle cruiser *Invincible*, apple of Fisher's eye; both were commissioned in 1908. *Invincible's* four 12-inch gun mountings were electrically operated, but the installation proved unsatisfactory and hydraulic systems were used in later ships.

Since 1900 the staff at *Vernon* had been busily evaluating and developing the Jackson and Marconi systems of wireless telegraphy. Trials had been carried out with thirty two Marconi sets leading to the issue of general working instructions applicable to both the Marconi and Jackson systems in HM ships. For a few months at the end of 1904 Henry Jackson himself became *Vernon's* commanding officer and he was able to supervise the full exploitation of the new radio instructional facilities provided by the arrival of *Warrior*. By 1906 activities in the Wireless Telegraphy Department had increased to such an extent that a special annexe had to be added to the *Vernon* Annual Report. The fitting out of ships with wireless equipment was proceeding apace and to operate it efficiently it was decided to institute permanent wireless operators. In a report by representatives of the Channel, Mediterranean and Atlantic Fleets, meeting on board the battleship *Exmouth* in early 1906, it was agreed that there were insufficient wireless operators for war purposes. It was proposed that signalmen trained in the fleet should requalify as wireless operators, but it had become the practice to send men to the wireless office as a form of punishment and it was natural, therefore, that signalmen did not relish the duty full time. The *Exmouth* conference decided that:

We have assumed that a separate branch is a necessity, that the case is an urgent one in which numbers must be rapidly increased. Therefore any system of training boys will be too lengthy for immediate requirements. Under these circumstances we propose that volunteers from any branch of the service (signalman, bluejacket, marine, stoker and so on) should be eligible for the new branch of wireless operator. The requirements for a candidate will be a good education in reading and writing, a good character and intelligence.

The conference further considered that:

Wireless operators should be solely under the control of the Torpedo Department.

Their recommendations were not confined to ratings. They concluded that:

An expert officer in wireless telegraphy should be attached to each fleet solely for this purpose. He should be made responsible for the training and efficiency for the operators in his fleet. We would recommend this officer should be a Torpedo Lieutenant with some sea experience as such, and be especially selected for his capabilities in wireless telegraphy.

By the outbreak of war in 1914 these recommendations had led to what was virtually a sub-specialisation of the Torpedo Branch. It was then only a matter of time before this subspecialisation broke away from its parent branch as the Torpedo Branch had parted company with the Gunnery Branch in 1876.

Torpedo Officers' inventiveness also involved them in the creation of yet another new branch of the Navy, aviation. *Vernon* showed an early interest in balloons and torpedomen were involved in private enterprise experiments with both lighter than air and heavier than air craft. Captain Reginald Bacon, as Director of Naval Ordnance, recommended that the Royal Navy build a rigid airship in 1908, long before the German Navy decided to buy a Zeppelin. When the contract was placed with Vickers of Barrow another torpedoman, Captain Murray Sueter, was made Inspecting Captain of Airships. In 1910 an Air Department was established at the Admiralty under the Assistant Director of Torpedoes. Sadly, this enterprise was to be ill rewarded.

Vickers' experience was more in heavy industrial production and the firm was used to matching large displacements against the waves, armour against shell, pressure hulls against the depths and hydraulics against recoil. This was not necessarily the appropriate background for a firm being asked to convert to light alloys and silken fabrics. Vickers encountered problems

'Mayfly' a costly blunder which broke her back without leaving her mooring

with unfamiliar alloys, complex stress calculations and an unending series of design alterations by the Admiralty. When the 'Mayfly', as she had become known, eventually emerged she met with instant disaster. After being unable to fly on her first outing due to excessive weight, her framework was lightened, so weakening her structure. Caught in a cross wind on her second outing in September 1911 she broke her back without ever leaving her mooring mast; she had cost the Naval Estimates £41,000. Lessons had been learned by Vickers, but the development of rigid airships for the Royal Navy never properly recovered. Not until 1913 did the Admiralty, noting the successful operation of the commercial Zeppelin services in Germany, give any further thought to the construction of rigid airships for the Royal Navy and no British rigid airship design proved successful until captured Zeppelins were copied late in the war.

The demise of the 'Mayfly' confirmed the opinion of Wilson, Fisher's successor as First Sea Lord, that aircraft were not a good idea, but the Royal Navy was already training its first pilots to fly aeroplanes. In October 1911, the first naval aeroplanes were purchased and a flying school established at the airfield at Eastchurch on the Isle of Sheppey. These activities were supervised by *Actaeon*, the Chatham torpedo school. In 1912 the Air Department was re-established as an independent organisation with Sueter in command and the strong backing of Winston Churchill, the dynamic First Lord. The enthusiasm of the young airmen was to be exploited to put the Royal Navy in the forefront of aviation. Given the influence of torpedomen in the new organisation a natural and early aim was the combination of aircraft and torpedoes. Small 14-inch Mks IX and X, developed for picket boats in the 1890s, were suitable for this duty and late in 1913 Lieutenant Arthur Longmore (later Air Chief Marshal Sir Arthur Longmore) took one into the air; the following year he carried out the first ever air torpedo drop. *Vernon* reported favourably upon the simple release gear which allowed torpedoes to be dropped successfully from heights of approximately 45 feet. By 1914 the Royal Naval Air Service was the largest naval air arm in the world and the most advanced in the use of heavier than air aircraft for both reconnaisance and combat purposes.

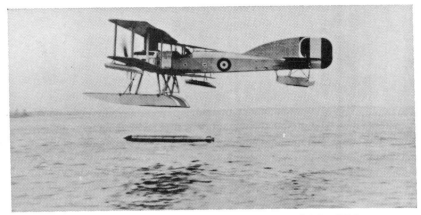

Short type 184 seaplane releasing 14-inch torpedo from height of 20 feet

Torpedomen also became involved in diving, although this remained the responsibility of the Gunnery Branch until 1944. The Torpedo Branch had always had to rely upon divers for many facets of underwater work and their early history cannot be ignored in the *Vernon* story. Diving and salvage had been a haphazard affair until the creation of the Admiralty Deep Diving Committee in 1906. At that time the greatest authenticated depth at which divers had done practical work in safety was 210 feet; this was accomplished by Lieutenant GCC Damant, Inspector of Diving in the Royal Navy and Gunner AY Catto. The operations were carried out under the personal supervision of Professor JS Haldane of Oxford University. The Deep Diving Committee consisted of Captain FT Hamilton, Professor Haldane, Captain Reginald Bacon and Captain Edgar Lees, the secretary being Staff Surgeon Oswald Reece, whilst Lieutenant Damant and Gunner Catto were appointed for the experimental work. Experiments showed how the dangers arising from the formation of bubbles of nitrogen in the blood and tissues of a diver ascending from deep water could best be overcome. A table was drawn up showing the limits of time on the bottom and the corresponding precautions recommended in ascending from different depths up to 210 feet. Diving could now take place with much greater safety up to this depth. Work could also go forward into the investigation of different gas mixtures to eliminate the presence of nitrogen and to examine the effect upon the human system at depths beyond 210 feet. By 1910 the physics and physiology of diving were well understood and documented in the Royal Navy's diving manuals.

These were issued by the Gunnery Branch and laid down strict rules regarding the selection of divers. The diving manual stated that divers:

should be steady men, of good character and good physique, capable of sustaining a good bodily strain ... and free from obesity. Particular attention is to be taken that he is free from any cardiac or pulmonary disease, that he suffers from no constitutional complaint, such as syphilis, albuminuria, urea, and shows no sign of middle ear disease; that there is no history of fits of any kind, and that he is not addicted to alcohol or smoking in excess. There should be no tendency to varicose veins or arterial degeneration.

Commander EAD Masterman and the Whitehead Department staff. Vernon 1911

Officers selected for training as divers came from the Gunnery and Torpedo Branches. Gunnery lieutenants were given a course of eight days and torpedo lieutenants a course of five days; Torpedo Officers were considered to be already fully conversant with the means of communication. Seamen and artificers qualifying as divers were given a course lasting forty days. The officers' course included general work down to 10 fathoms whereas the seamen and artificers' course required work to be done at 20 fathoms. Training of new recruits to diving took place in the diving tank developed at Whale Island for that purpose.

Vernon may not have had an official interest in diving beneath the waves but the establishment was very interested in listening to what went on there. Underwater sound seemed to have relevance to communications and navigation and possibly even to the detection of submarines and torpedoes. General interest in the subject led to a series of trials at *Vernon* using a hydrophone designed by Captain CA McEvoy. This design was abandoned in 1903 in favour of *Vernon's* own hydrophone. This consisted of a microphone secured to a mahogany sounding board fixed to the inside of an old hundred pound mine case. It was laid out at the Horsea range, the receiver being placed on board *Ariadne*. This arrangement worked satisfactorily for three months, it being possible to hear a torpedo run the whole length of the range. When it was taken up, the apparatus was found to be dry and clean inside.

The hydrophone was then laid out at the entrance to Porchester Creek, about 500 yards from the stern of *Ariadne*. Receivers were placed in her signal house and on the poop. A ship's bell was suspended from the derrick of a steam boat by a line marked in feet; another line was secured to the tongue of the bell. The boat then proceeded to a point nearly over the hydrophone, the bell was lowered 10 feet under water and the line pulled so as to strike eight bells. This was repeated at short intervals. The steam boat drifted slowly with the tide towards the mouth of the harbour. The bell could be heard until a distance of 1,000 yards had been reached: at this point other noises drowned it out. It was noted that at this range the workings of a mud dredger could be heard distinctly. *Vernon* reported that it had been difficult to obtain the direction of the sound, but it was suggested that it should be possible to overcome this difficulty by placing a microphone in the principal focus of a parabolic reflector.

In 1909, a committee had been formed under the chairmanship of the Captain of *Vernon* to consider the use of submarine signalling apparatus for navigational purposes and intership communications, but little thought appears to have been given to the possibility that the principles of the transmission of sound in water could be used for the detection of submarines. The American Submarine Signal Company and its British subsidiary, The British Submarine Signal Company, developed an intership and navigational system based upon the use of underwater bells and microphones and in 1911 thirty naval vessels were equipped with this primitive equipment. The British version had been equipped with an improved Hervey-Gardner microphone designed by Lieutenant RG Hervey, for the reception of navigational bell signals. It was also found to be marginally useful for the detection of ships' propeller noises, including those emitted by the very noisy German U-boats of that period. On the outbreak of war it was the only shipborne equipment available which, under ideal conditions, might detect submarines.

With such limited progress in submarine detection it was not surprising that the means of submarine destruction was in a similarly parlous state. *Vernon* carried out tests in 1900 with a 42 foot anti-submarine spar torpedo, the 'swinging outrigger'. It was secured by a wire strop at the stern of the carrying vessel with the head pointing forward carrying the charge. Resting on an inclined spar, the outrigger projected six feet outward from the gunwhale and downwards at an angle of about thirty degrees. Trials were carried out in a torpedo boat, six runs being satisfactorily carried out, the charge being ten to twelve feet deep when abeam. The gear was then transferred to the destroyer *Teazer*. Four runs were carried out at gradually increasing speeds, the spar breaking at 17.5 knots. Firing trials were then carried out using charges of 34.5 lbs of guncotton. *Teazer* was not damaged but the heel fittings to the spar were carried away by the recoil. The destroyer *Starfish* was fitted for further trials to be carried out in 1902, when the charge was increased to 51 lbs of guncotton and some improvement was made in preventing damage to the gear on firing. Although these trials continued for a number of years they were finally discontinued and general fitting of this gear to ships of the fleet was not proceeded with.

Whilst *Vernon* was carrying out trials with the swinging outrigger at Portsmouth, a method of using a towed torpedo against submarines was being developed by *Defiance* at Devonport. Experiments were carried out to tow the torpedo at a constant depth with varying speed. However, these trials met with no success and they were abandoned. The Royal Navy was destined to enter the First World War virtually unprepared for anti-submarine warfare.

The 1914 *Vernon* Annual Report reported favourably upon the Royal Navy's preparedness for war. Great progress had, indeed, been made in the development of torpedoes; the equipping of the fleet with wireless telegraphy was felt to be proceeding satisfactorly; British ships had good electrical arrangements. Few officers, however, understood how unprepared the Royal Navy was to face the German U-boats. The infant Naval Staff formed in the two years or so before the outbreak of war was still struggling to come to terms with the full impact of the revolutionary changes that had been in full swing for over half a century and which were still going on at an increasing pace. For too long the scene had been dominated by great personalities possessed of their own dogmatic opinions. On 4 August 4 1914 the time to test those opinions had come at last.

IN OCTOBER 1914 FISHER WAS RECALLED as First Sea Lord. He was soon writing, in typical style:

Our torpedoes seem to be filled with sawdust! There's a heavy reckoning coming to everyone connected with Vernon during the last four years. I hope to get a good many officers disgraced for it!

Charlton, the pre-war Assistant Director of Torpedoes was to be 'blown from a gun'. Fisher's outburst was both intemperate and unfair. If anyone was responsible for the Admiralty's inability to develop effective weapons it was he, who had so consistently opposed the creation of a Naval Staff. Nevertheless there had been torpedo failures, especially concerning torpedoes fired from submarines. Lieutenant Commander Godfrey Herbert in *D5* had succeeded in penetrating the screen of the German cruiser *Rostock* only to see two well aimed shots pass directly under the target without harming it. Ernest Leer, Captain of the *E4*, sighted the German submarine *U23* on the surface off Heligoland on 10 September 1914. His torpedo ran directly under the U-boat causing great concern on her bridge but failing to harm her. Then *E11*, commanded by Lieutenant Commander Martin Dunbar-Nasmith, sighted a German battleship: yet again the torpedoes ran under the target. Fisher was not the only senior officer to express dismay; Vice Admiral Sir David Beatty, commanding the battle cruiser force, wrote to Roger Keyes, the Commodore of Submarines:

It was a thousand pities you had not had submarines waiting for them. I sympathize with you and your fine fellows in the submarines for all their disappointments. What had gone wrong? I hear the damned torpedoes dived too deep.

These difficulties contrasted dramatically with the achievement of the German submarine *U9* in sinking the three armoured cruisers *Aboukir, Hogue* and *Cressy* in the afternoon of 22 September. The submarine threat to the Grand Fleet in its undefended base at Scapa Flow seemed so great that Admiral Sir John Jellicoe felt forced to withdraw for a time to Lough Swilly on the coast of Ireland. The torpedo threat had scored a significant strategical victory.

Despite the problems created by the departure of most of the establishment's officers to sea and their replacement by reservists, *Vernon* traced the main technical problem with the British submarine torpedoes to the single hydrostatic valve controlling the depth mechanism of the the older 18-inch Mk V* torpedo. But most submarines were fitted with later Mk VI and Mk VII* torpedoes which had double valves and any faults with these lay elsewhere, and *Vernon* advised the submariners that it was the way they treated their torpedoes that caused the difficulties. It was hard to maintain torpedoes in a good state of readiness when they were kept for any length of time in a submarine's flooded tubes; igniters became drowned and balance chambers and buoyancy chambers flooded (the specially designed Mk VIIIs were less prone to flooding). Instructions were therefore issued to exchange submarine torpedoes at least every three months and to increase the staff of depot ships for this purpose. These precautions solved the problems and *Vernon* was confident enough to call submariners' attention to the fact that it was undesirable to set torpedoes to run at a less than six feet owing to their liability to break surface should there be any sea or swell running.

The retired officers and men recalled to active service at *Vernon* had acquitted themselves well, and had not been panicked by Fisher's tantrums. The shortage of experienced staff and the need to retrain the men recalled to active service led to many problems, complicated by the Captain of *Vernon's* responsibility for the defence of the port. Captain Frederick L Field, a future First Sea Lord and *Vernon's* commanding officer for the first half of the war felt that this responsibility taxed the resources of the School to their utmost. The approach of winter weather aggravated an already difficult situation and revealed many flaws in the *Vernon's* organisation which had not been apparent in peacetime. It was fortunate that the emergency lieutenants, retired torpedo warrant officers and pensioner reserve higher torpedo ratings quickly responded to a brief course in modern torpedo work. Their ability to recall the practices and operation in vogue twenty or thirty years before proved invaluable, especially as many of the weapons and much of the equipment in the Reserve Fleet was of equally ancient vintage.

Hostilities also brought about a great increase in the use of wireless telegraphy which called for a stepping up of the training programme for telegraphists. The increasing need for the maintenance of electrical installations also led to a tremendous demand for skilled torpedo ratings. To cope with these huge training programmes, courses had to be severely curtailed and standards fell drastically as men had to complete their training at sea. The strain on *Vernon* emphasised the fact that certain activities of the torpedo branch had to be hived off, and in 1917 a new Signals Branch was formed with its own school in the Royal Naval Barracks at Portsmouth.

The Royal Navy's massively increased mining effort also strained *Vernon's* inadequate accommodation. No sooner had it been decided at the beginning of October 1914 to lay defensive fields at the southern end of the North Sea to protect the cross-channel communications of the British Expeditionary Force from submarines than trouble was experienced with mines exploding prematurely under the sterns of their layers. This problem was traced to the Mk II* pendulum pistols used and these were immediately withdrawn. The less sensitive Mk II inertia pistols remained in service until mid-1915. The improved Mk III Mine also had a premature explosion problem, if the firing lever became fouled in the mooring rope or sinker, damaging the shearing pin. The mine then exploded at a depth of five feet.

This problem was solved by the Apollo Safety Gear , named after the minelayer of that name. This was a soluble plug which prevented the firing mechanism from operating until the mine had reached its set depth. Originally the plug contained ordinary sugar. This caused a bizarre accident when a mine fitted with the gear exploded prematurely, happily with no damage to the minelayer or loss of life. The Board of Enquiry concluded that the sugar filling had been removed thus allowing the mine to be fired by a twisted firing arm. There was little doubt that mine handlers with a sweet tooth had been responsible. The sugar was replaced by less palatable ammonium chloride and the problem was solved. Another safety device added to the Mk III was the Woolwich Safety Gear which locked the firing mechanism for a few minutes after laying.

These precautions solved the problem of premature explosions satisfactorily and the *Vernon* Annual Report for 1917 proudly reported that over 10,000 Service Mines had been laid without incident. But there were also problems in making the mines detonate when struck by the enemy. Malfunction of the mooring rope safety gear prevented the firing caps of the mines from being fully pierced by the striker. If this were not enough the primers had a tendency to unscrew and fall out until set screws were introduced to pre-empt this problem. Trouble was also experienced with the parting of the mooring ropes until new techniques of laying with slack wires and the introduction of spring shackles between the mooring wires and mooring chains were introduced. *Vernon* carefully studied every failure, tried to rectify it and refused to face the fact that the MK III was a failure. Its firing mechanism was inherently faulty and would always be less efficient than the electro-chemical horn.

Vernon strongly challenged the view that German mines were in any way superior to the British. The 1915 report argued that:

The general superiority of the German mine had been freely stated in many quarters, and it has even been urged that the type should be adopted forthwith. Apart from the impracticability of adopting such a suggestion in war time, there is no evidence to show that the German mine possesses all the advantages claimed for it.
There is, in fact, evidence to show that it is not durable, and that failures of the firing gear are frequent. It must be remembered that any German mine found with its detonator still in place and its horn broken has failed to endure. There have been many instances of this.

Notable examples of the failure of German mines were given:

A fisherman came into Grimsby towing a German mine with all the horns knocked off, and explaining that as he had heard that these were the dangerous parts he had knocked them off with a boat hook. A fishing boat at night secured to what was thought to be a buoy but at daylight it turned out to be a German mine.
A mine was washed ashore on the Banff golf links ... much damaged with all paint washed off and four horns out of five broken...

Vernon was tragically wrong. The horned German mines were very effective. On 27 October 1914, during fleet exercises off the Irish Coast, the new battleship *Audacious* was shaken by an explosion which was first thought to be the shock from a collision at the stern. Soon the great ship was lying dead in the water. The remaining seven battleships in company, influenced no doubt by the recent loss of *Aboukir*, *Hogue* and *Cressy*, which had committed the cardinal error of stopping to give assistance, quickly dispersed leaving *Audacious* to attend to her wounds alone. The White Star liner *Olympic* appeared and tried to tow the battleship to a safe anchorage but all her efforts were in vain. The super-dreadnought wallowed and sank deeper into the water until it was considered necessary to abandon ship, and at 2100 there was

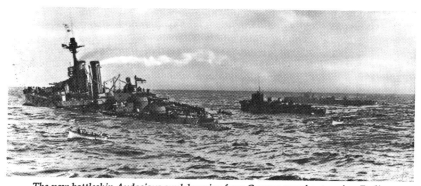

The new battleship Audacious sunk by mine from German merchant cruiser Berlin

an explosion, after which the 23,000 ton capital ship, which had been in commission for less than a year, disappeared. The mine had been laid by the armed merchant cruiser *Berlin*.

At the outbreak of war, Jellicoe had called for minesweepers to proceed ahead of the Grand Fleet, but soon realised that this would reduce its speed of advance to an impractical degree. He started, therefore, to press for the introduction of a minesweeping device which could be fitted to the units of the fleet themselves. Commander Cecil V Usborne of the battleship *Colossus* proposed trials of an apparatus which could deflect any mine not encountered head on: these were carried out with prototype equipment fitted to a picket boat, but though these were pursued with vigour, the materials available in the Grand Fleet proved unsatisfactory. Jellicoe then directed that the project should be discussed with Lieutenant Dennis Burney. When in command of the destroyer *Velox*, this young officer had submitted designs for an anti-submarine torpedo to be towed from destroyers. His device was to be fitted with hydro-vanes enabling it to be towed clear of the ship. Burney had been granted permission to experiment with the system and by the end of 1914 the preliminary experiments with wooden bodies were completed. Burney's anti-submarine sweep as fitted in destroyers was towed from the stern. Now it was redesigned as a minesweeping device towed from the bows and was given the name 'Paravane'. Paravane trials were transferred to *Vernon* where they proved entirely successful, and the device was fitted to all larger ships of the Royal Navy and to many merchant vessels.

On 1 November 1914, Jellicoe hastened from Lough Swilly to confer with the First Lord and the First Sea Lord about the serious shortage of trawlers, drifters and other patrol vessels for the protection of fleet bases. The Grand Fleet included only five minesweeping gunboats. As a result, the minesweeping force attached to the Fleet was steadily increased over the next two years. By July 1916 Scapa Flow and Cromarty boasted two flotillas of sloops and gunboats and two flotillas of a dozen trawlers each; in addition one flotilla of paddle minesweepers was based at Granton on the Firth of Forth to cover Rosyth based ships. During the war the total force of yachts, trawlers and drifters employed on patrol and on minesweeping duties increased from just over 700 in 1914 to 3,084 in November 1918. The gallantry and esprit de corps of the men who manned this huge force of auxiliary vessels were remarkable. Some were fishermen; others were merchant seamen of the Royal Naval Reserve or volunteers from the Royal Naval Volunteer Reserve. There were also retired regulars, amongst whom were several former flag officers who had volunteered to serve in lower ranks. 444 of these small ships were lost and 234 officers and 2,058 men gave their lives to keep the sea lanes open.

In the early days, the sweeping of moored contact mines was attempted by towing a ground chain from two spars set athwart the stern of the minesweeper. It was a time consuming and largely ineffective process and it soon became apparent that a wider loop was needed. This could be obtained by using a wire towed between two minesweepers with the help of otter boards used by trawlermen to keep open the mouths of their nets. This simple design frequently became snagged on rocks and wrecks on the seabed, but after extensive trials at *Vernon* this problem was overcome by the introduction of redesigned otter boards, known as kite otters.

Such was the basis of the British Type A sweep used for almost all the minesweeping carried out by the Royal Navy in the Great War. The sweepers themselves had to pass over the mines which meant that their draught had to be less than the depth of the mines below the surface, a condition which could only obtain near high water. In tideless waters with shallow mines this kind of sweeping was impossible. Minesweeping by the A sweep method was always a hazardous operation, but the gear was simple to operate, reliable and effective. It could be adjusted to any depth up to 50 fathoms or more without recovering the sweep.

Its chief disadvantages were that when sweeping in shallow water there was a possibility of the sweep fouling the bottom because of the sag of the sweep wire. Detecting the entry of mines into the sweep was difficult, mines could be dragged or even re-moored, especially when sweeping at slow speeds, and very efficient station keeping from the bridge and constant vigilance on the sweeping deck were necessary, while if the sweep wire parted the services of at least two, and possibly more, sweepers were lost until the situation had been rectified.

The principle of the A sweep was the same for all types of minesweeper. The kites by which the depth of the sweep was regulated were towed on a separate wire. The depth to which the kites dived depended upon both the amount of wire veered (i.e. paid out) and the speed of the sweeping ship; the longer the kite wire the deeper the sweep, the greater the sweeping speed the shallower the sweep. The sweep wire was coiled on a drum on a sweeping winch and, when sweeping, it was veered or hove in by the winch. With ships in pairs, the sweep wire started on the winch drum of one minesweeper, went through leads on deck, passed outboard through a fair lead or gallows block to the other ship and then inboard through a fair lead or gallows block to be secured to a steel slip. A snatch block was secured to the kite wire and then attached to the sweep wire in both ships, and the kite veered to the required depth. The sweep wire was serrated, a single strand of steel wire being laid counterwise to the lay of the ropes. This presented a rough outer surface to saw through mine mooring ropes as they ran along the wire. Sweeping was more effective against the tide especially if the sweepers could beat the tide by six knots or more. The A sweep was not too effective as a wire cutter and mines could be dragged into the centre of the sweep where they bumped against each other and exploded.

Later in the war an improved technique was developed, which could be used by one minesweeper alone. This was the 'Oropesa' sweep held at the correct depth by a kite-otter and taken out on the quarter of the sweeping vessel by another kite on its side or by a otter board supported by a float. At the end of the sweep a 'V' cutter severed the mooring ropes of mines that had not already had their cables cut by the sweep wire. This new sweep meant that operations could be carried out more easily, with greater reliability, and greater safety. High speed sweeping gear was also developed for use with destroyers.

Destroyer minesweepers had been first developed during the the Dardanelles campaign in early 1915. The Turks laid 344 German made 'Carbonit' contact mines in eleven lines to guard the straits and covered them with 74 light artillery pieces. Paravanes were not yet available and the difficult job of sweeping under fire was left to 21 former North Sea trawlers still manned by their fishermen crews. No more than seven minesweepers operated at any one time. The trawlers could not sweep against the strong Dardanelles currents; they had to get upstream of the minefields, join up their sweeps under fire and then come down with the current. When sweeping downstream the wires tended to ride over any mines they caught, and even if the sweeps caught a mine disposing of it under fire was near impossible. The minesweeping crews knew that the draught of their craft was greater than the depth of at least some of the mines and when a trawler hit a mine and sank on the night of 10 March the rest withdrew. The threat of the Turkish batteries was equally terrifying and on the following night the minesweepers simply turned tail and fled.

It was decided that the trawler crews should be stiffened by the assignment of a Naval officer together with a midshipman, a mate or warrant officer, a petty officer and a signalman. One volunteer was Lieutenant Commander WM Robinson, Torpedo Officer of the battleship *Vengeance*. He had already led a landing party to eliminate as many enemy batteries as possible, conducting himself with such valour that he was awarded the Victoria Cross. With such officers aboard the trawlers there was an improvement in the determination displayed by the minesweepers which were able to get well into the enemy minefields on the night of March 13-14. Despite much damage to sweep winches and kites, a little sweeping was accomplished but no amount of bravery and determination could achieve the impossible and the minesweepers once more were forced to withdraw.

It was then decided to try to silence the guns with a major fleet attack on 18 March. The inexperienced commander of the minesweepers thought that the area in the southern part of the Straits was clear of mines. Four had been caught and exploded there on the nights of the 15th and 16th but it seems to have been assumed that these were mines that had drifted down with the current . It is probable that a more experienced minesweeping commander would not have made that error. In fact, the mines were from a line laid parallel to the straits by the small Turkish steamer, *Nusret*, on the night of 7th-8th March. On the 18th, this one line of mines sank the French pre-dreadnought *Bouvet*, two British pre-dreadnoughts, *Irresistible* and *Ocean* and inflicted damage on the valuable battle-cruiser *Inflexible*. Once more the minesweepers were driven back by the Turkish batteries.

There was no alternative but to create a really effective minesweeping force. The trawlermen were allowed to return to the United Kingdom and 115 of them chose to do so. Some, however, decided to remain behind, determined to re-establish the reputation of the minesweepers' crews. Officers and men were selected from amongst the survivors of *Ocean* and *Irresistible* to man the trawler minesweepers but more important than that was the suggestion of Lieutenant Francis Sandford, Torpedo Officer of the sunken *Irresistible*, that destroyers be used as fast minesweepers. Sandford had commanded the only pair of trawlers to succeed in sweeping on the night of 13-14 March and knew all the difficulties facing the slow minesweepers. Orders were sent to Malta on the 19th for heavy sweeps to equip eight *'Beagle'* class destroyers which were converted by 4 April. Eight more *'Beagles'* were available by the 14th, and two days later eight fleet minesweepers requested from the Grand Fleet also arrived. In addition six *'River'* class destroyers and four torpedo boats were fitted with light sweeps for use as mine seekers, and a flotilla of picket boats was equipped with explosive sweeps. Captain Algernon Heneage, a distinguished torpedoman and commanding officer of the battleship *Albion* was given command of the minesweeping forces with Sandford on his staff. The light cruiser *Sapphire* became the mother ship for the minesweepers.

With professional leadership and the right equipment the mines could now be dealt with, but the Allies were committed to landing troops and the Dardanelles campaign had become hostage to the success or failure of operations ashore that soon degenerated into stalemate. When the landings took place at the end of April the destroyer minesweepers demonstrated what they might have achieved in March, but it was all too late and the minesweeping forces were denied the opportunity to make a decisive contribution to forcing the straits. Their role changed to that of supporting the land offensive.

For torpedomen, the failure of the campaign was a bitter pill, success had been so close wherever they had been involved. 18-inch torpedoes had been used by British submarines in a successful campaign to interdict Turkish supply lines in the Sea of Marmora. When one boat, *E15*, was marooned at Kephez Point, picket boats armed with small 14-inch RGF Mk X torpedoes were used to wreck her. These small torpedoes were also used in pioneering seaplane attacks on Turkish shipping, a milestone in naval aviation.

The Dardanelles fiasco was further proof of the power of the mine. It confirmed the wisdom of the decision to improve Britain's own mining capability. By 1915, *Vernon* was fully involved, not only in improving the troublesome British mines and their sinkers, but also in training the great number of officers and men required to lay them and maintain the new defensive minefields. In November 1914, the decision of 1903 to abandon coastal minefields was reversed as the strategic premises upon which had been based were altered by the German conquest of most of the Belgian Coast. Controlled mines had to be improvised using old 76 lb electro-contact mine cases with new 150 lb gun cotton fillings, until more 500 lb observation mines could be made; these re-appeared in 1915. A Directorate of Defensive Mining was established at the Admiralty and retired Torpedo Officers and ratings who remembered the old days before 1903 recruited to maintain the mines. Day to day watch keeping was provided by the specially raised and trained

'Royal Marine Submarine Miners'. The first controlled minefield was laid at Blyth in November 1914 with the mining party supplied by *Vernon*. It was soon followed by others at the mouths of the Tyne, the Tay, the Wear and at Hooton Head. Two electro-contact minefields were laid by January 1915 to defend the fleet anchorage at Scapa Flow.

In January 1915 the first offensive British minefield was laid in the Heligoland Bight by the cruiser minelayers *Apollo*, *Naiad*, *Latona* and *Iphigenia*. The following month, after laying more defensive fields in the southern North Sea, the slow cruiser minelayers were paid off and replaced by six faster and more capacious converted merchantmen. The best of the new vessels were the *Princess Irene* and *Princess Margaret*, 6,000 ton 23 knot coastal passenger steamers designed for the Canadian Pacific Railway; each could carry 500 mines. The others were the 12,000 ton liner *Orvieto* with a capacity of 1,200 mines, the 21 knot cross-channel steamers *Paris* and *Biarritz* and the 4,300 ton *Angora* originally employed on the Calcutta-Rangoon run and with a capacity of 300 mines. There was little offensive British minelaying while *Vernon* supervised the commissioning of the new minelayers and in the first half of 1915 only two fields were laid, between the Frisian Islands and the Danish coast.

Then disaster struck. On 27 May 1915, *Princess Irene*, temporary flagship of the Captain in Charge of Minelayers (CCML) was devastated by an internal explosion whilst in harbour at Sheerness. All on board were lost save one. She and her sister ship were fitted for the new 'British Elia' mines These had been developed by Vickers, based on the concept of an Italian officer, Commander Elia, but modified to prevent premature explosion. The

British Elia mines on quarter deck of the cruiser Ariadne. She was sunk by UC65 on 20 July 1917

Elia had been considered by *Vernon* in 1901 but was found to be too complicated. The Elia mine under trial was cocked by its own buoyancy when it was struck, and disconnected from its mooring rope. The British Elia incorporated a pistol activated by a firing lever beneath the mine. It was available in the early months of the war and made up half the Admiralty's orders for new mines. Not properly tested and laid at night, when its performance could not be monitored, it was used in the early 1915 fields. Trials were not carried out until June 1915 off the Goodwin Sands, using the newly converted trawler *Welbeckone*. To the horror of both the mine department at *Vernon* and the newly appointed and redesignated Captain (M), commanding the minelayers, it was found that the Elias had defective sinkers and did not take their depth properly. Offensive minelaying was suspended for two months and only defensive fields in the southern North Sea laid in July.

In August attempts to mine the Heligoland Bight began again but the operation got off to a bad start when German destroyers drove off *Princess Margaret* and and her escorting destroyers, damaging one of the latter. Despite this setback five more fields were successfully laid in the Bight in 1915 completing the line from the Lister Deep to Borkum Flat. A new mine, the DO, was also developed in 1915 based on a principle suggested by Lieutenant Sandford of Dardanelles fame. This was the 'oscillating' mine designed to rise and fall as its buoyancy was automatically controlled by a hydrostatic mechanism. It was only laid once and then not until January 1918 in the Heligoland Bight by a destroyer minelayer.

At the beginning of 1916, British mining policy was defined as the reinforcement of the offensive minefields in the Heligoland Bight on the routes leading north and west from the enemy's ports, and of the defensive minefields across the southern parts of the North Sea; the laying of deep mines, reinforced by mine nets, round the occupied part of the Belgian coast, and of deep and shallow independent minefields as required off the English and Scottish coasts, and mining the entrance to the Dardanelles.

If this programme was to be successfully carried out, it was vital to select the appropriate type of minelayer for the specific task. Minelaying in the Heligoland Bight was becoming increasingly hazardous for surface ships and special 'S' type mines were developed to be laid by submarine. These were equipped with German type Hertz horn firing gear; a submarine-laid oscillating mine the SO was also developed, although never used operationally. Six E-class submarines under construction were completed to carry twenty 'S' mines. The first, *E24*, was ready for service in February 1916, and after trials off Harwich she carried out her first minelaying trip to the Bight on the night of 27 March. Hers was a short career. On only her second mission she was lost in mysterious circumstances, probably to mines, perhaps her own. Three more submarines (*E41*, *E45* and *E46*) were commissioned as minelayers in 1916, and two more (*E34* and *E51*) in 1917. *E34* was also mined and sunk, on her twenty fourth trip to the Bight in July 1918.

In order to provide a more suitable surface vessel for Bight minelaying operations the new flotilla leader *Abdiel* was equipped to carry eighty mines and commissioned as a fast minelayer in March 1916. She and the submarines virtually monopolised the Bight operations for the rest of the year, although

Princess Margaret laid two fields and *Biarritz* one; a total of 17 fields with 1,782 mines were laid in the Bight in 1916. At the beginning of the year, the minesweeper *Gazelle*, converted to lay mines off the the Dardanelles, was replaced by *Perdita*, a 500 ton former merchantman, fitted out at Mudros to carry 100 mines. At home, in April, the unwieldy *Orvieto* was replaced by the handier 4,500 ton *Wahine*, formerly of the Union Shipping Company of New Zealand. Two more trawler minelayers were also commissioned in May and operational use of these little vessels began in the Spring of 1916.

The main minelaying task of 1916 was the 'Belgian Coast Zareba' a complex of mines, nets and buoys directed against German movements off the occupied coast. The nets were fitted with a new type of 65 lb electro-contact mine proposed by Wilson. The first fields were laid on Easter Monday, 24 April. The barrier was virtually complete by the end of May and was patrolled throughout the summer. The batteries energising the mines were housed in empty mine cases secured to the jackstays supporting the nets. Maintenance was far from easy in these enemy waters and it stretched the resourcefulness of the torpedomen involved.

By 1916, the minelaying programme had grown so great that it imposed a significant burden on both the munitions manufacturing capacity of the nation and *Vernon's* capacity to carry out development and trials. There was now not enough space in *Vernon* afloat, and it was decided that a mining establishment should be set up ashore, still as a branch of *Vernon* but at the Old Gun Wharf at Portsmouth. Rear Admiral Phipps Hornby was put in charge of organising the move which took place in December 1916 with the establishment of the 'Mining School'. This became responsible for the design, testing and development of mining materials. With ample space and a large new specialist staff concentrating wholly on the job and not distracted by diversions, a decisive improvement of Britain's mines now became a real possibility.

Much was known of German naval mines; four types were identified at the end of 1915 in the *Vernon* Annual Report. Mines were recovered by British minesweepers, often under the most perilous conditions. Two mines recovered by the minesweeper *Sagitta*, a converted yacht, were of more than average significance. The first was on the surface but still attached to its sinker, thus providing an opportunity for close examination. A motor boat was lowered to convey Stewart Garnett, the minesweeper's commanding officer, to the vicinity of the mine. Garnett, armed with a pair of pliers, leapt into the sea and swam to the mine. His examination revealed two wires exposed to the elements, and he promptly severed them. The mine was then lifted clear of the water by *Sagitta's* derrick before the detonator was removed and it was cut adrift from the mooring wire. The sinker side of the mooring wire was led to the windlass and an attempt was made to recover the sinker, but the wire parted. Then a second mine was found. The drill was repeated and the mine recovered, being rendered safe on this occasion by a rating, Alfred Evans. These turned out to be the latest German mines and the Mine Design Section drew up designs for a British copy, known as the H mine.

This was a great improvement on even the latest Mk IV version of the Service mechanical mine and, with the backing of the new organisation at the Gun Wharf, it was put into production in 1917 as the H.II, the first specimens being laid in the Heligoland Bight on 24 September 1917. This was part of a greatly intensified campaign in those waters. Doubts over the fate of the British mines laid in 1915-16 led to efforts being concentrated further out and the construction of a barrier from Terschelling to Horn's Reef. Mines were laid thickly and at shallow depths to catch minesweepers and patrol craft. German losses to British mines greatly increased during 1917, and the enemy minesweepers, which had little rest, began to suffer serious losses. The Germans became less and less inclined to venture far from their harbours; morale began to suffer and from the winter of 1917-18 onwards the Germans abandoned attempt to clear the minefields, concentrating their dwindling efforts on keeping narrowly swept routes open.

Other British mining initiatives were the construction of a mine and net barrage in the Dover straits in December 1916-February 1917. This was not a success however as the strong tidal currents displaced the mines and made maintenance of the barrage hazardous. After the loss of the tender *Albert* the mines were swept and the nets relaid in a new position to the south. Deep minefields were also laid in 1917 in the Channel, and in November 1917 construction began of a deep mine barrier between Folkestone and Cap Gris Nez; while deep and shallow fields were laid off the east coast. The minefields in the southern North Sea were also strengthened to protect the vital crossing to France, which was also defended by a new mined net system laid off the Belgian coast, supported by mines laid close to Zeebrugge. In the Mediterranean a deep mine barrier was laid to block the Dardanelles, mines were laid in the Mityleni Channel and in the Adriatic and a massive patrolled mine and net barrage established to block the Straits of Otranto. But despite all these efforts the movements of U-boats were not greatly inconvenienced.

To sustain this mining campaign required a greater allocation of vessels to the minelaying task. The old but large protected cruiser *Ariadne* was converted to a minelayer but her career was short and she was sunk by *UC65* off Beachy Head in July 1917. She was replaced by her sister *Amphitrite* in August . Eleven light cruisers and a dozen destroyers were fitted to act as temporary minelayers though not all carried out this role. Fourteen motor launches were fitted out as coastal minelayers, two for Mediterranean service, and nine coastal motor boats were converted to lay mines off the Belgian Coast. In October 1917 Captain (M) became Rear Admiral (M) with his headqurters at Grangemouth on the Firth of Forth.

In 1918, mining in the Bight was concentrated on blocking the swept routes. Submarines were used for this duty together with the minelaying destroyers of the Twentieth Flotilla, a mixed bag of a dozen boats of different classes formed in February 1918 and based at Immimgham . The flotilla's operations were often hazardous. On the night of 1-2 August 1918, the destroyers *Vanoc, Vanquisher, Vehement, Sandfly, Telemachus* and *Ariel*, each carrying forty H. II mines, sailed straight into a German minefield protecting the Bight. The first sign of trouble was an explosion and sheet of flame as *Vehement's* bows were blown off. Attempts were made to tow her clear but she had to be sunk. Then the older desroyer *Ariel*, last in line, hit another mine with catastrophic results. It exploded under the forward magazine and burst the boilers ; as the wreckage sank *Ariel's* depth charges, set for firing, also exploded, adding to the massacre of her crew. The four surviving ships retreated carefully out of danger. Unfortunately, this incident received insufficient study for it was to be repeated almost exactly less than a quarter of a century later.

1918 also saw the Anglo-American attempt made to lay a mine barrier from the Orkneys to Norway. Given the effort that went into this enterprise it was hardly a cost-effective use of resources. Work also went on to make the deep Channel barrier successful- which it began to be to a limited extent- and to lay shallow as well as deep fields to block the Dardanelles. The latter were successful, both the German ships handed over to the Turks,the cruiser *Breslau* and battlecruiser *Goeben*, being mined in late January, the cruiser fatally. Laying independent minefields off the British coast continued, one was a hundred miles long and fifteen miles wide, running from the coast north from Flamborough Head. New style controlled minefields using detector loops were established off Folkestone, Cap Gris Nez and Dungeness and the controlled minefields at Harwich and Scapa converted to this system. In the middle of 1918, a Rear Admiral Controlled Mining hoisted his flag at Dover. More minelayers were commissioned ranging, from the old battleship *London* to eight trawlers, for channel duty and five converted paddle steamers for the loop fields. Five improved L Class minelaying submarines were built.Twelve larger specialised minelaying CMBs were ordered and more merchantmen converted,but only seven of the CMBs were completed. By the end of the war there were 60,000 mines in stock, and 131,313 had been laid.

CMB minelayer at full speed

At Portsmouth, *Vernon* had played a continuous part in this massive campaign. The staff at the Gun Wharf began examining new and radical mine designs. It had long been appreciated that a mine lying on the bed of the ocean was far more difficult to sweep than a moored mine. If this type of mine was to be effective, however it would have to be exploded by the influence of the target rather than by physical contact. Towards the end of the war a new magnetic mine, called the M-sinker, was laid off the Belgian coast by destroyers of the Twentieth Flotilla. These first magnetic mines were of simple types employing a pair of compass needles which moved when a ship passed overhead, the mine exploding when the needles made an electrical contact. The four hundred M-sinker mines laid off Zeebrugge and Ostend each contained a charge of 1,000 lbs of TNT, the mechanism being set within a heavy concrete base unlikely to move in the strong tidal streams. An enemy destroyer and a submarine are known to have been sunk off Zeebrugge at this time, but it is not certain whether the minefield of M-sinkers was responsible. These mines were considered to be unsweepable and were, therefore, fitted with a time controlled self flooding device which renedered them harmless.

The Mining School was also investigating the possibility of producing an acoustically influenced mine. Experiments were well advanced by August 1918 with the intention of using acoustic units in moored mines. Soon all this valuable work was to be set aside and, in the financially stringent peacetime atmosphere, Britain allowed her lead to be dissipated. The Germans exploited these developments and carried on where the British had left off, and produced a deadly and efficient weapon for which Britain was completely unprepared at the outbreak of war in 1939.

Mine warfare was *Vernon's* greatest growth industry during the First World War but her more traditional activities went on also. All aspects of the establishment's activities were emphasised by the war. Within the huge Grand Fleet, the foundation stone of Britain's command of the sea, *Vernon's* graduates were preoccupied with torpedo and electrical duties. In the detached Battlecruiser Fleet at Rosyth the senior torpedo adviser on Admiral Beatty's staff was Commander the Hon. AR Plunkett, a founder member of the Naval Review and who later changed his name for inheritance reasons to Plunkett-Ernle-Erle-Drax. He monitored all reports coming in from the ships of the Battlecruiser Fleet and made certain that his Admiral and the Admiralty were fully acquainted with the state of torpedoes and electricity in that vital force, the spearhead of the entire Grand Fleet. He was undoubtedly a leading figure in the development of torpedo work in its widest sense during the crucial years of the war. He was quick to point out to Beatty if the torpedo efficiency of the fleet was being adversely affected by an attempt to rotate maintenance personel through various specialisations. The torpedo, he wrote was a very delicate instrument:

and requires to be handled by highly specialised men. To get the best result all really competent men who are now handling torpedoes should continue to do so, and should never do anything else, until the end of the war. The routine change rounds necessitated by the 'Jack of all trades' policy is most detrimental to efficiency.

Beatty scribbled 'What policy is this!?' and Plunkett got his way.

He next turned his attention towards the improvement of torpedo work in the three light cruiser squadrons attached to the battle-cruisers: the First equipped with newer '*Arethusa*' class ships and the Second and Third with pre-war '*Towns*'. The '*Arethusas*' had twin 21-inch tubes on each beam. Plunkett insisted that these be placed under a proper system of director control to work out the best angle for them, the correct range to set on the torpedoes (not more than 80-90 per cent the full range of the weapon) and the correct instructions for the Captain to turn to bring on the sights. The Admiralty were asked by telegraph to supply four directors, one for each ship. This was the first occasion on which an attempt had been made to centralise the control of the torpedoes and was the forerunner of all future torpedo control systems. The older cruisers had submerged torpedo tubes, one on each beam, and Plunkett had to work out how these could best be used at speed. He was fortunate that he had the powerful backing of Sir David Beatty in seeking Admiralty approval for the new methods.

Plunkett's electrical responsibilities were no less onerous. Electrical damage control had been given very little thought. In a memorandum issued in 1914 he had drawn the attention of commanding officers to the serious implications that could result from any dynamo damage, flooding in a dynamo space or a shell striking the ring mains. In order to familiarise ships' companies with electrical damage, he instituted a periodical test which required all dynamos to be stopped for five minutes. Experience obtained from these tests enabled alternative arrangements to be considered for lighting, telephone, fire control and firing circuits. Magazine lamps were fitted; at least one was to be kept burning continuously when action was imminent. Oil and candle lamps were also fitted and always to be kept burning when ships were firing their main armament. The Battlecruiser Fleet owed a great deal to Plunkett's thoroughness.

An interesting comparison can be made between the capital ships of the opposing navies in the First World War. The Royal Navy operated with an electrical capacity of only 750 kilowatts, even in the latest battleships of the 'Royal Sovereign' class. By 1914, the latest German battleships had achieved a rating of 2,040 kilowatts using six dynamos; the two German 15-inch gun battleships (Baden and Bayern) of 1916 were fitted with eight diesel dynamos with a total capacity of 2,400 kilowatts. As a general rule the ships on both sides during the First World War operated electrical systems which were severely flawed. Damage to any part of the ring main or to other circuits involved the maintenance staff in physically exhausting repairs, often working in areas which were extremely difficult of access. Almost all the equipment was vulnerable to damage by salt water and required constant vigilance.

The main clash between the battlefleets occurred off Jutland on 31 May 1916. This is not the place for a detailed account of the well chronicled battle, though it was fought with an awareness of the threat of underwater weapons. Vernon's main interest was in torpedo work that proved sadly inefficient. British destroyer attacks were carried out with great bravery but little tactical skill. Successes were scored, notably forcing the German battlecruisers to turn away at a vital moment just before they joined the main German fleet, and in sinking one of the least capable enemy battleships in the confused night melee as the Germans escaped. Nevertheless, the general performance was unsatisfactory. Neither side had employed effective tactics for the deployment of torpedoes in their destroyers, a failure which would greatly influence the development of ships, material, tactics and training during the twenty years before the next world war.

The torpedo armament of the British destroyers and their control arrangements had not been designed with mass attacks by torpedo carrying craft in mind. The 1917 Annual Report of the Torpedo Schools contained a lengthy analysis of the results of torpedo attacks by both sides. It makes dismal reading for it was the fear of torpedo attack, and not the actual use of torpedoes, that had had a significant effect. The successes scored by torpedoes were few but it was the Germans who were the less effective. Their destroyer flotillas carried out seven daylight attacks but only one torpedo, and that from the damaged cruiser *Wiesbaden*, hit a British capital ship, *Marlborough*. During the night action they were even less successful, being in the main unable to locate the British capital ships. The British flotillas consisted of some eighty ships, but many of them were new vessels not at the peak of efficiency. Their main training priority had been gunnery action defending the fleet from torpedo attack, and not in mounting torpedo attacks of their own.

About eighty torpedoes were fired by each side during the battle, but each regarded the successes obtained as a poor return for the effort. The Germans blamed their lack of success on their torpedoes which, they believed, had been set to run too deep. *Vernon's* analysis indicated that, although the British attacks had been pressed home gallantly, they had been unco-ordinated and delivered in insufficient strength. In future destroyer torpedo attacks would have to be carried out in force, deploying the largest possible number of torpedoes. The lesson was taken to heart and resulted in a great deal of time being spent between the two World Wars in training the British fleet to fight fleet actions more effectively.

After Jutland an officer of the 12th Destroyer Flotilla, serving in *Maenad* in the early hours of 1 June, wrote:

At about 2.15 a.m. we turned, and everyone was at pretty high tension waiting to sight the Germans as they appeared out of the haze. At 2.20 we sighted them and attacked. As soon as the attack started, one lost all sense of excitement, because things were happening. The Germans opened a fairly heavy fire on all of us, and right at the beginning hit the ONSLAUGHT, *which was quite close to us. We fired one torpedo at a German battleship of the 'KONIG' class about 4,000 yards off, but I do not know whether we hit. One torpedo from the flotilla certainly found a mark. The whole attack only lasted about five minutes, by which time we passed this division of German ships and lost sight of them.*

The destroyer fired only one torpedo in this important attack; indeed, only six of the sixteen boats of the flotilla fired, loosing off in all seventeen 21-inch Mk IIs. The flotilla was, however, lucky in that at least one found its mark; not, however, on one of the latest German dreadnoughts but on the old pre-dreadnought *Pommern* which blew up.

The German intention at Jutland had been to lure the Grand Fleet into U-boat traps to reduce its strength, and the High Sea Fleet came out again in August 1916 to repeat this gambit. Although U-boats sank two British cruisers, and a British submarine torpedoed a German battleship, the Germans were confirmed in their opinion that their only chance of victory at sea was to re-open the unrestricted U-boat campaign against merchant shipping that they had been forced to abandon because of American political pressure in 1915. This campaign came close to bringing Britain to her knees in 1917.

British efforts to best the U-boat were not well co-ordinated; several establishments were engaged in parallel research and development. The main establishment for the development of hydrophones was at Hawkcraig in Scotland, commanded by that inventive Torpedo Officer Commander (later acting Captain) CP Ryan, recalled to service from the Marconi Company. This establishment came under the new Anti Submarine Division of the Admiralty, set up to deal with the developing U-boat crisis at the end of 1916. By this time the work at Hawkcraig was beginning to bear fruit. The Mk II directional hydrophone was ordered in large numbers in 1917 for fitting in most patrol craft. By then Hawkcraig had been entrusted with the training of hydrophone operators and control officers. Next in importance to the training facilities there was the new Listening School and Experimental Station which had been established at Weymouth in August 1917, as HMS *Sarepta*. It was moved to new buildings at Portland in April 1918.

Some work on active echo ranging methods of detecting submarines was carried out at *Vernon* by Professor Horace Lamb, but this was moved to the new Signal School at Portsmouth in 1917. Work went on at the Gun Wharf on passive hydrophones but the main role of the Mining School in defeating the U-boat was its responsibility for the development of anti-submarine weapons. Trials at *Vernon* in 1916 showed that there was very little to be gained from continuing with the use of towed anti-submarine charges; the depth charge was the way ahead. By the beginning of 1917, two patterns were being supplied to the fleet; the Type D which contained a charge of 300 lbs of TNT and Type D* carrying 120 lbs. Unfortunately, both these types were in such short supply that only four of the former could be issued to each destroyer and only a few of the latter to selected trawlers and other patrol craft. The War Office was demanding more and more ammunition for the Western Front and was reluctant to agree to the diversion of munitions production capacity to meet naval demands. Conscription was having its effect; labour was short and where heavy work was concerned, female labour, which had been drafted in, could only partially compensate. It was not until the end of the year that depth charge production could provide thirty or forty for each destroyer. The shortage of depth charges was not the only problem. The early hydrostatically operated pistols exploded at such a shallow depth that full charge Type Ds could only be used by ships which could operate at high speed. A modified pistol was introduced which enabled relatively slow vessels to release depth charges without endangering themselves; the type D* with its reduced charge could now be abandoned.

In order to increase chances of hitting or at least menacing their targets, depth charges had to be delivered in complex patterns. A 300 lb depth charge had to explode within 14 feet of a submarine to ensure its destruction, or within 28 feet to force it to the surface. Firing in patterns required mortar like depth charge throwers. Early in 1917, Thornycroft delivered the first depth charge throwers to *Vernon* for trials, and they quickly proved a success. Deliveries began in July and by the end of 1917 they had been fitted to nearly all destroyers, one on each quarter. In the end, however, it was not these weapon developments in themselves but the reluctant re-adoption of the convoy system that defeated the German submarine offensive.

The slow but sure working of the convoy system tried the patience of those who wished for more 'offensive' solutions to the submarine menace. Such an officer was Roger Keyes, appointed to succeed Bacon in command of the Dover Patrol. He planned an assault on Zeebrugge with the object of blocking the channel leading from the Flanders U-boat bases. The story of the assault, carried out on St. George's Day 1918 is well known. Many trained in *Vernon* played their part in what was an heroic but, at best, only a partially successful assault. James Nathaniel Short, who died in 1983 aged 96, had a successful career as a torpedoman. He joined the Navy as a seaman boy, and progressed through the lower deck to Warrant rank, finally being promoted to Lieutenant Commander. At the time of the raid on Zeebrugge he was a Gunner(T) serving in the destroyer *Warwick*, flying the flag of Vice Admiral Sir Roger Keyes. *Warwick* was at the head of a flotilla of twelve destroyers towing two old C-class submarines each loaded with 5 tons of amatol, and accompanied by upwards of thirty motor launches and several coastal motor boats armed with torpedoes.

From the upper deck of the destroyer, Short witnessed the effect of the German gunfire on *Vindictive* as she approached the mole to disembark the landing party: he also saw the abortive attempts to position the three old cruisers *Thetis, Intrepid* and *Iphigenia* as blockships in the channel. The landing force had failed to silence the German guns, and terrible casualties were inflicted upon the men manning these three old blockships. Motor launches were able to bring the survivors from *Intrepid* and *Iphigenia* to *Warwick*, but all hands were lost as the *Thetis* disappeared beneath a deluge of fire from the shore batteries. Most of the survivors were terribly wounded and were given what aid that could be provided from the limited resources of the destroyer. Short remembered that Keyes spoke to each of them, assuring them that their efforts had not been in vain and that the assault on Zeebrugge would be recorded in naval annals as a great and glorious achievement. He recalled that the Admiral had promised that after the raiding parties had withdrawn from the mole, an opportunity would be given to see what sort of a dent their torpedoes had made in it. Unfortunately, *Warwick* was unable to fire her torpedoes, her tubes having become jammed after she had suffered mine damage to her stern.

The antithesis of blocking enemy submarines in their bases was preventing them from hitting ships with torpedoes, by trying to develop that time honoured concept, the anti-torpedo net. *Vernon* was responsible for testing this concept. The first attempt was the Actaeon high speed net developed by the torpedo school of that name. The object of this net was to deflect torpedoes downwards so they would pass underneath a ship, or to catch them by their propellers. A ship fitted with these nets was required to steam at not less than 8 knots, with the fore foot of the net held down by an otter board. Kites were attached to the centre and the after end of the net, and a footrope was weighted at intervals. Actaeon nets were first fitted to a merchant ship, *Navigator*, which was attacked by a U-boat in February 1918, as she made her first voyage with them after the trials by *Actaeon*. On the way down Channel from Sheerness the merchantman was struck amidships by a torpedo which exploded in the net. The ship sustained some buckling of the plates and a slight leak but she proceeded under her own speed to Weymouth, Devonport and then to Cardiff where the damage was repaired at a cost of £500.

The Admiralty was so impressed that orders were given for a number of merchant ships to be fitted. One of these, the *Stockwell*, whilst proceeding fully loaded from the Tyne was attacked by a submarine. The nets did not prevent her manoeuvering under full helm to avoid the torpedoes. Later the cutters, fitted to the deflecting wire on the foremost kite, cut adrift a German moored mine. The order was now given for two hundred ships to be fitted with the Actaeon high speed nets, but by then the end of the war was in sight, and by the time the armistice was signed only fourteen ships had been fitted.

Trials were also carried out with the Turnbull screen, developed by Mr. WR Turnbull, Chief Inspector of Messrs. Frederick Sage and Company of Peterborough. This was a screen of interwoven canvas and piano wire. It was kept out by booms with the foot kept down by kites, and was designed to detonate the warhead of a torpedo on contact with the net. On its *Vernon* trials, using an 18-inch Mk IV torpedo, the net was penetrated on each occasion and the torpedo struck the ship; it was duly abandoned as useless.

Coastal motor boats have already been mentioned in relation to mining, but they had been intended to carry torpedoes, and *Vernon* had played a major role in their development. It was in November 1915, that several officers suggested that racing hydroplane speedboats could be adapted to carry torpedoes. After discussions with J Thornycroft Limited, trials were carried out by *Vernon* to find the best method of launching the torpedoes from these flimsy craft. The original idea was that the hydroplane, on coming into range of the target, should turn stern on and discharge the torpedo towards the target over the stern. This idea was soon rejected on the grounds that the boat might run out of range before the torpedo was discharged and that good depth keeping would be difficult owing to the low velocity of discharge. A more practical method was soon found. The torpedo was launched tail first over the stern so that the discharged velocity was the speed of the boat less the velocity of the impulse needed to discharge it. Successful trials were carried out from an 18 knot boat, followed by further trials with a 30 knot hydroplane; the 18-inch Mk VIII torpedoes used ran successfully. A particularly encouraging result was that the depth taking was excellent.

Orders were placed in January 1916 for thirteen 40 foot boats, each carrying one torpedo and having a speed of 25 knots. In these boats the torpedo, resting on its side lugs on rails in a trough in the stern, was discharged by firing a charge of 1,000 grains of cordite into an explosion vessel. The gas from the explosion vessel forced out a ram which engaged the head of the torpedo and forced it down the trough. More boats were ordered, some with more powerful single engines capable of over 35 knots, and others with twin engines, being 55 foot boats capable of over forty knots once both the torpedoes had been released.

The first CMBs were intended for use in the Heligoland Bight but, because of bad weather these operations were never carried out and the boats were transferred to the Dover Command where they were employed against enemy vessels operating from Ostend and Zeebrugge. CMBs were vulnerable from air attack and best employed at night. On one occasion aircraft bombed Zeebrugge to smoke out the enemy destroyers, whilst the CMBs lay off the harbour entrance waiting for them to come out. On the first occasion on which this ploy was carried out, one German destroyer was sunk and another damaged. It was after the Armistice, however, that CMBs carried out their most successful attack, in an assault on the Bolshevik Fleet at Kronstadt in September 1919. After this they were sold or expended as targets and only one, *CMB12*, survived to 1935 to hand on the torch to the new generation of British Power Boat motor torpedo boats which returned to *Vernon* that year.

A more important high speed method of torpedo delivery, one that was to have a fundamental influence on naval warfare, was the aircraft. After the early experiments with 14-inch weapons orders were placed with Shorts for long range torpedo seaplanes to carry a larger, specially designed 1,000 lb 14-inch Mk IX torpedo. Development work took place at Felixtowe. By October 1916 the Mk IX was undergoing trials and that far-seeing torpedoman Commodore Sueter conceived of the idea of a higher performance aeroplane to carry the new weapon flying from ships. An order was placed with Sopwith forthwith and the new machine first flew in June 1917. Beatty, in command of the Grand Fleet since the end of 1916, was a great enthusiast for this aircraft, which could attack the enemy fleet in the harbours it was reluctant to leave, and asked for two hundred as soon as possible.

At the end of 1916, a torpedo seaplane school was started up at the seaplane base at Scapa Flow, but the need was for a training base for the crews of the new torpedo aeroplanes. Beatty preferred Rosyth as his main fleet base, and so the torpedo aeroplane base and school was established at East Fortune near the Firth of Forth. During April and May 1917, torpedo ratings were sent there from *Vernon*. Running of torpedoes was started that July, the sands at Bellhaven, near Dunbar, being used as a landing ground from which to operate aircraft and train the pilots.

Unfortunately, production of the new Sopwith (T) torpedo bomber was delayed. Christened the Cuckoo, because it was intended to lay its eggs in other people's nests, it had been designed in close consultation between Sopwith and Sueter. Although the order for the first hundred production aircraft was placed with Fairfields in October 1917 manufacture was delayed by the switch from the excellent 200-hp Hispano engine to a heavier, and less reliable, British Sunbeam Arab power plant. Shortly afterwards, another order for sixty Cuckoos was placed with the Pegler company and in February 1918 a further order for fifty with Blackburn, but deliveries did not begin until September 1918 and the first squadron embarked on board the new carrier *Argus* on 19 October 1918, less than a month before the Armistice.

The *Vernon* Annual Report of that year commented that:

The delays in production were to a great extent caused by the change from the Hispano engine to the Arab engine. The original drawings were also in many cases incorrect. This, combined with the fact that two of the firms making these machines had no previous aircraft experience, caused serious delays, with the result the machines were not ready for operations with the Fleet until the winter of 1918, when the fine weather had been lost.

With seven torpedo aeroplane squadrons planned, work began to set up another torpedo aeroplane school, nearer to *Vernon's* at Gosport. The new establishment would also house a torpedo aeroplane experimental squadron. In the meantime, to obtain proper test results, four Short 310 seaplanes carried out trials at Calshot in February 1918 to obtain records and information about the behaviour of torpedoes on entry after release from various heights and at various speeds. As was to be expected, a number of violent dives by the torpedoes were experienced but the trials team expressed satisfaction with the majority of runs. Only three torpedoes were lost, all because of the failure of the pneumatic release gear. These trials proved that a torpedo dropped at air speeds in excess of 70 mph or from higher than 20 feet was liable to incur damage and would be unlikely to run true.

Commander Peter Bethell's description of the problems concerned with the dropping of torpedoes from aircraft accurately summarises the difficulties that had to be solved:

Compared with the destroyer and submarine, the torpedo aircraft launches its missile at a fairly short range; the designer of the weapon is able, therefore, to economise in air-vessel weight, but other serious problems confront him. The worst is obviously that of gross poundage; but he cannot economise here by 'adding more lightness' in the traditional manner, because the aerial plunge is by far the most severe and testing form of torpedo discharge. The tactical demand is always for higher and faster dropping, and quite apart from the increased structural strength entailed, this calls for a separate study of the torpedo's aerial trajectory. The centre of pressure is usually in front of the centre of gravity; hence, unless some compensation is applied, the torpedo will go in tail first, a mode of entry that it resents most bitterly. This tendency was originally countered by fixing a wooden drogue abaft the propellers, which brought the centre of pressure aft and also prevented a deep dive on entry; the drogue was released automatically, either by a nut which unscrewed from the propeller shaft or by a dashpot mechanism.

In late 1917 it was felt that the normal 170 lbs warhead of the Mk IX torpedo would not be totally effective when used against German battleships. As a temporary measure its warhead was increased to 250 lbs but work began on a successor to the Cuckoo to carry the Mk VIII submarine torpedo with its 320 lbs head. The initial designs for this specification were none too promising being slower and clumsier than the handy Cuckoo.

The problems with naval aircraft reflected the general weaknesses of Britiain's aircraft procurement system. The Lloyd George Government was committed to solving these difficulties and felt a unified air service was the best way to go about it; Sueter and most of the naval airmen agreed. On 1 April 1918 the Royal Naval Air Service became part of the newly formed Royal Air Force, which assumed responsibility for the provision of all service aircraft, including those for the Royal Navy. Immediately the development of a vital component of Britain's naval capability became subject to the inevitable inter-service squabbling. The Admiralty would not provide officers for instructing RAF personnel in torpedo duties and *Vernon* had to train new RAF torpedo officers to do so. Before the war's end the preliminary training of torpedo pilots, what had originally been carried out in *Vernon*, had been transferred to the new lecture rooms and torpedo parting shop at RAF East Fortune. The RAF also began to train its own mechanics to maintain torpedoes and to supplement the twenty former RNAS torpedo ratings transferred in April.

Vernon's pioneering work in aircraft torpedoes contrasted strangely with the old hulks still afloat in Porchester Creek. A Torpedo Officer who qualified in the early months of 1918 described the torpedo school, a little inaccurately as :

... an old three-decker hulk which lies amidst the mud at the upper end of Portsmouth harbour. In actual fact she is four old ships - three connected together by bridges, and the fourth lashed alongside. For a big instructional school she suffers from the grave disadvantage of not being alongside a jetty.

This same officer remarked that work was fairly strenuous but very interesting. Nobody cared how hard they worked during the week for weekends were very generous- in usual contrast to the Gunnery School at Whale Island, where the weekend was severely curtailed. There was no doubt that the peacetime rivalry between *Vernon* and *Excellent* remained unaffected by the war years. Long torpedo course officers continued to bait the long gunnery course officers, asserting that the motto of the gunnery officer was, 'Guns, gaiters and guff', whilst the torpedomen remained, 'Cool, calm and collected'. Raids upon each others' establishments continued in the most friendly manner, almost as if the war did not exist.

From Porchester Creek, or from the Gun Wharf, the war at Portsmouth was chiefly visible in the form of small escort vessels shuttling in and out of the harbour to accompany the troop convoys across the Channel at night. Every evening they left and every morning at about 11 am they returned to fuel, ready to return to their cross Channel duties that evening. These small craft worked on a three week schedule, followed by a week's rest. Indeed, the pattern of life at Portsmouth became a routine of almost peacetime regularity. The escort vessels kept to their daily schedule and the dockyard workmen arrived as usual for work every morning. *Vernon's* log reflected steady, and sometimes monotous, daily activities which were untroubled by enemy action.At Portsmouth it was a very different war from the one which would call for such great sacrifices two decades later.

The staff at *Vernon* in that last year of the First World War was still dominated by officers and men called up for the duration. Sometimes these members of a former generation found difficulty in keeping up to date with new technology, and students who were often more conversant with the subjects than their teachers. On one occasion, an elderly Gunner was lecturing to a class of newly joined electrical artificers on the subject of 'simple cells'. One young man, bent upon exposing the limitations of the old man's knowledge of the subject, raised his hand and asked for a fuller explanation of alternating current. The elderly instructor was more familiar with seamanship than the theory of electricity. He was used to giving instructions to a boat's crew in strident terms and so, after a moment's reflection, he raised his voice to a full quarter deck roar, determined to silence his tormentor:

The exact understanding of an halternatin' current ain't rightly understood by only scientific men; but I sez as 'ow it's a positive current a-nippin' along a wire follered at a short relapse by a negative current a-nippin' along after it, but one don't never catch the other no how, savee?'

The heckler did not signify that he understood but he was effectively silenced!

The old *Vernon's* days were clearly numbered. The Mining School at the Gun Wharf, comfortable and with plenty of room to expand, was in sharp contrast to the ageing conglomeration of formerly proud warships squatting on the mud of Porchester Creek. *Vernon I's* once 'up to date' instructional facilities were badly in need of modernisation. *Vernon III*, the former *Warrior*, still provided a spacious hull for wireless telegraphy instruction, a large factory and a variety of other workshops but the third ship of the group *Vernon II*, the former *Marlborough*, had become overcrowded. In 1916, extra living accommodation was provided by the former second class cruiser *Furious*, now renamed *Forte*, which was moored alongside *Vernon III*. *Vernon IV*, the original frigate, *Vernon*, was now the practical workshop, moored on the east side of the creek, the sheds on her upper deck remembered for their silhouettes against the early morning light. The officers and men in this increasingly ramshackle empire looked with envy towards the distant lower reaches of Portsmouth Harbour and the inviting prospect of being more comfortably accommodated at the Old Gun Wharf, where the Mining School had been provided with fine new buildings, including a workshop and acetylene welding store, a mine assembly building, a bomb store, a generator house and a theatre. Surely after the war ..?

During the four years of that spreading conflict, 'The Great War', though much shorter than the long wars against Revolutionary and Napoleonic France, a radical change had taken place in the whole structure of the Royal Navy. Its leadership passed from the old Victorian and Edwardian oligarchy to an emerging staff structure which stretched from the Admiralty into every ship and establishment of the fleet. The Torpedo Branch and *Vernon* could not escape these changes. Before 1914, officers' careers rested on individual prowess and leadership, but the bitter experiences of the War had demonstrated the need for system and organisation. The new generation of officers was in no way less capable, and still included men of great character with the usual leaven of idiosyncratic individuals, but they would be harnessed in a staff organisation where the whole was greater than the sum of its parts. The hard won lessons of the war would be systematically learned as far as the financial stringecies of peacetime would allow. Sadly, shortage of both money and personnel would mean that some wartime lessons would also be forgotten.

The Torpedo Branch could contribute many fine officers to the new era. Herbert Richmond, promoted Commander in 1903 after only six years as a torpedo lieutenant and the Navy's leading intellectual and founder of the Naval Review; Dudley Pound, trusted and diligent staff officer, if somewhat prone to over centralisation; Algernon Willis, described by John Ouvry, the distinguished mining expert, as 'very clever, rather up in the clouds, very capable indeed'; Plunkett-Ernle-Erle-Drax, a foil to Richmond, and always searching for improvements to weapons, tactics and training as well as towards the more efficient use of electricity. These men and their colleagues would have the responsibility of distilling the experience of one war and preparing the Royal Navy for another.

WHILST THE GERMAN HIGH SEAS FLEET was surrendering in the Firth of Forth on 21 November 1918, an equally significant, if less public, surrender of the German submarines was taking place at Harwich. The High Seas Fleet had been the supreme threat, and the Grand Fleet, swinging at its moorings in Scapa Flow and the Firth of Forth, the only answer to it. But, under cover of those main fleets, the grim and equally important struggle against the U-boats had made the Grand Fleet's successful containment of the High Seas Fleet far less relevant. These momentous events seemed to be a satisfactory end to hostilities and for a while no-one suggested that Germany could again pose a threat to the British Empire. Naval policy makers and planners, therefore, were facing a more complicated and difficult situation than ever before. The types of forces they had to consider, and the kinds of threats against which they had to plan, were becoming more diverse. Providing all the necessary equipment would be expensive and obtaining resources difficult.

Only nine months later, on 15 August 1919, the Cabinet decreed that in the next financial year, the three services should base their estimates on the assumption ' that the British Empire would not be engaged in any great wars during the next ten years'. As Roskill opined:

This rule, which was wholly empirical and was not based on any scientific data, was to exert profound influence on all aspects of naval policy for the next decade and more.

Worse, it was:

in 1929 made automatically self-perpetuating i.e. on any given day it was to be assumed that no major war would take place for ten years.

This ludicrous notion was not abolished until late in 1932.

1914-18 had, supposedly, been the war to end wars and all politicians accepted the need to reduce the defence budget to the acceptable minimum. The Navy vote was grudgingly approved by Parliament and the Admiralty had perforce to give careful consideration to the manner in which it was spent. The lessons of war, so far as they had been learnt, would have pride of place in these considerations, but it was far from clear which were the most important and what were the correct conclusions to be drawn. Both the submarine and the new influence mine posed deadly potential perils to Britain's maritime lifelines but they were not necessarily uppermost in the minds of senior officers of the post-war Royal Navy. The main naval threats were now posed by the United States and Japan, both of whom deployed traditional battlefleets. Jutland had demonstrated considerable weaknesses in British doctrine and practice in fleet actions. It was hardly surprising, therefore, that naval planners concentrated on considering the manifold lessons of that battle and agonising upon the reasons why the German Fleet had not been destroyed in that epic encounter, all too often to the exclusion of thinking about newer problems or new aspects of other older ones.

The Navy's principal aim had still to be the containment and, if possible, the destruction of an enemy's fleet, the great columns of battleships supported by scouting lines of cruisers and defended by destroyer screens. Massed destroyer torpedo attacks upon opposing lines of battleships were regularly carried out during fleet exercises: never again would British destroyers perform as disappointingly as they had that night off the Jutland bank in the summer of 1916. The peril of the submarine and the drudgery of anti-submarine and mine warfare, though not entirely forgotten, scarcely competed with the imposing image of the battleships and the prospect of fleet actions fought with their great guns.

The Admiralty was convinced that one of the main lessons of the Great War was that the materiel departments were out of touch with the needs of the users. The shortcomings in guns, shells, torpedoes and mines, revealed by the test of action, caused a major revision in the organisation of the Naval Staff with the aim of getting it right next time - for a few in the service did not believe that the conclusion of the recent conflict had brought a lasting peace. The specialist schools had a key role to play in this process, carrying out sea trials and representing the opinion of the users to the relevant departments in Whitehall. The old *Vernon* was increasingly unsuitable for this enhanced role. The lack of space in the hulks for the installation of modern machinery, their unsuitability for scientific work, their generally inadequate accommodation and sanitation, their limited access, only by boat, and their rotting hulls made the move ashore imperative. The Gun Wharf site where the Mining School was already established seemed the obvious choice for a new *Vernon*.

The Gun Wharf was Portsmouth's ancient naval ordnance depot, dating back to 1662; the original buildings had been built on land reclaimed from the sea. At the beginning of the nineteenth century, during the Napoleonic Wars, a 'New Gun Wharf' was built to the south of the old. The Gun Wharf was originally a War Office responsibility but, with the growth of Admiralty responsibility for its own ordnance, naval stores began to appear. In the early 1890s, the Royal Artillery was turned out of its 'New Gun Wharf' and a strict line of demarcation established between the Naval 'New Gun Wharf' and the War Office's 'Old Gun Wharf'. Each had its own staff and Chief Ordnance Officer. When the Mining School was established on the New Gun Wharf during the First World War it took over the large gun shed next to which a new 'bomb store' and mine assembly building were constructed. The mine design department was established in the former smithy and the workshops built around it.

In 1919, the decision to move the rest of *Vernon* ashore was made and the entire Gun Wharf was taken over for the Torpedo School. As the War Office moved out of the Old Gun Wharf site, work began in 1921-2 to rebuild old store rooms into new ratings quarters and to build a wardroom and warrant officers' accommodation. On the New Gun Wharf side the old Sea Armoury became the Church and School building and the old Barracks Block the Electrical Experimental Department and Mining Lecture Rooms. In December 1922, a Portsmouth General Order designated the area the '*Vernon* shore establishment'. The same order named the North Pier '*Donegal* Pier', the South Pier '*Marlborough* Pier' and the area between '*Vernon* Creek'.

Almost as if their essence was being transferred ashore, the wooden hulks rapidly deteriorated. *Donegal* sprang a leak and began to sink at her moorings until she was rescued by the pumps of the dockyard tugs. This added to the pressure to move ashore, and on 2 October 1923 another order duly commissioned the shore establishment as HMS *Vernon* and authorised the commanding officer, Captain JD Allen CB, to transfer his pennant ashore. The new Whitehead accomodation in the south western corner of the Old Gunwharf was still not quite ready and the Whitehead Department continued to use the *Warrior* hulk, which was given back her old name. Traditionally the name of the establishment had also to be that of a real ship upon whose books the officers and men would officially be borne. The trawler minelayer *Strathcoe*, used as a tender by the new establishment was accordingly re-named *Vernon* for this purpose.

For the old frigate *Vernon*, it was the end of the line. She was towed back to to Woolwich, where ninety years after her launch there she was broken up at Castle's Yard. Her spirit was, however, preserved in some of her timbers which were included in the new shore establishment. Her figurehead was mounted in the grounds of the new *Vernon* with those of *Ariadne* and *Marlborough*. The panelling in the east wardroom ante room was cut from the frigate's main deck beams and stanchions; in the Mess itself the gallery was made from the mahogany poop and poop rails from *Marlborough*. In the new chapel, the altar was constructed from the *Vernon's* beams and the ridell-poles and altar rails from her capstan bars.

Donegal went, like *Vernon* , to the breakers yard but *Marlborough* followed her two predecessors to the bottom. In December 1924, the old first rate of 6,300 tons left Portsmouth under tow bound for Osea Island, Maldon, to be broken up. On board was a skeleton crew of seven men. Off the Owers Lightship, a violent gale swept down the Channel engulfing and flooding the old ship and leaving the two attendant tugs unable to save her. Tragically, the end came too quickly for the crew to be saved. Four of the skeleton crew, including the master, Mr F Simmons, were swept away. Another victim was the mate, Mr F Wheeler whose grandson, Mr A Wheeler, later served as a hall porter in the *Vernon* wardroom. Three survivors were rescued by the tug *Vanquisher*, whose master, Captain H Pascoe, reported the heroism of one of her crew, Cecil Stebbings. Ignoring the risk to his own life, he swam in the raging sea to a large piece of wreckage to which his uncle, James Stebbings, was clinging, having secured a line from the tug to his uncle and together they were hauled aboard.

The hulk *Forte* went for scrap but *Warrior* remained at Portsmouth for another five years. The Whitehead accommodation was completed within a few months and *Warrior* was declared redundant in March 1924. She was offered for sale but no one seems to have been interested in her scrap iron and she was converted into a mooring hulk for oilers. On 13 March 1929 she left Portsmouth for Llanion Cove near Milford Haven arriving two days later to rest in gentle obscurity for over fifty years. Then she was restored to her previous glory and placed on public view at Portsmouth, close to *Victory* and the Gun Wharf.

In order to maintain the traditions of the Torpedo Branch the new *Vernon* was filled with the names of ships that had played a part in the development of the torpedo in the Royal Navy. The wardroom block was *Ariadne*, the warrant officers' quarters *Defiance*, the CPOs' and POs' quarters *Actaeon* , the ratings quarters *Warrior*, the canteen *Hecla*, the sick bay *Florence Nightingale* and the mining buildings *Vulcan* and *Polyphemus*. By such means was the new generation reminded of its predecessors.

The move ashore from the *Vernon* hulks to the Gun Wharf had been accompanied by a review of all the attendant craft required to support the development and instructional programmes. The old *Vesuvius* was at last paid off after some forty-five years of service; her name lived on as the name of the Whitehead Experimental and Instructional Workshops. In her place the *Vernon* Flotilla was formed: by the end of the 1920s this consisted of five destroyers, the former monitors *Media* and *Minerva* and five trawlers. Four small 'M' class monitors were converted into minelayers in the early 1920s; one served as tender to *Defiance*, another at Malta and the other two with *Vernon*.

Great improvements in the training facilities and in the living conditions for seamen resulted from the move ashore. The conditions in *Vernon* afloat have been described by a leading torpedoman, AA Sewell, who returned from the China Squadron in 1921 to qualify as a Seaman Torpedoman in the *Vernon*, then still afloat in Porchester Creek. The deckheads seemed rather low and any daylight which filtered through to the broadside messes came from the old gunports. However, lighting was reasonably good being supplied from 16, 32 and 100 candle power carbon filament lamps. The young seamen were told not to grumble about the comparatively low deckhead

' . . . and so back to negative'. Elecdtrical instruction in Vernon circa 1920

heights because Nelson's Captain Hardy of the *Victory* had been a man of over six feet and he had coped very satisfactorily with much lower deckheads for very much longer than the ratings in the *Vernon* complex!

Sewell was enthusiastic about the standard of instruction, commenting that it started him (like many *Vernon* torpedomen) on a professional career as an electrician: he finished as chief electrician in a large factory. Much of Sewell's torpedo training was carried out aboard the destroyer *Vanoc* and in the light battlecruiser *Courageous* lying in reserve 'up the trot' in Porchester Creek before her conversion to an aircraft carrier in 1928. No doubt, like many seaman trainees, he appreciated being able to go ashore to the bright lights of Portsmouth and Southsea. The only interruption to this tranquil existence came during the great coal strike of 1921-22 when all instruction in *Vernon* ceased on the formation of armed platoons for the protection of the wireless station on Horsea Island. The platoons were accommodated in tents and carried out their duties in watches as in ship's routine. Their main responsibility was to guard the masts of the wireless station, which were vulnerable lattice frameworks. However, the interruption was short lived and after a few days they returned to the daily routine of *Vernon*. Sewell left *Vernon* in 1923 and returned when the move ashore had been made to what he described as a 'vast improvement on the old ships'.

Another junior torpedo rating of great character, Joe Davis, who retired from the Navy in 1960 as a Chief Petty Officer, Torpedo Anti-Submarine Instructor. He witnessed the transfer of the northern Gun Wharf site from Army to Navy control. As they departed, the Army left large quantities of furniture, desks, chairs and the like which were quickly 'acquired' by the Admiralty. Most of the buildings were dirty, shabby and full of rubbish. Duty watches and volunteers came ashore from the hulks to rectify the situation. There were skirmishes between soldiers and seamen as the latter inspected their new domicile and work places. Men under punishment, who would normally be undergoing vigorous rifle drill, were only too pleased to down their rifles in the dog watches and grab a paint brush. Even torpedomen from ships in the harbour helped out.

A warrant officer of the Army Pay Corps was sitting at his desk quietly writing when a leading torpedoman in charge of a small working party 'whipped' his desk and chair. The warrant officer lodged a protest but in vain. The working party retired silently. The warrant officer emptied his desk and withdrew mumbling dire threats. The furniture so acquired was taken to the Mining Department where it joined the long list of War Office property which had been 'borrowed'. Protests were made by the Army but an inspecting Torpedo Officer was heard to say that torpedomen were an uncouth lot and he would see what he could do about it. The matter was conveniently forgotten. The Army presence quietly faded away; and the main gate was taken over by the Royal Marine Police. All was now bustle and enthusiasm as buildings were prepared, cleaned and painted. As the various departments came ashore, life became increasingly busy. Every available man turned out to get the departments ready, whilst the long suffering men under punishment cleaned out and refurbished the very primitive sanitary arrangements. (They were modernised shortly afterwards.) It was a great tribute to Joe Davis and his fellow members of the lower-deck that they worked so hard to convert the *Vernon* ashore into what he described as: 'A home from home for sailors returning from two and a half years in ships'. The enthusiasm and high spirits are apparent in the pride with which he wrote: 'In October 1923, our Captain's pennant was hoisted with the white ensign flying, *Vernon* was ashore.'

Davis' observations did not end there. He went on to record that by the end of 1924 *Vernon* had settled comfortably into her peacetime routine. A Sea Cadet Unit was formed and, when an official band was refused, *Vernon* formed its own Blue Jacket Band; an achievement which was to do much for the morale of the establishment and the branch. The customary relaxed *Vernon* approach to discipline was maintained amidst the busy routine and the comings and goings-courses for seamen torpedomen, leading torpedomen and torpedo gunners mates; working parties; tenders' crews; drafts; mining trial parties; tube trials, net laying parties, torpedo trials parties and many others. This was a stabilising period when the football teams were formed, the wardroom staged plays, and Chief and Petty Officers had their dances and childrens' parties. According to Joe Davis, *Vernon* was a happy place in those peacetime years; it was then that the phrase ' a mild rebuke is better than an irksome task accomplished' was first heard.

One new recruit, Patrick Budge, who later became a Rear Admiral and one of the Royal Canadian Navy's leading torpedomen, welcomed the prospect of undergoing a seaman's course at *Vernon*. He described the establishment as: 'A new school in a particularly bright holiday type city so different from the dingy city of Chatham and the Edwardian barracks of HMS *Pembroke*.' It was indeed a change from the cramped quarters in his previous ship, the cruiser *Despatch*. Instead of sleeping and eating in the same mess deck, seamen were now accommodated in bright and airy dormitories fitted with beds, though some, including Budge, insisted that the beds were not as comfortable as 'slinging a hammock'! it was difficult for a young seaman to get used to these new conditions. Budge said: 'They did not provide the closeness of a mess where one ate and slept and was responsible for its cleanliness.'

The impression gained by Budge and other ratings who served at *Vernon* in the 1920s was that although discipline was not unduly strict, a vigorous routine was in force. The men were paraded daily at 'Divisions'; prayers were said and hymns sung and, afterwards, the ship's company marched down the road for 'colours'. Yet, on the whole, the relaxed atmosphere that had grown up whilst *Vernon* was afloat still remained ashore and, unlike in many similar establishments, the parade ground at *Vernon* was not sacred: it could be crossed at any time regardless of rank or rating. But Budge remembered that there was not enough contact between officers and men; the only officers encountered were those in charge of the courses. Nevertheless, there was a happy atmosphere with no chasing by a 'barrack guard'. Torpedomen disdained spit and polish; but there was always the danger that a relaxed attitude would degenerate into slackness and that the motto 'Swing it 'til Monday' would become a reality. The fact it never did is demonstrated by the clear evidence that the maintenance of the electrical installations in units of the fleet was so efficiently carried out by the torpedo branch. Often, in the smaller ships, only one seaman torpedoman was provided to maintain the ship's high and low power systems. It befell Budge to be one of these men.

He was drafted to the minesweeper *Badminton* at Portland where, in addition to his responsibility for the electrical installation, he was also required to man the 20-inch searchlight and to be on deck at every minesweeping exercise to learn minesweeping, including all the relevant flag signals.

During the General Strike of 1926 the daily routine of *Vernon* was again interrupted by the need to organise parties for general duties around the area, protecting vulnerable points, operating docks, guarding volunteers unloading foodships, working pumping or oil fuel stations and doing many things for which naval officers and men had not been trained. Ships of the flotilla attached to *Vernon* were sent to ports and strategic points around the coast to provide emergency electricity supplies and to carry out many other duties such as the distribution of yeast for bread making, and the movement of petrol from Thames Haven to distributing centres up river. Ratings from *Vernon* assisted in the manning of grain elevators, running the machinery of cold stores and operating the switchboards in power stations. Torpedo ratings took over thirty power stations including the vital installations at Ipswich and Gravesend. It was a strike breaking operation about which some naval ratings felt unhappy but though the miners held out for months, the general strike did not last long and all concerned were glad to return to the more agreeable surroundings of *Vernon*.

By the end of 1927 *Vernon* ashore had become the torpedoman's spiritual home to which most were glad to return. If anything, life became even more relaxed. The march to 'colours' every morning had ceased and, for the officers especially, life at *Vernon* became a comfortable and routine affair. The work of the Mining, Whitehead and Electrical Departments went on against a background of ceremonial and social occasions. In June 1927, *Vernon* was selected to mount the Royal Guard at the south railway jetty for the return of the Duke and Duchess of York in the battlecruiser *Renown* from their tour of Australia and New Zealand. The Blue Jacket Band performed at wardroom theatricals, the annual gymkhana and at the cricket matches which were played on the village green at Ebernoe, north of Petworth, the home of Admiral Heath who had qualified as a Torpedo Officer in 1887. *Vernon* as the home of 'Navy electrics', organised famous childrens' parties which were the envy of all other naval establishments in the command.

The increasing complexity of warships' electrical installations led to pressure for specialist electrical personnel. In 1918, a Directorate of Electrical Engineering was set up at the Admiralty, and in 1920 the Field-Waistell Committee (one officer the captain of *Vernon* 1914-16, the other Captain 1919-1920) recommended the introduction of an Electrical Branch. In the prevailing atmosphere of economy a complete new branch seemed inappropriate but a new type of specialist non-commissioned technical rating was an urgent necessity that could not be ignored. During the War, RNVR Electrical Officers had been recruited to assist Torpedo Officers in their electrical duties and it seemed probable that in the event of another war that process would have to be repeated. In the absence in peacetime of these electrical engineers, Electrical Artificers had perforce to fill a large and important gap. In 1922, the first such artificer apprentices were being trained at *Vernon* . The establishment's Electrical Department also carried out considerable experimental work and progress was made in improvements to the ring main systems in warships.

In 1924, an Admiralty committee again recommended the formation of an Electrical Branch with a Director of Electrical Engineering of Vice-Admiral rank, but the time still did not seem right to spend any money on this change. The new Electrical Artificers, however, soon proved their worth. Some qualified as Warrant Electricians and together they became a critical component of the Torpedo Branch throughout the inter-war and wartime years. Without them, torpedomen alone would not have been able to keep the weapons, control equipment and power supplies operating.

The professional standing of *Vernon's* Electrical Department rapidly obtained an enviable reputation both within the Navy and in the electrical industry. This was particularly true of its experimental and trials work. During 1921, trials were carried out to test the fire hazards posed by electric cables. The traditional electrical casing was easily melted by cordite flames: in some cases all insulation was consumed and cables were burnt through to the bare wires which could cause serious explosions. Explosions and cordite fires at Jutland had been blamed by the Grand Fleet's gunnery report on burning cables. It was concluded that if the flame could be prevented from coming into contact with the cable no damage would result from cordite blast, and the cables would not act as burning fuses. It was, therefore, decided that light steel guards should be fitted over the cables where they were liable to be exposed to cordite flames.

A little later representatives of electric light manufacturing companies visited *Vernon* at the invitation of the Admiralty to inspect the apparatus designed for the shock testing of metallic filament lamps. Indeed, throughout the 1920s a tremendous load devolved upon *Vernon* for investigation into a mass of low and high power electrical installations and equipment, ranging from synchronous systems, magnetic release firing gear and counter drum instruments, to rubber jointing materials and the use of anti-gas respirators with telephones. Trials were carried out to improve the general arrangement of dynamo supplies to the ring main; and trials were instituted to improve the power supples to searchlights and the performance of those essential aids to night actions.

It was concluded that the principal functions of the searchlight were:
(a) Illumination of the target between the firing of a star shell and the burst of the shell.
(b) General use when low clouds prevent the star shell being effective.
In view of the improvement of star shell for target illumination, it was decided to reduce the number of searchlights mounted in ships. Only four searchlights were now fitted in capital ships and two in cruisers but they were of greater power and the 48-inch projector became standard equipment. This searchlight could be used against aircraft, although it was designed primarily for horizontal or surface work. As the decade came to an end trials were being carried out to dispense with motor generators, searchlights in future taking their supply from the ring main system through a resistance.

The creation of the Signals Branch with its own School in Portsmouth in 1917 meant that *Vernon* no longer had responsibilities for wireless telegraphy. The Signals Branch also took over primary resposibility for underwater sound communications although there continued to be liaison with *Vernon* because of the latter's continued responsibility for hydrophones. The Mining

School maintained a Submarine Detection Section which continued to develop hydrophones and alternative forms of underwater detection and ranging. Ryan's establishment at Hawkcraig was closed down in 1919 and he moved to the Gun Wharf as Head of this Section for two years before he retired. In 1923, the Admiralty Experimental Station at Shandon on the Gareloch closed and its staff was relocated at the newly established Admiralty Research Laboratory at Teddington and the Signal and Mining Schools. These three establishments continued to work on submarine detection but *Vernon's* main task was the more mundane improvement of existing passive instruments rather than the development of the new active 'asdics' which was later to revolutionised submarine hunting. In the move ashore of the entire *Vernon* establishment, the Submarine Detection Section separated from the Mining Department, but its autonomous existence was short lived and in 1924 it seems to have been absorbed into *Vernon's* general scientific staff. It may be no coincidence that in October of that year Captain SD Tillard, the Captain A/S, the officer on the Naval Staff with responsibility for anti-submarine activities, wrote a paper complaining about the dispersion of A/S activities and the tendency for small research groups such as *Vernon's* to be lost in larger establishments.

In 1925, Tillard's submission was considered by a Committee at Portsmouth upon which *Vernon* was represented by Commander JP Farquharson; the Chairman was Rear Admiral WR Napier. The Napier Committee recommended asdic and hydrophone research be concentrated at the Anti-Submarine School at Portland. *Sarepta* , the 'Listening School', had closed in 1919 and its duties were assumed by the First Anti- Submarine Flotilla, a heterogeneous force of a whaler, PC boats and drifters, with the old cruiser *Gibraltar* as depot ship. The attempt to dispense with shore accommodation was not a success and the school ashore re-opened in 1920. It became an independent command, HMS *Osprey*, in 1924, and thanks to the Napier Committee's recommendations the home of virtually all research and development on anti- submarine detection. However, *Vernon's* Mining Department still had full responsibility for the development of anti-submarine weapons. The concentration of acoustic detection work at *Osprey* had positive results and the Royal Navy became a world leader in this area with its active 'Asdic' equipment, named for the Allied Submarine Detection Investigation Committee set up in 1918. There was, also, a negative impact; the divorce of sensor and weapon development meant that insufficient attention was given to the interface between asdics and depth charges. This created problems later that were only solved by the amalgamation of the Torpedo and Anti Submarine Branches, informally during World War Two and eventually in the setting up of the combined branch thereafter. For the time being the Type D depth charge seemed a satisfactory enough device.

The establishment of a Chemical Warfare Department compensated for the loss of hydrophone development in 1927. Soon the new department was carrying out a series of trials which led to the redesign of the gas respirator and alterations to British warships to exclude gas from between decks areas. Where it was necesssary to maintain continuous ventilation, such as boiler rooms and engine rooms, drills were carried out to familiarise ship's companies with the use of respirators under operational conditions. Using a 'Dart' torpedo bomber simulated mustard gas attacks were exercised at sea and trials were also carried out with chlorine gas released from cylinders on the quarter deck of the battlecruiser *Tiger*. Valuable information was obtained concerning the travel of gas clouds over the sea and training in mustard gas decontamination was introduced at *Vernon*. Other trials involved the production of vertical smoke curtains from aircraft, the use of smoke float bombs dropped by aircraft and the wider use of smoke.

With the move ashore of the rest of *Vernon*, the Mining School became the Mining and Anti-Mining Department of the Torpedo School. With its own experimental department it was responsible for research, development and design of all the Royal Navy's underwater weapons other than torpedoes as well as finding countermeasures to them. It inherited from the war a wealth of technical data and stocks of over sixty thousand efficient contact mines. However, the over-ambitious nature of much Allied mining in the war, especially the poor results obtained from the vast numbers of mines laid in the great Northern Barrage and in the Dover Strait, fostered doubts about the operational value of the mine. Fortunately, the pessimists did not prevail and, in spite of a considerable reduction in the staff of the Mining Deprtment, an efficient nucleus of scientific and design staff was retained under the Superintendent of Mine Design. The Admiralty was far from uninterested in the subject. Scarce resources were invested in a completely new 27 knot minelayer built on light cruiser lines. *Adventure* was commissioned in 1927 and replaced the last of the large wartime minelayers, *Princess Margaret*, sold in 1929.

Priority was given to improving the performance of the standard moored contact mine, the H.2. Trials were carried out with a new, more buoyant shape intended to reduce the tendency of the mine to dip in a current and to prevent it behaving erratically in heavy seas. Lighter mooring wires of the same strengths as those used hitherto were produced, thus further reducing the tendency to dip and allowing the depth to which the mines could be laid to be increased from 3,600 to 6,000 feet. A new mine resulted from these developments which became the standard British moored mine, the Mk XIV.

In 1890, a replaceable mine charge had been designed but the H.2 mine had retained a fixed explosive filling. Now a detachable charge case was incorporated in the Mk XIV which allowed for two different sizes of charge to be used, weighing 500 lbs and 320 lbs respectively. The smaller charge was needed to increase the air space in the mine and hence the positive buoyancy when laying the mine in great depths or strong tides. In the 1920s, priority was given to the contact mine rather than to the antenna or the influence mine. The antenna mine, a mine exploded by contact with a long antenna connected to it, was not developed except to examine its effectiveness and to investigate ways in which it could be swept.

Although the capabilities of influence mines had been demonstrated in the final stages of the Great War, so had their shortcomings. The M-Sinker was very prone to premature explosion, caused by the time taken for the mine's needle to settle down after laying. A safety mechanism had been added, consisting of a soluble plug which prevented the batteries being energised until it was estimated the needles would be settled. This protected the minelayers but it did not stop premature firings. On the second occasion when M-Sinkers were laid operationally fifty per cent of the field exploded before the minelaying flotilla had left the neighbourhood. The answer had not been found by the end of the war and the Mining Department still had much to do to perfect the firing mechanism of the British magnetic mine. Under these circumstances it was not surprising that magnetic mines were suspect.

During his time in the Anti - Submarine Detection Section Ryan encouraged the development of acoustically operated mines. He designed an acoustic attachment for buoyant mines, the CW Type-1, which was accepted into service. *Vernon's* scientific staff recruited the assistance of two Fellows of the Royal Society, Professors Horace Lamb and Augustus Love. Experiments were started to determine the acoustic signatures of submarines and surface vessels. A great deal of valuable information was obtained but the development of the acoustic mine was delayed by the Admiralty on the grounds that the magnetic mine would fire underneath a vessel under almost all conditions but the acoustic mine would generally fire astern and might do no damage.

After the decision to concentrate upon magnetic rather than acoustic mines, it was agreed that the buoyant magnetic mine should take precedence over the ground magnetic system. This decision was influenced by trials involving a former German U-boat, during which it was ascertained that an explosive charge of 500 lbs had a rapidly diminishing effect outside a range of 20 feet from the hull of the submarine. It was calculated that in the likely areas of operation of the U-boats they would seldom be proceeding at less than 20 feet from the sea bed. It followed that a non-contact anti U-boat mine should be of the buoyant moored type. A further consideration was that the magnetic moored mine overcame the problems of dip, caused by the variation in the depths of tidal waters and strong currents, which often rendered a contact mine ineffective. The decision, which reflected Britain's preoccupation with the mine as an anti U-boat device, meant that little attention was given to the magnetic ground mine and few trials were carried out to ascertain the effect of the explosion of a ground mine beneath surface ships. Had these trials been carried out, other than against sections of various types of ship, the devastating effect known as 'whipping' of the hull would have been discovered before the start of the next war in 1939.

Throughout the 1920s, work continued to establish the magnetic characteristics of ships and submarines, but full scale trials were not carried out because insufficient funds were made available to complete these investigations or to develop the ground magnetic mine. In spite of all these frustrations, what was learnt about the magnetic characteristics of ships and the design of magnetic mines proved to be of value during the German magnetic mining campaign in 1939.

In the development of all types of mine it was necessary to observe their performance. For this purpose a large mining trials tank was constructed at the Gun Wharf, 30 feet in diameter and 60 feet high. For the life of *Vernon* it remained a feature of the landscape of that part of Portsmouth. It was completed in June 1919 and very quickly proved its value in a large variety of trials. Trials could be carried out in a few hours which had hitherto taken days at sea. By means of portholes (seventy in number) it was possible to observe precisely the behaviour of material under test conditions.

The decision to make *Osprey* responsibile for submarine detection did not extend to detector loops. These were a simple systems of harbour defence which had been used increasingly in 1918 instead of traditional controlled minefields. A loop consisted of a multicore cable on the seabed. When a ship or submarine passed over it the induced current was recorded on a galvanometer in a shore station. Allied to a row of mines laid down the centre of the loop this provided a very effective means of harbour defence against surface vessels and submarines. The destruction of *UB116* in an attempt to penetrate Scapa Flow on 28 October 1918 was a classic example of this technique.

On 30th June 1924, a loop was laid at Portland from the trawler *Vernon*.This operation was accorded the maximum publicity within the Atlantic Fleet. The Fleet Torpedo Officer and as many torpedo officers as could be spared were embarked to see the first loop laid in the correct position in one day. A total of 8,000 yards of cable had been coiled in the hold of the trawler for laying by a party consisting of a Gunner (T), a Chief Petty Officer (Torpedo Gunner's Mate) and six Able Seamen. A Lieutenant Commander (T) was in charge of the operations. A second loop was laid the following day and the whole system was connected to a control station by three o'clock on 2nd July. A successful trial was carried out and a rocket was fired by the watch keeper in the control hut when the loop was activated. It was an impressive demonstration.

A team from *Vernon* was sent to investigate the working of loop detection and the changes in the magnetic state of vessels near to, and south of, the magnetic equator. The *Vernon* team took records of the magnetic signature of the cruiser *Dunedin* at Spithead as she passed over the defence loop. A further set of records was taken when *Dunedin* arrived at Sydney in Australia. Similar trials were carried out with the cruiser *Southampton* running over the loop at Trincomalee and again immediately on her arrival in the United Kingdom. From the analysis of these records it was possible to correlate the ship's magnetic signature with change of latitude and longitude.

'Department M' also turned its attention to the development of a sweep which could be used to clear buoyant magnetic mines. This was achieved by the conversion of an Oropesa sweep to take advantage of the principle that an electric current in a wire creates an electric field around it. Wires of the correct type, supplied with an alternating current and towed on the Oropesa principle, provided a magnetic impulse sufficient to actuate the magnetic mines of the period. By 1930, although under-funded and under-manned, the Mining and Anti-Mining Department at *Vernon* had made notable progress.

New challenges also confronted the Whitehead Department but it did not have the same authority as Department M possessed in mine warfare, or in the way in which the Royal Naval Torpedo Factory at Greenock maintained its supremacy in torpedo design. It was originally planned to give *Vernon* the same leading role in torpedo development as it possessed for mines but the Torpedo Experimental Department never received the required funds. Nevertheless an impressive torpedo testing range was established at the pier at Stokes Bay to the west of Portsmouth Harbour. A large compressor house and camp to acommodate sixty men was built. On the pier itself was a torpedo workshop fitted with overehead transporting runways, three ton lifting purchases and a narrow gauge railway system running through the shop to a three ton lifting crane on each side of the pier. It proved a useful and essential facility for experiments and the sea trials of the new weapons.

The Naval Staff's requirements for new and improved torpedoes led to the reconstitution in 1920 of the Torpedo Design Committee. Formed in 1887 it had last reported in 1904. The new committee was made up of representatives of the Director of Torpedoes and Mining, the Director of the Torpedo Division, the Director of Armament Supply, the Captain of *Vernon*, the Superintendent Royal Naval Torpedo Factory, the Superintendent of Torpedo Experiments and the Chief Inspector of Naval Ordnance. It was required by its terms of reference to clarify the staff requirements, co-ordinate experiments and prevent overlapping. In meeting these responsibilities it was authorised to co-opt the assistance of the Admiral (Submarines), Captain-in-Charge Coastal Motor Boats and the Air Officer Commanding Coastal Area, all key torpedo users.

When the committee first met on 15 September 1920 the newest weapon in the Royal Navy's torpedo armoury was 21-inch Mk V introduced in 1918. This torpedo had been designed to satisfy demands from sea for a torpedo capable of 29 knots for 15,000 yards and of being fired from existing surface tubes. It had been designed with negative buoyancy at ranges below 7,000 yards and was considered to be unsatisfactory for use in peacetime because practice runs were usually carried out at ranges of less than this figure; torpedoes would therefore be lost. The Committee directed that future designs should combine greater ranges with positive buoyancy. There were also considerable stocks of 21-inch Mk II* and IV* torpedoes. These were used by the latest submarines, which were equipped with tubes of this calibre. Work was already in hand to improve the ranges and speed settings of these older weapons.

Inevitably, thoughts turned to radical proposals to achieve the vastly increased ranges and speeds of torpedoes which were demanded. The first experiment involved the 'mocking up' of a 21-inch Mk IV* torpedo to a diameter of 26 inches from which data was obtained for the design of torpedoes of larger diameters than hitherto. As a result of these trials it was decided to proceed with the construction of experimental 24.5-inch torpedoes for use in the new battleships *Nelson* and *Rodney*.

An increase in size alone could not produce the torpedo improvements required and experiments began in great secrecy to produce new and improved forms of propulsion. Experiments were carried out to increase the ratio of fuel to air but this only resulted in a deposit of soot in the generator. Attention then turned to the quality of the air supply. The air vessel of the heater torpedo accounted for one third of the total weight of the weapon, but the air it contained was made up of only 21 per cent oxygen. The obvious answer to these problems was to increase the amount of oxygen and to find a more volatile fuel. Experiments were begun at *Vernon* in the early 1920s.

By 1926 the development of the 24.5-inch torpedo had reached the stage of manufacture. During November and December 1926 the Mk I underwent a series of trials from the destroyer *Vanoc* in the Clyde. A year later, when this giant enriched air torpedo was issued to *Nelson*, the concept of the 'big' torpedoes was no longer popular as their massive weight made them difficult to handle and unsuitable for use with collision heads. Hence only a limited number were manufactured for use in the battleships *Nelson* and *Rodney*.

In parallel with the enriched air fuelled torpedoes an examination was made of the use of hydrogen peroxide as a low pressure oxidant. It was, however, the use of enriched air which continued to find favour. Such was the secrecy which surrounded these trials that they were not reported in the *Vernon* Annual Reports until they were well advanced. By then, the enriched air 21-inch torpedo had completed its acceptance trials and was designated the 21-inch Mk VII. Sea trials were carried out in 1928 in the new cruisers *Berwick, Suffolk, Australia* and *Canberra* (the other three 'Kent' Class ships carried Mk V torpedoes with specially strengthened tails to cope with the ships' high freeboard). The Mk VII operated satisfactorily and in 1928 was accepted into service being issued to later eight-inch cruisers. Like the 24.5-inch MK Is, the 21-inch Mk VIIs were not outfitted with collision heads and, therefore, were not run to hit in the practice mode.

The Mk VII also shared the unpopularity of the larger enriched air weapon. Enriched air was a dangerously unstable substance and if it came in contact with oil it could explode with disastrous results; the torpedoes used an alcohol/water mix as fuel. The Mk VII's length of 25.5 feet made it difficult to handle and many a torpedoman's finger or toe were lost in the necessarily spotlessly clean torpedo workshops of 'County' class cruisers. But it was the constant need to avoid contact between the enriched air and 'torpoil' lubricant which made it so unpopular. Furthermore, the air vessels were subject to rapid corrosion. On the credit side, the use of enriched air provided a trackless wake , a valuable improvement over the conventional torpedo which it outperformed. At 33 knots the 21-inch Mk VII had a range of 16,000 yards.

The unpopularity of enriched air was not shared by all users. Shortly after the outbreak of war in 1939, *Rodney's* Torpedo Officer found that the oxygen making plant, which was used to manufacture enriched air for the torpedoes, had fallen into disuse. He persuaded a young Reserve Engineer officer to overhaul the plant and make it work. Thereafter, *Rodney's* oxygen plant was able to supply all her torpedo requirements as well as pure oxygen for medical and other purposes throughout the fleet at Scapa Flow. Early in the war the Mk VIIs in the British heavy cruisers were converted to run on natural air and shale oil which lowered their range to 5,700 yards at 35 knots. *Canberra* seems to have retained enriched air Mk VIIs until she was sunk in 1942 and *Australia* until she lost her tubes in a wartime refit.

Although the Royal Navy became disenchanted with enriched air, the Japanese, basing themselves on an erroneous report that the British had made the same move, went a stage further and developed a pure oxygen torpedo. Despite a series of fatal explosions they developed the world's most powerful and advanced torpedo. Known as the Type-93, 'Long Lance', its existence came as a great shock to the Allies during the Second World War. The Type-93 was a 24-inch torpedo, 30 feet in length: it carried a warhead of over 1,000 lbs of explosive, had neutral buoyancy and could be set at 49 knots for 24,000 yards and 36 knots for 43,000 yards.

Britain's torpedo designers had to look elsewhere for higher performance and better reliability. The obsolescent submarine torpedoes could not, in their opinion, be replaced with anything so inherently dangerous as the 21-

inch Mk VII. The best alternative was the burner cycle semi-internal combustion torpedo engine. This was a four cylinder radial fed with air from the main vessel. As before, fuel (initially shale oil, later paraffin) was burned in the air before it entered the engine but most of the oxygen was retained to be burned within the cylinders as more fuel was injected into them. Ignition was spontaneouus as in a diesel engine and exhaust gases were ejected through ports in the piston crown and cylinder liner into a hollow propellor shaft.

The new submarine torpedo appeared as the Type G and it had a five knot advantage over the MK IV at 5,000 yards. So was born the 21-inch Mk VIII, easy to maintain, rugged and reliable, and destined to remain in service for over half a century. Its success derived from the basic excellence of the engine which gave it good development potential. The initial Mk VIII had a range of 5,OOO yards at 40 knots and appeared in 1927; it went into service in the 'P' class submarines in 1930-31. A surface-launched burner-cycle torpedo was also developed as the Type-J to be fitted first to the new 6-inch gun light cruisers and then to the new destroyer flotillas from the 'D' class onwards. It entered service as the Mk IX in 1930; its range was 13,500 yards at 30 knots and 10,500 yards at 35.

While Torpedo Officers ashore were making important contributions to torpedo development, those at sea were continuing to carry out live runs with their torpedoes and to participate in fleet exercises with enthusiasm. Lieutenant Commander William Andrewes (later Admiral Sir William) was Torpedo Officer of *Warspite*, flagship of the Mediterranean Fleet. His diary entries for 1930 provide a useful insight into the tempo of life amongst torpedo departments in ships of the Royal Navy's premier fleet as it concentrated on improving its skills in fleet action. In February, Andrewes noted that for a few days he had been finishing off and despatching records and reports of exercises involving massed torpedo attacks by destroyers. At the same time he noted that the torpedo party had been allocated the task of painting the *Warspite's* funnel and searchlight platforms. These were the same men who went ashore that evening to rig the lights for a performance in the Royal Engineers' Theatre. The following day, at 10 o'clock, Andrewes visited the battleship *Royal Oak* to take part in an enquiry into the circumstances connected with the loss of two torpedoes during an exercise period. The Torpedo Officer of *Royal Oak* was CAL Mansergh, who also reached Flag rank.

Andrewes paid tribute to the officers and men of his department. He acknowledged that responsibility for electrical installations, both high and low power, together with that for the operation and maintenance of the torpedo armament, was an exacting job. He mentioned especially his Commissioned Gunner(T), Mr Pitts, who was a tower of strength and whose knowledge of the ship was prodigious. In those days officers and men were totally dedicated to the daily requirements of the Navy, it was the single most important factor in their lives, and there are still those brought up on the maxim that 'the Navy looks after its own'. On Sundays wives came on board for divisions and church. A choir was organised and Andrewes proudly reported that 'The singing is rather above the average ship's singing.' Soon *Warspite* was back at sea for Maditerranean Fleet manoeuvres in conjunction with the Atlantic Fleet; Andrewes wrote 'The situation is likely to be an interesting one as we are trying to prevent the junction of two parts of the Atlantic Fleet and bring one to action before it can obtain the support of the other.' In these exercises the Mediterranean Fleet explored the potential of torpedo carrying aircraft and, perhaps even more important, the improvement of night action. Here the comparatively short ranges at which the actions were to be fought meant that the combination of gun and torpedo could be exploited to the full.

Back home an officer of the Engineering Branch, who was to have a strong influence later on torpedo development, was having his first experience of *Vernon*. He was OW Phillips, later a Rear Admiral, and one of the most influential officers ever to have served in the Engineering Branch. In May 1926 he found himself appointed to the destroyer *Winchester*, leader of the *Vernon* Flotilla. She was commanded by HE Snepp and her First Lieutenant was Gerald Gladstone, later Admiral Sir Gerald. The five destroyers of the *Vernon* Flotilla took their turn as guard and emergency ships and the Commander-in-Chief Portsmouth often used *Winchester* for inspection trips within the command. Most of the time was spent carrying out high speed trials, testing torpedoes and other items of equipment.

In July 1926 the Prince of Wales (later King Edward VIII) embarked in *Winchester* for passage to the Isle of Wight, where he opened a hospital in Ventnor, carried out several engagements on the island and re-embarked in *Winchester* the next day at Cowes, where the Captain was instructed to take him to the South Railway Jetty in Portsmouth Harbour. Phillips recalled that when the destroyer arrived three minutes early, the Captain became the butt of royal reproof. The ship's company was, for once, glad to return to the daily round of torpedo running.

When *Winchester* became due for her first major refit Phillips demonstrated his professionalism and his extraordinary attention to detail. The ship had trimmed badly by the bow, a serious fault in a high speed ship and one which had been assessed as a defect peculiar to *Winchester*. But Phillips looked a bit more deeply into the matter. He managed to arrange for the main store room to be moved to the after part of the ship from its existing position under the forecastle. He then examined what had been carried in the store room and he was able to return tons of surplus material to the Superintendent of Naval Stores. Amongst these stores were fifty three hand lead lines, each weighing over 11 lbs. He then turned his attention to the paintwork. As an engineer, he was unimpressed by spit and polish and he was well aware that the lead paint and enamel which looked so smart were also extremely heavy. Tons of paint were removed before getting down to the rivetheads. Soon the bare metal appeared and it was possible to apply two coats of red lead before repainting. *Winchester's* ailment of trimming by the head was cured.

Phillips had by now gained an enviable reputation within the Torpedo Branch. No one was surprised when he became increasingly involved with it. His next appointment, after promotion to Commander, was as Engineer Overseer at Cammell Laird's Shipyard at Birkenhead where *Phoenix*, one of the new class of submarines, was being built. She was the first submarine for many years to have been built at the yard, and serious problems had arisen. Phillips' job was to 'encourage' the firm and get the boat away from dockyard hands. He soon found that most of the trouble was concerned with the piping and other arrangements around the torpedo tubes. The work had been badly done and Phillips referred to it as an 'appalling lash up'. He hurried down to *Vernon*, where he arranged for photographs to be taken of the torpedo tube compartments in the *Pandora*, a Vickers-built P-class submarine. This was followed by discussions with the Torpedo Tube Design Department in the dockyard at Portsmouth and in *Vernon* at 'a long seance to clear the administrative decks'. The next day, talking to the Director of Torpedoes and Mining at the Admiralty, he explained the situation and was able to obtain approval for extra expenditure to correct the problem at Cammell Laird.

From Cammell Laird Phillips expected to move on to Fort Blockhouse, HMS *Dolphin*, as Chief Engineer at the submarine base, but the day before he was due to take up his appointment he was informed that he should hurry down to Portsmouth and find himself a suitable house from which he could take up a job in the dockyard as designer of the Navy's torpedo tubes. He was thus destined to play an important part in the activities of the Torpedo Branch.

At *Vernon* the decade of the 1920s ended as it had had started, with relaxed routines and without too much thought of another world war. Soon the optimistic and peaceful atmosphere was to disappear from the Gun Wharf as it would from in the nation at large, but nobody could accuse the establishment of complacency even if visitors sometimes reported that, in comparision to the parade ground atmosphere at *Excellent*, the mood at *Vernon* seemed to be positively scholastic. Commander ED Webb, in his history of *Vernon*, commented:

After the Vernon moved ashore in October 1923, there followed a period of settling down and consolidation, and it is difficult to find much of historical interest until the middle thirties. There was a great deal happening but it was mainly unexciting routine.

This is not wholly fair. Perhaps to a young officer in the establishment on the training side, it may have appeared unexciting and 'routine'. Nevertheless, developments of some significance had been taking place that were to have a considerable influence in the future. Progress was being achieved with the first post-war influence mines, and with the vital problems of the magnetic signature of all types of ships. Investigations were being made into many aspects of electrical damage control and there were fundamental improvements in train in the design of torpedoes. The enriched air weapon had made its appearance, but been made almost immediately obsolete by a fundamental new development in torpedo engine design. Using this motor the 21-inch Mk VIII submarine torpedo, one of the best and most reliable torpedoes ever to be designed, had been developed and was entering service. Despite the outward appearance of unexciting routine, much solid work had been achieved in the whole field of reponsibilities over which *Vernon* still ranged. All had not been frivolity in the 'Cocktail Years'.

CHAPTER SIX
FROM PEACE TO WAR 1931 - 39

THE TROUBLED THIRTIES BEGAN for the Royal Navy with those now epoch-making events at Invergordon, where the Atlantic Fleet went on strike when it found out about the proposed pay cut for personnel on the 1919 rates of pay. It was a sorry story of mismanagement by the Government, the Board of Admiralty and, indeed, the Commander in Chief's office although chance and the accident of illness compounded the problem. It had a profound and shocking effect on the country at large and on Great Britain's standing abroad and it was the main reason for the country's abandonment of the Gold Standard. Fortunately, it was confined almost entirely to the Atlantic Fleet. The fleets abroad and, perhaps surprisingly, the establishments at home remained unaffected. One cause of the trouble was that there was all too little contact between officers and men, and Torpedo Officers, who prided themselves on their approachability, tended to get so wrapped up in their technical work that they were not always aware of what was going on around them.

As has always been the case, there was a much closer relationship between officers and men in small ships than in the larger ships in the Fleet. This was nowhere more clearly demonstrated than in the Atlantic Fleet Destroyer Command in which torpedomen figured prominently. On 11 September 1931, ring leaders from the insurrection at Invergordon hurried down to the canteen at Rosyth to address a meeting of seamen from the destroyers. They urged the men to return to their ships and refuse duty. One young leading seaman, a torpedoman from the destroyer *Vivien*, stood up to declare that he was in opposition to any such step being taken in destroyers, where the vast majority of men trusted their officers. He suggested it would be a far better thing to return to their ships and inform their officers immediately of all their complaints. Fortunately his resolution carried the day. On returning to his ship Leading Seaman Diable immediately roused his divisional officer, Lieutenant Roger Lewis, and informed him of the step he had taken. Lewis, who had already turned in for the night, listened to Diable who urged him 'To do something quickly, Sir'.

Lewis hastened to consult his Captain, and together they approached the Captain(D), Captain HD Pridham-Wippell, who, without further delay, hurried across the harbour by motorboat to discuss the situation with Commodore (D); the latter at once agreed that something urgent had to be done to represent the seamens' complaints. Before midnight a signal had been sent to all destroyers of the Atlantic Fleet putting the whole of the Destroyer Command out of routine and instructing divisional officers to take personal notes of the problems of all their men, so that a dossier could be sent to the Admiralty within forty eight hours to support the sailors' case. Soon Admiral Sir John Kelly, who had been specially appointed to command the Atlantic Fleet, appeared at Rosyth where he ordered the Destroyer Command to clear lower deck and to assemble ships' companies so that he could address them.

Lewis remembered vividly that he opened in strident terms.'Take a good look at me', he said, 'I am Darby Kelly, I have been appointed the new Commander-in-Chief by His Majesty the King personally. I am going to see to it that your problems are sorted out and this is being done in the Admiralty at the moment. I have been given a special request by the King today. Leading Seaman Diable step forward. The King has personally asked me to promote you to Petty Officer for what you did the other night, so you are now Petty Officer Diable, carry on.'

The men dispersed and returned to their ships, which soon sailed for their home ports. Many years later, after World War Two, Lewis was relating this story to a retired Chief Petty Officer at a time when the newspapers were full of the details of the scattering of the ashes of one of the ring-leaders of the Invergordon Mutiny. The Chief Petty Officer said, 'I knew Diable when he was Master-at-Arms in the barracks at Devonport'. So it seems that this key leading seaman survived the war and went on to the highest non-commissioned rank: it is pleasing to think that torpedomen were thus involved creditably in this lamentable interlude.

After Invergordon, a National Government, unusual in British history, continued for a time to pursue a policy of retrenchment. The cuts which resulted continued to inhibit developments in all branches of the Navy but, in spite of the meagre budget, progress continued to be made at *Vernon* and especially in the Electrical Department. The introduction of the '*County*' class cruisers into service at the end of the 1920s had seen the introduction of a number of significant changes in the use of electricity in the Royal Navy. Steam and hydraulic pipes had hitherto controlled most of the machinery outside the engine and boiler rooms but this now became dependent upon electric cables for its power supply. For the first time steering engines, gun turrets, salvage and fire pumps, and even engine room auxiliaries, were energised by electricity. These developments meant that *Vernon* became involved in trials to improve the flexibility of electrical supply systems: electrical failure might now put a ship out of action.

The ring main system had been introduced to reduce the number of cables passing through watertight bulkheads. The main was divided into sections corresponding to the number of dynamos, and the sections could be connected by hand worked switches should a dynamo fail or be out of use. Many improvements were now introduced, including the replacement of hand switches by ring main breakers electrically operated from a main switchboard. Even more important was the addition of a system of cross connections with hand worked switches so that each dynamo could feed into the main on either side of the ship; and groups of branch circuits could draw a supply from the opposite side of the ship if the main on their side was put out of action.

Torpedo officers serving in these new ships soon realised that if the benefits of replacing steam pipes by electric cables were to be realised, an emergency supply system of flexible cables to replace damaged cables would have to be provided. Unfortunately, the Electrical Engineering Department at the Admiralty considered that the alternative systems already provided were all that was required. Subsequent events, soon after the outbreak of the Second World War, showed once again that recommendations from sea should not be so lightly set aside.

The arrival in service of new classes of ship alerted the staff at *Vernon* to the importance of electrical hand-books for the guidance of their crews.

This was particularly important in the new ships where the main machinery had been sub-divided into independent units. Dynamos had been resited and the main electrical supply systems had been redesigned, but all that existed in the shape of an electrical manual in the early 1930s were two slim volumes. The first was a text book of electrical engineering with no particular application to the Navy and the second comprised a series of pamphlets dealing with high power equipment or main supply systems. To make matters worse, the Electrical Engineering Department at the Admiralty had no book writing section. Captains RB Miles and AU Willis, successive commanding officers of *Vernon* from 1934 to 1938, insisted there must be handbooks for the new and more complex supply systems. After lengthy discussions with the Director of Electrical Engineering and the Director of Torpedoes and Mining, it was agreed that *Vernon* should produce the new handbook and in 1936, Lieutenant PHF Colomb was appointed to undertake this work. He was an officer of outstanding intellectual capability whose ancestors, Sir John Colomb (late of the Royal Marines) and his brother Vice Admiral Phillip Colomb, had been able commentators on naval and maritime affairs.

Colomb had to deal with electrical systems which traced their development back to the beginning of the century. His meticulous and detailed study soon caused consternation at the Admiralty and at *Vernon*. He drew the attention of their Lordships to the departure in ships of the latest construction from the principles governing the electrical installations in the '*County*' class cruisers. He pointed out that ring main breakers had been inserted haphazardly with the possibility that damage in one section could put undamaged sections out of action. In the worst cases damage anywhere in the system could cause a complete blackout throughout the ship. Colomb's work led to the drawing up of a set of principles known as the 'Eighteen Points of Ring Main Design'. The ring main systems in ships under construction were as far as possible redesigned, but many ships at sea had been completed before remedial action could be taken.

Anxieties about the electrical systems were constantly being expressed by torpedomen at this time. They were particularly critical of the switch gear system which often operated incorrectly and caused many interruptions to the electrical supply. Early in 1938 the Commander-in-Chief Home Fleet informed the Admiralty of his concern and *Vernon* was instructed to carry out trials in *Nelson* in Portsmouth Dockyard. it soon became obvious that the switch gear was inherently defective. Present at the trials was Mr. Whipp, Managing Director of the firm Whipp and Bourne, switch gear manufacturers; in traditional engineering fashion, he demonstrated on the back of an envelope what was going wrong and how it could be cured. Shortly afterwards, Mr. Whipp's son arrived at *Vernon* with a set of modification parts. It was proved in another ship in the dockyard that the fitting of modified parts could easily be carried out by ships' electrical artificers. Successful full scale trials were carried out in the cruiser *London* in January 1939; the ship had just been decommissioned for a major rebuild. With the coming of the war, however, it was some two years before modification kits were available for all ships in the Fleet. This modification and the steady improvement of the electrical systems in ships of the Royal Navy owed much to the dedication of officers and men of the Electrical Department of *Vernon* during the inter-war years, but their work was soon to suffer a serious setback.

The Electrical Department was housed in Number 17 building, one of the old buildings on the 'New Gun Wharf' which had been built as a gun carriage store and artillery barracks. The walls of the ground floor retained ring bolts for horses and there was a magnificent wooden roof extending throughout the length of the building uninterrupted by partitions and lined with tarred felt. Even without the absence of fire hydrants the whole building presented a serious fire risk. From time to time wisps of smoke could be seen emerging from the roof, but nobody had thought to question why or to take any action to reduce a fire hazard which was a constant threat to the trials and experimental work of the Electrical Department.

The afternoon of 18 January 1935 was like that of any other Friday when considerations of a long weekend were uppermost in the minds of many of the officers and men at *Vernon*. As members of the Electrical and Mining Departments were leaving their offices in Number 17 Building they observed smoke coming from the roof, and a smell of burning pitch began to pervade the atmosphere. Friday evening lethargy and familiarity with the wisps of smoke from that building had produced a complacent attitude and it was not until flames had replaced the smoke, and the sound of crackling fire could be heard, that onlookers were persuaded that the building was well alight. The Royal Marine Police in the dockyard had recently formed a fire brigade which was soon in action with two engines. They were quickly followed by four appliances from the Portsmouth City Fire Brigade. *Vernon's* steam powered fire engine, affectionately known as the 'Bloodhound', raised steam as a matter of routine every Thursday, but this was Friday! Panic signals were sent out for the stoker responsible for raising steam and, after some delay, he was found at the scene of the fire, fighting the flames with buckets of water. The western part of the building was soon very seriously damaged. It was demolished and replaced by a two storey building known as 17A, better suited for its advanced instructional and experimental functions. A new building, No. 18, was erected behind No. 17 to test searchlight mirrors in less flammable surroundings.

Rearmament was in the air in 1935, but, for a few precious weeks, doubts and anxieties were forgotten. The national pride diverted thoughts towards the celebration of the Silver Jubilee of King George V, and in the service to preparations for His Majesty's Review of his Fleet at Spithead. *Vernon's* guests were privileged to watch the spectacle from the torpedo testing station at Stokes Bay, from which the Fleet could be seen drawn up in lines, together with ships from foreign navies. *Vernon's* organisation was, for once, found wanting. The guests arriving by car choked the narrow roads through Gosport, causing massive hold ups and criticism by the local authorities. But events of darker significance were stirring and *Vernon* was becoming increasingly active as she geared herself to meet the demands which a deteriorating situation and eventual war would impose.

The crisis with Italy over Ethiopia and the vulnerability of Malta to air attack caused the removal of Sir WW Fisher's Mediterranean Fleet to Alexandria. Contingency plans were drawn up to deal with a sudden outbreak of war, and by the time Italian troops invaded Abyssinia in the first week of October 1935, the Mediterranean Fleet was ready for all eventualities. This included the laying of harbour defences at Alexandria, no mean task and one for which *Vernon* was largely responsible. In the first week of September 1935, orders had been received in *Vernon* to equip, as a matter of great urgency, a controlled mining base capable of dealing with 192 mine units, an assembly station, 2 control stations, 150 miles of cable, relevant stores and boats, stowage for 48 miles of indicator loop and harbour defence asdic cable, associated gear and stores and accommodation for 43 officers and men. On 6 September, three ships were inspected: the SS *Atreus* of the Blue Funnel Line and the SS *Counsellor* and the SS *Tactician*, both of the Harrison Line. *Atreus* was selected, chiefly because of her existing accommodation, which included provision for nearly thirty passengers , with space for extension.

Atreus was an old ship, built in 1911, which had a displacement of 13,535 tons, a length of 441 feet, a cargo carrying capacity of 8,625 tons and a speed of 12 knots. It was of great importance that she was fitted with 2 powerful electric generators, 20 derricks of lifting capacities varying from 2 to 10 tons and one capable of lifting loads of 40 tons. As soon as the decision had been made to charter her, she was docked, cleaned and commissioned as a naval vessel, and was ready to sail by the evening of 9 September. Two days later she arrived at Portsmouth, where she berthed at the South Railway jetty. During the intervening five days plans had been drawn up at *Vernon* for the essential structural modifications, which were limited by the agreement that no bulkheads were to be pierced and that the alterations to the tank tops should be confined to the welding of angle lugs or cleats. One week later, all the essential alterations had been made and the ship was fully equipped, loaded and ready to sail. Soon after the full outfit of 192 mines had been loaded, Lieutenant Commander RW James, who had taken a leading part in the operation, had decided that it would be expedient to embark extra fire appliances.

As James sat in his office telephoning the order to the Naval Stores Officer, a civilian officer burst in, interrupting the telephone conversation: :'Keep cool! Don't get excited!' the civilian shouted.James assured the excited gentleman that he was:'Quite cool, thank you.''Well', was the reply, 'you won't be soon for there's a big fire in number 1 hold!'. Number 1 hold contained stores and equipment and 48 miles of anti-submarine cable. Immediately above it was a petrol tank, and astern of it, number 2 hold, containing 105 mine units. Number 1 hold had to be quickly and completely emptied before the fire could be extinguished but, in spite of this delay and the trauma it engendered, the programme was not interrupted and the ship sailed on time. (No enquiry was carried out and the cause of the fire was not revealed). The establishment of net and loop defences at the Mediterranean Fleet anchorage was of paramount importance. On 11 October 1935, two weeks after *Atreus* had arrived at Alexandria, two guard loops had been laid and were in operation controlled from a station ashore. It was a truly memorable achievement but one that was little appreciated.

A great gale in September 1935 seemed to signal the end of an era. It sent the massive elm on the wardroom lawn at *Vernon* crashing to the ground severing a water main, flooding the roadway and revealing the foundations of an ancient building and a spiral staircase. As the elm came down, more important events were unfolding, the decision was taken to re-activate a form of torpedo warfare that was dying out in the Royal Navy. The wartime coastal motor boats had become virtually extinct and Hubert Scott Paine of the British Power Boat Company persuaded the Controller of the Navy, Vice Admiral Sir Reginald Henderson, to order six new 60 foot 'motor torpedo boats' subject to the successful trials of the prototype. The new term MTB rather than CMB reflected the greater sea keeping qualities expected of the newly developed 'hard chine' hull of the MTBs developed from British Power Boat's RAF rescue boats. The Abyssinian crisis played a key role in this decision since, if successful, the boats were intended to help defend Malta from the now unfriendly Italians.

These first MTBs were powered by three Napier Lion aero-engines which gave them a top speed of about 38 knots. Two 18-inch torpedoes were loaded through long hatches in the deck above the engine room, and were stowed facing forward. Hinged outriggers provided extensions to the discharge rails abaft the boat's transom, and could be folded up when not in use. Doors were fitted over the stern apertures. When the boat was prepared for firing, the doors were opened and the outriggers were hinged down. The torpedoes were launched by accelerating the boat and thus allowing the torpedoes to roll backwards down the rails in the engine room into the sea. It was a most unsatisfactory arrangement: the torpedoes could not be fired with the boat stationary, the rails were flimsy and liable to buckle with the slightest motion, even in harbour, and loading was a tricky operation. Finally, the discharge was very unsatisfactory, for since the torpedo entered the water nearly stopped, depth taking was a chancy business. It was, in fact, considerably less reliable than the old trough discharge of the CMBs

Soon after the order for the boats had been placed, a docket arrived on the desk of Owen Phillips in the Admiralty Department of Torpedoes and Mining. Scott Paine was demanding a payment of £1,200 per boat for this torpedo launching equipment. Phillips was horrified both by the limitations which this gear placed upon the tactical manoeuverability of the MTBs and by the exorbitant charge being made for it. He considered it could be produced, With a little machining here and there, by the village blacksmith for £120 to £150 and at a handsome profit. He was determined that an incident like this should never occur again.

He sketched out the design of a very lightweight 21-inch torpedo tube, just stiff enough for a close fitting torpedo to be handled and hoisted in and out, which could be held by a side stop and fired ahead by a powder charge. The tube was kept splash tight by a ring fixed in the tube and sealing round the head of the torpedo. This seal acted as a gas check and gave a very good firing compression. The design was sent down to Portsmouth Dockyard where the prototypes were manufactured. These tubes were fitted in the bigger and better motor torpedo boats designed by Vospers of Portchester. Phillips was concerned that in Commander Webb's 'History of *Vernon*' it was claimed that these light construction torpedo tubes were a *Vernon* product for this was not so, to put the record straight Phillips wrote:

While I have no wish to denigrate the great contribution by Vernon to torpedo discharge, especially that of the late Mr WF Thain who would have provided the cordite or powder pocket discharges for the new ahead firing tubes in any case, ... in

the interest of truth it must be stated that the remainder of the design was initiated by the Admiralty and produced by the torpedo tube design officer in Portsmouth Dockyard.

Vernon was however given charge of MTB development. Lieutenant Commander GB Sayer, author of the first short history of the establishment, was re-appointed to *Vernon* to supervise the training of officers and men and the trials of *MTB1* (or *MTB01* as she was then numbered). In 1936 she became a common sight travelling at high speed around Spithead and the Solent and, when weather permitted, in the Channel. Extensive torpedo trials took place at Stokes Bay but the boat remained the property of British Power Boat. Then in June, the first two boats were temporarily commissioned, under Sayer's command, in order to provide a special demonstration for King Edward VIII.

It was an important occasion: contingents from *Dolphin* and the Royal Naval Hospital at Haslar joined the officers and men of *Vernon* drawn up on the football field for an inspection by the King, who was accompanied by the First Sea Lord (Admiral Sir Ernle Chatfield). On completion of the inspection the King boarded *MTB01* for high speed manoeuvres in Spithead, followed by an attack on the destroyer *Amazon* at which a torpedo was fired. Some consternation was caused as the two boats entered Portsmouth Harbour at 38 knots, rocking ships at anchor and causing their wash to thump up against the harbour walls in direct violation of the harbour regulations. The King was disembarked at Whale Island.

It was intended that the six MTBs would form the 1st MTB Flotilla under Sayer's command. As the boats completed their acceptance trials they were commissioned and began an intensive working up programme, operating as part of *Vernon's* flotilla. These craft appealed to the young and there were many volunteers to serve in them. They were given a high public profile; in April 1937 four escorted the Royal Barge as it carried the new King George VI and Queen Elizabeth by river to Greenwich to open the National Maritime Museum. Three MTBs were used at the Spithead Review carrying out patrol duties. As the First Flotilla was working up, the Controller, Henderson, paid a visit to inspect the boats on the slipway at Hythe. Sayer seized the opportunity to present to the Controller a picture entitled, 'Henderson's Half Dozen'. The picture had been drawn by Mrs. Sayer to demonstrate the advantages to mobility which would be conveyed by a depot ship. The Controller must have been impressed because very shortly afterwards the trawler *Aston Villa* was provided for this purpose and given the honoured torpedo name HMS *Vulcan* . In June 1937, *Vernon's* task with the First MTB Flotilla was complete, and it sailed from Portsmouth for Malta on 22 June, stopping at ten ports on the way. The voyage covered 2,323 miles. When the six reached Malta on the morning of 17 July, a week ahead of schedule, every engine was in full working order, 'a fitting and most satisfactory conclusion to the eighteen months' close interest , faith and parental devotion of HMS *Vernon*.'

The renewed interest in coastal craft led to the establishment at *Vernon* of a small section headed by a Commander and including two Engineer Officers, a Gunner (T) and a number of technical ratings. The early boats were far from satisfactory, but, despite their defects. twelve more were ordered from British Power Boat, six for Hong Kong to form the Second Flotilla and six for Singapore. Given the international situation this Third Flotilla was ordered instead to reinforce the First at Malta, not this time by the long sea route but through the inland waterways of France from the Channel ports to the Mediterranean, an adventure which was the envy of every young officer and rating in the Royal Navy. *Vernon* supervised the working up of these boats and the trials of a twin engined British Power Boat high speed motor minesweeper *MMS51*; she did not prove useful and was refitted as *MTB100* in 1939. The design was also made the basis of a new class of Motor Anti-Submarine Boat (MA/SB) armed with depth charges. *Vernon* had effectively become the parent establishment for coastal forces and tasked to carry out the trials of the new craft being submitted by the boat building companies. In order to provide more acommodation for MTB personnel at *Vernon* a new block, *Marlborough,* was built.

The *Vernon* staff were far from keen on the British Power Boat craft and preferred the rival design from Vosper of Portsmouth, who had built a 68 foot boat as a private venture(PV) in 1935-6. This was much stronger and heavier than the Hythe built vessels and , with some irony, was powered by three Italian Isotta-Fraschini engines; domestically built lightweight engines of sufficient power were not available. The original intended armament was a bow torpedo tube, but by the time the boat was taken over and commissioned as *MTB102* in early 1938, a stern trough arrangement had been adapted for the larger 21-inch torpedoes. This was soon replaced by two of Phillip's new tubes, one facing forward on each beam angled out from the centreline.

Vernon thus developed the classic British MTB which, slightly enlarged to over 70 feet, was ordered into limited production at Vosper's yard in Portsmouth and at Thornycroft's at Southampton. Scott Paine and British Power Boat produced a 70 foot design but, after thorough comparative trials at *Vernon*, it was turned down on grounds of hull weakness, despite its British Rolls Royce engines. Scott Paine took it to America where it became the basis of the American PT Boat. White's of Cowes produced an advanced hydrofoil that was delivered to *Vernon* as *MTB101* in 1939. There was no time to develop the design before war broke out and when orders for MTBs were expanded White's built standard 70 foot hard chine vessels.

Vernon continued to put its limited mine development resources into both the improvement of contact mines and the development of usable magnetic mines. Given the problems with British contact mines in the First World War it seemed negligent to ignore the possibility of improving the Mk XIV although, in retrospect, perhaps too much attention was lavished on painting the lily. Doubts still existed about the Hertz horn: it might not explode if given a very severe blow and it was vulnerable to near-by explosions. Perhaps more relevant, British industry was still having problems with production. A new, over complicated, electrical switch horn was therefore developed for the MK XV mine which proved unsuitable for quantity production; it was therefore simplified as the Mk XVII. The Mk XVI was a new contact mine for laying by the new generation of submarine minelayers of the *'Porpoise'* class; this mine reverted to the Hertz horn.

All this effort on contact mines did not mean that influence mines were neglected. Available efforts were , however, concentrated upon anti-submarine applications rather than anti-surface ship. In 1931 the dip needle method method of magnetic firing was abandoned in favour of the 'coiled rod' of special 'Mu-Metal' in which a current would be induced by the rate of change in the strength of magnetic field caused by a passing target. In 1933 trials were held at Portland, and after the submarines L19, L22, L53, and L71 had carried out a large number of runs over the trial devices, it was concluded that, with this class of submarine at a speed of 3-4 knots, the mines would be actuated at distances of approximately 5 feet.

In 1936, a team from *Vernon* sailed for Singapore where trials of magnetic mines were carried out in low magnetic latitudes; at home similar trials were continued at Portland. As a result an order was placed for six hundred M Mk I moored magnetic mines and and trials began with a magnetic ground mine to be laid by aircraft, the A Mk I. The M Mk I was in full production by September 1939 and the A mine was about to go into production The A Mk I was an anti-surface ship weapon and was found to have the following performance:

Target	Actuation Range Distance Beneath Keel
Destroyer	30 feet
Heavy Cruiser	50 feet
Battleship	55 feet

In 1935 the Mine Design Department at *Vernon* voiced concern about the magnetic mine threat. The following year the Admiralty set up an Anti-non-contact Mine Committee to look at the problems posed by sweeping such mines and protecting ships from them. As far as sweeping was concerned the normal Oropesa was adequate against moored magnetic mines but at some increased danger to the minesweeper. A sweep that was effective also against ground mines was also considered but the situation was made difficult by lack of knowledge of the precise charagteristics of the mines that might have to be swept. An electrical 'A' sweep had been used in 1918-19 to sweep British 'M' mines but in May 1939 it was decided to develop an alternative which would be cheap (in case it did not work!) and flexible. This was the Magnetic Sweep MkI consisting of thirty four 27inch magnets ten feet apart suspended on forty foot pendants from a 1 inch 'A' sweep wire carried between trawlers two hundred yards apart.

Within two months, i.e. in July 1939, a prototype with dummy magnets was being tested in the Solent by *Vernon's* Minesweeping Section. A proposed mine destructor ship converted by fitting a merchantman with a powerful magnet in the bows was also considered but such a vessel was deleted from the 1939 Estimates. British ground mines were not yet in service and the new Magnetic Sweep could deal with mines like them if and when required. With so much else on the Navy's plate and with little or no knowledge of German developments in this area, the Naval Staff decided that nothing further could be done until the situation was clarified after the declaration of war. This was obviously meaningless and Captain Denis Boyd, the commanding officer of *Vernon*, from April 1938 to November 1939, tried his best to get more resources allocated. Thoroughly frustrated he framed in his office the reply to his frequent requests more resources with which to perfect magnetic sweeps:

As this form of sweep is only required in war time it need not be developed in peace time.

This would have near-tragic consequences.

British moored magnetic mines were designed to be fired close to their target and *Vernon* therefore concentrated on magnetic conditions close to the ship. At this range absolute demagnetisation was considered to be impossible and therefore research went into over magnetisation to explode mines at safe distance. In 1937 the light cruiser *Curacoa* was fitted with coils which could be supplied with either AC or DC current so as to produce a magnetic field sufficient to activate an M Mk I at a safe distance from the ship. The problem with this approach was that the enemy could always reduce the sensitivity of his mines so attention turned back to demagnetization. Again, however not much of a practical nature could be done until the threat clarified.

It is important not to exagerate the Admiralty's lack of interest in mine warfare in these years. Seventeen of a new type of 800 ton minesweeper, the 'Halcyon' class, were produced and four new coastal minelayers were laid down to replace the remaining converted monitors. The first, *Plover*, was an 800 ton vessel that entered service as part of *Vernon's* flotilla in 1938. She was sent to the Mediterranean for deep minelaying trials and with no armament beyond side arms, her crew felt somewhat vulnerable when the Munich crisis mobilised the fleet. Of the three smaller 500 ton vessels laid down that year, two were intended for *Vernon* and the other for the China Station. More important, however was the decision to spend scarce shipbuilding money and resources on a new class of six ultra-fast 2,650 ton minelayers. The first two, *Abdiel* and *Manxman*, were laid down in March 1939.

In the years immediately preceding the outbreak of war *Vernon* was organised into three sections: Administration, Instructional and Sea Trials and Development. Each had its own Commander in charge, the head of the adminstrative section also being the Executive Officer of the establishment. Also at *Vernon*, although directly responsible to the Admiralty, was the Superintendent of Mine Design. The attempt to give *Vernon* similar responsibilities with torpedoes was finally abandoned in 1936 and the Torpedo Experimental Department left for the Royal Naval Torpedo Factory at Greenock. *Vernon's* Whitehead department took over Stokes Bay and remained responsible for much of the running carried out by the Superintendent of Torpedo Experiments. To support the establishment the destroyers of the *Vernon* flotilla were kept busy. In the middle of 1938, there were seven, *Winchester, Wrestler, Skate, Amazon, Ambush, Ambuscade* and *Acheron*. At the end of 1938 the 300 ton minelaying tender *Skylark* replaced the former *Strathcoe* as the name ship *Vernon*.

The Captain of *Vernon* remained a key figure in the world of torpedoes, mines and naval electrics. Denis Boyd's predecessor was a Torpedo Officer who was to attain the highest rank in the Service. Algernon U Willis was a far-sighted officer who demanded the highest standards of efficiency and who had an eye for detail. Regarded with apprehension by his subordinates and envy by his contemporaries, he was known throughout the service as 'Algy'. His leadership made a major contribution to *Vernon's* being ready to face the test of war.

During Willis' period of command the administrative side of *Vernon* had to provide accommodation for a rapidly increasing number of men under instruction. At the same time the establishment had to play its part on the many ceremonial occasions attending the Coronation Year of 1937. Commander Webb's account is of interest:

1937 was Coronation Year and a time of great activity for Vernon. A strong contingent under arms went to London to line the streets during the procession, and was allotted a strategic point in Whitehall close to the Admiralty Arch. During the Spithead Review period, all foreign libertymen passed through Vernon, with times suitably staggered to avoid the Germans meeting the Russians and the Russians meeting the Japanese. It was amusing to see the Russians landing from their drifter in the early morning, bound for the Tower of London or some other capitalist stronghold. Immediately on landing there was one cigarette all round and the air was filled with Eastern perfume. The next moment they had all fallen in and were marching smartly to the gate in their blue and white striped flannels, specially bought for the occasion and reminiscent of Tsarist days. The Germans, too, from the Graf Spee had a special walking-out dress, with round jackets and trousers fitting very tightly across the seat.

In common with the other shore establishments, *Vernon* held a cocktail party and a dinner party. The senior foreigner at the dinner was a Russian Engineer Captain and it sounded novel to hear him propose the King's health. To mark the occasion a most ambitious review was produced by the Commander, ACG Madden, who conducted the orchestra, while his wife's sister coached the ballet. Several engagements resulted and even some weddings.

On the day of the Spithead Review, many important people passed through *Vernon* to embark, including Prince Bernhard and Princess Juliana. Cars were heavily labelled and scrutinized. Suddenly a small car with no label at all dared to enter and was swept to one side under close arrest. On being asked his business, the driver replied in a hoarse whisper, 'We've come for the 'arp'. The harp had been specially acquired for the orchestra to improve the more soulful moments of the ballet.'

The glitter of the Coronation ceremonial only served to emphasise the tremendous problem facing the Instructional Department. The *Vernon* Annual Report of 1936 stated:

Owing to the expansion of the Fleet the numbers of Leading Torpedomen and Seamen Torpedomen allowed by Vote 8 were increased in April. No increase in the number of Torpedo Gunners Mates was allowed. These increases had been difficult to meet due to the lack of suitably recommended candidates, which in turn is due to an extreme shortage of Able Seamen in the service as a whole.

It had been hoped to rate enough Seamen Torpedomen to fill gaps, but the numbers rated had been too small to have any effect. In 1937, the number of torpedo ratings of all rates was again increased considerably; the numbers trained going up from 450 in 1936 to 670 in 1937, but still there was a shortfall. Matters were no better in the provision of electrical artificers for the Fleet and many of these skilled ratings were coming to the end of their engagements. It was soon necessary to reduce the numbers carried in the Home Fleet destroyers and all depot ships. By the Autumn of 1938, fears were being expressed that in 1939 and 1940 some ships would have to be de-commissioned because of the serious shortage of electrical artificers.

The crisis was not confined to the Instructional Department; the pressure on the other sections was equally great. The Superintendent of Torpedo Experiments carried out 4-5,000 runs a year and *Vernon* was responsible for many of these, either at Stokes Bay or at the new trials and base facilities at Bincleaves in Weymouth Bay, opened in 1934. Both the Mk VIII and IX were steadily improved. The former progressed through the MK VIII* with its strengthened air vessel and longer range to the Mk VIII** that was about to enter service in 1939. This had larger propellers and could run 7,000 yards at 41 knots and 5,000 at 43.5. The Mk IX went through a similar process and the MK IX** could make 15,000 yards at 35 knots and 11,000 yards at 41; it entered service with the latest destroyers in 1939.

Development of aerial torpedoes was a major problem in the 1930s, the Stokes Bay facility becoming increasingly monopolised by aircraft torpedo running. What made the problem so difficult was that both the Admiralty and the Air Ministry were involved. The bureaucratic rivalry between the two had several results, not least the provision of separate RAF torpedo hoisting and transport facilities at Stokes Bay. In the 1920s an uneasy system of dual Admiralty- Air Ministry control had been worked out for ship-borne aircraft but land based maritime squadrons remained under complete RAF control.

In the early 1930s ship and shore based torpedo bomber squadrons carried the old 18-inch Mk VIIs and VIIIs. These old heater weapons were obsolescent by 1929 when the decision was made to go ahead with the development of a new specially designed aircraft torpedo. An 18-inch Type-K was designed using the new burner cycle engine but the RAF did not like its size or weight. A major problem in RN-RAF relations at this time was that because of a failure to understand each other's environment, the Admiralty asked for impractical aircraft and the Air Ministry impractical naval weapons. The Air Ministry forwarded an over-ambitious requirement for a much lighter torpedo to be of 14 inches diameter and a maximum weight of 1,000 lbs. The performance required was 1,200 yards at 35 knots carrying a warhead containing 200 lbs of explosive. It was designated the Type-O. The nearest the Admiralty could come to this specification was a lightweight 18-inch torpedo of 900 lbs weight with a 184 lbs warhead. Its speed was however only 30 knots for a range of 1,200 yards and the Air Ministry rejected it. The Admiralty pointed out that the only path to improvement would be to use aluminium construction for the afterbody and tail, but that there was no experience of combined steel and aluminium construction. Trials were eventually carried out using a light alloy known as 'Wilmil' but the Air Ministry finally agreed that there was no practical alternative to the development of the Type K.

Even using more conventional technology it was not easy to combine a weight of no more than 1,500 lb with a charge of 465 lb and a performance of 1,500 yards at 40 knots and 4,000 yards at 25 knots, the whole being capable of being dropped at 100 ft at a speed of 150 knots. It was with the Type K that several advances were made into the problem of obtaining stable flight for the torpedo in the air. Comparatively large aerofoil surfaces of light construction were tried fixed to the tail, but these broke off on hitting the water. During 1934 and 1935, the *Vernon* Torpedo Trials Team carried out trials at Stokes Bay of an air tail invented by Captain J A Bull of the Royal Norwegian Navy. It consisted of two light wooden and canvas flaps attached to the horizontal rudders, which were operated by the torpedo's servo motor. On entry into the water the flaps broke away and a clutch connected the servo motor to the depth keeping mechanism for the next stage of the weapon's journey. An improved tail based upon this design was adopted for service.

The Type K was accepted into service as the Mk XI in 1936 but it was still unsatisfactory and was soon replaced by the improved Mk XII with a longer, lower pressure air vessel and a shorter, stronger balance chamber. Playing a leading role in the trials with air dropped torpedoes was John Hext Lewes who had been serving as Torpedo Officer of the cruiser *London* before being appointed to the *Vernon* Sea Trials Section for the specific purpose of working on the improvement of the air dropped weapons. Lewes was left very much to himself at Stokes Bay and the trials went forward successfully, and without interruption. From the outset the intention had been that Lewes should take the Mk XII to sea in *Courageous*, now an aircraft carrier, with a vested interest to see that it did not fail. This was important, since at the time very little importance was attached by aircrews to the tactical aspects of launching a torpedo successfully from aircraft.

When Lewes became Torpedo Officer of the aircraft carrier *Courageous*, he relieved Jock Hughes-Hallett, another Torpedo Officer whose personality was later to be indelibly imprinted upon the future of the Royal Navy's underwater weapons branches. Lewes inherited a variety of ingenious developments which had been originated by his predecessor. These included aircraft sector lights, night landing illuminations and a torpedo aiming camera. It was at the time when new types of Torpedo Spotter Reconnaissance (TSR) aircraft were coming into service, the Swordfish and the less popular Shark. It soon became apparent that the pilots found it difficult to take seriously any comments from a non-flier such as Lewes, despite his insistence on flying as much as he possibly could to support his detailed investigation into the tactical aspects of launching torpedoes from the air, and in the development of attack angles for the delivery of the torpedoes against fleet units. Using a complicated gunnery analysis system he estimated the number of hits obtained by an attack by twenty aircraft on the *Courageous* during one Spring cruise. He believed that eight of the twenty torpedoes launched would have found the target, which had failed to take effective avoiding action. The lessons learned from such exercises as this showed conclusively that the aircraft-launched torpedo now constituted a deadly menace to capital ships, and that a great deal could be done to frustrate attacks by torpedo-carrying aircraft by taking avoiding action in a carefully prescribed manner. Unfortunately the Admiralty did not act positively to develop a standardised evasive manoeuvring doctrine based on these lessons. Lewes, commenting upon the later loss of the *Prince of Wales* and *Repulse*, remarked:

The Prince of Wales presented herself as perfectly as she could to the Japanese attack whereas the commanding officer of the REPULSE did everything he could correctly and avoided the torpedoes for quite a long time until he was overwhelmed. If you look at the story of that battle, the PRINCE OF WALES turned wrong every time, REPULSE turned correctly every time.

Lewes was very appreciative of the inventiveness of Hughes-Hallett, particularly of his development of a torpedo sight. It was a crude development, but the best thing available then to assist the pilot of an aircraft in his final approach to the target. It consisted of a metal bar supporting a row of electric bulbs, each bulb representing a different speed of the target. All that was required of the pilot was to estimate the speed and switch to whichever electric bulb represented it. It was crude but as good an indication of the deflection as could be expect to give to a busy pilot who was almost totally engaged in manoeuvring his aircraft.

According to Lewes, progress at all levels was impeded by the continued system of RN/RAF dual control which he later referred to as a 'criminal and terrible' system. It must have been frustrating indeed for ship's officers, such as Lewes, when Fleet Air Arm pilots used their privileged status to ignore naval advice and demands. As he later complained:

The moment the aircraft and crews went ashore they cocked a snook at the captain of the carrier and he had no control over them whatsoever.

The perspective of the flyers themselves was a little different. Those Naval officers of all branches who were given flying experience in the Fleet Air Arm found the situation to their taste and were not conscious of any rift between RN and RAF personnel: the latter appeared to be as keen and efficient as their naval colleagues. It was mainly at the higher levels and especially within the Ministries at Whitehall that rivalry and vested interest combined to thwart the professional enthusiasm of the junior ranks.

The impasse over aircraft and weapons went on, even after the decision was taken in 1937 to begin a two year process of trasferring the Fleet Air Arm to Admiralty control. The Admiralty believed that it would be possible to develop a carrier borne torpedo-carrying aircraft which would be able to deliver a torpedo weighing approximately 1,900 lbs. A prototype torpedo of 1,870 lbs was accordingly developed for trials. But, the Air Ministry stated it was not possible to produce a carrier borne aircraft which would be able to carry it and the project was dropped. Meanwhile the Royal Air Force's demand for a lightweight torpedo continued to be resisted by the Navy, which believed that the use of special metals presented unacceptable constructional difficulties. Although these lightweight torpedoes were developed and produced for trials they did not enter service and had been abandoned by 1939. So it was that the Fleet Air Arm went to war with the slow Swordfish biplane, the best that could be done to meet the Admiralty's demanding requirement for a combined torpedo bombing, spotting and reconnaissance (TSR) aircraft. Both it and the RAF's own equally slow and shorter ranged Vildebeeste torpedo bombers carried the 18inch Mk XII which was being given greater striking power with a new 'Duplex' pistol. This was a magnetic exploder using the Coiled Rod (CR) principle of British magnetic

Admiral Sir Denis Boyd. The inspired captain of Vernon 1938-39

mines. It was at an advanced stage of development by the outbreak of war.

For most of the lower deck, inter-service bickering went on almost unnoticed. Chief Petty Officer Joe Davis, describing his experiences at *Vernon* in the 1930s, gives an interesting insight into the way the new burner cycle torpedoes were treated at *Vernon*, Davis recalling that:

The Mk IX was hidden in a classroom, 56 building Mohawk , and kept locked. I was qualifying LTO at the time, and was very interested (bare details were given to the class) but I wanted to know more and one day I volunteered as an Acting Leading Seaman to take charge of a window cleaning party. Given the key to the classroom I was able to inspect and check up details, this information was invaluable to me as I was shortly afterwards drafted to the cruiser GLASGOW *which carried the Mk IX. I was put in charge of tubes, the servicing space and the Whitehead room.*

The enthusiasm of the torpedo ratings and their esprit de corps were reflected in his next words:

We worked on the parting shop, all white enamel paint, the armoured deck was polished and the non-slip strips were burnished as was all the copper funnels and bright work, it became a show place and the Torpedo Lieutenants and Gunners from other ships who came to us inspected it all, it wasn't very popular with the other torpedomen, but when it came for them to do their routines I obtained permission to go aboard their ships and work with them very successfully and was plied with much rum!!'

Dennis Boyd relieved Algy Willis as the Captain of *Vernon* on 21 April 1938. Lewes, back at the establishment as the new First Lieutenant, remarked that:

VERNON, under Dennis Boyd was a lively place, he was a tremendous chap. It is relevant to the atmosphere at the time that he always went to mass at 8 o'clock every morning, he was a devout Roman Catholic. He always attended the parade service every Sunday, if he did not agree with the sermon he did not hesitate to tell the chaplain and if there was not a parson available he would take the service himself. He was a man for whom I had enormous admiration and with whom I had a very warm relationship.

Lewes had reported for duty on a Friday evening in the latter half of September 1938, during the Munich crisis. He was greeted by the Commander, AF de Salis, with the news that he was expected to take charge of the digging of the trenches to be used as air raid shelters. Immediately the sense of rivalry between the Torpedo and Gunnery Schools resulted in a race to see which establishment could complete the best trenches in the quickest time. All was fair in love and war. Dennis Boyd had anticipated this development and had sent de Salis into the dockyard to draw shovels and spades.Finding only 130 available he signed for the lot and brought them back to *Vernon*, By the time the order was given to start digging, Lewes had drawn up a plan for the trenches which avoided digging up the football field. Soon a platform was rigged for the band and they played continuously whilst the sailors dug, each trench being left to the initiative of a Leading Torpedoman.

Vernon was commended for its outstanding organisation but, in truth, it was the fact that they had purloined the only spades which led to their victory over the Gunnery School. For many years Lewes was to tell the story of how he and the Captain visited Whale Island on the completion of the *Vernon* trenches. Supervised by the Gunnery Branch, the trenches were laid out in immaculate parallel lines and dug to the strictest and most specific instructions, in sharp contrast to the *Vernon* organisation where each trench had been left to the initiative of an LTO. It was an interesting illustration of the equally excellent, but very different, approaches of the Gunnery and Torpedo Branches: the Gunnery Branch strictly and smartly following orders; the Torpedo Branch laying down general instructions and leaving it to the initiative of torpedomen to do the job. (The Army might have commented that digging trenches haphazardly or in straight lines are neither very good from a strictly military point of view).

Munich revealed that there were no plans for the deployment of Britain's stock of mines. The Directorate of Torpedoes and Mining thought *Vernon* had plans for mining the Dover straits but Boyd denied any knowledge of them. The only officer who might have known was in *Plover* in the Mediterranean. Little more had in fact been done than give information on a 'hypothetical minefield' for a Staff College scheme. Work therefore began after the crisis to draw up proper plans for a Dover Barrage but the work was hampered by doubts as to whether the required destroyer flotilla or two converted ferries would actually be made available.

Munich also made the Commander in Chief, Portsmouth (Admiral the Earl of Cork and Orrery), concerned about the defence of the port against an enemy mining campaign. He sent for Boyd to discuss what he considered to be a shortfall in the minesweeping force which should be allocated to the port on the outbreak of war. It would be a dangerous period and the country could not afford to have one of its principal naval ports closed by enemy mining at such a critical time. Boyd was told to organise a force which could fill this gap: how he was to do it was left to him. On his return to *Vernon*, he sent for Lewes and told him that the Commander in Chief required *Vernon* to organise a force able to keep the approach channels to the port clear of mines for the first month of the war. Furthermore, within *Vernon*, Lewes was to be responsible for establishing this unofficial and, presumably, volunteer mine sweeping body. Lewes was stunned, 'How on earth am I going to do that?', he said. Dennis Boyd replied, 'I suggest that you go round the pubs in Gosport one Sunday afternoon canvassing.'

Lewes' first step was:

To contact the two young Blakes of the famous Gosport based sailmakers, Ratsey and Lapthorn, and a young solicitor called Glanville.

John Glanville had been something of a thorn in the side of the naval hierarchy since 1936 when he had decided that he would like to be a member of the Royal Naval Volunteer Reserve. He had been turned down by Commodore Lord Howe for membership of the Sussex Division whose headquarters were at Hove. He had then approached the Member of Parliament for Portsmouth North, Admiral of the Fleet Sir Roger Keyes, without success until, much to his surprise he received a letter from the MP informing him of the formation of the Royal Naval Volunteer Supplementary Reserve. He immediately applied for membership and was accepted. Unfortunately, the First Lord of the Admiralty, Sir Samuel Hoare, had announced the formation of the Supplementary Reserve without consultation with the Board and no funds were available for training.

After a great deal of frustration and rejection by the Admiral Commanding Reserves, Admiral Sir Henry Studholme-Brownrig, Glanville and other members of the RNVSR in Portsmouth met at the Royal Albert Yacht Club under the chairmanship of Mr JV Bullin. They formed themselves into a group known as the Portsmouth Unit of the RNVSR which would met once a week at the Royal Albert Yacht Club. The meetings took place but nothing else happened. A further visit was made to Roger Keyes to enquire whether something could be done in view of the mounting tension and the possible outbreak of war. Keyes replied that it was now a matter for the Admiralty.

Commodore Howe was informed and in due course passed the reports submitted by the Portsmouth Unit of the RNVSR to the Admiral Commanding Reserves. Like a large broody hen the Admiral sat upon the report and, after a considerable lapse of time, the Unit received the following result of the Admiral's lengthy gestation:

It was noticed that the organizing secretary had visited a Member of Parliament upon a Service matter and whereas the Admiral Commanding Reserves did not in any way wish to interfere with the rights of members of the Reserves as civilians he would like it to be known that as members of the Reserves they were expected to conduct themselves as such and not expected to see Members of Parliament about Service matters.

In spite of Glanville's further appeals for help, Studholme-Brownrig adamantly refused to back the venture, but a chance meeting between Glanville and Rear Admiral R Leatham, the Chief of Staff to the Commander-in-Chief, Portsmouth, brought about a miraculous change of circumstances. The C-in-C invited Glanville to a meeting with the commanding officers of ships and establishments in the Portsmouth Command. Thereafter, offers of assistance for the thirty strong volunteer unit flooded in. When the Commander-in-Chief came to consider the need for an interim minesweeping force he informed Glanville that he had arranged for the unit to be turned over to the Captain of *Vernon* to form the nucleus of a minesweeping party. Meanwhile, instructions had been given for two trawlers to be taken out of reserve and fitted out for instructional purposes.

At *Vernon*, Lewes was glad to receive from Glanville a list of names and addresses to supplement the list which had already been drawn up. Lewes now dined certain yachtsmen who it was thought might be interested in joining this somewhat exclusive and unusual new club. Boyd attended the dinner and warned the diners that they might find themselves in the Tower of London for piracy or high treason but, if so, they would be in good company for the Commander in Chief would be there too. In spite of this warning, volunteers flocked to *Vernon* to serve in what was to be known as the *Vernon* Auxiliary Company.

Before long the VAC was ready to man the two trawlers, *Hornbeam* and *Hawthorn*. In one of the trawlers the Captain had a Sea Scout as signalman, a greyhound race track engineer as leading seaman, a milk roundsman as a wireman, a timber merchant as a winch man, a yacht hand as coxswain and Portsmouth Gas Company men as stokers. In spite of their enthusiasm, their assortment of privately acquired working dress gave them a piratical appearance. After a while it was considered that the lack of uniform was not befitting His Majesty's Ships, particularly on leaving and entering harbour. A uniform was devised consisting, for officers, of blue reefers, grey flannel trousers and black shoes, all privately purchased since no pay or allowances had been authorised, and, for ratings, uniforms supplied from naval stores with the cap tallies inscribed 'VAC'.

In the six months after Munich, the VAC took over complete responsibility for manning and operating the two trawlers; by June 1939 two more vessels had been taken over. They all operated every Sunday and went on a week's cruise with the Fifth Minesweeping Flotilla at Portland. As a special honour, the VAC manned part of the route in the dockyard along which the King and Queen drove to embark for their visit to Canada; they were described to the King as the latest addition to his fighting forces. In August 1939, the trawlers took their place in the Reserve Fleet Review at Weymouth when their commanding officers were presented to the King. In the wardroom of the Reserve Fleet flagship *Effingham* one of the commanding officers was mistaken, in his VAC uniform, for the attache of a foreign naval power!

A few days before mobilisation the VAC was called up as planned, and was given the task of training regular RNVR officers in minesweeping duties. Soon, however, the unit began to break up as members were called away for further training at HMS *King Alfred* at Hove, which had become the central depot for all hostilities only officers. The VAC had completed its task successfully, and the members had good cause to be proud of their achievement.

As war became imminent preparations were made to place the *Vernon* on a war footing. Partial mobilisation of the Reserve Fleet involved the staff in a major operation, receiving large numbers of reservists and arranging for their drafting to ships being brought forward. Plans were drawn up for the dispersal of the trials departments, and officers and men undergoing training were quickly reallocated to ships commissioning from reserve. Commander Webb wrote:

Although part of the Reserve Fleet was commissioned before mid-summer, general mobilisation was delayed until the last practicable moment. After the experience gained during the Munich crisis things went quickly and smoothly. The gym was rigged with canvas screens and barriers, to form a route to ensure that men were seen by the right people in the right order. The South Gate was opened at 0800 to admit a number who had travelled all night. Fortunately, a stall had been set up in the garage entrance, with hot drinks and sandwiches. The stream of arrivals was most intresting to watch, two at least arrived in large cars driven by chauffeurs, others in well kept No1 uniforms. A few had gone downhill since leaving the service and turned up in poor clothes and in poor condition. There were very few, if any, absentees, other than those sick or whose address had recently been changed.

There were, however, a large number of men who owned 'one man' businesses, shops, garages and so on, which had taken all their savings and several years to build up and which their wives, often with small children, could not carry on. An immediate Commander/Captain's request table was set up in the afternoon for 'urgent compassionate leave' and advice. The men were very soon drafted to the Reserve Fleet or to make peace complements up to war strength. It was often very difficult to fill the non-substantive vacancies with the most suitable qualified men; particularly with the LTO rating, whose knowledge was expected to cover such a wide range of subjects and who found himself the senior torpedoman in the smaller ships.

Everyone was cheerful and reasonably happy; sad at leaving settled home and jobs but realizing that war was inevitable and had to be got on with.'

Now, as war approached, the spirit of the old Torpedo Branch came to the fore: the team had lost none of the creative enthusiasm inherited from the beginnings in Victoria's reign. It was this teamwork that brought all the resources to bear where they were most needed, on some of the most serious problems that the Navy and the nation had ever had to face.

On 2 September 1939, officers and men read on the front page of the Daily Express that there would be no war. The next day thousands of men waited in their ships to hear the German Government's reply to the Anglo-French ultimatum. Many still remember the feelings of that fateful hour. One of them, a young future Torpedo Officer, was standing alone on the quarterdeck of the cruiser *Frobisher*. The sound of Neville Chamberlain's voice, announcing Germany's refusal to withdraw from Poland and the inevitable consequences, filtered through from the radio in the Captain's cabin. In the still air of that September morning, in the upper reaches of Portsmouth Harbour, the unreality of the situation numbed the senses. Suddenly the future, which seemed to be so predictable, was now uncertain and fraught with danger. *Vernon's* finest hour was approaching faster than anyone thought.

GERMANY BEGAN THE WAR WITH A stock of 20,000 moored contact mines and 1,500 magnetic ground mines. The latter were new, and only a few were available for immediate laying; *Vernon* had no intelligence on them and there was no organisation tasked for their recovery and investigation. Commander Guy Sayer, in charge of *Vernon*'s Mining Department, had only one Lieutenant Commander for depth charge and demolition work and two Lieutenant Commanders and one Lieutenant for mining matters. It was fortunate that the calibre of these torpedomen enabled Britain to overcome the first crisis of the naval war.

Given the small numbers of operational submarines and other naval units available to Germany at the outbreak of war, mines, especially the new magnetic variety, should have been her major means of striking at Britain's vital shipping. They were laid by small coastal U-boats from the start. On 10 September, the steamer *Magdepur* was sunk by an underwater explosion whilst in convoy off Orford Ness, an area which had already been swept of moored mines. Convoys were immediately diverted from the area but six days later, off the East coast, the SS *City of Paris* was seriously damaged by a similar underwater explosion. She was abandoned but did not sink; her crew returned on board next day and she steamed slowly to London. There she was dry docked and it became clear that she had been damaged by an influence mine. The hull had not been penetrated as it would have been by the explosion of a moored mine but a great deal of internal damage had been caused. The working of this influence mine was a mystery; most experts diagnosed magnetic actuation but others suspected acoustic operation.

The officer at *Vernon* with gretest experience of non-contact mines was Lieutenant Commander JGD Ouvry. A diffident and quietly spoken man, he was no obvious leader of men and had been passed over for promotion, despite distinguished service in the First World War as a young minelaying officer in the light cruiser minelayer *Inconstant*. Ouvry's careful attention to detail and his intimate knowledge of the minelaying instructions resulted in his ship's outstanding success off the German coast. Ouvry was intuitively intelligent, quietly efficient and self effacing. Speaking of himself, he once remarked that he was 'neither pretty, intelligent nor brave', though, he conceded that he had a special gift: steady nerves and an equally steady hand. This, he explained, was because he was so intent upon the job that had to be done that his mind dwelt upon the problem of keeping his hand steady; sudden movements might well induce electric currents with disastrous results.

The Mining Department was soon strengthened by three able officers of the Royal Naval Volunteer Reserve ; Geoffrey Hodges, a master from Winchester College, John Cameron, a King's Counsel (later Lord Cameron) and Selby Armitage, another barrister. After a three week course in controlled mining under the able and wise guidance of Commander GE ('Porky') Veale and Chief Petty Officer Coope, the trio had approached Veale to ask that they should be attached to a department which was actively involved on war work.

All three were therefore attached to the Mining Department , Cameron as assistant to Sayer, and Armitage to Ouvry. Soon Armitage and Cameron moved to the Admiralty and were replaced at *Vernon* by Lieutenant Goodman RNVR and Lieutenant M. Griffith RNVR, the latter the former editor of Yachting Monthly.

The first priority was to find out as much as possible about German mines by recovering examples, in particular examples of the mysterious influence mines. Between 19 and 22 September Ouvry supervised a major search off Orford Ness in an area that had been well swept by the fleet minesweepers based at Harwich. The *Vernon* team, consisting of Ouvry, Chief Petty Officer Baldwin and Able Seamen Vearncombe and Boobier, embarked in the trawler minesweepers *Mastiff* and *Cedar* and proceeded to the vicinity of the wreck of the *Magdepur* but their attempts to find mines of any kind were a complete failure. Early in October the trawler *Tokyo*, whilst fishing off the Swarte Bank, swept up two moored mines in her trawl. It was quickly slipped and *Tokyo* returned to Grimsby to report the incident. Then, on 8-9 October Lieutenant J.E.M. Glenny tried to locate and recover a moored mine reported near Swansea but had no better luck.

Not until 12 October, over a month into the war, were Ouvry and his team able to render safe a German contact mine washed up at Bridlington. Two days later a rendering mines safe service (RMS) was established by *Vernon* on the Yorkshire Coast when CPO Baldwin began operations between Scarborough and Spurn Head. German moored mines now began to be washed ashore in quantity on the east coast beaches. Torn by a storm from the German defensive minefield in the Heligoland Bight, they had been blown across the North Sea. They were of the standard German EMC and EMD contact type (known to *Vernon* as the GY and GX respectively) and presented no difficulty for the teams from *Vernon*. About 200 were rendered safe in October and November; Armitage was transferred from *Vernon* for this task and Glenny was involved also . Further south Lieutenant Commander RB Edwards, a retired torpedo officer recalled to service with the Nore Command, recovered a new contact mine at Baker's Score on the North Norfolk Coast. It was a UMA anti-submarine mine, later designated GZ by *Vernon*, and its switch was set to the position that should have exploded it as soon as it broke free. Edwards bravely ignored standing instructions to coutermine all unexploded mines found set like this as it was clearly a new type. The weapon was duly rended safe.

Still no influence mine turned up. Exploratory sweeping for magnetic mines began, using *Vernon*'s first operational Magnetic Sweep MkI deployed by Lieutenant Commander FC Husband-Clutton, head of the minesweeping section at the outbreak of war. A successful explosion off the Scarweather Light Vessel near Swansea on 20 October seemed to confirm the magnetic hypothesis but this was an isolated success. It was later found that the 27inch magnets had to be closer together and trailed at least fout feet from the bottom to be reliably effective against the German mines.

Even if the mystery mines were magnetic their detailed 'firing rules' would have to be worked out before effective countermeasures could be developed. In September and October 1939, mines accounted for almost 60,000 tons of Allied merchant shipping, compared to almost 290,000 tons lost directly to submarines. The Germans, however, noted the vulnerability of the British to their new mines and stepped up laying. German destroyers and motor torpedo boats joined in the minelaying offensive from 17 October. A clue to the new methods of laying came on 25 October, when a float used to lower the mines to the sea bed, and adorned by a rude message to the First Lord of the Admiralty, was discovered off the Lincolnshire coast at Mablethorpe. Glenny, who discovered the 'Churchill Float', thought it might be evidence of aerial minelaying from seaplanes on the water. However they were delivered, the threat from German mines soon became pressing indeed. In November, mines took the lead as the main threat to Allied sea communications. Some 27 merchant ships of 121,000 tons were sunk.

On 13 November the cruiser minelayer *Adventure* was severely damaged by a mine off the Tongue Light Vessel in the Thames Estuary and her escorting destroyer *Blanche* was sunk. Sayer sent for a retired officer who had been recalled to *Vernon*, Commander CE Hamond. He was the only officer at the establishment with knowledge of trawling and Sayer ordered him to develop a trawl net to recover bottom mines. Hamond discussed the problem with Skipper Reynolds of the trawler *Dorienta* and together they designed suitable equipment. This was fitted to the trawler *Cape Spartel* and sent to the area in which *Adventure* had been damaged. Glenny was put in charge of the operation as Sayer wanted Hamond back at *Vernon* as soon as possible. Glenny and Hamond travelled to Sheerness where they met Ouvry who was to act as danlayer in the trawler *Mastiff*. *Cape Spartel* arrived on 18 November The operation began on Monday 20 November; it quickly ended in disaster when *Mastiff* was mined and sunk, and six lives were lost to no avail. At 1900 that evening Hamond and Glenny reported to the Admiralty, where they were interviewed by Churchill, and Admiral Sir Dudley Pound, the First Sea Lord. Pound ordered Hamond to fit out non-magnetic wooden drifters at Lowestoft for further trials with his gear.

Earlier that fateful Monday morning Boyd had been at the Admiralty and and he and Pound had agreed that everything depended upon the early recovery of a German influence mine. There then entered upon the scene another distinguished torpedo officer, who was to play a key role in this task. On the outbreak of war Lieutenant Commander Roger Lewis had been re-appointed from Torpedo Officer of *Warspite* to stand by at *Vernon* where he was not to remain idle for very long. He had only recently been promoted and his reputation as a tough and reliable character commended him as Torpedo Officer on the staff of Rear Admiral AL St G Lyster, preparing block ships for use at Zeebrugge and Ostend, and training a demolition party to blow up the harbour installations there. It had been intended to carry out this operation with the help of the Belgians once the Germans invaded, which was expected in mid-November. The Germans however had not obliged and the blockships were reduced from immediate to four hours notice on 20 November. Lewis and the commanding officers of the two blocking forces took the opportunity to travel to London to report to Lyster. At lunch Lewis was informed that Lyster had been ordered to turn his attention to searching for the new mystery mines, and that Lewis, as the Torpedo Officer on his staff, would be the key figure.

Cameron came up from *Vernon* and his analytical legal training combined with Lewis's practical experience and organisational ability produced a comprehensive nine point programme:

1) The characteristics of ships reported sunk or damaged by the weapon were to be carefully analysed.
2) The reported movements of enemy aircraft in areas discovered to contain the mines were also to be carefully examined.
3) Senior survivors of mined ships were to be interviewed.
4) Ships damaged were to be visited by members of Lewis's team.
5) Personal visits would also be made to areas where mines were reported laid in the hope of obtaining sufficient information to organise a dive.
6) All intelligence on German mines and mining held by Naval Intelligence Department was to be carefully reviewed.
7) A questionnaire was to be issued to all British consuls and agents in neutral countries adjacent to Germany to elicit more information.
8) All German patents on magnetic and acoustic properties were to be examined.
9) All British firms in touch with Germany pre-war were to be interrogated for any useful leads.

In order to collate and analyse the information, reinforcements in the shape of six RNVR sub-lieutenats trained as barristers were sent up from *Vernon* to work under Captain Barratt. Armitage was also posted from *Vernon* to work for Lyster and Lewis. On Tuesday 21 November Cameron left for the Firth of Forth where the new cruiser *Belfast* had just been seriously damaged by a mystery influence mine. Further south, the destroyer *Gipsy* was also mined and sunk that day and merchant shipping was being seriously delayed. That night news arrived at the Admiralty of aircraft laying mines off the Humber, Harwich and Southend. At 0300 on Wednesday morning Lewis drove to Southend; Armitage went to the Humber and Barratt to Harwich.

This new aerial mining offensive was the brainchild of Raeder, the C-in-C of the German navy who was anxious to press ahead with the mining capaign while Britain had no antidote. Contrary to the wishes of Goering who wanted to delay an aerial mining campaign until enough weapons were available for a mass attack, the German Navy organised a force of nine Luftwaffe Heinkel 59 float planes, already under its tactical command, to undertake limited aerial minelaying in the Thames Estuary. On the evening of 20 November the nine lumbering biplanes took off, each carrying two magnetic mines. The operation was poorly planned; faulty navigation caused five of the aircraft to return to base without releasing any weapons and the remaining four laid seven mines. The Heinkels met with more success on the following night. The masters of the merchant ships anchored in the Thames Estuary reported seeing low flying aircraft dropping what looked like hammocks suspended from parachutes.

Lewis was informed of the mysterious parachutes when he interviewed the masters at Southend on 22 November. This was the first hard intelligence that the Germans were employing air dropped mines. Merchant seamen had seen similar parachute drops in the Baltic but Naval Technical Intelligence had not associated these with mines. Lewis was able to obtain the approximate position of four mines and some information on laying techniques but he lacked firm information and decided to return to the Admiralty where he was told to get some rest after his long day. He left for the Naval and Military Club at 2300 but was almost immediately recalled by telephone. Southend had reported mines dropped near the pier above the low water mark. The Heinkels had been engaged by Lewis machine gunners specially posted by the Naval Officer in Charge Southend at the end of the pier after the first reports of aerial minelaying. Other machine gunners were placed on the ships trapped by the mines in the area. As naval personnel these gunners were not subject to the standing ban on engaging suspected enemy aircraft without the permission of air defence headquarters at Uxbridge. Their fire played a crucial role; the crew of one Heinkel jettisoned a brace of mines close to the shore off Shoeburyness.

At the Admiralty Lewis met Ouvry and told him that a car and driver had been ordered for 0100. Ouvry had been wakened at 0300 the previous morning by a policeman banging on the door of his house in Fareham with a message from *Vernon* that he should contact Sayer as soon as possible. Captain Boyd had rung his Commander 'M' at 0215 saying that mines were being dropped by air and that his most suitable officer should be sent to London to aid in the effort to 'catch a mine alive and probe its secret'. Sayer had earmarked Ouvry for this duty and sent a car to bring him to *Vernon*. There he briefed him and, as Sayer later remembered, 'told him briefly of the dangerous job of work in store for him. I don't think either of us had any illusions as to the possible consequences and it was not a pleasant order to give.' The car then took Ouvry to the station to catch the earliest possible train to London, where he was to report to the minesweeping department at the Admiralty. No useful news came in on 22 November from Lewis, Armitage or Barratt and Ouvry had returned to his room at the Victoria Hotel in Northumberland Avenue. Just after midnight he was recalled by telephone and left so hastily that he left his secret 'Rendering Mines Safe' notes on the dressing table. Worrying about this kept him awake on the back seat of the Naval car as it rushed through the night to Southend; a 'grand' drive as Lewis remembered it from his position in the front passenger's seat navigating the driver along a familiar route, 'we crashed fifteen red lights before getting out of London'! Making final arramngements had delayed departure until 0130; *Vernon* was contacted and ordered to send up the special mine recovery party with non-magnetic tools. The Naval Control Service at Southend was told to arrange lights, securing gear and a photographer.

The car arrived at the Naval Control Service Headquarters at Southend at 0330, only half an hour before high water. It picked up Commander Bowles of the Control Service staff and an apprehensive civilian photographer. Ouvry and Lewis were also told that the mines by the pier were non-existent but that the Army at Shoeburyness claimed that they had found one in front of their battery. There Commander RFPL Maton RN , a gunnery specialist was serving as the Naval Experimental Officer on the artillery ranges. Maton was a contemporary of Lyster's and had been personally ordered by his old friend to give every possible assistance to the *Vernon* team. Maton threw himself into the task with great energy and enthusiasm; when Ouvry and Lewis arrived he had already organised a party of soldiers equipped with lights, ropes and stakes and his civilian photographer. With the soldiers in the rear illuminating the path by Aldis lamp Lewis and Ouvry trudged across the mudflats in the darkness and the rain. Eventually , a cylindrical shape was seen lying partially embedded in the mud. Ouvry, meticulous about detail, had previously insisted that all metal objects, such as money or cigarette cases which the party were carrying, should be discarded and that metal buttons should be removed.

When the object was sighted in the mud Ouvry told the party to remain well clear while he and Lewis advanced to investigate. A preliminary examination established that the thing was approximately 7 feet in length and 2 feet in diameter, with tubular horns on the nose and a large spring inside a hollow tail; it was constructed of a light aluminium type alloy. There was no indication as to whether this mine was of the magnetic or acoustic type. Speaking in subdued tones to avoid exciting any acoustic vibrator, Ouvry and Lewis continued their examination. They identified a housing containing the hydrostatic valve but were puzzled by a polished aluminium fitting secured by a screwed ring sealed with tallow. This seemed the likely position of the primer and detonator and with a sheet of signal pad Lewis took an impression of the ring so that Commander Maton could have a brass spanner and pins made in his workshop before the mine was uncovered again at the next low tide. The next task was to secure it against the incoming water and the soldiers tethered it with hemp lines secured to wooden stakes driven into the ground. Meanwhile, Ouvry instructed the now terrified photographer to take a comprehensive range of flash pictures of the mine. On their way back to the shoreline they were diverted by a mysterious light on the shore. This disappeared but the party discovered the parachute lying spread out on the sand and recovered it. Maton took Bowles, Ouvry and Lewis to his home at 0600, where they all enjoyed an excellent breakfast. Shortly afterwards they received a message that a second mine had been sighted about 300 yards from the first. The officers drove to the location but despite wading out into the advancing tide could not locate the mine which was already covered. They decided to wait until the tide began to fall before dealing with both mines.

This gave Ouvry and Lewis enough time to return to Southend to frame a preliminary report and to send it immediately by hand of officer to the Admiralty, accompanied by copies of the flash photographs. By 1300, when the falling tide had uncovered both mines, a party of soldiers and the range's crane equipped recovery vehicle had assembled. Leaving the official Army photographer to take a series of daylight photographs of the first mine, Ouvry and Lewis examined the second which, firmly held by its horns, was still lying the way it had fallen, at a different angle from the first. A large plate was exposed which lead Ouvry to believe that it concealed a second hydro-static valve. At this juncture the mine recovery party from *Vernon* arrived with a set of non-magnetic tools to augment the spanner and pins made overnight by Maton's team. All was now ready to tackle the first mine which was the less damaged of the pair.

The first problem for Ouvry and Lewis was to identify the purposes of the tubular horns and the massive phosphor-bronze spring. It was soon agreed that the horns were not dangerous, and intended only to prevent the mine from rolling with the tide. The hollow tail and its spring were concerned solely with the ejection of the parachute. For the two Torpedo Officers it was a time for constant vigilance. It was still not clear whether this was an acoustic or a magnetic mine. The former might be actuated by any loud noise, and the latter by the proximity of metal or, indeed, by any rapid movement of its own shell. A further worry was that the Germans, in their anxiety to protect their secret, might have installed a booby trap. Chief Petty Officer Baldwin and Able Seaman Vearncombe had arrived with the team from *Vernon*. Both were steady and reliable torpedomen who greatly impressed Maton with the quiet and efficient way they got on with their duties under conditions of great stress. Ouvry summed it up some forty six years later; 'They never flinched, they just got on with the job.'

Surveying that scene on the deserted mudflats at Shoeburyness on 24 November 1939, Ouvry decided that he and CPO Baldwin would tackle mine number one whilst Lewis and Vearncombe kept in communication from the safety of the foreshore with field telephones borrowed from the range. A sequence of events was arranged which could be reported so that the procedure could be corrected in later operations should anything go wrong. According to plan, Ouvry and Baldwin first tackled the screwed ring which secured the aluminium fitting close to the nose of the mine. The brass makeshift tools made in Maton's workshop were intended for application to this screwed ring but on examination it was found that one of the holes intended for a pin was masked by a copper strip. Ouvry instructed Baldwin to bend the strip back, but in his enthusiasm the Chief Petty Officer began to tear it off, until Ouvry told him to stop. As it turned out, if he had not done so both of them would, in Ouvry's words, have been 'blown to kingdom come'. The strip activated the mine's bomb fuse and had not been removed as the mines had been jettisoned rather than dropped. Ouvry later confessed that

One of the Shoeburyness mines. 24 November 1939

at this stage he said a prayer. All was now ready for the application of Maton's four brass pins and their spanner handle, and the keep ring unscrewed quite easily. Using a brass rod Ouvry was able very carefully to prise out of the mine a fitting which he saw contained a detonator. Convinced that the main danger was now over, Ouvry signalled to Lewis to come to the scene to take the detonator ashore to be photographed. Lewis and Vearncombe then joined Ouvry and Baldwin to help man-handle the mine so as to get the primer out of the pocket and to reach the various other pockets and fittings still buried in the sand. Doctor AB Wood of the Mine Design Department had now arrived and he followed Lewis and Vearncombe across the mudflats to a position whence he could monitor the proceedings.

With the aid of a rope Ouvry, Lewis, Baldwin and Vearncombe managed to turn the mine over. The loose primer discs were extracted but the plate covering the suspected hydrostatic valve proved difficult to budge, despite the attentions of a hammer and screwdriver. Attention then turned to a plate directly opposite the suspected hydrostatic valve. Feeling confident that the mine was now probably safe, they unscrewed the plate which exposed a 'circular screwed bung with four recesses'. No special spanners had

Baldwin, Vearncombe and AN Other with an early German mine

been manufactured for this fitting and, as the mine was now considered safe, considerable force was again applied. The 'bung' was removed to reveal another screwed plate with two terminals and two pairs of leads one of which diappeared into the nose of the mine. This was diagnosed as the mine's battery. The leads were parted by twisting and the plate was unscrewed with the aid of a non-magnetic screwdriver. Ouvry and Lewis were 'rather surprised' to find that they had in their hands not a battery but a carrier for the electric detonator of the type used in the standard German moored mines. The pair were considerably relieved that they had succeded in removing such a potentially dangerous fitting by such crude methods. Ouvry felt momentary relief and exhilaration; they were 'on top of the world,' he later recalled.

This detonator's primer was still firmly fixed in the mine and could only be removed by turning the mine over again so that it could be approached from the opposite side through another, larger, suspected hydrostatic valve plate found on the underside of the mine. This plate was removed and the normal switch gear of German mines found, within together with a heavy cylinder with a hydrostatic valve at one end and five leads going off into the mine. The leads were cut and the cylinder removed. Finally attention returned to the original suspected hydrostatic valve plate. A considerable amount of force was required to free the fitting, and when it did come clear it came with a rush, propelled by a long phosphor-bronze spring which was later discovered to be part of a a hydrostatically operated primer release gear. The spring flew through the air into the mud; the second primer was then easily removed. All that now remained was one more plate. Before removing it the recovery vehicle was sent for so that the mine could moved as soon as possible. The last extraction revealed a copper diaphragm and Wood immediately diagnosed acoustic firing. The mine was taken ashore by the recovery vehicle and placed on a wooden pallet.

The rising tide now made it too late to recover the second mine. The primers, detonators and other trophies were each carried ashore in turn for storage in the police lodge. When the cylindrical fitting containing the hydrostatic valve was laid down on the beach for the first time it started to tick. There was a rapid retirement from the area but it was soon found that the weight of the fitting had been thrown on to the protruding hydrostatic valve spindle, setting the clock in motion. It was by this time quite harmless. At 1700 on 24 November, Ouvry asked Southend to signal the Admiralty that one had been recovered intact. Lewis returned to London to report to Admiral Lyster. He was taken by car to the station where he boarded a train to London at 2100, saying that he would be at the Admiralty about ninety minutes later.

On arrival in Whitehall he was told that Lyster had tried to keep the meeting a small one but that the First Lord had insisted on attending and that it would be a major occasion. He apologised as he knew that Lewis had not been to bed for four days. Churchill and about sixty senior officers assembled in room 60, the Admiralty Cinema, at 2300 on 24 November. The large, solid and reliable Lewis, aptly known as 'Bull' to his fellow officers, was seated beteween Churchill and Pound. He had agreed with Ouvry to inform the meeting that:

a) They did not think that the mine was magnetic.
b) They did not understand the cylindrical mechanism, which afterwards was found to be a bomb fuse. The reasons for thinking it was acoustic were:
1. It was known that the Italians were developing acoustic mines.
2. They had found the large copper diaphragm (actually covering a filling hole) in the nose.
3. The leads from the detonator disappeared into the nose in the direction of the copper diaphragm.

Churchill interrogated Lewis intensively about how the characteristics of the mine and how it had been dismantled. He summed up in typical style: "...you have dissected this monster, divided it into pieces and now you can examine it at leisure.'

Lewis then added his personal opinion that he thought the mine was actuated by magnetic as well as acoustic influence. The Director of Scientific Research suggested that one means was used to prime the mine and the other to fire it. This was the only minuted contribution to the meeting not made by Lewis or Churchill. Shortly afterwards the First Lord drew proceedings to a conclusion as follows:

We cannot carry on any further at the moment. We have got our prize, as good a ship as ever sailed the seas, and we owe a great deal to the public spirit of Lieutenant Commander Lewis and his colleague Lieutenant Commander Ouvry who have been up against it today. They have given us a lot of most valuable particulars which the science of the VERNON *and the Admiralty will employ to the full.*

Ouvry's mine is loaded onto truck for delivery to Vernon

The mine and parachute left for *Vernon* in a naval lorry at 0900 the following morning, 25 November. Ouvry and HJ Taylor of the Mine Design Department then left for Woolwich, taking with them the mysterious aluminium fitting first removed from the mine. There a series of X-ray photographs were taken, but they did not reveal the secret within the container. However, the detonator envelope was unscrewed and left at Woolwich for analysis of its contents. Without further delay Ouvry and Taylor returned to *Vernon* where the fuse was stripped and examined. It was found to be a device for enabling the mine to be used as a large delayed action bomb. It proved to be an adaption of the standard bomb fuse used by the Luftwaffe, and designed around a patent brought out by the company Rheinmetall in 1932. This was a valuable discovery which was to pay dividends when the Luftwaffe started to use these mines for blast effect during the 'Blitz'.

At 1600 on 25 November the mine arrived at *Vernon* where work was started immediately to dismantle it. Inside was found an elaborate aluminium casing mounted in rubber, which was turned over to Doctor Wood for immediate examination. Churchill sent word that the answer to the problem was to be found without delay and that work was to proceed night and day to this end. The First Lord was not disappointed, within twelve hours the Admiralty was informed that, contrary to the views of the officers who had dismantled it, it was indeed a magnetic mine. This diagnosis was an outstanding achievement by the Mine and Mine Design Departments of *Vernon*. Sayer reported that he:

had made various preparations for the reception and examination of our prize. It was decided to carry out the post mortem in the non-magnetic laboratory building, where operations could proceed behind locked doors and, we hoped, with a minimum of disturbance. Sentries were detailed to guard the door and a small team of experts chosen to do the job. These consisted of Dr AB Wood, Messrs Kelly and Shaw (all of the Mine Design Department) and CH PO Baldwin and myself of 'M' Department. A recorder was also detailed to keep tally of what was done, and others were co-opted from time to time as required, such as the VERNON *photographer and various skilled workmen from the MD Department. On arrival the mine was shifted out of the lorry and placed on the operating table, the doors were locked and the team started in. The stripping and examination went on continuously throughout the night and I shall never forget some of the incidents - the first conviction on the part of the scientists that it was an acoustic mine - the excitement of stripping the bomb fuse which was still in a partially 'alive' state - the ingenious and plausible excuses of some who wanted 'just to have a look' - the arguments and discussions - and finally the gradual piecing together of the why and wherefore of the whole infernal bag of tricks. By 0200/24 the main secret had been laid bare, and I was able to 'phone direct to the Admiralty the brief but certain news that it was a magnetic mine and operated by vertical magnetism.*

Ouvry and Lewis had thought it proper that no attempt should be made to recover the second mine on the mud at Shoeburyness until the *Vernon* examination of the first mine had been completed. It was, therefore, not until ten o'clock in the morning of Saturday 25th that Glenny was sent to Shoeburyness with Baldwin and Vearncombe to tackle it. They had spent most of the Friday night and early Saturday morning examining the mechanism of Ouvry's mine and they set off feeling reasonably confident that they could cope with the mine still in the mud. Once again Maton provided splendid assistance, enabling swift progress to be made although the hastily manufactured non-magnetic tools seemed to delight in slipping and turning at the edges. When the detonator had been removed the bung and cover plate were carefully replaced before the mine was covered by the incoming tide. However, there was still time to remove the bomb fuse if the mine could be rolled over. This proved more difficult than had been expected, the hollow horn protusions around the nose being firmly embedded in the wet sand. Nine men working with hand spikes as levers were unable to move it but, fortunately, Maton was at hand with the recovery vehicle to which a rope was attached, the other end being secured to the mine which rolled over obediently.

Now some anxiety began to be felt by Glenny and Baldwin. They noticed that there was no tear off copper tab on the bomb fuse and with the knowledge which they now had of the type of fuse it seemed strange that the mine had not detonated on impact. With darkness setting in and the tide coming in fast they began to work feverishly. Spanners did not work too well and the keep ring on the bomb fuse moved only half a turn and then stopped. As they moved the spanner to try again there was a sharp 'click'; they glanced at each other and without a word both left the scene as rapidly as possible. The soldiers who had been helping and standing some 400 yards away, also vanished into the gathering darkness and nothing more was seen of them that night. For what seemed an age, the two torpedomen stopped and waited. Nothing happened. The mine was still there, sitting in the water and just visible. They did not take long to decide that they would be better off for a hot bath and a good dinner, so collecting their belongings they retraced their steps and decided to complete the job at dawn the following morning.

The task was completed without further incident and the mine loaded on to a lorry for transport to *Vernon* where it arrived later that day. But what was the noise that had caused them to abandon the work on the previous day? Lewis had arrived in time to help with the final stages of the operation, and said that in his opinion the 'click' had been caused by no more than the corner of Glenny's oilskin flapping against the mine!

Satisfied with the progress with the second mine, Lewis hurried down to Gravesend where another mine had been reported on Mucking Flats. The search proved both unpleasant and abortive, but on his return to the Admiralty Lewis found that Churchill had started powerful arrangements for finding countermeasures to the magnetic mine. Rear Admiral W.F. Wake-Walker, the Flag Officer in command of minelaying, was placed in charge of magnetic mine countermeasures and Lyster's investigation organisation absorbed into the new organisation. Lewis had to go back to Sheerness to look after his primary responsibilities, the blockships and their demolition parties, but he also helped with the experimental sweeping operations in the Thames Estuary

It was *Vernon* , however, that was in direct charge of developing the key countermeasure to the magnetic mine, making the ships themselves undetectable by the mines' magnetic sensors. The principle was well known and after the Munich crisis in 1938 experiments in changing a ship's magnetism using electrified coils had been carried out at the Admiralty Research Laboratory. Captain Boyd at *Vernon* had studied this work and thought it had potential but in November 1939 was about to leave the establishment; he needed to leave a trusted and able Torpedo Officer to find practical means of following up the initial experiments. Boyd decided to recall his able former First Lieutenant, John Hext Lewes, who had just been made an Acting Commander and appointed to take over the old destroyer *Shikari* refitting at Devonport.

Boyd was being dined out of *Vernon* the day Lewes arrived. At the dinner in *Vernon*'s wardroom he greeted his former subordinate with an apology for recalling him from such an attractive command and wasted no time confronting him with his new task. Boyd's instructions were brief. Referring to the Research Laboratory trials he said, 'Here is an idea which there may be nothing in. If there is anything in it, it is very big. Find out at once on a full scale and drive the scientists.' Lewes set about the task that very night. He was soon provided with a trawler and a working party, and was authorised to call upon the assistance of the civilian technical staff of the Superintendent of Mine Design.

It had been found that the German magnetic mines recovered by Ouvry, Lewis and Glenny were operated by the vertical component of a ship's magnetic field. It was, therefore, the original intention of the *Vernon* trials to reverse this vertical component. The polarity of a ship's magnetism depends upon its position in relation to the earth's magnetic field while under construction : each ship has a a different magnetic signature depending upon the orientation of the slipway upon which she was built. Some method of measuring these individual magnetic signatures was therefore an essential first step and a magnetic measuring unit operating a spot of light galvanometer was laid in Portsmouth Harbour off *Vernon* pier. Three horizontal coils carrying electrical current were assembled around the hull of Lewes' trawler, and trial runs over the measuring unit were instituted which were an immediate success. Lewes' team demonstrated that they could reverse the magnetic field under the trawler and so give protection against the mine recovered at Shoeburyness. Within forty eight hours orders were given for all minesweeping trawlers to be fitted with these coils.

So far so good. But Lewes was aware that this was not enough. Twelve more of these primitive measuring units were laid on the sea bottom in the Solent, close by the *Vernon* experimental establishment at Stokes Bay. With galvanometers installed in a hut ashore, this magnetic range was ready by December to measure the effectiveness of a three coil 'demagnetisation' system fitted in a small merchant ship. The results gave an indication of the strength of the coils required to give protection to the ship, but it was a hit and miss affair. The ad hoc nature of the trials programme brought Lewes into conflict with his scientific colleagues. Lewes was trained in decision making on the basis of limited data; the scientists were trained in arriving at conclusions on the basis of long and painstaking research. The synthesis of this potentially disastrous dialectic was helped by the arrival of Edward ('Teddy') Bullard, later Sir Edward Bullard FRS, who knew that the crisis demanded the speedy solutions that could only be obtained by a more pragmatic approach.

Another new member of Lewes' team was Sub lieutenant Lochner RNVR, seconded from 'Q' ships. He had submitted a paper suggesting a horizontal coil similar to that being used in Lewes' trials, and he had also estimated the strength of current required which he thought necessitated a a coil twelve times the depth of the hull in feet. Lewes then met the East coast shipowners at the Ministry of Shipping. When he proposed that their merchantmen should be fitted with coils supplied with electric current from the ships' own power sources he met with instant opposition. The owners said that it was quite out of the question to supply the quantities of power required. Fortunately, a number of 5 kilowatt generators were available which could power the coils in the merchantmen chosen to be fitted with the coils. Their masters showed little confidence in this new fangled system of defence against magnetic mines; they gained rather more when, at the end of her voyage, a ship anchored in the Humber and switched off her coils, and a mine on the seabed beneath her immediately exploded!

It soon became apparent that Lochner's estimate of the power required to operate the coils was considerably underestimated. Once again the ship owners protested when Lewes raised the coil strength safety factor by stages to 20 and 24 times the depth of the hull. However, a powerful figure at the highest level swept away all opposition. Each day a report recording the work of the previous twenty four hours in countering the magnetic mine was forwarded by courier to the Admiralty; by midnight it was on Churchill's desk. Admiral Wake-Walker described his meetings with the First Lord as 'shattering' but, for Lewes, Churchill's intervention was a godsend. He was able to overcome many dockyard difficulties by reminding those concerned that he had to report to the First Lord each evening; an implicit threat to say that a dockyard department had not tried hard enough was sufficient to obtain all the support that was needed. Some 2,000 merchant ships had been fitted with coils by May 1940.

With the merchant ship programme well under way, Lewes was able to turn his attention to the equally urgent problem of the protection of major warships. In December, the cruiser *Manchester*, flying the flag of Rear Admiral Geoffrey Layton, was allocated for trials over the Stokes Bay range. The flagship's Torpedo Officer was instructed to rig the trial coils. Before he could do so he had to face the wrath of his admiral who remarked, 'If their Lordships think we are better employed on this nonsense than chasing Germans in the North Sea so be it, but by God I'll see that you don't waste time.' For four days the ship ran trials over the Stokes Bay range, but the results proved inconclusive. More calculations were required and the cruiser's sailing was delayed. Eventually, however, the trials were successful and the way was open to fit all major warships with what soon became definitively known as 'degaussing' coils.

The degaussing group of the Mine Sweeping Section rapidly outgrew its parent. The two attics which it had occupied in No 21 Building at *Vernon* were no longer adequate, but finding this new home proved to be unexpectedly difficult. Lewes had his eye on the ballroom and offices at the Clarence Pier close to the entrance to Portsmouth Harbour, but somewhere a strong personality was arguing that a fun fair and dance hall were vital to the morale of the citizens of Portsmouth and that of the sailors on shore leave. Lieutenant GAJ Goodhart, who had recently been appointed as an assistant to Lewes, was selected to call on the manager of the pier, and to tell him that it was being requisitioned by the Navy. The manager turned out to be small in stature but no easy pushover; it was Billy Butlin (later Sir Billy Butlin of Holiday Camp fame). However, the matter was settled amicably and the Navy got its way and the accomodation it needed.

Teddy Bullard's scientists and the *Vernon* degaussing team were now working together in complete harmony. Lewes said that he had once heard someone describe Bullard as the most inspired guesser he had ever met. 'Bullard would reach a correct conclusion on little more than half the data really required.' Once Bullard got going it was no longer a matter of driving the scientist but rather 'of running as hard as one could to keep him in sight.' For his part, Bullard said that degaussing was the only piece of research in which he had reached more than one hundred per cent of his expectations.

With success came the rapid setting up of degaussing ranges around the United Kingdom, and subsequently around the world. These measured the magnetic signatures of ships and asessed their safety factors. To man the new ranges many accomplished men came forward, among them famous scientists such as Henry Hulme, the assistant to the Astronomer Royal and future head of the Atomic Weapon Research Establishment at Aldermaston. Perhaps the most eminent was Lieutenant Commander CF Goodeve RNVR. On the outbreak of war, he had been given a roving commission as technical assistant to the Captain of *Vernon*. Given a free hand, Goodeve was able to apply himself to the degaussing problem. Indeed, it he who invented the name 'degaussing' as a means of confusing inquisitive people as to the purpose of the programme.

Goodeve developed an effective method by which the magnetic signature of a small ship could be changed. This consisted of raising a horizontal cable carrying a heavy current around the ships' hull. This had the effect of neutralising the normal magnetic polarity and was introduced in time to treat the vessels used for the Dunkirk evacuation. Known as 'wiping', this procedure became a normal part of the preparation of small ships for war service.

In the course of difficult trials fitting a degaussing coil to an old destroyer, a member of the team involved, Sub Lieutenant Payne RNVR, suggested that the permanent magnetism built into a ship could be altered by introducing a heavy current flashed through an external and temporary coil. A trial was immediately carried out with such successful results that the system, known as 'Deperming' was subsequently applied on a large scale. It could not achieve the permanent protection of proper degaussing equipment but it allowed degaussing to be carried out with greater accuracy.

Meanwhile, the Admiralty, anxious and impatient to find out whether the Germans were using other types of influence mines, instructed Hamond to repeat the operation to attempt to recover specimens by ground trawls. Early in December 1939, he left for Ramsgate in charge of six wooden drifters. There he met Glenny and Armitage who were told to find and prepare a suitable place for landing the nets and any finds. A suitable site was found at Palm Bay, close to Foreness. 'TM 2' was a disastrous operation, for the drifters were poorly manned, leaky and dirty. They managed to dredge up one mine, but it exploded in the trawl, sinking the drifter *Ray of Hope* with the loss of fifteen lives. Another trawler, the *Jacketa*, caught fire on Christmas night, and this destroyed the after part of the ship. As a result, trawling for mines in this way was abandoned. Hammond and his assistant, Lieutenant CWA Chapel RNVR had performed gallantly during these abortive operations and were awarded the Distinguished Service Order and the Distinguished Service Cross respectively.

Another type of magnetic mine was however discovered in December. Again, Roger Lewis was involved, although not so directly as he would have liked. The mine had been reported to C- in-C Nore and Lewis sent an officer and a CPO to investigate the vague initial sighting. They reported that it was indeed a magnetic mine but failed to tell Lewis that it was twice the size of the Shoeburyness weapons. Preoccupied with minesweeping experiments and with no tools available, Lewis reported the mine to *Vernon* for disposal. Glenny and Armitage duly arrived and on 7 December rendered the mine safe and brought it back to *Vernon*. It was a parachute mine but of a new type, almost twice the size of the Shoeburyness mines; it was therefore designated Type 'B'. The German designation was LMB and its firing mechanism was similar to the LMAs already recovered.

Lewis was frustrated at being 'done out of this mine' but the magnetic minesweeping experiments he was supervising were beginning to bear fruit. *Vernon* had set up a separate Minesweeping Section under Commander R Oliver Bellasis and a number of alternative approaches to the problem were being tried. An electrical coil was fitted into a barge supplied by the Royal Naval Armament Depot at Upnor. It was connected to a 17kw generator in the drifter *Feaco*, commanded by Lieutenant GP Kilroy. who towed it to an area off Holehaven where Lewis knew that the Germans had laid several mines. *Feaco* was immediately successful in detonating a mine on 3rd December and the system was rushed into production as the Skid. This was a wooden catamaran about 20 feet square in which was mounted a large electrical coil. A 75kw generator was mounted in a trawler or drifter which supplied current to the Skid through an electric cable lashed to the three inch flexible steel wire tow rope. This was sufficient to produce from the Skid's electrical coil a magnetic field equivalent to that of a cruiser or a large liner. Soon 45 of these unwieldy sweeps were in operation around the coasts of Great Britain but they soon became unpopular. With a following wind and sea, the Skid would come racing towards the towing vessel, forcing it to take emergency action to avoid a collision. Suddenly, the tow rope would take the strain again. Often, with an almighty 'twang', it parted leaving the Skid floating aimlessly about. Then it had to be recovered before setting about the lengthy job of splicing the towing hawser and repairing the electric cable. After two such annoying incidents Sub Lieutenant Sworder, one of the officers in charge of a Skid sweep, came up with his own solution; 'to avoid losing our 'Skid' in rough weather we attached a harness to it with buffer springs which I found in an old railway yard in Birkenhead. A half hundredweight sinker was then shackled half way down the tow between the ship and Skid. This seemed to do the trick...'

Another problem was that if a mine was detonated the Skid was destroyed and the towing vessel was also in danger. In the Mersey one of the trawlers managed to detonate a magnetic mine using her Skid, but in doing so she received damage requiring her to be beached. She was quickly repaired and, on her return to the Mersey, was cheered by other ships using the river which gave the little ship credit for having saved the new aircraft carrier *Illustrious* which had been routed down an alternative channel. This indeed was the key to the Skid's utility. Rather than sweep mines, Skid fitted trawlers and drifters could identify safe passages and they played a significant role in getting coastal shipping moving again after the crisis of November-December 1939. Development of *Vernon*'s Magnetic Sweep continued. In December 1939 it began to be fitted in minesweepers with seventy 27 inch magnets each ten feet apart. Weights trailing along the bottom ensured that the magnets remained at the correct depth. Two inch sweep wire was used to allow sweeping by trawlers and drifters up to 1.5 cables (300 yards) apart. Unfortunately, the new Magnetic Sweep remained less effective than expected. A clue to the reason why was provided when a smaller variant was provided to Lieutenant WG Wheeler RAN, sent by *Vernon* to the Thames Estuary to clear the channel of two magnetic mines holding up a large number of ships. Wheeler, whose Government had insisted he stay in Britain to complete the Long Torpedo Course, had been supplied with a short magnetic sweep with six 27 inch magnets, to be towed them from the sterns of two bawleys, hired with their local crews at Southend. He achieved no success towing the magnets at the long scope instructed by the Admiralty. In Webb's words, 'bored by this, he shortened the scope and blew up both mines before evening'. The boats were damaged but Wheeler was ecstatic. He send a cryptic signal to Boyd at the Admiralty, which read, 'W W S S H H'. This caused much confusion while the staff attempted to unravel the meaning. Eventually decoded, it read 'Wheeler Wins. Southend Safe. Heil Hitler'.

Experience and knowledge gleaned at *Vernon* from the mine recovered by Ouvry and Lewis allowed further modifications to the Magnetic Sweep to produce the MkII*** which used larger, 72 inch bar magnets. This made the sweep much more effective but did nothing to make it easier to operate. The unfortunate seamen charged with this difficult task christened the magnetic sweep the 'Bo'sun's Nightmare'. They disliked the many tangles which always took place as they paid out the heavy clanking bars of iron over the stern. If a mine was detonated bars would be blown away and the sweep would have to be repaired. Nevertheless, in the winter of 1939-40 a large number were pressed hurriedly into service.

An alternative pre-war solution was to put huge electro-magnets in the bows of 2-3,000 ton ships, of sufficient strength to detonate mines at a safe distance ahead. Wartime necessity now overcame peacetime parsimony and a mine destructor ship, *Borde* was hurriedly improvised. Being a collier, with her engines and bridge accommodation right aft, she was eminently suitable for conversion to her new role. A 450 ton horizontal magnet, 105 feet long and 5 feet in diameter, was fitted in her fore hold. The magnet consisted of a coil of 317,000 ampere turns, the foremost end of which was raised through 9 degrees. Power was supplied by a 300kw diesel generator. Later the magnet was supplied with alternating current by motor alternators running off the DC generators. This proved to be a wise precaution when the Germans altered the polarity of their mines. The *Borde's* sweeping speed was limited to a maximum of 6 knots. With Churchill's enthusiastic backing the conversion work was hastened and on New Years Eve 1939, *Borde* sailed from Portsmouth for trials in the Barrow Deep, the shipping channel to the north of the Thames Estuary. As she steamed up the Deep at 5 knots she was accompanied by a rescue drifter and a motor launch carrying mine countermeasure experts. The trial was a complete success: during the afternoon of 4 January 1940 a magnetic mine was detonated 150 feet ahead of the ship. As the *Borde* steamed through the column of water thrown up by the exploding mine, equipment, furniture and crockery were thrown around, and the switches controlling the current to the windings of the magnet were blown off. This was a serious matter as it exposed the ship to possible destruction by any other mine which she might encounter before she could restore the current to the magnet. With this success behind her, *Borde* was ordered to sweep the channel close to the Downs where she immediately destroyed two more mines.

Strange things began to happen on board this little ship. The mighty magnet in the forehold magnetised the whole ship. All objects made of ferrous metal were thrown around, with spanners leaping from men's pockets, and spoons and forks clinging together as if for protection. Worst of all, watches died an ignominious death. On 8 March, *Borde's* commanding officer, Lieutenant Commander Hudson, was awarded the Distinguished Service Order; the First Lieutenant, Lieutenant Morris, received the Distinguished Service Cross; and four of the crew the Distinguished Service Medal. In a short time the ship had disposed of twenty three magnetic mines and had been declared by Churchill, who visited her, as 'the most valuable ship in the Navy.'

The success of *Borde* led to the conversion of nine more colliers. Among these was *Corburn*, commanded by Lieutenant Commander Mark Welby. She was despatched to Loch Ewe to clear the mines from the field which had damaged *Nelson*. These mines had been laid in deeper water than those encountered by *Borde* in the Barrow Deep and in the Straits of Dover. This meant that they exploded much closer ahead of *Corburn*. She was, therefore, ordered to proceed to Stokes Bay for trials and investigation by the *Vernon* Mine Sweeping Department. But the situation on the Continent had taken a serious turn. The Germans were advancing into France, and to deny the use of the Channel ports to the Allies they had carried out a mining campaign.

Corburn was diverted to Le Havre, which had been heavily infested with mines of a much greater explosive content than usual. She successfully detonated a number until, on 21 May 1940, the circuit breakers carrying the current from the alternators to the magnet were thrown off by the explosion of a mine. So close had the mines been laid that, in spite of the *Corburn's* engines having been put full astern, she drifted over the next mine which detonated immediately under her, cutting her in half and sending her to the bottom. The crew scrambled ashore whence they were able to escape to Britain before the Germans arrived at Le Havre. Lieutenant Commander Welby remained behind to organise minesweeping by two small trawlers. Sadly he was killed during these operations.

Apart from the loss of her experienced Captain, the destruction of the *Corburn* was serious for another reason: she had sunk in shallow water and it was comparatively easy for the Germans to investigate her secrets. As a result of this, they developed the Period Delay Mechanism which allowed the mine to be actuated by several pulses from the mine destructor ship's magnet before detonating. This placed all mine destructor ships at risk, and so their short lived usefulness was now at an end. Some were converted into minesweepers but the original mine destructor ship, *Borde*, was so heavily magnetised that even the most dedicated efforts by the degaussing teams failed to return her to her normal state of magnetism. She was converted to a minesweeper depot ship and made her way to North Africa where she became a well known sight amongst the little ships. At the end of the war she asserted her personality by refusing to be consigned to the breakers yard,

Wellington 'Flying Wedding Ring' over the Suez Canal 1942

foundering on her way there.

Aircraft were also used in the attempt to find answers to the magnetic mine. Experiments with horizontal electro-magnets carried by torpedo bombers in their weapon racks and vertical magnets in the bomb bay of an obsolete Harrow bomber proved unsuccessful. External coils seemed to offer a more likely solution. To carry them a number of obsolescent Wellington MkI bombers and four more modern MkIA machines were made available by the Royal Air Force for conversion to flying minesweepers. The more modern machines were able to carry a load of 8,000 lbs, permitting a vast coil 48 feet in diameter, containing 64 turns of wire, to be slung beneath the fuselage. The coil was activated by a 35kw generator, driven by a Ford V8 engine, producing a coil strength of 22,400 ampere turns. The older aircraft were limited to a load of 7,500 lbs., but it was found that improved performance could be obtained by using a 90kw generator set driven by a Gypsy Queen aircraft engine. This provided an improved performance, the coil delivering a massive 30,000 ampere turns. Some success was achieved, a mine being detonated for the first time on 8 January 1940. The torpedo officer attached was Lieutenant R Cooper, a former pilot in the Fleet Air Arm who had been a member of the 1939 *Vernon* long course.

While the airborne trials were in progress, the Mine Sweeping Department sought other aircraft which might be suitable in this role. There were obvious attractions in the use of flying boats, and a design was drawn up for *Golden Hind*, one of the Short Empire G Type flying boats. Although the *Golden Hind* sweeper would have been able to produce a coil strength of 81,000 ampere turns the scheme had to be abandoned because of the expense of producing enough of these aircraft.

In the absence of any alternative aircraft the trials of the 'DWI' (as they were called) Wellington minesweepers were treated as a matter of urgency. Simultaneously, the original boats of the First MTB Flotilla were hastily pressed into service as 'DWI Marker Boats'. On at least one occasion an apprehensive MTB crew watched fascinated as the aircraft swept overhead at 70 feet, forgetting to switch off its 'ring', and nearly blowing the unfortunate craft out of the water. Before the experiment ended a few former MTBs were fitted with a 40 foot mast from which flew a large black flag to help the aircraft maintain its line.

The very narrow lane swept by a single aircraft was of little use for clearing a channel, and attempts were made to fly several aircraft in formation at about 100 feet at a speed of 140 knots. The Royal Air Force very quickly decided that formation flying at those heights above the sea was impracticable. This limited the utility of airborne minesweeping and only eleven Wellington aircraft were converted. Five were flown to Egypt for use in the Suez Canal area where they became known as 'Flying Wedding Rings'. Flying low and fast over the Canal they achieved some successes but it was a hazardous affair. If the aircraft proceeded too slowly at such low altitudes the explosion of a mine was liable to lift the tail, with disastrous results. The success rate of the Wellingtons was small for the effort expended, but in the narrow waters of the Canal every positive contribution was important in the struggle to keep this essential waterway open. By the end of 1940 the remaining minesweeping Wellingtons had been converted for other duties.

'Flying wedding rings' were not the most unlikely mine countermeasures suggested at this time. *Vernon* received many suggestions from members of the public. Hodges and Cameron were given the job of reading through the suggestions on behalf of Sayer. Any that were of merit were forwarded to the Director of Torpedoes and Mines at the Admiralty. For many months a proposal known as the 'flat fish' project became the source of much light hearted banter. It was as much as the staff could do to keep this 'secret weapon' to themselves. The headmaster of a well known school suggested that shoals of flat fish should be captured alive. They would be fitted with small magnets, intended to detonate the mines, before being released in danger areas. The suggestion duly found its way to the staff of the Director of Torpedoes and Mines where, in mock seriousness, an official reply was concocted. The letter congratulated the headmaster. It was, it asserted, an impressive idea and the Second Sea Lord's Office (responsible for personnel) had now been approached with a view to recruiting for this hazardous service a special new branch of the Navy to be known as Sub Lieutenant (Flat Fish) RNVR. Since, however, no Sub Lieutenant (Flat Fish) who faithfully carried out his duty could expect to return from a successful mission there would be only one rank in the branch and no pension rights. Perhaps fortunately, the reply was never despatched.

Degaussing was one aspect of the real answer to the peril of the magnetic mine. The other was the creation of a practical sweep. In October 1939, even before the first mine was recovered, the Minesweeping Department at *Vernon* began to recreate the First World War concept of an electrical sweep. Lieutenant Commander TGP Crick and Lieutenant GP Kilroy were employed upon the trials. Work began to to prepare two trawlers to carry an electric 'AA' sweep but while this was going on *Vernon* produced a rather different 'lash up' towed between two drifters. The generator ship towed two wires lashed together; one ended in a 30 foot bared tail acting as a positive electrode and the other was connected to an ordinary wire pendant towed by the other drifter: the wire was then bared and trailed 30 feet astern to act as the other electrode. The sweep actuated the first German mine encountered but it had to pass close by to be effective and had a number of other problems.

Instead work was concentrated on overcoming the various problems being encountered with the Electric 'AA'. In its final form this consisted of two armoured cables towed between two trawlers. Otter boards kept the cables close to the bottom and floats were attached to the sweep wires to give positive buoyancy and prevent sagging. Each trawler had its generator connected in series to send a 300 amp current through the wires. The foremost wire was connected positive in the port ship and negative in the starboard. The after wire was connected up in the opposite direction so as to increase the vertical component of the earth's magnetic field between the wires. The sweep was effective against both polarities of vertical magnetism, mines actuated by horizontal magnetism and buoyant mines. It only required a 35 kilwatt generator and could therefore be operated by existing minesweeping trawlers. The first sweep was ready in March 1940 when three pairs of trawlers were fitted with the Electric 'AA'. Operational use, however, demonstrated two defects. The low current meant that the cables had to pass close to the mines and the floats supporting them were badly damaged each time a mine was detonated. This meant the sweep had to be recovered on each occasion. Secondly, irreparable damage was done should a moored mine be encountered. However, the Electric 'AA' did have some success and it proved its worth in the specialist role of sweeping magnetic mines in river estuaries where the depth and salinity of the water was much reduced. A 'Baby AA' was produced for use with drifters but was abandoned at the trials stage.

A less vulnerable electrical sweep directed specifically against the German mine was the answer and it was Goodeve, who had contributed so much to the development of degaussing, who made the breakthrough. He turned his attention to the investigation of the magnetic field created by a current passing through the sea between buoyant insulated cables towed astern of two ships in line abreast. After Goodeve had carried out preliminary calculations, trials were held by Lieutenant RGM Collins, in charge of the project, on the Canoe Lake at Southsea which, being fed with salt water from Spithead, provided a suitable environment. Two insulated cables were suspended from floats and fed with power supplied from army searchlight generators. The trials were immediately successful. If the electrical cables could be given positive buoyancy they could be used to sweep a channel without fouling obstacles in their path, such as moored mines. Next handling trials were carried out in Portsmouth Harbour. A solid copper cable, one square inch in section and rubber sheathed, was supported by logs and scaffolding poles provided by a Portsmouth firm of builders. It could not have been a more awkward affair and the cable, logs and scaffolding poles drifted across Portsmouth Harbour. One end fouled *Vernon* Pier and the other ran aground on Dolphin Point. Vessels plying their lawful trade between Portsmouth and the Isle of Wight became entangled in what was now virtually a barrage. It took some time to untangle the Isle of Wight car ferry from this unholy mess. Webb remarked, 'It was at this time suggested that the harbour defence experts might be interested in the Project.'

In spite of these difficulties, enough information had been obtained from the trials to justify the fitting out of two Dutch tugs, *Salvo* and *Servitor*, for sea trials with the new sweeps in the Thames Estuary as part of Lewis's efforts. Each was fitted with a 35kw 110 volt generator and a large battery composed of 126 banks of lead acid cells in series, each bank consisting of three 6 volt car batteries in parallel. Power was fed from the generators to the batteries which were intermittently discharged through the sweep by means of a breaker actuated by a synchronised time switch. In this manner a pulse of 3000 amperes was drawn from the batteries for 5 seconds in each minute allowing the battery to be recharged by the generator for the following 55 seconds. All wiring in the ship which carried the main current was paired to avoid a magnetic field being built around the ship. The sweep itself was composed of a pair of cables, one long and the other short, lashed together for the entire length of the shorter cable and each terminating in a fifty foot electrode. *Salvo* and *Servitor* were also each fitted with early and primitive degaussing coils.

While *Salvo* and *Servitor* were being fitted out, the sweeps, complete with logs, had been sent to Sheerness where Lewis was waiting to take charge of the trials. On arrival the 'Great Snakes', as they had become known, were assembled on the beach at the Isle of Grain before being moved to buoys in the river to await the arrival of the two tugs. The operation was not a success. They became fouled in the groynes on the beach at Sheerness and when they finally reached their destination became entangled with a minesweeping trawler which, in Lewis' words, 'created an awful mess'.

When Collins arrived with *Salvo* and *Servitor* the trials began immediately in the crowded waterways and the strong tides of the Thames estuary. The tugs were accompanied by a motor boat, from which Lewis and his assistant, Sub Lieutenant Ashworth, observed events. Ashworth was one of the many RNVR electrical officers selected by Goodeve to expedite the development of these new and revolutionary mine countermeasures. Lewis had assured the Clacton beach seamen who manned the boat that they were viewing the proceedings from a safe distance. They had faith in Lewis and accepted his assurance, but the truth was that a disaster might have followed had the sweep detonated a mine. The trials party would have felt even more insecure had they realised that in the haste to get ready for the trials the degaussing coils in the tugs had been connected the wrong way round. Fortunately no mines were encountered on this occasion but sufficient evidence was collected to show that the sweeps generated the required magnetic field. Indeed the results were impressive enough to justify an order being given for the conversion of fifty trawlers to tow the 'LL' or Double L Sweep as it was called. However, there still remained the problem of producing a more practical floating cable.

At lunch in *Vernon* a Canadian Sub Lieutenant claimed that the dredgers on the Great Lakes were supplied with electric power carried by buoyant cables. Goodeve and Collins immediately passed this information to both Callender's and Henly's, the cable companies who were working on the project. The Sub Lieutenant's story turned out to be inaccurate: the Canadian cable was also floated out to the dredgers suspended from logs. Nevertheless, by the end of January 1940 the first experimental length of buoyant cable was delivered by Callender's and transported to Brightlingsea, where *Salvo* and *Servitor* were now attached to what had become Lewis' Experimental Minesweeping Flotilla. The cable used tennis balls housed in cylinders to give buoyancy. With Lewis and Collins embarked, the pair of tugs set out on 10 February 1940 for trials in the swept channel.

When close to the Hazeborough Light Ship, with a snow storm swirling around them, the first successful explosion of a mine by a Double L sweep was achieved. With the existing design the short leg of the sweep was only 50 yards long, so the effect on the tugs was dramatic if not disastrous. The mine went up in 17 fathoms, 30 yards away. The stern of the *Servitor* was lifted into the air and the boiler jumped off its seating, bending the base of the funnel before righting itself. As Lewis and Collins were not sure where a mine should be detonated relative to the sweepers, all men on duty were told to remain on the upper deck to avoid them being trapped below should the worst occur. It was bitterly cold, and most of them had taken shelter in the forepeak. When the mine went up, most of the iron castings on board fractured and a fresh water tank on the forepeak bulkhead burst with alarming effect. The sheltering men emerged through a manhole with great velocity. Although both tugs were damaged, they were able to make their way safely back to Harwich to report the success of the Double L.

Together with the development of degaussing the Double L sweep was the greatest single step forward in the battle against the magnetic mine and one of the greatest successes for *Vernon* and her people. The trials had shown the need for longer cables and the Mk 1 Double L was lengthened to 125 yards for the shorter leg and 525 for the long. This was intended for tugs but the Mk II intended for trawlers was similar. The Mk III intended for the new motor minesweepers had a 200 yard short portion of tail as did the Mk V intended for larger fleet minesweepers; power outputs were increased to 108kw and 140kw respectively. The MK V could be used at eleven knots against 7-8 knots for the lower powered versions. The V8 car engines used to provide power in the initial trials had proved barely adequate and had been cooled by water hoses, despite the snow storm raging at the time. Diesel generators were installed in later outfits.

One reason for the higher power demands was the discovery that the Germans had produced mines with alternative polarities, south pole down instead of north. This required double pulsing and colour coding, red and blue, was introduced on the lights that co-ordinated the pulsing between the ships. Later automatic 'slave gear' using a sensitive relay activated by the potential difference across the electrodes in the 'master' ship mechanised the synbchronisation problem successfully. Proper floating cable also appeared which made the tennis balls redundant. The first production Mk 1* Double L sweeps went into service in March 1940 and within a year many more minesweepers were fitted.

So the peril of the magnetic mine faded as the various British coutermeasures began to take effect and the German effort slackened because of shortage of mines. In December the situation was still serious with 33 merchant ships of 82,712 tons sunk , a second month in which the U-boats were less successful. But the corner was turned decisively in 1940; in what the new head of M Section, Commander Geoffrey Thistleton-Smith, remembered as the 'active and arduous' first four months months of that year mines accounted for a steadily reducing number of Allied merchantmen, in April 1940 eleven ships of only 19,799 tons. The first phase of the battle for Britain's sea communications had been won and the U- boat would now be the main threat to Britain's sea communications for the remainder of the war.

Vernon's role was central role to Britain's struggle for survival. Not only had it diagnosed the threat but it spent the busiest months in its history degaussing ships and producing magnetic sweeps. As this activity got underway, on 19 December 1939, the King visited the establishment to present the first naval decorations of the war. Ouvry and Lewis were made members of the Distinguished Service Order, Glenny was awarded the Distinguished Service Cross and CPO Baldwin and AB Vearncombe were awarded Distinguished Service Medals. The visit was kept as secret as possible and Lewis had been summoned from his work in the Thames Estuary to attend a 'conference'. He had no proper uniform for an investiture and had to dash into Gieves just before it closed to commandeer a surgeon commander's half finished jacket. The obliging tailors altered the jacket to loan it to Lewis the following day and he was also able to borrow a set of smart trousers and a cap from friends. After the investiture Gieves sewed the DSO ribbon onto Lewis' own jacket without charge. It had been a close run thing, but then so had saving Britain from the magnetic mine. Ouvry and Lewis and Vernon as a whole had been lucky; the right people had been in the right places at the right times. Hitler's bad luck, however, was not to be relied upon, as the events of 1940 and 1941 would prove.

THE EARLY SUCCESSES IN FINDING German mines and rendering them safe were only the start of a continuing campaign of mine disposal. Thistleton-Smith's Mining Department continued to play the key role in this effort. It was always a hazardous business as was tragically shown early in the new year of 1940. The British defensive minefield of moored mines laid in the approaches to the Firth of Forth was suffering from a number of faulty moorings. Scores of mines were washed ashore causing great danger to shipping. The local Rendering Mine Safe parties were overwhelmed and Chief Petty Officer Baldwin was sent north to assist and advise. On arrival he was appalled by the carelessness with which the local authorities were going about the job of disposal. Small craft of all kinds had been rounded up to search for these mines and were towing them inshore where they were manoeuvred under a davit and lifted out on to the jetty still in a live condition. Disaster was not long in coming. A small drifter was despatched to collect mines taking with her fourteen Royal Naval Volunteer Reserve Sub Lieutenants under instruction. On sighting a mine a 'messenger' was hooked on to it before hoisting the deadly load clear of the water. As the lifting progressed the mine's broken mooring rope became fouled somewhere below the waterline: it was pulled taut, thus arming the mine. As it was swung inboard the mine bumped against the ship's side and exploded, flattening the superstructure of the

Baldwin preparing countermining charge

Lieutenant Geoffrey Hodges supervising the removal of a mine from a residential area

drifter and killing everybody on the upper deck, including Chief Petty officer Baldwin and the fourteen Sub Lieutenants. Only the engine room crew survivied to tell the story. It was a sad loss, not only of so many young lives but of that very gallant man Chief Petty Officer Baldwin DSM.

The Admiralty commented thus: 'The fact that Chief Petty Officer

Baldwin, perhaps the most experienced Petty Officer in mining in the Service at the time, should have been present and assenting to such dangerous procedure, emphasises the importance of impressing on all personnel that in handling explosives the greatest care should invariably be exercised.'

On the other hand, early 1940 saw the recovery of another German 'B' magnetic mine, although not without difficulty. It was discovered in the Whitstable oyster beds on 28 January. The inexperienced Hodges was given the job since Ouvry had influenza and Glenny was at Falmouth. Accompanied by CPO Ellingworth and AB Hurlstone - and a driver who had also succumbed to influenza and was far from well - Hodges set off on an adventurous drive through snow and ice. Taking the wheel, he piloted the party to his parents' home in Kent, where they spent the night before tackling the snowdrifts. Exhausted, they arrived at the 'Blue Anchor' inn at Seasalter after dark on the 29th.

The *Vernon* party were led out to the mine the following morning. As Hodges described it:

The scene was memorable, as the coast was deep in snow, and we waded through great drifts of frozen foam to reach the waters on which was a top covering of slushy ice. The mine was found down by the nose 15 degrees with the parachute container just awash, and after examining it Ellingworth and I agreed that the bomb fuse should be tackled as soon as it came clear of the water. The tear off strip had gone and although the keep ring turned fairly easily, the bomb fuse would not come out. This, even for a beginner, was a little upsetting. It was said that the bomb fuse took 20 secs. to fire after operation and with this for comfort I put my foot on the mine, and by hard and steady pull got the bomb fuse out, called up Ellingworth and handed him the trophy. Next came the primer release. This would not shift with the pin spanner so I used the screwdriver as a punch and the spanner as a hammer but could not drive the screw round. I called up Ellingworth but our combined efforts failed to loosen the thread. By this time we had both lost all feeling in our hands and the tide was rising. Our thigh boots were shipping icy water which warned us of the advancing tide and we had to retreat defeated.

The tide prevented further efforts and a dejected Hodges and his team made the long, cold and difficult journey back to Portsmouth. They returned on 10 February but their attempts to tow the mine to shallower water met with no success. A third attempt was made on the 26th when Hodges came armed with a special lifting clamp and a new and heavier spanner for removing the primer release gear. As on the previous occasions he was assisted by a working party from Chatham. There were also two officers from the Chatham torpedo school, Lieutenant Commander Obbard and Lieutenant West and the latter used a large hammer, 'The Chatham Persuader', to help Hodges finally loosen the primer release gear. The primer was finally 'persuaded' to come out and the Chatham men fixed cask floats to the mine so it could be towed to the shore at high tide. Still, however, Hodges' luck was out; when the men returned after breakfast they found the floats had broken away. The next day the party stood by as the tide rose, and the floats stayed attached. The mine was towed to Whitstable harbour and its detonator removed prior to transport to *Vernon*. When the mine was dismantled it was found that it had not worked because the clock hydrostat was jammed with sand, which explained the its passivity under the many blows it received.

Hodges had another lucky escape on an off-duty Saturday, 6 April, when he had been keen enough to accompany Glenny to Dover to investigate a mysterious float, which turned out to be the first example of German explosive sweep cutter to fall into British hands. Hodges reported that:

we found a conical float complete with mechanism and piece of mooring wire, but we also found that a member of the depot staff had begun to unfit it , had disliked the look of it, had re-assembled it and, most serious of all, could not be sure in what position the square handed spindle had been found originally...The mechanism when withdrawn and partly taken down appeared to have a charge that we estimated at two or three pounds of Hexanite, and had a hydrostatic valve that seemed to be the key to the situation. During our work we partly uncovered this diaphragm which was seen to be rising slowly up, but Glenny, who knew the danger gave me hardly any indication of what he feared beyond suggesting that I might absent myself. The depot official took the hint. This phase over, we decided to pull out the whole hydrostatic valve by a cord from a safe distance. The first attempt failed and so did the second, and we were fixing the mechanism more firmly for another pull when our friend, who was already walking back, caught his foot in the cord, stumbled and jerked out the valve completely under our noses. At this point VA Dover arrived to see how we had got on and the depot man served us cups of tea. On his departure and after discussion Glenny decided to unfit the charge so that we might lower the tension a bit. The depot official, who was clearly anxious for us, murmured something about getting a tool for us and went out. We took the plunge and unfitted the head. This revealed the striker forward though when it moved we could not say. The workshop staff at VERNON *said later that it failed to fire because the striker was bent and could only slide forward slowly to bury itself slowly. Perhaps this occurred when the hydrostatic valve was jerked out....*

If *Vernon* was to keep up with the German mine designers it needed a steady supply of their latest mines. By early 1940 only air dropped mines had been recovered but it was known that U-boats were now probably the main mine layers. The mine recovery drifters became more efficient and continued their work, their strength expanded to two flotillas, each of five drifters and an echo-sounding yacht. A search for submarine mines was concentrated off Falmouth but everything recovered turned out to be nothing more lethal than rocks or old anchors; larger items, including perhaps mines, broke the nets. The crews of these mine recovery flotillas were brave men as was shown at Dunkirk (see chapter 9) but throughout their five years' existence, they were rewarded by the recovery of only one mine and that for the loss of three vessels with most of their crews. Armitage and Glenny were distracted from their main duties by their appointment as advisers to the flotilla Commanding Officers. Luckily for *Vernon* a chance encounter in late April 1940 between British destroyers and two apparently Dutch trawlers off the coast of Norway led to submarine type mines soon falling into British hands.

In late April two trawlers flying the Dutch flag were found on examination to be armed enemy ships. One was sunk and the crew of the second ignored the scuttling charge in one of the magazines and surrendered. On the 29th, Glenny was ordered to Scapa Flow where the captured ship, the *Polares*, was awaiting inspection. A preliminary examination had revealed that she carried two 21-inch torpedoes fitted in concealed bow tubes, five mines, twelve depth charges, two field guns, one 4.1-inch ship's gun (camouflaged as a boat), several light and heavy machine guns, large quantities of ammunition and many cases of stores containing binoculars, compasses etc. The vessel was also fitted with a direction finding set, hydrophones and echo-sounding gear. Furthermore, the crew of forty were well stocked with quantities of food purloined from the newly conquered Danes, including hams and a great deal of butter. For Glenny, however, by far the most important discoveries were the five mines, lashed on deck under a fish trawl. He immediately diagnosed them by the shape and fittings as being of the hitherto mysterious type designed for laying from submarine torpedo tubes.

Given the unknown nature of these weapons Glenny decided to remove one from the ship for exploratory stripping and examination. A trawler, *Cape Nyemetzki*, was put at his disposal and, with the rest of the fleet at a safe distance, the tricky work began, everything being recorded by a fleet photographer from *Rodney*, called in aboard an accompanying drifter at the appropriate moments in the sequence of operations. Glenny first removed the coverplate and, to his consternation, the cover bung, electric detonator and two spring arming devices bounded out onto his chest. These proved to be the same as in the 'A' and 'B' mines but when he shone a torch into the mine he was further disconcerted to see that the leads from the detonator ran in the opposite direction to that expected. He decided therefore to change his plans and to remove next the end hemispherical cover. This revealed a familiar magnetic unit but it was suspended in the mine in a new way. Glenny gave the mine a thorough internal examination, removing various plates and bars and also the primer. Having satisfied himself that the mine contained no more surprises he removed all the mines and the depth charges for transport to *Vernon*. *Cape Nyemetzki* arrived at Thurso with her explosive cargo on 3 May and the mines and charges were loaded into a special van which arrived at Portsmouth two days later. *Vernon* gave the 'S' mines a thorough examination, finding that the available intelligence information on them was, in fact, remarkably accurate. The German designation for these weapons was TMB; they were 7.6 feet long, 21-inches in diameter and contained about 1,000 lbs of Hexanite explosive.

Another new type of mine turned up at the same time. A German minelaying aircraft crashed at Clacton on 31 April. Lewis, still with the experimental minesweepers but now based at Brightlingsea, felt the massive explosion which was traced to Clacton. Lieutenant Forman was sent to investigate and discovered an object which the ARP wardens thought was the cistern of the house demolished by the aircraft; Forman, a Mine Recovery Officer, was not so sure, so he decided to phone *Vernon*. Ouvry, accompanied by Hodges, immediately left for Clacton. Meanwhile, Lieutenant Ryan, at the Admiralty, had been informed and he let Lewis know that he was on his way. Lewis picked him up at Wivenhoe station and together they arrived at the crash site while Forman was away phoning *Vernon*. Lewis immediately recognised the 'cistern' as a mine, apparently a type 'B' and without delay borrowed some tools from a garage and rendered it safe. Forman was 'rather upset' on his return to find the job already done, and when Ouvry arrived he was not entirely pleased to be told that the mine had been rendered safe, towed away by a brakedown van, loaded onto a privately owned lorry and carried to Portsmouth. There had been a deal of duplication of effort which Ouvry was determined should not be repeated. However, when the *Vernon* team arrived they were mollified by a fine meal of plover's eggs collected by the minesweeping flotilla.

Vernon found that the mine was a new kind of LMB with a more dangerous type of bomb fuse and , more importantly, a magnetic exploding device that could work on reverse polarity. This weapon was indeed set to 'blue', ie south pole down. A similar 'C' mine, as the British coded it, this time set to 'red', north pole down like earlier mines, was recovered from Maplin Sands a week later after being rendered safe by Lewis, Sub Lieutenant King RNVR (a locally based officer who had rendered British mines safe), Sub Lieutenant Goodman from *Vernon* and two RMS torpedo gunners' mates, one from *Vernon* and the other from Brightlingsea. The group saw the dawn as they stood in shallow water a mile and a half from the shore. Lewis took out the bomb fuse under water. Shortly afterwards the fuse exploded; there were no ill effects but if it had gone off inside the mine it would have been the end of the five men. Instead the process of rendering the mine safe was completed and it was floated ashore for dispatch to *Vernon*. A similar improved version of the smaller air dropped mine, the LMA, was recovered by Glenny on the mud flats in Liverpool Bay on 21 July. It was coded 'D' and Glenny received a well earned DSO for his excellent work.

In May 1940 an Enemy Mining Section had been set up as part of the Mining department at *Vernon*, specially tasked with the recovery and disposal of new kinds of mine. The following month one of the earliest essays in modern style minehunting using divers was attempted. On 6 June a report was received that an enemy aircraft had dropped a mine off Poole Bar Buoy. It came at a time when it was essential to keep the approaches to Poole Harbour open during the attempted St Valery evacuation and it was decided to use both echo-sounding ships. Divers would classify contacts found by the yachts and if a mine was was found a specially trained *Vernon* diver would render it safe under water. Two days later, *Esmeralda* and *Sir Sydney* began operations with a mobile diving unit from *Excellent* standing by. After a false start which turned up three mystery contacts the operation was resumed on 13 June under Armitage's direction. The following day, Diver A.R. Knight reported that one of the contacts found in the initial search was indeed a Type 'C' mine, lying in 7 fathoms at an angle of about 30 degrees to the bottom and swinging gently in the ebb stream.

The first and most dangerous job was to secure and buoy the mine. Glenny was despatched to take charge of the operation and on 14th June *Vernon*'s divers started work. One of them, Able Seaman R.G.Tawn, found the mine lying flat on the bottom with the lifting lug on top. His first job was to fit a specially adapted motor horn to the bomb fuse. The object of this device was to keep pressure on the hydrostat in the bomb fuse to prevent it firing as it was brought to the surface. After attaching the horn, he removed the fuse which was brought safely to the surface. Unfortunately, as the mine was being towed ashore by a fishing boat it exploded, happily without ill effects to the boat. Diver Tawn was awarded a well deserved DSM. Sadly he was killed in another incident late in the war. He was a very brave man.

Less lucky was the the commanding officer of the former yacht, *Campeador V*, Commander C.H. Davey, whose First Lieutenant was Surgeon Rear Admiral J.R. Muir, long retired, well seasoned in years and serving as a Temporary Lieutenant RNVR. In June 1940 the little ship was employed patrolling in Spithead and the Solent where her nightly duty was to look out for enemy aircraft laying mines. On that summer's night two mines were spotted being released, and their position was noted carefully. The yacht decided to anchor close to for the night, ready to direct the recovery team to the spot. Tragically, as the tide turned the following morning, the little ship swung over one of the mines which exploded, blowing her to pieces with the loss of all but two of the ship's company. It was a sad loss of so many lives, caused by a misplaced sense of duty allied to a lack of understanding of the need to maintain vigilance at all times.

On 4 August another serious and tragic incident occurred, this time in *Vernon* itself. An aircraft mine had been discovered buried in a field near Birchington in Kent and Hodges and Chief Petty Officer Wheeler were despatched to investigate. At the site they met Lieutenant West and a working party from the Chatham Torpedo School. West appeared to be a trifle jealous of the presence of the *Vernon* team, and insisted that the removal of the mine was his responsibility. Hodges wished to dig it out but West proposed to extract it by tractor and the first afternoon and evening were wasted on three such attempts. Eventually the mine was dug out under the direction of the *Vernon* team. Rollers were positioned under it and it eventually emerged from the mud. It proved to be a Type 'C' which was loaded on to *Vernon's* three ton lorry for transport back to Portsmouth where it arrived at 2200 o'clock that evening after a rapid journey.

Next morning Hodges, after satisfying himself that dismantling the mine was well in hand, left for the armament depot at Priddy's Hard, accompanied by Lieutenant Forest USN, one of the American officers then secretly attached to the Royal Navy. They had just cast off when a large explosion took place and they saw the roof of the mining shed disintegrating. At that same moment Thistleton-Smith was sitting at his desk. Seconds later Dr. Wood came to tell him that there had been an explosion in the mining shed. They hurried to the scene where blackened and burned men were being taken away. The roof had gone and glass lay everywhere. One contorted and horribly blackened man had been flung into a corner and a shocked sailor was collecting the bloody and charred remains of another, putting them on a trolley. Thistleton-Smith turned from the sickening scene. Mr. R.A. Cook (Commissioned Gunner 'T') was dying, and Petty Officer Fletcher had been blown to pieces. Nobody seemed to know the whereabouts of Glenny. Later he was found to be in the sickbay badly burned and shocked. He had been lucky as he had been standing only a few feet behind Fletcher as he had lifted off the rear door of the mine. There had been a whirring noise followed by a blinding flash and a deafening roar.

One officer and four ratings had died and others were seriously injured, but it was clear that the charge that had caused the explosion had been placed for a purpose. The Germans had been determined to hide some new device in the mine and it was imperative to find out what this was. Dr. Wood arrived to take charge of the minute search. Matter is indestructable. Every little piece of the mine was collected and reconstruction work to unmask the secret began. It was soon established that the booby trap was was an electrically fired 2-lb charge, the circuit of which was completed by the withdrawal of a stud attached to the rear door; it had been intended to protect a 'period delay mechanism', in other words a ship counter that allowed a prearranged number of ships or sweeps to pass over the mine without it exploding. The German attempt to protect this secret had failed and although the lives of five skilled, experienced and brave men had been lost, a greater tragedy had been averted by the fact that the 2-lb charge was not arranged to fire the mine's 1500 lbs main charge. Henceforth, every care would have to be taken to detect booby traps before attempting to strip a mine. These small explosive charges became known as 'Prevention of Stripping Equipment' (P.S.E.)

It was also decided that mine stripping could no longer take place at *Vernon*. An investigation range was required, remote from vital service installations and the general public yet within easy reach of Portsmouth. There were a number of false starts - a large bunker at the Portsmouth end of Hayling Island golf course, the yacht club at Sandy Point and then the chalk pits at Paulsgrove. Finally Ouvry found the best site yet, a disused lime works near the little village of Buriton. It had the advantage of having only one entrance and being sufficiently rugged to dissuade most prowlers from making any unauthorised entrance. It came into use in October 1940 and was

Able Seaman S J Tuckwell - veteran of the Great War and hero of World War II

unofficially christened HMS *Mirtle* after the initials Mine Investigation Range (MIR).

Immediately after the explosion in the mining shed at *Vernon*, steps had been taken to improve the X-ray techniques, by introducing portable radio-active radon gas sources, so that the interior of the mine could be examined without removing any of the exterior fittings. It was then possible for the staff at *Mirtle*, assisted by the Mine Design Department, to identify any unusual circuitry or fittings. Access to the mine then had to be obtained by remote control; this was achieved by the use of an ingenious machine designed and produced at the National Physical Laboratory which, running on compressed air, could cut a hole in a mine shell and be controlled from a safe distance. This technique borrowed the surgical description and became known as 'trepanning'. Other improvements included, remote, non-magnetic 'crystal' microphones for listening to clocks; remote digging and lining of shafts to attend to buried bombs and mines; liquid oxygen to fast freeze battery operated fuses; and curvilinear shaped-charge techniques for explosive separation of booby traps from the main charge.

These developments came just in time as the Germans started a campaign in August to intimidate the RMS teams by using special booby trap devices in what *Vernon* designated 'E' mines. One was dropped inland of Portsmouth and the other near Portland in order to entice the RMS teams to their doom. Shortly after midnight on the 16th an aircraft circled low, over North Boarhunt, near Southwick in Hampshire. Through the thick ground mist a green flash was observed followed shortly by an explosion. The Home Guard on duty in the area reported that the explosion had been noisy and accompanied by a bright flash but there had been little or no shock. Thistleton-Smith was staying at the Red Lion Hotel in Petersfield at the time and was awakened at 02.30 to answer the telephone. The call was from C-in-C Portsmouth's staff to inform him that a mine had been dropped near Bere Farm at North Boarhunt and to ask if *Vernon* would deal with it. As soon as it was light he set out to find the mine. Following the direction given by the village grocer's boy he soon found the police constable on guard who led him to the spot. It was an unusual sight that greeted him. There was no crater and only a small area of burnt grass with the ground around covered with pieces of explosive. Some little way from the mine lay a heavy cylinder. A deposit of yellow explosive on its outside showed it to have been fitted into the main charge: but why had the latter not exploded?

Thistleton-Smith returned to *Vernon* to obtain help and later he, Ouvry and Walden of the Mine Design Department revisited the scene. A hurried reconstruction showed clearly that there had been an electrically operated booby trap designed to explode when the rear door came off. The cylinder which had been found beside the mine appeared to have fitted in a central hole in the rear end of the main charge and was obviously the explosive for the booby trap. There was no sign of any sort of mine actuating gear, and no magnetic unit or anything of the kind in its place. The mine had quite obviously been planted with the object of destroying the people who were sent to investigate it.

Later that day, the existence of a German anti-personnel campaign was confirmed. A signal was received that a mine had been found lying undamaged on the slopes of a grass field about one and a half miles from Piddlehinton in the Dorsetshire countryside. It was far from the sea and a long way from the nearest military objective. On a fine night with a full moon and with little or no mist it could be assumed that the mine had been dropped in that spot for a specific purpose. On examination it was noted that the mine was similar to a normal 'D'; it had the normal primer release, and the plate over the detonator was visible, but there was no place for fitting either a clock or a bomb fuse. In fact the shell of the mine had been specially made for the job.

When Thistleton-Smith and Armitage arrived at the scene it was guarded by the local soldiery and Mr. Fish, the village constable. After confirming there was no sound of ticking, photographs were taken and as rolling had not had any effect on the mine so far, it was rolled over once more to reveal its under side. The X-ray machine was not due until the following day and in order to prevent the device being exploded by some timing device , Thistleton-Smith instructed Armitage to remove the main detonator and primer, which was done without any difficulty. Thistleton-Smith then returned to *Vernon* leaving Armitage and Walden to await the arrival of the X-ray machine and the trepanning instrument that was being hastily assembled. It was built in a mere 72 hours and arrived with its designer, Mr Bradley from the National Physical Laboratory, on 21 August.

That day Armitage hurried back to *Vernon* with the X-ray photographs, which were studied with great care. It was decided to use the trepanning instrument to cut a four-inch hole in the end of the battery section of the mine. This would allow the leads going away to the electrically fired auxiliary charge to be cut. The initial cutting operation was not a success and Thistleton-Smith returned on the 23rd to take charge. He found another cutting operation about to begin. As the Commander (M) vividly remembered.:

The next few hours were most exciting. The high wail of the cutter, our retirement to the little trench shelter dug by the soldiers in the neighbouring field, the eager approach after each cut to see what mysteries were revealed, and the usual disappointment when we found there was still a long way to go...At last the cutter got through on one side, and Walden enthusiastically set to work with a bit of hacksaw. It was at this stage, when we were all keyed up, that first I and then Walden, then all of us smelt burning. 'Pitch' said Walden. 'It's getting worse' said I. We prepared to run and leave it for awhile. As iI turned I found a cloud of smoke coming from my jacket pocket - I had done the usual silly thing with a pipe.

The hole was well positioned, although the hacksaw blade had had to be used to reveal the leads coming away from the battery so they could be cut and insulated. Thistleton - Smith again takes up the tale:

I was pretty certain now that we had isolated the primer in the rear end of the charge, and that we were left with a separate charge in the rear compartment - a mechanically fired charge. Photographs showed this to be very complicated and gave little guidance as how best to tackle it, the air was exhausted and the cutter badly in need of modification; it was getting late and we had already been five days on the job. All these things decided me to use plastic explosive to make a hole in the rear door through which we should be able to see mechanical gear.

Chief Petty Officer Thorns was already 'itching to use' this and soon he was ready, the detonator being inserted in the two inch circle of plastic explosive on the rear door of the mine. The fuse was lit and the team retired to await the explosion which duly occurred at the appropriate moment. Thistleton-Smith leapt from the trench eager to inspect the hidden secrets but when he was only fifty yards away from the mine there was another explosion which threw everyone to the ground. By the greatest of good fortune nobody was seriously hurt. Armitage and Walden were disappointed to lose the mine but Thistleton-Smith was of the opinion that its dismantling would have been very difficult and perhaps not worth the trouble; the devices were clearly special weapons and not part of the main campaign. In any case the mechanism of the mines could be reconstructed from the X-ray pictures. Indeed, no more 'E' mines were found but every member of the RMS organisation was doubly aware of the need to take careful precautions against booby traps.

There was more than enough to keep the *Vernon* RMS team occupied as the enemy mining campaign was kept up. In August 1940 there were four officers available for operations, RS Armitage, HE Wadsley, GA Hodges and D Speirs who was commanding officer of the Portsmouth mine recovery division. In addition there were MW Griffiths and CWA Chapple in charge of mine recovery divisions at Brightlingsea and Rosyth respectively. Armitage led a campaign agaist a mine that had dropped in *Vernon*'s mining trial ground in mid-August bringing trial work to a stop. A new floatation bag attached by a diver was used to lift the mine from the sea bed and although it sank again later it was eventually rendered safe.

Hodges was sent to neutral Eire to help with a mine in Dungarven Bay, with Mr Thompson of the Mine Design Department and CPO Salter. The group was briefed at the Admiralty on how to act as plain clothes 'engineers'. Hodges soon found that he was at cross purposes with the Irish authorities:

Admiralty wanted all possible information without revealing to anybody the method of tackling German mines; and the Eire Authorities wanted the beast removed and to learn how to deal with any further mines that might be laid. Thus they had the goods and we had the knowledge.

The Irish reports suggested that the mine was an interesting one and frank talking between Hodges and both the Irish Army officer in charge (Major Lawler) and Sir Grant Murphy at the British Embassy cleared the air for trust and co-operation. The mine had not been marked well by the Irish Army and was hard to locate. With the tide coming in it was vital to recover it quickly. Four Irish sailors- including Mr Power, an ex-Royal Navy *Vernon* trained CPO, Hodges, Salter and Thompson floated the mine off and it was towed ashore by a lorry. Hodges identified it while it was still in the water as a 'C' mine with a new small brown disc fitted into the top of the bomb fuse. The bomb fuse fusing link and safety clips, of a new double design for both primer and bomb fuse, were inadvertently pulled off during the beaching operation.

Vernon, worried about 'E' mines, cautioned extra care in the RMS operation and Hodges took more than 4 hours for the eight stage process, beginning with the bomb fuse and ending with the rear door. The actions were explained to Lawler and an Irish armament officer as Thompson checked to see whether the mine held any more surprises, which it did not. The Irish Army then recovered the mine and the *Vernon* group returned to Holyhead as incognito as they had come, being delayed 24 hours by the Irish authorities' confusion over ferry sailing times. The Irish Government released the interesting new bomb fuse, safety clips and fusing links to Britain and they arrived at *Vernon* where it was found they had seized up. It had been an excellent example of Anglo-Irish co-operation.

Magnetic ground mines tended to predominate that summer but a new enemy type of sea mine turned up in September 1940, the EMD antenna mine, designated the German 'X' mine by *Vernon*. The first of this type was spotted off Portsmouth by the minesweeping trawler *Cypress* whose commanding officer, Lieutenant Commander Lawson, saw that it had a green 'hat' type of mounting on the top so he did not sink it. The mine recovery organisation was called in from *Vernon* and Hamond was put in charge. Using a grapnel sweep he managed to tow the mine towards the shore but he had problems with the shallow water and had to anchor it after dark. After safely putting it ashore on Ryde Sands the next day, Hamond was lent the two minesweepers *Cedar* and *Cypress* to find another mine. Speirs was also in attendence with the mine recovery drifter *Frons Olivae*. Another was found but attempts to cut its mooring wire failed and it was dragged towards the shore. This again proved to be far from the simple operation expected and Hamond used the drifter's dinghy personally to shackle the mine to a dan buoy. Hamond gave Speirs the task of unshackling this mine on 7 September but unfortunately the latter got into difficulties and was forced to take hold of the mine by its contact horns to stop his boat brushing into it. Hamond came across in *Cypress'* dinghy to sort the situation out and the mine was soon in tow of *Frons Olivae* en route for Ryde sands. Hamond made a number of other attempts to capture a mine complete with sinker but these all failed. Nevertheless the mines already obtained were rendered safe and dismantled. They were found to contain very intricate clocks set to explode the mines after a period in the water. The Portsmouth mines were timed to explode on September 15, a possible indicator of the last expected potential invasion date.

No invasion occurred and the Germans resorted to night bombing. Among the weapons they used were magnetic mines converted to huge blast bombs by using the bomb fuses originally designed to prevent mines inadvertently dropped on land from falling into enemy hands. Perhaps because their fall was cushioned by a parachute a large percentage of these 'land mines' failed to explode and *Vernon* initially had the task of dealing with most of them. Two were found at Edmonton on the night of September 15-16th. The news was sent to *Vernon* where Thistleton-Smith was staying as the invasion seemed likely. When awakened by Hodges at 0400 with news of the mines he decided to take the '1st Team' with him, ie. Armitage and Hodges. The first mine, a 'C' was in some tennis courts in the middle of a recreation ground. Another was in the back yard of a terrace house whose terrified inhabitants had clearly beat a hasty retreat; the table was still laid for supper. Armitage duly rendered the tennis court mine safe and then took over from Hodges in the back yard. One mine had exploded to great effect but the local inhabitants made clear their gratitude to the naval officers who had saved them from further destruction.

On the following night more mines were dropped and Armitage, Speirs, Sub Lieutenant HE Wadsley and Hodges were sent up to the capital to deal with them. Chatham also contributed Lieutenant Commanders Ryan and Obbard. A mine at Woolwich was found already partly made safe by an old pupil of Hodges, Sub Lt Danckwerts. This keen young officer had also already worked on a mine at Kidbrooke Park to which Armitage and Wadsley had been sent. All the more experienced officers could do was remove the clocks from the two mines and ask the Admiralty to caution young Danckwerts not to be too ambitious. Hodges and Spiers moved on to Swanley and Dartford, making safe a mine at each place. Armitage and Wadsley had a narrow escape when the mine they were working on began its firing sequence; the officers were able to get clear, though Armitage was knocked down at 30 yards. Despite their narrow escape both officers reported for duty at the Admiralty on the morning of 19 September.

Speirs and Hodges, assisted by CPO Godwin were allocated four mines, two at Hammersmith, one at Barnes and a fourth at Willesden. On of the Hammersmith pair went off before the team got to it; the second proved remarkably trouble-free despite being jammed on a staircase with a most inaccessible bomb fuse. Hodges and Speirs went on to Barnes where Hodges was in the midst of removing the bomb fuse when the he heard the whirr of it beginning to activate. He was only able to get 35 yards from the weapon, a 'D' type, before it went off. Hodges was taken to hospital with injured ears and suffering from shock. Speirs took on the Willesden mine alone. Others were not so lucky. That week, both Ryan and Ellingworth were killed: Hodges had worked with the latter on his first mine in January 1940.

More RMS officers were urgently needed and Commander Obbard, officer in charge of the Chatham Torpedo School was ordered to London. Three types 'C' were allocated to him, two at Cold Norton and the other near Epping, and a type 'D' at Chelmsford. Obbard had not got the bulb safety horn intended for removal of the bomb fuses of these mines and instead used a long length of cord with a noose at one end. Despite some rather unco-operative police in Chelmsford all the mines were rendered safe. Six more were also dealt with in the Epping area on 21 September. Two proved in Obbard's words 'interesting'; his language typifies the cool courage of these pioneering RMS officers:

One had been dropped in a tank trap at Lodge Road, Upshire Turning. It was standing vertically and was embedded in the clay. In consequence minor digging operations had to be carried out to obtain access to the bomb fuse. The fuse and gaine fired on withdrawal, which gave quite a thrill to all concerned, especially the Police. The other had been dropped on a railway embankment at Stonard's Hill, Epping, and was lying between the permanent way and the edge of the embankment. The German ground staff had carefully painted on it 'Aus Liebe'. The embankment at this place is between fifteen and twenty feet high and the mine was lying so the bomb fuse was not accessible. Rolling the mine inboard, ie. towards the permanent way, did not give access to the fuse either, as the mine fouled the railway line before the fuse became clear. Consequently the mine had to be rolled outboard, and although the greatest care was exercised, the mine took charge of us both and rolled down the embankment. However the result of this accident was not disastrous. I was not quite so sure about the state of my personal linen, but after a pause in which we both smoked a cigarette the mine was rendered safe.

Obbard returned to Chatham after reporting to the Admiralty and later received the George Medal, along with Hodges, Wadsley and Speirs. Several King's Commendations for bravery were bestowed upon the hard worked teams, including one to Lieutenant Commander Ashe Lincoln for the first G type magnetic. The George Cross, which was instituted on 23 September 1940, went to Armitage, the late Lt Commander Ryan and Danckwerts. Ouvry and Lewis had received their Distinguished Service Orders earlier in the war because they were regarded as not entitled to the Victoria Cross since that supreme award being reserved for bravery literally in face of the enemy. It was to end this anomaly that the George Cross was instituted. Ouvry was offered the opportunity to exchange his Distinguished Service Order for the George Cross but he declined: for some unknown reason the offer never reached Lewis who would have accepted it. It is a pity that the service of these two very brave did men did not receive the fullest possible recognition; it should not be overlooked that His Majesty decided to confer the awards to all concerned at an investiture specially held in *Vernon* on 19 December 1939.

Ouvry was not directly involved in these initial London events although he trained the volunteers from *King Alfred* the RNVR training establishment at Hove, who came forward in large numbers to swell the ranks of RMS personnel. Although it was officially under Armitage, Ouvry also kept an eye on Buriton which was a hive of activity. From late October mines came there for stripping but soon a purpose-built X-ray machine, costing £10,000, was installed. German mines began to come in at such a rate that at any one time there were over 150 on the site. The mines and their stripped carcases had to be kept well separated so as to avoid the tremendous explosion that would have caused serious damage and casualties for miles around had one detonated. The call eventually came for empty mine shells and work began to empty the carcases by boiling the explosive from the mine case allowing it to escape from the access plug through which it had originally been inserted. The explosive, freed from the confines of the mine shell, could now be safely burnt on site. The initial steaming out went on over one intensive week as the establishment was invaded by 'numbers of unearthly machines and teams of busy enthusiasts.'

The massive quantities of explosive being disposed of made Buriton a dangerous place. Security was good but not perfect. Ouvry was alerted to this danger by a serious breach of security which involved a number of schoolboys from Petersfield. Six Italian mines had been received at the range and had been placed apart from the German mines ready for stripping, but the activities of the range personnel had been observed by these young miscreants who, on the following night, climbed down on to the range, removed the explosive from the Italian mines in the manner in which they had observed and proceeded to burn it. Hitherto the range had been locked at night but guards had not been mounted. Henceforward guards remained on duty at all hours.

In the days following the initial mining of London the Mine Design Workshops at Portsmouth were kept busy expanding the stock of tools used to render mines safe. The land mine campaign, however, required a separate RMS organisation at the Admiralty and Captain CNE Currie RN was called in to take charge of it. This became the Land Incidents Section (LIS) and took over the rendering safe task for mines of known design found ashore. *Vernon's* Mining Department remained, as the main base for RMS work. The Enemy Mining Section had the task of recovering and rendering safe all mines of a new type found on shore in in the United Kingdom as well as all ground mines found under water and thus likely to be active. It was responsible, in co-ordination with the similar section of the Mine Design Department, for producing the techniques for rendering safe all types of enemy mines and writing manuals on how to do so, for training personnel in dealing with influence mines and dealing with all mines washed ashore in the Portsmouth Command (other commands had their own RMS organisations for dealing with routine mines).

By April 1941 the Mining Department was playing these vital roles in Britain's defence from a new home. *Vernon*(M) had moved to West Leigh Cottage at Havant.

His Majesty the King presents the first Naval Honours of the war in HMS Vernon,
December 19th, 1939

DURING THE EARLY MONTHS OF THE WAR many new courses were introduced at *Vernon* and RNVR officers began to take the Torpedo Officers Long Course, a prelude to service as torpedo and Electrical Officers in the fleet. Training of seamen torpedomen was trasferred to *St Vincent* in Gosport which reduced congestion at the Gun Wharf. At the end of 1939 *Vernon* shed its responsibility for MTBs which moved across the harbour to Gosport and the old CMB base at *Hornet*. The Whitehead Department lost its destroyers but continued to carry out torpedo discharge trials at Bincleaves for destroyers, submarines and MTBs. The latest variants of the Mk VIII and IX torpedoes were coming into service equipped with the troublesome duplex magnetic pistol and air blast gyroscopes. The electrical department was beginning its systematic electrical investigations of damaged warships and a foretaste of things to come was provided when an anti-submarine attack teacher was installed. The war was beginning to seem almost routine. Then, in the late spring, the 'Phoney War' suddenly came to an end.

On the night of 10 May 1940, the German army invaded Belgium, Holland and Luxemburg under cover of air attacks of overwhelming strength, and British and French forces moved into Belgium ready to challenge the German advance. But by the end of May the Belgian army had surrendered, the French armies were shattered and in headlong retreat, and a large part of the British Expeditionary Force was fighting a rearguard action within the perimeter of the defensive positions at Dunkirk. It was now the task of the Royal Navy to extricate as many of the Allied forces as possible before the Germans could break through the defences.

Vernon was responsible for 'wiping' all the vessels mobilised at Portsmouth for the evacuation. Working parties from the establishment laboured day and night in the Dockyard struggling with enormous 'wiping' cables and *Vernon's* boats and tenders were manned and sent off to Dover via Newhaven. Other torpedomen from *Vernon* were used to man the Dutch 'schuyts' at Poole, while officers on the Long Course were flown by Albacore torpedo bomber to Hawkinge for duty on the Dunkirk beaches, to which they sailed in destroyers from Dover and were landed by motorboat. *Vernon* became the centre of intense activity co-ordinated by the Executive Officer, Commander SH Paton, helped by the newly installed loudspeaker system. Webb provides a description of *Vernon* during those desperate days:

The Commander oscillated between the east ante-room and the hall and called out officers as the boats were reported ready from the pierhead or as requests were received for officers from the Commander-in-Chief. The mess caterer, John Canty, and his store keeper kitted them up with haversacks of bully beef and biscuits, pusser's dirk, cigarettes and matches, and with water bottles and revolvers. Some who accepted the pusser's dirk unwillingly said afterwards it was the most useful thing out of everything they took. In the hall porter's office was a young Leading Seaman, too young to have even his first badge. He was qualifying for LTO and swotting at his manual, quite unmoved. As the commander threw messages at him - 'I want to speak to So-and-So' - he put down his manual, looked up the officer's name in the card index, dialled his home number, gave the message, and went on reading. At intervals he interrupted his studies to broadcast. A message that would have taken some sorting out without the broadcaster was a signal from the Commander-in-Chief calling for an RNR with an Extra Master's ticket. This was broadcast, and within two minutes there were six in the hall. The revolving light-tight door at the Ward Room entrance paid for itself that night, as things could be controlled in a calm, fully-lit hall instead of in a windy blackness. Meanwhile the Chief Routine Officer was collecting crews in WARRIOR Block in much the same manner.

At Ramsgate were the drifters, *Lord Cavan, Silver Dawn, Fisher Boy, Jacketa* and *Formidable*, under the command of Lieutenant Commander AJ Cubison, waiting for orders to recover German ground mines by trawling. They were commanded by Royal Naval Reserve skippers, all fishermen from the Hull and Grimsby deep sea fishing fleets. Each ship had a crew of ten; a mate, a chief engineer, cook, signalman, four deckhands and two stokers. The name *Formidable* had been reserved for the new aircraft carrier under construction and the name of the drifter was changed to *Fidget*, much to the annoyance of the skipper.

With the situation at Dunkirk detoriating rapidly, Cubison was instructed to stand by to assist in the evacuation. Armitage, the second in command, was under orders to return to *Vernon* but he contrived to remain with the flotilla, particularly as it seemed unlikely that the little ships would be able to make more than one visit to the beaches. They had been given the job of acting as ferries between Dunkirk harbour and the larger ships lying in the approaches. At 1630 on the afternoon of 28 May the flotilla, led by the *Lord Cavan*, sailed from Ramsgate and proceeded at full speed towards Dunkirk where it arrived at 2200. As they approached the flames of burning buildings and ammunition dumps illuminated the night sky. Inside the harbour all was quiet, although wreckage littered the entrance.

As soon as each drifter had embarked one hundred and fifty men from the East Mole they tried to transfer the troops onto larger ships in the roadstead. In the dark and confusion it only proved possible to transfer a few loads. Cubison decided that it would be best to take the soldiers direct to Ramsgate. The drifters left Dunkirk at 0230 and arrived at at Ramsgate without further incident. There the ships were cleaned and refuelled and, with the exception of *Lord Cavan* which had remained at Dunkirk, the four drifters were ready to sail again at 0500, accompanied by the 80 foot echo-sounding yacht *Bystander*. They were back at Dunkirk by 1030, by which time many more fires were blazing and the air was thick with smoke from burning oil.

Armitage, in charge of the four drifters and the yacht, was surprised to find no sign of other shipping and, with the sound of small arms fire from the harbour, concluded that the Germans must be in possession of the port. Alongside the East Mole was a troopship which Armstrong approached in the *Fidget* to get news of the situation. The troopship's electric bells were ringing, there was no sign of life and she was sinking. In the absence of other ships, Armitage decided to lead his little force into the harbour. Securing alongside the jetty, he stepped ashore to find the mole littered with equipment and suitcases but the whole place was deserted, except for the armed boarding vessel *King Orry* whose crew informed him that there had been a severe bombing attack; the destroyer *Grenade* had been hit, she was burning fiercely and the sound of small arms fire was caused by her ammunition exploding.

The Captain of *King Orry*, which had been badly damaged, was anxious to escape but no sooner had she cleared the harbour in the strong running tide than she rolled over and sank. *Bystander* picked up thirty two of her crew and with fifty soldiers already embarked, made her way back to Ramsgate. By now the drifters were waiting at the inner end of the mole anxious to embark as many soldiers as possible before the ebbing tide grounded them. There was no sign of life, so Armitage decided to land and find the Army. Before long he found an officer and asked for a thousand men as quickly as possible, but they only drifted down the mole in small parties. The whole business seemed interminably slow. Armitage remarked:

At a time like this knowledge of the Taoist philosophy of indifference is an advantage, nothing more can be done so you are free to sit on the sandbag and stare at the scenery.

After what seemed a lifetime, the loading was completed. Surprisingly, there were no accidents, although it had been necessary for soldiers with full kit to climb down ladders from the top of the mole to the wheelhouse of each drifter. The soldiers, weakened by lack of sleep, could hardly make the descent but the sailors rallied round and the tired men were half rolled and half lifted from the wheelhouse roof to the deck. From time to time bombing caused delays, but the drifters suffered no damage and by 0230 on Thursday 30 May the last ships were away, each carrying 180 soldiers.

If it had not been for the unintentional but sustained efforts of a friendly destroyer to sink *Fidget*, the return journey to Ramsgate would have been without incident. When scarcely a mile out of Dunkirk in the narrow western channel, a fast moving destroyer was sighted dead ahead at no great distance. Since *Fidget* fully loaded could not make more than six knots little could be done to get out of the way. Armitage ordered a turn to starboard in accordance with the rule of the road, sounded his siren and flashed a light but it was to no avail; the destroyer ploughed down upon her. At the last moment, fearing that *Fidget* was going to be cut in half, Armitage rang down full speed astern. The destroyer struck a glancing blow with the side of her bow, causing the drifter to bounce down her side. The soldiers remained remarkably calm, except for two who jumped overboard and were later recovered by the destroyer. To Armitage's surprise *Fidget* suffered little damage but it might have been much worse. The drifters reached Ramsgate at 0900 , where they disembarked their passengers. There was now no time to consider a plan of campaign; each ship began to act independently and by 1800 they had sailed again for Dunkirk where they arrived at 2330.

On that last evening of the evacuation Armitage found that the harbour was full of large ships and as it seemed that the drifters might cause confusion, he ordered them to proceed to the beaches. In the darkness and without lights, taking soundings until they were as close inshore as possible, they steamed slowly east as far as La Panne. There was still no sign of life till they were halfway on their return leg when they heard shouting coming from the shore. *Fidget* anchored and lowered her boat, but having been badly maintained, it filled and sank, but they found and secured an empty skiff.

Armitage and one member of the crew rowed ashore where they found a solitary soldier who said there were about forty others nearby. Only seven at a time could be embarked in the skiff and it was a difficult task to relaunch it each time. It was made harder by occasional shells which dropped too close for comfort. The long row back with a strong cross tide running proved too hazardous and Armitage decided to abandon the skiff and to find some more practical way of embarking the waiting soldiers. *Fidget* was, however, not the only ship of the evacuation force which was in trouble.

The Vernon drifter Fidget bringing home soldiers from Dunkirk 26 May 1940

Armitage soon came upon the Eastbourne beach excursion boat *Enchantress* which, having no charts on board, had found its way from Dover by following a tug. Her captain kept close to *Fidget* but Armitage lost sight of her and later she was later sunk. On finding no more soldiers for evacuation during the night, Armitage concluded that the operation was over, but with daylight he met a large motor barge which he asked to stand by and help him load *Fidget* with troops from the beaches. By 0600, large numbers of men were sighted standing patiently in the water. The German shelling was comparatively ineffective in the area but enemy aircraft made occasional bombing runs. Most of the noise was caused by the pom pom fire from the destroyers. Armitage kept *Fidget* in just sufficient depth of water in the ebb tide, sending the barge in on the end of a grass line attached to *Fidget's* winch. As soon as the barge was full it was hauled off, secured and the men disembarked. The instructions from the Naval Officer In Charge (NOIC) at Ramsgate had been that the drifters should limit their loads to about one hundred men, but by this time Armitage knew that they could carry twice as many and on this occasion he took on the whole barge load which was a little over three hundred. This was undoubtedly the limit and reluctantly he had to send back a number of men who had swum out whilst loading was taking place. Armitage remarked that:

They were amazingly philosophical about it and went back with cheerful comments on the wetness of the water.

Fidget made her way slowly back to Ramsgate, arriving there at 1400 on the afternoon of Friday the 31st. Armitage took pity upon a Colonel of the Highland Light Infantry whom he had found sitting drying out his trousers. He took him to the wheelhouse and gave him a tot of whisky. A year later Armitage ran into him again, by which time he was a Brigadier. He told Armitage that the wife a brother officer who had been on board had had a daughter shortly after returning and had insisted on her being christened *Fidget*. It was as well that the drifter's name had been changed from *Formidable*!

Fisher Boy, Jacketa and *Fidget* were ready again for another trip to the beaches, and at nine o'clock next morning they were away again. *Silver Dawn* had dropped out with a smashed propeller, having lost a blade on some wreckage in Dunkirk harbour, but the skipper had managed to get her back with over three hundred men on board. In addition to the three drifters, Armitage had collected three large motor boats commanded by Royal Naval Reserve officers. By now the drifters had perfected their method of embarkation using grass lines; and the new officers, who had not been to the beaches before in their boats, were instructed in their use. Things turned out differently.

Ten miles short of Dunkirk, the drifters came upon a large troopship, *Scotia*, lying on her side and burning after five direct bomb hits. A destroyer which had gone alongside signalled the drifters to close in, but as they approached the wreck the German aircraft returned to machine gun the troops in the water, most of whom were French. The drifters set about picking them up, the ships' companies jumping onto the upturned boats and wreckage to pass lines around those of the wounded who were unable to help themselves. When the last survivor had been recovered the drifters returned to Ramsgate in company with the homeward bound evacuation force. The journey was punctuated by attacks by enemy bombers, but their bombs fell harmlessly into the sea.

The heroic action of the *Vernon* drifters was now at an end. The official figure of troops brought off by the four vessels was four thousand and eighty five. The record for a single trip was held by *Silver Dawn* with three hundred and twelve. *Lord Cavan*, which had stayed in Dunkirk was sunk by shell fire, but Cubison and his crew returned safely. The crews had acquitted themselves tirelessly and gallantly under trying conditions, even though towards the end they had found difficulty in keeping awake. There had been no time for relaxation as, despite the calm weather, there had been a great deal of sickness amongst the soldiers so that when in harbour the time had been spent in cleaning ship, refuelling and carrying out repairs. Throughout the whole operation the crews remained keen for another trip, none more so than the cooks who succeeded in producing tea and food for the majority of the soldiers. This meant victualling over one hundred men from a galley equipped for twelve. *Vernon* could be rightly proud of its drifters and their crews. Cubison, Armitage and the skippers had shown that their skills were not confined to the business of mine recovery, and the seamen had shown a great deal of ingenuity in adapting the meagre resources available to the task of evacuating soldiers from the harbour and the beaches at Dunkirk.

The fall of Dunkirk was followed by an attempt to evacuate the Fifty First (Highland) Division from St Valery. Craft from *Vernon* were involved in this operation on 11 and 12 June 1940 but fog intervened and before the ships could make the harbour the Germans had reached the cliffs to the south and the beach was under direct fire. Now all that was left was for *Vernon* demolition parties to visit the remaining continental ports to destroy stores and dock installations. A party, under Commander CD Howard-Johnston, a future Captain of *Vernon*, embarked in the sloop *Wild Swan* for St. Malo with eight tons of explosive. After completing their demolition tasks they escaped via the Channel Islands just ahead of the advancing Germans.

At *Vernon* everyone was on the alert for parachutists. The threat of invasion brought with it added responsibilities for anti-invasion measures at the ports. Plans were made for the destruction of the cranes and jetties at *Vernon* Creek, although the charges were not laid as the danger of air raids seemed greater than that of invasion. *Vernon*'s demolition parties were soon touring the south coast, laying charges at many piers and jetties, sometimes to the annoyance of the Army who often proceeded to remove them. *Vernon* formed a branch of the Home Guard, or as they were originally known, the 'Dockyard Defence Volunteers'. Commanded by retired Vice Admiral N.A. Sullivan, the unit was formed from civilians in the Mine Design Department. Dressed in brown boiler suits with naval webbing they formed a guard of honour for the King when he visited Portsmouth on 25 July 1940.

Vernon was used as a transit station for French civilian and naval refugees who arrived at Portsmouth, she also provided boarding parties for the seizure of French ships in Portsmouth Harbour in the early hours of 3 July. The *Vernon* men faced no serious difficulties and brought the surprised French ships companies back to temporary acommodation in No 50 Building at *Vernon*.

The threat of invasion and the air raids led to *Vernon*'s departments seeking safer acommodation elsewhere, and as the mining offensive was making Portland untenable, submarine and destroyer torpedo discharge trials were transferred to Loch Long, leaving the Bincleaves range responsible only for MTB trials.

During the Battle of Britain in August 1940, the Luftwaffe concentrated their daylight attacks in the Portsmouth area against the neighbouring airfields, but on the 12th bombs fell around *Vernon* in Queen Street, St. George's Square, Penny Street and off Donegal Pier. Twelve days later, the Germans switched their attention to the dockyard, bringing *Vernon* under direct attack. Bombs fell on Alexandra Building, which housed the electrical instructional section, and on the trenches which had been constructed during the Munich crisis and which were now used as air raid shelters. Fortunately, at tea time on Saturdays, *Vernon* was relatively empty and casualties were limited to six ratings, who were slightly injured. 17A building and Marlborough Pier were near missed.

The growing threat to Portsmouth focussed attention upon the safety of the departments which were particularly vital to the war effort. At the end of August the Superintendant of Mine Design moved to Leigh Park House near Havant, and the Degaussing Department was despatched to Ardencaple House opposite Helensburgh on the Firth of Clyde, to which the Clarence Pier team moved on the 15 September. Twenty five naval officers, fifty sailors, twenty Wrens and over a hundred civilians left by a special train via Bristol for their new headquarters. Meanwhile, on the 7th, church bells started ringing (the acknowledged call to arms instituted by the Government), all leave was cancelled, the general recall was issued and the armed forces along the coast stood ready for the invasion. It was a false alarm, and as Webb wrote in his history of *Vernon*: 'Although there was a splendid organisation for starting the bells, it appears that no provision had been made for stopping them'.

By the end of September, the Royal Air Force had driven the Luftwaffe from the daylight skies and 'The Blitz' by night commenced in earnest. The German bombing of Portsmouth confirmed the policy of dispersion and probably helped rather than hindered the war effort. On 7 October, during an evening raid producing showers of incendiary bombs, the duty officer in *Vernon* placed his telescope to his blind eye in the true Nelsonic tradition. No bombs had fallen on *Vernon* but Portsmouth Grammar School was burning fiercely. The school housed *Vernon*'s instructional drawing office and some of the electrical instruction facilities. It seemed logical that *Vernon*'s fire fighting facilities should proceed to the scene of the fire. He pretended ignorance of the Commander-in-Chief's standing order that appliances were not to leave the establishment without orders from headquarters, and *Vernon*'s trailer pumps, under Chief Petty Officer Tanner, saved the Grammar School buildings. An official reprimand from the Commander-in-Chief duly arrived, but was followed the next morning by a letter of commendation from the Admiralty praising the prompt action which saved the Grammar School from total destruction! Commander HR Bennett, who was responsible for air raid precautions, finding these two letters on his desk, was faced with a dilemma. He took the easy way out by sending both letters without comment to the Commander-in-Chief's air raid precautions officer. No more was heard of the matter!

Bennett had been painstaking in his preparations. The *Vernon* fire crew had been trained by the City of Portsmouth Fire Brigade and they dealt most competently with many large and dangerous fires. Bennett's precautions were also noteworthy in many other respects: he had noticed that the essential water, gas and electricity supplies to the establishment approached through the main gate and were, therefore, liable to be cut off by a single bomb burst. A second water main and alternative electricity supplies were laid through the South Gate, and the air raid precaution parties at *Vernon* were forbidden to use fire hydrants. Their water supply had to come from the sea: this was achieved by pumping sea water via a canvas tank to the buildings furthest from the *Vernon* creek. Bennett's foresight and imagination were to pay dividends.

During December, a series of disastrous incendiary raids halted instructional activities. On 5 December, Alexandra Building, which had been damaged earlier, was completely burnt out; but the indomitable Chief Petty Officer Tanner was once again the Duty Fire Chief and saw that the fire was prevented from spreading to other buildings. An air raid shelter was hit and the adjoining seamens' living quarters in Warrior Block were severely damaged. Two ratings were killed and ten were injured. Two other bombs landed in *Vernon* that night but they did little damage.

Lieutenant Commander Lloyd I Jones, Royal Canadian Navy, who was then on a Gunner (T) course at *Vernon*, had reason to remember the raids. On the night of 7 December, some time after supper, the red air raid alarm sounded. His action station was with the fire party at the main entrance to Warrior Block. On this occasion it was a lone bomber which approached from the south at high speed and at low level. After releasing a stick of bombs it turned and disappeared southward. The first bomb hit *Vernon* Pier causing some damage; the second hit the Electrical School which began to burn fiercely, and by 0400 on the morning of 8 December, was completely consumed; a third bomb entered through the south side of Warrior Block and destroyed several seamens' messes, killing and wounding nineteen men, most of whom belonged to the fire party. The telephone in Warrior Block, located in the main entrance, remained intact and survivors were able to report the incident to the damage control headquarters. Army lorries were quickly on the scene to collect the wounded. The loss of life and limb, tragic though it seemed, was little compared to what was to come.

Lloyd Jones was still accommodated at *Vernon* on 10 January 1941. That night, under a full moon, there was a massive raid during which two waves of bombers deluged the city with high explosive and incendiary bombs. A major target was the large electrical power plant located just to the east of *Vernon* which was knocked out in the first hour. Thousands of incendiary bombs and hundreds of explosive bombs were dropped on Portsmouth. After the power station had been dealt with the aircraft began to approach from the west in single file, dropping their bombs in sticks. Bombs fell on the dockyard, the harbour railway station, and *Vernon* where they overshot Warrior Block and landed in the playing field, which soon became full of craters. The Captain's and Commander's houses were both heavily damaged.

There was a lull just before midnight. Then the raid resumed with increased intensity. Just before dawn it suddenly ceased and the noise faded away; but the huge fires continued to burn. The water pressure had fallen so low that the City Fire Brigade found great difficulty in dealing with the multitude of fires. Two of *Vernon*'s air raid shelters were destroyed, but they were empty as everyone was fire-fighting. One bomb landed in the wardroom garden, blowing the ornamental cupid off his pedestal and breaking his basin but causing surprisingly little other damage. Once again, Chief Petty Officer Tanner was to the fore, saving many buildings at *Vernon* by adhering strictly to the policy of always drawing water from the creek in preference to the hydrants. London Fire Brigade units, immobilised close by on the Hard by lack of water from the hydrants and a low tide, were redirected by Commander Paton to the ferry approach where the tide was high enough for them to obtain water supplies.

In spite of the severity of the raid, there were very few casualties in

Vernon. Only four men were slightly injured but the establishment was out of action for several days. Webb wrote:

The wardroom had bought a large oil stove for emergencies, and after the January raid this stove produced hot drinks, soup, tea, etc. for the whole of Vernon - about one thousand five hundred officers and men. Fresh water came by boat from Whale Island. there was one shady candle for each mess and no water for washing. Life was dirty and miserable for several days, but fortunately there were no follow-up raids during January or February. March was to see a resumption of the ferocious attacks upon Portsmouth..

On the night of 9-10 March 1941 a full moon brought a devastating raid on Portsmouth. Two high explosive bombs fell on *Vernon* demolishing the Captain's House and wounding Captain B Egerton, Boyd's successor. Another wrecked Princess Margaret Building and badly damaged No. 21 Building. The Mine Design Workshops and the shipwright's shop were also damaged and water from the ruptured mining tank flooded the area around. Incendiary bombs gutted the upper floor of Forte Building. Two AFS men were killed by a bomb along with a Petty Officer pensioner. Fourteen were injured, including Commander Veale who was temporarily blinded by an incendiary he was tackling on the top floor of the mining tank.

The Germans came back the following night and Lloyd Jones carried with him for the rest of his life memories of that devastating raid. It was of the same proportions as that of 10 January, but there were fewer incendiaries and many more high explosive bombs, all of which seemed to be heavier than in the past. He was in a brick air raid shelter, near the Whitehead Building and parallel to the wall of a War Department property. The shelter was full. As the raid increased in intensity the lights in the shelter went out. Someone shouted: 'Go over to Dido Building and see if they can put the lights on'. Jones volunteered to go. He ran to the Dido Building, normally used for torpedo instruction, and now the damage control headquarters. He asked the senior rating on duty, Chief Petty Officer Best, if the light switch for his shelter was on; Best remade the switch and Jones ran back to the shelter, pursued by the sound of an aircraft in a power dive towards the building. He managed to dive into the shelter just as the whole edifice trembled and twisted as if in an earthquake. The night was full of dust and the noise of falling masonry and human suffering. Slowly a light off-shore wind blew the dust away sufficiently to see what had happened. Dido Building had disappeared. Where it had stood was a rectangle of rubble standing eight feet high. Beneath it one hundred and forty people lay buried. Lloyd Jones and a few others ran to the rubble where they met Lieutenant Commander FB Caldwell RCN and a Scottish electrical artificer also called Jones, who was shouting orders. Voices could be heard coming from beneath the rubble. As more helpers arrived they began to pick up the bricks in front and threw them to the rear. Before long they came upon the body of Chief Petty Officer Best, the first of many who died in Dido building.

The sickbay, damaged by the blast, had been evacuated and the wounded had to be carried to the two underground shelters. Already there were wounded from the Mining Building which had been hit by a 500 lb.

bomb. Meanwhile, Lloyd Jones and others continued feverishly to clear the rubble from the ruins of *Dido* Building. Commander Holmes, who had been working in the Low Power Department, was dragged alive from the rubble. The rescuers spoke in hushed voices, murmuring that Holmes had been a scientist in peacetime. Such irrelevant details seemed pointless but the tittle tattle seemed to ease the tension.

Lloyd Jones helped to carry Holmes to the sickbay shelter where the injured were lifted on to bunks. There he met another Canadian, R Malin, who had been injured in the Mining Building blast. They teamed up with a third compatriot, a Gunner(T) trainee called Slater, and began searching for medical attendants and doctors. They found them working in two surface shelters, unaware of the destruction of Dido Building. They were soon at work taking care of the injured. Whilst the rescuers dug feverishly at the rubble, a bomber was hit and burst into flames. It appeared to be falling towards *Vernon*. Luckily it cleared the roof tops and hit the harbour waters about mid channel. A cheer went up from the rescue party. Soon the injured were being passed down to the boats for transport to Gosport and then by road to the Royal Naval Hospital at Haslar.

Just before dawn the raid ceased. A great silence and a gentle sea breeze came with the dawn; only the sound of bricks being thrown clear of the rubble disturbed the morning twilight. Caldwell turned to Lloyd Jones, 'Can you hear an aircraft?'. They looked south across the harbour in time to see a single aircraft, a few thousand feet up, coming towards *Vernon*. It dropped a bomb, turned and fled back to France. The bomb struck Haslar hospital, causing *Vernon*'s injured to be sent to inland hospitals.

Vernon was a desolate sight. Dido Building had been well built, the walls were two to three feet thick, and where they had stood several huge steel beams remained resting on the columns which had supported the upper floors. Nothing was left of the instructional equipment. The submerged torpedo tubes which had been installed on the ground floor had only recently been replaced by a 'mock-up' of a Swordfish torpedo bomber. It had not survived the force of the explosion. Lloyd Jones and Caldwell stood silently beside the wreckage. They had liked the idea of naming buildings after ships rather than simply numbering them as they did in Canada. They hoped that the history of the old Building would be written and that a new Dido Building would be erected somewhere. There were one hundred and forty people on duty in Dido, only forty came out alive. Two months later some of the survivors, still on sick leave, returned to *Vernon* of their own free will, to renew acquaintances and friendships. Unashamed tears were shed for their companions who had perished that night.

The struggle to contain the fires at *Vernon* and the efforts to save lives brought forth many tales of courage and escapes. Lieutenant Commander Macdonald, the Senior Air Raid Precautions Officer, had a miraculous escape at the southern air raid headquarters. He had been standing at the entrance to the building, giving instructions to another officer to investigate a communications failure with northern headquarters, and was about to leave when the raid intensified. Tracer ammunition began to fly everywhere, some of it horizontally, causing Macdonald to go back to the office. As he did so he heard bombs starting to fall and it seemed certain that they would land close by. One crashed through the roof of the building, exploding on the first floor with a bang and a flash. Fortunately, only the primer exploded and little damage was done. It landed on one of the instructional exhibits, a mine sinker. Why the main charge of the bomb failed to explode was never discovered.

The southern headquarters staff, still stunned by the effects of the explosion, received a visit from the Captain who was bandaged about the head but in good heart. With Macdonald still in action and required to stay at headquarters, the injured Captain went to the site of the building, where he was astonished to meet the Commander-in-Chief, Admiral Sir William ('Bubbles') James whose house in the dockyard had also been hit. It had not deterred James from making a tour of inspection of his command, and he had been well pleased to find Egerton directing operations. However, one glance at the devastation had persuaded him that the establishment should be evacuated immediately by all instructional, trials and development activities vital to the war effort. Already the constant air raid alerts and consequent lack of sleep were making both trials and training impossible. Most departments had evacuation plans and the decision to move was taken at a meeting in the Mining Office in No21 Building. As Webb put it; 'Any doubts were set at rest by a delay-action bomb going off in the power station block, and the meeting was concluded under the table.'

Lloyd Jones and Slater were billeted in the Portsmouth suburbs. They helped in the evacuation of the establishment but had almost completed their courses, they were anxious to get back to sea. They asked 'Porky' Veale, whose sight had been restored and who was still in charge of training, if arrangements could be made for them to do their final examinations. Veale readily agreed and the examination was conducted in a room in the Chief Petty Officers' mess. There were no doors or windows and the table had to be swept clean of brick dust before they could start writing. The next day each gave a twenty minute lecture on fire control systems to six Commanders. This was followed by an oral examination in low power, but by that time they were both so tired through lack of sleep that they found it difficult to keep their eyes open. In spite of all their tribulations, the two Canadians satisfied their examiners and were promoted Acting Gunners(T), Royal Canadian Navy.

The newly appointed executive officer, Commander KHT Peard, had been wounded in Dido and his duties were assumed by Commander Oliver-Bellasis, the officer in charge of the Mine Sweeping Department. Until the arrival a month later of Commander R Heathcote, he was faced with the task of finding new premises for all the departments still at Vernon. The Trials Departments went first. In April the Mining Department took over West Leigh to be close to the Mine Design Dept; the Electrical Department moved to East Leigh House nearby. Two days before the move the house was rocked by the explosion of two German land mines. The locals suspected a deliberate attack and were suspicious of their new neighbours who seemed to attract trouble. Mining Trials were moved to ranges at Arrochar on Loch Long and Weston-super-Mare. The Controlled Mining Department was established at Hillside House, Purbrook and in the Lennox garage at Southsea.

The Whitehead Department moved to the Royal Naval Torpedo Factory at Alexandria, on the extensive site of the former Argyll motor factory, and not far from the Torpedo Discharge Trials staff on Loch Long.

Most of the Whitehead equipment trials staff were moved to a house in Carlisle, but Stokes Bay remained open for both aircraft torpedo trials and ships building at southern yards. The Mine Sweeping Department also went to Scotland, to Kimmerghame House at Fettes College. The Department was installed by April and for reasons of security adopted the adress PO Box 10, Edinburgh. It was close to Port Edgar where the four experimental drifters were sent and where a small sound range was set up. Clarence Pier sound range was replaced by one established off Innellan Pier in the Firth of Clyde. By July 1941 the new range was in full use, busily measuring the sounds emitted by warships and merchant vessels.

The newly formed Acoustic Sweeps Section, which had been set up at Clarence Pier, had suffered the loss of much valuable equipment when the pier was destroyed by fire. Before going to Kimmerghame House, it had moved to the Alberta Hotel in Southsea, where a new section, known as the Future Sweeps Section, was formed, under Lieutenant RGM Collins, to develop countermeasures for new types of mine which the enemy might contrive.

The Instructional Book Production Department, which had moved in the early part of 1940 to acommodation on the South Parade at Southsea then moved to a country house named Ryecroft at Ropleigh near Alresford. Where, however were the main training and instructional sides of *Vernon* to go? A large evacuated boarding school seemed most suitable and eventually the famous girls' public school at Roedean near Brighton was chosen. The young ladies had moved to Keswick early in the war and the buildings lent to the nation. The London Scottish were using part of the buildings for training when the first reconnaissance party from *Vernon* arrived in March 1941 on the way back from a visit to Eastbourne College. The Brighton area seemed most suitable for the new *Vernon* as there was a direct current supply for the ring main model and for other items of electrical equipment transferred from Portsmouth.

After an encouraging preliminary report *Vernon*'s civilian Chief Draughtsman, Mr Croucher, and a photographer, Mr Clements, were sent to obtain a full report on the buildings within twenty four hours. The drawings of the school were photographed at the school's architects in Brighton and on the basis of this information a decision was taken to begin the move to Roedean without waiting for official approval. The Army was not keen to hand the school over to the Navy but found it hard to object to the suggestion that *Vernon* take over those parts of the building that were not being used. A policy of infiltration was decided upon and Lieutenant JR Carr led an advance guard of trainee artificers and mechanics to Roedean. After a meeting with the Army and interested authorities, chaired by Commander Oliver-Bellasis, the party began its work helped by local contractors. As work was completed on each section, Carr telephoned *Vernon* to send men to occupy them. They arrived fully kitted and self-supporting for at least four days. Trucks brought in food and essential supplies from *Vernon*, and Portsmouth Dockyard provided furniture and stores. Before approval for the move was given the Navy already outnumbered the Army at Roedean School!

The school was spacious but still more accomodation was needed, especially for Electrical and Whitehead instruction. This had therefore to be requisitioned in Brighton, where the 'Grand' Garage became the High Power Practical Workshop and the 'Dreadnought' Garage the Whitehead Instructional Workshop in which a large air compressor from *Vernon* was installed. An old people's home in Brighton became Wrens' Quarters.

The London Scottish remained confident that the Admiralty would not give their approval, but eventually the navy's complete occupation of the school was agreed in Whitehall, thanks to the advocacy of the Second Sea Lord, Sir Charles Little. (The London Scottish threatened to camp out in tents but they found new accommodation at a hotel in Rottingdean). The White Ensign was hoisted on 31 May 1941, and Captain Egerton, Commander Heathcote and the administration was officially installed. It took time for *Vernon (R)*, as the establishment became known, to become operational and *Defiance* at Plymouth had to take more than its normal share of training. Before the end of the year *Vernon(R)* had expanded into the freshly completed buildings at the St Dunstan's Home for the blind at Ovingdean. This housed High Power electrical instructional facilities, Sub-Lieutenants' Accommodation and the Central Pay Accounts. Chief Petty Officers' and Petty Officers' quarters were established at the Children's Summer House, Rottingdean. By the end of 1941 there were 150 officers, about 1,000 ratings and 100 Wrens housed in Roedean and its surrounding buildings.

The battered *Vernon (P)* on the Gun Wharf at Portsmouth continued a twilight existence as an accommodation barracks, administered from Roedean but with Commander LHT Hallebone in charge. He tried successfully to maintain the morale among the men and women quartered there by keeping as many old *Vernon* traditions as possible. The only torpedomen using *Vernon (P)'s* acommodation were those still employed in the Mining Shed, in the Controlled Mining Department at Lennox Garage and in a mine disposal team. The establishment also housed the Command Fire Fighting School. Not until 1943 would the torpedomen start to return to the Gun Wharf in larger numbers but the traditions and spirit of the old *Vernon* remained.

In September 1940, a number of mysterious explosions began to take place around the coast, and it was soon apparent that the Germans were using a new type of influence mine, which might be the acoustic mine that Ouvry and Lewis thought they had found the previous November. These mines had been developed for anti- submarine purposes during the First World War but the consensus of opinion among British naval scientists was that the noise output from a normal ship was not enough to fire a mine with a sufficient degree of reliability, if at all. Evidence of these doubts was contained in a paper which, after the war, was kept framed on the desk of Lieutenant Commander KS Main, then Commanding Officer of the Minesweeping Experimental Flotilla at Port Edgar. The Director of Minesweeping, anxious that steps should be taken to prepare the Navy for other types of influence mine, had asked the Head of the Royal Naval Scientific Service what alternative forms of actuation were possible. The reply stated that a careful study had been made of the underwater sounds transmitted from a ship which were of a nature and intensity which precluded them from being used to operate a mine mechanism. Two weeks after this was written, a ship became the first victim of an acoustic mine. Fortunately for the Allies, *Vernon's* Mining Department was not caught napping.

Pre-eminent among those responsible for this work was Dr TF Gaskell. Shortly before war began he and Bullard had established very close relationships with the Royal Navy's Hydrographic Department, and with the outbreak of war they had become familiar with the asdic control trials being conducted at Portland. When they joined the Sweeping or 'S' section of the *Vernon* Mining Department, at the Assembly Rooms attached to the Clarence Pier, they brought with them detailed knowledge of the behaviour of sound in water. Their first notable achievement was the development of a quartz hydrophone, which enabled them to make accurate measurements of the sound output from the ships operating over the sound range in Spithead. They soon found themselves at odds with those who considered the production of an acoustically operated mine by the enemy was unlikely.

German naval scientists were already aware that acoustic mines were perfectly practical and they had every incentive to take this new path as they knew by March 1940 that *Vernon* had mastered the magnetic mine. Although they continued to produce more sensitive and more intricate magnetic mine circuits throughout the war, their attention now turned to the production of an acoustic firing system for their standard LM and TM series influence mines. Production began in July 1940 and the first German acoustic mine was laid on 28 August. Correctly degaussed ships of different classes and proceeding at different speeds began to detonate mines at varying distances. *Vernon* immediately suspected that the enemy was using an acoustic mine. Bullard and Gaskell had expected this move, and had an idea as to the best answer but before they could produce an effective sweep they needed proof of the existence of a real acoustic threat. Also, although they were convinced that the best and simplest answer to such mines was a generator of 'white noise' over a relatively broad frequency band, it would also be helpful to know the exact frequencies being used by the enemy.

The situation resembled that of a year ago when the German magnetic mine made its sudden appearance, little could be done to deal with the new weapon until a specimen was avalable for study. The Germans, 'once bitten', were determined to protect their secret by forbidding the crews of aircraft carrying acoustic LM mines to fly over the land, and by ordering the mines to be laid well clear of the coast. On the night of Sunday 27 October someone blundered: an acoustic LMB mine was dropped by an enemy aircraft in about 25 feet of water in the entrance to the River Ogmore, near Porthcawl in South Wales. It was uncovered at low water when it was examined by Lieutenant S Baker RNVR and Sub Lieutenant Cummins RNVR. They had been sent from the Admiralty RMS Organisation after an initial investigation by Lieutenant Commander Chapple RNVR who happened to be on leave in Cardiff. It seemed at first to be a familiar 'C', but it was noticed that the mine had an unusual identification number painted on it, L d335. It was also found that the release mechanism on the primer had failed. Baker and Cummins removed the bomb fuse, detonator, clock and primer in accordance with normal procedure. The clock was found to be of the normal kind but instead of the usual four leads leading to the battery and detonator, Baker and Cummins found six.

As far as could be seen, the mine had been rendered safe and on 30 October it was sent by lorry to *Vernon*'s X-ray photography range, then still at Sandy Point, Hayling Island as the intended X-ray building at Buriton was not yet complete. The six lead clock bomb fuse and primer release gear were taken to *Vernon* for close examination. The X-rays were inspected by Armitage and Walden of the Mine Design Department. They saw immediately that the arrangement of the components bore little resemblance to that of previous aircraft mines. They also noted that the the mine was fitted with an extra anti-stripping mechanism, so arranged as to complete an electric circuit and detonate an auxiliary charge on removal of the rear door. It looked as though a period delay mechanism was fitted and there was a mysterious opaque mass situated in the middle of the compartment.

The usual ticking was absent; all Armitage and Walden could hear was a faint and irregular high pitched click. Past experience suggested that, if the clock mechanism found by X-ray had the same time period set as discovered in other mines, the auxiliary charge would detonate some time during the night of Saturday 2/Sunday 3 November. It was now late afternoon on the 31st October. Glenny was put in charge and the mysterious mine was moved to the recovery range at Buriton. A 4 inch diameter hole was cut over the auxiliary charge by the remote controlled trepanning equipment. The detonator was successfully removed but it was found that the faint clicking noise was being made by an unseen clock. An anxious hour passed while three more holes were cut, to reveal a clockwork mechanism and two more batteries, one of which accounted for the large black mass shown by the photographs of the centre of the unit. All seemed to be going well until a screw was found located in the centre of the rear door. It seemed to be almost certain that a mechanically operated destructive device was in place. As the clock had been disconnected from the mine, darkness had fallen and the day's rain had drenched everyone,

Glenny considered it best to leave the mine to be dealt with next day.

When work began again the following morning a probing hole revealed that no destructive device was present, and the clock had stopped. The rear door was removed, but to be on the safe side, special gear was used which had been designed to hold the door tight while the securing nuts were withdrawn. The door was then released and pulled off from a distance. At 1300 the actuating circuit was dispatched to *Vernon*. The new 'C' variant was indeed found to be acoustically operated. The pick-up unit consisted of a carbon microphone with a small cantilever on a spring to provide amplification. It was Gaskell's responsibility to lock away this precious piece of apparatus in a safe overnight before proceeding the next day to install it in a German mine casing in which it was lowered into the water. It was subjected to various frequencies and intensities of sound from which it was established that the Germans had selected an operating frequency of around of 250 cycles per second, middle C. The problem was now to find a practical noise making device which could be installed in the minesweepers.

Tea time for Lieutenant Peter Bathurst and colleagues from Edinburgh PO Box 10

The Underwater Weapons Establishment at Osprey wished to develop tuned noise makers, but Bullard and Gaskell had a more practical solution, a simple 'white noise' generator covering a wide frequency spectrum. Their idea was to use a pneumatic riveting hammer/ road drill made by a firm named Kango. This could deliver twenty blows per second and could be arranged to strike a water loaded steel diaphragm; the noise making characteristics of such a diaphragm were already known and Bullard and Gaskell now worked hard to design a practical white noise sweeping gear. The sensitivity of the mine was found to vary over a wide range, depending upon such factors as the length of time it had been laid, and the nature of the sea bed upon which it lay. It was soon apparent that the sound source to be produced by the sweep had to have a considerably greater margin of power than was at first thought necessary. The designers also had to consider the heavy damping exerted upon oscillators in water, the substantial amounts of power required to produce the required noise levels and the heavy stresses exerted upon the component parts.

Nevertheless, with the head start provided by their previous work the SA Sweep Type 'A' Mark I was at sea by December 1940. It consisted of an electric Kango hammer which beat upon a diaphragm fitted in a tank filled with water and situated in the bow of the sweeper. Power was delivered from the ship's lighting dynamo to drive the hammers. It was essential that those handling the sweep should be properly trained and made aware that the safety of the sweeper depended largely upon the correct adjustment of the hammer in relation to the diaphragm, and the maintenance of the required electrical motive force at the hammer terminals.

The sweeps were not in service a moment too soon. On the night of 12-13 December 1940 the Germans carried out a major minelaying operation in the Thames estuary off Southend. It was a deliberate attempt to close the river and most of the weapons laid were acoustic. Only three minesweepers had been fitted with acoustic sweeps but they were able to clear the waters off Southend sufficiently for convoys to move again. If the Germans had not revealed their hand a few weeks before it might well have been a different story.

One of the minesweepers engaged in this sweeping operation was damaged and this demonstrated a fault in the design of the the SA Sweep Type 'A' Mark I. It exploded mines too close for comfort. There were two approaches to solving this problem. One was to mount the hammer remotely from the ship's hull and at a greater depth. In the SA Sweep Type 'A' Mark II, the hammer was placed in a conical steel box mounted upon an 'A' frame over the fore foot of the sweeper. When required the box could be lowered to a depth of 12 feet below the surface, with the diaphragm facing forward and its axis horizontal. The other approach was to increase the power of the hull mounted sweep by using two hammers each with a larger diaphragm; this was the SA Sweep Type 'A' Mk III. The Mk III was the less successful of the two and was taken out of service by 1943, while Mk IIs remained in use until the end of the war. From late 1942 the main acoustic sweep became the Mk IV which had a spring hammer in a conical box towed from a short frame amidships or, in motor minesweepers, from davits on the foredeck.   T h e rapid development of acoustic sweeps was another notable success for *Vernon*. 224 acoustic sweeps were at sea by mid-January. Eventually the Kango hammer As were joined by the alternative Cs mounted mainly in warships other than minesweepers and consisting of Fessenden oscillators mounted in the bows. By the second anniversary of the outbreak of war, 962 acoustic mines had been swept in home waters as against 1,262 magnetic and 818 contact mines. This success was all the more creditable when it is considered that it was carried out at the height of the German 'Blitz'.

On the night of 9-10 March 1941, the mining tank at *Vernon* was rigged for some important experiments the following morning. The precious German acoustic mine unit was placed upon the wooden platform which raised and lowered articles within the tank. The aim was to establish the effect of various frequencies of sound on the unit at different depths. That night, as we have seen , the Luftwaffe made a heavy raid, and at dawn Gaskell was confronted with a tank with no water in it and with his precious German acoustic mine lying at the bottom. His irreplaceable equipment 'had shrapnel holes all over it'. All morning he contemplated the scene with dismay, until the head of the Minesweeping Department Commander Oliver-Bellasis, took pity upon him and led him off to the wardroom for a consoling drink. Suitably fortified, he returned later to pick up the pieces.

Worse was soon to follow. At Clarence Pier, all was prepared for a visit by the First Sea Lord, Admiral Sir Dudley Pound. Gaskell had worked late into the previous night to prepare for the visit and, in particular, to ensure that all the equipment concerned with picking up the sound of the relevant frequency was in good working order. The last thing he did that night was to make recordings of the long range pick up of all the sounds emanating from a vessel operating off Spithead together with the background noise. All was in immaculate working order. Then, in Gaskell's own words, 'They bombed the thing to bits. The next morning we had about six burnt out ends of cable. It was sad really. The First Sea Lord did not bother to come down.' A more important loss perhaps was the archive that had been built up on the performance of underwater sound in different frequency ranges.

That was the end of the Clarence Pier operation but with the move to Edinburgh, the Minesweeping Department expanded rapidly. An early addition to the team was a group of mainly Royal Naval Reserve officers and men, who were assembled to oversee the fitting out of the minesweepers. They were known affectionately as the 'Apostles'. Also established, at Port Edgar on the Firth of Forth, was the Experimental Minesweeping Flotilla consisting of four drifters, two yachts and a 55 foot MTB. They were joined later by the destroyers *Witch* and *Sabre* and a number of motor minesweepers.

1941 saw the minesweeping force get the measure of the mining threat. In the Spring two flotillas of valuable *Halcyon* Class fleet minesweepers had to be withdrawn for escort duties in the Western Approaches leaving only four large minesweepers based at Harwich. However, the situation improved with the delivery of new motor minesweepers and *Bangor* class fleet mine-sweepers. SA acoustic sweeps also proved effective additions to escort destroyers operating off the East Coast, allowing them to sweep ahead of coastal convoys. The training of personnel for the rapidly increasing minesweeping forces was transferred from Portsmouth to Port Edgar, where, during the course of the war, large numbers of officers and men were trained and kept up to date with the frequently changing mine countermeasures.

German thoroughness in classifying their enormous array of devices had, perforce, to be matched at Kimmerghame House, where they were designated in alphabetical sequence based on size and general characteristics:

A - 550 kg LMA air dropped parachute magnetic influence mine.
B - 960 kg LMB air dropped parachute magnetic influence mine.

C - modified LMB, later fitted with acoustic, magnetic/acoustic, or magnetic/pressure circuits.

D - modified LMA later fitted with acoustic or magnetic/acoustic firing.

E - booby trap mines used in 1940 based on the LMA.

G - 1,000 kg BM 1000 air dropped mines first recovered 1941; no parachute; various forms of actuation, magnetic, magnetic/acoustic and later acoustic/pressure.

H - 'Turtle', RMA hemispherical ground magnetic mine laid by surface craft from 1939.

I - RMH wooden cased rectangular box shaped ground mine, surface ship laid.

J - Small spherical mine with one horn and 12 kg. charge.

K - 'Katie', KMA ground contact coast defence mine; 75 kg charge in concrete base.

L - Designation apparently used for moored contact mine with 110 kg charge and for a drifting contact river mine with a 12 kg charge.

M - BMC air dropped moored contact mine introduced mid 1943.

N - TMC enlarged ground influence mine for laying by submarines, charge circa 900 kg., introduced 1940, magnetic, acoustic or combined actuation.

O - moored influence mines for laying from vertical tubes of special mine laying U-boats or (O*) from surface craft, 350 kg. charge.

P - LMF 1050 kg. moored influence mine introduced in 1943 for laying by 'E'-boats and aircraft.

Q - FMC shallow water contact mine with five horns and 40 kg. charge.

R - UMB moored anti submarine mine with 40 kg charge and five Herz and three switch horns.

S - TMB submarine laid influence mine with charge of circa 500 kg., same actuation as N.

T - TMA moored magnetic mine withdrawn from service in 1941.

U - EMA oval moored contact mine with 150 kg charge.

V - Antenna mines of the EM series.

X - EMD spherical moored contact mine with 150 kg charge.

Y - EMC spherical moored contact mine with 300 kg. charge.

Z - UMA anti submarine moored contact mine like R but with with 30 kg charge.

If all this were not enough, there were variations to each type of mine. For example, a new acoustic mechanism appeared in July 1941. It differed from the original in having increased sensitivity and a ship counter but without an arming delay clock. In 1941 the Germans expanded their influence mining campaign to the Mediterranean. Both Malta and the Suez Canal suffered, the situation in Egypt being particularly serious. When the Germans dropped their first mines into the Canal on 30 January 1941, there were only three Double L sweepers available. Urgent steps had to be taken to augment the available Wellington and LL sweepers, whose combined strength was quite inadequate for the purpose. Lieutenant Commander JF Duckworth, the torpedo officer on the staff of Vice Admiral Sir James Pipon, Senior Naval Officer Suez Canal, set about supervising the conversion of some of the canal hoppers for sweeping magnetic mines and the creation of an organisation for spotting the exact location at which individual mines were dropped. The teams of mine spotters were not popular with the Army as they absorbed three and a half battalions of British troops. Meanwhile, however, the immediate need was for increased anti-aircraft defences and Admiral Pipon despatched Lieutenant Commander Duckworth to argue his case at the Army Headquarters in Cairo. As a result more anti-aircraft guns were allocated to the defence of the Canal, but the situation was still critical. There was an urgent need to bring into the Mediterranean *Formidable*, waiting in the Red Sea to relieve the damaged carrier *Illustrious*, and for the latter to get away to the United States for repairs. The carrier *Eagle* was also locked up in the Mediterranean though she was required in the Indian Ocean and South Atlantic to search for German surface raiders.

The sweepers alone could not guarantee that the canal would be cleared of mines. It was, therefore, necessary for the mine watchers to take the bearings of the falling mines so that divers could locate them. The mines were then dragged to the Canal banks where they were disposed of. It became an increasingly hazardous business as the Germans began to drop acoustic as well as magnetic mines. As a temporary measure two high speed motor boats, which had been employed on the Canal as despatch vessels, were taken over and manned by naval personnel. Driven at high speed up and down the Canal, these small craft succeeded in exploding a number of mines but eventually the inevitable happened.

Lieutenant Commander M.C.Giles (later Rear Admiral Sir Morgan Morgan-Giles) was a torpedo officer engaged in trials in the Suez Canal area. He was watching from the bank when a mine exploded immediately beneath one of the small boats, completely shattering it. Fragments of the hull, engines and bodies were flung into the air. He sprinted to the nearest Suez Canal Station to obtain a boat to go to the scene. One was quickly supplied, but he was temporarily delayed by a French clerk of the Suez Canal Company who ran after him insisting that he should sign a receipt; Giles brushed him aside. Further delay was caused by the Arab crew, who stopped the boat to recover an object on the surface which flashed in the sunlight. For a moment it looked as though they had found a survivor but it turned out to be a large fish stunned by the explosion, which the crew wished to recover for their lunch. Miraculously, the Petty Officer who had been coxswain of the destroyed boat survived but the remainder were never found. Giles recalled that 'there was just a lot of scum and bits of wood that had comprised this little boat, nothing bigger than a pencil remained'.

The urgency of the situation prompted a number of bizarre suggestions for keeping the Canal clear. Some were immediately discarded, such as the training of dolphins to find the mines or the provision of glass bottomed boats. The legendary Jim Irish was recruited to find Egyptian skin divers to assist the Naval divers in the location and recovery of the mines. Their performance was not always in accordance with their instructions. One one occasion Duckworth observed that whilst one skin diver was operating correctly, the other six were merely jumping over the side of the boat and splashing around for a while before returning aboard, breathing heavily and towelling themselves down. It was found that none of these men were divers: they had been recruited by the artful Jim Irish only to boost his commission. Nevertheless, the work of the Naval and Egyptian divers was essential to the success of the operation to keep the Canal clear of mines. Their work was punctuated at regular intervals by excitement and apprehension. A Canadian diver named Cook was using the standard 'motor horn' safety device to remove the hydrostatic valve from a mine. He reappeared on the surface, waving the horn and complaining bitterly that 'the bloody Germans' had 'fitted the wrong screw thread...'.

Another proposal for keeping the Canal clear of influence mines involved the use of giant drogues which were intended to be dragged along the bottom of the Canal to remove the mines physically. As the drogues proved difficult to tow, an attempt was made to drag them from the bank, using tow ropes led through snatch blocks and pulled by camels. However, the camels were reluctant to co-operate and the project was abandoned.

Attention now centred upon another scheme, the evidence of which is still apparent in the Suez Canal. The whole area of the Canal was to be netted so that when an air raid took place a hole in the net would denote where a mine had been dropped. Admiral Andrew Cunningham, the C-in-C, supported the project; he believed that it was one a sailor could understand. But his staff calculated that a million miles of cod line would be required to make the netting. A compromise was reached and it was decided to net a small section of the Canal; a substantial order for cod line was placed in India. Eventually, long after the threat to the Suez Canal had disappeared and the war had gone from the Canal area, the nets became available. They were stretched across the Canal and trials begun on an experimental section. They were marred by tragedy when a Gunner(T), endeavouring to secure the nets from a boat, was drowned when it capsized and he became entangled in the net. This tragedy was followed by a fiasco. Bedouin Arabs appeared during the night and stole the lines which were intended for hauling the net across the Canal with the result that it could not be hauled clear to make way for approaching convoys.

The immediate mining crisis had been overcome by March 1941 but it took continuous efforts to keep the Suez Canal open as long as German minelaying aircraft remained in range. Closures were, however, limited to 24 hours or so. During the first two years of the war some 28 magnetic and 2 acoustic mines were swept in the Suez Canal; in the Mediterranean theatre the minesweepers accounted for 63 more magnetic mines, 28 acoustic and 71 contact.

Hidden in the Mine Sweeping Section at *Vernon* when it was transferred to Scotland were two American naval officers who had joined secretly before their country had entered the war. They wore plain clothes and were listed as members of the civilian staff. In Edinburgh a number of temporary reserve officers with special qualifications were also appointed to the staff, one of whom was Lieutenant Peter Bathurst. He had been one of a number of civilians in the days before the war who had received a grant from the Admiralty to purchase and operate radio transmitters and receivers. When war broke out, he had been sent as a telegraphist to a trawler in the north western approaches, where it was not long before his leadership qualities were recognised. At the officer training depot, Bathurst qualified top of his class, and when a signal was received from *Vernon* requesting the appointment of a 'House Trained Officer' as Secretary to the Commander Minesweeping at PO Box 10, he was soon on his way to Edinburgh where he found himself employed shuffling officers' expense claims in the Commander's office. It was apparent that he had a technical aptitude and intellectual capacity which would make him a valuable asset to the trials sections and he was reappointed to the SW Section as a trials officer, a job requiring a great deal of resourcefulness - particularly where it was necessary to circumvent the regulations without actually breaking them.

The need to go through offical channels to obtain special equipment could often be overcome by a visit to Port Edgar where, in the rigging shop presided over by two experienced seamen, Lieutenant Bowden and Chief Petty Officer Savage, an enormous amount of skilled splicing of heavy wire for the many items of towed equipment was carried out. The rigging shop could also manufacture a wide range of devices and had acquired an extensive stock of surplus material which lurked invitingly. Savage, a character who lingered long in the memories of the occupants of Kimmerghame House, had retired from the Royal Navy after many years of service but, after a period in the Royal Dockyards, was recalled in 1939. His experience as a seaman and in the dockyard meant that he could turn his hand to almost any task of improvisation and invention. Undecorated and uncomplaining, he was typical of the many ratings who worked tirelessly to keep the Royal Navy a step ahead of the Germans in the often unpredictable, always dangerous and frequently changing mining contest.

In the Minesweeping Department there developed a team spirit and lively sense of humour which never wavered and which was assisted by the naval tendency to capitalise upon any eccentricity. Nicknames were given and accepted without rancour. Dr. Edward Bullard was known variously and affectionately as the 'Cunning Kango' and the 'Button Booted Boffin'. A naval officer who had the habit of wearing a much battered hat became known as 'T-Cosy Dunne'. Two scientists working diligently on a highly secret project were christened 'Humguffin and Snook'; the unfortunate representative of the Royal Corps of Naval Constructors, guilty only of wearing an Anthony Eden homburg was known as 'The Black Hat'.

This team spirit was due largely to the influence of the two men who were consecutive heads of the scientific staff. First was Bullard, who laid the groundwork upon which co-operation flourished. Then came Edward Collingwood (later Sir Edward Collingwood). The son of an army family, he was also a collateral descendant of the Nelson's second in command at Trafalgar. After cadet time at Osborne and Dartmouth he was appointed to the battleship named after his illustrious ancestor. While recovering from accidental injuries he underwent a 'Pauline conversion to Mathematics'. Invalided out, Collingwood went to Cambridge where he became a university lecturer and, in 1930, Steward of Trinity. Family affairs returned him to his native and beloved Northumberland of which he was High Sheriff in 1937, but despite an allegiance to the local yeomanry, he was persuaded by Bullard to rejoin the naval service in 1940. He was promoted Captain RNVR in 1944, which he said 'gave me more pleasure than anything except, perhaps, being elected FRS'. He was appointed to the Minesweeping Department as its scientific head, and he soon gained the respect of the naval and civilian staff, proving to be a brilliant manager of the mixed group of scientists and technicians who were not subject to, and had little regard for, naval discipline and customs. He was regarded by everyone at Kimmerghame House as guide, mentor and friend, as well as their much respected scientific leader. The highly professional, but relaxed, atmosphere at PO Box 10 continued the tolerant, hard working and good humoured approach to work which could be traced back to the earliest days of *Vernon* and the Torpedo Branch.

PO Box 10 Edinburgh was divided into five sections:

Section SA	Acoustic
Section SL	Electric
Section SW	Wire
Section SF	Future Sweep
Section SM	Mathematical Appraisal and Theoretical

The head of each was a torpedo and electrical specialist, judged to be of superior intellectual ability.

Amongst these was Lieutenant Nigel Tibbits. Towards the end of 1941 he disappeared from his office at Kimmerghame House and for a while the reason remained a mystery. He had, in fact, been seconded to a force commanded by Commander RED Ryder which was preparing to attack St. Nazaire. . The expedition aimed to destroy the gates of the only dry dock on the Atlantic coast where the battleship *Tirpitz* could be repaired and

Campbeltown at St Nazaire in the sluice Normandie before exploding with the sluice gate

depended for its success on the former US destroyer *Campbeltown* being able to ram the dock. Tibbits was responsible for installing a large demolition charge fitted in her bow. She was successfully wedged in position to explode the demolition charge against the dock gates, but Tibbits was captured after leaping ashore with a landing party to destroy the dock machinery. From the scanty evidence available, it is apparent that he was taken back to *Campbeltown* with a large party of German officers and technicians intent on inspecting the stranded destroyer. There is no doubt that they pressed him to reveal the whereabouts of the fuse and detonator. This Tibbits resolutely refused to do though he knew that at any moment the demolition charge would explode. He stood his ground and lost his life. By this one act of supreme bravery, Tibbits took his place on the list of the most honoured Torpedo Officers though he received no posthumous award. He was not only a very brave man, but also one of outstanding ability. His devotion to duty was an inspiration to all his colleagues in the Torpedo Branch, and especially to those at Kimmerghame House.

The maintenance, development and trials of the acoustic mine sweeps became the responsibility of the SA Section, which had access to the valuable facilities of the new sound range at Inellan on the Clyde. The existing sweeps could cope with the magnetic and acoustic mines discovered so far but the SF department were considering the Germans' next step - a mine operated by combined magnetic-acoustic signals. The Germans first started using this type in the summer of 1941. It was triggered magnetically but actuated by the acoustic unit. This meant that a much more sensitive magnetic setting could be used, thus endangering ships which had been partially but not completely degaussed. The Germans were confident that the magnetic-acoustic unit would play havoc amongst ships operating on the continental shelf. They took steps to protect the mine unit with an anti-stripping device which consisted of photo-electric cells in a compartment which was normally covered by a large manganese steel dome. This meant that the mines could not be rendered safe in daylight or normal artificial light. However, a booby trap of this kind had long been anticipated, and steps were always taken as a precaution against this eventuality. Thus, when on 5 September 1941 a magnetic/acoustic mine was recovered, it was successfully rendered safe and its secrets uncovered despite the presence of the anti-stripping device; it was given the name 'Sammy'. PO Box 10 already prepared for the challenge soon devised an effective sweeping procedure using LL and SA A MK II sweeps.

The advent of the acoustic mine alerted Kimmerghame House to the need for the most careful measurement of the magnetic and acoustic signatures of all ships and, in particular, of minesweepers. Since the introduction of acoustic sweeps, the only means of checking the adjustment of sweep gear had been by testing each one against a replica of the German acoustic mine unit. Although it had given good service as an indicator, it was in no sense a measuring device; and, in view of the wide possibilities of variations in mine design, minesweeping bases were equipped for sound analysis using quartz hydrophones.

Accurate and up-to date records were important to PO Box 10, especially to the working of the SF Section, under Lieutenant KS Main. He received all reports about ships damaged below the waterline and an effort was made to deduce the type of weapon which had caused the incident. The mathematics of 'inverse probability' were used to try to deduce fairly accurately which of a possible number of causes was responsible for the damage. Less successful were the attempts to detect any change in the sensitivity of the settings or the actuating mechanisms of enemy mines so that new countermeasures could be introduced. A record of all enemy mines swept by magnetic and acoustic sweeps was received by the section and plotted on a large wall diagram. But, apart from indicating the areas of activity, it failed to produce a consistent pattern upon which an analysis could be made. It was soon realised that any change in enemy tactics was bound to be masked by the random behaviour of existing mines in various depths and by varying sea conditions. Future trends would, therefore, have to be guessed by the experts, who undertook a careful examination of all possible developments such as changes of polarity or field direction, a change of sound frequency in acoustic mines, exploitation of the galvanic effects known to exist in the vicinity of a ship (underwater electrical potential), the use of hydrodynamic effects and the use of all these in combination. It was a formidable task, but the section was well endowed with scientific and mathematical talent.

Intelligence reports from British agents and members of the Resistance in Europe often contained messages and diagrams made by the foreign workers forced to labour in the German factories making components for enemy weapons. Bravely and secretly smuggled out, these precious documents were hastily written on scraps of paper and cigarette packets, often using the old German script. It fell to the SF Section to translate most of these fragments before they made any sense. Although some yielded a great deal of important information, the Section had to guard against the planting of misinformation by the enemy. They suspected such a spoof when much effort went into developing a sweep to deal with a mine reported to use reflected high frequency sound. This seemed a rather dubious device as in order to trigger the transmission of the high frequency sound beam it would need to contain its own more conventional magnetic or acoustic enabling mechanism. Nevertheless a 'WIP Sweep', using an array of reflecting neoprene tails, was designed but it was never required.

It was important that the Mine Design Department at West Leigh should keep the SF Section informed of their own 'dirty tricks'. This led to some of the few light hearted interludes in what was otherwise a serious and dangerous trial of strength. On one occasion, rumours filtered through from West Leigh that a mine had been laid deliberately on a drying bank off the German coast. It had contained a highly complicated spoof actuating mechanism constructed from the components of a broken radio gramophone in the works canteen. At Christmas, the British mine designers perpetrated a seasonable, if less fearsome trick, when a mine was laid which contained a spoof actuating mechanism consisting of a slice of Christmas pudding and a piece of holly!

The Germans introduced two new types of influence mechanism, both in the late Summer of 1943. One was a magnetic/acoustic circuit first encountered in the Mediterranean. The microphones needed to be activated for 15 seconds before the magnetic trigger became effective. If the latter was not actuated the whole mine became dormant. Despite this sophistication, mines fitted with this circuit still proved vulnerable to the LL and SA Mk IV sweeps used in combination. In home waters the Germans tried a new purely acoustic unit, the A104. This had a ship counter and was also supposed to discriminate between the sounds of ships and acoustic sweeps. It did not work as intended but it was a warning to PO Box 10 as to what it might expect in the future

The public continued to bombard the Service Ministries with ideas and inventions. Those concerned with mining or minesweeping were passed to the SF Section for evaluation. Main, who was head of this section between 1943 and 1945, commented that:

most were impractical but occasionally valid suggestions were received. Some of these suggestions were eminently workable but the writers had to be fobbed off politely because of the high security risk involved in telling them the true value of their ideas. In particular, I recall a plumber in Helston who described, with complete accuracy, the principle which ultimately rang the death knell for conventional methods of minesweeping.

This warning foreshadowed the introduction of mines using a completely new influence, the change in water pressure on the sea bed created by a ship moving overhead. The Germans had been aware of this possibility since early in 1940, when Korvettenkapitan Fett had drawn attention to British work in the First World War on the pressure signatures of canal barges. An experimental pressure detonator was produced and fitted to a ground mine designed to fire as the result of the sustained drop in pressure produced by the velocity of the water as it passed beneath the ship. The trials were successful, but, as no means of sweeping this new secret weapons could be devised, fears were expressed in Berlin that if this mine was recovered by the British it could be used with devastating effect against the Germans, particularly in the Baltic. Therefore its development was not encouraged, but by the end of 1943 the Luftwaffe had developed a pressure/magnetic version of the 'C' and a pressure/acoustic 'G'. In both a reduction in pressure of 1.5 inches present for about eight seconds activated the alternative trigger; in the acoustic mine there was a delay of thirty seconds before the mine reverted to normal. The use of these weapons was strictly forbidden until the time seemed right.

In Edinburgh, the SF and SM Sections were becoming increasingly concerned about the unsweepable characteristics of pressure mines. The Helston plumber had served to heighten their awareness by pointing out that when water passes through a pipe the pressure on the walls of the pipe depends on its velocity; and if this is increased sufficiently, pressure drops to such an extent that a pipe is no longer needed to contain it. It is an effect which every fireman and gardener experiences when water is passed through a nozzle at the end of a hose. It was soon established that when a ship proceeding in fairly shallow water passes over a pressure detecting device, the pressure on the seabed drops and the fall in pressure is maintained during the passage of the whole length of the ship. A simple diaphragm firing device could work on this principle. What worried the SF Section was that there was no way of simulating this effect except by displacing the same amount of water as that displaced by the ship. There appeared to be no simple answer. It seemed that the perfect mine actuating mechanism had been discovered.

As a matter of urgency, attention was focussed upon production of a displacement sweep. The first was a huge canvas drogue called a 'Drachen', which contained the same mass of water as a ship's hull. It was towed down the swept channel by a tug whose pressure signature was insufficient to actuate a mine. It was effective but, as it was destroyed every time it exploded a mine, it was a very costly way in which to sweep them! When a 'Drachen' and its tow line became entangled in the propellors of the trials destroyer *Witch*, the project was abandoned.

Trials were now concentrated upon the mine destructor ships, *Cyrus* and *Cybele*. Converted merchantmen, they were given buoyant bow and stern sections and a midship honeycomb framework with hinged bottom plates. The theory was that the underwater explosion would lift the hinged plates and the force of the explosion would be vented upwards and away, after which the bottom plates would fall back and it was hoped that the ship would be undamaged, ready for the next mine. A midship section was built for testing to destruction by the SF Section. The result was disastrous. The bottom plates were torn away and the honeycomb structure damaged beyond repair. In spite of this failure, the two so-called 'Stirling Craft' were completed.

The introduction of the pressure mine, which became known as the 'Oyster', meant that the existing mining and mine countermeasures trial ranges were unsuitable. A new range was established at Falmouth, to which *Cyrus* and *Cybele* were ordered. The voyage from Merseyside, where they were converted, was hazardous and filled with incident. On the way down

Creating a pressure wave at the Falmouth Range

the west coast, the tug towing *Cyrus* reported that it had been found necessary to take shelter off Lundy Island. The unfortunate skipper signalled the Admiralty that *Cyrus* had insisted upon circling the tug, wrapping the towing wire around her. Bathurst, who had moved to the Falmouth range, remarked that *Cyrus* and *Cybele* invariably reacted to being towed by 'attempting to field at cover point'. Even when towed by two tugs, *Cyrus*'s speed was hardly above 3 knots and the pressure signals produced were correspondingly disappointing. *Cybele* failed to reach Falmouth at all and was eventually sold to the breakers yard. The 'Stirling Craft' trials were abandoned.

The American 'Egg Crate'

Amongst the large number of devices which underwent trials at Falmouth was the American 'Egg Crate'. It consisted of flotation tanks with large vents between them, the whole structure measuring 45 feet square by 28 feet deep. It was a cumbersome construction which, towed by two *Bangor* class minesweepers, made fifty slow circuits of the range at never more than walking pace. With the arrival of two of the Admiralty's most powerful tugs of the *Samsonia* class, a sweeping speed of 4 knots was achieved. Although the 'Egg Crate' was a much more manoeuvrable pressure sweep than *Cyrus* and *Cybele*, its swept path was too narrow for any practical use.

As the 'Oyster' mine might have a combined magnetic circuit, trials were carried out at Falmouth to determine whether LL sweeps and pressure waves could be phased effectively. A number of proposals were considered amongst which was an exciting trial involving a destroyer and steam gunboats manoeuvring at high speed. The destroyer, steaming at 28 knots, created a large pressure wave by applying 30 degrees of helm. At the same time, the steam gunboats proceeded ahead of the destroyer streaming LL sweeps. It was too complicated a manoeuvre to be of much practical value and it was made all the more difficult by the precise timing which it required. However, the SGBs had a potential on their own as pressure wave making mine sweepers, and they were given a very unpopular role as mine countermeasures vessels. They operated in threes with the central boat fitted with an LL tail and a 75 kW generator and the other two single L tails and lower powered generators. The central boat also used an acoustic sweep.

By May 1944, a large stock of 'Oyster' mines had been built up in France but the German high command decided to keep them in reserve until the advent of invasion. This was a mistake as the time to use the mines was when the great fleet was gathering in the Solent southwards into Saint Helen's Roads, where the ships were so densely packed that they could barely swing clear of each other. The Germans had only to lay a mixture of influence mines of various types to cause chaos. The waters could not be swept with so many ships in the anchorage, and if the ships had been required to get under way in the midst of a mining scare, only confusion and disaster could have followed.

Only two attempts were made to lay mines in the invasion anchorage, on 28 April and 15 May 1944. The mines dropped in the first raid fell well clear into the Needles Channel whose strong tide took them into shallow water where they exploded harmlessly. The raid on 15 May was equally unsuccessful. It was broken up by fighters and aborted by a smoke screen. The only other mines which the enemy succeeded in releasing landed on the shore and were rendered safe.

The immediate and extensive use of 'Oyster' mines off the beaches might have proved disastrous to the Normandy landings in their crucial opening hours, but, shortly before 'D' Day, Goering ordered the two thousand 'Oyster' mines which had been stored in France as a precaution against the invasion, to be returned to Magdeburg where they arrived on 4 June. This order had been influenced by German intelligence, which had advised that the stock of mines in France, at Le Mans, was in danger of being overrun before they could be used. The German High Command - correctly as it turned out - also considered that 'Oyster' mines would be only of limited use on the expected invasion beaches due to the swell effect and unfavourable depth of water. So it was that, when the order came to lay the mines in the path of the invasion fleet, none were available.

The mines arrived back in France between 11 and 14 June, and 400 pressure mines were laid off the beaches in the six weeks after 'D' Day. The first pair of 'Oyster' mines was recovered at Fluc-Sur-Mer on 22 June. On examination at *Vernon* they were discovered to be combined acoustic/pressure devices and were coded AP Mk I (the German designation was AD104). To the relief of Kimmerghame House they proved to be vulnerable to the contingency countermeasures that had already been prepared. A list of safe speeds was issued to the invasion forces for various depths of water. Also, as expected, the mines were kept continuously activated by the succession of drops in pressure in the swell off the beaches. This made them vulnerable to simple acoustic sweeps, and swell recorders were installed in the invasion area to warn the minesweepers when the correct conditions existed for acoustic sweeping.

To reinforce the SGBs, the large Fairmile 'D' MTBs were employed in threes, towing noise makers; occasionally with an SGB as centre boat. The system was effective, clearing a path two cables wide, but the sea conditions usually produced sufficient swell to actuate the pressure units and the MTBs were seldom needed. The persistent rough weather off Normandy in June and July meant that normal acoustic sweeping was adequate. On 24 July, the first magnetic/pressure mine was recovered and it was found that its pressure unit was not subject to swell effect; making the MTB and SGB sweepers ineffective. The only protection available to shipping was slow speed and good degaussing. If such mines were to be permanently neutralised they would have to be located on the sea bed and countermined where they lay, ie 'hunted' rather than 'swept'.

The SF Section in Edinburgh examined the possibilities of mechanical and acoustic methods of locating objects on the seabed. The first of these was known as the 'Snag Locator Sweep', but it was yet another 'Bosun's Nightmare'. Designed to deal with non-ferrous metal mine cases, it consisted of an

A-Sweep, towed between two ships from which trailed a weighted insulated cable containing projecting spikes of stainless 'Staybrite' steel. When a spike touched a metal object, a galvanic signal was received in the sweeper. A marker buoy was dropped to mark its location and a diver was sent down to locate the mine and lay countermining charges.

Unfortunately, the spikes could not distinguish between ferrous and non-ferrous metal, and when tested in the Solent the mass of old iron on the bottom rendered the 'Snag Locator Sweep' impracticable. Further experiments with a second type of bottom sweep of a more sophisticated nature were needed. Instead of the 'Staybrite' steel spikes, the sweeper trailed exciter coils over the bottom, each coil carrying a high frequency alternating current inducing eddy currents in the sea. Any object protruding into the otherwise uniform ambient conditions produced a positive signal for a non-ferrous object and a negative signal for a ferrous one. The sweep was given the descriptive name the 'Conductor Inductor Spar Sweep'. In its final form it consisted of a 31 foot spar towed beneath a motor fishing vessel, with sixteen tails containing the small induction coils spaced 2 feet apart, giving it a very limited swept path. It was, however, valuable for use in confined waters, such as in canals, docks and basins.

Both these sweeps were in use at the end of the war. The 'Snag Locator Sweep' had the advantage of its wide swept path, but it was difficult to handle and required a run of about 3 miles to stream or recover, and at least half a mile beyond the end of a leg for turning at the end of laps. Furthermore, it could not be handled efficiently in winds above force four, and its use was not recommended in a tideway.

These towed mine location devices were expensive, hard to handle and of questionable efficiency. Priority was therefore given to the development of acoustic means of detection and classification of dormant underwater objects. Some experience of this technique had been gained early in the war when the Southampton based echo-sounder yacht, *Sir Echo*, had carried out trials off Sheerness. These trials had been continued by the mine recovrery flotillas notably by Lieutenant Commander Callieu in the yacht *Esmeralda*, but his efforts were limited by the primitive equipment then available. The normal navigational echo-sounding sets were not satisfactory for the location of small objects such as mines on the bottom, but when three sets were employed simultaneously, improved results were obtained giving a swept path of about 50 feet. Quite obviously, something better than this was needed if this means of minehunting was to be a practical proposition.

The development of high definition sonar was a priority on both sides of the Atlantic, and it was not long before a system, designed by the General Electric Company in the United States, became available for trials by the SF Section. The American company, anxious to sell its wares, designed a target to be laid on the seabed consisting of a large board with reflecting metal studs arranged in the form of the letters GEC. It was suspected that the dimensions of the metal studs were specially chosen to reflect the exact frequency of the minehunting sonar. The sonar certainly produced an accurate picture in the form of the letters on a cathode ray tube and, under very favourable conditions, other objects on the bottom could be identified by shape and dimension, but the equipment, still in its infancy, required highly skilled maintenance and operation. Towards the end of the war, *Vernon* recommended that it should be used in combination with the 'Snag Locator Sweep'.

Another important part of the work of the SF Section was the study of countermeasures to torpedoes, a subject of constant concern to Winston Churchill, both as First Lord and then as Prime Minister. A system was devised consisting of paravanes streamed from the bow of a merchant ship; attached to the paravanes were long snakes containing hydrophones, whilst further snakes containing explosives were towed from positions half way along the paravanes' towing wires. The intention was that as a torpedo crossed the line of hydrophones, the sound of its propellers would trigger the explosive charges and destroy the torpedo before it struck the ship. It was an alarming 'bunch of knitting' calculated to frighten any sailor. When, at Liverpool, Main met the first ship fitted with this device, he found the Master seated in a cabin with a very white face and a glass of Bourbon. Halfway across the Atlantic the ship had run into heavy weather, causing one of the paravanes to porpoise and run into the side of the ship. The explosive snake had wrapped itself around the ship's single propeller and for the rest of the voyage the Master had heard it being flailed round and round under his stern, banging insistently against the hull. Although he had been able to switch off the firing circuits, the crew had waited, nervously expecting the explosive snake to detonate. Not surprisingly, further development of this device was abandoned!

In the Summer of 1943, Lieutenant WFH Lamacraft was appointed to the SF Section to reinforce the team engaged upon the development of anti-torpedo measures. Under his control these now took a less dangerous course. The new project linked the detection of torpedoes by sonar with a fire control system designed to place an explosive charge in the path of the oncoming torpedo. Provided with a number of British torpedoes, Lamacraft carried out static trials in the Firth of Forth to determine the extent and nature of damage caused at various ranges by a variety of explosive charges. Later, similar trials were carried out at the Arrochar torpedo range on Loch Long using captured German torpedoes. Each torpedo was fired through a large mesh net of copper wire. The passage of the torpedo triggered a galvanic signal which in turn activated an explosive charge. It was expected that the detonation would damage the torpedo and stop it where it could be recovered for examination. Unfortunately, these trials were beset with many tribulations and had not reached fruition by the end of the war when they were discontinued. One of the problems was the tendency of torpedoes to run out of control down the loch. On one occasion an errant weapon beached itself in an elderly lady's garden.

Amongst the information which came from Allied agents on the Continent in 1943 was news the Germans had designed an acoustically operated homing torpedo. If this were true it would pose a serious threat, particularly to convoy escorts which were expected to be specially targeted. The SF Section soon found itself heavily involved in the search for effective countermeasures. It was important that a decoy should be devised as quickly as possible which would make a loud noise in the water at the correct frequencies to deflect the torpedo. Research was conducted in the United Kingdom and the United States, and it was from the latter that information came which led to the development of a towed device. Professor Theodore Von Karman had demonstrated that a tethered cylinder in a water stream oscillates from side to side. It was obvious that if two cylinders were towed together astern of a ship they would collide with a force depending upon the velocity of the water flow, and in so doing would make a great deal of noise. It was not long before a prototype decoy had been constructed, consisting of two parallel metal bars.

In spite of the apparent importance of this project it was given a low priority by the Ministry of Supply. Fortunately, however, the Admiralty had provided the Superintendent of Mine Design with an unusually generous fund for experimental work. Well aware of the dire consequences if an answer to the acoustic torpedo was not found quickly, the Mine design department made sufficient funds available for experimental work and the initial manufacturing costs.

The prototype decoys, code named 'Foxer', were sent for sea trials in *Sabre* and *Witch*, with Bathurst as the trials officer. Days were spent testing the various designs to ensure that they did not self destruct after a few hours of towing. Chrome-vanadium steel was selected for the manufacture of the bars; and, as an added precaution, they were constructed so that they would rotate and vary the point of impact. It was just in time: final trials were underway at sea when on 20 September 1943 a frigate engaged in convoy duties was struck by a homing torpedo. The news was transmitted to Commander Fuller, the Commander M/S, at a dinner party in the North British Hotel in Edinburgh, which had been organised to welcome his relief, Commander Fisher. Escorted by the police, the staff of the SF Section and all those who had been involved in the development of 'Foxer', rushed back to Kimmerghame House where an immediate programme for the mass production of 'Foxers' was put in hand.

It was a formidable achievement but, as little was known of the actual operating characteristics of the German homing torpedo, it was not certain how effective the 'Foxer' would be. Until more intelligence was obtained about the enemy weapon it was decided that two decoys would have to be towed, one on either quarter of the ship, and for this purpose it would be necessary to design diverters. The Admiralty recommended that old World War I paravanes would serve, but they were very heavy and had depth control mechanism which depended upon the use of scarce and costly mercury to operate the hydroplanes. The SM Section produced in a very short time a light and entirely effective alternative form of diverter at a fraction of the cost. However, the twin decoys posed operational problems. A single 'Foxer' was screened from the ship's sonar by her wake, but the twin 'Foxers had no such protection. They caused considerable interference and the yards of wire and quantities of heavy metal posed severe handling problems.

The twin 'Foxer' was without any doubt effective, but a far simpler device was urgently needed. Its unpopularity and the difficulty of operating it led to the decision to concentrate upon the single version, known as the 'Uni-Foxer'. This was soon justified when it emerged from intelligence reports and experience that the German T5 Zaunkonig 1 Torpedo (which was given the name 'Gnat' by the Allies) was a far simpler device than had been imagined. Its listening pattern made it vulnerable to capture by the 'Uni-Foxer', around which it weaved in a figure of eight pattern once it was trapped. It was a timely and remarkable achievement for *Vernon*.

At the Admiralty, consideration was given to ways in which a ship could dodge the 'Gnat'. A manoeuvre was devised by Commander R Portlock which combined an interruption in the ship's noise output with a sudden drastic alteration of course. It became known as the 'Step Aside' manoeuvre. When a 'Gnat' attack was suspected, engines were stopped and the wheel was put hard over until the way was off the ship. The original course and speed were then resumed. This countermeasure was used in conjunction with three different towed noise makers: the British 'Uni-Foxer', the American FXR and the Canadian CAT gear. These devices, together with the 'Step Aside' manoeuvre, reduced the 'Gnat' to the category of a nuisance weapon. However, the Admiralty was aware that the enemy would not be content to rely upon the early versions of the 'Gnat', and that it would not be long before the convoys would have to face more effective homing torpedoes. Furthermore, it would be necessary to design and to bring into service as soon as possible a decoy which would greatly reduce the interference to the ship's sonar. PO Box 10 experimented with 'Expendible Noise Makers' (ENMs) dropped or projected overboard when a homing torpedo attack was ecpected.

The best known of the ENMs was the 'Publican'. It had originally been designed for use in submarines, where it was discharged from the torpedo tubes as a jamming device for German sonar. In the surface vessel version it was fired by rocket. Lieutenant JLM Joly, who relieved Main as head of the SF Section, described 'Publican' as being 'so fantastic as to be funny'. At the top of its trajectory the device was ejected from its container and descended by parachute. On entering the water, its ammonium nitrate cartridge was ignited, the gases passing into a pneumatic hammer box and thence out through a cloth exhaust tube wound around the wire suspending the noise maker from the parachute. The exhaust gas kept the parachute inflated so that it floated on the surface, keeping the noise maker suspended at a selected depth for three minutes, after which it sank. Probably the most dangerous aspect of this 'Boffin's brainchild' was that it had become a project of great interest to the Prime Minister who was pressing for it to become operational. Encouraged by Churchill's interest, sustained efforts were made to overcome the many problems which beset it. One special problem was the erratic combustion of the ammonium nitrate composition which aggravated the numerous mechanical difficulties. So great was the priority given to 'Publican' that a flotilla of escort ships was instructed to develop tactics for its use (and measures to protect its ships and the convoy from 'Publican's' eccentricities). It came as a relief when the proposed manufacturer reported that it would operate reliably only if it was manufactured to very tight tolerances, and consequently it would be virtually impossible to manufacture it in quantity. Although, after many problems, three thousand 'Publican' ENMs were manufactured they proved totally useless. The project died a natural death, to the relief of all concerned.

Another volatile substance used in association with work on explosive noise makers was thermite. Some two years earlier Main had visited the Nobel Factory at Ardeer to solicit the help of the company's research department. He had an entertaining day talking to a number of chemists, some of whom lacked fingers or had powder blackened faces. They recommended that the SF Section should carry out experiments using thermite, a particularly pernicious concoction containing magnesium and sodium, and which was used in incendiary bombs. A number of semi-explosive devices using thermite were manufactured and sent for trials in a pond at Port Edgar to determine their underwater sound output. The trials proved abortive, and Main received a number of superficial burns on the hands. The doctors recommended that the burns should be treated with gentian violet; this remedy resulted in him becoming known at Kimmerghame House as the Purple Emperor. The staff was inclined to be sympathetic until he appeared one day with a blue face having to admit he had been trying to rekindle the 'Ideal' boiler at his home with a paraffin soaked rag!

Explosive sweeps were used in 1944 when the Germans introduced a device, known as the A105 firing mechanism, that was immune to the continuous sound transmitted by existing types of SA sweep. Three types of explosive sweep were installed, each with a different explosive charge dispensed through a firing tube, and calibrated to produce the required pulsed sound effects. These simple dispensers proved to be very effective.

The Minesweeping Department was at the centre of a world wide minesweeping organisation that grew massively in the war years. At the beginning of September 1939, there were only 21 fleet minesweepers in commission in the Commonwealth navies and 40 trawlers taken up from trade and manned by Royal Naval Reserve personnel. It was a pitifully small force, trained only in the use of wire sweeps. As the minesweeping force expanded, ratings were drawn from the Royal Naval Patrol Service, a group initially made up of professional fishermen but later augmented from all walks of life. It soon became apparent that the mine countermeasures task would involve reserve officers and men being trained in complex electrical and tactical work, as well as in practical seamanship. During the five years of the war, four thousand and fifty officers and thirteen thousand ratings were trained at *Lochinvar*, and large numbers were sent untrained direct to the operational ships to gain experience on the job.

Some 43,000 officers and men were serving in minesweeping at the height of the war but only 3 per cent came from the RN; the rest were from the RNR and RNVR. The minesweepers were truly a citizen force among whom a high state of morale rapidly developed which was maintained throughout the long years of conflict. Friendly rivalry was commonplace and it became the practice for a chevron to be painted on the funnel of a sweeper for each mine swept. There was, therefore, fierce competition to display the most chevrons. Feelings ran high when sweepers in adjacent areas accused each other of poaching but such competition encouraged good performance. The minesweeper crews dealt with over sixteen thousand mines over six years of war for the loss of 316 minesweepers. In September 1944 there were 949 minesweepers in commission of which 124 were large fleet minesweepers, 220 were motor minesweepers, 81 were American lend-lease 'British Yard Minesweepers', 247 were oropesa trawlers and 166 were LL trawlers and drifters. All mines but one variant of the new pressure mine could be swept and techniques were being developed to deal with that. It was a notable achievement for all the *Vernon* people involved.

On 1 October 1944, diving became a responsibilty of the Torpedo Branch. For some time the branch had been the principal users of divers and underwater salvage techniques, and the change had become inevitable, especially when the retreating Germans began the systematic laying of mines with time fuses and explosive booby traps in the abandoned ports. These could only be cleared by specially trained divers. Moreover, the advent of mines with long time clocks and unsweepable pressure mechanisms pointed to the crucial role of divers in future mine hunting. As mine countermeasures now promised to be the the main role of naval divers it made sense to transfer diving from the Gunnery Branch to that primarily concerned with mine warfare and explosives.

Before 1944, *Vernon* had been allowed two divers and they had been employed laying the degaussing range off Clarence Pier. They were the responsibility of a Commissioned Gunner (T) who was known as the 'Worm Gunner', because his principal duty was to look after *Vernon*'s grounds! Leading Seaman (later Lieutenant Commander) WB Filer, who was one of the two divers at the time recalls:

When he became agitated, as he occasaionally did, he would produce a signed certificate with proof of his sanity. He had apparently received treatment on that score which, for a serving officer, was rare in those days!

Filer and his colleague assisted two Australian officers, Lieutenant Commander JS Mould RANVR and Lieutenant LV Goldsworthy RANVR, working on the design of a self contained diving dress for mine clearance divers. These activities were not given special priority and the *Vernon* divers were also employed on maintenance duties at the submarine base, *Dolphin*.

Other divers trained in working with explosives were used in RMS operations around the coast and in the London docks but their activities were restrained by their clumsy and heavy 'hard hat' diving gear with air lines that had been standard equipment in the Royal Navy for several generations. In 1941, after the successful attack by Italian Maiale 'Human Torpedoes' on the Mediterranean Fleet at Alexandria, the modern self contained diving suit abandoned by one of the Italians was sent for analysis to the United Kingdom. A similar suit was developed by Commander Geoffrey Sladen and Siebe Gorman. Although it was used successfully it developed an unfortunate reputation as the 'Clammy Death'.

The Admiralty Research Laboratory at Teddington and the Admiralty Experimental Diving Unit at Tolworth under the direction of Commander WO Shelford and Surgeon Lieutenant Commander KW Donald, were both involved and a British diver, Lieutenant Commander Anderson, assisted the Australians in determining the correct air mixture for the new breathing equipment which they were devising for mine recovery work. The modified 'Salvus' fire fighting breathing unit was adopted using oxygen enriched air supplied from a portable bottle. The exhaled mixture was purified by a chemical carbon dioxide absorbent before being returned to the breathing circuit.

This breathing set and the 'Clammy Death' suit made underwater explosive disposal much more practical. Their introduction came just in time, as the Germans prepared plans for the immobilisation of the ports left as they retreated. In addition to laying all types of mines in the approaches and harbours, they planned to destroy jetties and equipment, plant booby traps and underwater obstructions, and scuttle all ships and small craft which could not be evacuated. Working in appalling conditions amongst the wreckage and in the mud, divers would have to be trained to deal with all manner of underwater hazards in addition to their trade as mine clearance divers. For this purpose the famous 'P' parties were formed. They were composed of personnel from most of the Commonwealth nations. Among the most decorated of the Commonwealth contingent were the four Australians, Lieutenant Commander JS Mould, Lieutenant Commander LV Goldsworthy, Lieutenant Commander G Gosse and Lieutenant HR Syme. Previously these officers had figured prominently in the RMS campaign, and between them had been awarded, in addition to a George Cross each, three George Medals, a DSC and an MBE.

What was in store was revealed during the Eighth Army's advance from El Alamein. A small team of mine disposal ratings under two officers, Lieutenant GH Goodman RNVR and Lieutenant GF Gutteridge RNR, had been detached from Rear Admiral, Alexandria's staff and charged with the responsibility of being the first naval personnel into each of the newly occupied Western Desert ports. Goodman was already an experienced Mine Disposal Officer having been in charge of the release of 'R' mines into the Rhine during Operation Royal Marine in May 1940. With his colleague, Gutteridge, they formed an excellent team.

At Bardia, Sollum, Mersa Matruh and Benghazi they were faced with booby traps, tank and anti-personnel mines, demolition charges, depth charges and naval mines. Being without diving equipment they were obliged to swim down to investigate underwater hazards.   At the end of the only serviceable jetty at Sollum, they found two depth charges placed in about 15 feet of water. Gutteridge, swimming down, discovered two wires leading into the silt and ending in a red coverplate at one end. On removing the coverplate the mechanism inside started to tick, but when Gutteridge pulled on a chrome plated spindle the ticking stopped. Becoming short of breath he surfaced and clambered up a rusty ladder, before covering one hundred yards in record time. The expected explosion did not take place, and the depth charges were successfully removed. At Tobruk, Gutteridge and his team were sent to investigate a 'ticking' at Navy House. They searched room by room and cellar by cellar. It was a wet, smelly and lonely business. Eventually the 'ticking' was traced to a halyard block on the flagmast. Moving in the wind it was striking the mast, sixty times a minute! At Benghazi, Gutteridge and his driver were caught by a booby trap. Both received second degree burns which required treatment at a field hospital. They then drove the 600 miles back to Alexandria.

One of the early pioneers in harbour clearance was the South African Navy's salvage vessel, *Gamtoos*. She was a small coaster belonging to the

Durban sugar magnate, Sir Charles Smith. Launched in 1936, this 797 ton ship was a comparatively new vessel of superior seaworthiness. In late 1942, at the request of the British Mediterranean Naval Command for a harbour clearance and salvage vessel, *Gamtoos* was requisitioned and fitted out with workshops, salvage equipment and accommodation for a crew of 8 officers and 47 men, including 5 divers. Two weeks before Alamein, she was on her way to the Mediterranean where she arrived on 20 December 1942, ready to embark upon urgent salvage work at Port Said. A month later she was anchored in Homs Bay waiting for the Eighth Army to enter Tripoli; and on 26 January 1943, her divers began cutting away obstructions and salvaging the wrecks in the harbour. This was only the beginning, and the little South African ship received a personal letter of congratulations from the Commander of the Eighth Army, General Montgomery, before following the advance of the Allied armies to Italy and eventually to Southern France. How much of *Gamtoos*' experience was passed on to the 'P' parties is not known.

By late 1942, Lewis had become Staff Torpedo Officer to Admiral Cunningham who had been appointed to command the naval side of the North African landings. Lewis was allocated two mine- and two bomb disposal officers. As soon as ports became available these officers were stationed with the port parties at Algiers, Bougie, Philipville and Bone. Bizerta proved especially difficult to clear as the Germans laid many mines with no actuating mechanism other than six day clocks. After the defeat of the Afrika Corps, this small team was reinforced. One new arrival was Lieutenant LK Crabb, fresh from encounters with Italian underwater saboteurs at Gibraltar.

One of the most outstanding feats of harbour clearance was carried out by members of Naval Party 1500 at Messina. On 23 August 1943, Lieutenant Ferminger and four of this unit were killed attempting to clear depth charges from a jetty. Lieutenant John Bridge RNVR and another team were sent to survey the area. They found more depth charges fitted with the mechanisms which had wiped out Ferminger's party. On 31 August 1943 Bridge dived for over six hours to assess the situation.

The next day, sheer legs were rigged so that individual depth charges could be lifted as they were rendered safe. The wire ropes holding the depth charges underwater were severed by remote control using small amounts of explosive. The depth charges separated in 'the most desirable way possible'. With the aid of a volunteer, Able Seaman Peters, Bridge was able to fix four hooks to the depth charges and their firing mechanism, which were then lifted on to the jetty and rendered safe. With the secret of the firing mechanism discovered, it was possible to remove all other depth charges from the harbour. By 1130 on the morning of Thursday 2 September, Messina Harbour had been cleared and was ready to receive shipping. At 0400 the next day, the invasion of Italy commenced, and John Bridge was awarded the George Cross. He also accumulated two bars to his subsequent George Medal, and became the most decorated member of the RMS branch.

On 2 December 1943, twelve Junkers 88 bombed the Italian port of Bari. Lieutenant Commander GV Corbett, the Torpedo Officer of the Coastal Forces depot ship *Vienna*, had to turn quickly from consideration of torpedoes and mines to face an unexpected catastrophe. Two convoys which had recently reach Bari were the targets for the bombers. The first ship to be hit was a tanker which sank, spilling its load of oil fuel into the harbour, followed almost at once by the gigantic explosion of an ammunition ship. It had been loaded with a cargo of shells filled with mustard gas, on their way to the front as a precaution against the use of gas by the enemy. The liquified gas poured onto the surface of the water, already covered in a layer of oil. Into this deadly mixture rained burning debris from other ships. Survivors attempting to swim to safety became covered in oil and mustard gas. Corbett was the first to notice the smell of the gas. Collecting as many survivors as possible, he insisted that they should be scrubbed instead of being wrapped in blankets. It was not popular but it saved a number of lives. The less fortunate were transported, still covered in oil and mustard gas, to be attended to in hospital, where doctors and nurses in turn became affected by the gas. That night seventeen ships were sunk and a thousand men lost their lives.

Morgan Giles, who had moved to a new appointment at Bari was instructed to evacuate all the ships still afloat. This was no easy task as very few of them had steam to work their capstans let alone to get underway. He had to organise demolition teams to cut the cables of these ships before they could be moved. The job was eventually completed and the harbour cleared. The events at Bari were a reminder of the wide diversity of a torpedoman's qualifications.

As the Allied armies advanced in Italy they were accompanied by two Naval Mine and Bomb Disposal Units. Equipped with tents and radios, they advanced up the east and west coasts close behind the advancing land forces. Working closely with *Gamtoos* and independently organised salvage teams, they had often to deal with extraneous, but frequently important, explosive discoveries. At Messina they rendered safe, contrary to Lewis' firm instructions, an Italian air launched 'circling torpedo' which had landed on the roof of a building required by the Eighth Army as a hospital. During the campaign Danckwerts, one of the original team of four, suffered serious injuries to his feet which caused him to be rushed to an Army field hospital. Fearing the onset of gangrene, and with amputation a strong possibility, the doctors ordered the injured feet to be encased in plaster of Paris. Later, Danckwerts noticed maggots emerging from the plaster. Horrified, he demanded that it should be removed. Apprehension turned to delight when healthy feet were revealed. The objects of his revulsion had devoured the purulent flesh.

While Danckwerts remained immobilised, other members of Lewis' team accompanied the Army to Anzio where they dealt with the first captured 'Biber' one man submersible. This consisted, in effect, of two torpedoes, one equipped with a cockpit for the diver who controlled the device and the other slung beneath it with a warhead . It had run onto the beach and its diver had surrendered. Its capture had been reported to the Admiralty which ordered that it should be put upon a cruiser and sent back to the United Kingdom. Lewis, aware that these weapons could be used with great effect, and concerned that any delay might prove dangerous to the Allied forces during the invasion of Europe, considered that an assessment of its capabilities should be carried out immediately. He asked permission from the C-in-C, Sir John Cunningham, to carry out trials at Malta, where the Torpedo Depot could make good any damage and where the services of the Torpedo Officer of the Third Submarine Flotilla could be obtained. He assured the Commander-in-Chief that he would be able to prepare a comprehensive trials report, containing complete details, drawings and performance figures, in time for distribution to to the Fleet before the invasion of Europe. The Commander-in-Chief agreed, and Lewis made arrangements for the weapon to be transported to Malta where he made contact with his submarine colleague , Lieutenant HF Fewins, who joined enthusiastically in making arrangements for the trials.

The Torpedo Depot replaced the cracked dome of the cockpit with one salvaged from a Wellington bomber. Fewins was equipped with a Davis escape apparatus, and with some trepidation, mounted the upper torpedo and took the device to sea. He drove it out of the Grand Harbour into a choppy sea, which very nearly capsized the unwieldy craft. However, the trials were successfully completed, including an assessment of the limiting sea conditions. Such early pioneers as Eardley Wilmot, Wilson and Sturdee would have been proud of Fewins.

In Sardinia, Lewis' team took possession of the first specimen of the German glider bomb, the Hs 293. Crabb's experience in dealing with the Italian underwater saboteurs at Gibraltar also proved invaluble in disposal work , especially at La Spezia where the unit discovered a new bilge keel clamp mine which detonated if unscrewed by the diver. This problem was overcome by burning out the section of bilge keel using underwater cutting equipment. At Leghorn, Lewis and Lieutenant Commander Plowman, a Tasmanian, found that the Germans had planted bundles of magnetic mines in various parts of the harbour with their anti-countermining switches wrongly assembled. If left in that state they could have been detonated by the many large dispersal charges being exploded to clear the wrecks. So large were these charges that on one occasion a lighthouse was accidentally demolished. It had been planned for press photographers to witness the explosion from the 'safety' of the lighthouse, but fortunately for the photographers the boat taking them there failed to start. The many and varied experiences of the Mine and Bomb Disposal Units in the Mediterranean were of inestimable assistance in the formation of the 'P' parties, which began, after the Bizerta experience, under the direction of, Commander CE Hamond, responsible for the mine location organisation around the coasts of Britain. In July 1943, the Admiralty, at Hamond's request, called for volunteers from the lower deck 'for a hazardous operation'. The response was immediate, and Hamond was able to select enough volunteers to form two 'P' parties, each consisting of two officers and approximately forty ratings. In each party half were young ratings to be trained as divers, while the other half, consisting of older men, were responsible for maintenance and support duties. In each party one officer was prepared to dive and deal with any lethal objects reported by the divers. Rendering mines safe in the depths and in the darkness, surrounded by mud and wreckage was only part of the problem; thorough searching for mines was as big a challenge. A new method had to be devised as normal shot ropes and distance lines soon became snagged in the murky, muddy and littered bottoms of harbours.

Two ship's lifeboats were allocated to each party and, after having laid out two anchors at right angles to the quay about three or four hundred feet apart, the boats were moored fore and aft to the anchor warps, with bows on to the quay. Three shot ropes were lowered from each lifeboat and jackstays were laid along the bottom between the two craft. One end of each jackstay was attached to a shot, and the lines were passed through a shackle on the shot under the other boat and then back to the first boat. It was thus possible to hold the jackstays taut and straight on the bottom. One breast anchor was laid from each boat on the opposite side to the jackstays to take the lateral strain. It was first envisaged that the diving work would have to be carried out under enemy fire or with enemy attack imminent. It was, therefore, proposed to use only three divers in the water at any one time. Each diver descended to his shot and, holding a jackstay in his right hand, he searched an estimated width of three feet as he moved towards the other shot. When he reached the second shot he crossed over his jackstay and returned in the same fashion, so that on return to his starting point each diver covered an area six feet wide by three or four hundred feet long. When there was no visibility the jackstays were placed six feet apart and this distance was increased according to the visibility. Later, when it was discovered that diving could usually be carried out without interference from the enemy, it was possible, with the help of the Army, to make use of Bailey Bridge pontoons which increased the number of divers operating at any time from ten to fifteen. It was not necessary to use either pontoons or lifeboats when working in enclosed places where it was possible to run jackstays from side to side of the dock.

By 6 June 1944, the two 'P' parties were highly trained, their complement having settled down at two officers, one of whom was trained and experienced in either bomb disposal or rendering mines safe, 1 petty officer, 2 leading seamen, 17 other maintenance hands and 15 divers. During training it was found that specialisation in various jobs added to the speed and efficiency of the work. Specialisation fell under three different headings:

(a) Benchwork: The care, maintenance and preparation of diving equipment.
(b) Seamanship: The mooring of pontoons, rigging of jackstays, sheerlegs and dinghy work.
(c) Dressing: Dressing of the diver and general attendance: assistance in getting in and out of the water.

After operational experience the complement of each 'P' party was increased to 3 officers, 20 divers, 15 maintenance hands, 4 Royal Marine drivers, 1 sick berth attendant and 1 cook.

On D Day, the two 'P' parties, Nos 1571 and 1572, waited ready for action. Their training had been intense and they were now skilled in diving maintenance work, mine and bomb recognition, the avoidance of booby traps, the use of automatic weapons, fieldwork - and in tying bends and hitches whilst blindfolded. All members were young men at the peak of physical fitness but this did not mean that they were willing to forego certain traditional aspects of naval life. The 'grog' list of Naval Party 1571 showed that out of forty two eligible ratings only three volunteered to forego their daily tot. (Seventeen men, being under the age of twenty, were not entitled to the daily issue.)

On 25 June 1944, the 'P' parties started operations. A small group went to Ouistreham to clear the Caen Canal in preparation for the opening of the port. The remainder of the two parties, under a Canadian officer, Lieutenant Commander Harris, made their way to Cherbourg, ready to start operations as soon as the port had been cleared of the Germans. With the assistance of a third 'P' party, No 1503, the Cherbourg clearances were completed in a much shorter time than had been expected, in spite of determined efforts by the Germans to wreck the port. An incident involving the experienced diver, MH Woods, illustrates the hazards encountered in what was considered to be a routine clearance.

Stranded on the bottom at the Quai Homet was a dry dock with its machinery destroyed. The first searches were carried out in the vicinity of the dock, with the divers attached to buoyant floats to indicate their positions rather than the usual lifelines. Woods was one of those working in close proximity to the scuttled dock when the maintenance hands noticed that his float had stopped moving. Harris ordered them to give one pull on the line to ask the diver if he was in difficulties. There was no reply. After two more attempts, the order was given to recover the diver but the united efforts of two ratings failed to bring him to the surface. Almost immmediately, Woods was sighted on the surface some yards away. He reported that he had discovered an enemy remote control mine which he had marked with his float line. Consequently, the recovery team had been trying to lift a two ton mine by pulling on the float! As soon as Harris had assessed the situation he dived on the mine, disconnected it from its electric cable and rendered it safe. Woods received the George Medal for his part in this operation.

To the east, the small party under Lieutenant W. Bailey had landed with the invasion forces on 'Sword' beach. Under fire, they had transported their equipment to Ouistreham at the mouth of the Caen Canal. Here Bailey's party carried out an examination of the lock gates which controlled the water level inside the Caen Canal. They found that the Germans had connected a number of demolition charges to the underwater sections of the gates and had wired them to explode when the gates were opened. Small drifters, positioned at each end of the lock and loaded with explosives, had been arranged to detonate at the same time as the underwater charges. With only minutes to spare before the enemy started to shell and mortar the area, Bailey succeeded in removing all the charges. They were then obliged to abandon the area and to take shelter in the army slit trenches. When the enemy onslaught had diminished, the section returned to continue the search but nothing more was found.

The clearance of the harbour at Cherbourg and the Caen Canal had enabled supply ships to enter. Now the 'P' parties were given the task of removing booby traps from the vessels captured in the ports. When this had been done, the ports were able to resume normal working. There is no doubt that the 'P' parties played an important part in the success of the Allies' first offensive; but so intense had been their work that the Medical Officer was obliged to introduce a strict roster of rest periods. 'P' Parties 1571, 1572 and Bailey's element, which became a separate party numbered 1574, returned to England for a short leave period. When they returned, they had been strengthened and were beginning to have even more of a Commonwealth flavour. 'P' Party 1574 now had the services of a South African, Lieutenant G Casey; a brave and competent officer, he was greatly missed when he was killed driving to Bremen from the British Army Headquarters at Minden. The first Dutch party, number 3006, had also been formed under the command of Lieutenant Commander JJC Korthals-Altes, Royal Netherlands Navy.

As the five parties, four British and one Dutch, moved along the coastline of Europe, the ports of Caen, Boulogne, Calais, Brest, Dieppe, Le Havre and Rouen were all cleared; new types of ground mines, demolition charges and jettisoned enemy equipment were successfully recovered. The parties often worked in appalling conditions of ice and thick mud, but the teams pressed on, knowing that the advance of the armies depended on the ports being cleared of all obstacles as quickly as possible. With the armies advancing towards Germany, Antwerp was cleared and by the end of December, Terneuzen, Zeebrugge, the South Beveland Canal and Flushing were all free of mines and obstructions. By the Spring of 1945 six 'P' parties were operational.

The most notable feature of this gruelling and dangerous work was the manner in which the observance of standing orders enabled it to be completed with no loss of life through diving accidents, either in training or during operations. This was achieved in spite of the fact that the German naval mine experts, questioned after their surrender, stated that some of their latest mines could neither be swept nor recovered without exploding. The constant danger and the often gruesome surroundings which the divers accepted as their daily lot were described by Gosse, the commander of Naval Party 1571. The procedure was for the clearance divers to locate a mine and then report the find to the officer, who then dived to the spot to render the mine harmless or to explode it if it was safe to do so. On this occasion it was a 'G' type pressure mine. Gosse reported, 'I had seen bits of one before but this was quite different from the one I had seen.' The mine was resting on a body but Gosse was used to working with 'plenty of rubbish and bodies in the harbour' and 'did not worry about this. It was very dark and I had to work by sense of touch in about two feet of mud. It was quite cold too and a little lonely. I took the primer off and brought the mine up to the surface. It was like taking a sparking plug out of a car. You can do it in the dark if you know what you are looking for!' Throughout this hazardous incident Gosse was 'tended' by his second in command, Gutteridge, who had dealt with 'G' type mines ashore at Tobruk.

There were advantages in being attached to one of the 'P' parties. Higher authority, recognising that a difficult job was being well done, was inclined to leave well alone. At Bremen, which was an American supply 'enclave', NP 1571 became an American Command Task Force. As such, Lieutenant WK Heath RNVR and Petty Officer C Webb (known to the sailors as 'Pop') were assigned by the American admiral to drill his strongly democratic sailors on the parade ground. The admiral also developed a taste for the luxuries of the 'P' parties wardroom facilities. He found these preferable to standing in a 'chow line' and sharing the latrines with his troops, on a park bench in the open, with the seat slats knocked out. The four young officers of NP 1571 enjoyed a tented wardroom, a 'liberated' antique table and damask cloth, elegant glassware and silver, Marine drivers as mess stewards, and three course hot meals instead of 'K' rations.

These privileges were not undeserved as the operations of the 'P' parties demanded continuous self discipline and steady nerves. The experiences of the nineteen year old diver, Eric Maydon, attached to NP 1571 were typical. As the party approached Ostend, men could be seen working to clear away the havoc left by the enemy. Bridges were being repaired, railway tracks laid and preparations were in hand to transport the vital supplies required by the armies. It was a daunting sight. Cranes still lay sprawled on the docksides, breakwaters had been torn apart, barges and freighters rested on their sides and mines on the harbour bottom had not been located. On one occasion 57 'C' and 'G' type magnetic/acoustic/pressure mines were located.

Maydon had been an Admiralty clerk when he responded to the call for volunteers for secret and dangerous work. He was soon to know just how accurate that description was. On what was a typical day, he was pulling his way laboriously along the jackstay, groping ahead with his hands in the mud and total darkness, until he came across a soft object on the bottom. Running his hands over it he decided that it was a dead horse! Then his hands touched upon a metal object with sharp sides. After a while wondering whether it was a mine, he identified it as a German helmet; and so the search continued. On the surface Pop Webb waited to help divers take off their suits and prepare them for another dive. There were many like Pop upon whom the divers relied to make sure that they had complied with all the regulations, particularly with the requirement to come back to the surface when their absolute maximum of forty five minutes had been completed. Identifying mines, dead horses, corpses and wrecks by touch was the usual daily task, and these young men certainly deserved a lot more than a hot cup of tea when they came to the surface, however welcome that might have been!

Training for the 'P' Parties was the main responsibility of the branch of *Vernon* set up in response to the decision to transfer all Navy diving to the Torpedo Branch. In November 1944 Commander AR Alston opened *Vernon(D)*, a central diving training school and experimental station at Brixham in Devon. The Superintendent of Diving, whose responsibilities included the co-ordination of training and research and development, also moved to Brixham, with *Tedworth*, the Navy's deep diving tender. At first the accommodation was dispersed around the town, the Commanding Officer being housed in the Berryhead Hotel, while the Superintendent of Diving had an office on the other side of the harbour. The base offices were located in a row of requisitioned terraces, and the ratings were accommodated in several Nissen huts and a former holiday camp at St. Mary's Bay. Webb states:

The officers lived in the Northcliffe Hotel where they were petted and spoiled by the proprietress, Mrs Silley. Later, they acquired Wolborough, a pleasant house with extensive grounds overlooking the harbour. Hand-picked WRNS cooks and stewards came from Devonport, and the wardroom developed into a show place where traditional VERNON *hospitality was dispensed to many visitors.*

With this secure base supporting them, the work of the 'P' parties proceeded with growing efficiency. Extraordinary feats of bravery and endurance became commonplace. Improvisation and the acceptance of the macabre were matters of daily routine. On one occasion a diver surfaced and reported to Gosse that he had found the body of a civilian. When Gosse asked him how, in the darkness and covered in mud, he could tell that it was a civilian. He replied that the corpse was wearing trousers with turn ups. There were not many who could better Gosse for ingenuity or sheer cold blooded bravery. When rendering three pressure mines safe he found that when wearing a new diving dress designed recently at Brixham he could not maintain negative buoyancy. He therefore secured one end of a line around his neck and the other to the mine upon which he was working. With his legs lifted above his head he continued to work moored to the mine.

In the latter part of 1944 and early in 1945, it was decided to form two new parties for service in the Far East. These were formed in June 1945, commanded by Gosse and another Australian, Lieutenant M Batterham; but VJ Day came before the teams could go to work. With the coming of peace, a small 'P' party was formed under the command of a third Australian, Lieutenant W Jackson, to clear any suspected residual bombs and mines in British ports. A typical operation took place in Manchester where the merchant ship *Pacific Pioneer* had been holed by a 500 lb. bomb and had settled on the dock bottom. It was considered that there was little chance that the bomb could still be dangerous but the Ship Canal Company asked for the search to be made. In three days the divers crawled over 100 yards of the dock's bottom groping in four feet of mud. They found no bomb, but plenty of bottles, scrap iron and other sundry objects. In other searches they found rings, watches and wallets but they usually yielded nothing but frozen hands and broken finger nails.

Across the English Channel, the French Navy was facing the huge task of clearing and reconstructing the ports and harbours. Gutteridge and eight divers were sent on loan to assist in removing mines from France's third largest harbour at Dunkirk; but it was soon realised that in the immediate post war period the French Navy had no mine clearance capability, very few supplies and transport and, consequently, no immediate hope of searching

Lieutenant Gordon Gutteridge and a 'P' Party diver in a Sladen 'Clammy Death' suit at Dunkirk 1945

the vast area of this wreck and debris strewn port. Gutteridge proposed that a large British 'P' party should be formed to tackle the task, and the Admiralty reacted positively and immediately.

The largest of all the 'P' parties, NP2444, was commissioned with a complement of 4 officers, 1 sick berth attendant, 1 cook and 40 divers, mostly experienced. Everyone in NP2444 was qualified to dive, including the cook and the sick berth attendant. Their adventures form a fitting end to the story of the 'P' parties. NP2444 found that Dunkirk contained nearly two thousand German prisoners of war who were requisitioned to provide drivers, boats crews, cooks, stokers for barrack room heating, staff for servicing diving equipment and diver handlers. Among the prisoners was a former commanding officer of a midget submarine. His craft had been employed shipping butter and other supplies into the Dunkirk enclave. Known as 'Oscar', he became one of NP2444's most resolute divers.

Every day no less than thirty divers attempted the difficult task of searching for mines amidst the wreckage and debris. Nowhere was there space to conduct a clear search but most of the known mines were located and disposed of. One was found accidentally when it exploded under a steel caisson while it was under tow. Eventually it was possible to berth a motor minesweeper alongside the knuckle at the harbour entrance and days were spent towing the end of its LL sweep around the harbour. A mine was detonated by this ad hoc arrangement.

NP2444 was under the supervision of the Commander Minesweeping, Dover who, unwittingly, provided some light relief from the hard task of diving and mine disposal. He had recently been provided with a new Humber staff car, of which he was immensely proud. The car was for use during his visits to France and it was on one of these occasions when its brakes failed. It was handed to prisoner of war mechanics with instructions to fix it. This they proceeded to do by driving it into a 20 foot cast iron lamp standard, which fell upon the car breaking all the windows and creasing the roof. The Commander M/S was due back in forty eight hours. The mechanics were given a choice of repairing the damage in thirty six hours or, metaphorically speaking, face the firing squad. The Army Supply Department in Lille supplied six new windows and Chief Petty Officer Gribben, in charge of divers, liberated a gallon of royal blue enamel. On time, the car was delivered to Commander M/S who comented upon the smart appearance of his staff car. On this high note diving operations at Dunkirk ended on 18 March 1946.

At the end of September 1945, *Vernon*(D) closed and, with the end of NP2444's operations in March 1946, one of the most courageous episodes in the whole history of the Torpedo Branch came to an end. In all, the 'P' parties carried out more than 780 days of work in actual diving. They searched an area of more than 26 million square feet; travelled more than 1,600 miles underwater; and dealt with 219 mines, 121 explosive charges and one V2 rocket. When *Vernon* (D) closed the Commanding Officer received a signal from the First Sea Lord:

On closing down your establishment at Brixham, I should like to express to you and your staff my admiration of the splendid work done by 'P' parties. The ingenuity shown and the courage displayed contributed materially to the success of the

Although the 'P' parties had been trained to clear harbours it did not relieve torpedomen of their responsibility for demolitions and the rendering safe of underwater weapons. The countless occasions when ship's torpedo staff were called upon to carry out these hazardous duties remain largely unrecorded, but two exceptional incidents make an appropriate finale to this chapter.

On March 24 1942 two survivors of a four ship convoy bringing supplies and ammunition reached a hard pressed Malta. Off-loading continued in spite of the continuous air bombardment until one ship was sunk and the other, the Norwegian *Talabot*, caught fire. The flames spread until the harbour was threatened with a massive explosion. It became imperative that the ship should be scuttled and the task was undertaken by seamen from the cruiser *Penelope* led by their torpedo officer, Lieutenant Dennis Copperwheat. The heat was so intense that the demolition charges could not be placed inside the ship and they had to be secured to the ship's side. Coperwheat's team suceeded in this task and, after telling the others to take cover, he detonated the charges electrically from the shore, forty yards from the ship. He was injured in the explosion but survived to be awarded the George Cross.

In late 1945 the Sixth Minesweeping Flotilla was supporting the British forces re-occupying Singapore and Malaya. For many weeks after the Japanese surrender the minesweepers settled into a sweeping routine clearing the channels around Singapore. Ashore, the Army had set about clearing and examining the vast stocks of arms and equipment left behind by the Japanese and at Penang they discovered a major Japanese mine and torpedo depot. Naval assistance was requested and the Flotilla's Torpedo Officer, Lieutenant PLR Needham, was called upon to supervise the rendering safe and disposal of the Japanese weapons.

Needham and his senior torpedo rating went to Penang, where they were confronted by workshops, stores, magazines and storesheds filled with row upon row of buoyant mines on their sinkers, torpedo bodies, warheads and large numbers of primers, pistols and detonators. It was a daunting prospect. They had no instruction books, no tools and very little detailed knowledge of the weapons which confronted them. Even more worrying was the possibility that the Japanese had booby trapped the depot before their departure. Hours of cautious inspection persuaded Needham that it would be safe to dismantle a mine to find out how it worked. He was relieved to find that Japanese mines were very similar to British, primed but without their detonators.

The torpedo warheads were more difficult. He did not know what type of pistols were used or how they were fitted. There was a likely looking pocket near the front end of each warhead. In order to discover the truth, Needham sat astride a warhead thumping the locking ring with a hammer and chisel until it unscrewed. He was startled when he lifted out an inertia pistol with detonators fitted!

A week's hard grind followed before everything was safe and ready for removal in the largest barge which Needham could commandeer. The load included a hundred or so mines, dozens of torpedoes, boxes of ammunition, primers and detonators, bundles of explosives of various sorts and a collection of 'dangerous objects'. The weapons were prepared for destruction using the Japanese primers fitted with British detonators. When ready, the barge was towed out to sea but one problem remained. How were the detonators to be fired? A clock was clearly required and the only suitable one was in the Coxswain's office in the Minesweeping Flotilla leader. It was purloined, and with one wire going to the battery tied to the minute hand and the other wire attached to a nail driven into a block of wood on which the clock lay all was ready. Needham wired up the initiating charge, the battery and Coxswain's clock before returning to the tug to beat a hasty retreat. Thirty minutes later, as timed, there was a mighty explosion which was heard all over Penang! Very deservedly, Needham was awarded the Distinguished Service Cross.

This brings us from disposal to demolition. The mining department at *Vernon* was in charge of all static explosive charges for naval use, ashore, on or under the sea. In the early part of the war anti-invasion and immobilisation charges were developed, especially in the Portsmouth Command area. Extra personnel were drafted to the Mining Department at *Vernon*, where commercial explosives, fuses and detonators were tested as replacements for service explosives. A standard set of shore explosive charges began to be issued in October 1940 to augment depth charges which were being used for demolition puposes. By the summer of 1941, the new commercial demolition charges, fuses and detonators came into large scale service and in the autumn work began with Combined Operations HQ on investigations and trials into assault demolition.

In 1942, *Vernon* was also involved in developing weapons for the midget underwater craft developed for attacks on enemy vessels in harbour. In January, Flag Officer Submarines asked *Vernon*(M) for advice, trials and the development of maintenance drills for the 4,000 lb side charges for the projected X-Craft midget submarines. These charges were developed during 1941 and were used in the successful attack on *Tirpitz* in September 1943. In the meantime development began of detachable, time fused warheads with 590 lb charges for the 'Chariot' human torpedoes. The staff requirement was issued in April 1942, and the first attempt to use the system was made at the end of October 1942 in the abortive attack on *Tirpitz*, Operation 'Title'. The chariots' Explosive System was not considered fully proven until December when more chariots were deployed to the Mediterranean. Two were successfully used the following month to sink the unfinished Italian cruiser *Ulpio Traiano* and a troop transport in Palermo harbour. In 1944 another Italian cruiser, *Bolzano* under German control at La Spezia was sunk by another chariot. Both chariots and X-Craft also used limpet mines; Leading Seaman Magennis, XE-3's diver, and his commanding officer, Lt. Ian Fraser RNVR, won the VC for their successful attack on the cruiser *Takao* in Singapore Harbour in July 1945. A 425 lb charge was also developed for the one man Welman Craft to be used by Army divers but the only attempt to use it failed and the project was cancelled.

The Normandy landings saw the culmination of more than two year's work by the demolition section at *Vernon*. In March 1942, the investigation into assault demolition suggested a number of options including the throwing and placing of time-fused depth charges, firing torpedoes, pattern bombing by aircraft and placing of small charges by swimmers. Combined Operations Headquarters assumed responsibility for implementation of these proposals but representatives of *Vernon* were members of the inter-service Allied Joint Demolition Committee, which met regularly until the middle of 1944, and sponsored a new Demolitions Handbook . The work of the committee was summarised by one of *Vernon*'s representatives:

priority was to devise a means for demolishing obstructions expected on the D Day beaches. This involved several days of paddling on the sands and sunbathing at East Head near the Witterings, waiting for the tide to be right for the bang. I believe that the Captain (M), had to use all his tact in persuadng Winston Churchill's special advisers that some of the hare-brained ideas sent down for trial would be infinitely more dangerous to the landing craft than the beach obstructions.

Improvements in shaped charges provided demolition personnel with a directional cutting capability. Better scuttling charges were also produced and advice issued to the fleet on how best to use charges to deter swimmers and human torpedo crews. Equipment was also designed for Allied underwater swimmers including that used by the 'P' parties for countermining and clearance. Beach mine clearance charges were developed as was a a new line charge with sixty 14 oz. blocks of TNT which,from November 1944, replaced the old TNT hose. This was so successful that it was adopted for general naval use.

One of the requirements for the Normandy landings that had to be met by June 1944 was the scuttling of blockships to be used as Mulberry harbour breakwaters. Plans were prepared by the demolition team at *Vernon(M)* between February and June 1944. One officer involved in implementing them was Needham, then Head of the Underwater Weapons Section at *Defiance*. He was allocated the job of preparing the old French battleship *Courbet* for scuttling. Taking his two senior instructors with him, a survey of the old ship was carried out. They clambered over the vast, dark, empty hull from the double bottoms up to the bridge and decided how they were to accomplish the task of sinking her quickly on an even keel. They divided the ship into eight vertical sections and in each section a hole was cut in the inner skin of the double bottom so that charges could be placed directly on to the outer plating. Each charge consisted of 50 lbs of TNT made up of two 25 lb charges. One charge was rigged to be fired electrically and the other by 'Cordtex'. The charges were then heavily tamped with sandbags. Holes were cut in all watertight bulkheads.

The electric firing cables were joined and led to the armoured conning tower below the bridge, where they were connected to two 12 volt batteries and a firing switch. The 'Cordtex' was well separated from the electric wiring and was arranged in a ring main thus providing a back up if electrical initiation failed. Needham was not informed whether his preparations for scuttling *Courbet* had been successful, but the wreck rests off Arromanches to this day, a silent monument to the effectiveness of the procedures developed by a small but vital group of torpedomen.

During the build up to 'D' day *Vernon* provided important back up facilities. Much of Force S intended for 'Sword' Beach, under the command of a torpedoman, Rear Admiral AG Talbot, was accommodated on the Gun wharf. Special courses were laid on for beach clearance parties and the Whitehead Jetty was used as extra accommodation for coastal forces required to cover the landings and which were too numerous for *Hornet*. When the plans of the landing beaches arrived they were so bulky that they had to be kept in Warrior Block under special guard. Security was tight and when Churchill and General Smuts arrived to visit the beaches the Officer of the Watch sent the distinguished party to the offices of the C-in-C as he was not authorised to divulge information about the embarkation to anyone. The only real hitch was the delay caused by the weather and in his signal Talbot apologised to *Vernon* for having to 'swing it till Monday'!

CHAPTER TWELVE
TOOTH FOR TOOTH AND EYE FOR EYE

WHILE AN UNREMITTING BATTLE WAS being fought to defeat the German mines a massive British minelaying campaign was taking shape. Pre-war plans were to restore the First World War barrages in the Dover Straits and across the northern North Sea, to lay a field between the Bass Rock and North Berwick to protect the Firth of Forth and to begin offensive minelaying in the Heligoland Bight. Stocks of moored contact mines had been built up during the inter-war years, and 20,000 were on hand around the world. A large proportion were old First World War H.II mines but there were also the improved switch horn mines developed in the years since 1918.

The surface minelaying force immediately available and loaded at the outbreak of war consisted of the 6,750 ton cruiser minelayer *Adventure*; the destroyers *Esk* and *Express*; and *Plover*, the small coastal minelayer of 800 tons which had been attached to the *Vernon* for instructional purposes and which was standing by to lay the Firth of Forth field. On 3 September 1939 she laid the first mines of the war and then moved south to join *Adventure* in laying the Dover Barrage. Conversion of two train ferries *Hampton* and *Shepperton* had already begun during the run up to 3 September and the operation began on 11 September. 3,000 H.IIs were laid in the Goodwins-Dyck Barrage over the following five days. *Hampton* and *Shepperton* then laid more H.IIs between Folkestone and Cap Gris Nez. The barrage was effective and after two U-boats were sunk they stopped using this route to the Western Approaches, being forced to transit north about until France surrendered and her west coast ports became available.

A large area of the Heligoland Bight was declared 'dangerous to shipping' and *Esk* and *Express* began operations from Immingham to lay mines in the area. The two destoyers then joined *Adventure* in laying the East Coast Barrage on 27 November, and were responsible for a declared minefield off the Yorkshire coast while *Adventure* laid a deep, undeclared anti-submarine field off Flamborough Head intended to trap submarines rounding the promontory. On 2 December an area off the Thames Estuary was declared dangerous, a minefield having been laid by *Hampton*. This was also an anti-submarine measure but fears grew about the activities of surface ships and on 23 December an extended area from Rattray Head to the Thames was declared to be dangerous to shipping. In order to give substance to this the newly converted Bank Line steamer *Teviot Bank* laid dummy mines down the middle of the area. These dummy mines, which were easily produced, inexpensive and quickly prepared, were programmed to break surface at half tide where they could be sighted by enemy reconnaissance aircraft and neutral fishing vessels. Throughout the bitter winter of 1939 another converted minelayer, the former LMS ferry *Princess Victoria*, the destroyers and *Hampton* laid deep anti U-boat minefields in the focal areas to the north and south of the declared line. In May, after the fall of the Netherlands, the minelaying forces were reinforced by the modern Dutch minelayer *Willem van der Zaan*. The completion of the defensive minefields was largely responsible for the cessation of enemy surface and submarine minelaying operations in the area.

Although the destroyers took part in laying the barrage, they were essentially fast offensive minelayers, part of a reconstituted Twentieth Destroyer Flotilla. They had been built to allow for rapid alteration to fast minelayers and just before the war they had been converted to their minelaying role at Swan Hunter's Yard at Wallsend-on-Tyne. This involved fitting mining rails running aft on each side from their after funnels to short projecting sponsons. These ships had a designed speed of 36 knots but to maintain it with a maximum load of sixty mines, weighing over 100 tons, two of their 4.7-inch guns and the two quadruple 21-inch torpedo mountings had to be removed. The after mast was replaced by a light tripod which did not require the shrouds which interfered with the mining rails. A 3-inch anti aircraft gun was fitted in place of the torpedo tubes, a wooden dummy gun graced the after gun deck, and a 4.7-inch gun and torpedo tubes were portrayed on canvas screens in the after part of the ship.

From the earliest days of the war, *Esk* and *Express* had laid mines in the vicinity of Terschelling. These operations had been carried out on moonless nights after high speed passages. The ships' companies stood up manfully to these dangerous and disagreeable conditions, during which both watches were closed up at action stations for between twenty and thirty six hours, often in bad weather and rough seas which made the use of high speed a dangerous business. It soon became obvious that wooden guns and canvas screens were of little value and they were not replaced when they were swept away by the almost permanant inrush of the waves. There were, however, a number of occasions when the screens were used to hoodwink enemy agents. Before sailing at dusk, screens were rigged portraying a full load of mines. When darkness fell the destroyers anchored for the night. Before returning to the harbour the following morning the screens were removed, revealing the empty mining decks.

Esk and *Express* were soon joined by the rest of the Flotilla, the destroyers *Ivanhoe, Icarus, Intrepid* and *Impulsive,* all modified in the same manner as the two 'E's. In April the destroyers were used to lay the minefields in Norwegian waters that marked the start of the Norwegian campaign. When the Germans invaded Holland, the flotilla was laying mines in the Elbe Estuary, and was not available to take an immediate part in the operations intended to provide cover for Dutch and Allied ships escaping from ports in the Low Countries. However, on 10 May, with the Germans already smashing their way through Holland, *Princess Victoria,* escorted by *Express, Intrepid* and *Esk,* succeeded in laying a minefield without interference from the enemy, thus allowing the Admiralty to issue a warning to shipping which deterred the Germans from interfering with the exodus from Dutch and Belgian ports. *Princess Victoria* did not long survive this operation. A week later she was herself mined and sunk off the Humber, but by that time had laid 2,756 mines in twelve operations.

By this time magnetic mines and the aircraft to lay them were available and it would have been prudent to cease using the fast minelayers for operations off the enemy coast. The lessons of history were plain; the minelaying destroyers *Vehement* and *Ariel* had been lost in 1918 when they ran into an unexpected enemy minefield (see Chapter 4). Now a similar fate awaited *Esk* and *Ivanhoe.* On the night of 31 August 1940, *Express, Esk, Ivanhoe,*

Icarus and *Intrepid* sailed from the Humber bound for a minelaying operation in the Heligoland Bight. The flotilla, led by Commander Bickford in *Express*, streamed paravanes and proceeded as usual for their operational destination. On passage Bickford received instructions that after laying the mines they were to prepare to engage an enemy force that might be in the vicinity, and 'not to lack daring' which seemed somewhat offensive advice. Twenty minutes later, when 40 miles from the dropping point, *Express*'s paravane cut a mine mooring wire, detonating the mine and destroying the paravane. Minutes later, *Express* struck a mine, which killed Bickford, exploded the forward magazine and blew off the whole fore part of the ship.

Express after being mined in the North Sea

The next half hour re-enacted the stark story of the loss of the two earlier members of the Twentieth Flotilla. Once again a British destroyer's siren wailed eerily in the darkness, while the stricken ship was illuminated by the flames which rose from her. Then *Esk* suffered the same fate, broke in half and sank. *Ivanhoe* came alongside *Express* to remove survivors but moments later she struck a mine. She could not be saved and eventually she sank. In the darkness the crews of the three destroyers swam in the oil-covered sea, grabbing whatever they could find to keep them afloat. After an agonising ordeal lasting several days, survivors were picked up by German trawlers. Of the three mined destroyers only *Express* survived; her remains taken in tow by the destroyers *Javelin* and *Kelvin*. She was later fitted with a new bow and rejoined the fleet in the winter of 1941. The effectiveness of the field previously laid had prompted this devastating German retaliation. The remaining minelaying destroyers continued to operate until they were returned to fleet duties in April 1941; they were replaced by the new fast minelayers.

The six *Porpoise* class submarine minelayers which carried sixty Mk XVI or XVII contact mines installed in mine rails laid along the pressure hull and enclosed by high casings were also available in the early months of the war.. They were employed laying minefields in the Baltic and off the German coast. The operations of these boats were hazardous. In May 1940, *Seal* embarked upon a particularly dangerous operation in the treacherous waters of the Kattegat, at the entrance to the Baltic. One field was laid successfully, but when withdrawing from the area, *Seal* was damaged and trapped by a German minefield which forced her to bottom in 22 fathoms. When she finally freed herself, she was found to be uncontrollable. With her crew exhausted and pressure gone from the hydraulic system, there was no escape and *Seal* was captured. Three more submarine minelayers were sunk in the following two months. The arrival of the Free French minelaying submarine *Rubis* was therefore especially welcome. She was equipped with Vickers T III mines and carried out 28 minelaying patrols, during which she laid 683 mines, costing the enemy 14 supply ships, 7 anti-submarine vessels and minesweepers, and damage to other vessels. *Rubis* was the most successful minelaying submarine of the war.

The introduction of the M Mark II influence mine for discharge from submarine torpedo tubes gave the specialist minelayers a new capability and ordinary 'S' and 'T' Class submarines a new minelaying potential. *Cachalot* was sunk in the Mediterranean in 1941 but the surviving pair, *Porpoise* and *Rorqual*, continued to lay mines and to supply the island fortress of Malta. They were later deployed to the Far East where *Porpoise* was sunk in January 1945. *Rorqual* survived the war, but only because a U-boat captain mistook the large and unusual silhouette of the minelayer for an aircraft carrier. He set his torpedoes to run deep and they passed under the submarine. *Rorqual* laid almost 1,300 mines.

The staff of the Mining Department at *Vernon* were faced with a formidable instructional and training task in support of mining operations. In the early months the training of officers and men for this task was inhibited by the rapid turn-over of staff, when retired and reserve officers had to be absorbed into the system. But by the summer of 1940 the task was well in hand and during the first eighteen months of the war over two thousand officers and men completed training in mining and minesweeping. Despite the removal of minesweeping training to *Lochinvar*, training in all branches of minelaying, recovery and disposal continued to be a *Vernon* responsibility. Meanwhile the Mine Design Department had moved to Leigh Park House, Havant, followed by the Mining Department's arrival at nearby West Leigh. Leigh Park was responsible for the design of material to meet staff requirements, while West Leigh, *Vernon* (M), was responsible for ensuring that material was in all respects satisfactory under service conditions.

Procedures were worked out to maintain the close touch between Leigh Park House and *Vernon*(M) that had been taken for granted on the Gun Wharf. To ensure that British mining operations should not be carried out in a haphazard manner, a section was also created in the Admiralty charged with the production of the staff requirements for mines to be used against a variety of targets. Its Director was Captain J S Cowie, who subsequently wrote extensively about his experiences.

At Leigh Park House a formidable team of Royal Naval scientists was assembled, among them Gaskell, who came down from Edinburgh to take charge of the composite acoustic and magnetic mine development. His arrival provided a close link between the scientific staffs at Leigh Park House and Kimmerghame House. Gradually, the Mine Design Department extended its activities to include all underwater explosives. Among those responsible in this enlarged area was HJ Taylor, who had been involved in the development of the depth charge in the First World War. He was still designing underwater firing mechanisms which could not be countermined, and concentrated on relays and explosive devices to be used in beach clearance. With this accumulated knowledge and experience, the Mine Design Department and the Mining Department were to prove more than a match for the Germans in this 'tit for tat' struggle.

Before the war it had been suggested that the 'Northern Barrage' be relaid - the massive minefield laid across the northern exits of the North Sea in 1918. Churchill supported the idea and in October 1939 Rear Admiral Wake-Walker was made responsible for closing the gap between Scotland and Norway. In 1918 the barrage had been been laid largely by the United States Navy. Now alone, the Royal Navy was faced with a formidable task, although the monitoring of the minefield could now be carried out by aircraft. A great deal was expected of this field but World War I experience had shown that, massive as it might be, a northern mine barrage could only be a deterrent, and not a barrier against enemy submarines and surface craft. In order to compensate for the smaller number of mines to be laid the new Mk XIX anti-submarine contact mines were replaced by Mk XX antenna mines. They had been developed in a very short time using the Mk XVII case, and orders for 60,000 had been placed with three contractors familiar with mass production methods, Pressed Steel, Briggs Motor Bodies and Wolseley Motors. A base was established at Kyle of Lochalsh on the west coast of Scotland, to which the mines and the sinkers were transported as they came off the production lines. Five merchant ships were taken up and converted: *Southern Prince, Port Napier, Port Quebec, Agememnon,* and *Menestheus,* each with a capacity of 440-560 mines. The total capacity of the force was 2,600 Mk XXs.

A start to the minelaying campaign was contemplated for the early summer, but in April the German invasion of Norway put paid to the original plan. The only alternative was to examine the feasability of laying mines between the Orkneys and Iceland. Here the length of the minefield would be nearly 500 miles, and the depth of water in which the mines would have to be laid was up to 500 fathoms. Furthermore, great currents flowed in this northern extremity of the Atlantic and for a large part of the year the seas were inhospitable. In spite of these formidable obstacles it was decided to go ahead and in June 1940, despite pre-occupations elsewhere, the five converted merchantmen were became the First Minelaying Squadron, and Wake-Walker hoisted his flag in *Southern Prince.* He was later reinforced by *Adventure* which also gave anti-aircraft protection.

In accordance with international law an area dangerous to shipping was declared in July 1940 which embraced all the waters between Scotland and Iceland, and Iceland and Greenland. The laying and maintaining of this giant minefield then became a continuous commitment, which required the presence of cruiser and destroyer escorts for the minelayers. It was a slow and hazardous business, made all the more onerous by the loss of *Port Napier.* The harrowing story of her loss was relieved only by the bravery of the ship's mining party. On the night of 27 November 1940 a fierce gale battered the waters of Lochalsh, causing *Port Napier* to drag her anchors. Being a twin screw diesel ship she was soon underway and heading for a safer anchorage, but she was blown across the bows of a collier whose anchor cables fouled her screws. Together, the ships drifted towards the Skye side of the loch where at last their anchors held firm.

As dawn broke the remainder of the squadron proceeded to the minefield, leaving *Port Napier* to refuel and to shed the collier's cables. As pumping of fuel oil began a fire started in the engine room. It was soon out of control. Immediately above the engine room the two mine decks were fully loaded with mines which had been prepared for launching. Faced with an impending disaster the mining party set about removing the detonators. The remainder of the ship's company abandoned ship and steps were taken to evacuate the inhabitants of the small town of Kyle and to clear all shipping from the vicinity. When the mining decks became unbearably hot, the mining party was forced to abandon the ship. Later, when it appeared that the fire had died down, the mining party returned and an attempt was made to discharge the mines by the stern chute, but the smoke and heat forced them once more to leave the ship. Moments later there was an enormous explosion which blew out part of the port side of the ship and broke her back. She rolled over and sank, part of the wreck being visible at low water.

A wreck buoy was moored over the grave of the *Port Napier*, where she remained a menace to shipping until, in 1952, the mines and the wreck were removed in a memorable salvage operation. Later in the war, an attempt had been made to salvage her side plating and phosphor-bronze propellers. Disaster nearly befell the salvage parties when a diver attempted to clear the cables fouling the propellers by exploding a small charge. When the charge was detonated it countermined a mine lying on the bottom, sinking the diving boat and damaging the salvage ship. The salvage operation was abandoned.

Laying and maintaining this widespread system of minefields, now extended into the Denmark Strait between Iceland and Greenland, was a severe strain on the country's resources at a very difficult time and there were considerable contemporary doubts as to whether the effort was really justified. The First Sea Lord, Sir Dudley Pound, was adamant that the Admiralty would never have been forgiven if it had not tried to restore the Northern Barrage. But its effectiveness was not helped by defective equipment. The Mk XX was not a good mine having been rushed into service without proper trials at *Vernon*. In January 1943 laying was stopped and attention concentrated on deep fields of moored magnetic mines laid along the passages deemed most likely to be used by U-boats.

Wake-Walker's ships were also needed for other duties. In 1940 they laid a field of Mk XXs near the north western approaches shipping routes, to which *Adventure* and *Plover* later added anti-submarine contact mines. In August, they laid a contact field across St George's Channel as an anti-invasion measure and a Mk XIX contact mine anti-submarine field off Cape Wrath. The ships of the First Minelaying Squadron laid a total of 110,000 mines in often atrocious and always dangerous conditions.

The converted merchant ships were sometimes reinforced by   fast minelayers of the *Abdiel* Class. The first four, *Abdiel*, *Latona*, *Manxman* and *Welshman*, each capable of almost 40 knots and carrying over 150 mines, were completed between April and August 1941. *Abdiel* laid her first field in enemy waters even before she had completed her acceptance trials. The high speed and carrying capacity of these ships meant that they were often used for ancillary purposes, such as fast troop and supply ships.

Admiral Somerville in command of Force H in the western Mediterranean conceived a daring plan to use one of these ships, disguised as a large French destroyer, to lay mines off Leghorn. On 14 August 1941, the commanding officer of *Manxman* at Kyle of Lochalsh received orders to camouflage his ship to resemble the French ship *Leopard*. The order seemed to be unreasonable, since apart from each having three funnels there were many differences between the ships. However the challenge was accepted; it was fun, it was mysterious and it was a change from wartime routine. The ship's company, with the help of the First Minelaying Squadron , achieved a surprisingly reasonable likeness to *Leopard* using paint, spars and canvas. All on board joined in the charade and, appropriately dressed, they went about their business in the guise of French seamen.

After loading at Milford Haven, *Manxman* proceeded to Gibraltar where she took on board the final orders for the operation before a quick dash northwards between the Spanish coast and the Balearic Islands, and thence to within sight of the French Riviera. Here she was sighted by three enemy aircraft but, perhaps deceived by the camouflage, they took no action. *Manxman* arrived off Leghorn on schedule, where a mixed minefield of moored contact, magnetic and delayed release mines was laid. The high speed return journey to Gibraltar was uneventful, and *Manxman* was soon back at Kyle of Lochalsh ready to carry out, with *Welshman*, further minelaying operations off the coasts of Norway and Brittany, and in the Bay of Biscay.

During the magnetic mine crisis in 1939 Winston Churchill had recalled the idea of retaliatory mining; he suggested releasing fluvial contact mines in the Rhine at Strasburg, so that they would float down into the German reaches of the river. These R Type 1 mines consisted of a 15 inch sphere containing a 25 lb. TNT charge. Approximately 28,000 were manufactured in three different versions: a simple floating contact mine, a contact mine trailing a slipper sinker and a third known as the Slug, which oscillated between the surface and the river bed. They were designed to be floated down the river just below the surface and to explode on contact with shipping, bridges and other stationary obstacles.

In March 1940, some 2,000 of these mines had ben collected on French soil, ready to start 'Operation Royal Marine'. The French Government, always cautious during the phoney war and desperately worried about German retaliation from the air, gave an uncompromising refusal to allow this kind of strategic action to be taken. Had it been able to make up its mind to take aggressive action against a common enemy, significant damage to the German lines of communication might have resulted. When the German attack on the Low Countries began, 'Operation Royal Marine' was eventually sanctioned. Over 1,700 mines were launched into the Rhine, halting all movement between Karlsruhe and Mainz for a time. The preparation of these mines was supervised by Lieutenant GH Goodman RNVR, who found himself cut off by the advancing German armies. After a difficult journey he was able to make his way back to the United Kingdom, where he became one of the first Mine Disposal Officers attached to the Land Incident Section. Goodman was over forty years of age and was known to his colleagues as

'Granny' because of his deliberate, very cautious approach to anything likely to explode. This was in sharp contrast to the intrepid manner in which some mine disposal teams regarded unexploded devices. Throughout the war he was to be a tower of strength in the mine disposal organisation until, on VE Day, he was killed in the detonation of a German mine depot. This very gallant officer was awarded the George Cross for defusing an Italian so-called self destroying Surface Torpedo on 15 January 1942 just after one had killed the Torpedo Officer of *Medway*.

The 'R' mines were used for anti-invasion purposes but were prone to accidental explosion. *Vernon* vetoed their proposed use later in the war by defensively equipped merchantships (DEMS)

In 1940, the British A Mark I magnetic mine became available designed to be released from 18inch Mk XI torpedo dropping gear, but there was little chance that naval aircraft such as the Swordfish would be able to operate within range of powerful shore based air forces; only Coastal Command Beauforts had the range and speed to undertake minelaying sorties in enemy waters. However, the A MkI mine was adapted for use in the larger aircraft of Bomber Command by replacing the ballistic tail by a parachute. This allowed it to be dropped from greater heights and at greater speeds, and it also reduced the overall length of the mine, thus facilitating stowage in bomb racks. The campaign got under way on the night of April 13/14 when Hampdens of 5 Group laid A Mk Is in the Great Belt, Little Belt and the Sound. Two nights later Coastal Command Beauforts laid mines in the Jade Estuary.

The advance of the Germans into the Low Countries and Northern France allowed shore based Fleet Air Arm aircraft to join in the mining campaign. Hodges was sent by *Vernon* to Detling in Kent, where Lieutenant Commander Esmonde's Swordfish squadron was based. The squadron personnel were completely unfamiliar with mines, and Esmonde's aircraft had not been fitted to carry them. Hodges could not help remarking that it was an odd situation. Here was a Swordfish squadron required at short notice to carry a weapon about which the personnel were completly ignorant, and the Naval officer sent to advise them had only recently been a schoolmaster. It was much to their credit that after thirty six hours of hard work, without outside assistance, all the squadron's aircraft had been modified to carry 'A' mines. As soon as this work had been completed, the Swordfish were sent on their first mining operations off Boulogne. The fall of France also saw carrier based Swordfish lay mines off Oran to contain the French fleet but their contribution to a lamentable operation was a failure because the mines had not been prepared properly.

Vernon had not been allowed to test the 'A' mine and on examining a specimen considered it badly designed and inherently dangerous. Torpedo Officers were flown to the various air stations to brief RAF armament personnel about their new weapons. In the Autumn of 1940 a series of disastrous accidents occurred when mines exploded as they were being prepared for laying, or on one occasion on release. It was found that it was possible for the safety fork to seem to be in position when the switch was at 'fire'; movement would then set the mine off. The dropping accident was caused by the sudden deceleration caused by the opening of the parachute which closed the inertia operated impact fuse in the mine.

As a result of these disasters Torpedo Gunner's Mates were lent to Bomber Command and Hodges was based in Lincolnshire for a time to supervise arrangements in 5 Group. He reported that he was deeply impressed by the morale, gallantry and efficiency of the air and ground crews. After a few months he was certain that there was little more that he could teach them. Unfortunately constant changes made to the mines meant that RAF armourers were sometimes badly briefed and disastrous accidents continued to occur. At Scampton, the temporary absence of the Chief Torpedo Gunner's Mate contributed to a major explosion that demolished an entire bomb store being used for mines.

In early 1942, a dash up the Channel from Brest back to Germany by the *Scharnhorst*, *Gneisenau* and *Prinz Eugen* was anticipated and minefields were laid to trap the German ships. This was a fully co-ordinated operation; *Plover* strengthened the Dover barrage with moored magnetic mines, *Manxman* and *Welsman* laid twelve fields of moored contact, magnetic and delayed release mines mines off the northern coast of France and 5 Group carried out a daring daylight operation to lay a minefield off the Frisian Coast. One of *Plover*'s mines damaged a German destroyer during the preparations for the operation. Intensive sweeping neutralised the fast minelayers' fields when the Germans mounted the daring voyage that February but one of the minesweepers escorting the capital ships was sunk. It was the RAF's minefield that achieved success to redeem the fiasco of the squadron's undetected escape from Brest and the subsequent failure to stop the passage of the German warships. Their mines caused serious damage to *Scharnhorst* and *Gneisenau* and the latter never went to sea again.

In February 1942 Air Marshal Sir Arthur Harris became Commander-in-Chief, Bomber Command. He began to involve more of his groups in the minelaying offensive. He also arranged for the appointment of a Captain, Royal Navy, to his staff. It was an important appointment soon repeated at the appropriate level at each Group Headquarters. A generally harmonious system developed by which the overall minelaying plans were formulated at the Admiralty, whilst detailed planning and execution of the operations rested with Bomber Command. A major mining offensive began using mines of increasing complexity. The A Mk I was joined by the Mks II, III, and IV variously altered to allow for easier mass production. A smaller MK V was also introduced designed to fit a 1,000 lb bomb rack. A twin engined Hampden could only carry one mine but the four engined Halifax could carry two. *Vernon* soon suggested how this could be doubled again to four. The more powerful Lancasters bombers could carry up to six mines.

The first acoustic mines were introduced in August 1942. The devices seemed too simple and Cowie had difficulty in persuading the planners that the surprise effect would be significant. When the first 500 mines were laid over two nights the Admiralty minelaying staff was vindicated; the simple acoustic mines created chaos and inflicted serious casualties. At the same time, magnetic firing was improved by requiring two actuations, one to put the detonator in circuit and the other to fire the mine. If no second actuation was received within between six to sixteen seconds then the mine did not explode. This made countermeasures more difficult. Combined magnetic and acoustic firing was also developed.

Cowie's team passed their staff requirements to the mine designers at Leigh Park House, where the new circuits were quickly put together in box assemblies. The difficulty lay in providing these boxes quickly and accurately in the relatively small numbers required. The problem was solved in January 1943 by setting up an organisation, known as MX, for the rapid design and production of small numbers of these special 'tailored assemblies'. In was housed in the former Mine Design machine shop in No. 38 Building at *Vernon*, Portsmouth. Here the combined team of designers and naval officers developed the new circuits in a format suitable for fitting into standard mine casings. The work force which assembled these mine circuits consisted entirely of women of the Womens' Royal Naval Service. Very soon the MX Department was producing fifty mines a week for despatch by the Armament Supply Department to selected airfields.

To use Cowie's own words, 'the object of the designer is to produce a mine which will either make use of the enemy's sweeping technique or one which would detect the difference between a minesweeper and a normal ship'. Air reconnaissance established that the Germans provided an escort of one minesweeper proceeding ahead of U-boats or surface vessels leaving the Biscay ports. The distance between the minesweeper and the escorted vessel was always the same. It was, therefore, possible to design a firing circuit timed to operate on the second impulse, thus allowing the minesweeper to pass over the mine without detonating it and leaving the escorted vessel to do so. If either the speed or spacing of the vessels was not in accordance with the usual practice the mine reverted to normal stand-by mode. It was not long before the Germans diagnosed the problem, and reacted by adding extra escorting minesweepers or two 'Sperrbrechers' (mine exploding ships similar to *Borde*). As the number of escorts changed, MX produced assemblies to match, until this approach had to be changed when the required assemblies became too big for the mine casings.

Vernon MX Wrens 1943-45

Other circuits could distinguish between the different intensities of sweeping influences and the magnetic or acoustic signature of a normal ship or submarine. When the Germans tried countermining explosions to deal with acoustic mines, MX produced circuits that could differentiate between the different sound characteristics. And so the battle of wits went on. By the time that the battle had been won, the 63 WRNS employed in the Mine Design machine shop at *Vernon* had produced 7,638 mine circuits. These bright young women, knowing that they were doing an important job of work, did much to keep the fighting spirit alive in *Vernon(P)* during those difficult years.

During 1943, *Vernon*'s battered home at Portsmouth began to come alive again. The MX Wrens were followed by the Mining Instructional Department which came back from Roedean in the autumn and established themselves in their old home in 17a Building. Electrical and anti-submarine training were stepped up. In view of the returning importance of the parent establishment at Portsmouth, the post of commanding officer was upgraded in the summer of 1943 from Commander to Captain, when Commander Hollebone was succeeded by Captain FHG Ree.

At Leigh Park House, 1943 was proving to be an interesting but sometimes frustrating year for Gaskell and his colleagues. They were particularly concerned to exploit the growing efficiency of the RAF in laying mines accurately in the focal areas around the enemy ports and harbours. Gaskell and an RAF colleague, Wing Commander Collier, were enthusiastic about the use of small acoustic mines in river estuaries where the muddy bottoms made acoustic sweeping extremely difficult. Unfortunately they encountered great obstacles. Captain Abbot, the naval officer in charge of procurement of mines at the Admiralty in Bath, was reluctant to order special mines exclusively for the Royal Air Force and without his support Gaskell and Collier had little chance of realising their ambitions, particularly when the Ministry of Supply considered that their request for only 500 of these mines was uneconomical, and that to manufacture a larger number would be a waste of important industrial effort. Later when the centre of operations moved to the Far East, Collier continued to press for a supply of small air dropped acoustic mines for use in the Burma theatre of war, but in vain. A small, 500 lb acoustic Mk VIII* was designed but never used.

The use of the growing family of influence mines continued to be stepped up. The H2S navigational radar greatly increased the accuracy with which mines were laid and casualties to the dropping aircraft were minimised by modifying mines for release up to 15,000 feet; Lancasters began to operate in this way in 1944. Special low level missions were carried out when necessary. The mining of the enemy's inland waterways sometimes required such tactics and were considered to be of such importance that it formed part of the 1943-44 Strategic Warfare Plan. Lancasters dropped mines into the Konigsberg Canal in April 1944 and the following month Mosquitoes carried out a successful mission against the Kiel Canal. About 100 specially shortened mines Mks I-IV and VII were developed for the Mosquito canal missions with special fusing to allow them to be dropped in water only ten feet deep at speeds of 300 miles per hour. MX provided the assemblies and MX Wrens went to the airfields to supervise the loading of the aircraft with the special mines.

Supplies for the Axis campaign in Southern Russia and the flow of Romanian oil to the German industrial heartland were both dependent upon the uninterrupted use of the River Danube. The strategic importance of the river had long been appreciated by the Yugoslav partisans - and indeed by the British Government before that - and they had carried out a number of minor raids upon shipping. The British naval liason officer with the partisans was Lieutenant Commander Alexander Glen (later Sir Alexander Glen). He was well acquainted with both Admiral Sir John Cunningham aand Air Marshal Sir John Slessor, the Allied Naval and Air Commanders-in-Chief concerned with these operations, and he found no difficulty in persuading them that an early start should be made to the Danube mining campaign. In May an RAF/ USAAF bomber force began a comprehensive series of minelaying operations from bases in Italy. Detailed preparation of the mines was carried out by Cowie in London and the *Vernon* MX unit.

Lewis, now a Commander and Mediterranean Fleet Torpedo Officer, was determined that the mines should be properly prepared. From a disabled cruiser he 'dragged out' an assistant, Lieutenant IR Johnston, for liaison with the Allied Mediterranean Air Force. The British Wellingtons could carry the large magnetic-acoustic Mks I, II and IV mines but the American Liberators could only carry the smaller 1000 lb A Mk V and 500 lb A Mk VIII mines specially developed to fit in normal bomb racks. The latter mines were fitted with simple magnetic pistols only but this did not reduce the effectiveness of the mining campaign, which was helped by the Germans who showed an unusual and sustained ineptitude in dealing with it. By October 1944, over 1,200 mines had been laid in the Danube; between April and August 1944, 90 per cent of the traffic was stopped; 45 tugs and steamers and 150 tankers were sunk. Panic ensued, causing large scale desertion amongst river craft crews. The passage of tankers was so reduced that only 35,000 tons per month of Romanian oil got through to Germany instead of the normal 200,000 tons. Vital supplies for the German forces in the Crimea were stopped and statistically the mining of the Danube became the most effective mining campaign of the entire war. It was also the most economical in terms of aircraft losses.

HMS Apollo 1945

225

The major mining operation to cover the Normandy landings involved almost all existing means of mine laying; 1,3,4,5 and 6 Groups Bomber Command, the minelayers *Apollo* and *Plover*, five MTB flotillas and four motor launch flotillas. *Apollo* was one of two new fast minelayers laid down in late 1941; the second was *Ariadne*. The ships had proved useful as high speed transports for special missions as well as in their primary function; indeed *Latona*, one of the original quartet, had been sunk in the Mediterranean in 1941 without ever laying a mine. It was as well that two new examples of the type were built as *Welshman* was torpedoed on her way back from a mining mission in the Sicilian Channel and *Abdiel* was mined while being used as a high speed troop transport. Both these losses ocurred in 1943; *Welshman* laid 3,000 mines, and *Abdiel* 2,000.

Coastal forces craft had started minelaying in early 1941 operating first from Dover and then from Nore Command bases further north. Specialities of these small minelayers were the Mk XXV and MK XXVII 'snagline' mines with a floating line attached to one of the switch horns of a contact mine. These were designed to catch enemy motor torpedo boats ('E' Boats) and other small coastal craft. British MTBs also laid American mines in the Mediterranean.

The mining contribution to 'Overlord', Operation 'Maple', was designed to protect the invasion forces and landings themselves without compromising their security or endangering Allied shipping. This required delayed arming and accurate sterilising of mines at the right time. New variations introduced specially for 'Maple' were dual magnetic/low frequency acoustic actuators that were virtually impossible to sweep without specialised and clumsy equipment; MK XVII acoustic moored mines designed to deal with enemy coastal forces and the 2,000 lb A Mk VI dual magnetic and acoustic mines dropped from aircraft. The operation began on 17 April and 7,000 mines were laid, 4,000 of them by Bomber Command. About 100 enemy vessels were sunk or damaged. An officer from *Vernon(M)* was attached to the Staff of C-in-C Portsmouth to cordinate 'Maple' with 'Overlord'. It had been planned well in advance but nevertheless there were problems in getting all the equipment prepared, especially the new devices. As the history of the Mining Department put it:

As the target date approached VERNON *heard of one trouble and another which might postpone the date on which mines would be ready for her to carry out production trials. Each rumour had to be investigated and unfortunately some proved to be correct and* VERNON *had, eventually, to declare that no further postponement of her trials would be possible if the mines were to be used in the operation and to advise that unless an unqualified acceptance of the date was given the use of other mines would be recommended. The assembly of mines for trial...was interrupted by the absence of various components.* VERNON's *motor transport and officers' private cars were used to collect them.*

When, after all this effort, the new mines were finally dispatched to the bomber groups an officer from *Vernon* went to check that all was satisfactory. It was not. There was a shortage of lugs and appropriate securing screws for the new Mk VIs and it needed considerable efforts on the part of the *Vernon(M)* officer to obtain them in time. The good relations previously established between *Vernon*, the Naval personnel serving at the bomber bases and the RAF was fully exploited in this rush to prepare the new weapons for use.

Other *Vernon* contributions to 'Overlord' were the testing of an underwater beacon, the PM 830 Buoy, and the training of coastal forces personnel in the laying and use of this important aid to navigation. This work was carried out in great secrecy and the buoys played an important part on 'D' Day.

1945 saw the aerial mining campaign make its final contribution to victory in Europe when it interfered with the training of crews for the new generation of fast battery driven U-boats in the Baltic. The entry into service of these revolutionary new units, the ancestors of all post-war conventional submarines, would have caused serious problems for Allied escort forces and the whole Allied cause, even at this late stage of the war. Meanwhile, operations against Japan were stepped up. Allied mining had an enormous effect on Japan's vital sea communications and British mines and minelaying aircraft, ships and submarines played a part in the offensive. Of the 321 Japanese ships lost to mines 21 were sunk in British minefields. *Vernon* formed two Mobile Mine Units to test and maintain mines in the Far East and these had just been readied for service when the war came to an unexpectedly early close.

Over the entire war, British mines sank almost 1,050 German and Italian vessels; this was nearly twice the number of British ships sunk by German mines and about equivalent to the total Allied losses to German mining. Bearing in mind the much greater numbers of Allied ships the exchange ratio is very favourable. Aircraft laid mines sank the lion's share, 864, surface ships sank 125 and submarines 59. The Mine Design Department and *Vernon* had acquitted themselves well in a very effective partnership. As the history of *Vernon* Mining Department put it:

It may be said that Superintendant of Mine Design and VERNON(M) *were father and mother to the mines, and saw to it that their family had good health and good manners. As with many married couples, occasional differences took place but these did not lead to proceedings in court (Admiralty and Divorce).*

Cowie summed it all up simply and directly, 'the cold fact remains, our mines defeated their mining organisation.'

CHAPTER THIRTEEN

TORPEDOES AND TORPEDOMEN AT WAR

THE HAVOC WROUGHT BY THE TORPEDO armament of submarines during the First World War had not been matched by the performance of torpedo carrying surface and air craft, especially at Jutland, where the threat of torpedo attacks had been more significant than the damage which they inflicted. The battle left no doubt in the minds of tacticians that torpdoes needed to be fired in much larger quantities, at closer ranges and in ways that made avoidance more difficult. These opinions dominated tactical thinking and material development during the inter-war years. Massed destroyer attacks by day and night were exercised by the new generation of destroyers, which were armed with eight or ten torpedo tubes rather than four or six. By the outbreak of war advances had been made in technology and tactics and improved torpedoes had been introduced. On 3 September 1939 the Royal Navy had 7,100 torpedoes although less than half were of modern construction. The oxygen enriched air torpedo, the 21-inch Mark VII was being converted to natural air propulsion and only *Rodney* and *Nelson* retained enriched air torpedoes in the 24.5-inch Mark I.

Some old torpedoes were still being issued to the fleet. The 21-inch Mark II which dated back to the years before the First World War went to some submarines and to old destroyers including the four-funnel destroyers transferred from the United States Navy. The principal torpedo in use during the First World War, the 21-inch Mark IV and its immediate successor the Mk V, formed the main bulk of the old stocks and were used in older destroyers, submarines and MTBs. A few old 18-inch torpedoes of Mks VII, VIII and XI were also used by MTBs and aircraft.

Eventually all these obsolescent torpedoes began to be replaced in submarines and MTBs with larger tubes by the 21-inch Mk VIII, in cruisers and destroyers by the 21-inch Mk IX and in aircraft and some MTBs by the 18-inch Mks XII and XV. The 21-inch Mk VIII would be used during the war in greater numbers than any other torpedo; 3,732 were expended by September 1944, amounting to 56.4 per cent of total torpedo expenditure. Production of torpedoes of all types was only 80 per month in September 1939, but wartime manufacture was carried out by a number of British, Commonwealth and American contractors until, in March 1942, production outstripped use. In early 1944, 800 torpedoes a month were being produced.

Before the production and distribution problems were fully solved , the supply of 21-inch Mk VIII torpedoes occasionally failed to meet the demands, particularly in the Mediterranean in 1943 when the submarines were expending torpedoes faster than they could be brought to Allied bases in North Africa. Lewis, the Staff Torpedo Officer, found it increasingly difficult to meet the Commander-in-Chief's requirement that submarines should always carry their full outfit. This meant that those submarines which were fitted with tubes outside the pressure hull, as well as the normal number inside, required seventeen weapons. The problem reached its peak when a submarine, due to sail for its patrol area in forty eight hours, was still six torpedoes short. Lewis arranged for a vessel carrying torpedoes to be diverted to Bougie, where they were transferred to a coaster for transport to Algiers. The remaining three torpedoes were collected by Fleet Air Arm lorries so as not to have 'all the eggs in one basket'. The following day the coaster was torpedoed and sunk and the lorries lost their way and drove over a cliff. Lewis was summoned to appear before a wrathful Cunningham, in the presence of General Dwight D. Eisenhower and Air Marshal Sir Arthur Tedder. Lewis was dismayed, but the tragi-comedy of the occasion and the expression on his face saved the situation. The three leaders burst into laughter and expressed sympathy with his predicament and efforts. All six torpedoes were recovered later, but whether the submarine sailed with its full outfit of torpedoes is not recorded.

Mk XII Torpedo fitted with a MAT IV tail loaded on a Mk II Barracuda

British torpedoes in 1939 were uncomplicated and reliable and were progressively improved throughout the war. Only the Mk XII air dropped weapon needed replacement because of the need for higher speed and range; the 18-inch MK XV could run 2500 yards at 40 knots as opposed to 1500 yards by its predecessor. Because of their smaller warheads, priority was given to providing the 18-inch weapons with magnetic pistols fused to go off under their targets. The Duplex CR pistols developed to achieve this proved troublesome in service, despite their success at Taranto in November 1940. The pistols were subject to premature firing and an annoying reluctance to explode under their intended targets. They were activated when the torpedo passed under a ship by the current created in a coil wound around a mu-metal rod. But they were easily countered by degaussing unless the torpedo passed very close. The premature firing was caused by the earth's magnetic field if the torpedo made a sharp movement. At the end of 1943 it was finally decided to abandon the Duplex CR and rely on contact pistols for airborne torpedoes. An improved magnetic pistol, the CCR (Compensated Coil Rod) was developed to overcame the problems of the Duplex but it only proved practical to fit it to 21-inch weapons.

Vernon's Whitehead department in its new accommodation at Alexandria in Dunbartonshire was the key establishment for maintaining torpedo operational standards. As well as trying to perfect the magnetic pistol and keep torpedoes watertight in flooded submarine tubes, it had to ensure quality control among the various manufacturers as they in turn struggled with declining standards of materials and workmanship. The advent of significant numbers of variously equipped Allied ships and submarines complicated the difficult logistic problem. The 21-inch Whitehead wet heater torpedoes used in these Allied vessels were collectively designated Mk X which ran to five variants. Some Dutch submarines were even outfitted with German G7a torpedoes captured in two supply ships. These torpedoes had to be converted to run on new fuel and did not prove entirely satisfactory and were eventually replaced by the latest British Mk VIIIs. Alexandria was hard pressed to carry out all the equipment trials and had to be supported by a trials team based at Aglionby Street, Carlisle. Bincleaves remained an out-station for MTB torpedo trials and Stokes Bay for aircraft drops until D-Day preparations caused the latter to move north to less satisfactory acommodation at Crail. Most discharge trials were, however, carried out at Arrochar where acommodation was increased: submarines of several nationalities could be seen at work in Loch Long. Trials with destroyers were also carried out in the broader waters of the Firth of Clyde including the development of angling gear, which allowed a torpedo's course to be kept contiuously up to date in the tube thus allowing the ship or submarine to choose its angle of approach to the target. Britain had lagged behind German and American practice in this regard in 1939.

Life in the Sea Trials Section at *Vernon* sometimes seemed dull and remote, a sharp contrast to the drama of life in the Mining and Minesweeping Departments. Lieutenant Commander RC Didham, who served throughout the war in the Torpedo Tube and Firing Gear Section, remembered:

It had always been like that in the Whitehead Department during the war. There was meticulous attention to detail and a determination that when the equipment went to sea it should not fail in the heat of action.

It never did. It is a tribute above all to *Vernon*'s trials staff that British torpedoes never suffered from the disastrous failures that beset German and American weapons at various points in the war.

Torpedo development was the responsibility of the Torpedo Experimental Establishment at Greenock. With the success of the burner cycle Mks VIII and IX and their steady incremental development not much priority was given to the development of an electrically propelled torpedo to match the German G7e. In 1942, with a clear need for trackless torpedoes in the Mediteranean, work was pushed ahead with a little more vigour and in May 1943, the first prototype was available for trials. By this time the need for special torpedoes for Mediterranean operations had diminished and the first production weapon was not delivered till August 1944. Designated the 21-inch Mark XI, none ever saw service given their limited performance, (5,500 yards at 25 knots compared to 5,000 yards at over 45 knots for the Mk VIII). Greenock also experimented with advanced 'monofuels' for torpedo engines, but in the wartime context there seemed little need for such advanced technology while perfectly adequate weapons of more conventional design available.

In one area, however, the weapons were not quite adequate; the greatly improved anti-aircraft armaments of ships were making aircraft launched torpedo attack increasingly hazardous. A torpedo with a still longer range and greater speed than the 18-inch Mk XV would have helped, but it was doubtful whether this was a technically feasible proposition. A weapon which could be released from outside the accurate range of AA fire was needed. In the fleet carrier *Furious*, which was employed in 1943 and 1944 in strikes against German coastal traffic in the Norwegian Leads, it was decided to experiment with a jet assisted glider torpedo designed in the ship's own torpedo workshop. Its design included a winged main body, driven in both air and water by a solid fuel propellant. It was intended to be released from height of 3,000 feet and a range of 2,500 yards. A model was constructed and despatched to the Admiralty. The Torpedo Officer was congratulated for his foresight and imagination, but nothing more was heard of the proposal. In fact, in 1942 Greenock had already experimented with an egg shaped jet propelled torpedo of rather similar concept but the Naval Staff had not been interested.

Much more interest was shown in the development of acoustic homing torpedoes for use by aircraft. Thought had been given before the war to the development of such a weapon but the tactical justification, that it would enable aircraft to drop from a safer zone ahead of the target, was not taken seriously, as mass attacks using conventional torpedoes were preferred. In 1940, the appearance of the German acoustic mine reawakened interest and, under pressure from Churchill, both the Torpedo Experimental Establishment at Greenock and the S Section of the Mine Design Department at Leigh Park began to re-examine the development of a homing torpedo, and by the end of 1942 designs were well advanced for the manufacture of an active air dropped prototype, code named Bowler. The design incorporated two quartz transducers, one on each side of the torpedo, producing sound beams at right angles to it. 'Bowler' was intended to be dropped ahead of the target which it detected at ranges of up to 100 yards. The torpedo would then steer towards the target, striking it broadside on. This design was abandoned when it was found that it was subject to premature turns caused by the explosion either of other torpedoes or deliberate countermeasures.

All was not lost by the failure of Bowler. The lessons learnt were incorporated in a new design for use with the tried and reliable 21-inch Mk VIII and Mk IX torpedoes from submarines and surface ships. This design incorporated an amplitude comparison system, based upon a transmitter and receiver made of quartz crystals, contained in an oil filled dome fitted to the nose of the torpedo. Named Trumper, it was intended to engage the target from an angle at a much improved range from the target. Work was carried out in conjunction with GEC at Wembley and initial trials proved encouraging, but the war ended before 'Trumper' could be proved and put into production.

The Royal Air Force carried out its own investigations into air launched homing torpedoes. A team led by Squadron Leader JW Robertson, who later became a senior scientist at the Torpedo Experimental Establishment at Greenock, was responsible for the research in co-operation with the General Electric Company, and designed an active homing torpedo based on the 18-inch Mk XV. The acoustics were designed by the Underwater Research Establishment at Fairlie, where it had moved from Portland. When asked to name the device, they chose Joker, which proved an apt designation since soon afterwards sea trials revealed that the weapon was much troubled by reverberation, self noise and the shock of water entry. In December 1943 it was abandoned in favour of 'Dealer', a new electrically propelled weapon. This incorporated many novel ideas and abandoned several of the accepted principles of torpedo design. Instead of the hydrostatic and pendulum arrangements which had evolved from Robert Whitehead's secrets, the design team chose to alter the centre of gravity by moving the main battery longitudinally. The torpedo was driven by two propellers, one on each side of the vertical fin. It was steered was by varying the voltage supplied to the separate motors for each propeller. It was surprising that such a novel design could have been brought to the manufacturing stage, but before the end of the war the Royal Naval Torpedo Factory had produced one hundred Dealers. None of them saw action and all were scrapped.

While the British struggled to produce an effective homing torpedo the Americans were making steady progress. In December 1942, WW Jackson of Fairlie went to America to keep the United States Navy up to date with British developments. In April 1943 Gaskell, Spends and Naval and Air Force technicians were sent by the Mine Design Department to study progress made by the Americans. This had resulted in the development of the torpedo code named Fido, which went into service as the air launched Mk 24 torpedo (in the American series) . It was a simple device with a maximum speed of 12 knots, considered sufficient to deal with a submerged submarine. Its existence was so secret that it was always referred to in signals as an air launched anti-submarine mine. By 1943, the Mk 24 torpedo had been issued to the Royal Navy and the Royal Air Force and it had achieved its first successes. When undergoing trials with the Royal Navy, it was launched from an aircraft from the aircraft carrier *Biter*; the torpedo ran awry and finished up by chasing *Biter*, which had not taken proper precautionery measures. Thus, goes the story, was 'The *Biter* bit'!

Although the development of more advanced weapons proved difficult, maintaining high standards of efficiency with less sophisticated equipment was carried out more successfully and this was ultimately more important. A regular supply of personnel trained to a very high standard was maintained by *Vernon(R)* throughout the war, despite the large numbers of personnel passing through - at its peak the school was home to 250 officers, 1,500 ratings and 600 Wrens. Those responsible for maintaining the standards made no headlines but their dedication deserves special mention. Nobody who underwent courses at *Vernon (R)* found the routine drab and the instruction or training never lagged behind the requirements of the Fleet.

As a contrast to the attention paid to Portsmouth the enemy seemed to have had little interest in Brighton and only a few scattered incidents occurred. In the Summer of 1943, when Captain Egerton was being relieved by Captain HE Morse, the farewell photograph of all the officers was rudely interrupted by two waves of enemy fighters. The photographer collapsed into the rose bed enveloped in his black cloth, but the cannon shells that splattered the concourse caused no injury or serious damage. The only casualty was a civilian draughtsman, who had gone for a walk along the cliffs and was killed by one of the bombs dropped by the passing aircraft. Casualties during the whole war at Roedean were few: a Sub Lieutenant was killed when enemy fighters bombed the hostel at the Marine Gate Hotel in the summer of 1942 and, when the St. Dunstan's Home for the Blind at Ovingdean was requisitioned for high power electrical instruction, a young seaman was killed by a stray machine gun bullet fired by a tip and run raider.

It was not only Royal Naval personnel who had lasting memories of their time under instruction at Roedean school. Many Commonwealth and Allied personnel have been heard to boast that they are 'old boys' from Roedean. The Commonwealth and foreign students never forgot the rotund figure of Commander 'Porky' Veale, the officer in charge of the Instructional Department. He was not always popular with his contemporaries but his eccentricities made certain that he was well remembered and made up for his tendency to give quick and sometimes cruel answers to any questions which he considered to be silly or misdirected. He was an integral part of an atmosphere at *Vernon(R)* that was was remarkably happy and harmonious. This was in the best traditions of the Torpedo Branch and helped maintain the high level of co-operation which existed throughout the war between the uniformed torpedo officers and the scientists and technicians in the research and development establishments. It also eased the way for those officers in 1941 and 1942 who had been directed into the Torpedo Branch without volunteering. They often arrived at Roedean in a negative state of mind, but before many weeks had passed the combined influence of Veale and the sensitive and hard working Commander CM (Monty) Donner had brought about a remarkable change of attitude. There were few who left *Vernon(R)* without being enthusiastic members of the Torpedo Branch. Early in 1943 the shortage of volunteers had ceased and new recruits were readily forthcoming for the remaining war years.

Another well remembered figure at *Vernon(R)* was Lieutenant Commander Robin Buckley. He had been Torpedo Officer of the cruiser *York* at Suda Bay, Crete on 12 March 1941, when she was seriously damaged and later abandoned after being attacked by Italian explosive motor boats. One of the boats was beached and it was while Buckley was attempting to render the explosives safe that a detonator exploded, blinding him for life. In spite of this he became, with the assistance of his wife who was a WRNS officer, a most accomplished and knowledgeable lecturer. It was this redoubtable spirit which ensured that officers and men left *Vernon(R)* inspired and well trained.

There is ample evidence that British torpedoes and torpedomen performed well in the Second World War. In the First Battle of Narvik Lieutenant George Heppel, the Torpedo Officer of Captain Warburton-Lee's Second Destroyer Flotilla, showed considerable initiative, courage and determination. He and Paymaster Lieutenant Geoffrey Stanning were put ashore at the Tranoy Pilot Station to find out the strength of the German forces at

Narvik. They reported that approximately six German destroyers had gone up the fjord. On receiving this estimate, Warburton-Lee signalled his intention to attack at dawn. Heppel was given the job of breaking the news to the off-watch members of the ship's company. As he left the mess deck the ship's loudspeakers broadcast the popular song, 'It's a lovely day tomorrow'.

When the crowded harbour of Narvik came into sight, Heppel turned to Warburton-Lee and remarked, 'There's a torpedo target such as I've never seen in my life!'. 'Well, get on with it then!', was the reply. Warburton-Lee had achieved complete surprise. Heppel remembered that the most important lesson of the First World War was, 'never fire torpedoes in penny numbers' and, with *Hardy* turning gently, he prepared to fire a full salvo but only three Mk IXs were launched in a narrow fan at the destroyer *Wilhelm Heidkamp*. One hit and blew off the German destroyer's stern, another destroyed the bows of a merchantman. Only the forward tubes had been brought to bear and there was a misunderstanding over whether the fourth torpedo had fired, which it had not. When more targets presented themselves Heppel ordered his after tubes turned to engage, no easy task in the cold, snowy conditions. There was almost a disaster when Heppel fired the first tube before the quadruple mounting was properly locked in position; happily the torpedo missed the superstructure. With the mounting properly locked the last three torpedoes were fired but they hit the quays. Such fumbling was the natural result of inexperience; this was the destroyers' first real torpedo action of the war.

Hunter, the next in line, fired all her eight MK IXs into the harbour, creating chaos among the merchantmen at anchor there. Then Lt John Burfield, the Torpedo Control Officer of *Havock* fired a salvo of four Mk IXs all of which found a mark, two on merchantmen and two on the destroyer *Anton Schmitt*. The explosion of the second Mk IX on the latter so shook the nearby destroyer *Hermann Kunne* that her engines seized. Finally *Hotspur* fired a salvo of four Mk IXs that dealt with two more merchantmen. It was a formidable demonstration of the power of British torpedoes, especially when *Diether von Roeder* tried to exploit its facility to angle its torpedoes to fire a spread of eight G 7as while still stopped. The attack was a dismal failure caused by the G 7a's poor depth keeping and ineffective fuses, both contact and magnetic. The torpedoes that ran on the surface were avoided and the majority that ran too deep did not explode, despite passing right under the British destroyers. Two ran up the beach at Ankenes.

In all the five destroyers made three attacking runs and *Hostile* managed to add four of her Mk IXs as a final contribution to the torpedo bombardment. Another German torpedo counter attack out of the harbour was as ineffective as the first but as as the British destroyers withdrew they were engaged from two directions by five German destroyers. At last the Germans scored a success with their torpedoes and *Hunter* was crippled; she later sank after being in collision with *Hotspur*. *Hardy* was also seriously damaged by gunfire which killed Warburton-Lee. Stanning, with great coolness, took over control on the bridge and successfully beached the ship. Heppel, who was uninjured, fired the only remaining torpedo at a German destroyer, and then took charge of the ship's company as they abandoned ship. He was responsible for saving a number of lives and was seen encouraging the weaker swimmers in the icy water. After seeing that the survivors were being cared for by the kind villagers of Virek, Heppel returned to the still burning wreck of *Hardy* to bring off the wounded officers and to destroy the safes in the Captain's cabin. During the next few days he marched her men 15 miles to the town of Ballengen, where the wounded were taken to hospital.

When, three days later, the battleship *Warspite* and her escorting destroyers were advancing up the fjord to complete the destruction of the German squadron, Heppel was looking for a craft in which he could search for the British force. With the help of a Norwegian fishing vessel he was able to seize a German motorboat in Ofotfjord, in which he was able to make contact with *Warspite*. Thanks to Heppel's unceasing endeavours and example, *Hardy's* survivors were picked up by the destroyer *Ivanhoe*. Stanning, who also distinguished himself, was quick to recognise the significant part played by Heppel and, many years later, W Pulford, one of *Hardy's* Leading Torpedo Operators, wrote, 'of those who have survived the passage of time, none will forget the outstanding courage, with complete disregard for his own personal safety, of the man who made our rescue possible ... the man known as "Torps".

Just over six months later another torpedo attack on an enemy in harbour had even greater strategic results. In November 1940 the Commander-in-Chief Mediterranean Fleet, Admiral Sir Andrew Cunningham, was faced with an Italian Fleet that was numerically superior in capital ships. The best option to even the odds seemed to be a night attack on the Italian fleet

Swordfish torpedo bombers from Illustrious

base at Taranto using Swordfish torpedo bombers. The Italians were confident that such an attack was impossible as the depth of water in the harbour at Taranto was never more than 42 feet but AL St G Lyster the Rear Admiral Aircraft Carriers, flying his flag in *Illustrious*, was confident of success. As captain of *Glorious* he had considered such an attack in 1938 when war between Britain and Italy had seemed likely. The new Mk XII torpedoes did not dive deeply after launch and Lyster and his aircrew thought they were quite usable in Taranto's shallows. Now, just over two years later the idea was resurrected. Lyster had the full co-operation and support of his Flag Captain, none other than Boyd, commanding officer at *Vernon* until the previous year. As Captains of the Gunnery and Torpedo Schools at Portsmouth Lyster and Boyd had become close friends, and had shown how well the Gunnery and Torpedo Branches could work together.

The attack was in two waves, the first of twelve aircraft and the second of nine aircraft. Six of each wave carried torpedoes, the rest bombs. The torpedoes were armed with a mix of duplex and contact pistols but in the calm waters and low latitude of the Taranto anchorage the former type worked

The Italian battleship Cavour sunk by Swordfish aircraft at Taranto 7 November 1940

well. One launched by a Swordfish of the first wave exploded under the battleship *Cavour* and sank her. Two more Mk XIIs with contact pistols damaged the larger *Littorio*. In the second wave a Duplex headed Mk XII exploded under *Caio Duilio* which had to be beached to prevent her sinking. Another contact-headed torpedo damaged *Littorio*: she was only out of action for three months but it took until June 1941 to repair *Duilio*, and *Cavour* never sailed again. The strength of the Italian battle fleet had been halved, for the cost of two Swordfish and their crews, a remarkable victory made possible by the skill of the pilots, the durability of the aircraft, and the reliability of British torpedoes. *Illustrious's* torpedo party had prepared their weapons with skill and efficiency.

The Mk XII scored another vital success on 26 May 1941 when one exploded on the stern of the battleship *Bismarck* slowing her down and jamming her steering gear to an extent which allowed *King George V* and *Rodney* to catch and destroy the German capital ship. The Duplex heads had inadvertently helped prevent a disaster earlier that day when the Swordfish pilots from *Ark Royal* had carried out an attack on the cruiser *Sheffield* which was shadowing *Bismarck*. A number of premature explosions had helped the British cruiser avoid the attacks and also demonstrated the unsuitability of the influence pistols in the rough seas and higher latitudes of the North Atlantic. Torpedoes played little role in actually sinking the German ship which was shattered by heavy gunfire. Lewis, now torpedo officer of *Rodney*, persuaded Captain Dalrymple-Hamilton to let him fire the ship's stock of 24.5 inch torpedoes at *Bismarck*. This was the only occasion they were used in action, but no hits were scored. The German battleship had been pounded by gunfire until she could scarcely retaliate before the final coup de grace was delivered by the cruiser *Dorsetshire*, which put a 21-inch torpedo into each side of the burning hulk.

Later that year, on the night of 13 December 1941, one of the most successful torpedo actions of the war was fought by the destroyers *Sikh*, *Legion*, *Maori* and *Isaac Sweers*, under the command of Commander GH Stokes in *Sikh*. On passage from Gibraltar to Malta they were directed to attack the Italian 6-inch gun cruisers *Alberto di Gusisano* and *Alberico da Barbiano* carrying supplies to North Africa. The destroyers hugged the Tunisian coast to avoid the minefields in the Sicilian Channel and as they rounded Cape Bon found the Italian cruisers coming north. Fearing attack from Malta the Italians had decided to abandon the mission. The dark outline of the shore behind them gave the Allied destroyers cover but not much sea room for the turn required to spread their torpedoes. *Sikh* eventually fired all four of her Mk IXs at *Barbiano*, the leading ship, at a range of 1,500 yards and scored two hits. *Legion* also engaged *Barbiano* as her captain Commander RF Jessel thought *Sikh* would follow normal practice and engage the second ship in line. He hit *Barbiano* with the first of two torpedoes but then checked fire, and started a second firing swing aimed at the *Gusisano*. This shift of target while firing seems to have been unique in the annals of torpedo warfare, at least in the Royal Navy. One of the six Mk IXs hit the second cruiser and started a fatal fire. The four destroyers entered Grand Harbour at dawn next day to the cheers of the population of Malta.

A year later, an especially significant torpedo action occurred in the waters climes of the Barents Sea. On 30 December 1942, a U-boat operating south of Bear Island reported a lightly escorted convoy bound for North Russia. The German Commander in North Norway ordered the cruiser *Hipper*, flagship of Vice Admiral Kummetz, and the pocket battleship *Lutzow* escorted by six destroyers to sail and intercept the convoy. It was JW-51B, escorted by the destroyers *Onslow*, the ship of the Senior Officer of the escort, Captain R. St. V. Sherbrooke, *Oribi*, *Obedient*, *Orwell* and *Obdurate*. The gun armament of the ships was particularly poor, most being equipped only with four old 4-inch anti-aircraft guns. But all carried their full outfit of eight Mk IX torpedoes. The other ships of the escort were the destroyer *Achates*, the corvettes *Rhododendron* and *Hyderabad*, the minesweeper *Bramble* and the trawlers *Vizalma* and *Ocean Gem*. Unknown to Kummetz, two 6-inch gun cruisers *Sheffield* and *Jamaica* under the command of Rear Admiral RL Burnett, were also providing cover for the convoy.

Kummetz had devised a good plan in which *Hipper* and three destroyers would attack the convoy at first light, drawing off the escorts and driving the the merchant ships towards *Lutzow* and the remaining three destroyers. As dawn broke on New Year's Eve, JW-51B was faced with a difficult situation. At 0820, the corvette *Hyderabad* sighted two destroyers which were taken to be Russian reinforcements for the escort. Sherbrooke was not satisfied and instructed *Obdurate* to investigate. It was not long before the escort commander's fears were confirmed. At 0930 the Germans opened fire. Sherbrooke signalled his destroyers to join him as he placed his ships between the convoy and the enemy, which was soon identified as *Hipper*. The cruiser's fire was directed against *Achates*, which was hit before *Hipper* shifted fire to *Onslow* at a range of 5• miles. The story is now taken up by the Flotilla Torpedo Officer and second in command of *Onslow*, Lieutenant Commander TJG Marchant.

Marchant had qualified as a Torpedo Officer in 1935: he had served in the battleship *Royal Sovereign*, and then for three years on Atlantic convoys before being appointed to the *Onslow* when she was building at John Brown's Yard on the Clyde. In her he had taken part in a number of Arctic and Malta convoys. His account of his part in the Battle of the Barents Sea gives a vivid insight into the experience of Torpedo Officers in action at that time in World War II. He was on the bridge as Officer of the Watch during the middle watch (midnight to 0400) so that Captain Sherbrooke got some rest. At the end of the middle watch on New Year's Eve, Marchant had gone to his cabin after a quiet night but he was soon awakened by the Navigating Officer, who said that things were warming up and that the Captain wanted Marchant on the bridge. His cabin being situated over the port propeller, he noticed that the ship was picking up speed. As he arrived on the bridge, *Onslow* was swinging on to a westerly course into the leaden, snow-laden cloud base over a smooth and oily swell. Almost immediately, Marchant sighted a dark blurred object off the starboard bow which seemed to be bows-on and bigger than a destroyer. He reported the sighting to Sherbrooke, who altered course towards it. The looming silhouette turned sharply to port and fired a broadside from four twin-turrets. Marchant called out '*Hipper!*' and the Captain came round to starboard to a parallel course of approximately northeast and, at the same time, altered the course of the convoy to the southeast. Torpedo control signals were passed to *Orwell* which was following astern.

It had always been Sherbrooke's intention to keep his ships between a raider and the convoy, and this he did. Meanwhile, *Hipper* continued to fire at the convoy with little success for the best part of an hour and a half, while Sherbrooke's destroyers followed a parallel course, continuing to fire at *Hipper* and pushing her away from the convoy, giving nothing to starboard and thrusting to port whenever she turned away. She had three destroyers following close astern, each with heavier guns than the British but they kept station on *Hipper* and took no part in the action. The action continued with Sherbrooke always thrusting towards the enemy as opportunities arose; it was a tactic which had often been discussed and about which Marchant observed, 'It had always been said that the greatest advantage of the torpedo in the circumstances was to use it as a threat to *Hipper* which had superior speed and freedom of movement.' It was this constant pressure away from the convoy and towards *Hipper* that persuaded Kummetz that he was being led into a trap and, in accordance with his instructions to avoid damage to his ships, he continued to edge away from the threat. At 1010, realising that the convoy was out of range, he shifted target to the leading destroyer.

Sherbrooke and Marchant observed *Hipper's* fall of shot, which was soon perfect for line if not for range, although the first four salvos pitched ahead of and over the British ships. Sherbrooke, as he looked forward, told the navigator to steer for the splashes and to wriggle along the mean line of advance. Marchant, counting the salvos turned to tell Sherbrooke that the one screaming over the ship was the fifth, when a shell struck the top of the funnel, riddling the director and the radar hut and sending a splinter which took out Sherbrooke's left eye and laid it out on his duffle coat, giving Marchant an unpleasant shock as he turned to acknowledge Sherbrooke's remark.

It was evident that Sherbrooke would have to go below to receive medical attention, which he reluctantly agreed to do, but not before he had given the order to turn away and reduce speed. Seeing that *Onslow* was well alight forward, he made a signal to Lieutenant Commander Kinloch, in *Obedient*, to take over command of the escort and to maintain a course towards the head of the convoy. As all wireless aerials had been destroyed, it was decided to rig a jury-aerial and to home Burnett, with his two cruisers towards *Onslow* from their estimated position some 40 or 50 miles to the north.

As *Onslow* limped to the head of the convoy of the starboard beam of the Commodore, the ship's company fought the fires forward and assessed the damage. She was down by the bows and listing, but the speed of the convoy enable her to maintain station. The weather had not changed and there were heavy patches of fog and low cloud. At 1120, Kummetz's plan began to bear fruit. On the bridge of *Onslow* they sighted, approaching silently out of the mist on the starboard bow, the daunting silhouette of *Lutzow* at a range of about 6,000 yards and steering north northwest. They watched, deeply conscious of their predicament. If they could see *Lutzow*, surely the enemy could see Onslow and the forty ships with her? They just stopped breathing, did nothing and waited for the first broadside. Onslow's bridge was silent with anticipation, but nothing happened! As quietly as she slid into view, *Lutzow* slid out, a ghost ship if ever there was one. Many prayers went aloft during those tense moments.

Achates, which had been sent to reinforce *Onslow* at the head of the convoy, was heavily damaged by *Hipper*, and her Captain killed. After gallantly continuing to lay a smoke screen between the enemy and the convoy, she finally succumbed. The minesweeper *Bramble* was sunk by the German destroyers *Eckholdt* and *Beitzen*, but as they withdrew they mistook *Sheffield* and *Jamaica* for their own heavy ships. *Eckholdt* was sunk by the British cruisers but *Beitzen* escaped unharmed. When *Sheffield* and *Jamaica* arrived, *Hipper* was firing on *Obedient* and did not notice the British cruisers until a 6-inch projectile fired at a range of over 6 miles crashed into her superstructure. When *Hipper* had been hit twice more, Kummetz, true to his instructions to avoid damage, decided to terminate the operation and return with his ships to the safety of Altenfjord.

During that afternoon, the fires in *Onslow* were got under control, the list was reduced and the bow was lifted by pumping out flooded compartments. The principal damage and casualties had been caused by two 8-inch shells hitting forward of the bridge. The engine room department and the damage control parties did well during those few hours. Marchant, now in command, realised that *Onslow* was of no practical use to the convoy and considered that her safety was now paramount. He decided to leave the convoy and to proceed at *Onslow's* best speed of 15 knots, hoping to make the Kola Inlet while the quiet weather lasted. She made port early on the following day, in the middle of an air raid, and secured alongside Vaenga Jetty. Sherbrooke and the other wounded were sent to a nearby Royal Naval Hospital, which had been set up some months previously in a disused Russian warehouse. He was later sent home in the destroyer *Oribi*, together with members of the flotilla staff.

Tom Marchant was very typical of his generation of Torpedo Officers, and what follows was his story. At Vaenga, at that time of year, only a light grey smudge would appear on the horizon for about thirty minutes between noon and 1300. Surrounded by this gloom, Marchant was soon in for a surprise. Resting after the battle and the gruelling passage, he was called from his bunk by the quartermaster to speak to a lady. Pulling on his jacket, he opened the door to reveal an attractive woman with shoulder length blonde hair, dressed in a long naval greatcoat with scarlet between four gold shoulder straps, who said that she was the Principal Surveyor and that she had come to see the damage. The Gunnery Officer willingly accompanied her on her inspection, and on completion she and two other Russian officers had tea in Marchant's cabin. Five days later she was back asking for another meeting at which she said that *Onslow* would be repaired at Rostov a mile or two up the river. However, some minutes earlier, another surveyor had told Marchant that repairs would be carried out at Vaenga. On his seeking confirmation, the beautiful Nina merely spread her hands, palms upwards and with a shrug of her attractive shoulders added, 'Ah well, if he says so, then maybe!'

Eventually the work was carried out at Rostov, where a box like structure was spot-welded from the bridge forward. All this was done by women, with trigger-happy sentries at each gangway day and night. On completion, *Onslow* returned to Vaenga to await a homeward bound convoy. But she had to face one more danger before she could sail. At Vaenga, in the gloomy half-light at midday, the Germans staged daily air raids. One Sunday, Marchant had just finished a church service in the shell of the forward mess deck, which still smelt strongly of burnt debris and cordite, and was making his way aft, when he felt a sudden irresistable urge to move the ship. On gaining the quarterdeck, he noticed that a Russian merchantman had anchored nearby and, sensing that it would be a likely target for the German aircraft, he immediately asked his Engineer Officer how soon he could let him have steam to shift berth. Neither the Chief nor the First Lieutenant could understand why Marchant felt it necessary to move the ship but, nevertheless, the latter assembled the cable party on the foc'sle. At 1130 Onslow moved 50 yards to a fresh anchorage. As the manoeuvre was being completed, sounds could be heard of a dog-fight overhead. Within seconds with an ear splitting crescendo, one of the aircraft came crashing down from 10,000 feet, plunging with a devastating thump into the sea on the spot that *Onslow* had vacated minutes before. There is no doubt that the ship would not have survived had Marchant not moved her.

Onslow finally sailed with a homeward bound convoy until it had passed Bear Island, when she proceeded independently to Scapa Flow. As she approached her destination, *Duke of York* was sighted, escorted by three destroyers, and made the signal: 'Pass close to me'. The battleship had cleared lower deck, and with her upper deck crowded with her ship's company was an impressive sight as her Captain called for three cheers for *Onslow*. As the destroyer approached Hoxa Gate, the Commander-in-Chief Home Fleet signalled: 'Pass around the fleet before proceeding to your berth alongside *Tyne*'. All ships of the Home Fleet, big and small, paid tribute to the battered destroyer. As she passed the gate, the trawler attending the gate made the signal: 'Proud to open the gate for you'. Then the battleship *Malaya*, on her way out of harbour, repeated the tribute of the *Duke of York*. Marchant instructed his ship's company to 'just stand there and take it'.

After a slightly hazardous passage of the narrow waters of the Weddel Sound *Onslow* secured alongside *Tyne* on time at 1030 to be visited immediately by Admiral Burnett. It was the end of an action about which the Commander-in-Chief Home Fleet, Admiral Sir John Tovey, was later to say:

The Battle of the Barents Sea was one of the finest examples in either of the two World Wars of how to handle destroyers and cruisers in action with heavier forces. Captain Sherbrooke saved his convoy by going straight into attack his far heavier enemy, using his guns to do what damage they could but relying on his torpedoes, the real menace to the heavier ships, to deter them from closing the convoy.

The Battle of the Barents Sea was not of major significance if it were to be judged by the damage inflicted by the opposing forces, but that would be to underestimate totally the effect which it had upon the morale of the naval forces on both sides and upon the course of the war. When the news reached Hitler he flew into a great rage, demanding the abolition of the German Navy's surface forces, a step which was strongly opposed by Raeder. Faced with Hitler's antagonism, Raeder resigned in disgust and was replaced by Doenitz who managed to persuade the Fuhrer to keep some of the surface units in service.

Almost a year after Sherbrooke's victory the battleship *Scharnhorst* met her end on Boxing Day 1943, in part thanks to the torpedoes of the cruisers *Sheffield*, *Belfast*, *Norfolk* and *Jamaica*, and their eight destroyers, *Savage*, *Saumarez*, *Scorpion*, *Stord* (Royal Norwegian Navy), *Opportune*, *Virago*, *Musketeer* and *Matchless*. In the action the Home Fleet made intelligent use of its superior radar. *Scharnhorst* was taken by surprise, pursued and finally despatched by a combination of the heavy gunfire from the battleship *Duke of York* and torpedoes delivered, almost at will, by the British cruisers and destroyers. The pattern of destroyer attacks had now entered a new phase. It was no longer the practice for flotillas of destroyers to bear down upon the enemy to deliver their torpedoes en masse and usually from one sector. With the introduction of centimetric radar, it was now possible to plot the position, course and speed of the enemy in the comparative comfort of an operations room and to co-ordinate simultaneous torpedo attacks delivered by destroyers from different directions. In a 'star' attack ships were allocated sectors from which to carry out their attacks as co-ordinated by signal from the leader's Operations Room. Only at the last moment did control revert to the bridges of the destroyers where the torpedo sights remained.

This was the last significant surface torpedo action of the war, indeed the last in the history of the Royal Navy. Intimately involved in it was Lieutenant Douglas Stobie, who qualified as a Torpedo Officer in June 1943, one of the 'pressed men' who had not volunteered for the torpedo branch. He initially regarded his duties as the provider of underwater ordnance and electricity as neither glamorous nor exciting but, on his own admission, his gloomy prediction was wrong. His first appointment on completion of his course was as Flotilla Torpedo Officer of the Twenty Sixth Destroyer Flotilla, consisting of the new 'V' class destroyers under construction in the north of England. Stobie always considered his appointment to be a great piece of luck, not only because they were fleet destroyers, but also because the flotilla was to see a great deal of action under the command of a very distinguished officer, Captain Manley L Power. By 1945, Power's flotilla was serving with the East Indies Fleet based at Trincomalee whose task was to harass the lines of communication of the retreating Japanese.

Intelligence was received that the Japanese intended to sail the heavy cruiser *Haguro* and supporting units to cover the evacuation of troops from the Andaman and Nicobar Islands. An interception operation, code named 'Dukedom' , was therefore planned under Vice Admiral HTC Walker, commanding a force which included the battleships *Queen Elizabeth* and *Richelieu*, cruisers and the four escort carriers of the Twenty First Carrier Squadron. Superimposed upon 'Dukedom' was another plan designed to permit ships of the force to take action against subsidiary targets. Code named 'Mitre', it covered sweeps into the Andaman Sea by air and surface forces. As part of this plan Power, in *Saumarez*, was proceeding in company with *Venus, Virago, Vigilant* and *Verulam* on an anti-shipping sweep. He had been keeping in close touch with enemy reports being made by submarines and aircraft. These had included sightings of the *Haguro* and the destroyer *Kamikaze* and he was convinced that these two units were proceeding under cover of the monsoon weather to support the Japanese evacuation operations. He was, therefore, surprised to receive a signal from the Commander-in-Chief to abandon Operation Mitre. He doubted the authenticity of the aircraft enemy report upon which this decision had been based and he decided to press on along an interception course towards the estimated position of the two Japanese warships. Power received no immediate reply to a signal to the C-in-C questioning the abandonment of 'Mitre' but, an hour later, an Avenger aircraft intercepted *Haguro* and made a definite sighting report. Power's stand had been vindicated and he was instructed to proceed to intercept and destroy the enemy ships.

In *Saumarez* the Operations Room team had reached a high state of efficiency. Here, at last, were concentrated all the lessons learnt during the war in the conduct of operations. Destroyers now had an Action Information Organisation which could collect data from a variety of sensors. In charge of the Operations Room team was the Flotilla Anti-Submarine Officer, Lieutenant Reay Parkinson. Assisting him was the Flotilla Torpedo Officer, Lieutenant D. Stobie. Both these officers requalified after the war as Torpedo Anti-Submarine specialists and Stobie later commanded *Vernon*. The operations teams in the ships of the flotilla had also been exercised until they had reached the pitch of perfection demanded by Power. He glared down ominously from his 6 feet 5 inches upon anyone who did not come up to the high standards which he expected. Throughout the flotilla he was regarded with great respect, which augured well for the outcome of this last action between surface forces of World War II.

On the afternoon of 15 May 1945, Power signalled to the flotilla his intention to carry out a night attack upon the enemy force. He realised that against such a powerful adversary he had no alternative. *Haguro* mounted five twin 8-inch gun turrets and eight 24-inch torpedo tubes for oxygen fuelled 'Long Lance' torpedoes. *Kamikaze* was an easier target. She was an old destroyer converted for escort work with three 4.7-inch guns. Her torpedo tubes had been removed and replaced by anti-aircraft armament.

As darkness descended upon the Twenty Sixth Flotilla, ships' companies prepared for action and donned anti-flash gear. Radar operators scanned their screens anxiously until at 2240 Ordinary Seaman Poole in the Operations Room of *Venus*, detected a small blip on his screen. The range of the detection was well beyond that normally accepted as the maximum for Radar Type 293 and the command doubted its veracity. However, Poole was adamant and was able to persuade his Commanding Officer, Commander de Chair, that he had a solid contact. Power ordered *Venus* to close and investigate. On the assumption that Poole was correct a plot was built up which indicated that *Haguro* was now heading for Singapore. At midnight, *Saumarez* made radar contact and the flotilla prepared for a 'star' attack with torpedoes. The timing of the attack was dictated by the need to wait for *Venus* to rejoin, and was set for 0100 on 16 May.

There was a tactical weakness in the 'star' attack concept which was inclined to leave ships attacking from the rear of the target engaging in a stern chase. This was twice the fate of *Saumarez* and the carefully planned 'star' disintegrated leaving her in *Vigilant*'s sector. The situation was further complicted by a breakdown in the timing of the attacks. In the melee which resulted, *Saumarez* was hit by *Haguro*'s 8-inch guns, but not before she had launched her MK IXs, three of which hit the doomed Japanese cruiser. *Verulam*, under cover of *Saumarez*' action, was able to fire torpedoes undetected, hitting *Haguro* again. *Venus*, *Vigilant* and *Virago* pressed home their attacks whilst jostling for position. *Venus* and *Virago* co-operated well and both obtained hits. However, in the confusion of the action, all that could be fairly said was that the credit for *Haguro*'s destruction was shared by the entire flotilla.

No account of surface torpedo warfare would be complete without mention of light coastal craft, the MTBs and their adversaries, the German E-boats. In the early days of the locomotive torpedo, Sleeman had advised young officers to seek glory through service in torpedo boats. That 'glory' now waited in the narrow seas between the United Kingdom and the European mainland. MTBs, manned by regular and reserve officers and men, began to operate from bases at Dover, Felixstowe and Harwich using the original 60 foot British Power Boats. They were soon replaced by 70 foot boats designed and built by Vosper's.

Although a building programme for the new boats had been approved some senior officers doubted that MTBs gave value for money; and since *Vernon* had reliquished resposibilty for training, a tendency had developed at *Hornet* to pitchfork crews into their boats untrained in their weapons and in the handling of these high speed coastal craft. Only one training boat was provided, the experimental *MTB102*, which was completely insufficient to provide anything but sporadic and unscheduled instruction which did little to develop the professionalism, steady nerves and tactical awareness which were later to be the hall-mark of successful coastal force officers. The training of ratings was no better, but their enthusiasm helped them to benefit from experience on the job. There was a great deal of room for improvement, and two contrasting actions illustrate the change which took place.

On 16 September 1940, *MTB29*, Lieutenant Commander A.B.Cole; *MTB30*, Lieutenant D Jermain; and *MTB32*, Lieutenant E N Poland, sailed from Felixstowe bound for Dover. On arrival they refuelled and at dusk left, without formal briefing, for their patrol area off Cap Gris Nez. Poland had only recently arrived at Felixstowe where he had assumed command of *MTB32* without having any experience or instruction in the armament or the engines. As a regular officer he was expected to compensate for inexperience by calling upon his basic training. That night, the sea was calm and the visibility good when they arrived off Gris Nez, where they cut main engines and patrolled at slow speed on their Ford V8 engines. Soon, they sighted the outlines of two large ocean going trawlers. Cole was immediately suspicious that they might be British minelayers; he ordered the MTBs to cut their engines and lie silently in the calm sea while he signalled Flag Officer, Dover. When he received clearance to attack, he called the boats as close as possible, and conducted an oral briefing, shouting instructions. *MTB29* and *MTB30* were to attack leaving *MTB32* in reserve. Poland interpreted his instructions liberally and followed the others into the attack. Both trawlers had quite clearly mistaken the MTBs for E boats, and only at the last moment did they open fire when it was too late to save them from being sunk. The attack was hailed as a great success but it had been sheer luck that the enemy had been surprised by the apparently unaggressive manoeuvres of the MTBs, it did little to dissuade the doubters who were refering to coastal craft as 'Costly Farces'.

Steps were taken to weld coastal forces into a single organisation and a base was set up at Fort William where a training flotilla was established. In November 1940, Rear Admiral Piers K Kekewich was appointed as Flag Officer Coastal Forces and in 1942 a working up base was set up at Weymouth, although by that time coastal forces had achieved a high standard of efficiency thanks to such flotilla commanding officers as Lieutenant Commander EN Pumphrey. In September 1941, almost exactly a year after Cole's action, he was at Dover commanding the 6th MTB Flotilla, when intelligence was received that a convoy was about to leave Boulogne. This time there was no need to set up a patrol area. Pumphrey was able to give his MTBs precise instructions to intercept the convoy off Cap Blanc Nez. *MTB35* (Pumphrey), *MTB218* (Lieutenant CE Bonnell Royal Canadian Navy) and *MTB54* (Lieutenant Per Danielsen Royal Norwegian Navy) proceeded at dusk to engage the convoy.

Patrolling adjacent to the Varne Shallows were two Motor Gun Boats commanded by Lieutenant Stewart Gould, one of the most colourful characters in Coastal Forces. His escapades ashore and afloat were well known and he was respected by officers and men for his courage and powers of leadership. On this occasion he had to make the best of two underpowered boats, each armed with an Oerlikon gun, eight .303 Lewis guns and depth charges. Gould regarded the pitiful performance of his MGBs as a challenge. He remarked that they were so slow that there was no question of running away, the only viable alternative on sighting E boats was to attack. Among his practiced tactics was a plan to release a depth charge about one hundred yards ahead of an enemy vessel and then to lead it over the explosion. It was a manoeuvre which was to prove very effective when he was called to the support of Pumphrey's MTBs,

In contrast Pumphrey's Packard powered MTBs were fast and manouverable. Each carried two 21inch MkVIII torpedoes, a twin 0.5inch powered worked machine gun and .303 inch Lewis guns. Even so they were outgunned by the E boats which carried 37mm gas operated air-cooled automatic guns. After reducing speed and proceeding on one engine using the silencer, the MTBs had not long to wait before they sighted the convoy escorted by armed trawlers and E boats. The enemy was unaware of the presence of the MTBs but they had dropped astern and Pumphrey was obliged to make use of full power to gain bearing. He fired two torpedoes: one misfired, the other hit the rear ship of the convoy. MTB 218 had fired but missed, and she withdrew. MTB 54 then joined Pumphrey and the two MTBs proceeded at full power to regain firing positions from inshore of the convoy.

Further south Gould had been told to go to Pumphrey's assistance. As he approached the convoy he observed high speed craft which he took to be the MTBs, but he was greeted by a hail of bullets which wounded his Lewis gunners and put an engine out of action. Undismayed, Gould pressed home his attack to close range before releasing a depth charge. It knocked out an E boat and caused havoc among the remainder who he left firing wildly ay each other. This action diverted attention from the two MTBs which were able to fire torpedoes, two of which hit their targets. *MTB218 and MTB54* returned safely to Dover but Pumphrey's boat was badly hit and had to be beached after an adventurous return journey.

Pumphrey's action was one of the first of many fought by coastal craft in the narrow seas around Britain and in the Mediterranean. They were often bloody affairs fought at short range by leaders such as Lieutenant Commanders Peter Scott and Robert Hichens, and Lieutenants Peter Dickens, Christopher Dreyer, Tim Bligh and Stewart Gould. Hichens and Gould were killed in 1943, the latter in a gallant daylight attack on a destroyer escorted convoy off Cape Bon. Most of his contemporaries hoped that his extraordinary gallantry would be recognised by the posthumous award of the Victoria Cross, but this was not to be.

Another gallant daylight action fought by destroyers, MTBs and Swordfish must be mentioned, even though, in the face of superior fire power and overwhelming shore based air forces, it was a failure. The vulnerability of destroyers and MTBs to attack by aircraft and the close range weapons of capital ships was no more clearly illustrated than during the abortive attempts to intercept the battlecruisers *Scharnhorst* and *Gneisenau* and the cruiser *Prinz Eugen* during their Channel dash in February 1942.

On 12 February, five MTBs under Pumphrey waited at Dover. The news he received was not encouraging. The three German warships were approaching escorted by a large screen of destroyers, E boats, S boats and fighter aircraft. He could see no way in which his MTBs could approach close enough in daylight and it was now too late to intercept by night. The five MTBs sailed and made straight for the German formation but they could only fire torpedoes from long range and the enemy had no difficulty in avoiding them. Immediately, one of the German destroyers turned in pursuit but just in time Gould arrived with MGB43 and MGB41. Once again he pressed on towards the enemy forcing him to turn away in anticipation of torpedo attack. All that was left for the MTBs was to pick up the survivors of the equally abortive attack by Lieutenant Commander E Esmonde's Swordfish torpedo bombers.

It was not only the MTBs and Swordfish which failed that day. At Harwich, Captain Mark Pizey, a torpedoman, was waiting in command of a destroyer force made up of old V and W class destroyers of the 21st and 22nd Destroyer Flotillas. He had been alerted ten days earlier to the possibility of a channel dash by the German heavy ships and, in anticipation, all confidential books had been landed, semi-armour piercing shells had been provided to replace the high explosive anti-E boat projectiles, and torpedoes had been prepared for firing. It came as a shock when at noon on 12 February a signal was received saying that the German ships were passing Boulogne. *Campbell*, *Vivacious*, *Worcester*, *Mackay*, *Whitshed* and *Walpole* proceeded immediately with the intention of attacking against overwhelming odds. The prospect was almost unbelievably risky, no wonder Pizey called it 'The Charge of the Old Brigade'. When two large echoes appeared on *Campbell's* type 21 radar, Pizey turned to close the contacts. Half an hour later, gun flashes to starboard

The Charge of the Old Brigade 12 February 1942

revealed the presence of a German destroyer and it soon became apparent that they were behind the enemy's destroyer screen. As they turned to close the German heavy ships the rising sea came in green onto the bridge, dimming the gun director telescopes and hampering the guns' crews. In *Mackay*, the after gun took the full force of the turbulent waves, the ramming tool was washed overboard and the captain of the gun was knocked insensible. The First Lieutenant leapt to the assistance of the gun's crew and loaded the gun by hand. In spite of these adverse conditions, *Mackay's* guns crews managed to fire fifty semi armour piercing shells.

Pizey's destroyers pressed home their attacks under heavy fire, zig-zagging all the time to minimise the chances of being hit. *Campbell, Vivacious* and *Worcester* closed to 3,300 yards when *Campbell* turned and fired torpedoes. *Vivacious* and *Worcester* continued to close the enemy unaware that *Campbell* had fired. *Vivacious* fired first and was lucky to escape damage, but *Worcester* at 2,400 yards was a 'sitting duck' and was hit twice in the boiler rooms. She managed to fire her torpedoes in local control, but she was soon lying stopped broadside on to a rough sea and still under heavy fire. The wounded were put into rafts and were picked up by *Campbell* and *Vivacious*. At 1515 *Worcester* had put out the fires and raised steam. Meanwhile, *Mackay*, *Whitshed* and *Walpole* had fired torpedoes from 3,800 yards before retiring behind smoke, believing that they had obtained a torpedo hit. The truth was that all the British torpedoes fired that day failed to find their mark. All the gallantry in the world could not compensate for the bungling of the high command!

Whether they were victories or gallant failures, Sherbrooke's action, the sinking of the *Haguro*, the MTB operations and the 'Charge of the Old Brigade' proved one old lesson. Plans often go awry, but men, well led, highly trained and with faith in their weapons, can turn the tide of victory. *Vernon*, and all the Royal Navy's weapons schools, sought to produce such men and to provide the weapons they needed. These actions, for which descriptions were provided by participating torpedomen, provide a fitting climax to the end of one era in torpedo warfare and the beginning of another.

Surface actions during the war were influenced progressively and significantly by the introduction of improved voice radio communications, radar and direction finding equipment. Until late in 1942 control was exercised by the command, virtually always on open bridges, using visual communications. A year later control had begun to pass to operations teams in the protection of Action Information Centres. In May 1945, in the *Haguro* action, Power was served by a highly skilled team, operating in a comparatively sophisticated centre and led by the Anti-Submarine and Torpedo Officers. It was a development which led after the war to the argument that the officer in control of the operations team did not need the depth of technical knowledge provided by the specialist Long Courses. This argument prevailed and led to the introduction of the Principal Warfare Officer qualification in 1974.

THE THREAT OF DEFEAT BY THE U-BOATS in 1917 had convinced the Admiralty of the need to introduce convoys and of the importance of effective countermeasures, by sea and from the air. Their reaction was to establish an Anti-Submarine Branch with its headquarters in HMS *Osprey* at Portland. The branch was quick to develop a firm liaison with the scientists working to produce the first Asdic sets but, despite this acknowledgement of the submarine danger, the branch remained unfashionable in the minds of the ambitious. Its creation also meant that the Mining Department at *Vernon* was left with the responsibility for the provision of anti-submarine weapons and training of personnel without being involved in the development, use and maintenance of detection equipment, or the evolution of A/S strategy and tactics. This directly contradicted the usual practice in the Royal Navy of the closest possible liaison between the user and the provider. It was not a satisfactory arrangement and it led to many misunderstandings and inefficiencies on the outbreak of war and for some time afterwards.

One fundamental problem was that the efficiency of Asdic had been grossly overestimated. It suited both the A/S Branch and the Naval Staff to do so; the former to expand its small stock of prestige in the Service, the latter to be able to concentrate on apparently more pressing and interesting matters than the arcane novelties of anti-submarine warfare. If Asdic worked, why spend more scarce resources on it ? Many demonstrations were laid on to prove that Asdic had reduced the submarine to impotence; it was described as the underwater eye that stripped from the submarine its cloak of invisibility which had been its principal weapon. Insufficient attention was paid to the experience of *Havock* and *Basilisk* which had become targets for Italian submarines while on the Nyon Patrol in 1937. Neither British destroyer had been able to maintain Asdic contact with her attacker. In *Havock's* case the Italian submarine *Iride* fired torpedoes which narrowly missed. *Havock* had immediately counter-attacked but she soon lost Asdic contact and *Iride* had no difficulty in escaping.

No development of depth charges, throwers or rails took place in the inter-war years and no new A/S weapons were contemplated. A staff of only a Lieutenant Commander, a Gunner (T) and a Torpedo Gunner's Mate were in charge of sea trials for depth charges and their pistols, and they also had to cover other underwater demolition charges. 1939, therefore, found anti-submarine vessels having to rely upon primitive weapons little better than those which had existed in 1918. The Mark VII depth charge was essentially the same as the Type D of the First World War. It contained an explosive charge of 290 lbs of Amatol and was fitted with a pistol operated by a hydrostatic valve fed through a variable leak hole, allowing for six depth settings from 50-500 feet. One of *Vernon's* first wartime tasks was to set up an equipment trials organisation at the ports where the reserve A/S trawlers were being fitted out with asdic and Mk VIIs.

The events of September 1939, notably the sinking of the carrier *Courageous* which was ill-advised employed on anti-U-boat 'hunting' patrol, dispelled the illusion that Asdic alone provided the answer to the U-boats. Divided rsponsibility, however, blunted the British response. Anti-submarine weapons were not central to *Vernon's* interests in those busy days when every effort in the Mining Department was put into overcoming the menace of the magnetic mine. More importantly, *Vernon*, which was supposed to represent the user's interest throughout underwater weapons development and production, was institutionally separated from both sets of users of anti-submarine weapons, which included not only the Royal Navy's Anti-Submarine Branch but also Royal Air Force Coastal Command. There had been a series of informal monthly meetings between *Osprey* and *Vernon* held shortly before the war but these seem to have ceased after September 1939 as each establishment became preoccupied with its own war work. There was no liaison between *Vernon* and the Anti-Submarine Department Scientists after the latter were evacuated to a new Anti-Submarine Experimental Establishment at Fairlie in Scotland in 1940. The RAF had rebuffed suggestions from *Vernon* that an air dropped depth charge might be a useful addition to their inventory of air dropped weapons.

Even before the sinking of *Courageous* it had become clear that the time fused 100-lb anti-submarine bombs developed by the Air Ministry were ineffective against submarines and dangerous to the aircraft that dropped them. On 5 September an RAF Anson swooped on the submarine *Sealion* in the North Sea and dropped two A/S bombs. The weapons bounced on the surface initiating the fuses but bringing them up under the aircraft where they exploded, forcing the Anson to ditch. On this occasion it was as well that the bombs proved ineffective agaist this British submarine. But when dropped on U-boats the bombs were equally useless, and dangerous to the users, accounting for two Royal Navy Skuas and an RAF Anson on 14-15 September.

Hardly surprisingly, Boyd was asked by a concerned member of the Air Staff why a depth charge had not been produced for use by aircraft. He replied that *Vernon* had never been asked for one but he could have it designed within one week. The Staff Requirement eventually came in March 1940, after Boyd's departure, and the project was delayed further by the Air Ministry deciding in April that it did not want depth charges after all. There were indeed several difficulties to be overcome. Not only did a new pistol have to be designed that could be pre-set for depth before the charge was loaded on to the aircraft and would not be prone to explosion in the event of forced landings but the bulky Mk VII depth charge was difficult to marry to existing bomb bays and bomb release gear. It could only be dropped at low speed and low altitude, hardly the most desirable conditions for an attacking aircraft.

Coastal Command, however, frustrated by the poor performance of its A/S bombs, sent an urgent 'SOS' via the Air Staff to the Admiralty in June 1940. Development began, almost immediately, of the new pistol for the Mk VII and new smaller depth charge for aircraft that could carry a 250-lb bomb. By September, the new Mk X pistol was ready, but difficulties in carrying the weapon and general shortages of Mk VII charges delayed the general service use of the air dropped version until Spring 1941. Even then the large 450 lb charge fitted with an aerodynamic detachable nose amd tail was restricted to a dropping height of 100 feet at speeds not in excess of 100 knots; even with this limitation the Mk X pistol proved to have a high failure rate.

The new smaller charge, the Mk VIII, was ready by May 1941. Its diameter was limited to 11 inches and length to 38 inches. This ruled out the fitting of the Mk VII type 'through' primer charge which could be inserted after the pistol was fitted. Instead a new 'blind' primer tube was used in which the primer had to be inserted before the pistol. The new weapon was tested at double the limits of the Mk VII but showed a tendency to tumble and ricochet on hitting the water. A new cylindrical tail solved the problem and the Mk VIII entered service in May.

Both the Mk VII Airborne and the Mk VIII proved a disappointment; U-boats were attacked and straddled but escaped. The newly founded Operational Research Section of Coastal Command soon diagnosed the problem as not one of the weapons themseves but in the way they were being used. The Mk X pistols were being set too deep, 100-150 ft, when virtually all submarines were being attacked either on the surface or very close to it. Immediately the Mk Xs were altered to their minimum depth, 50 ft, a relic of the pistol's ancestry as fifty feet was the minimum depth any surface ship could drop a depth charge; an aircraft, however, required a much shallower setting. By mid-1941 *Vernon* (M) had developed a close relationship with the Armaments Directorate of the Ministry of Aircraft Production. This provided a ready channel of communication with the users in Coastal Command and in October 1941 development began of a Mk XII pistol with a setting of of 25 ft; it entered service with both charges the following month. In order to improve both reliability and dropping height, development of a still further improved pistol was immediately begun and this began to be fitted from March 1942. This allowed a 50 percent increase in dropping height and speed for the Mk VII Airborne.

The transformation in effectiveness was was not quite as great as Coastal Command had hoped. The Mk VIII depth charges sank too fast and carried a bubble of air down with them which caused them to explode rather deeper than intended, outside the lethal radius of the relatively small charges they carried. The Mk VIIs did not share this problem as not only was their lethal radius bigger but the nose and tail fittings had always broken away on impact with the water. In January 1942, development began of a new small charge with concave nose and new Mk III tail that would also break off on entry. The Mk XIs appeared in May 1942 and proved a great success; they went off at a 'genuine 25 ft setting'. Still further improved depth charge pistols for air dropped weapons, the Mk XVI, which combined this setting with improved safety and the Mk XIV that was redesigned to allow greater speed and height of release, entered service in July and September 1942 respectively. With the latest pistols the Mk VIII charge could be dropped at up to 750 ft and 175 knots and the Mk XI at up to 1250 ft and 250 knots. Once the right bureaucratic mechanisms had been worked out *Vernon(M)* could respond quickly to the demands of Coastal Command but the delays in opening these channels meant that it took until mid 1942 for British anti-submarine aircraft to grow fully effective teeth.

Surface ships, therefore, were the major U-boat killers in the early years of the war. When a submerged U-boat was detected by Asdic, the ship turned towards the contact, closing the range and then running in on a collision course. When the transmission from the Asdic set and the echo coincided, the Asdic operator reported 'instant echoes'. Contact was then lost as the ship passed over the target and the depth charge pattern was laid. The standard pattern was five charges, three laid in line by a stern mounted rack and one on each side using Mk II Thornycroft depth charge throwers.

Because the early Asdic sets had no means of determining depth, the settings on the depth charges had to be made by guesswork. There was a rule of thumb method of measuring depth which was based upon an assessment of the range at which contact with the target was lost. This theory was based upon the fact that the lobe pattern of the Asdic beam was such that when the target passed under it and contact was lost the range was less than three to six times the depth of the target. Since it was safe to assume that the submarine would not be at a greater depth than 300 feet, a depth setting on the depth charge of 150 feet would be a reasonable guess. Anti-submarine tactics and methods of attack in the early months of the war were based upon a primitive understanding of the problem. It was not surprising that less than five per cent of attacks sank a U-boat.

It might have been assumed that, as more experience was obtained, the average skill of Asdic operators would increase and attacks would be made with greater accuracy but, because of the inevitable dilution of peace-time trained personnel with new, less well trained operators , the contrary was true. There was, therefore, an urgent need to improve the effectiveness

Starling's depth charge crew leave a visiting card

of depth charges and the way they were used. One obvious solution was to increase the number of depth charges which could be laid in a single pattern. This was achieved by doubling the number of depth charge rails and adding up to three more throwers each side; this allowed patterns of ten or fourteen charges. In order to increase the volume of water covered by the charges still further a new Mk VII Heavy depth charge was introduced at the end of 1940. A cast iron weight fixed to one end gave a sinking speed through the water of 16.5 feet per second, compared with 10 feet per second of the standard Mk VII; a new Mk IX pistol gave depth settings down to 550 feet. In a ten-charge pattern, which became the standard the heavy charge was set 100 feet or more deeper than the pistols in normal Mk VII charges. This gave a layering effect which greatly increased the lethality of the pattern; success rates became 20 per cent, a four fold increase.

The new multi-charge patterns created problems of congestion and handling on board. To help solve these difficulties a new Depth Charge Thrower Mk IV was developed with a piston type non-expendable carrier. It went to sea for the first time in the escort destroyer *Winchelsea* in September 1941. It was fitted into other escorts as quickly as possible. Another development begun in 1941 to increase lethality was a 2,000 lbs 'blockbuster' depth charge that could be fired from a 21-inch torpedo tube (for comparison, a Mk VII had a 290 lb charge). The Mk X was given a slow sinking speed to allow the destroyer to get safely away from the explosion. It entered service in March 1942 but its high minimum safe speed led to few being used in action. When it was used , however, it had a fifty per cent kill rate, a proportion *Vernon* thought 'very satisfactory'.

Improvements in depth charges were indeed welcome but it was no secret that the key to fundamental improvement in A/S tactics was finding some way of engaging the submarine while the escort was still in sonar contact. This required an ahead thrown weapon and such a device, using small contact charges, on the lines of the First World War anti-submarine howitzers, had first been considered by scientists at *Osprey* in 1938 and discussed with *Vernon* at pre-war monthly meetings. After communications with *Vernon* had broken down The Underwater Research Establishment at Fairlie completed the design of what came to be known as the 'Fairlie Mortar'. Two sets of ten barrelled mortars with movable, stabilised barrels would be positioned one on each side of the escort vesel's fo'c'sle. Each bomb would contain 20 lbs of explosive fused for contact. A number of alternative approaches to projecting the bombs were tried and Fairlie enlisted the Chief Scientist Propulsive Devices Establishment (CSPDE) to develop rocket projectiles, the Chief Superintendent of Dockyards (CS of D) a spigot mortar, and the Miscellaneous Weapons Development Department (DMWD) an alternative spigot projector based on an army design. All these weapons were contact fused but at the beginning of 1940 Fairlie also began to work with Vickers on triple barrelled mortar for depth charges.

All this seems to have been done with the responsible establishment at *Vernon* in complete ignorance, communications with the A/S Department's technical developments having broken down after *Osprey*'s scientists moved to Scotland. *Vernon* , of course, had ideas of its own and encouraged its long standing supplier Thornycroft to design a five barrelled trainable thrower known as 'The Five Wise Virgins', with a range of 200 yards for mounting on an escort's fo'c's'le. At the end of 1940, the Admiralty began to impose some order on this increasingly chaotic situation. The Directorate of Naval Ordnance held a first co-ordination meeting in January 1941 and the Controller ensured that the authority of the Directorate of Torpedoes and Mines and *Vernon(M)* was progressively re-asserted. The 'Five Wise Virgins' was tested in the destroyer *Whitehall* in July 1941 and a smaller version fitted to a corvette shortly afterwards but, despite its connections with the project, *Vernon* decided against fixed long range mortars. They were not stabilised, they required considerable stiffening work on the ships, and the depth charges they would throw had unreliable pistols. Work at Leigh Park began on a new weapon, Squid, that would be free of these problems.

In the meantime, DMWD, set up in 1940 under Commander Charles Goodeve, fresh from his degaussing work, developed an army spigot mortar into the multiple Hedgehog, incorporating design features from the abandoned Fairlie Mortar. Hedgehog ran its first sea trials in 1941 in the destroyer escort *Westcott*. The weapon projected twenty four contact fused explosive charges, each containing 30 lbs of TNT. The bombs landed in a 40 yard diameter circle about 200 yards ahead of the firing ship. Electric motors allowed training through a narrow arc of 20 degrees and simple 'follow the pointer' gyro gear was later introduced to compensate for roll.

In early 1942, even before the roll stabilisation system was perfected, Hedghog was deemed ready for service. The Superintendent of Mine Design was put in charge of production, and *Vernon(M)* made responsible for sea trials. As many vessels as possible were fitted and Hedhehog was at sea in 100 ships by the end of 1942. A few were of a new 'split' design that allowed retention of the entire forward gun armament in ships that needed it. 'Split Hedgehog' first went to sea in the former Admiralty yacht *Enchantress* in July 1942 and was introduced operationally the following year.

With the accelerated programme, *Vernon(M)* could not ensure the complete safety of Hedgehog. It had taken over another establishment's weapon and important safety requirements where overlooked. In the autumn of 1943, a serious explosion occurred during the firing of a salvo in the destroyer *Escapade*. Most of the projectiles in the mounting detonated prematurely, resulting in twenty fatal casualties on the bridge, the forecastle mess decks and amongst the Hedgehog crew. The devastation caused was so great that no positive evidence could be produced to account for the accident. Detailed examination was however made of many thousands of live projectile fuses and a tentative diagnosis made. The accident was almost certainly caused by an ill fitting plug, which should have rendered the projectile safe whilst it was on the mounting. The plug easily became loose, thereby rendering the fuse partially armed. As a result of this accident, a grub screw was introduced to provide a more definite lock.

More important, however, was Hedgehog's failure as a U-boat killer. In theory, its chance of sinking a U-boat with a single Hedgehog attack had been calculated at 50-60 per cent but it was not until November 1942, and after numerous attacks, that the first Hedgehog kill was recorded. During the following year Hedgehog's operational success was less than 10 per cent, ie half the theoretical probability of a pattern of ten depth charges. Ships companies disliked Hedgehog because its bombs did not explode unless it hit a target and when it killed it gave few of the tell-tale signs of a depth charge attack. *Vernon(M)* began a propaganda campaign to increase confidence and an equally intensive effort to deal with teething problems with mountings and fuses.

The success of the staffs at Havant in producing and fitting Hedgehog to escort vessels had far outstripped the training which was required to familiarise the ships' anti-submarine teams. This problem was exacerbated by the large number of new officers and men being drafted into the still expanding escort force. In order to find out the real situation an enquiry was carried out in the Hedgehog fitted ships operating from the convoy escort base at Londonderry. This re-emphasised the need for better training for the Asdic and weapon teams to improve tactics and maintenance. An Asdic bearing recorder helped improve fire control and the operational successes of the Hedgehog were gradually increased until by the second half of 1944 the probability of success reached almost 30 per cent.

The introduction of Hedgehog brought about a radical change in the Torpedo Branch. Drill had traditionally been an anathema to torpedomen, but now the Hedgehog weapons' crews were drilled as expertly as any gun's crew, and control drill was exercised regularly on board each ship. Ashore, Hedgehog mountings were set up and made to roll realistically: they were connected to mobile anti-submarine teachers, in which emphasis was laid on giving the proper control orders in a Hedgehog attack. Every Commanding Officer was required to attend lectures on the operation of the weapon, its limitations and its advantages in an attack on the shallow submarine. During exercises, every ship carried out at least two Hedgehog attacks, using full patterns of practice projectiles. By such means confidence in the weapon was greatly improved, and so were the results obtained. Commanding Officers soon learnt that to obtain success with Hedgehog, attacks had to be conducted in absolute quietness, the Asdic team being isolated from outside noise and interference and in good communications with the Commanding Officer.

In September 1941, explosive trials carried out by the Director of Naval Ordnance had cast doubt upon the ability of the Hedgehog projectile to rupture the pressure hull of the submarine. This unwelcome news prompted a staff requirement for an ahead-thrown weapon projecting a contact explosive charge twice the size of the Hedgehog projectile. The Fairlie Mortar was resurrected in a new and larger form, called Parsnip. Work on this project proceeded throughout 1942 and, in February 1943, the prototype was fitted in the destroyer *Ambuscade*. It consisted of two fabricated steel units, each of ten barrels. The units, which were located on each side of the forecastle, fired a half circular pattern with the centre 250 yards ahead of the mounting. The mountings were power stabilised and could be trained either side of the bow to a maximum of 20 degrees. The total weight of the projectile was 120 lbs, containing 65 lbs of explosive.

The trials of Parsnip were successful but it was shelved. Closer examination of the Hedgehog projectile had established that doubts about its power were groundless. Moreover, the work at Leigh Park on Squid made a larger contact weapon redundant and user reaction to Hedgehog made investment in a new device that did not create satisfying explosions undesirable. Squid consisted of three barrels of 12-inch bore built into a gyro stabilised mounting. The weapon fired a triangular pattern of depth charges ahead of the ship; the triangle had 40 yard sides and its centre was normally about 275 yards from the bow. Normally two mountings were carried, the bombs of each being set to 60 ft apart in depth to cover a greater volume. Each finned charge contained just over 200 lbs of explosive fused by a clockwork mechanism set automatically by the ship's Type 147 depth measuring sonar designed to support the system.

Although prototype trials at Thornycroft's Woolston range were not yet complete, the need for the new weapon seemed so great that sea trials were started in *Ambuscade* in May 1943 and production orders were placed before either of these sets of trials were completed. The first production mounting was fitted to the new 'Castle' class corvette, *Hadleigh Castle* completed in September 1943. Only twelve months had passed since development work had started at Leigh Park. Single Squids were fitted to new construction *Castle* class corvettes and twins to new *Loch* class frigates from April 1944. Between sixty and seventy ships were equipped with Squid including one destroyer, *Escapade* that received a twin mounting at the beginning of 1945. Once again it took time to get the new ahead throwing weapon fully operational and the first kill was not scored until 31 July when *Loch Killin* sank *U333*. A week later the same ship sank *U736*; three Squid patterns had disposed of two U-boats. The success rate in late 1944 was eighteen per cent for single Squid and twice that for double Squid; by 1945 all Squid fitted ships were scoring 60 per cent success rates per attack.

Although Hedgehog and Squid helped to maintain Allied supremacy over the U-boats, they arrived too late to be a decisive factor in the victory in the North Atlantic in 1943, which was due mainly to the introduction of long range aircraft to cover the mid-Atlantic 'gap', the concentration of escorts allowed by larger convoys and the insight into German U-boat activities provided by code-breaking. As well as providing aircraft with the means to kill U-boats, *Vernon's* main contribution was probably in ensuring maximum efficiency in the use of depth charges with the introduction of new equipment and techniques for loading, handling and training. August 1942, had seen the introduction of 'Depth Charge Drillers' to help train crews at escort bases, and firing clocks and depth setting order instruments in the escorts.

The division between Torpedomen and the Anti-Submarine Branch cast its shadow over the requirement for better training and operational practice. The Anti-Submarine Branch had never been regarded as a high road to promotion and it was natural that it would seek to exploit its new-found position in the forefront of the British war effort at sea by asserting control of all aspects of anti-submarine warfare, including the development and maintenance of anti-submarine weapons and the training of personnel to use them. These ambitions were strongly resisted at *Vernon*, where any intrusion into the torpedomen's responsibilites were resented. Lieutenant GR Grocock, who qualified as a Torpedo Officer at *Vernon* in 1941, recalls the unhappy situation which existed.

By the time Grocock was appointed to the Mining Instructional Section, the idiosyncratic Porky Veale was in charge. Veale was the very last person to accept any criticism of *Vernon's* instructional techniques, especially from another specialist branch. The contention was that torpedo ratings were leaving *Vernon* improperly trained in depth charge drill. There were several reasons for this unfortunate state of affairs. Training in anti-submarine weapons was not accorded the high priority that it should have had; and secondly, what training there was, was concentrated upon the construction, design, and maintenance of depth charges, depth charge rails and depth charge throwers. It was considered that responsibility for firing the throwers and operating the depth charge rails lay with the ships' A/S teams. Furthermore, drill and maintenance would be of little value if the depth charge could not be aimed accurately, and little or no thought had been given in *Vernon* to this important aspect of the problem; it was assumed that the charge sank at a uniform speed and straight to its detonating point. This assumption led to great inaccuracy and it was not until 1942 that trials to ascertain the trajectory of depth charges were carried out.

In the early years of the war, training in anti-submarine weapons at *Vernon* did little credit to anyone; and it was fortunate that, in due course, a major row ensued which resulted in considerable improvements in all aspects of anti-submarine weapon training. However, torpedomen found that they had to tread warily where their responsibilities marched with those of the anti-submarine specialists. Typical of these occasions was the experience of Grocock when appointed as Torpedo Training Officer on the staff of Commodore Western Approaches at Londonderry. On arrival, in March 1943, he was told by the Torpedo Officer already on the staff that the appointment of a Training Officer had been made in response to complaints by the Anti-Submarine Branch that the Torpedo branch was only interested in the maintenance of anti-submarine weapons and that it took no interest in the training of personnel to use them. Grocock found that there was some justification in this claim, but it was not solely the fault of the Torpedo Branch. Indeed, there were no facilities available for training crews in the use of the new Hedgehog weapon, and no lecture rooms were provided in which to give the necessary instruction. He took steps to have a Hedgehog drill equipment erected alongside the depth charge driller; but he had to appear before the Commander-in-Chief Western Approaches in order to obtain financial approval for these improvements. Meanwhile, Commodore Simpson, Commodore Western Approaches, expressed his opinion that it was more logical for anti-submarine weapon training to be carried out by the Anti-Submarine Officer, leaving the torpedomen responsible only for maintenance. Grocock successfully resisted this suggestion, but he reported that he had a 'rough ride'.

Grocock's enthusiasm resulted in his appointment to the staff of the Commodore Western Isles at Tobermory, where all newly commissioned escort vessels proceeded for a working-up period under the eagle eye of one of the most feared and respected torpedomen, Vice Admiral Sir Gilbert Stephenson. Stephenson had retired from the Royal Navy in 1928 with the rank of Rear Admiral. During the First World War his enormous energy had been wasted in trying to make the Otranto Barrage prevent the U-boats from leaving the Adriatic. When war broke out in 1939, he was one of the many senior officers to be appointed as Commodores in Charge of Convoys though he was soon recalled to set up an organisation to administer anti-submarine patrols off the coast of Norway. The German invasion of that country ended any thought of that job and he found himself responding to the First Sea Lord's instructions to set up a working-up base for escort vessels at Quiberon Bay on the French coast near Lorient. Once again, the Germans got there first and it was decided to establish the working-up base at Tobermory.

Before long the reputation of this little man was known throughout the Western Approaches. He glared, rugged and stern faced, at new arrivals while the tufts of hair on his cheek bones added to his fierce countenance. He was already known to his contemporaries as 'Buggy' or 'Monkey' Stephenson, but it was not long before the ceaseless and tremendous energy with which he approached his task had earned him the title of 'Terror of Tobermory'. Every student of the Battle of the Atlantic is aware of the many and legendary tales told about this remarkable officer. There is no doubt that he is counted as one of the great characters of the Royal Navy but, equally, if less well appreciated, is that his often unconventional approach to this important training and working-up task was, equally without doubt, responsible for achieving the high standard of efficiency of the Allied escort vessels which, until the end of the war, maintained the upper hand in the struggle against the U-boats. His task was to ensure that properly trained and motivated ships' companies were ready to be go into battle in the shortest possible time. In this task, he was completely successful, and his fame will last as long as there is a Royal Navy.

In order to instil a sense of urgency into the ship's companies of vessels working-up at Tobermory, Stephenson continually devised, for the whole five years of his time in command, a series of evolutions and tests for which he became famous. Grocock, fresh from his unhappy experiences at London-derry, went to Tobermory, apprehensive about meeting this already legendary figure and wondering how he would react to Stephenson's style of command. He comforted himself with the thought that, after all, Stephenson was a Torpedo Officer and that he would welcome one of his branch which had so far not been represented on his staff. When Grocock presented himself to the Commodore he was confronted with a frown and a stony silence which lasted for several minutes. Standing awkwardly, shifting his weight from one foot to the other, the young Torpedo Officer waited for the Commodore to welcome him to the staff. Without looking up from a paper which he was studying, he remarked coldly, 'I did not ask for a 'T'. I do not want a 'T. How long will it take you to become A/S?'

Grocock left the Commodore's cabin downhearted but determined that the Torpedo Branch would establish its position at Tobermory as the authority responsible for the maintenance and operation of anti-submarine weapons. He became the butt of many of the Commodore's asides and witticisms but 'although the ground shook at times', the Commodore was eventually persuaded that a Torpedo Officer on his staff was useful. When the first Squid-fitted ship arrived to work up at Tobermory, Grocock was well acquainted with the weapon and was finally able to consolidate his position. It was just as well, for at that time the enemy started to use the Gnat homing torpedo in the Western Approaches and the Foxer was developed and fitted for use by all ships. This turn of events led to the appointment of a Torpedo Officer, Commnader DF Fuller, to the staff of the Commander-in-Chief

Western Approaches and, from that time onwards, there was no more argument about the division of responsibility for anti-submarine affairs.

As well as the introduction of Squid and Foxer, 1943 saw improvement in depth charges and their use. The fourteen charge pattern was found to be inefficient because of the mechnical damage it caused to the depth charge pistols, and a new drill for the release of patterns was developed. The effectiveness of the standard Mk VII charges was also improved by the introduction of the Minol II explosive in the Mk VII*, which was given to as many escorts as possible. This improved charge was fitted for use with primer fitting safety gear which *Vernon(M)* had devised in the previous summer. Extra deep settings were introduced for the Mk IX pistol in the Mk VII depth charge and a similar modification was added to the Mk X 'blockbuster'

By 1944, the escort forces were operating with their 'tails up' with ample equipment and excellent training. Air/sea co-operation was extremely effective and the air dropped Mk XI depth charge proved itself more effective than ever. It was adopted by the Americans and fitted with a new Mk IV tail and new pistols to allow arming in flight. To deal with the threat from midget submarines a small depth charge with a 55 lb charge, the Mk XII, was developed for use by coastal forces. A larger version with a 120 lb charge was introduced for offensive use against enemy convoys. Early 1945 saw *Vernon(M)* involved in a range of developments; power stabilisation for Hedgehog, fast sinking charges, a Mk V depth charge thrower, a twin pistol air dropped depth charge to cope with Schnorkel fitted U-boats and improved pistols for surface dropped charges. None were, however, adopted by the war's end.

Vernon played a part in the development of another key anti-submarine development, the Leigh light. As a result of suggestions put forward by Squadron Leader Humphrey De Vere Leigh and supported by *Vernon's* Electrical Department, *Vernon* was asked, in early 1941, to assist in the development of a suitable searchlight for anti-submarine work in large Royal Air Force bombers. At the time, bombers employed on anti-submarine Atlantic patrols had radar equipment which allowed them to approach to about one mile from a submarine with considerable accuracy but then without a means of sighting the target, they were unable to attack. Flares had proved unsatisfactory and nothing less than a searchlight appeared to be the solution to the problem. The only suitable searchlight available was the naval 20-inch Mk IV, which was adapted to fit into a 24-inch projector and to operate on the 150 amp electrical current available in the aircraft. In February 1941 the first Wellington was equipped and was ready for trials. It was immediately successful and a large number of other aircraft were equipped. This success was followed by the development of a self-contained searchlight unit built into a nacelle for use by flying boats and other types of aircraft. In *Vernon* further development was carried out to keep the diameter of the searchlight down to a minimum. The rapid development of a searchlight for use in anti-submarine aircraft was due to the close liaison between the Royal Air Force and *Vernon*.

Vernon produced originally two versions of the modified 20-inch Mk IV searchlight. The first supplies of these two types were provided by *Vernon* by conversion of lamps from Admiralty stocks. The Electrical Department converted ninety four lamps to tide over the interim period before the

Leigh light could be put into production by contractors. The spread of the beam from these searchlights was insufficient for the more inexperienced air crews to pick up the target. Work was, therefore, carried out at *Vernon* to provide a diverging lens which would be interchangeable with the existing front glass to give a horizontal spread of 10 to 12 degrees. This greatly enhanced the chances of picking up a target in the beam.

The success of the Leigh light in Coastal Command aircraft was soon apparent, and it was not long before a proposal was received from the Director of Anti-Submarine Warfare for a light which could be carried by Swordfish aircraft operating from escort carriers. In very quick time, the design had been completed of a small spherical searchlight which was known as the Pumpkin. It was 19 inches in diameter and had a 16 inch reflector. The total weight of the equipment, including the battery and fixing arrangements, was 200 lbs. By removing the torpedo crutches from the aircraft, the net additional weight was 130 lbs. and a Swordfish, fitted with Pumpkin, could still carry its full load of six 250 lb depth charges.

A final anti U-boat device developed by *Vernon* which deserves mention originated in another Churchillian memo to the First Sea Lord on 21 September 1939, written after his visit that day to *Vernon*:

Deputy Chief of the Naval Staff and I were much impressed with the so-called Actaeon net against torpedoes on which the VERNON are keen. This net was introduced at the end of the late war. It is a skirt or petticoat which is only effective when the vessel is in motion. The VERNON declare that a vessel can steam 18 knots with it on. The LACONIA is to be tried out with one. The net is of thin wire and large mesh. It should be easy to make in large quantities very quickly. I suggest that this is a matter of the highest urgency and significance. it should be fitted on merchant ships, liners, and also, indeed, above all upon ships of war having solitary missions without destroyer protection. Could not a committee be formed before the week is out which would grip this idea, already so far advanced by the naval authorities, and see whether it cannot be brought into the forefront of our immediate war preparations. If it is right, it would require a very large-scale application.

It was not quite as easy as Churchill had imagined. A garage in Southsea was taken over for the design of nets capable of dealing with 21-inch torpedoes and the liner *Queen of Bermuda* was used for experiments before the end of 1939. Designs were sent to the Admiralty and in January 1942, a new and much more improved net underwent successful trials. In anticipation of success, arrangements had been made in the previous August with the United States to equip fifty merchantmen which were being built in American yards. Eventually, hundreds of merchant ships were so fitted but only fifteen were saved by the nets, which were abandoned in 1944. They were unpopular with merchant seamen as they interfered with the life-saving arrangements and the loading and discharging of cargo, although anything which would contribute in a material way to the defence of the ship against U-boat attack was tolerated. In British merchant ships, virtually new crews might be signed on for every voyage. This meant that new net handling teams might have to be trained each time a merchant ship sailed. The nets themselves had a limited life and they were only streamed if the presence of U-boats was known or strongly suspected.

In 1945, the Germans introduced new submarines of radically improved design capable of high underwater speeds. The Anti-Submarine Branch was faced with the task of devising new tactics for dealing with them. Detection equipment with much enhanced performance would need to be brought into service as quickly as possible. In the weapons field, the Torpedo Branch were confronted with an equally urgent task. The range and performance of Hedgehog and Squid would no longer be adequate. Consequently, in the final days of hostilities, scientists at the Mine Design Department were considering how a mounting similar to the Squid could be trained by tilting the cradles out of the vertical plane and, at the same time, compensate for the rolling and pitching of the ship. One of these scientists was still contemplating this problem whilst lying in his bath. Eyeing the male profile objectively, he began to move his hips and thighs as if they were a model of the forepart of an anti-submarine vessel. The male appendage became an anti-submarine mortar. It is claimed that the results of the ad hoc experiment led, in due course, to the development of the Limbo three- barrelled mortar, which eventually replaced the Squid!

Although the negative results of the division between the Anti-Submarine and Torpedo branches had been overcome in great measure by the time the Battle of the Atlantic was won the challenge of the new submarine only emphasised the need for a combined Branch. This, and the creation of a separate Electrical Branch was announced in Admiraly Fleet Order 1012/45. Implementing this order, which caused considerable resentment amongst the existing branches, would prove almost as difficult as winning the Battle of the Atlantic.

THE TORPEDO BRANCH HAD ALWAYS been closely associated with submariners and its future would make it even more dependent upon this relationship. In 1907 Fisher had drawn attention to this deadly partnership, which was to persist throughout two world wars and beyond. The role of torpedomen in submarine operations was vital; if they failed to supply and maintain efficient torpedoes, a submarine would be largely ineffective, even if in other respects it had both a strategic and tactical advantage over surface vessels. The truth of this statement was dramatically demonstrated when at the outbreak of the Second World War, when German torpedoes proved to be disastrously defective. The supply of reliable and effective torpedoes for British submarines should have been assured by the successful trials of the 21-inch Mk VIII torpedo in 1928; but good house-keeping seemed to justify making use of the large stocks of 21-inch Mk II and Mk IV torpedoes of First World War design. Until production of the Mk VIII could be stepped up, it was necessary to call upon these reserves and some were fitted with larger warheads from later marks of torpedo to increase their striking power.

From the submariner's point of view the completion of a successful torpedo attack upon a selected target involved both tactics and fire control. In both world wars the torpedoes with which British submarines were armed required an approach 'unseen and undetected' to a position 1200 yards or so roughly on the beam of the target, with the bow pointing some 10 to 20 degrees ahead of it (depending upon target's course and speed). Using the Captain's estimations of target and movement, obtained by a combination of hand plotting of successive bearings by periscope or Asdic and observation of the target's bow wave and other factors, the fire control instrument (affectionately known as the 'fruit machine' calculated the amount of 'aim-off' (Director Angle or DA) required. This was then set on the periscope, and when the point of aim chosen on the selected target crossed the hairline the order was given to fire. The torpedoes, hand set to run at a depth appropriate to the target, were fired in a straight running hosepipe salvo of two or more. Firing intervals were governed by the lateral 'spread' required to allow for errors in the estimation of the course and speed of the target. The lesson of the First World War was that the maximum number of torpedoes should be available to strike against fast moving and well protected targets. British submarines from the 1920s onwards were given six internal tubes facing forward and the 'T' class submarines launched from 1937 onwards had in addition four external tubes (two of these were later turned to face aft together with a fifth external tube). The smaller 'S' and 'U' class boats built at the same time as the 'T's carried six tubes forward, two mounted externally in the early 'U's although these were removed in most later boats of the class as they interfered with sea keeping on the surface. Once external tubes were fired they could not be reloaded until the boat returned to base. The more important the target the larger the salvo fired. The aim was to ensure at least one hit on a small target, perhaps two on a larger.

As submarines grew in size it was realised that it would be difficult to manoeuvre into a good firing position relative to the target while trying to reduce the chance of sonar detection by remaining end-on, or nearly so, to the nearest screening vessel. Hence there arose a demand for the facility of 'angling' the gyros of the torpedoes before firing, so that they would, after launch, turn to take up the desired course. Accordingly, the Control System Submarine Mk II, was developed which allowed angled fire with the Mk VIII** torpedo up to 50 degrees right and left. Unfortunately the equipment was not perfected in time to be used in the war and British submariners remained at a significant disadvantage compared to the Germans and the Americans who both employed torpedo angling gear in their boats.

Bearing in mind that equipment was already in use in the surface fleet to give a mechanical solution to the gunnery problem, it is reasonable to expect that *Vernon* would have designed a machine which would generate a quick and up-to-date torpedo fire control solution based upon a continuous feed into the machine of the submarine's angle on the target's bow, the target's speed and the running speed of the torpedo. However, all that was available to the submarine until 1937 was a rudimentary type of calculator known as the ISWAS, on which the necessary settings were made by hand, and the director angle read off a pointer. By 1938 the ISWAS had been replaced by the mechanical 'Fruit Machine' using estimated target data. This was obtained (a) by plotting successive true bearings of the target, (b) by using either an estimated range or one observed by periscope range-finder (itself dependent upon the accuracy of the masthead or funnel to waterline height of the target), (c) by counting revolutions per minute of the target's propellers. Most submarine captains made their own combinations of all three parameters in their minds. The firing interval depended upon the number of torpedoes in the salvo and the enemy's speed. An aid to solving the spread and spacing problem was provided in the shape of the Greek Slide Rule named after Lieutenant Commander Tsoukalas, an officer of the Greek Navy who introduced improvements to its design.

The crews of British submarines were all volunteers. They were competent and well trained, and all the commanding officers had undergone a demanding three months' course to qualify them for command of a submarine. Known as the 'Perisher', this eliminated those officers who found it difficult to remain cool and collected at the periscope when directing a torpedo attack and could not maintain in their minds a constant and accurate picture of the situation on the surface.

In the early years of the Submarine Branch, it had been torpedomen who were principally involved in its development. As the branch acquired its own identity within the Royal Navy, the role of torpedomen was reduced but they continued to carry out vital tasks both in support and in the submarines themselves. Where a flotilla of submarines was based upon a depot ship, the Flotilla Torpedo Officer combined his electrical duties on board her with his responsibilites for the supply, preparation and maintenance of all underwater weapons and equipment for each submarine. It was essential that the torpedoes embarked in submarines should require only the minimum of attention after preparation in the depot ship. For this reason there was always the closest liaison between the depot ship's Torpedo Officer and staff and the Torpedo Gunner's Mates of the submarines who were responsible for the final adjustments to the torpedoes before they were loaded into the tubes.

It was not only the torpedoes that required constant attention and careful maintenance. The depot ship staff was also responsible for ensuring that the torpedo tubes underwent their regular firing tests, a task which sometimes involved the staff in working very long hours. On two occasions, mistakes made by the overworked staff nearly led to disasters. In Scotland, at the Holy Loch, near the end of a tiring day, a warrant officer was carrying out firing tests in the submarine *Thule*. It was, perhaps, the very repetitive nature of the task that caused the nearly fatal error. It was routine procedure before loading torpedoes to carry out water shots in the empty submerged tubes and air shots in the external tubes. It was mandatory to ensure that the number of tubes which had been loaded was counted carefully. On this occasion, the officer concerned emerged from the submarine after-hatch to check that everything was clear before carrying out the air shot. The flotilla Gunner (T), who was standing nearby on the deck of the depot ship, noticed with horror that there was a torpedo in the tube. He shouted, 'You got a fish in the tube', to which the reply was, 'No I havent', and the officer disappeared below. He then fired the tube. Close by were the depot ships *Forth*, *Titania*, a floating dock and some merchant ships. The torpedo behaved impeccably, missing all the ships and passing under a civilian rowing boat. The unfortunate man rowed frantically as he disappeared in a cloud of spray. When he emerged from it, he was still labouring frantically at his oars. The torpedo continued on its way until it ran ashore at Sandbank where its warhead performed impeccably. Windows were broken and the Admiralty was later besieged by extravagant claims for damages.

A similar incident occurred at Trincomalee, when *Severn* was carrying out air shots alongside the depot ship *Wu Chang*. Tests still had to be completed on numbers 5 and 6 tubes. The test on number 5 tube was successfully carried out and the torpedo was loaded into it. In the heat of the day and at the end of a prolonged series of tests, the officer in charge had a temporary mental aberration. Instead of carrying out the next air shot, on number 6 tube, he repeated it on number 5. The torpedo leapt from the tube and raced across the harbour for 200 yards, at which stage it struck a tanker between the bow and amidships and exploded. It was a 21-inch Mk VIII torpedo fitted with a warhead with a duplex pistol which, on this occasion, had been set to contact only. With such a short run the warhead pistol should not have armed, but it appears to have exploded, luckily causing only a a a comparatively small hole in the tanker. When the explosion occurred Lieutenant JRH Bull, the commanding officer of *Severn*, was in the depot ship. Having been informed in his cabin that he had just torpedoed a tanker, he hurried to report to Captain (S) whom he found pacing the quarterdeck of *Adamant*. Observing Bull approaching at the double the Captain halted and before Bull could collect himself said, 'You have something to tell me, Bull!!'. It was fortunate that the incidents in *Thule* and *Severn* did not result in serious damage or fatalities.

There was always the possibility that an unsuccessful torpedo attack by a submarine could be attributed to the malfunction of the torpedo itself but Mk VIII in its various modifications proved a very reliable weapon and failures were usually due to poor preparation. Even this was rare enough, but one example took place in July 1942 in the Mediterranean, when *Traveller* left the hurriedly established submarine base at Haifa in Palestine for a war patrol in the Adriatic. As she passed through the Strait of Oranto she fired at a 2,000 ton vessel but her torpedoes missed. Again and again she encountered enemy vessels and again and again the torpedoes missed. The Commanding Officer and his crew were dismayed when a perfect opportunity to sink the ex-Yugoslav cruiser *Dalmacija* failed, presumably because of defective torpedoes. A few days later *Traveller* attacked an Italian submarine and again the torpedoes missed. There is no record of an enquiry being carried out; it can only be surmised that the lack of adequate facilities at Haifa for servicing torpedo gyros caused errors in alignment, so that the torpedoes did not run straight. The supporting evidence is that they appeared to run at their set depth and their engines operated satisfactorily.

The Mediterranean was the most important theatre of operations for British submarines. In an area where the air threat usually made surface operations hazardous, and where Britain was trying to deny an enemy the use of the sea, submarines were especially useful. It was unfortunate that they had to berth and to work in the clear and often shallow waters of that sea. In April 1941, the intensity of the war at sea in this theatre caused many logistical problems. The short supply of torpedoes caused deep anxiety, requiring the use of 21-inch Mk IV torpedoes of ancient vintage. Once loaded into torpedo tubes no further adjustment of their depth and speed settings could be made and given their age it was not surprising that the gyros in some developed errors which were difficult to adjust. This led to a number of incidents which had an adverse effect upon the morale of the submarine crews. Lieutenant Commander MD Wanklyn, who achieved fame in *Upholder*, experienced one of these problems when on patrol off Cape Bon in the first weeks of April 1941. He had been involved in two attacks on convoys, but one was unproductive because it had been carried out at very long range, and the other because the torpedo tracks were sighted, allowing the enemy to take avoiding action. That night Wanklyn carried out an unsuccesful attack on a merchant ship. He could not surface to bring his gun to bear because one of the torpedoes was wandering out of control, causing *Upholder* to dive deep to avoid it. It was an unsatisfctory ending to what might have been a very successful operation.

In the following September, there occurred an incident which caused a twofold problem for Captain GWG Simpson, commanding the Tenth Submarine Flotilla at Malta. He had an armaments crisis and a complicated moral issue with which he confronted his Commanding Officers. On 17 September intelligence arrived that three large ships were about to leave Italian ports, carrying troop reinforcements for Rommel's forces in North Africa. *Upholder*, *Upright*, *Unbeaten* and *Ursula* were sailed immediately to intercept the convoy before it could reach Tripoli. In a brilliant surface attack at night *Upholder*, from a range of 3,000 yards, torpedoed and sank the troop ships *Neptunia* and *Oceania*, big ships of some 20,000 tons. They were loaded with troop reinforcements for Rommel in the Western Desert. Over 5,000 were drowned. The escorting destroyers gathered round picking up survivors and very soon their decks were jammed with soldiers. *Unbeaten*, which was the nearest of the British submarines, had the opportunity to attack these four destroyers but the Commanding Officer was motivated by feelings of compassion for the survivors and did not press home the attack. *Upright*, whose Commanding Officer was concerned with doing as much damage to the enemy as possible, could only stand by helplessly. Of the four submarines, his was the only one which was armed with the old 21-inch Mk IVs. They were set to a depth of 24 feet and could not be adjusted to the 10 feet which was required to sink the destroyers. Consequently, a large number of enemy soldiers were spared to reinforce Rommel's armies in the Western desert and to inflict casualties upon our own troops in the desert war. Although the sinking of *Neptunia* and *Oceania* was a considerable victory, the failure to provide all submarines with the torpedoes which were needed to carry out their task had denied the submarines of the Tenth Submarine Flotilla an even greater triumph.

The loading of torpedoes into the submarines was an arduous task, which had to be carried out without the benfit of the shelters. Alfred Gower, a Seaman Torpedoman who served in a number of submarines, remembered that under the conditions prevailing, loading topedoes was 'bloody hard work'. It was an understatement, especially when air raids added to the hazards. Eric France, a Telegraphist serving in *Trident*, described the operation as follows:

Inside the upper casing were stowed trestles and a track of L shaped iron. The track was bolted to a fixed track through the forward hatch into the fore ends of the boat. The torpedo workshop staff would wheel the fish out to a position where it could be lifted into the submarine. The torpedo was fitted with a kind of body belt around the fish which had a small free running wheel on either side. Nose and tail lines were secured and held by men at each end of the torpedo. As the crane began to lift it, these men would use their lines to stop the fish from swinging about. As the crane swung its load over the side above the boat, these lines would be thrown to two men on the submarine casing, who carried out exactly the same job to stop the torpedo swivelling around. The crane continued lowering until the wheels on the body belt were settled squarely in the L track. The nose line was then passed into the boat and held by a man there, and the crane then continued lowering until the fish was settled onto the track, when the crane cable was released and withdrawn back up the jib. Inside the boat, if the tube needed a reload, the Torpedo Gunner's Mate and his torpedomen serviced the fish, then it was slid into the tube by means of a block and tackle. If it was not required in the tube it was secured in the rack, pushed back to the boat's side and anchored there. This process continued until all torpedoes were stowed, then the railway was dismantled and replaced in the casing and well and truly secured.

From 1941 to 1944, the Tenth S/M Flotilla was composed entirely of the small U-class boats. Of the thirty four of these submarines which served in the flotilla, eleven were lost, two in the harbour at Malta. They sank 648,629 tons of enemy shipping and damaged 400,480 tons. After the Italian surrender the flotilla operated from Maddalena in Sardinia from December 1943 until the end of submarine operations in the Mediterranean. The torpedo workshops at Malta prepared and repaired 1,790 torpedoes of which 1,289 were expended in attacks upon enemy shipping. 335 certain and 30 probable hits were

Italian cruiser Muzio Attendolo damaged by torpedo from submarine Unbroken

obtained, making a success rate of 28.2 per cent. This compares very favourably with the wartime average of 22.6 per cent. During the four years when the flotilla operated from Malta the special relationship between submariners and torpedomen flourished. Many years later Vice Admiral Sir Ian McGeoch, who served in the submarine *Ursula* in Malta in 1941-42, wrote: 'I would like to pay the greatest possible tribute to Mr. AT Warne, Gunner (T), and his team at the Torpedo Depot which supported the Tenth Flotilla at Malta. He and they were fantastic, given the apalling and dangerous conditions'.

In home waters too British submariners were well served by the Torpedo Branch. There were a number of failures of the ancient Mk II and Mk IV torpedoes but there were none of the total failures of torpedoes which afflicted the German U-boats. Nevertheless, some senior submariners claimed that the provision of efficient duplex pistols would have resulted in many more sinkings, and would have materially affected the course of the war. Trials of a Compensated Coil Rod pistol for the Mk VIII** torpedo began in submarines in 1942 but were delayed by the loss of the *Vernon* trials officer with all his records in an air crash within sight of Plymouth breakwater. Trials began again in December 1943 in the First Submarine Flotilla operating from Beirut. The Tenth Flotilla received them some four months later. These pistols proved troublesome and on a few occasions positive menaces to the submarine when unrelated failures in the mechanism of the torpedo caused wandering or circling. This situation occurred when *P34* fired a torpedo fitted with a CCR pistol. The first that the submarine's crew knew that something was wrong was when they heard the unmistakable noise of the torpedo's propellers circling close to the submarine. Many hearts beat rapidly until the sound faded into the distance. When P34 retunred to Malta, her 'third hand' and Torpedo Officer, Lieutenant TS Weston, chided the base Torpedo Officer about this rogue torpedo. Lieutenant OPJ Bennett, who had relieved Warne could only 'laugh about it in an understanding way'.

Despite these problems, however, the CCR pistols proved effective; 35.7 per cent of the first 250 expended obtained hits compared with 22.2 per cent hits for contact exploders. *Ultor*, commanded by Lieutenant GE Hunt, a very successful submarine commanding officer, obtained a number of creditable performances using the CCR pistols. On one occasion he fired the torpedoes at a range of 1,000 yards and noted that one ran directly under the target exploding amidships. The ship's back was broken immediately and the bow and stern rose vertically and she sank amidst a flurry of steam and water. A few days later the CCR pistols again performed impeccably when *Ultor* attacked a heavily laden lighter accompanied by an R boat.

Unfortunately, though, in August 1944 the pistols began to suffer a number of failures that shook confidence in them. First, *Unswerving* was denied a successful attack when achieving an excellent firing position against a merchant ship in the Aegean Sea. A salvo of four torpedoes was fired from 1,400 yards and an explosion was heard which was assumed to be a hit on the target. Then three more explosions were heard which corresponded to the torpedoes reaching the end of their runs. But the target was unharmed and reached its destination safely; the commanding officer in his patrol report stated bitterly that he now had no faith in non-contact pistols.

Then *Sickle* operating out of Beirut observed a laden lighter escorted by armed caiques. A perfect firing position was achieved and four torpedoes were fired spread over the lengths of the lighter and one caique. Shortly after the discharge of the third torpedo a large explosion took place 300 yards ahead of *Sickle*. It was probably the second torpedo. Not only was the submarine endangered by the premature explosion of the CCR pistol, but it also affected the running of the other torpedoes, which missed the target.

On the last day of the same month *Vox*, operating in the Aegean, sighted a merchant vessel and fired four torpedoes: one broke surface and exploded prematurely and the others missed. As a result of these and other failures, commanding officers of submarines now lost all confidence in the CCR pistols. To compensate for their lack of success they now began to use depth settings as small as 2 feet, and to set their CCRs for contact only. Furthermore, in their determination to achieve success they began to press home their attacks to very short range. Lieutenant JM Michell, commanding *Vox*, reported that his failure to inflict damage with his torpedoes was due to his getting too close for the torpedoes to take their depth satisfactorily, owing to his determination to get in to short range. On 28 September 1944, Flag Officer Submarines, (Rear Admiral GE Creasey, himself an experienced Torpedo Officer) decided that the growing number of CCR pistol failures could no longer be tolerated; the failures were discussed and he decided to impose an embargo upon their use.

The news of was received with dismay in *Vernon* because careful consideration had been given to the trials of these pistols and to the preparation of instructions for their use. A determined effort was made to find the cause of these failures and it was not long before the reasons became apparent. Torpedomen in depot ships and bases in the various theatres of war had not been trained to deal with such delicate and comparatively complex instruments, nor were torpedo workshops equipped to the required standards. The vulnerability of the CCR pistols had, in fact, already been recognised in the preparation instructions which read: 'It must be clearly understood by all persons handling the CCR non-contact pistol that this type of pistol is more complicated and more delicate than the impact pistols previously fitted to British torpedoes'. The Torpedo Officer was clearly told to ensure that the ratings responsible for the preparation of the pistols followed meticulously the instructions contained in the handbook. These represented a major change; the previously acceptable tolerances of a simple mechanism had been replaced by the precision of a higher technology. Although the CCR pistol was inherently robust if treated with ordinary care the insulation resistance of the pistol wiring and contacts was so reduced by dampness that it was liable to become unstable. Even the perspiration from the hands could adversely affect it. Having defined the problem, *Vernon* insisted that the pistol was reintroduced and it became standard by the beginning of 1945 where maintenance facilities were adequate.

With the concentration of the numbers of British and Allied submarines in Trincomalee, operations began under tropical conditions and in the shallow waters close to the Japanes occupied territories in Burma, Malaya and the Dutch East Indies. In these waters, targets were mainly small craft carrying supplies to the Japanese armies in Burma and many were intercepted and sunk by gunfire. However, several successes were achieved against enemy warships and submarines. On 8th June 1945, *Trenchant* carried out one of the most exceptional torpedo attacks of the war. In flat calm seas she intercepted and sank the Japanese heavy cruiser *Ashigara*. Her commanding officer, Commander AR Hezlet, was determined to score a success against this important target and to use almost every torpedo available. He fired a full spread of eight Mk VIIIs from his bow tubes and then turned to fire two stern tubes. He scored five hits with his first salvo at 4,000 yards, and before the last pair arrived the *Ashigara* rolled over and sank. This remarkably successful and skilful attack was a fitting end to the wartime campaigns of the British submarines.

Torpedomen serving in submarines were part of a close knit crew bound together by the intimacy of their quarters, the ever present danger of their task and the uniform excellence of their leadership. There can be no better example of the reactions of a Senior Torpedoman in submarines than that of Chief Petty Officer SC Kaye, who was awarded the Distinguished Service Medal. At the outbreak of war Kaye was serving in the World War I submarine *L26* as a Leading Torpedoman responsible for the electrical circuits. When the message was received that Great Britain was at war with Germany, the old submarine was already on patrol off Heligoland.

Life in the L class was not as uncomfortable as might have been expected because the two beam torpedo tubes, with which the submarine had originally been equipped, had been removed cosiderably increasing the space available as living quarters. The declaration of war was accepted by *L26's* crew with equanimity as they continued to carry out their duties as though they were on a peacetime exercise. The move from Blyth to Dundee, with the remainder of the flotilla, was followed by a number of uneventful patrols off Norway. No targets were encountered and no torpedoes fired before Kaye moved on to a modern submarine, *Seawolf*. Before joining, he qualified as a Torpedo Gunner's Mate at *Vernon* during the 'Blitz'.

Seawolf gave her new Torpedo Gunner's Mate a challenge. She was the first British submarine to be fitted with high pressure torpedo firing gear. In previous submarines, the air with which the torpedoes were discharged from the tubes was contained in a large reservoir below the torpedo tubes at a relatively low pressure of about 200 lbs per square inch. In *Seawolf* the very high air pressure at some 3,000 lbs per square inch was contained in a much smaller reservoir. This new equipment had to be tested every day whilst at sea. It performed satisfactorily, and while Kaye was in *Seawolf* he encountered no difficulties with it.

Torpedoes loaded but not fired could not be left in a flooded tube for more than five days: they then had to be withdrawn to check the air pressures and the gyros for water tightness. This led inevitably to their maintenance at sea, an operation unpopular with the crew whose living quarters were in the fore ends. Furthermore, the hauling in and out of the torpedoes required the participation of all available hands, a greasy, oily and tiring business.

During Kaye's time in *Seawolf*, torpedoes were fired only once. On 30 July 1941, intelligence was received while patrolling off Brest, that a U-boat would be transitting the Bay of Biscay on its way back to its base. *Seawolf* was ordered to intercept and in due course she found her quarry and attacked. A full spread of six torpedoes was fired and four separate explosions were heard. *Seawolf's* ship's company was convinced that the U-boat had been sunk, but on return to base at Devonport the destruction of the U-boat was not confirmed. According to post war records, the U-boat was the *U562* which was undamaged. The torpedoes must have exploded harmlessly at the end of their runs.

On *Seawolf's* return to Devonport, Kaye was sent north to Vickers Armstrong at Barrow-in-Furness to stand by the larger submarine *Turbulent*. Her captain was Commander JW Linton. Known as 'Tubby', he was one of the most popular officers in the submarine service as well as being one of the most highly decorated. He was both physically and mentally tough; he had been one of the Royal Navy's most promising rugby players. The entire ship's company had joined by October 1941, and *Turbulent* carried out working up exercises at Dunoon before proceeding to Gibraltar, for further working up off the east coast of Spain. After a visit to Gibraltar to re-embark spare equipment she sailed for Alexandria to join the First Submarine Flotilla.

On passage, she was diverted to patrol off Crete where she was sighted by aircraft and depth charged by small anti-submarine vessels. Members of the crew were unmoved by the inaccurate attacks and were undecided how many depth charges had been dropped. Some estimates were as high as one hundred and twenty, but Kaye's recollection was that it was more like sixty or seventy. Linton was anxious that the crew should be usefully employed during depth charging, rather than merely sitting tight during the attack, and appointed Kaye to be the official counter of depth charges.

The submarine received a warm welcome at Alexandria, where friendships were renewed and anecdotes exchanged. This comradeship was particularly strong among the submariners, who considered themselves to be of one brotherhood to which they referred as 'The Trade'. *Turbulent's* first patrol from Alexandria was in the Aegean, where the targets were mainly caiques carrying personnel, ammunition and other supplies between enemy occupied islands. These small vessels, not worth a torpedo, were destroyed by gunfire. It was not long before the crew christened their Captain, 'Six Gun Linton'

Turbulent was at sea on 30 June 1942, when *U372* sank the submarine depot ship *Medway* and, in common with the remainder of the First Submarine Flotilla, was suddenly without a base. The only solution was to remain on patrol while a temporary base was set up in Beirut. This was a period of great difficulty for the Torpedo Branch. Stocks of Mk VIII torpedoes had been severely reduced by losses in *Medway*, and there were only primitive facilities available on the quayside at Beirut to prepare those still available some of which had been recovered floating in the sea.

Of all the parts of a torpedo the most vulnerable is the gyro which must be kept free of dust and dirt: now the electrical artificer responsible for the maintenance and preparation of gyros had to make do with the corner of an engineer's workshop, which was partitioned off with tarpaulins. There was no doubt that some of the torpedo failures which followed the loss of *Medway* were due to these primitive conditions at Beirut. Fortunately, better conditions were soon established in a warehouse close to the docks.

Turbulent was fitted with the standard armament of a 'T' class boat, eleven torpedo tubes, six reloadable tubes in the fore ends and five external tubes of which three faced aft and two forward. The external tubes were of the tight fitting type which meant that when the bow cap was opened the tube did not flood. The six internal tubes were of the loose fitting type from which a torpedo could be withdrawn for maintenance in the submarine. Six spare torpedoes were carried for the internal tubes. Linton showed his consideration for his crew by allowing two torpedoes to be withdrawn from the tubes at a time during patrols so that the torpedomen would be free in harbour to take advantage of their rest periods.

The total involvement of a submarine's crew in attacks is well illustrated by Kaye's account of *Turbulent's* operation against the Italian supply traffic to Benghazi between 14 and 29 May 1942:

This patrol off Benghazi was really good, plenty of fun and activity in it. Plenty of actual attacks on the surface and submerged. We were close inshore off Benghazi when we saw a convoy entering Benghazi harbour, and the skipper said, 'It won't be long before they'll be leaving to return to Italy and I propose to attack when it gets dark'. So we remained submerged until it had become nightfall, then we surfaced and waited out in the darkness until the convoy left. It comprised of three merchant ships and two destroyers. We trailed this convoy as it left Benghazi and, later on, about three o'clock in the morning, we carried out a surface attack on the convoy. We fired torpedoes, we sank one of the merchant ships, and the another one, it was the middle one, and also hit one of the escorts. We were on the point of firing at the third merchant ship when the other destroyer, which was at the head of the convoy, spotted us and turned completely round and came at us full bore to try and ram and sink us. He did not, but it caused us to crash dive. The last to leave the bridge, of course, whenever we were on the surface and had to dive was the Captain.. On this occasion, when he observed the destroyer about to come at us full speed, he cleared the bridge of all the look-outs and then would have followed them down but, unfortunately, one of the look-outs let his binoculars slip over the rim of the conning tower hatch as he was going down the ladder. They were tight round his neck, he struggled, got his head free and fell down the hatch, through the lower lid and into the control room, and would have had a very serious accident if the Chief Electrical Artificer, who was at the bottom of the hatch, had not thrown himself at the falling body like a rugby tackle, and then pushed him on to the deck in the control room. This all takes a lot of time to tell but it happened in fractions of seconds. All the others on the bridge, except the Captain, managed to get down into the control room, but by the time the Captain got inside the upper lid and was attempting to close it, we were going down rapidly to 90 feet, which was the depth we normally went to for depth charging, and it takes only a few seconds to get down from the surface to periscope depth. When Linton got inside the upper lid and tried to close it down, he could not get the clips on because the straps on this rating's binoculars were over the rim of the hatch; well, Captain Linton just hung on to the two clips which should have made the lid watertight and with the weight of his body kept it sufficiently closed to stop the whole of the conning tower flooding. As we went deeper, the external pressure of the water assisted to close the lid on the leather straps of the binoculars and he did get the clips on eventually. By this time, the conning tower was half full of water because, as soon as the water had started coming through the lower lid from the conning tower into the control room, they had shut the lower lid for safety. Eventually we were down at 90 feet, all serene, nice and quiet, the destroyer had not even dropped depth charges, and in the control room they heard a thud, thud, thud. They immediately realised that, although there must have been a hell of a lot of water in the conning tower, Captain Linton was still there. The upper lid must, of course, be shut! There was, in fact, so much water in the conning tower, it was half full, that the long handle that was on the lower hatch, and you can get good leverage on it, could not be opened from inside the submarine, so the pump was put on and a lot of the water was pumped from the conning tower into the bilges of the submarine, until eventually they could open the lower lid, down into the submarine came Captain Linton looking like the proverbial drowned rat. I can only relate what went on now from what I was told, because I was nice and dry in the fore ends by the torpedoes. It appears that the Captain, having got safely inside the boat, the lower lid was closed again and the Captain enquired from the First Lieutenant what the situation was, and was told that everything was closed down for depth charging. Captain Linton then turned round and said, 'Who was the bloody fool that left his binoculars on the upper lid?' Looking round, and don't forget that he was a United Services rugger player, and a jolly good tackler, there was no answer. He repeated his question, and still got no answer. He was wringing his hands as though he would tear the submarine apart, until there was a small voice from the

Linton said, 'Do you know that you frightened every man in this submarine?' Fortunately, Linton had a sense of humour, and the young man was not severely punished.

Kaye went on to give a close insight into the state of mind of the torpedo ratings in *Turbulent*:

When we were diving we, the four torpedomen in the fore ends, in the torpedo compartment, were isolated from all the others. Although the bulk head doors were not closed except when we shut them in an emergency, we never heard any dissension from anyone at all. Captain Linton was liked by every single man.

One of Kaye's clearest memories was that during this particular patrol off Benghazi, a United States Navy officer was borne to obtain experience. He was so impressed by what he saw that when he returned to Alexandria he asked that he should be allowed to stay in *Turbulent* for a further patrol, but this was not allowed. Kaye recalled that the American officer later commanded the American submarine *Kingfisher*, lost in action in the Pacific.

Kaye remembered another remarkable incident during the same patrol. *Turbulent* intercepted another convoy and carried out a surface attack in which a merchant ship was sunk. The submarine then dived and carried out a further attack in which one of the torpedoes had a gyro failure. The noise of this torpedo circling around overhead was described as being 'like a Junkers 88 roaring down and attacking'. Usually a torpedo with a gyro failure will continue circling until it eventually sinks and the warhead explodes on hitting the bottom. On this occasion, the explosion came fairly shortly after discharge and was for a moment mistaken for a depth charge. However, Kaye claims that it ran straight up the stern of an attacking destroyer and hit it between the propellers, sinking it.

On the same patrol, a U-boat was sighted and claimed sunk. It had been sighted by the perpetrator of the binocular incident, as a result of which the young rating had his stoppage of leave cancelled. The significance of this simple story is that it was remembered over forty years later by a Chief Petty Officer of the *Turbulent's* crew: It still reflects the close understanding between officers and men who endured hardship and danger together. Unfortunately, there is no record of a U-boat having been sunk at this time and place. Kaye's last patrol in *Turbulent* began just before Christmas 1942, when she left Beirut bound for Malta carrying supplies of all kinds, including Christmas puddings and all the other paraphernalia of the festive season. After unloading stores and equipment at Malta, *Turbulent* headed for patrol off the coast of Sardinia. Although one ship was sunk, it was not a particularly successful patrol.

Kaye was now struck down by severe rheumatism, which led to him being invalided. In March 1943 he was undergoing treatment in South Africa when the news arrived that *Turbulent* had been sunk by convoy escorts off Bastia. During his command of *Turbulent*, Linton had sunk a destroyer and thirteen supply ships, and also destroyed three trains on the mainland of Italy by gunfire. He had been awarded the Victoria Cross. Kay's memoir gives a first hand insight into the life of a torpedoman in a successful submarine.

272

During the Second World War, 5,121 torpedoes were fired by British submarines and those of her European Allies. 1,040 hits were obtained and 95 probable hits. When it is borne in mind that these Allied submarines were operating in difficult conditions such as off the Norwegian coast or in the clear waters of the Mediterranean, often close to enemy occupied territory, a percentage of certain and probable hits of 22.6 per cent is highly creditable. The decision to concentrate upon the production of the well tried and tested 21-inch Mk VIII torpedo was thoroughly justified and it proved the key to the success of British submarines. Although the techniques of its operation were significantly cruder than in German or American submarines there was no record of a significant torpedo crisis as suffered by both those submarine services.

W<small>HEN ELECTRICITY WAS REGARDED</small> as a mysterious force the development, trials, installation, operation and maintenance of electrical equipment in ships of the Royal Navy had devolved upon the Torpedo Branch. It seemed a logical decision at the time that the officer who knew all about the batteries which supplied low power for the operation of telephones and the elctrical detonation of mines should also be responsible for the high power required to light the incandescent light bulbs which replaced the oil lamps and candles. In the 1870s, even the most farsighted would not have predicted that within a quarter of a century *Vernon* and the Torpedo Branch would be involved in the development, trials and operations of telephones, searchlights, batteries, dynamos, electrical hand lamps, electric motors, incandescent lamps, electric semaphores, gunnery control circuits and electrical circuits in general. This process continued through the first quarter of the twentieth century: by the end of the First World War, torpedomen had become technicians as much as seamen, with electrical responsibilities that gave them, in large measure, control of the quality of life in the fleet.

However, electrical installations were essentially simple and designed to be operated by a variety of non-technical officers and men. During the First World War, and for a few years after, the high power supply in ships was used for lighting and ventilation while equipment vital to the fighting capability of the ship, such as fire control and gunfiring circuits, were supplied at low power (22 volts), for which batteries were provided in case the main supply failed. There were also a number of hand worked emergency arrangements. In this system a failure of the main electrical supply, though very inconvenient, did not put a ship out of action. The organisation within ships of the Royal Navy appeared to work well and there was very little pressure for change, in spite of the 1920 Field-Waistell Committee which recommended the formation of a separate Electrical Branch.

Almost imperceptibly during the inter-war years the Torpedo Branch's electrical duties became more complicated and demanding. New ships, entering service from 1925 onwards, were no longer equipped with steam and hydraulically operated auxiliary machinery, which depended upon lengths of piping vulnerable to action damage and which were difficult to repair. All machinery outside the engine and boiler rooms was driven by electric motors; and for the first time steering engines, gun turrets, salvage and fire pumps and many important engine room auxiliaries were dependent upon the supply of electricity. The Royal Navy continued to rely upon the tried and tested direct current system rather than adopt the alternative of alternating current. Despite the growing complexity of the electical installations of new construction between the wars, the Torpedo Branch remained responsible for all electrical supplies outside the engine and boiler rooms.

To give Torpedo Officers the necessary knowledge to meet these responsibilities the pre-war one year's qualifying course, known as the 'Long T Course', began with a period of six months at the Royal Naval College Greenwich, where the students took a refresher course in mathematics and physics which included an introduction to electrical theory. A few out of those who obtained high marks during the 'Long T Course' returned later to Greenwich to undergo an advanced course in electrical theory.

The study of electrical theory in both the normal and advanced courses was severely limited. Professor Haigh, in charge of electrical instruction at Greenwich, told the students that they would have to cram into three months knowledge which was normally imparted to electrical engineering students in a University over two years. Paradoxically, perhaps the electrical training given to ratings was more thorough, but they tended to become specialised in either low power or high power duties. The training given to electrical artificers was particularly good and in all major war vessels, the Gunner (T) and the Warrant Electrician provided the expertise without which the Torpedo Officer could not have fulfilled his responsibilities. In destroyers and other small vessels, the Gunner (T) alone was in charge of the electrical installations. With well trained officers and ratings, the Torpedo Branch was not hard pressed to meet its shipboard responsibilities in September 1939. But all was not well.

The loss of *Courageous* and *Royal Oak,* followed by severe damage to the minelayer *Adventure* and the cruiser *Belfast* by magnetic mine, revealed severe deficiencies in the design of the electrical supply systems in all four ships. In each there had been a total failure of electrical supply. A team was set up at *Vernon* to investigate the causes. The services of a young scientist, Dr J Cowan, were called upon; after consultation with Haigh, Cowan carried out a series of experiments using small explosive charges in one of the basins in Portsmouth Dockyard. Now thoroughly conversant with the characteristics of the shock produced by non-contact underwater explosions, he sought to discover the reasons for the severe damage caused to the mountings of a wide variety of electrical equipment, including dynamos. Unfortunately, the Electrical Engineering Department at the Admiralty, which had been responsible for the design of the mountings, was staffed largely by technical personnel who had not served at sea and who, therefore, had been unfamiliar with action damage.

This was another side effect of the failure to create a proper Naval Electrical Branch. During the inter-war years the electrical engineers had developed and relied upon a shock testing machine which was designed to deal with the shock produced by gun blast. Their reaction to Cowan's proposals for a new machine, designed to react to the effects of non-contact underwater explosions, was hostile. The Electrical Engineers favoured a policy of strengthening equipment to withstand shock rather than protecting it. Undeterred by this opposition, Cowan proceeded to design a more appropriate shock testing machine, and very soon his theories were being enthusiastically taken up by the Engineer-in-Chief's department. New mountings for the protection of main and auxiliary machinery against shock were developed but Admiralty opposition delayed them being fitted to ships under refit and new construction.

It might be supposed that in a gunnery dominated Navy, the electrical supplies in its ships would have been proof against crippling damage by gunfire. It soon became apparent after the Battle of the River Plate that the systems in cruisers were extremely vulnerable and that an emergency electrical supply system was urgently needed. This was another requirement which had been resisted before the war as being an unnecessary duplication. Belatedly, and with ill grace, approval was given for all ships to be fitted with emergency systems as quickly as possible. During the Norwegian campaign, many destroyers were damaged and investigations by *Vernon* showed that their electrical supply systems were as unsatisfactory as the cruisers. Very soon a completely new system had been designed which incorporated many improvements for protection against damage from bomb splinters and shell fire.

The division between the Torpedomen and Electrical Engineers had other bad effects. The system for identifying and correcting electrical faults in ships was time-wasting and inefficient. Prior to 1937, the Electrical Engineering Department at the Admiralty had been responsible for the design and development of high power systems while the Torpedo and Mining Department had responsibility for low power control systems, which were mainly concerned with gunnery control, auxiliary machinery and communications. In 1937, the Electrical Engineering Department assumed responsibility for all electrical matters, but *Vernon* remained responsible for sea trials and liaison with the fleet whose opinion was submitted in half yearly electrical reports forwarded to *Vernon* by Torpedo Officers afloat. An analysis of all these reports was made by *Vernon* and forwarded, via the Director of Torpedoes and Mining, to the Department of Electrical Engineering. At half yearly intervals, meetings were held between DTM, DEE, *Vernon* and representatives from the fleet to reach decisions regarding the various recommendations. It was a long and laborious procedure which inevitably caused delays of at least one year before anything could be achieved.

During the war, members of the *Vernon* Electrical Department visited ships immediately upon their return to harbour, to discuss damage to equipment and any lessons learnt in damage control before memories of the incidents had faded. If these discussions were to be of any value it was imperative that the torpedo personnel, particularly the Torpedo Officers in the larger ships, should have a thorough knowledge of their electrical installations. Before long, it became apparent that some Torpedo Officers were ill prepared to meet these stringent requirements. Very early in the war, Torpedo Officers who had undergone only a shortened wartime 'Long T Course' found themselves having to teach themselves some of the rudiments of their trade whilst in positions of considerable responsibility at sea.

Lieutenant GAJ Goodhart, remarking upon his wartime service said:

After about six months in the VERNON Mining Department I was appointed 'T' of AJAX. Having done all of six weeks training in electrics - high and low power, it was quite a shock to find myself responsible for everything electric, and everything except the main steam engines seemed to be and indeed was electrical. Luckily I had a first class Warrant Electrician who, I believe, later became a Commander (L).

It was a feeling shared by many of Goodhart's contemporaries who had undergone high and low power training at *Vernon(R)*. The instructional staff was very competent, but Torpedo Officers were urgently needed at sea and there was no time to go very deeply into the theory of electrical supply systems in the fleet. However, one of the most important improvements in the course was the inclusion of electrical damage control, which, in time of war, is ultimately the Torpedo Officer's most vital electrical commitment.

The consequences of the inadequate war time training of Torpedo Officers were, to some extent, redressed by the loyalty, support and aptitude of their staffs. This applied especially to the Electrical Artificers, whose training had not suffered to the same degree. From their ranks emerged the invaluable and highly experienced Warrant Electricians. With the Gunners(T) they had to bear an increasing burden of responsibility for the electrical integrity of ships during the war years.

Electrical Artificers were craftsmen of a very high standard who were also required to be electrical technicians capable of locating and repairing faults in a wide range of electrical equipment from heavy machinery to delicate instruments. The combined experience and capabilities of Electrical Artificers and torpedo ratings had so far borne the test of time; but the rapid introduction of high technology equipment posed a serious problem for officers and ratings alike. It was not a situation which could be allowed to continue. To complicate matters further, the war found Torpedo Officers expected to shoulder their electrical responsibilities in addition to demanding seaman duties, and the maintenance of more and more new kinds of weapons and equipment. All too often these duties conflicted, to the detriment of the efficiency of the ship when faced with the crisis of damage from enemy action.

In many of the major units of the fleet which had been built between 1906 and 1920, the electrical ring main was constructed in sections which were connected together by links or switches and it was not possible to run all the dynamos in parallel because one short circuit would cause all the dynamos to fail on overload. In ships designed between the wars, breakers fitted with overload release gear were inserted between adjacent sections. Thus, the only dynamo to come off an overload would be the one feeding the damaged section. However, trials carried out in the cruiser *London* in January 1939 revealed that when a section became very heavily overloaded any of the ring main and supply breakers was liable to open. Therefore, at the outbreak of war, all major war vessels designed between the wars were instructed to run their ring main systems in separate sections, with one dynamo in each section. This arrangement, which continued until ships could be modified, meant that the full back-up potential of the complete system of four or six dynamos could not be realised.

With the knowledge supplied by the annual electrical reports from the ships, the Electrical Department at *Vernon* was able to take a leading part in developing improvements to the ring main system. Immediately before the war the '*Vernon* proposals' were published in the form of an imaginary cruiser's electrical system, embodying the establishment's ideas on ring mains and emergency cables developed from the annual reports. The principal recommendations included:

1. Vitally important ring main breakers to be duplicated.
2. Fairly important breakers to be grouped and given emergency feed.
3. Emergency cables to be provided and bulkhead terminals to be fitted.
4. Important services to have a reel of cable alongside them of such a length

that it would reach the main run emergency cable.
5. Services in the engine room to have emergency cables capable of running to the nearest emergency terminal.
6. Emergency fuse boards to be supplied to each repair party.

The proposals ended with an important proviso:

It is emphasised that the emergency system must not be run prior to action. It must be kept reeled up to a required stop and it is not intended that the system should be capable of supplying the whole ship. The system is intended to provide a flexible means of supply to any individual service.

Examination of reports of action damage reveal that these proposals were far sighted and it was unfortunate that many of them had not been implemented before the war became a much more heated conflict. To complicate the situation further, ships were faced with conflicting instructions. A Confidential Admiralty Fleet Order gave instructions for running ring mains complete under action conditions, while the *Vernon* pamphlet issued in March 1939 advised ships to keep their ring mains in sections pending the fitting of modified overload devices to the ring main switch gear. It soon became apparent that the term 'under action conditions' had caused misunderstanding. To an older generation this meant a gun action between opposing surface vessels, and it was not understood that it was necessary for the electrical installations to be in a high degree of readiness when danger from mines or torpedoes existed, even if the possibility of close encounter with the enemy was remote. It was not long before near misses by heavy bombs and underwater explosions revealed that ring main supply breakers were liable to open under these conditions and thus cause serious interference with the electrical supplies. Modifications were quickly designed and fitted and the need to operate under conditions of full electrical readiness at sea was soon appreciated.

The difficulties which faced the Torpedo Branch in fulfilling its electrical responsibilties and the growing need for a specialist Electrical Branch can be most easily traced through the action damage reports at various stages of the war. There is no doubt that old attitudes prevailed during the Second World War's early months. This is no more clearly demonstrated than in the case of *Belfast* which, as we have seen, was mined and seriously damaged on 21 November 1939. She was about to carry out gunnery exercises in the vicinity of May Island in the Firth of Forth, in company with the cruiser *Southampton* and a target tug. The atmosphere on board was relaxed and as the ships were close to their base the only dangers seemed to be from submarines and mines, and as a precaution paravanes had been streamed. It had been considered unnecessary to have the ships at action stations and damage control parties, including those required for electrical repairs, were not closed up.

On 4 November, the German submarine *U-21* had laid a minefield, not of the conventional moored contact type as expected by the British, but of the far more deadly magnetic ground mines. At that stage of the war British warships had no protection against influence mines and when *Belfast*, proceeding at 17 knots, was swinging after nearly completing a turn she detonated a mine almost under the centre of the ship, slightly to starboard and just abaft the aircraft hangar. The damage that resulted was far more severe and of a different type from that experienced before. There was little flooding, but a length of the keel seemed to have been pushed into the ship and the upper deck was buckled just as though the two ends of the ship had been pressed downward and pivoted at this point. The main shock was preceded by a briefer but severe one. Two torpedomen in the bows were hurled into the air and severely injured; throughout the ship men and equipment were thrown about by the force of the impact. Alongside, a huge column of water shot up abreast the foremast and came down again abreast Y turret. The next few minutes were bedlam as men staggered to their feet and tried to shake off the effects of the shock.

In spite of the severe damage, the ship remained watertight and the only flooding experienced was from oil fuel which leaked into the spaces where ring main breakers and low power controls were situated. Notwithstanding the oil fuel, the ring main and all electrical gear in these compartments, including the low power battery supplying the telephone system, continued to function correctly. But the electrical supply system proved vulnerable, although there were three running dynamos and one under repair. Immediately after the explosion, a complete blackout followed, the dynamos having been isolated by the ring main breakers all of which came off due to the shock. Number four dynamo appeared to be undamaged. Number two dynamo, which was diesel driven, was belching smoke and flame from a cracked exhaust pipe. The watch keeper, holed up in the complete darkness, shut down the machine. The remaining dynamo that had been running, number one, was turbo-driven and situated in the forward boiler room. It was severely damaged and had also been shut down. The loss of the dynamos had a knock-on effect because number one had been feeding the low power generator supplying the telephone exchange and the gunnery control systems. Fortunately, the telephone system was operated on a battery supply floating on the generator, and thus continued to operate; but the watch keeper in the exchange, alarmed by the darkness and the shock of the explosions, scrambled towards the upper deck until he was confronted by a Leading Torpedoman who ordered him back to his post. When he arrived the switchboard was jammed by a multitude of calls. He realised that the hand sets must have been shaken off and he redeemed himself by arranging for messages to be sent around the ship to have them replaced. Thus restored, the telephone system worked without interruption. Had an automatic secondary lighting system been installed, the tendency to evacuate compartments would have been greatly reduced and communications might have been restored far more quickly and efficiently.

In the gunnery transmitting station the low power Electrical Artificer was attending to a fault when he felt a shock which made him sag at the knees. Two seconds later the main shock caused the transmitting station to move up and down throwing him on to his face. In the next compartment the master gyro compass was unshipped and hurled to the deck, as was the after gyro compass.

At the main switchboard the watch keeper was concussed; when interrogated he could recall nothing about his having left the compartment. For some time after the explosion the switchboard was left unattended and the first person to reach it was the Torpedo Officer. He had been on the quarterdeck when he felt the preliminary shock just before he was hurled to the deck by the shattering crash of the main explosion. As he lay on the deck, the ship heaved up and down and it was some minutes before he could get to his feet and make his way forward. Almost immediately a huge column of water fell alongside the after gun turrets as he made his way towards the main switchboard through the darkness which now enveloped everything below decks. He at once attempted to restore power by closing ring main breakers, but there was no response. Soon, however, the Chief Electrical Artificer arrived at the switchboard and between them they were able to assess the situation. By that time, the watch keeper had recovered and returned, allowing the Chief Electrical Artificer to make his way aft to recock the fuse release switches. Ten minutes had passed since the explosion and before the Commissioned Electrician was able to make his way to the switchboard and restore power from number two dynamo. It had been restarted by an Engine Room Artificer, who displaying great courage and initiative, had gone down to the dynamo room immediately after the explosion.

He had encountered some difficulty in restarting this diesel driven dynamo owing to a leak in the air system controlling the starter, and he had to recharge the air bottles before proceeding. It was fortunate that the diesel dynamo was working. The Engineer Commander was doubtful about maintaining steam for the steam turbo dynamos and had ordered them to be closed down. All oil suction pipes had been broken and the engine room department was having great difficulty in maintaining steam from one boiler by means of a hand pump.

Vernon's verdict was that the electrical installation had stood up well to the tremendous shaking, but that power would have been restored far more quickly had there been a satisfactory secondary lighting system. Even in 1939 it was archaic that the secondary lighting system which had been installed in this modern cruiser consisted of oil lamps. In the event, those that were lit, particularly in the dynamo rooms, were either blown out or smashed by the force of the explosion. Battery driven lamps, known as Oldhams' lamps, had been situated strategically around the ship but in the darkness they were hard to find before they could be switched on.

The damage caused to *Belfast* was the first experience the Royal Navy had of the havoc caused by the explosion of an influence mine at close quarters. This incident, in the early weeks of the war, drew attention to the need to have an electrical repair organisation which could be brought into action at the shortest possible notice.

Only seven weeks later, while the reports of the damage to *Belfast* were being analysed, another non-contact mine exploded under *Nelson* in the approaches to Loch Ewe. The ship, which was proceeding at 13 knots and about to enter harbour in 19 fathoms of water, exploded a mine which lifted the whole fore part of the 35,000 ton battleship about three feet, shaking her violently, particularly in the unarmoured parts forward and aft. In this large ship comparatively little electrical damage was suffered and in accordance with the ship's organisation, all electrical repair parties closed up immediately after the explosion. The Warrant Electrician made his way quickly to the switchboard where he ascertained that all supplies were normal. Shortly, however, number one dynamo came off on overload, and for a while the damage control parties found difficulty in locating the whereabouts of the damage. Consequently, the causes of electrical breakdown which now began to occur were difficult to find. The main capstan motor and the starboard cable holder motor were out of action until an emergency lead was run from the port motor starter to the starboard starter. This damage prevented the ship from anchoring for three hours. Once again, the urgent need for strategically placed emergency leads was amply demonstrated.

Throughout the first year of the war the shortcomings of the electrical installations in all ships became increasingly apparent. In the closing days of April 1940, the sloop *Pelican* was secured alongside in the harbour at Lerwick (in the Shetland Islands). She had been dive bombed on 22 April off Aandalsnes and was struck on the quarterdeck, losing the stern. However, all three dynamos remained in working order and it should have been possible to restore electrical supplies to the surviving part of the ship, had not bomb splinters passed through the switchboard room, demolishing the de-gaussing switchboard. damaging the main switchboard and short circuiting all electrical supplies. Although all three dynamos were in working order, no electrical power could be taken from them and the only source of power available was from 22 volt batteries. It was not until some hours later that the Electrical Artificer was able to borrow flexible cables from another ship, and could rig temporary power supplies direct from the dynamos to important services. *Vernon's* investigating team reported that:

The complete disablement of the high power system by two or three splinters shows the necessity for making adequate emergency arrangements in this type of ship as well as in all others.

On the anniversary of the outbreak of war, the armed merchant cruiser *Scythia* was escorting the Dakar Intervention Force accompanied by the cruiser *Fiji*. The force was intercepted by *U32* which fired torpedoes and claimed to have hit *Scythia*. She had, in fact, hit *Fiji*, wrecking a boiler room, causing the ship to list to port and letting the sea surge in through the damaged port sides, flooding the Marines' barracks to a depth of two feet. By this stage in the war, a damage control headquarters had been established and electrical repair parties closed up under an Electrical Artificer at the main switchboard. Flexwell emergency lighting circuits, fed from each side of the ring main, were available, backed up by 150 torches distributed around the ship in racks. However, the task facing the electrical repair parties was formidable. When 'A' boiler room failed, steam driving the prime movers of numbers one and two dynamos was interrupted and power failed throughout the forward half of the ship. The Electrical Artificer on the switchboard had been thrown to the deck by the explosion. In the darkness, with the gyro and steering motor alarm bells ringing eerily, he attempted to restore power by closing a ring main breaker from the switchcboard. Unfortunately, a 40 amp fuse had blown so that no supply was available to the ring main breaker. He was faced with no choice. Unable to establish contact with the repair party he decided to go himself and close the ring main breaker locally. He had to force his way in the darkness through the crowded mess decks, through a number of watertight doors which had been closed and through the Marines' flooded barracks. It was a nightmare journey but he succeeded in his task and returned to the switchboard. Meanwhile, the amidship electrical repair party had managed to reconnect electrical supplies from another dynamo and so restore power to three quarters of the ship. Although the initial failure of power supplies caused the low power generators to fail, the majority of the telephones remained in action supplied by the batteries.

The electrical repair parties worked all night. Twelve hours after the torpedo had struck, the Marines' barracks were drained and most low power systems had been restored. Furthermore, the 40 foot strip of degaussing which had been blown away was replaced by new cable which was run around the upper deck in place of the damaged coil. The torpedo department, operating as an important part of the ship's damage control organisation, had performed impeccably and, in many cases, with considerable courage. *Vernon's* examining party reported:

The supply system in Fiji and the damage sustained is typical of conditions under which, given correct sequence operation of the switch gear, it would be preferable to run with the system split fore and aft with pairs of dynamos on each side. If this had been done, no blackout would have occurred in the forward part of the ship, the work of the men in the forward engine room would have been greatly assisted and the task of the Electrical Artificer in charge of the switchboard would have been simplified. It must also be remembered the complete lighting failure has an adverse effect on morale, giving the impression that very severe damage must have occurred and so making men reluctant to remain at their posts below decks. This would be minimised by automatic emergency lanterns, the fitting of which to all ships should be expedited.

Each case of war damage to ships reinforced the lesson of the dependance of the Torpedo Officer on the skill and dedication of his staff. As *Vernon* commented:

It is clear that urgent switching operations, particularly if local control becomes more general, are more quickly and readily carried out if electrical complements are adequate. For efficiency, an officer or senior rating in charge with a watch keeper and a messenger at the main switchboard, at least two repair parties, and a party in each engine room competent to take over control of the dynamos at a moment's notice, are the minimum requirements. A watch keeper is also essential in the forward and after low power rooms and any modifications, such as the provision of an escape hatch, to this end should be given high priority. The design of future installations should aim at being operable by a number of men under war conditions rather than under peace conditions which has been allowed undue consideration in the past.

Vernon's reports reflected adversely upon the system for the design of ships. The Naval Staff left details to the Naval Constructors and Electrical Engineers to draw up the detailed arrangements and they were inclined to place important machinery in small compartments below the waterline, where access was always awkward, and escape in the event of emergency was hazardous. Torpedomen had insufficient influence. This was unfortunate as the sailors understood the real and imagined horrors of being caught below decks in a ship listing and in danger of sinking, and the added nightmare of being entombed in an air pocket in a ship lying on the bed of the ocean. Such considerations are vital to the efficient working of a ship, as we have seen in the examples of the desertion of switchboards by watch keepers in the immediate aftermath of violent explosions. In the case of the *Ark Royal*, the desire to save life was given priority over the urgent need to restore power to the ring main in order to save the ship. This decision contributed to the loss of this important ship.

On 13 November 1941, *Ark Royal*, in company with other ships of Force H from Gibraltar, was returning to base from Operation Perpetual. Just after 1530, when steaming at 18 knots, she was struck by a torpedo on the starboard side. A huge column of water rose up and acrid smoke smothered the bridge as the bomb lift doors were blown open. The ship whipped violently and aircraft on the fore-end of the flight deck were thrown into the air. *U-81* had fired a four torpedo spread at long range at the battleship *Malaya*. The U-boat's crew had waited patiently for seven minutes before they heard two detonations. The fact was that only one torpedo had hit, and that struck *Ark Royal* and not *Malaya*. For *U81* it was a desperately lucky miss which earned stardom for Friedrich Guggenberger, her Commanding Officer.

Perhaps because *Ark Royal* had led such a charmed life, or maybe because Force H was so close to Gibraltar, no recognised electrical organisation was in force and no damage control or electrical repair parties were closed up. Furthermore, in the main switchboard, where under normal steaming conditions in wartime, a senior rating would be the watch keeper, only a junior rating was in charge. The ring main had been split fore and aft with numbers three and four dynamos supplying the starboard side and numbers one and two the port side. To make matters worse, the modifications to the electrical organisation and equipment resulting from the damage to *Belfast* and *Fiji* had not been carried out nor received on board. Particularly damaging was the failure to install an emergency electrical supply system. The only provisions made for an emergency was the supply of emergency lanterns and portable floodlights.

When the torpedo struck, power failed on the starboard side of the ring main and in some sections of the port side. In the forward part of the ship, the lights fed from the starboard side of the system dimmed before the whole section was plunged into darkness. Although numbers three and five dynamos kept running, they were isolated by the ring main breakers which were opened by the direct effect of the explosion. Similarly, on the port side, ring main breakers opened and all communications from the bridge failed immediately due to the flooding of the main exchange and the telephone battery in one of the low power rooms. However, all was not lost. Although the starboard boiler room had been flooded almost immediately, steam was still available in the port boiler room. The Warrant Electrician, who was on the bridge at the time of the explosion, immediately set about rigging the emergency floodlights to restore lighting to the engine rooms, while the Commissioned Gunner (T) supervised the rigging of emergency telephones between the bridge and the engine room. Unfortunately, some of the emergency telephones which had been provided were found to be defective and this seriously prolonged the operation with disastrous results.

Only twenty minutes after the torpedo had struck, the Captain decided that it would be wise to evacuate as many of the ship's company as was possible. Accordingly, hands were piped to abandon ship stations and the repair parties to muster on the flight deck. Due to the breakdown in communications and the need to rely upon word of mouth to pass on the order to go to abandon ship stations, the instructions for the repair parties to remain on board and to muster on the flight deck was not understood. When the destroyer *Legion* came alongside, the Torpedo Officer and most of the electrical repair parties left the ship. To make matters worse, the watch keepers on number two dynamo stopped their machine, thus cutting off all electrical supplies to *Ark Royal's* forward parts. Under these circumstances, the situation deteroriated steadily with electrical repairs depending upon the initiative of the Commissioned Gunner (T) and the few torpedo ratings who remained on board. With the departure of *Legion* all steam and, therefore, all electrical power failed due to loss of feed water in the port boiler room, the sole boiler room available. Under these circumstances the flooding in the forward part of the ship increased. The two 150 ton pumps which were provided to deal with this type of emergency were in a cross-passage which had been rendered inaccessible.

Ark Royal sinking after being hit by a single torpedo

The battle to save this valuable ship was now in the hands of parties from other ships. The destroyer *Laforey* came alongside at 1730 and started to supply electric power and feedwater to the port boiler rooms. Fifteen minutes later a party from the cruiser *Hermione*, under the charge of her Torpedo Officer, Lieutenant GR Heppel arrived with four portable pumps. Using power from the destroyer, Heppel was able to supply the portable pumps and emergency lighting. Accompanied by members of his torpedo party, he made his way below decks in the darkness with the ship 'lolling' alarmingly. They were able to restart number six dynamo and soon the engine fans were working fed by emergency leads. Heppel, who it will be recalled had distinguished himself in the destroyer *Hardy* during the first battle of Narvik, seemed to be getting on top of the flooding. With steam raised and number six dynamo operating satisfactorily, electrical supplies were flowing comparatively freely, allowing the connection to *Laforey* to be disconnected. In the meantime, a signal had been sent to *Legion* to return the repair parties to *Ark Royal*, but this important step took two hours to organise and it was not until 2140 that the Torpedo Officer, Warrant Electrician, Electrical Lieutenant RNVR and a number of ratings returned to the carrier. For a while it seemed as though the repair parties were winning the battle but, in the early hours of the morning, water in the funnel uptake prevented the escape of funnel gases from the port boilers and this led to a total failure of power. *Laforey* returned alongside and again supplied power to the portable pumps, but they could not cope with the flooding. At 0415 next day the ship was abandoned and she sank at 0613.

The loss of such an important ship, especially when she could have been saved by better organisation and understanding of the electrical problems of running a major warship, had added significantly to the demand for a separate electrical department. In most large warships the organisation of the electrical section of the torpedo department was holding its own during a period of rapid change. However, the Torpedo Officer had other duties to perform, both within the torpedo department and as a seaman officer. In some ships he was the senior Lieutenant Commander; indeed, the more important the ship, the more senior the Torpedo Officer. Therefore, where the electrical organisation was most complicated, he was likely to have other duties which affected his overall efficiency as a torpedo specialist and diverted his attention from his electrical responsibilities.

The report on the loss of the *Ark Royal* stated:

In an aircraft carrier which carried a large number of torpedo planes the Torpedo Officer's job, the maintenance of torpedoes and training of pilots in their use, is a full time one and must inevitably take up most of his time and interest in what, after all, is one of the primary objects of an aircraft carrier. Prior to the war ARK ROYAL carried a second Torpedo Officer who was employed principally on electrical duties.

The war complement of *Ark Royal* included an Electrical Lieutenant RNVR who had little experience afloat. He was considered by *Vernon* to be an inadequate substitute for a qualified Torpedo Officer with many years service. Subsequent events were to show that this was a serious underestimate of the potential of these young Electrical Officers.

The failures in the electrical organisation of *Ark Royal* were many and varied but all were fundamental:

(a) No repair parties were closed up.

(b) No organisation existed for restoring power by local control. Thus important circuits were left unconnected in spite of their being largely undamaged portions of the ring main which could have been connected to the ample supply of dynamos left running after the explosion.

(c) The after breaker room was padlocked and had to be sawn open in order to approach and make the breakers.

(d) The telephone from the bridge to the engine room had been moved to the crow's nest so that lookouts could inform the engine room if they were making smoke. Thus, after the explosion contact could not be made between the bridge and the engine room.

(e) The evacuation of the Torpedo and Electrical Officers and repair parties only twenty minutes after the explosion was a major error with disastrous consequences.

(f) The Torpedo Officer, for one reason or another, was not in control of electrical damage control.

The loss of *Ark Royal* constituted a watershed in the affairs of the Torpedo Branch. Only the need to concentrate all efforts upon operations prevented the immediate establishment of a separate Electrical Branch and a reconsideration of the future of the other responsibilitiess of the Torpedo Branch. Meanwhile, the Torpedo Branch had to adjust itself to the increasing complexity of electrical equipment carried in warships.

Reports of damage to major units of the fleet continued to criticise the efficiency of ships' electrical organisations. On 29 March 1942, the cruiser *Trinidad* was on convoy escort duties off the Norwegian coast when she was involved in action with enemy light forces. The ship was hit twice by small calibre shells and later by a torpedo. Electrical repair parties were closed up with the Commissioned Electrician in charge at the main switchboard. Careful attention had been given to communications between the electrical repair parties so as to lessen congestion on the main exchange should damage occur. The small calibre shells inflicted some damage which was easily contained, but when a torpedo struck the port side one of the boiler rooms was badly damaged, the lower steering position was flooded and, worst of all, the damage control headquarters was soon under water killing all the occupants. The Commissioned Electrician took charge of the electrical situation from the secondary damage control headquarters in the forward engine rooms. To correct the list, an operation which took three hours was then carried out during which counter flooding was authorised and oil fuel was transferred from the port to the starboard side of the ship. This restored the ship to an even keel and she was able to proceed to Murmansk, where she remained for six weeks for repairs to the hull before sailing on 13 May for permanent repairs in the U.S.A. On the 14th she was seriously damaged by an enemy aircraft; a stick of three bombs caused a disastrous fire which became out of control causing the ship to be abandoned and sunk by her escort next day. Throughout the two actions, the electrical repair parties performed their duties impeccably and the *Vernon* report stated, 'In the circumstances the organisation worked extremely well and reflects credit on all concerned'. It was unfortunate that the torpedo which hit her was a Mk IX which she had fired at the German destroyers on 29 March. As Admiral Tovey said it was cruel luck that a ship which had fought off the enemy should torpedo herself.

When *Liverpool*, escorting a Mediterranean convoy south of Sardinia in Operation Harpoon on 14 June 1942, was torpedoed by aircraft, the damage control organisation of the ship was able to deal with the serious damage which followed. By now, war experience had led to the standardisation of the organisation of repair parties and their preparedness for action. *Vernon* reported:

Very considerable thought had been devoted to the training and organisation of the electrical repair parties. Each electrical section headquarters was provided with a large perspective diagram of the section of the ship showing the relative position of the compartments and the position of all important electrical gear, bulkhead terminals, permanent emergency cables, etc. It is considered that the time and trouble expended on training was well repaid. The electrical situation was very well handled in spite of serious damage and unforeseen failures of materials. The high standard reached in a ship so recently re-commissioned reflects credit on all concerned.

We have seen how in *Ark Royal* an Electrical Lieutenant RNVR had been apponted Assistant Torpedo Officer. It was an expedient which was to be used increasingly to support torpedo, signals and anti-submarine specialists, ashore and afloat. They soon began to take direct responsibility for equipment in areas of new technology in which regular service officers and ratings had very little experience; radar, voice communications at very high radio frequencies, integrated wireless communication systems, the application of electronics in the fields of gunnery and torpedo fire control, Asdics, homing weapons and influence mines, and all aspects of mine countermeasures. The officers and men needed to fill these roles had to be trained quickly because the equipment had to be brought into service with all speed.

A clear distinction has to be made between the Volunteer Reserve officers who joined the Navy as seamen and, as such, qualified as Torpedo Officers, and the young electrical engineers who were recruited and served in the technical ranks as Electrical Officers. The role of the latter became increasingly important in the increasingly electronically-dependant Navy. They became responsible to the Torpedo Officer for the maintenance of the wide variety of electronic equipment upon which the fighting efficiency of the ship relied. The rapidity with which the change came about can be gauged from the fact that, by the end of 1943, capital ships and carriers were fitted with more than a dozen different types of radars; for surface and air warning, navigation, gunnery control and IFF (Identification Friend or Foe). These required at least three radar qualified Electrical Officers and supporting staff.

At the shore establishments the numbers of officers and ratings under training had to be stepped up, particularly at *Vernon* and at the Devonport and Chatham Torpedo Schools. Still not enough men were being trained to meet the demands of the fleet. Some of the shortfall was made up by the training of WRNS in electrical and weapon maintenance and repair. In order to expedite the training of women, Wrens joined *Vernon* from the Governemnt Training Centre at Hounslow in increasing numbers.

Before long they were taking electrical courses identical to those undertaken by Leading Torpedo Operators. They were not employed in ships at sea but they carried out important routines in harbour on destroyers and smaller ships: they were not qualified in high power distribution systems in cruisers and larger ships , but a special course in alternating current circuits trained them to be employed in the growing commitment to American-built frigates. Throughout their courses and subsequently in their employment in the fleet, Wrens maintained a very high standard of work and enthusiasm. There is no doubt that without them the Torpedo Branch would have been very hard-pressed to meet its commitments.

It was not only the training at home which had to be increased. In November 1941, owing to the long delays in sea passages to and from the United Kingdom,it was decided to increase the scope of training in the Mediterranean and to build a Torpedo School at Alexandria. When the staff for the school arrived in April 1942, accommodation was found in two substantial buildings known as the Villa Laurens and the Ramleh Primary School at San Stephano. Two months later the new Torpedo School was commissioned as HMS *Pharos*, under the command of Acting Commander HC Stock. A training target of forty Seamen Torpedomen and twelve Leading Torpedo Operators monthly was given, but no sooner had training begun when bad news was received from the Western Desert. Allied forces had been driven back to El Alamein and, under the threat of the early occupation of Alexandria by the Germans, the school was paid off on 28 June 1942. The staff and those under training were sent to Durban, followed a few weeks later by the stores and equipment. A temporary Torpedo School was set up at Pietermaritzburg while a new school was built at Wentworth near Durban; this finally opened as HMS *Assegai* in April 1943.

At a time when new ships were arriving in the Mediterranean equipped with the latest electronic equipment, replacement ratings trained in low power at *Pharos* and *Assegai* and associated establishments were invaluable assets. In October 1943, an officer of the South African Naval Forces, Lieutenant Commander RMO Simpson, who had taken the Long Torpedo Course at *Vernon(R)*, assumed duties as commanding officer of *Assegai*. The school achieved a very high standard and was being provided with the latest training aids. However, the war in the Mediterranean was beginning to flow in favour of the Allies and, as success followed success, ships moved to other stations around the world and the need for *Assegai* diminished, so that by June 1944 she had been paid off. From January 1941, when overseas torpedo training began at Alexandria until *Assegai* closed, 6,855 officers and men went through on courses. That this training could continue with such efficiency and so promptly after Allied forces were driven back to El Alamein was due to the efficiency and enthusiasm of all concerned. The importance to the war effort of the part played by the South African Naval Forces should be noted. Without them the temporary home at Pietermaritzburg could not have been brought into operation so quickly when the demands of the Mediterranean Fleet were at their peak.

By the time Operation Overlord had been launched against the

Normandy beaches in June 1944 and the Allied land forces had begun to advance through Europe the time seemed at last ripe for the consideration of the formation of an an Electrical Branch. To prepare the way for this major reorganisation, a committee was set up under the chairmanship of Rear Admiral HC Phillips (later Vice Admiral Sir Henry Phillips). One thing which accelerated such radical developments was a report from *Vernon* on the loss of the cruiser *Spartan* on 29 January 1944 to a German Hs 293 guided missile off the Anzio beach-head. It was a report which combined the consequences of an attack by weapons of new technology and the failure of the electrical damage control arrangements.

In the opinion of *Vernon's* examining team, personnel were in a semi-dazed state through lack of sleep and blast shock, a situation in which it was essential that there should be good communications and that the men should be confident in their leadership. The main switchboard had been demolished by the initial hit and the Warrant Electrician had been killed. In his absence there was a lack of direction given to the electrical repair parties and watch keepers. *Vernon*'s Report stated:

Having no instructions and nothing to get on with they wandered more or less at random, either in search of occupation or with no definite aim and were hence impossible to find had they been required for an organised effort, such as making up the ring main in local control had power been restored.........It is essential if men are to work below decks with any degree of confidence in badly listed and blacked-out ships, that they should know that the live central authority is fully in touch with the situation and will warn them in time to make good their escape should abandonment of the ship become necessary. Should they lack the feeling of security afforded by good communication, the average person is apt to seek employment on the upper deck, and, once there, it requires a considerable effort of will power to take them below decks when there is no light other than the feeble illumination of emergency lighting.

In *Spartan*, overall control appears to have broken down simply because the complement of ships at that time did not allow sufficient flexibility amongst the officers responsible for the electrical efficiency of the ship. The officer in charge of the electrical department was the Torpedo Officer, but in *Spartan* both he and the Gunner (T) were required for other duties at action stations, leaving only the Warrant Electrician for electrical duties and he had been killed. The situation was made worse by the fact that the Torpedo Officer was also the First Lieutenant and consequently had to take over for the Commander, who had been killed, whereas he should have been free to take charge of his department.

It would be wrong to suppose that the lessons learnt from such damage control reports were the dominant factors influencing the considerations of the Phillips Committee, but they focussed attention upon the shortcomings of the existing electrical organisation. Much more important was the deployment and development of a growing range of electronic equipment operated and maintained by a large body of officers and men who had joined the Navy for the period of hostilities. It was essential for the future efficiency of the Navy that a considerable number of them should be encouraged to transfer to permanent careers in the new Electrical Branch.

The Phillips report did not outline in detail the form which the new Electrical Branch should take, but it did give sufficient guidance for preliminary steps to be taken to provide the personnel which would in due course be required. Fleet orders were issued calling for volunteers from suitably qualified regular and reserve officers to form the nucleus of the new Electrical Branch, which was established in late 1945 under the direction of Rear Admiral SL Bateman who took up his post on 1 January 1946.

Meanwhile, in February 1945, the Board of Admiralty had set up a steering committee 'to make recommendations to put into effect the decisions of the Board to insitute an Electrical Branch of the Navy which will ultimately be able to absorb the present department of the Director of Electrical Engineering, also having regard to the report made by Rear Admiral Phillips on 15th March 1944 and the Board's conclusion thereon'. Rear Admiral GB Middleton was appointed as chairman of the steering committee.

They rendered a comprehensive report delineating in detail the scope and responsibility of the Electrical Branch, its personnel structure, training requirements and precisely how it should be set up, drawing its resources from the current organisations with responsibilites in the field of electrical engineering. A large proportion of the officers came from the wartime Royal Naval Volunteer Reserve, and it was considered important that there should be a hard core of experienced regular officers, provided by former Torpedo Officers who saw in the new branch an opportunity to exercise their preference for a career with a technical background. A number of Warrant Electricians were commissioned in recognition of the great debt which the Navy owed to these highly trained and devoted officers. The rating structure was supplied from the already well established Electrical Artificers and those ratings from the Torpedo and Signals Branches who had ben concerned with the maintenance and preparation of electrical and electronic equipment.

It was understandable that these sweeping changes in the organisation of the Royal Navy were not always popular amongst the officers and men of the Torpedo Branch. Nine years before, in 1936, Admiral Sir Charles Lambe, then serving as Commander of *Vernon*, had predicted the inevitability of these developments. However, those who had trained as Torpedo Officers, and who had served at sea during the war in charge of the electrical installations of the ships of the fleet, were in some cases reluctant to give up their responsibilities. Furthermore, some of them found it difficult to see how the traditional attitudes within those ships could be maintained by a branch which depended in the main upon the transfer of 'hostilities only' officers and men. Hence for a short time Torpedo Officers were reluctant to turn over their responsibilities to officers of the Electrical Branch. Sometimes they resented the fact that in cruisers and larger ships, a Commander (L) was appointed to take charge of an electrical department in which previously a Torpedo Officer of the rank of Lieutenant or Lieutenant Commander had performed not only in the electrical duties but those concerned with the weapons of his branch as well. Such a prejudiced outlook soon vanished as mutual respect was established.

Torpedomen could be proud of their achievements in the development and maintenance of the electrical facilities in ships of the Royal Navy. Inevitably, in war the main objective had been to keep the ships running and to be able to introduce up-to-date weapons and equipment with the minimum of disruption. This had been achieved, although the installation of some essential electrical systems had been slow to follow. There were many examples where, under war conditions, means could not be found to make these alterations. Such a case concerned the fore and aft cable runs sited along the ships' side passages. These were particularly vulnerable to action damage. Quite often minor damage had resulted in considerable disruption which would have been avoided if the electrical cables had been run down the centre of the ship. Equally frustrating was the delay in installing newly rated systems in which the electrical power should be twice the estimated action/salvage load, with half the capacity provided by diesel generators. Both these critical requirements had long been called for by torpedomen.

When the war ended the Torpedo Branch had to face the inevitable outcome. Bereft of its electrical responsibilites, it would be merged with the Anti-Submarine Branch. Any differences which torpedomen might have with the Electrical Branch would soon disappear in the tribulations which would accompany the marriage.

THE END OF THE WAR FOUND THE Torpedo Branch still responsible for the distribution of high and low power electricity in ships, but torpedo officers had increasingly to depend upon RNVR Electrical Officers to provide the expertise needed to deal with weapons and equipment using advanced technology. It was a situation which also confronted the Signal and Anti-Submarine Branches which had responsibilities for the proper functioning of radar and asdics. There was, therefore, a certain amount of common ground between the Torpedo and Anti-Submarine Branches, but the latter guarded jealously their domination in anti-submarine escorts and they resented the Torpedo Branch's hold on the development and operation of anti-submarine weapons, although the exigencies of the war had produced a tacit truce.

Meanwhile *Vernon* had begun to return to the Gun Wharf at Portsmouth. In the Spring of 1943, Seamen Torpedomen from HMS *St Vincent* recommenced training in *Vernon(P)*, as did Wiremen(L), Torpedo Coxswains and Junior Probationary Electrical Mechanics (JPEMs). That autumn the Mining Instructional Department returned to Building 17A from Roedean. As a precursor of things to come officers of the anti-submarine Long Course at *Osprey* began to attend *Vernon(P)* for a week's course in Anti-Submarine weapons. RAF officers were also seen in the mess as they passed through on a mining course. In October 1944, HM the King visited the establishment to mark the twenty first anniversary of *Vernon* ashore. Among those on parade were contingents from *St Vincent* (complete with WRNS band), *Hornet* and *Dolphin*.

Plans were approved before the end of the war - and before the branch reorganisation was finalised- to rebuild the establishment as rapidly as possible and before peacetime economies and cuts began to bite. Two large buildings, West Block and North Block, were to be built for instuctional purposes on the south side of the Creek. Work began as soon as possible, the north wing of Vulcan was demolished and pile driving began, inevitably to the discomfort of those working close by. Given their proposed, size considerable care was taken with the design and materials of these new buildings. Working drawings were well advanced by VJ Day. Much additional new construction was planned. On the north side of the creek a large PO's and Chiefs' acommodation block was to be built on the sites of the former Dido and Mohawk buildings and the main boiler house. This would be demolished along with Donegal House that would make room for an extension to the Wardroom. A new Chapel was planned and No17 building was to be rebuilt with a new attack teacher. A new Polyphemus Block was to house the Mine Design Department, A/S weapons and engineers' and shipwrights' workshops. A new   Inflexible Block would cater for electrics and there was to be a new Captain's House, gymnasium, swimming bath, tennis and squash courts, sports pavilion, garages and boiler house. The decision to reorganise the branches would obviously have an impact on these plans but they also proved hopelessly ambitious for the straitened circumstances of post-war Britain.

By the end of May 1945, the instructional load at *Vernon(R)* had been much reduced and the school authorities wanted their buildings back. 7 June 1945 was the last day of naval instruction. Over the next few weeks ninety two 5 ton lorry loads of *Vernon's* instructional equipment were shifted from Brighton to Portsmouth, and by the middle of July the Navy had left: the girls public school reopened in January 1946, and a few weeks later Captain NV Grace, accompanied by a number of officers and their wives, attended chapel at Roedean.

During *Vernon's* occupation of the school buildings, a fund had been collected for the completion of marble panelling in the chapel and a cheque presented to the Headmistress enabled the work to go ahead. The School Council elected Captain Grace as a governor, a pleasing gesture and fortunately a purely honorary post, which was just as well for he was faced by mounting problems at *Vernon*, particularly with the inrush of personnel from ships and establishments being paid off or reduced to their peacetime complements. The influx caused a temporary but enormous overbearing of officers and men. When Commander GC Blundell arrived on 4 March 1946 to relieve Commander DG Clark as the establishment's Executive Officer, the return to *Vernon* at Portsmouth was in full flood and the need to restore the establishment to normal standards of peacetime efficiency was growing daily more urgent. A little space was provided when the MX organisation was wound up October 1945 but it was hardly enough.

To provide emergency acommodation and instructional space it had already been necessary to allocate the old battleships *Malaya* and *Ramillies* to *Vernon*. With 6-inch gun batteries removed, and classrooms built in the casemates, the two battleships were commissioned on 15 May 1945 as *Vernon II*, and moored alongside one another in Fareham Lake. Thus after twenty two years a part of *Vernon* was once more afloat.

On its return from Roedean and HMS *Marlborough* at Eastbourne, Whitehead Instruction was set up in Vesuvius and Mohawk buildings, and the trials part of the Whitehead Department also came home in June 1946, having left Alexandria in August 1945 and spent the intervening months in Eastern House, Alverstoke, near Stokes Bay. The torpedo trials organisations at Stokes Bay and Carlisle closed down on 1 February 1946. Post war experimental torpedo running and first of class discharge trials were carried out at Bincleaves (Portland) and Arrochar on Loch Long. Instead of moving to *Vernon*, minesweeping remained at *Lochinvar* at Port Edgar. The book production department returned from Ropley in April 1946 and the Mining Department began to return in July although the controlled mining organisation went to a new home at *Defiance* at Devonport.

Electrical training was shed as quickly as possible. Electrical instruction at Roedean first went to temporary accommodation in *Marlborough* at Eastbourne College as the new electrical training establishment was prepared at Fareham as HMS *Collingwood*. What had formerly been *Vernon's* Electrical Department remained at Havant until it was able to take up its new quarters there: in August 1946, all electrical instruction ceased at *Vernon* and the department moved to the new Electrical Branch headquarters in *Collingwood*. RNVR Torpedo Officers with electrical specialisation were demobilised or transferred to the new 'L' branch where many prospered. Torpedomen were left with a soul-searching decision whether to hang on to their Seaman status and hope for the best in a reducing navy which was becoming increasingly technologically orientated, or to transfer to a new Electrical Branch, not fully qualified as electrical engineers, but bringing to the new branch a much needed knowledge of the sea and ships and their administration. They would thus improve their chances of promotion but they would surrender any chance of a sea-going command.

Those who chose to remain found the Gun Wharf a depressing place. The buildings were drab, the roads were in a state of disrepair and were blocked by dockyard rubbish; and the 'swing it 'til Monday' attitude of all personnel, in the worse sense of the phrase, was pervasive. But, most important of all, the new unified Torpedo and Anti-Submarine Branch which was due to be officially formed in October 1946 in accordance with the previous year's order was being accepted with sullen indifference by many officers and men. Resentment was felt particularly keenly in the Anti-Submarine Branch. Being concerned principally with the operation of small ships, the relationship between officer and men in the branch was particularly close. Officers resented those from another branch intruding on their chances of small ship commands. Under these circumstances a free and easy attitude had grown up over the years which combined with a keen sense of achievement at the defeat of the U-boats.

The ratings were user/maintainers who were proud of their technical knowledge. Gordon Hayman, a Submarine Detector Instructor with a distinguished war career for which he had been awarded the British Empire Medal, wrote:

I and others, could fill a huge blackboard with the electrical circuits of any anti-submarine instrument or set that existed, all from memory. Over the years, we had learnt to love the electrics and electronics and committed them to memory.

They were resentful that, unlike the torpedo ratings, they were not offered the opportunity to transfer to the Electrical Branch. In Hayman's opinion, the cream of the senior torpedo ratings had transferred to the Electrical Branch and those that remained lacked the training and technical knowledge prevalent in the Anti-Submarine Branch. It was, of course, an allegation which was strongly denied by torpedomen. The hostility, real or imagined, ran deep. Hayman confessed that when Submarine Detector Instructors were obliged to convert to Torpedo Anti-Submarine Instructor the reception given to their instructors was quite often unfriendly and uncompromising.. In Hayman's course, the Torpedo Gunner's Mate was reputed not to know his job and to be unable to answer simple technical questions. Further irritation was caused by the introduction of early morning training, where Petty Officers were taught to throw a hand lead line, a skill which most of them had acquired when they were junior ratings. Worst of all, they were driven close to mutiny by the Chief Gunnery Instructor who had been brought in to smarten the drill and general demeanour of the new Torpedo Anti-Submarine ratings. It was not a policy which was welcomed by what Hayman referred to as the 'gentle pingers'.

The discipline of the parade ground was foreign to these small ship men and rightly or wrongly it was deeply resented. Under these circumstances, Blundell was faced with a totally unacceptable situation both as regards the state of the establishment and the morale of the officers and men who were to form the Torpedo Anti-Submarine Branch.

The introduction of a Chief Gunnery Instructor was with hindsight, a mistake. His presence in *Vernon* offended both Anti-Submarine and Torpedo Ratings. Its one redeeming feature was that the common hatred of the situation was a unifying force between the ratings of the two branches. Chief Petty Officer Joe Davies, one of the senior Torpedo Instructors, had been sent to Whale Island for a parade training course and had come top of his class. On return to *Vernon*, he found that the Chief Gunnery Instructor was in charge of the parade ground and was President of the Chief Petty Officers' Mess. For a mild and kindly man Joe Davies' comments upon this situation are unprintable. Hayman remarked:

It seemed to the 'gentle pingers' that the Chief GI who ruled the parade ground was specially selected from the Portsmouth Glass House warders. He had a particularly glittering eye which seemed to swivel in all directions at once. Even so he was almost felled by a rifle flung at him by a frustrated leading seaman during a drill session on parade ground.

Over forty years later Hayman still harboured this resentment, he said:

I suspect that the other SDIs like me, had enjoyed great partnerships with their A/S officers before, during and after World War II. In Vernon wardroom they leaked the fact that they were suffering too but advised us to stick it because there was an iron fist and it would be used unsparingly. So we graduated from our quiet world into the realm of explosives and underwater weapons. Hatefully, regretfully, but we did. So in 1987 the fleet has an Underwater Branch second to none in the world.

The Torpedo and Anti-Submarine Branches had each emerged from the war justly proud of their achievements, knowing that the relationships between officers and men in both branches were particularly close and that their expertise and resourcefulness were second to none. Inevitably this justifiable pride brought forth a measure of resistance to change, but this was mitigated by many of the younger Torpedo Officers being 'Hostilities Only' RNVRs and electrical specialists to boot. Conservatism from Torpedo Officers thus tended to come at *Vernon* and elsewhere from a few pertinaceous elderly officers who did not take kindly to the intrusion into their alma mater of officers from another branch. They were, however, greatly in the minority, as were those officers of the Anti-Submarine Branch who were openly opposed to the merger.

The memories of this difficult period of Lieutenant Commander DD MacFarlan, a well known Torpedo Officer, give an excellent impression of the problems faced by both torpedomen and their Anti-Submarine colleagues in coming to terms with what was not entirely jokingly known as 'perversion':

..to receive in your mail...a letter..asking you if you wanted to pervert to TAS or become an electrician was somewhat traumatic. When I was thirteen, father ordered

'right turn, double march into the Navy' and from then on my ambition was to command a ship and this took precedence over the unlikely event of ever becoming an Admiral. By turning over to the new Electrical Branch there were were obviously brass hats for the picking in the early stages as knowledge of the Navy and its administration would obviously be needed while the graduate technological whizz-kids were settling in. I had joined to be a seaman officer and trained and lived as one and elected to stay one. I believe that the severance of 'T' from the Electrical has had a very profound effect on the torpedoman and 'tasman's' status on board. Up till now the Gunnery and Torpedo Officers were both powers in the ship controlling the bulk of the Seaman complement. Guns took charge of of all ceremonial and waggled the so called main armament to his heart's content while Torps, as well as his pieces of weaponry had much to do with the comfort of all those on board - ventilation, lighting, heating, telephones and power for the armaments. From the time of the split the TAS Officer was in his element during underwater exercises but otherwise became a general dogsbody.

MacFarlan went to *Osprey* for the conversion course where:

...we were immediately subjected to a hymn of hate from our course officer who typified those pingers who were all against the merger mainly for fear of losing hold of their pinging commands. Many others took a broader view and were friendly. The first whoop of joy came from our course officer when two of us failed our audiometer test...My pitch discrimination was below par and I had an uncomfortable 48 hours wondering what the future might hold.

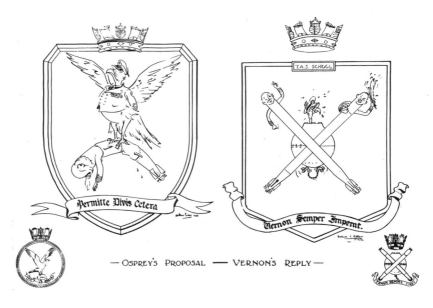

— OSPREY'S PROPOSAL — VERNON'S REPLY —

Opposing views of the marriage of the Torpedo and Anti-Submarine branches

Happily the Captain of *Vernon* came to the rescue and decided that a TAS officer was not an Asdic operator and that MacFarlan was to continue the course.

It was not, therefore, an easy situation which greeted Commander Blundell when he arrived at *Vernon* to relieve Clark. Under the benign and paternal captaincy of Grace, it was hard for Blundell to introduce the sweeping changes that were necessary, and he looked forward with mixed feelings towards the appointment of Captain J. Hughes-Hallett, whose repuation as an aggressive, talented and ruthless reformer was already the main topic of conversation in the wardroom and senior rates' messes. Some of the older officers who were serving out their time in *Vernon* were heard to make remarks which were sheer bravado. They were, they said, 'not going to be put upon by this upstart', but put upon they were. Within weeks of Hughes-Hallett's arrival on 20 June 1946 many of these officers who were surplus to *Vernon's* requirements, and who had come to the end of their careers, were on their way to retirement.

It was not long before the easy and relaxed tempo of the Grace regime was replaced by bustle and change. From the window of his office in the Administration Building, Hughes-Hallett looked out upon a scene of devastation and disorder. It was not long before his reputation for direct action and the avoidance of red tape was being demonstrated. Blundell had been frustrated by the dockyard's indifference to the rubbish and other obstructions on the roads. He was authorised by Hughes-Hallett to inform the dockyard that unless it was removed within a few days it would be embarked in vessels of the *Vernon* Flotilla and dumped in the Channel. The dockyard took immediate action.

Discipline was tightened up and standing orders were strictly enforced. For some, the new atmosphere at *Vernon* was far too similar to the regime at Whale Island; and across the water at *Dolphin*, the Submarine Base, complaints began to be heard that access through *Vernon* to *Dolphin's* liberty boats at Marlborough Pier was being impeded. However, Blundell was determined that nothing should stand in the way of the creation of a thoroughly professional approach to the important responsibilities thrust upon the emerging Torpedo Anti-Submarine Branch.

In his pursuit of excellence Blundell believed in making informal rounds on his own. On one of these excursions, on a Sunday morning, he visited the Petty Officers' mess and found half of them still in their bunks. He quickly had them turned out and issued orders which put an end to this practice. A visit to the wardroom in the small hours revealed officers sleeping on the settees. They came from *Dolphin* and *Hornet*, had missed the last boat to Gosport the previous evening and were in the habit of sleeping in *Vernon's* wardroom. These incidents reeked of the old attitude to the weekend of which Hughes-Hallett was determined to rid the TAS Branch. He vowed that *Vernon* should have a reputation for smartness and efficiency at least equal to that of the Gunnery School, if not better. A stop was soon put to the habit of officers of other establishments using *Vernon* as an overnight haven, but in some ways it was counter-productive as it impaired the long standing reputation of *Vernon* as the Navy's most relaxed and friendly establishment.

Blundell was glad for the support which he received from Hughes-

Hallett in eradicating these problems, but he found his Captain's attitude to his Executive Officer hard to bear. Most Captains were only too willing to delegate authority to their Executive Officer for the day to day running of the ship or establishment. It was a team affair, a partnership between the Executive Officer and his Commanding Officer in which the latter only interfered if he sensed that things were going wrong. There was no such team spirit with Hughes-Hallett; he chased and chivvied Blundell, expecting him to achieve miracles of reorganisation in the minimum of time. Blundell soon became an expert in assessing the Captain's moods. If he was sitting quietly at his desk it was usually the signal for a long dissertation upon his recent ideas and the action which he required to be taken. If, on the other hand, he was pacing up and down, or rolling a pencil between his hands, it was the signal that he was going to carry on at Blundell about something that had gone wrong, however minute it might be. On these occasions, he left Blundell standing and never once offered him a chair. In stature, Hughes-Hallett was a small man, quite similar in build to Napoleon whom he admired immensely. On the other hand, he was not enthusiastic about Nelson whom he considered to be too soft.

This autocratic Captain was a confirmed bachelor who had difficulty in coming to terms with the presence of women in the establishment. For the whole period of his command he never once visited the WRNS quarters. Two incidents illustrate this idiosyncrasy. The Captain and the Commander had on one occasion been carrying out rounds in an area which included male and female heads (lavatories) and office accommodation. A member of the Wrens, who was in the ladies' heads, and a Petty Officer who was in the mens' heads, on hearing the bugle announcing the arrival of 'rounds', had quickly adjusted their dress and were running to get back to their offices. Hughes-Hallett, on spotting the fleeing couple, turned red with annoyance but said nothing until his return to his office when he pressed the buzzer to summon the Commander. He greeted Blundell's arrival with the words,

Commander did you see that incident this morning at rounds?

Blundell was not quite sure what incident, but he replied,
Yes Sir, of course.

Well Commander, said Hughes-Hallett, *I want all the trees, shrubs and long grass removed in that area so that these incidents cannot occur in future.*

On another occasion a dance for the ship's company was arranged at *Vernon*. This amenity was greatly valued in the aftermath of war in Portsmouth and Southsea, since the air raids had destroyed most of the clubs, theatres, cinemas and dance halls. After these dances, which usually ended well before midnight, the sailors were given the chance to say farewell to their partners at the main gates to the establishment. This meant that for half an hour or so sailors and their girlfriends could be seen walking down the road leading to the main gate. On the night in question the Captain, returning in his car from his residence in Sussex, encountered many sailors and their girlfriends, some in their last embrace before parting. Next morning, Blundell had no sooner reached his office than the Captain's buzzer sounded non-stop. It was for just such an occasion that he had a peephole made through which he could observe the Captain seated at his desk. By this means he was able to see that the Captain was rubbing his pencil feverishly between his hands, in obvious agitation. Immediately Blundell had entered the Captain's office he was greeted with excited rhetoric:

Commander you won't believe it, I happened to enter VERNON *just at the time the dance you organised on the parade ground was ended and believe it or not Commander, the road was littered with sailors and their girl friends copulating in the main drive, Commander.*

Blundell was for a moment overcome with surprise, but with great tact, he replied:

Good Lord, I am so sorry. I will deal with that Sir.

Alright Commander but in future I want the main drive properly lit all along the base so that it will discourage this dreadful practice.

The Commander, looking suitably impressed, replied,

Thank you very much indeed Sir' and duly left the Captain's office.

The importance of the amalgamation of the Torpedo and Anti-Submarine Branches had prompted the Admiralty to appoint an assistant to Hughes-Hallett to ensure that the merger was brought about efficiently and expeditiously. The officer appointed was Commander Roger Welby, who was given the acting rank of Captain while holding the appointment. This provided Hughes-Hallett with an assistant with sufficient seniority to get things done and to take charge of the new instructional and training programmes. However, in those early days of the merger there was only one anti-submarine specialist on the staff of *Vernon*, Lieutenant PD Sturdee. He was well placed to judge the attitudes of officers and men towards the merger, but he found himself looked upon as something of a traitor when he visited *Osprey*. This attitude was displayed mainly by the older anti-submarine specialists, whereas the younger officers of both branches were more adaptable and mindful of the origins of the Anti-Submarine Branch which were rooted in the Torpedo Branch during the First World War. They understood the anomalies which had been created by the separation of responsibilities for weapons and detection equipment.

Shortly after his arrival at *Vernon*, Hughes-Hallett sent for Sturdee to discuss the establishment of anti-submarine training facilities. Hughes-Hallett was acknowledged to be a man with a very firm grasp of tactical and technical detail but he was unfamiliar with anti-submarine equipment. Enthusiastic, and anxious to achieve his objectives, he swept aside criticism and ignored those who urged caution, but when faced by firm and logical arguments he was prepared to listen. When Sturdee arrived in the Captain's office he was informed that the decision had been made to introduce anti-submarine training to *Vernon* and that all that was required was to set up an Asdic dome in a suitable building and to get on with the instruction. Sturdee explained that there was rather more to anti-submarine warfare and Asdics than just setting up an Asdic dome. Hughes-Hallett was impressed by Sturdee's frank and measured arguments; supported by Welby, he instructed Sturdee to draw up a programme of work and a list of equipment required to make an early start with anti-submarine warfare training at *Vernon*.

Hughes-Hallett's character is embellished by so many stories and anecdotes that it would be dangerously wrong to trivialise or obscure the significance of the leadership, drive and determination with which he directed the merger of the two branches. His enthusiasm for cycling and his possession of a ten-speed bicycle, his occasionally sardonic sense of humour and the ideas which emerged daily from his fertile imagination could be the subject of an entire biography. Most of his ideas were practical and useful, but from time to time he veered into the realms of absurdity, as when he suggested to Lieutenant Commander EW Ridley that useful information could be gleaned from experiments with the transmission of sound in a liquid of constant viscosity and that a likely liquid would be treacle! His staff had learnt to separate the excellent ideas from the eccentric, and the suggestion that large quantities of treacle should be purchased was quietly forgotten, by which time Highes-Hallett had moved on to the consideration of more immediate problems.

There was no doubt that Hughes-Hallett was one of the most important figures in the whole history of the Torpedo, Torpedo Anti-Submarine and Mine Clearance and Diving Branches of the Royal Navy. It has been said that he was the only man who could have merged the Torpedo and Anti-Submarine Branches with such efficiency and in such a short time; but Blundell, who knew him better than anyone else, believes, whilst recognising Hughes-Hallett's outstanding contribution to the Torpedo Anti-Submarine Branch, that a man of more human character but blessed with equal drive and energy could have been found amongst the list of senior Captains of the Royal Navy.

In spite of his awe inspiring presence and undoubted ruthlessness Hughes-Hallett was intensely loyal to his staff and backed them to the hilt if he felt that they were carrying out their duties with enthusiasm and to the best of their ability. Lieutenant EN Poland was impressed and sustained by this unequivocal loyalty. He had been sent to the Surrey Docks in the Thames with instructions to collect two 45 foot former German torpedo recovery vessels and to bring them round to Portsmouth. After forty eight hours to accustom the crews to these diesel engined craft, they sailed and berthed for the night at Sheerness dockyard. The following morning at 0700, an intention to sail signal was sent. When no reply had been received at 0745 the craft proceeded to sea. While rounding the North Foreland, they ran into the teeth of a Force 8 gale and, with some difficulty, reached the sanctuary of Dover Harbour where a signal from the Commander-in-Chief Nore was waiting, calling upon Poland to render his reasons in writing for leaving Sheerness contrary to orders. Poland replied drawing attention to his intention to sail signal. He almost immediately received a copy of a signal from the Captain of *Vernon* to the Commander-in-Chief Nore which read:

With respect consider your signal of ... could adversely affect the sense of initiative in a young officer.

When the two vessels arrived at Portsmouth, Hughes-Hallett was at the jetty to meet them with two words: *Well done.*

Throughout the period of unification, controversy continued as to whether *Osprey* at Portland or *Vernon* at Portsmouth should be the principal Torpedo Anti-Submarine School. It was a complex issue exacerbated by the underlying opposition to the merger from a significant minority. Even without this emotionally charged atmosphere, the amalgamation of these two seaman branches would have been a formidable task. That it was completed without lasting recriminations was a tribute to the determination of those who realised that there was no practical alternative. For many months, however, the relegation of *Osprey* to a reduced, albeit important, role caused bitterness among former anti-submarine specialists who saw themselves losing their hard won identity in the larger and more complex torpedo world.

Blundell had his difficulties as President of the wardroom mess where many of the Anti-Submarine Officers, quite naturally considered that *Osprey* had a much better run and more intimate wardroom mess. The wardroom mess suggestion book for that period, if it could be found, would provide some interesting and revealing information.

Osprey did offer some advantages as a training centre. The establishment itself was situated close to, and overlooking, the wide waters surrounding Portland Bill which provided excellent and easily approachable exercise areas. But Portland was relatively remote from a naval base and power and if the Torpedo Anti-Submarine Branch was to compete with other specialist branches, it was essential that it should have its headquarters at Portsmouth. Hughes-Hallett had to fight hard for that decision to be made and throughout he was particularly careful not to be influenced in any way by his torpedo background. It had not been easy going, and for a while it seemed that *Osprey* might indeed become the principal Torpedo School. Plans for *Malaya* and *Ramillies* to be towed to Portland to provide overflow accommodation and instructional facilities failed, partly because of the financial implications and partly because of the combined opposition of Flag Officer Submarines, Flag Officer (Air) Home, and the commanding officers of *Excellent* and *Dryad* who wrote to the Commander-in-Chief Portsmouth that they thought it vital that the Central TAS School should be at Portsmouth. So it was that *Vernon* became the headquarters of the new TAS Branch.

Hughes-Hallett urgently needed more training space so he sent for Blundell and Sturdee and told them that the top floor of Warrior Block together with Nos 49 and 50 Buildings were were to be converted immediately into classrooms for anti-submarine instruction. There was, as Blundell pointed out, no official authority to carry out these alterations nor were there any official funds available to do so. Nevertheless, like all Hughes-Hallett's ideas, it had to be acted upon immediately. No plans or lists of equipment existed but they were quickly drawn up and a list of equipment was prepared. These lists were soon given official status but the problem of finance remained. With the tacit support of the Commander in Chief, the dockyard work force, already working in *Vernon*, reacted enthusiastically, but still the money had to be found. This came from an unlikely source.

During those days of rationing, the Government encouraged the production of pigs fed upon waste food. Navy, Army and Air Force establishments produced large quantities of waste food products which, if not channelled in the direction of pig production, would be disposed of as garbage. Consequently, in most well run establishments, the food was carefully graded to make sure that there no injurious products in it, particularly tea leaves, government crockery and cutlery, or razor blades. Thus cleansed, *Vernon*'s pig swill was sold to a pig farmer on the east side of Portsea Island. Because of the severe shortage of pig food *Vernon* received a very good price for this by-product, producing a pig fund which was entirely under the control of the Commander. Neither the Captain, the Commander-in-Chief nor the Chancellor of the Exchequer had any influence over the manner in which it was spent. It provided flowers to brighten the ratings' dreary quarters, glass for new greenhouses, uniforms for *Vernon*'s civilian boat crews, and material for building the new Anti-Submarine School!

The war years had seen a proliferation of training establishments and a major priority in the immediate post-war years was to find a better balance between the adminstrative tail of the Navy and the operational fleet. In addition as much manpower as possible had to be demobilised in order to restore the nation's economic health. For the first time the word 'rationalisation' was heard. In 1946 all Portsmouth naval establishments' boats were withdrawn and replaced by civilian boats from a dockyard pool. This paid no regard to the overall organisation of the establisments which depended to a large degree upon the flexible use of their boats. Furthermore, the smartness and efficiency of a ship or establishment is reflected in their boats, and the idea of the *Vernon* being served at the whim and fancy of a central boat pool was quite unacceptable. The battle for the retention of *Vernon*'s boats was eventually won, but civilan crews were to be provided and it was for these that the 'pig fund' paid for smart uniforms. The boats were drab and no allowance was made for paint. Blundell overcame this by visiting his friends in ships in the dockyard who were prepared to give him the necessary enamel and paint, which he smuggled round the harbour into *Vernon*. Such mundane matters as this, which bear heavily upon the morale of men at the shore training establishments, are often lost sight of at the Admiralty where life is dominated by problems which seem of a different order.

A new and more streamlined organisation was developed for the new *Vernon*. There were to be three main departments:

(a) The Adminstrative Department. This was administered by the Commander, who was responsible for the running of the establishment in accordance with the King's Regulations and Admiralty Instructions. The department was also very closely bound up with the Instructional Department. For every course of instruction a Course Officer was appointed responsible to the Commander for the discipline and welfare of the men and women undergoing instruction.

(b) The Instructional Department, under Commander (TAS). This appointment took the place of the old title, Commander (Instructional). The

Commander (TAS) was responsible for the co-ordination of the instruction carried out in all Torpedo Anti-Submarine Schools. A 'Deputy Executive Officer' (DXO) was responsible to the Commander for all instruction in *Vernon* and for parades, drills and disciplinary training. The war years had seen many changes in instructional techniques. There had been significant technological advances in the design of instructional equipment and it was found necessary to establish a Training Development Section to supervise the introduction of working sectional models, film strips and many other training aids. One of the weaknesses in the pre-war instruction at *Vernon* had been the tendency to appoint specialist officers and ratings as instructors without any regard to their ability to teach. This had now changed and courses were introduced to train new staff in instructional technique. The demand for instructional books, pamphlets and drawings increased dramatically and the Book Production Section, the Instructional Drawing Office and the Photographic Section, were combined into a Publication Section within the Instructional Department.

(c) Sea Trials and Development Department. Before and during the war, sea trials and development had been divided into four separate departments dealing with torpedoes, mining, minesweeping and electrical matters. Electrical, Minesweeping and Controlled Mining trials were now at other establishments, and chemical warfare had been transferred to the Gunnery Branch, leaving the remainder of *Vernon* sea trials and development responsibilities to be amalgamated under a single Sea Trials and Development Department. The department was again organised into four sections; Torpedo, Mining, Underwater Defence and Diving (transferred from the Gunnery Branch in 1944). The two latter sections were new to *Vernon*, the Underwater Defence Section being responsible for the co-ordination of the development and sea trials of anti-submarine and anti-torpedo equipment after it had passed the experimental stage. The department was housed under one roof and all sections were served by a single trials office. It was soon found that the operational control of all weapons and equipment of the Torpedo Anti-Submarine Branch had reached a stage of electrical and electronic complexity that required its own trials section. Hence, in 1948 a Control Section was added. Until then the sections, although using the same trials office, had worked as separate units and it was not until 1948 that the whole department came under the direction of a Commander (Trials), initially Commander RA Villiers.

MacFarlan was an early member of the new Sea Trials Department. As he later recalled he was caught up in the post-war revolution in the management of naval operations:

Having survived my perversion course, I was delighted to be appointed back to Vernon to relieve Charles Cameron in the Torpedo Control Section, Sea Trials. Not being convinced myself I found it hard to convince the Senior Officers Technical Course, mostly salty old destroyer captains, that the enclosed bridge and operations room were the best place in which to fight the battle. As well as the requirements of input and output to and from the electronic plotting machines in the Ops Room for the prosecution of underwater warfare, the section carried out theoretical investiga-

tions on the optimum shape of convoys against torpedo attack, the probabilities of our submarine torpedoes against U-boats, (and)the merits of German LUT torpedoes against our own (future) pattern runners.

Part of that revolution was the new TAS Branch itself. It was offically inaugurated on 10 October 1946 and the first long TAS Course began at *Vernon* in 1947. Hughes-Hallett was not put off by the hostility shown to a Chief Gunnery Instructor, indeed he was all the more determined that the new branch should present a smart image to the Navy and to the public. He, therefore, requested the appointment of an officer of commissioned warrant rank from the Gunnery School to take charge of parade ground drill and the general smartness of officers and men as they went about their business on a daily basis. Blundell and many other officers believed that Mr Rose, for that was his name, immaculately dressed in the gunnery style, including gaiters, performed an absolutely essential role in the development of the new branch. He was greeted with the same animosity as the Chief Gunnery Instructor by ratings of both the Torpedo and the Anti-Submarine Branches who had been used to a far more relaxed atmosphere at *Osprey* and *Vernon*. The appointment of this officer will remain a bone of contention in spite of the fact that he carried out his duties with great tact and good sense.

It was not only Mr Rose who was held in awe. The Captain was considered by the majority of officers and men serving in *Vernon* as something of a tyrant and they nick-named him 'Hughes-Hitler'. The fact that he was a bachelor and had his quarters in the battleship *Ramillies* in Fareham Lake was something of a relief to *Vernon*. In the old battleship he had a formidable companion who commanded the *Vernon* II complex. Commander Anthony Miers VC, DSO was one of the nation's great submarine heroes, though his reputation has recently been disputed, and a man entirely equal to Hughes-Hallett in ruthlessness and determination. The two were well matched and there was no doubt that Miers had a quietening effect upon the Captain's ebullient character. Nevertheless, so great was the impetus which sprang from Hughes-Hallett's tireless spirit and restless mind that most of the obstacles to the successful development of the new branch were quickly swept aside.

Hughes-Hallet's unothodox methods of increasing his instructional accommodation were brought about in part by the break-down of the elaborate 1945 scheme to rebuild the esablishment. The immediate post-war years were even more austere than expected. Industrial renewal and housing the people were, quite reasonably, the Government's priorities and *Vernon's* new permanent buildings were a long way off. They were to be steel framed and steel was in such short supply that its allocation was directly in the hands of the Prime Minister. Other expedients had to be resorted to in order to comply with the Admiralty directive to have TAS instruction under way by April 1947. Five large huts in *Hornet* were taken over for the training of Third Class Rates and the theoretical instruction of all TAS ratings. This cut down on the boat work required to get to and from *Vernon* II. When accommodation at *Hornet* was reduced in mid-1947, alternative acommodation was found in huts in Clarence Barracks, until in June 1948 four huts called 'Pound' in honour of the former First Sea Lord were completed in *Vernon* on the site of the bombed Dido Building. The creation of hutted accommodation in Gosport had allowed *Malaya* to be replaced by a smaller and newer ship, the reserve *Royalist* which could provide her own power. *Vernon*'s sea training tasks , incuding torpedo running after October 1947, were transferred to *Osprey* where the Anti-Submarine Tactical Unit had moved back from its wartime acommodation at Dunoon. Two minesweepers, *Pluto* and *Fancy*, were provided to take classes along the coast between the establishments, passages that allowed minesweeping training on the way. This cut a week off the course. The old Coastal Forces torpedo parting shop at Portland Dockyard was used for the torpedo preparation and routines. *Lochinvar* carried out additional minesweeping training until No 18 building at *Vernon* was converted for this purpose in early 1948.

The establishment also carried out a number of miscellaneous training duties. Instructor Officers entered through *Vernon II* and Portsmouth Division Royal Marine recruits did three weeks seamanship training there. Sea Cadets came to *Vernon II* for a week's acquaint and Hughes-Hallett encouraged forty schoolboys from Midland towns to spend two nights there in a scheme funded by the Ministry of Labour. TAS training of National Service and Special Service new entries was carried out at *Vernon* between April and November 1947 and 1,600 ratings passed through the establishment before the commitment ceased. At the beginning of 1948 *Ramillies* paid off and was de-stored in a day to protect her stores from theft. She was replaced by the frigate *Modeste* but *Vernon II* ceased to exist. There was a scheme to return *Royalist* to the Reserve Fleet but she was saved for *Vernon* because of her Royal Marine training functions. With the departure of *Ramillies* the Captain moved ashore to the former WRNS quarters at Donegal House after the building had been briefly used to house the Senior Officers Technical Course. Hughes-Hallett moved in in February 1948 only shortly before being relieved by Captain WJC Robertson on 18 May. By then the formation of the new TAS branch was well under way. Some torpedo and anti-submarine specialists were waiting to carry out the conversion course to TAS, and this process was not completed until 1950.

A rating's perspective of life at *Vernon* at this time has been given by Fleet Chief Petty Officer JE Adams. He qualified at *Vernon* in the Autumn of 1947 as a Torpedo Detection Rating Third Class (TD3). As a young rating, his opinion of the Hughes-Hallett regime was in sharp contrast to those of the senior Torpedo and Anti-Submarine ratings who were serving in *Vernon* at that time. Without wartime experience, and having spent time in a battleship, followed by four weeks of gunnery instruction at Whale Island, he suffered from none of the inhibitions of the old Torpedo and Anti-Submarine ratings who so strongly resented Hughes-Hallett's vision of the new and meticulously smart TAS Branch. After a long and distinguished career in the post-war Navy, Adams could remember clearly and without rancour the names of the officers who were responsible for the establishment of the Torpedo Anti-Submarine Branch. He commented:

HMS VERNON was complemented with Captain Hughes-Hallett, Commander Carver, Lieutenant Commander Kimpton, Lieutenant Creswell and Mr Rose, the Parade Ground Gunner, to name but a few to frighten any young ordinary seaman.

There any hint of criticism ended. Adams was one of a new generation which accepted without question the new and brisker tempo of life at *Vernon*. For these young men of the new electronic age the approach of the old torpedomen had gone forever, with the concept of the 'gentle pingers' so dear to the hearts of Hayman and his contemporaries. These formerly desirable and worthy standards had served the Navy well but now they had to give way to the demands of the rapidly changing environment.

In Adams' recollections, the sheer amount of knowledge required was hard for a young rating to grasp, particularly at a time when manual and aural skills were still at a premium. Junior ratings were being given their first experience of co-ordinating eyes, ears and hands to work together to operate the control training unit of an Asdic Type 144, the improved set introduced in 1942. This was not an easy task, and it took years for an Asdic operator to become fully proficient in controlling the transducer training movement blind-folded, and to become part of the control team in a modern anti-submarine vessel.

Anti-submarine weapons instruction centred around depth charges, Hedgehog and Squid. Frequently important visitors would be invited to witness Squid drill to see how adept a crew was in the art of muzzle loading. All that Adams could remember about Hedgehog was that it was a dangerous weapon which was inclined to misfire.

The smarter and more vigorous environment at *Vernon*, was epitomised by the improved standards of drill and dress. This tended not to be noticed by the individual courses. Their more lasting memories were of the sea training in the minesweepers of the *Vernon* Squadron and anti-submarine instruction in the Portland based Second Training Squadron of *Castle* class frigates. Adams' course officer, a rugged A/S Bosun, made a strong impression 'standing on the bridge of HMS *Leeds Castle*, dressed in a sheepskin Liberty bodice, hurling abuse at the unfortunate seasick sailors'. Fortunately, most of the class survived his harangue and only two were deemed 'unfit for small ships'. Also well remembered were the few days which were spent in instruction in Seaward Defence, mainly because of the two eccentric characters in charge of the classes on board *Vernon's* two small mining tenders. These two Chief Petty Officers were seamen of the old school who, in teaching the students how to lay a 'back to back loop', earned the unforgettable names 'Seaweed Brown' and 'Loopie Coop'.

The breadth of knowledge which a TD 3 was expected to absorb was more than it had ever been. In the Torpedo Section he was expected to understand the rudiments of torpedo control, and the theory of sound, magnetism, electric motors and trigonometry as well as to be able to strip a torpedo, reassemble it and carry out important routines. The anti-submarine instruction contained an electronic element of increasing complexity. More and more technically complicated devices had to be understood into which the instructors inserted sticky tape conveniently placed behind the contacts to provide malfunctions which the trainees were required to detect and remedy.

An account of these formative years would not be complete without a mention of the social life of *Vernon* which played such an important part in establishing the esprit de corps of the new branch. A happy and efficient environment in which to live was essential, particularly during the first year of traumatic change when acrimonious discussion was liable to occur in the living quarters of officers and men. In Blundell the wardroom had a firm President who nevertheless had the good humour and patience to discuss the multitude of suggestions which cluttered the mess suggestion book. Service in the wardroom, was, however, the primary responsibility of John Canty. This unassuming, quiet man, small of stature, had been the mess caterer for a number of years. Unable to enter the Navy as a seaman because of defective eyesight he had joined the Paymaster Branch from which he had retired in 1929 as a Paymaster Lieutenant. At that time he was serving in the Victualling Office of *Vernon* and it was appropriate that he should be offered the post of mess caterer in the wardroom. From that moment he became what Blundell described as 'the greatest servant *Vernon* ever had'. Unmarried, he gave his whole life to the promotion, well being and efficient running of the *Vernon* wardroom mess. The standards of efficiency which he sought he had inherited from his father who, as a Petty Officer in the Victorian navy, had served in the Royal Yacht. In spite of all the difficulties during the war years, Canty made certain that the standards of service in the *Vernon* wardroom were the best that rationing would allow.

Not least amongst his achievements was an inspired intervention which pre-dated his appointment as mess caterer. In 1921, during the preparation for the move from the old hulks to the Gunwharf, Canty was a Stores Chief Petty Officer. He discovered that the Executive Officer was anxious to instal ship-type tip up wash-hand basins in the officers' cabins. Canty gently reminded the Commander that, now that *Vernon* was ashore, hot and cold running water was available. This timely intervention prevented the new officers' mess being equipped with ancient washing arrangements and no running water in the cabins.

One of the mysteries surrounding John Canty was that as a rating in the Supply Branch he had been awarded the Distinguished Service Medal and Bar. It was typical of the man that he never boasted about this remarkable achievement which took place during the First World War. In addition to his two DSMs, he was awarded the Albert Medal. Blundell remarked that although his time as Huges-Hallett's Commander was the most harassing and demanding in his whole naval career, one of those who gave him the greatest support was John Canty. Not only was Canty an extremely able man but he was also one of the kindest, always willing to do almost anything that he was asked by officers in the wardroom. He was a man of the greatest integrity at a time of tremendous temptation in the catering trade during the period of rationing of foodstuffs and clothing. Fiddling the rations was an almost daily occurence and one which, like smuggling during the eighteenth century, was regarded in some quarters as an almost honourable pastime. There were many incidents in the Portsmouth Command of the daily evasion of the rationing regulations; there was one senior officer serving in the Royal Naval Barracks who always had a large ham available at his home. It was common knolwedge that it had been supplied by the barracks wardroom mess caterers. This was only one example of the many 'rackets' which were continuously going on, a black market that flourished upon bribery with the concomitant threat of blackmail. Scandals erupted in more than one barracks in the Portsmouth Command . It was fortunate for *Vernon* that they had in Canty a man of such tremendous integrity. He never entered the black market or bribed anyone for increases in *Vernon's* rations and he never granted anyone a favour in that respect.

One of Canty's greatest achievements was concerned with the wardroom mess silver. On the outbreak of war the Wardroom Mess Committee had decided that all the most valuable items should be stored at Curtis's warhouse in Portsmouth, where it remained even when, in 1940 and 1941, Portsmouth was heavily blitzed. It might have been prudent to remove the silver from the Portsmouth area entirely, but before this could be done the warehouse was bombed and burnt to the ground. The silver was contained in a safe which in the conflagration had become so hot that its contents melted into a single lump. Thus the trophies assembled over many years were lost forever. After the war, the ingot was returned to *Vernon* and was sold to provide a small nucleus for the purchase of new mess silver. Blundell, as Mess President, gave full authority to Canty to use mess funds to augment the meagre nucleus. Over the next few years Canty was able to purchase the fine pieces of silver which graced the table on post-war guest nights. This former member of the Supply Branch played a vital part in the creation of the Torpedo Anti-Submarine Branch. He ensured that *Vernon* was regarded by the officers of the new branch as their spiritual home with the same fervour as that displayed by the old Torpedo Branch. In recognition of Canty's great contribution to the life of *Vernon*, an ante-room in the wardroom was named after him.

The *Vernon* Sea Trials and Development Department was the link between the fleet and the research and development establishments. These were controlled by the new Admiralty Department responsible for the development, manufacture and procurement of underwater weapons. After the war the responsibilities for torpedo and anti-submarine warfare at the Admiralty were divided between a number of Directorates and Departments. On the material side procurement was the task of the Anti-Submarine Material and the Torpedoes and Mining Departments at Bath . These were now amalgamated into one department known as the Underwater Weapons Department. In London, several divisions of the Naval Staff had been responsible for policy decisions regarding torpedoes, mines, anti-submarine weapons, anti-submarine material amd the prosecution of the undersea war; their responsibilities were now combined in one division under the Director of Torpedo Anti-Submarine and Mine Warfare (DTASW).

Most of the anti-submarine warfare research and development during the war had been carried out at the Anti-Submarine Experimental Establishment at Fairlie. On 28 February 1946, the Fairlie establishment was closed and the 134 members of staff and their families were transported by special train from their Scottish retreat to the more familiar Dorset countryside. The sight that greeted them at Portland was enough to dampen the spirits of even the most hardy! The establishment had been partly blitzed during the war and what had been left standing was more like a run down inner city tenement than a government development establishment. These partially derelict buildings had to accommodate not only the original staff but also the additional personnel recruited during the wartime years at Fairlie. To these were added the staff of the Directorate of Anti-Submarine Material who joined them from Bath. However, with the addition of some temporary buildings, and the advantage of the high priority which was still accorded to anti-submarine weapons, the staff were able to settle down into their old home, His Majesty's Underwater Development Establishment (HMUDE) in 1947. Some of Fairlie's scientists were trasferred to the Torpedo Experimental Establishment (TEE) which continued its work at Greenock. The Mine Design Department, so long a part of the *Vernon* scene, became the Admiralty Mining Establishment that remained at Havant; a new building was designed and built for the reduced staff in the grounds of West Leigh House.

By the end of the 1940s, the Torpedo Anti-Submarine Branch had acquired some maturity. The conflicts of opinion which had attended its creation were largely forgotten and progress was being made through the steady work of DTASW, the Underwater Weapons Department, HMUDE and the other research and development establishments. With the Cold War developing there was no danger of relapsing into the stupor of a long peace. This was nowhere truer than at *Vernon*, where the accelerating speed of technical developments was causing frequent reassessments of the plans for the development of weapons and equipment. *Vernon* and her people had to adapt themselves to the need to keep closely in touch with scientific developments and the progress of weapon technology at home and abroad.

THE PREVIOUS CHAPTER COVERED THE political and domestic problems involved in the creation of the Torpedo Anti-Submarine Branch. These were not the only problems that it faced. Many critics doubted the continued need for traditional naval forces in the nuclear era. It was assumed that any future aggression by one of the major powers would evoke the use of atomic weapons. The Soviet Union surprised British planners by exploding her first nuclear weapon in 1949. If the ports were going to be destroyed in the nuclear exchange the defence of shipping might be pointless. Until the development of hydrogen bombs in the mid-1950s, and to some extent thereafter, the Admiralty could argue that the initial nuclear exchange might well not be decisive and that the defence of sea communications would still be vital. Convoy escort would thus still be the key both to Britain's survival and to any hope of victory. But the huge fleet of escort vessels assembled during the war was a rapidly wasting asset. The Soviet Union was known to have taken over the latest types of high speed German submarine in 1945; these made the old, slow wartime escort vessels obsolescent. Meanwhile the Royal Navy continued to be deployed in far distant places safeguarding British lives and property. Thus on one hand the Government was obliged to maintain a large fleet and to undertake a considerable programme of building, while on the other, given the United Kingdom's post-war economic problems, it had to seek drastic economies. It all made a desperately difficult environment in which to develop a comprehensive set of capabilities for underwater warfare.

Minesweeping, too often the cinderella of underwater warfare priorites, had not stopped with the end of the War. The sea beds were still littered with mines and an international organisation was set up to provide machinery for the direction of policy and general control of mine clearance operations in European waters . The Central Board of Control for this organisation operated through four zone boards; Eastern Atlantic; Mediterranean; Barents, Baltic and Black Seas; and Kattegat, Baltic Straits and Approaches.

The minesweepers required to undertake this massive task were supplied from the navies of the European allies, the former Axis powers and Sweden. The United States were represented on the Central Board but took no part in the operations - a sign of the neglect of mine countermeasures operations that was to have serious effects on US Naval operations over the next four decades and enhance the importance of British and other Allied efforts.

During the war the Germans had laid approximately 126,000 mines and over 32,000 sweep destructors in the Eastern Atlantic Zone. In the Mediterranean they and the Italians laid a further 100,000 mines of all types. In the same area the British laid 255,000 mines giving a total of 480,000 mines to be accounted for before these waters could be declared safe. It was calculated that 20,000 mines had been swept in these zones during the war and an unknown number destroyed by other means.

Tremendous problems faced the minesweepers, particularly in areas where there were mixed minefields of moored and ground mines. Nearly all minefields were protected by moored anti-sweep devices, such as static and explosive obstructors and empty mine cases moored with five inch chain. The ground mines were fitted with period delay mechanisms which meant that the same area had to be swept up to fifteen times.

British minesweepers were involved in the clearance of mines in the Eastern Atlantic and Mediterranean Zones. In the former, 586 British minesweepers were operating in September 1945, but with rapid demobilisation this force had dwindled to 237 within six months. In the Mediterranean there were 211 British minesweepers in November 1945, but only 82 remained four months later. In contrast, the Germans started in the Northern Area with 196 minesweepers and by March 1946 they outnumbered the British. The transfer of mine clearance responsibilities to the former Axis powers continued in the Mediterranean where the Italians increased their minesweeping force from 42 to 71 during the same period. British minesweepers, however, continued to achieve a very high level of success. They swept more mines in proportion to their numbers than the other nations as they swept fields which were already well known to them, such as the ground mine areas on the east coast of England from the Humber to the Dover Straits, and the deep minefields in the English Channel and off Ireland. The mine clearance programme in the Mediterranean was also a predominantly British operation. Royal Navy minesweepers swept moored minefields in the Sicilian Channel and off Tripoli, and mixed minefields in the approach to Trieste.

Vernon was kept busy training new personnel for this gigantic task, in analysing the results of the sweeps and in the development of new equipment required to sweep mines fitted with the complicated circuits which had been developed by the end of the war. At the height of the post-war mine clearance programme the British minesweeping forces consisted of 234 vessels, of which 62 were *Algerine* class fleet minesweepers which were suitable only for sweeping moored mines. The job of hunting for the much more dangerous ground mines was left to the fleet of 126 wooden minesweepers. These were of three types, the 292 ton American built BYMS, the 165 ton MMS(1) and the 255 ton MMS(2).

Although a new post-war fleet minesweeper was designed, the Royal Navy concentrated on replacing the smaller coastal minesweepers and inshore mine countermeasures vessels. Their shallow draught made them less vulnerable to moored mines, while their low displacement made pressure mines less of a threat. They were also easier to build from non-ferrous materials, a necessity given the capacity of the latest Soviet mines to work on very small peak fields, thus defeating degaussing. Three classes were planned ,and the programme was given a crucial push when the outbreak of the Korean war in 1950 threatened a Soviet mining offensive at least as formidable as the Germans' campaign in 1939-40 . These vessels were the Royal Navy's top priority in the Korean War rearmament and even more would have been built if the Admiralty had not had to sacrifice the programme to maintain its carrier fleet at the end of the Government's review of defence policy in 1954.

Their chacteristics were:

Displacement		Length Overall	Beam	Draught	Speed	Number Built
Ton	360 tons	153	27.7	8.2	15 knots	117
Ham	120 tons	106.5 - 107.5	21-22	5.5-5.75	14 knots	93
Ley	123 tons	106.75	21.75	5.5	14 knots	10

They were originally to have a most unimaginative set of names combining colours with various insects and birds but happily more euphonious place names were chosen with the relevant final syllable. 'Hams' and 'Leys' were built for inshore work as minesweepers and mine location vessels respectively. The 'Leys' as minehunters proved more useful in the mine countermesures role, but Brinkley and Brenchley of the First Minhunter Squadron from 1962 to 1965, were also used for various auxiliary and tender duties as was the fate of the more numerous Ham class sweepers, many of which went straight into reserve. Most important, however. were the 'Tons', officially 'coastal minesweepers' but capable of global deployment. Like most of the smaller vessels (some 'Hams' were entirely wooden) they were built of wood with aluminium superstructures and were fitted with Eddy Current Compensation gear. Strict attention to the control of ferrous metal carried on board ensured that they were virtually invulnerable to magnetic mines. But they were relatively noisy and the early practice of streaming acoustic sweeps such as the Acoustic Hammer (AH) and lower frequency Acoustic Displacer (AD) abeam from derricks posed unacceptable risks. In any case Minefield Game Theory showed that all minesweepers would eventually be sunk by all acoustic mines working on a wide band of frequencies. Thus by 1961 the Combined Towed Acoustic Sweep had been evolved which allowed the towing of the AD under a float some way astern. This was done in combination with the Magnetic Loop Sweep with Pipe Noisemakers attached to it to cover the required acoustic spectrum. This was effective in sweeping most types of magnetic, acoustic and combined magnetic/acoustic mine assemblies.

But all this still left the pressure mine unsweepable. It had, therefore, to be 'hunted'. It was fortunate that the Royal Navy had already carried out research at Fairlie during the war into the use of extremely short asdic transmission pulses for the detection of 'bottomed' submarines. In due course, this research led to the development of the Asdic Type 162 'Cockchafer' for the detection of wrecks and ground mines. It was, however, only partially successful and a detection device with far higher resolution was required. In the early 1950s, a former Post Office scientist, DG Tucker, was employed at Portland leading a minehunting project team which developed an improved version known as the Asdic Type 179, which was fitted in British mine location vessels (as they were then known) for some years after the war.

At the same time a far more complicated system was being investigated by the Admiralty Research Laboratory at Teddington. This asdic, Type 178X, a joint venture by Portland and Plessey Cottage Laboratories, proved to be a step too far and never went to sea. The problem was complicated; it involved finding operating frequencies which would be high enough to reveal detail of objects detected on the bottom of the sea and, at the same time, to allow the ship to stand off at a sufficient distance to avoid being damaged by the detonation of any mine which had been located. So many different frequencies were explored that the research team trying to develop a successor to both 178 and 179 named their prototype mine detection asdic the EFFIE (Every F... Frequency in Existence). This was fitted to the former 'Miner' class controlled minelayer *Gossamer* whose successful trials led to the development of the extremely successful Type 193. This had a search frequency of 100 KHz and a classification frequency of 300 KHz, giving a search range of around 600 metres, a classification range of 250 metres

A pre-production set was fitted to *Shoulton* which carried it to the USA in 1959-60 for comparative trials with the US Navy's minehunting system. This was followed by a refit and a European sales and demonstration tour in 1961-62. After evaluation in *Shoulton*, the 193 was fitted to sixteen Royal Navy 'Tons', beginning with *Kirkliston* in 1964. The new emphasis on hunting with the need to use human divers for classification and counter mining led to the allocation of the Diving Trials Ship *Reclaim* to *Lochinvar* in 1960 as 'Mine Countermeasures Support and Diving Trials Ship' and then the creation of the combined Mine Warfare and Clearance Diving Branch of the Royal Navy on 25 February 1966.

A number of major mine countermeasures operations had been carried out in the decade or so before this merger. In 1956, the Suez Crisis, (Operation 'Musketeer'), had demanded a major minesweeping effort by the fifteen Ton class minesweepers of the 104th and 105th Minesweeping Squadrons under the command of Captain M/S Mediterranean. A swept channel was provided for the amphibious assault against moored and magnetic mines. Minesweeping went on after the assault in danger areas and anchorages. Home station and Mediterranean Clearance Diving Teams, an assault team and a French team cleared the beaches and harbours and helped to salvage the ships sunk by the Egyptians in the Canal.

In 1963, cable laying off Esbjerg and Borkum required major mine clearance efforts. In the former area Operation 'Clear Road' required nine 'Tons', the buoy layer *Laymoor* and diving ship *Reclaim*. In the Borkum area, Operation 'Cable Way', *Reclaim* was joined by the first Minehunting Squadron, *Shoulton*, *Brenchley* and *Brinkley*, fourteen 'Tons', including the five RNR vessels of the 10th Minesweeper Squadron, and *Bossington* and *Sheraton* of *Vernon's* own 5th MSS. No mines were found on these operations, but the same year, during Operation 'Ice Scot' carried out in two wartime convoy anchorages off Iceland, *Reclaim* and the four 'Tons' of the 2nd MSS found four old British Mk 14 controlled mines.

Minesweeping and minehunting had to take their place alongside the responses to the other naval threats facing the North Atlantic Treaty Organisation. From its inception in 1949 Britain and her NATO allies had to deal with a growing fleet of Soviet submarines which promised to restore the U-boat peril at its early 1943 worst. Moreover, the cruisers that Stalin built primarily as status symbols also had to be taken seriously as a new generation of potential surface raiders. Advanced torpedoes were clearly required by the Royal Navy but the story of post-war British torpedo development was little short of disastrous.

The end of the war had seen the appointment of Dr. Burns as Chief Scientist at the Torpedo Experimental Establishment at Greenock. He used his fertile imagination to initiate a series of weapons of truly revolutionary design:

Zonal - A ship launched winged weapon intended to skim across the sea at low altitude powered by a ducted propellor and then enter the water when its wings would fold and the weapon would continue at sixty knots with active homing.

Zoster - An air launched version of Zonal.

Zombi - A submarine launched 30-inch weapon capable of homing down to 1,000 ft.

Zeta - An air launched anti-submarine weapon.

Dewlap - A 21-inch surface skimming winged weapon for use by motor torpedo boats.

Burns' tenure as the Chief Scientist at TEE Greenock was short. His colleagues had little faith in his 'flights of fancy' and 'science fiction' projects. To them, the whole approach was unrealistic. Too much money and too many man hours were wasted in paper designs without any research or development into components of the required size or performance. Some of the technical problems of these weapons would have taxed the technology of the 1990s. To develop the correct shape for these weapons hydrodynamic research was carried out at the Glen Fruin water tank, the wind tunnel of the Blackburn Aircraft Company and the cavitation tunnel at Haslar, but in general they were little more than an expensive way of providing training for drawing office staff. They were at last cancelled in 1949. Lewis, who became the Superintendent of Torpedo Experiment and Design at Greenock the following year, considered that Dr Burns and his Z weapons were far ahead of their time and that it was ill advised to attempt such a huge leap in weapon development, especially in the financial circumstances of a nation in the grip of post-war austerity.

The need to save money also dictated a conservative design for a high performance pattern running torpedo designed to use hydrogen peroxide fuel, as pioneered by the Germans. It was decided to convert the old Mk 8 design (Arabic numerals were adopted in 1950) despite the fact that nearly all the materials used in the Mk 8 were incompatible with the highly corrosive and dangerous HTP. The project was known as Ferry, and after much metallurgical research to produce compatible components twelve torpedoes were assembled at the Torpedo Experimental Establishment and a series of very successful trials were carried out. In 1953, these torpedoes, now called Fancy SR were issued to the submarine depot ship *Maidstone*. Backed by meticulously prepared maintenance instructions and careful supervision these torpedoes remained in use for two years. They performed well but on 16 June 1955, whilst one was being struck down through the loading hatch of *Sidon* at Portland, a tremendous explosion sank the submarine and killed thirteen officers and men. The cause of the tragedy was HTP leaking and coming into contact with oil of some kind. Work continued on the 21-inch Mk 12, as it had become, but a further explosion on the Arrochar range and the rigorous safety standards required caused its abandonment at the beginning of 1959. The problem was not so much the HTP fuel but the need to put enough resources into designing a torpedo that could use it safely. The Royal Swedish

Navy acquired details of the Mark 12 torpedo and of the disaster enquiry and used British experience to design a modern HTP torpedo, the Tp 61, which has earned a reputation for high speed and reliability.

British resources were spread too thinly over too many projects. Despite the expensive diversion of the Z weapons some work was being done on practical homing torpedoes. The wartime 'Dealer' became 'Bidder A', part of a project to develop a passive homing, electrically powered, torpedo for use from surface ships or submarines. The novel features of the earlier weapon were replaced as 'Bidder' became a 21-inch weapon propelled by conventional contra rotating screws and a silver zinc battery. It eventually reached production in the 1950s as the Mk 20 (S) for submarines and the Mk 20 (E) for frigates. Matched to an elaborate fire control system it was mounted in rearwards facing tubes in the new generation of frigates but unfortunately it proved both too slow to catch nuclear powered submarines and too insensitive to deal with conventionally powered boats unless they were snorting at periscope depth. It was withdrawn from frigates in the early 1960s but was kept as a last ditch anti-escort weapon for submarines until 1982.

The Mk 20 was also used for wire guided torpedo experiments which followed earlier work by Post Office engineers fitting German equipment to the 21-inch Mk 11. In 1951, Flag Officer Submarines, (Rear Admiral Simpson, who had commanded the Tenth Submarine Flotilla in Malta during the war), attended a trial at the Bincleaves Torpedo Range of such a weapon fitted with 3000 yards of cable. It was fired into Portland Harbour set to run at a depth of 3 feet and tracked by a powerful head lamp fitted in the practice head. Simpson took over the controls and conned it round the harbour back to the base. The results were impressive enough to justify further development in co-operation with Vickers Armstrong. Work went on for five more years but the system, code named 'Mackle' and based on the Mk 20, had a very complex guidance system . The contract with Vickers was terminated and the project became 'Grog'. In view of the lack of cohesion demonstrared by the programme so far the name was considered to be appropriate. The system was simplified and the first 'Grog' torpedoes were ordered for trials in 1959. The system eventually entered service as the 21-inch Mk 23 torpedo in 1966 but further delays in fitting the asociated submarine torpedo control system TCSS-9 delayed full operational capability until 1971.

Mk 23 was a slow passive homer, only suitable for use against submarines. To engage surface ships British submariners had still to make do with the old reliable Mk 8. This was improved still further , being given at last the facility for gyro angle to be set on discharge; the final version was designated 'Mk 8** Mod 4 Cable Set'.

If British heavy torpedo development was a troubled tale the story for air dropped weapons was happier, if only at the outset. Squadron Leader Robertson, the designer of the wartime 'Dealer' joined TEE and developed Dealer B as an 18-inch passive homer with conventional twin screw propulsion. Trials against submarine targets in 1953 obtained such a high hit rate that Captain NA Copeman of *Vernon* announced that a new era had dawned in naval warfare; the submarine was no longer secure. In June 1954, approval was given for the torpedo to enter service as the 18-inch Mark 30 but this success was short lived.

As part of the Conservative Government's repeated attempts to cut defence expenditure between 1952 and 1958, an informal agreement was made with the USA that the UK would give up developing and producing lightweight torpedoes and rely on American supply. The money allocated to producing a Mk 30 Mod 1, which would have been the best weapon of its type in the world, was diverted to buying less effective active homing American Mk 43s. This was intended to be a stop gap order until the American Mark 44 could be supplied but this was not available until the 1960s when it was built under license in Britain. In 1956, a contract was placed with the Plessey Company for 'anglicisation' of the Mark 43 but it remained a singularly unsuccessful weapon with a hit rate some four times worse than the Mark 30 even in its original form. Perhaps TEE's biggest success was therefore not developed to its fullest potential.

One reason for this decision was the priority still given to 'Pentane', a heavy active homing air dropped weapon designed to deal with high performance submarines. 'Pentane' had begun in 1947 with TEE personnel being transferred to the Admiralty Research Laboratory at Teddington to work on the project. It became top priority after the abandonment of the 'Z' weapons but, nevertheless, it took until 1954 to decide on the design. By then it was being left behind by developments elsewhere. The helicopter was emerging as the main naval anti-submarine air platform which meant that lightweight torpedoes were becoming of greater importance. Nevertheless work went on until 1958 when Pentane was finally cancelled on the grounds that its search rate was too slow for nuclear powered submarines. By that time the only aircraft that could have carried the large and bulky 21-inch weapon was the RAF's Shackleton. Moreover, as part of the last and most stringent period of the defence review process the Naval Staff had decided in 1957 to follow the logic of their informal agreement with the Americans and stop work on all air dropped torpedoes.

Over £1.7 million had been spent on 'Pentane' and the naval and scientific staff at TEE pressed hard for the development of a submarine launched high test peroxide version. They believed that such a torpedo would put Britain in the forefront of torpedo development and that it would be far superior to the wire guided torpedoes upon which research and development were being concentrated; but the 1957 decision also saw the end of another TEE project, the 'Negress' 14-inch and 12-inch anti-submarine weapons. Also cancelled in the 1950s was the abortive rocket propelled 'Bootleg', a final attempt to give aircraft an underwater attack weapon. The decision was taken to rely on the new 'Red Beard' tactical nuclear bomb for use against major surface targets.

With the licence-built Mk 44 finally coming into service in the mid 1960s the decision of the previous decade was reversed. A long term staff target was drawn up for an advanced air dropped torpedo, but it was cancelled in 1970 and the American Mk 46 Mod 2 procured to fill the gap until the new British long term project came to fruition (see chapter 21).

It is easy to blame this poor record on Government parsimony and Admiralty bureaucracy. While Superintendent of Torpedo Experiment and Design at TEE, Lewis had experience of both. Every item of expenditure was scrutinised no matter how small. Only £200 per annum was allocated for university participation in the establishment's work and this was to be cut by 25 per cent. Lewis protested and was supported by Captain Guy Sayer now Director of Underwater Weapons. The TEE Budget was approved subject to a cut of ten per cent in areas decided locally. Local initiative was not always appreciated, however. In March 1950 Lewis had predicted an overspend and had taken action. As he later remembered:

so...I bought some £50,000 worth of silver from Johnson Mathey. We knew we wanted more silver for 'Pentane's' sea water battery and the Stock Exchange was sure that silver prices would rise. I was quite severely reprimanded for issuing the money in that year's budget but it saved the Navy nearly all that sum, as silver prices did rise and we used the silver. Naval and military department accountancy proved to be a crippling and stultifying obstruction to all Naval development organisations.

But that is not the whole story. The shortages of resources reflected failure in management and communication. The old days of *Vernon* running a tight knit development programme with user and designer in close harmony had been replaced by a high technology world where scientists went their own way, too often divorced from the joint realities of user needs on the one hand and financially constrained higher policy on the other. Yet to be fair to all participants in this sad tale, these were hard times. Naval tactics were being transformed more quickly than in any previous peacetime period, perhaps more quickly than ever before. Not for nothing were staff requirements constantly changing, to the despair of research and development staffs. At the same time Britain was having to come to terms with an equally rapid revolution in her world strategic and economic position. As governments of both the main political parties tried to find the least unfavourable balance of policies they inevitably tried do too much with too little, only to be forced into cuts when it became clear that too much was being attempted. The war had misled the Naval scientists, members of the 'Royal Naval Scientific Service' (RNSS) since 1946. They too often believed that any good idea would be funded; but it would not be and could not be. The only pity was that this was not recognised earlier and that greater discipline was not exerted on all those involved in British high technology defence projects, not the discipline of penny-pinching but that of a limited series of weapons programmes that were practical and which could be afforded.

Attempts were made to improve the organisational structure of weapons development. A combined Underwater Weapons Establishment was set up at Portland in 1959 (See Chapter 19) but this did not solve the problem of the balance of responsibility between the RNSS and the uniformed branches. Some naval officers still regarded all scientists as rather mad and best employed on purely scientific matters. But , within the RNSS, it was considered there was too much emphasis on the advancement of individuals for their scientific attainments rather than their leadership qualities. This had been to the detriment of project management and had resulted in the late arrival of equipment in the fleet, if it arrived at all. It fuelled accusations that the scientists were more interested in their projects and in working on the frontiers of knowledge than in getting equipment to the ships at sea.

An investigating committee, of which the principal members were Sir

John Carroll, Deputy Controller for Research and Development and the former Director of Underwater Weapons, Rear Admiral D Cawthra, reported early in 1964. Their principal recommendation was to give the Chief Scientists of the two main research and development establishments autonomy by making them Directors in their own spheres. The naval Directors of the weapons departments at the Admiralty were now required to concentrate upon the co-ordination of all programmes as they affected the design and equipping of ships and submarines. The responsibility for research and development was transferred to the new RNSS Directors.

This was an improvement but it did not solve the problems of torpedo development. A new wire guided weapon called 'Ongar', intended for use against both surface and submarine targets had been under development since 1958. It was an advanced device, electrically driven with two speeds and directed by information passed along the wire from a tactical data handling system. The target would be acquired by a passive sensor which would pass target information to a computer in the submarine, fed by data collected by the active sensor in the torpedo, to obtain data upon which to calculate the best interception course. The aim was to guide the torpedo to a position close to the target where the torpex explosive filled warhead would be detonated by influence fuses. The warhead was also provided with an impact pistol. Ongar became the Mk 24 but its acceptance trials in 1969 were a total disaster. The enquiry which followed helped lead to further re-organisation and the creation in 1972 of a Director Underwater Weapons Projects Naval separate from the Director of AUWE. Industry was now relied upon to produce the required weapons. Vickers had closed down their torpedo interests after an unsuccessful venture in the 1960s and the Royal Naval Torpedo Factory was sold to Plessey in 1970. The Torpedo Projects Executive formed by the new Projects Directorate chose General Electric to rectify faults with the Mk 24 but the sad saga of disappointed expectations was to continue into the 1980s (see Chapter 21). The Mk 8 had to soldier on as the primary means for a British submarine to attack an enemy surface ship.

Submarines had not been major anti-submarine weapons platforms during the Second World War but they emerged as such after 1945. Some crucial and pioneering trials were carried out in 1948 in the quiet waters off Rothesay. The engineering and TAS personnel of the submarine depot ship *Montclare* prepared the submarines *Alcide* and *Truncheon* for a series of exercises to investigate the effectiveness of submarines in the anti-submarine role. *Alcide* had been selected because she was equipped with the experimental double transducer 152X asdic with an extra 30 Khz transducer added to standard 129 submarine asdic: *Truncheon* was fitted with a normal 129, and, for trials purposes, with the American JT precision tracking hydrophone. These were the best asdic and hydrophone equipments available in the Third S/M Flotilla but they were totally insufficient to provide accurate control information for firing torpedoes in a submarine versus submarine encounter.

Truncheon was prepared for the trials by the removal of her gun, external torpedo tubes and any other-noise making fittings on the exterior of the hull. Little could be done internally to improve the inadequate and poorly situated asdic cabinet. During the trial, 32 attacks were carried out by *Truncheon* against *Alcide*, and 17 by the latter on the former. The trials team which conducted the exercise and carried out the ananlyses consisted of the commanding officers of *Truncheon* and *Alcide* (Lieutenant Commanders RF Park and WTJ Fox) the Flotilla Torpedo Anti-Submarine officer (Lieutenant Commander EN Poland) and the trials officer (Lieutenant Commander JM Michell). The submarine commanding officers were highly skilled, and had considerable war experience. The team was given a free hand to extemporise and to develop new tactics and procedures. 34% of *Truncheon's* attacks and 29% of *Alcide's* were deemed successful. Many of the statistics were inaccurate but the trials had demonstrated that, given the correct equipment and weapons, submarines could be very potent anti-submarine vessels. However, the Naval Staff, which did not examine the results until the middle of 1951, contented themselves with saying:

It is clear from the report that submarines with the present standard of equipment can only be expected to have limited success when employed in their anti-submarine role.

Later that year further trials were carried out involving *Truncheon, Tireless* and *Tally Ho*, which only confirmed what had already been known. Three valuable years had been lost. Fortunately work had already started in January 1950 to modify submarines of the T class along the lines of the advanced German submarines of 1945. In 1951 the first of these transformed submarines were returning to service. A new era in submarine and anti-submarine warfare had began in which silent underwater running at much higher speeds and for much longer periods were to be expected. The enhanced anti-submarine capability in submarines demanded that they should be fitted with greatly improved submarine detection equipment with both active and passive capabilities.

Great hopes attended Type 171, a submarine version of the new surface vessel Type 170. It was fitted for trials in *Thermopylae* in 1953 but was soon found to need the kind of computer support that could not be easily fitted into a submarine. The new Type 718 precision tracking hydrophone was developed into a low power Type 187 active/passive asdic set that entered service in 1958. This was intended primarily for passive use along with the new Type 186, code-named 'Knout' and introduced into service two years before. Based on German wartime research, it consisted of a pair of hydrophone arrays on each side of the submarine. The 186 and 187 equipped both the new *Porpoise* Class submarines primarily designed for anti-submarine operations that entered service from 1958 and the improved *Oberon* class that followed in 1961. Two years later the first Royal Navy nuclear powered hunter/killer submarine was commissioned carrying a powerful and revolutionary new set, the 2001. This had a large conformal array on the bows and was capable of long range detection in both the active and passive modes.

The 1950s and 1960s also saw significant improvements in shipborne hull-mounted sonar. By 1950, asdic equipment designed to detect older conventionally powered submarines had become inadequate and a new concept was introduced in which the transducer had four equal parts, the horizontal pair for determining bearing and the vertical ones for depth. Known as 'Four Square', this sonar was developed in conjunction with the improved depth charge mortar, code-named Limbo.

When, in 1948, Limbo and the Four Square asdic were combined in a single staff requirement, the new project was launched under the leadership of Peter Ward, one of UDE's scientists at Portland. This was the first time that a concerted effort had been made to obviate the human element by automating the whole procedure from detection to attack. Limbo, which became the Mortar Mark 10, was designed at the Underwater Countermeasures and Weapons Establishment and was a three barrelled weapon with a range of 400 to 1,000 yards. Its associated 'Four Square' asdic, the Type 170, obtained its information by phase comparison of returning echoes between the top and bottom and the left and right segments of a transducer steerable in azimuth and depth, allowing operators to track a target and produce smoothed fire control quantities. The asdic Type 170/Mortar Mark 10 system was installed in the destroyer *Scorpion* commanded by the distinguished submariner, Captain AR('Baldy') Hezlet. It had many advantages over asdic Types 144/147 and Squid, but it would be no match for nuclear powered submarines when they came into service in the Soviet Fleet.

In 1950, work started at the Underwater Weapons Development Establishment at Portland and the Plessey Company's Cottage Laboratories on the development of a high powered, relatively low frequncy asdic to meet a staff requirement for a minimum range of between 8,000 and 10,000 yards. The new asdic, known as Type 177, was first tested with a 170 transducer in the frigate *Brocklesby* in 1954 and a full prototype went to sea in the frigate *Undaunted* in 1955 for exercise against the American nuclear submarine *Nautilus*. It proved its capability and was accepted for service in 1957.

During this period asdics became increasingly complex. The early small transducers of a single homogenous form, using low power and high frequencies in the 20 to 30 kilohertz range, were replaced by the much larger composite transducers using high power and low frequencies of 5 to 10 kilohertz not subject to so much absorption in sea water. In earlier sonars, beam forming was merely a product of the relationship between the size of the transducer and the operating frequency, obeying well known antenna laws. With composite transducers and modern electronics using lag-lines, electronic beam forming became possible allowing multiple beams in azimuth, better bearing discrimination and also an application of target doppler analysis techniques. Type 177 produced a 40 degree swept area using five transmission and four reception beams and had to be stepped in azimuth to achieve the required coverage. It also possessed a range recorder which used electronic styli on electrically sensitive paper in the conventional manner, but which printed the returns from four beams and three different pulse lengths and sub-frequencies. This paper could be marked by electric pencil with time, bearing and other comments by the operator, then dried and stored, and this became a powerful post exercise analysis tool allowing, for instance, quantification of missed opportunities.

Type 177 was replaced in the 1960s in the new *Leander* class frigates by Type 184. This was a scanning sonar with an all-round look composed of a number of beams, a high power and a low power mode, operating on two frequencies, but which did not have a permanent recording facility. Both sonars had range settings of five, ten and twenty thousand yards, a considerable increase on the two to three thousand yard capability of ship-borne sonars installed so far. The volume of electronic cabinets within the ship was multiplied by a factor of perhaps sixty, a volume much reduced by solid state modifications to the Type 184.

During World War II, the development of asdics and anti-submarine weapons had been inhibited by the division of responsibility between the Torpedo and Anti-Submarine Branches. Fortunately, the leading scientists in both research and development were well aware of the importance of integrated detection and weapon systems and, as early as 1938, BS Smith had impressed upon the staff at Portland the importance of this concept. With the introduction of Asdic Type 177 an integrated weapon system became essential in order to exploit the much greater detection ranges.

Peter Ward, the project leader in the development of the Type 170, and later the division leader charged with the overall rsponsibility for the development of Type 177 was probably the most experienced scientist working in the field of anti-submarine weapons. In 1988, in an interview with Captain WDS White, he re-emphasised the importance which naval scientists had always placed upon the development of integrated anti-submarine detection and attack systems.

It was not long before it was recognised that Limbo was incompatible with the much longer detection ranges being obtained by Types 177 and 184; these were measured in miles rather than yards and submarines had to be attacked before they could use their high speed and deep diving capabilities to close their targets. At the Admiralty the Undersea Warfare Division of the Naval Staff examined projects undertaken by the nations of both NATO and the Commonwealth, in an effort to solve this problem. The Americans were developing a rocket propelled ballistic missile known as Asroc which carried either a nuclear depth charge or a lightweight homing torpedo to a range of 7 miles. The French preferred a winged and guided drone, called Malafon, carrying a torpedo to a range of 8 miles. In Australia, another winged vehicle, carrying an accoustic homing torpedo to a range of 11 miles, was being investigated. The origins of this system can be traced back to a conference held in Australia in October 1958 organised by the Commonwealth Advisory Committee on Defence Science. This conference coincided with the appointment of Peter Ward as Scientific Advisor to the Royal Australian Navy and Director of their research programme. In this capacity he was a founder member of the project to develop a long range Anti-Submarine system.

During demonstrations at this conference the Australian developed Army anti-tank missile, Malkara, was fired at the rocket test range at Woomera, and the possibility of a scaled up version for the Navy was mentioned. A Royal Australian Navy staff requirement was prepared, under the name Ikara, for a torpedo carrying missile which could be tracked and guided in flight to maximum range of over 10 miles. The staff requirement was approved by the Australian Defence Department in 1960, This was judged to be the most suitable for the Royal Navy's requirements and a joint undertaking to develop the weapon was agreed with the Australian Government. Attempts were also made, unsuccessfully, to interest NATO navies. However, the United States Navy agreed to help in torpedo procurement and, with the United Kingdom, made support information freely available.

Development proceeded apace and in 1963 the complete Ikara system, comprising 35 tons of complex electronic, explosive and engineering equipment came together for the first time in Australia's new Type 12 frigate *Stuart*. Successful sea trials were carried out and the Royal Navy, impressed by the proved capability of Ikara and the possibility of future development, decided to adopt a version of the system for fitting in the Type 82 guided missile destroyers then being designed to escort the proposed new aircraft carrier CVA 01. When, after a bitter dispute between the Royal Navy and the Royal Air Force, CVA01 was abandoned, consideration was given to other economies which could be made in the much reduced shipbuilding programme. Amongst these was a proposal to cancel the Ikara project but it was prevented by the memorandum of undertanding with Australia. The procurement programme was greatly reduced and the system was adapted for use in the modernised *Leander* class frigates and the large destroyer *Bristol*, sole survivor of the Type 82 programme. The Royal Navy's Ikara, which eventually entered service in *Leander* class frigates, was designed to carry the United States Mark 46 homing torpedo that had been adopted by the Royal Navy for delivery also from helicopters and surface ships. The Ikara missile system took some fifteen years to evolve from its origins to its final testing in *Bristol* at the American Autec sound range in the Bahamas in November 1973.

Ikara had a competitor, the helicopter, which between the mid-1950s and the early 1970s became the key anti-submarine system for surface ships of all sizes. The Match System (Manned Torpedo Helicopter) was fitted to frigates of the *Tribal* and *Leander* classes in the 1960s to allow them to exploit their 177 and 184 hull mounted sonars to the full. Larger helicopters with sonar capability of their own became standard for anti-submarine duties in large destroyers, cruisers and even aircraft carriers. During the war Anti-Submarine Branch officers had not been closely associated with the Fleet Air Arm, but Torpedo Officers had served in aircraft carriers. After the war, therefore, the new Torpedo Anti-Submarine Branch was able to appoint officers with air experience to a number of sensitive posts. One of these was as the Torpedo Anti-Submarine specialist on the staff of the Air Warfare Division of the Naval Staff.

Since the early years of the war much thought had been given to the possibility of towing an asdic transducer at a distance from the noise created by the ship's passage through the water and below the surface layer. Given a helicopter with sufficient lifting capacity and endurance, the possibility of designing a dipping asdic to be carried by helicopters seemed to show great promise. The first trials started in America in 1947 and the following year the first practical system was produced, the AQS-1. In Britain 1947 had seen the first steps in producing a dipping asdic for use by helicopters: this emerged as Asdic Type 194, a UK version of the early American AQS. But it was not until 1951 that the Air Warfare Division came to grips with the practical problems of developing an ASW helicopter squadron. When, in the early months of 1951, Poland became the Torpedo Anti-Submarine specialist on the staff of the Air Warfare Division of the Admiralty, he found a great deal of cynicism concerning the potential of the helicopter for anti-submarine warfare, but he was fortunate in having a colleague who was quick to grasp the importance of this development. Commander AWF Sutton was an observer with a great deal of wartime experience. With his support and with the backing of the Deputy Director, Captain RM Smeeton (later Vice Admiral Sir Richard Smeeton) the project began to take shape, and encouragement now came from another and unexpected source.

Osprey, the old headquarters establishment of the Anti-Submarine Branch was now well established as the Anti-Submarine Training Establishment. In command in the latter half of 1951 was an officer of outstanding ability who was to go on to the higher ranks of the service, Captain JB Frewen, fresh from command of the frigate *Mounts Bay*. His energy, foresight and imagination were focused on the tactical implications of the introduction of nuclear powered submarines. He was concerned by the lack of information in the fleet and training establishments about the steps being taken to deal with this critical threat to sea communications. Among the developments of which he had knowledge, he felt that the Anti-Submarine Warfare helicopter showed great promise. That autumn he invited Poland to *Osprey* to speak to his staff: when he arrived he found himself facing most of the flag officers and nearly all the captains available from the Portsmouth Command. The lecture and the discussions which followed were to have far reaching effects. Captain CD Howard-Johnston, the Captain of *Vernon* was there and was to take a

The first helicopter to be equipped with submarine detection equipment for the Royal Navy

leading role in the anti-submarine warfare helicopter project. The interest in the project which had been generated in the Air Warfare Division of the Naval Staff was sufficient for the authorisation of funds for the allocation of aircraft and personnel, though it was not until the following September of 1952 that Howard-Johnston was able to appoint a trials officer. That month he sent

Lieutenant RS Browning to join a naval pilot, Lieutenant H Phillips and an observer, Lieutenant FW Burgess, at the Royal Naval Air Station at Gosport to carry out trials on an American built Sikorsky S-55 helicopter (number WW 339) fitted with an AQS-4 dipping sonar and owned by the Westland Aircraft Company.

Although Browning now became, in effect, the first TAS/Observer, his appointment as such was not recognised and he was not granted flying pay in spite of all the efforts of Lieutenant Commander JR Blake, the TAS Officer on the staff of Flag Officer (Air)(Home). The refusal to recognise Browning's position as a member of an air crew was not surprising since qualified pilots and observers of the Fleet Air Arm were jealous of their qualifications and not anxious to encourage an officer from another branch to infringe their positions. However, when Browning was joined by two TAS ratings, Petty Officer R Surtees and Leading Seaman J Odell, he was able to obtain flying pay for them. There followed eighteen months of hard work to prove the viability of the helicopter and the sonar. On completion of the trials, Browning was summoned to the Admiralty to report to the Director of the Air Warfare Division, who enquired when the trials were going to start! Browning's answer was to hand him the trials report, advocating the use of ASW helicopters as an important addition to the Navy's ASW armoury.

Throughout the trials, John Frewen and *Osprey* had continued to give whole hearted support, particularly when the helicopter was operating from a field at Chickerell; this extended to the provision of a rum ration for the two air crew! The trials depended for their successful completion upon the enthusiastic support of a small number of officers who were convinced that the helicopter had an important role to play in anti-submarine warfare. Amongst them were Blake at the Headquarters of Flag Officer (Air)(Home) and Captain TWB Shaw commanding the Royal Naval Air Station at Eglinton, where, in 1954, the trials team was based whilst carrying out operations in the North Atlantic from the aircraft repair carrier *Perseus*. With aircraft, equipment and crew pushed to the limit, and beset by some of the worst weather the North Atlantic could produce, the trials were completed in the scheduled time by dint of sheer determination and improvisation. This extended to providing a rear view mirror for Browning, so that he could operate the asdic and navigate when in the hover, at a height of about 10 feet above the waves and keep a look out for a rogue wave coming in and endangering the tail rotor!

In September 1953, after the initial trials with the single S55 helicopter (705 Squadron, X Flight), a full squadron of eight HO4S3 helicopters was delivered from the United States to form 706 Squadron. It was still necessary to extemporise as the aircraft were received as troop carriers and had to be converted to the anti-submarine warfare role by the Trials and Development Unit at the Royal Naval Air Station at Gosport, HMS *Sultan*. Electrical junk shops in Portsmouth were searched to find 15 pin plugs for the asdic cabling. It is greatly to the credit of Browning and his colleagues that the trials were successfully completed. The tactics and procedures which they developed under difficult conditions were so sound that they were scarcely altered over the next three decades. In March 1954 845 Squadron commissioned as the Royal Navy's first operational anti-submarine helicopter squadron and in 1958 it was decided to abandon fixed wing carrier borne A/S aircraft. The

Whirlwind, Wessex and Sea King became progressively the fleet's primary anti-submarine aircraft. A new advanced lower frequency medium range 195 dipping sonar was developed and introduced in the mid-1960s. Tactics were developed to exploit the inherent unpredictability in positioning of the dipping helicopter and the latter became an integral part of the fleet.

The evolution of dipping asdic for helicopters proceeded in parallel with the development of variable depth asdics designed to be towed at the optimum depth by surface anti-submarine escorts. Project Beta commenced at Portland in 1954 and resulted in the production of a prototype known as Asdic Type 192. It was installed in the trials frigate *Brocklesby* but was so heavy and unwieldy that the towing vessel was endangered. After a series of misadventures the project was abandoned and in its stead the Royal Navy adopted the Canadian variable depth sonar, which in the anglicised version was designated Asdic Type 199.

Type 199 was purchased in 1960 as an 'Asdic' but entered service in 1968 as a 'Sonar'. The American term was adopted in 1963 despite the understandable reluctance of many Commonwealth officers, particularly TAS officers with A/S backgrounds. The advantages of standardisation within NATO were, however obvious. British members of the various NATO staffs were often chided for hanging on to a word which had not been adopted by any of the other allied nations. The lack of standardisation complicated correspondence whether by letter or by signal and amongst the new generation the word asdic was no longer regarded with the reverence with which it had previously been held. Poland, who as a Captain was appointed Director of Undersea Warfare in the latter part of 1962, was confronted with a bulky staff docket on the subject. Many of the entries forecast dismay being caused amongst all ranks and ratings but when the decision to standardise terminology was promulgated there was barely a word of protest.

The Admiralty never gave up improving its expertise in underwater warfare in the post war period, even when it seemed that such operations might be made irrelevant by a vast thermonuclear cataclysm. The advent of nuclear stalemate from the end of the 1950s onwards vindicated the Admiralty's prudent instincts. Conventional naval operations were re-emphasised as part of a strategy of 'Flexible Response' finally adopted by NATO at the end of 1967. Although much new equipment was in service by then it was the training and user trials conducted by *Vernon* that had made Royal Navy expertise in underwater warfare still second to none in the world. The post war naval revolution was continuing however and operations were fast outgrowing the relatively narrow bounds of the TAS branch and its schools, while, more expensive projects were competing for a naval vote that was beginning to decline significantly in real terms. 'Rationalisation' was in the air and *Vernon*, despite all its successes , was doomed.

WAR IN THE FAR EAST HALTED ANY suggestion of disarmament and *Vernon's* training commitments increased, requiring the appointment of a Lieutenant Commander (Training) to assist the Commander (TAS), who had to spend much of his time visiting other establishments. Formerly the Deputy Executive Officer had combined administrative duties with the organisation of instruction but these latter duties passed to the new post and the DXO was redesignated First Lieutenant. A Reserves Course Officer was also appointed to deal with the rapid growth of reserve minesweeping personnel intended for the new generation MCM vessels. In March 1951 MCM training came south from Lochinvar and a new section was formed in the Trials Department. Later in that year the seaward defence organisation at Devonport was wound up, the material side coming to *Vernon*. In the continued absence of new permanent building more huts were obtained from various establishments to house the new departments. In 1952 degaussing, a Dept of Underwater Warfare responsibility, returned to *Vernon* which also assumed responsibility for all Portsmouth's degaussing ranges; these eventually passed to C-in C Portsmouth's control.

The ratings' structure of the TAS Branch was revised in the light of experience. It had soon become clear that the original intention of combining the specialist qualifications of the Torpedo and Anti-Submarine Branches was impractical. Instead the second and third class rates were divided into three sub groups:

Control Ratings (UC)
Weapons Ratings (UW)
Mine Sweeping, Mine Laying and Seaward Defence Ratings (MD)

Although this was a practical solution it was not popular, if choice had been the main criteria many would have volunteered for the seamanship orientated mine warfare qualification, which included the ever popular demolition instruction, during which afternoons were spent in practical work on Farlington Marshes where, before laying and detonating a charge, it was necessary to drive away the cows. Many stories have been told of adventures on the Marshes, starting with the introduction of demolition training for WRNS. The officer in charge failed to warn the young women about the importance of wearing trousers with the result that they burnt their nylons with the sugar and sulphuric acid solutions in the explosives. Many years later, Chief Petty Officer RV Jackson, a senior instructor in the Mine and Mine Disposal Section, recalled that the amount of explosive allowed to be used at any one time was set at a single one and a quarter pound charge. Larger charges caused annoyance to the families living in houses known as 'Retired Admirals 'Row', bordering on the Marshes.

On his return to *Vernon* after a day's instruction on the Marshes, Jackson once found himself on a charge, accused of having violated standing orders and of having disturbed numerous residents of the Farlington area at various times during that afternoon. He returned to his class, checked all equipment back into the stores and dismissed the class. He was puzzled by the reports of 'big bangs', and he was certain that his class had done nothing to 'violate standing orders'. Later that evening, when listening to the six-o-clock news on the radio, he heard that a new air speed record had been set by a test pilot flying over Hampshire, breaking the sound barrier. Jackson received an apology from the complainants, but objections to the noise continued and the training area for demolitions was moved to Flowerdown, north of Winchester.

Sometimes the TAS Branch's demolition responsibilities involved *Vernon* in more serious controversy. In 1949, the growing crisis in the Far East had yet to attract the attention of the press and public, for whom local events often took precedence. The affair of the old wooden man of war, *Implacable*, was one. Conservation was not yet a matter of great concern to those who controlled the Navy's finances, either locally or in Whitehall, and they were unmoved by the fate of a redundant and decaying training ship.

Opposite *Vernon*, across the water between Fort Blockhouse and Gosport, lay the old two decker 74 gun ship of the line, *Implacable*, originally the French *Duguay Trouin*, built in 1800 and taken at Trafalgar. After service in the Royal Navy, she became a boys training ship from 1855 to 1908, when she was condemned as unsafe, but she was saved by a petition and turned over to the dockyard for preservation in 1912. Together with *Foudroyant*, she was used by the Society for Nautical Research as a holiday training ship for young people. In 1943 she was placed in a basin in Portsmouth dockyard for adaption to Naval training and was commissioned in June that year. After the war she was found to be too badly decayed for return to the Society for Nautical Research and she remained rotting at her mooring until 1949, when the Manager of the Construction Department in Portsmouth Dockyard, unmoved by sentimental rhetoric, reported her condition to the Commander-in-Chief, Portsmouth, who happened to be the navy's most senior torpedoman, Admiral Sir Algernon Willis. He advised the Admiralty that as *Implacable* was surplus to requirements she should be taken out to sea and scuttled. There was an immediate outcry, followed by pleas and protestations from many sources, particularly from the distinguished marine painter, Colonel Wyllie, in a series of letters to the Portsmouth Evening News. A project to remove her to Greenwich was backed by the London County Council and a number of heritage concerns; but after a further survey of the hull, the scheme was deemed to be impractical as the ship was in an advanced stage of decay and the money to make her good was not available.

On 10 October 1949, Admiral Willis informed Colonel Wyllie that it was intended to scuttle *Implacable* off the approaches to Spithead on the first weather suitable day after 30 November, and invited him to witness the event from the destroyer *Finisterre*. To the Captain of *Vernon*, Captain WJ Robertson, fell the onerous task of scuttling this fine old ship. The sizes of the demolition charges were carefully calculated and they were placed in strategic positions, but at the last moment, to make certain that nothing went wrong, the weight of explosives was increased! *Implacable* was towed to Spithead in readiness, but it was discovered that sections of the carefully laid copper demolition cable had been stolen and it had to be replaced in a hurry.

Before long, the distinguished gathering aboard *Finisterre* assembled to witness the end of the old ship. The charges were fired. Holes were blown in the hull; it sank rapidly. But the effect of the increased charges was to separate the hull from the upper deck which was left heaving gently on the swell. It became a temporary navigational hazard which had to be dealt with separately. Neither the loss of this ancient warship, nor the manner of her going, have been forgotten. Many years later, the World Ship Trust, which had been set up to preserve ships of historical interest around the world, struck a bronze medal featuring the stern of *Implacable*, under which were the words '*Implacable* Never Again'.

By 1952, the only ratings who were qualified in all the responsibilities of the branch were Torpedo Anti-Submarine Instructors (TASIs). The Mine Laying and Seaward Defence qualification was soon abandoned when it was found that the narrowness of the field was restricting the holders to small specialised craft with consequent career disadvantages. All TAS ratings were once again trained in MD subjects until this work was absorbed into the new Mine Warfare and Clearance Diving Branch in 1966.

In 1953 *Vernon*'s central position made her once more a centre of great activities on the occasion of the Coronation Review. She was the landing place for all foreign officers and ratings, for whom it was necessary to provide information in eleven different languages displayed on over a hundred different notice boards. During Coronation week, over 45,000 liberty men passed through *Vernon* and the Stokes Bay torpedo landing pier. *Vernon* was also the embarkation point for VIPs including diplomats, statesmen. military

The Vernon Main Gate dressed for the Coronation Review 1953

leaders and other famous figures. There were a number of difficult situations including one occasion when fifteen foreign flag officers arrived simultaneously to call upon Commander-in-Chief Portsmouth. The control of their barges in *Vernon* Creek called for a cool head, a knowledge of protocol and a great deal of tact!

Vernon became the Fleet Mail Office for all the ships assembled for the Review. The gymnasium was converted into a post office which handled a million letters and parcels during the week: mail was distributed to the ships by nine minesweepers, and it also provided facilities for the press. Finally, the establishment acted as host to a major foreign warship, the French flagship, *Montcalm*, whose officers and ratings were shown every form of hospitality. On the day of the Review, 1,000 VIPs were embarked from the quarter deck of *Vernon* in three hours. They included three royal families, all the ambassadors to the Court of St James and many public figures. Training continued uninterrupted by the additional duties imposed upon officers with such titles as Coroff, Embarkoff, Parkoff and Securoff: inevitably they were referred to as the 'Russian Corps'.

1953 saw the first 'Families Day' at *Vernon* and also the beginning of 'General Drills' in place of a Ceremonial Divisions. As Webb described it:

The entire establishment turned out for the competitions which were designed to stimulate quick thinking, resource and ingenuity. Many of them presented a startling departure from old time drills. Wrens were told to...become a guard of honour...Civilians found themselves frying an omelette on the quarterdeck. A lively and enthusiastic half day was enjoyed by all, and General Drill day was repeated as often as wholesale dislocation could be arranged.

The ships and vessels attached to the establishment also changed as time went by. In 1950 the Reserve Fleet finally reclaimed *Royalist* and *Modeste*. Both were to return later to active service; *Royalist* was modernised and then served from 1957 to 1967 with the Royal New Zealand Navy, and *Modeste* served in the Far East and the Mediterranean in 1953-58. In the *Vernon* Squadron in July 1948, *Fancy* had been replaced by *Welfare* which had reciprocating engines rather than turbines and was therefore more handy for manoeuvring. *Welfare* was transferred to *Lochinvar* as Minesweeping Experimental ship in 1951 and was replaced by *Marvel*. *Pluto* remained a member of the squadron from 1947 to the end of 1954, carrying out trials of the Squid fitted *Algerine*. She then went into reserve, replaced until the middle of 1956 by *Lysander*. In 1954 the first of the new coastal minesweepers, *Coniston* and the first inshore sweeper, *Inglesham* arrived for acceptance trials, and the establishment was allocated two vessels of each class. *Bodenham* and *Brigham* joined in 1954 and stayed for two years joining their sisters in operational reserve. At the end of 1956 there were four *Tons* class at *Vernon, Caunton, Gavinton, Laleston* and *Sheraton*. Despite their continued value for M/S and A/S training, *Lysander* and *Marvel* were scrapped in 1957-8 with the rapid run-down of the fleet minesweeper force as the *Tons* were delivered.

The mining tenders *Plover, Nightingale* and *Vesuvius* remained despite attempts to get them replaced by more modern war-built controlled minelayers of the *Miner* class. Conversion of the latter to their new role was not considered worthwhile as they would have to be converted back in time of crisis. As it was 'Miners' were based at *Vernon* from 1950 as a result of the Korean War and the build up of the seaward defence organisation at Portsmouth. The vessels were attached for 'general administration and organisation' but were used also for seaward defence training. In 1955 it was finally decided to replace *Nightingale* and *Vesuvius* with *Miner III* and *Miner IV* ; *Plover* was given a refit for further service although when she returned she was put under the C-in-C's command where she was served for another decade.

Ashore, the Commander (TAS) was redesignated Commander (Training) in 1953 and No 43 Building was enlarged to take a Type 170/Mk 10 Mortar combination. Huts were provided for the existing tenants, the Experimental Diving Unit (see next chapter). The long planned rebuiding programme did not begin until the following year with a start made on North Block and the demolition of No 56 Building to make way for the new Chiefs' acommodation.

In 1954, a Committee on Officer Structure and Training (COST) was set up under the chairmanship of Vice Admiral Sir Aubrey Mansergh, himself a torpedoman and one of the few officers of any branch to be awarded the DSC as a Midshipman. The Mansergh Committee Report was accepted by the Board of Admiralty in the latter part of 1955 and the findings were issued as Admiralty Fleet Order 1/56 in January 1956. This created a General List of all officers drawn from the Executive, Engineering, Electrical, Supply and Secretariat, and Instructor Branches. The non-executive officers removed the coloured distinction cloth from their stripes and took their place alongside seaman officers in a common seniority list. The new structure caused some anomalies but there was little ill feeling at *Vernon*. The reactions to the Admiralty Fleet order were well summarised by Commander Charles Emerson when he wrote:

The disappearance of the coloured specialist stripes made quite a big difference to the 'Schoolies' course (Instructor Officers). We had a particularly good course as far as games players were concerned. Gerry Tordoff played cricket for his county; and he and another of his colleagues, named Senior, were both good football players who earned their places in the team. These bright and athletic young men were in strong competition with the long TAS course as the social Lions in the ward room, and I felt the disappearance of their blue stripe had been a considerable boost to their confidence. From my own point of view, I was still second in command, but Maurice McMullen, our Captain (S), with four executive stripes, was occasionally invited to take divisions and similar functions. Shortly before, when Captain Copeman had been ill with a bad back there had been no question as to who took his place, particularly when George Creasy inspected VERNON *, but at that time the coloured stripes were still being worn. This change did not cause me any any concern, I merely list it as an historical event. Morris McMullen was a splendid messmate and always accompanied me on away guest night dinners, and gave splendid support in all ways.*

All would have been well if the Mansergh Committee's Report had only recommended the change of name from Executive Branch to Seaman Specialisation, but, in view of the limited number of jobs in command or second in command at sea, the Board decided to create a special Post List for the ranks of Commander and Captain. Those selected for the Post List would be available for those prized jobs at sea whereas the remainder of the officers of the Seaman Specialisation remained on the General List. The effect was immediate; those who had been selected for the Post List (which soon became known as the Wet List) thought they had been appointed to an elite body whereas their less fortunate colleagues seemed doomed on the Dry List to a career driving desks and forever labelled as second class citizens. There was an immediate clamour by some Dry officers for reconsideration and a number of cases of officers on the Wet List who were agreeable to swop with members of the Dry List. The Admiralty was, however, adamant; neither reconsideration nor swops would be allowed. Assignment to the Dry List hit TAS officers disproportionately and it came as a great relief when in 1969 this damaging and unfair system of classifying Seaman Commanders was abolished.

At the end of the 1950s the Admiralty recognised that the training establishments were too large and influential and that there was some duplication of effort. The Captains of such establishments believed that although there was some truth in the allegations, they were exaggerated. Their efforts to maintain the status quo were, however, frustrated by the appointment of a new Director General of Training, a flag officer under whose aegis a 'rationalisation' programme was started aimed at the diminution in the powers of individual specialist schools such as *Vernon* and *Excellent* . The former was in a particularly vulnerable position; in spite of having direct access to the harbour with base maintenance facilities, there was no room for further expansion and the school was thus unlikely to become the new centralised training establishment. The arrival of a radically minded Commander in Chief at Portsmouth, Admiral Sir Alexander Bingley, brought added pressure for rationalisation. A greater degree of co-operation during the officers' long courses was introduced and for the first time there was talk of creating a unified operations branch and of abolishing the seaman sub-specialisation branches. The Captains of the training establishments were in general agreement but were concerned that naval officers in Whitehall would find it difficult to hold their own without the benefit of at least some training in a specific operational discipline. In 1961 *Osprey* closed down as an A/S school and all shore training came to *Vernon* along with the various caravans containing mobile teachers.

Rationalisation in the 1950s and early '60s also affected the other establishments with which *Vernon* and her people were connected. During the war years the research and development of underwater weapons and equipment had become widely dispersed, geographically and administratively. It was an arrangement which was essential for survival under the threat of enemy action, but it was unrealistic, unnecessary and unacceptable with the financial restraints of peace. As part of the attempt to impose more order in underwater weapons developments, the establishments involved were rationalised. The main development and design of torpedoes went on at the Torpedo Experimental Establishment at Greenock in a building of palatial proportions containing very large and commodious offices and research facilties of which only half were used. It was close to the torpedo testing range at Arrochar on Loch Long but its distance from *Vernon* meant that officers of the Sea Trials Section were obliged to travel by the night train to Scotland to carry out a day's work before returning by the following night train to the south of England. This remoteness applied equally to the location of the other associated research establishments. Torpedo tube development took place at the Underwater Weapons Launching Establishment (UWLE) at Ferndown near Poole in Dorset, acoustic developments were the responsibility of the Underwater Weapons Development Establishment (HMUDE) at Portland, while anti-submarine weapons, mines and mine countermeasures were still the responsibility of the sucessor of the old Mine Design Department, renamed the Underwater Countermeasures Weapons Establishment, at West Leigh House.

Concentration of these weapons establishments was discussed and Portland seemed the obvious place. In 1958, Captain WDS White was appointed as Captain of UCWE at Havant, with the special responsibility of supervising the moves to Portland and the creation of the new Underwater Weapons Establishment. It was no easy task as there was much opposition to change, and had it not been for the determination of Captain RE Portlock, the Director of Torpedo and Anti-Submarine Warfare and his Assistant Director, Captain OHM St J Steiner, the whole centralisation scheme might have foundered. Opposition to the move arose mainly from a reluctance to move from areas to which staff and families had become accustomed. While some individuals were willing to change jobs, and even welcomed it in the interests of progress, the majority disliked change and sought arguments against it. White fully understood the human aspects of the moves; the uprooting of families, changes of schooling for children, moves to places with different customs, a change from familiar surroundings to the unknown. If the staffs at Havant and Poole found cause to argue it was nothing to the complaints from the Scots at Greenock who found the change to southern England a much greater wrench.

There were some good arguments against moving the Torpedo Experimental Establishment south. Lewis, who had served at TEE as Superintendent of Torpedo Experiment and Design pointed to TEE's proximity to deep sheltered waters in the Scottish lochs and the Clyde estuary, and to the submarine base at Faslane. He drew the attention of the Admiralty to the excellence of the facilities at TEE and, most importantly, to the finest naval deep water exercise areas just off the establishment's doorstep to which the Navy would have to return in the event of another European war. These were cogent arguments, but those for rationalisation were stronger and the move to Portland went ahead. White and the Chief Scientist at UCWE spent many long hours dealing with the teething problems of the new organisation but in March 1959 all was ready and the Underwater Launching and the Underwater Countermeasures and Weapons Establishments came together in the Underwater Weapons Establishment (UWE) under the same roof as the Admiralty Gunnery Establishment at Portland. The logic was carried to its conclusion in 1962 when UWE was combined administratively with HMUDE as the Admiralty Underwater Weapons Establishment; the surface interests of the Gunnery Establishment passed to the new Admiralty Surface Weapons Establishment at Portsmouth. This concentration of underwater weapons research and development at Portland reflected the growing influence of the

Royal Navy's scientists, and the greatly reduced participation of *Vernon* in the development of weapons and equipment: it required a greater effort by the Sea Trials Department to maintain a close liaison and understanding.

Between 1958 and 1966 the *Vernon* Squadron was reinforced and given an operational role as the Fifth Minesweeper Squadron. In 1958 *Caunton, Gavinton, Sheraton* and *Laleston* were joined by *Beachampton* and *Bossington* and in 1959 by *Monkton*. In 1963 *Gavinton* was replaced by *Repton* and over the following two years *Beachampton, Bossington, Laleston, Monkton* and *Sheraton* were replaced by *Lewiston* and *Wiston*. Fifth MSS was under its own senior officer and kept everyone in touch with the sea; it was a happy squadron which seemed to attract and cultivate colourful characters.

One of these was a Lieutenant Commander DG Sherrard. After assuming command of *Gavinton*, he was allowed twenty four hours to acquaint himself with the ship which included a quick trip to sea to learn ship handling. He had never been in charge of anything bigger than a battleship's launch, nor had he been a First Lieutenant: for him being on the bridge in command of a ship preparing for sea was a novel experience. Within a few days *Gavinton* was ordered to proceed to Southampton to pick up sea cadets for passage to Cowes for a big parade attended by the Commander-in-Chief. The cadets returned just after low water and asked to be taken home. *Gavinton* backed out and turned on engines in the river which was hardly wider than she was long. Shortly after the coxswain had been given a course to steer down the harbour the steering gear was found not to be working. *Gavinton* felt her way past the floating bridge and out through the crowded holiday harbour steering on two main engines, two black balls at the mast, and keeping a sharp lookout for the Commander-in-Chief's barge. They saw it well ahead but the barge went by without comment from the Admiral. Once in open water it was discovered that one of the sea cadets had removed the pin that connected the steering equipment to the rudders!

The minesweepers occasionally provided a service for the other training establishments. Early one morning, Sherrard was woken by the telephone ringing in the flat outside his cabin. It was the Training Commander at *Mercury*, reporting that it was blowing very hard in the vicinity of the Signals School near Petersfield, and asking whether the minesweepers were game to go to sea with his trainees. Sherrard replied immmediately that nothing ever stopped them going to sea but as soon as he had replaced the receiver of the telephone and put his head out through the screen door, he was 'almost blown into the scuppers'. All four minesweepers sailed, with *Gavinton* the last to leave the dockside. By watching the other three carefully Sherrard was able to ensure that *Gavinton* was the only ship not damaged leaving her berth. Once clear of the harbour the Communications Course Officers were so seasick as the minesweepers rolled 35 degrees in the lee of the Isle of Wight that they might just as well not have come.

It was not an occasion when *Gavinton's* popular cook could provide a good meal, although he succeeded in doing so in almost all weather conditions. This exceptional rating used to send what he called 'the Captain's trough' to the bridge when at sea. It was a curious victualling store which resembled a jerrycan without a handle. In it was put the whole meal, the sweet at the bottom, main course in the middle and soup on top, although on some occasions the weather was so bad that it only started that way. The Captain used to wedge himself between the pelorus and the binnacle and shovel it in quickly while it was still hot.

The Squadron provided tactical training at sea in minesweeping and mine countermeasures. Sea experience was a vital part of the curriculum for all classes at *Vernon*, particularly in anti-submarine training where it was carried out in co-operation with the Flag Officer Sea Training and the Second Training Squadron at Portland and, in the case of advanced courses, with the Joint Anti-Submarine School and the Third Training Squadron at Londonderry. Under the impetus of this large training programme, additional instructional facilities continued to be provided at *Vernon*, including a splendid auditorium in the Creasy Block, which was especially suitable for presentations to numerous parties of visiting VIPs and senior courses such as the Imperial Defence College.

In 1959, Captain EA Blundell was relieved by Morgan-Giles (later Rear Admiral Sir Morgan Morgan-Giles) who in turn was succeeded by Captain HL Lloyd at the begining of 1961. Under these distinguished torpedomen, and despite threats of closure, the throughput of trainees continued in the order of 1,000 officers and 3,000 ratings each year.

Training had continued at *Vernon* in surface torpedo attack, although vulnerability to radar directed gunfire meant that fewer ships carried torpedo tubes. The Cyclorama Attack Teacher, completed in December 1947, therefore remained in use. As MacFarlan remembered, its bridge resembled:

'one of the most sick-making machines from a fun-fair, and the Wall of Death structure around it provided the Section Officer a perfect track on which to try his jet propelled toy motor cars.

It was removed in 1966 with the end of surface ship torpedoes. Another casualty of the end of traditional ship torpedoes was the 21-inch quadruple mounting on *Vernon*'s quarter deck. This, as MacFarlan remembered:

caused at least one dyed-in-the-wool torpedoman to change his will. He had hoped that he would be finally fired into Portsmouth Harbour with the Training Commander in charge of Tube Drill.

Traditional torpedo warfare was abandoned as naval warfare became ever more three-dimensional and complex. A tactical teacher in Anti-Submarine operations had been in operation since 1948. It was a considerable improvement over the old tactical floor on which staff had to crawl about on their hands and knees to bring the picture up to date. Senior officers were introduced to anti-submarine tactical games in which they could suffer the ignominy of being sunk if they made tactical errors. The dexterity of Wren plotters writing backwards on the reverse of a perspex screen was a sight not easily forgotten; it was also an asset in the investigation of tactical problems. It was modernised in the 1960s with automatic plotting for control and command modules and facilities for introducing air, surface and underwater targets. It was an integral part of the Pre-Commissioning Training (PCT) and Command Team Training (CTT) that was introduced in the 1960s. By the

Vernon shortly before rationalisation and closure in 1986

middle of that decade seven instructional sections were being administered by the Commander (Training) working closely with the Director of Studies, an Instructor Commander:

Anti-Submarine (supported by mobile trainers)
Diving
Mining and Mine Countermeasures
Mine Disposal
Tactical
Theory
Weapons (both torpedoes and anti-submarine devices).

The advent of the Director of Studies resulted from the academic part of the long TAS course moving to *Vernon* from Greenwich. The Sea Trials Department under Commander (Trials) continued to work from 17a Building, carrying out trials in association with AUWE at Portland. The department, which was of considerable importance to research and development, seemed to be on the periphery of the general life of *Vernon*. As the Captain, ('Harpy') Lloyd, remarked, 'their work did not as a rule impinge much upon everyday activity'.

1963 saw the end of the Admiralty as a Department of State and its replacement by a unified Ministry of Defence of which the Navy was but one of three service departments, MOD(N), although HM the Queen assumed the ancient title of Lord High Admiral. Their Lordships disappeared and their Letters Patent were cancelled. Just before this, Admiral Bingley had been relieved by one of the Navy's most popular Flag Officers, a submariner, Admiral Sir Wilfred Woods. He took a very positive, yet friendly, interest in the many shore training establishments under his command. His critical eye quickly spotted the large numbers of supporting staff, both Wrens and civilians, needed to regulate and administer pay, clothing, sleeping and feeding arrangements for the large fluctuating complement of each establishment. There were also skilled and semi-skilled men, shipwrights and electrical and mechanical engineers essential for the many sophisticated trainers, weapons and equipment systems. Each establishment also had its own medical staff. Bingley therefore issued orders requiring the Captains of the schools to surrender some of their autonomy. Thereafter, the periodical meetings of the Captains of the Seaman Sub-Specialist Schools, which occurred several times a year and were chaired by the Chief of Staff of the Commander-in-Chief, took on a new significance. In London, the Director General of Naval Training, on his departure in January 1965 after two and a half years, wrote:

It has been a period of changing requirements and shifted emphasis to meet ever increasing demands for know how and skills in maritime and fighting sciences and techniques. The wind of change continues to blow at Force 9, and there is no doubt in my mind that with ... the advances in technical know how, changes in the next few years will continue to be even more far reaching than they have been up till now.

Professor Parkinson remarked that the completion of great programmes usually heralds the end of their original functions. This was certainly true of *Vernon* where, in the early 1960s, building recommenced after another dormant period. Work forged ahead with what was now known as the Creasy Block, accommodation was modernised, the canteen was built and the old iron chimney, climbed by so many generations of long course officers, was demolished to make way for a fine new brick structure. All this was amid fresh talk of closure but it was not taken seriously. There was even talk of a replacement for the Captain's house. The Captain's occupation of the old Chaplain's residence by the main entrance was so public that one incumbent complained that he was saluted by a passing sailor though the window while downing a pre-prandial gin. Various plans were discussed, including a modern house on the quayside overlooking the harbour, but the foundations posed a tricky problem and the cost would have been exorbitant: the plans were shelved indefinitely.

By 1966 a new Captain, RE Lloyd, was in residence. A defence review was being carried out by the Wilson Government but Captain Lloyd was optimistic about the prospects, as whatever the size and shape of the fleet there would still be demand for TAS and Mine Clearance and Diving (MCD) personnel (DCI 278/66 of that year had introduced the MCD officer as a specialist in clearance diving, mining, mine counteremeasures, bomb and mine disposal and demolitions). Since the early 1960s cross training had been encouraged, submariners were attending the Long TAS Course, and Air Observers were continuing to take the tactical though not the materiel part of the long course. *Vernon* had lost its MCM Squadron but it picked up several new craft. *Miner III* that had survived as training tender for the clearance divers after *Miner IV* had gone for disposal in 1961 was replaced by the converted *Laleston*. The 1st Fast Patrol Boat Squadron that had been at *Dolphin* after *Hornet's* closure also came to *Vernon*.

The cross training showed that the old 'tribal' loyalties were disappearing: in 1967 the introduction into service of a new simulator at *Dryad* began the gradual removal of anti-submarine Command Training away from *Vernon*. The concept of a Command Team instead of a Commanding Officer supported by a constellation of specialist officers was taking root. Perhaps not insignificantly, in 1966, (which was also the centenary year of the Whitehead torpedo), the head of the *Vernon* figurehead fell off and had to be refitted.

It was becoming operationally necessary for surface ships to operate in a defence or two-watch system with a capability to respond instantaneously to any threat and with a facility to go to Action Stations with minimum disruption if necessary. Thus throughout the 1960s, as a reflection of the increasing complexity of shipborne equipment, there arose the need for watchkeeping Operation Room Officers, authorised to act on behalf of the Command, conversant with all forms of naval operations above or below water and with the tactical employment of maritime aviation and of electronic warfare equipment. Much of this cross-training was acquired on-the-job at sea in an unstructured manner. There was an evident need for something better; on the horizon were integrated and computerised Action Information Systems (CAAIS and ADAWS) which would require the same types of user knowledge from all sub-specialised seamen, officers and ratings, and for which the shore-based training simulators would be very expensive. Already present was the threat from surface-to-surface and air-to-surface missiles which demanded instant tactical reactions. An evolutionary approach to this problem was already increasing the cross training components in each of the specialist courses with 'common time' in Action Speed Tactical teachers aimed at working up Command Teams. However, largely at the instigation of Admiral of the Fleet Sir Edward Ashmore, based on his experience as Flag Officer Second in Command, Far East Fleet, and as a result of his continuing involvement as Vice Chief of the Naval Staff, it was decided to go for radical solutions.

A Seaman Sub-Specialist Working Party (SSSWP) was set up to study the whole purpose and structure of sub-specialisation and to recommend changes accordingly. The members set about their task with vigour and had soon visited all schools. The responsibilities and career structures of TAS Officers posed a particularly difficult problem. The morale of the branch was high, but as a sub-specialist the TAS Officer suffered from the same handicap to his career as his torpedo predecessors. He had to be certain that he was employed on seaman's general duties for long enough to catch the eye of his superiors. Meanwhile, weapons and equipment systems were becoming progressively more sophisticated and training in all appropriate techniques was already expensive and time consuming. Strong opinions were held, but the most favoured solution was to reduce the number of seamen sub-specialists drastically and to give all seaman officers a more general training in tactics and the operational control of weapons systems. The new Principal Warfare Officers (PWOs) trained to a common standard would devolve more authority to qualified ratings. Fleet trials in *Achilles* and *Jupiter* proved the concept and the TAS Long Course was phased out in 1972.

Another change was an integral part of this process. Before the setting up of the TAS branch its two constituents were responsible for the maintenance of their own weapons and equipment, assisted as necessary by Electrical Artificers (who were 'T' Branch anyway). These responsibilities gradually shifted away from *Vernon* . At first the Ordnance Branch took over the weapons in the workshops and display room, and eventually, in 1970, maintenance of the the Mk 8 heavyweight torpedoes went over to *Dolphin*; the Mk 24 remained at *Vernon* as a new Mk 24 instructional wing had been installed less than five years before. Lightweight torpedoes became *Collingwood's* responsibility as the 'L' branch became responsible for maintaining all related equipment such as weapons launchers, control gear etc.

Another casualty of rationalisation was the Joint Anti-Submarine School at Londonderry in Northern Ireland which since 1948, had been running courses in advanced anti-submarine warfare and had earned an enviable reputation based on professional expertise and a happy symbiosis between the Royal Navy and the Royal Air Force, both of which contributed Directors at four stripe rank and whose staff worked together on the tactical problems of the day. Nearby, RAF Ballykelly provided a base for naval anti-submarine helicopters and maritime patrol aircraft of many nations. Submarines of the Royal Navy were readily available from the base at Faslane in Scotland or from Portsmouth; additionally submarines from other NATO nations could be supported, or at least made comfortable, alongside HMS *Stalker*, a small support vessel in the naval base compound near the town on the west bank of the River Foyle. Berths were available for frigates and destroyers either at Londonderry or at a fuelling depot at Lisahally further down the river. These facilities, coupled to the fact that the local sea areas were quiet and not much used by merchant ship traffic, and that deep water over the edge of the continental shelf was available within one hundred miles of the Loch Foyle buoy enabled a systematiic approach to training and tactical development. Courses involving all anti-submarine disciplines were founded on classroom instruction, tactical floor discussion, graduated exercises at sea and subsequent de-briefing and analysis. In 1961 the Operational Evaluation Group was inaugurated at Londonderry in support of the School, and over the years until its move in 1969 to Northwood, the headquarters of Commander in Chief Fleet, it produced some excellent work. Topics such as the tactical evaluation of the medium range sonars, the employment of the nuclear submarine in the escort role, were studied and the results analised to a depth rarely achieved before or since. Besides comparatively routine training courses, the combination of the Joint Anti-Submarine School and the Operational Evaluation Group planned and executed a number of valuable and advanced experimental exercises, often away from these northern waters, at Gibraltar or in the Mediterranean. Much tactical doctrine was evolved, a creditable proportion of which took its place in NATO publications.

But it was evident that while occasional surface actions were subjected to the same depth of rigorous analysis, the totality of naval warfare was not being evaluated. While the Londonderry Squadron, proudly bearing the Red Hand of Ulster on their funnels, were widely acknowledged as the 'creme de la creme' of the Royal Navy and, indeed European, anti-submarine experts, it was not until about 1966 that the first crude steps were taken to subject the surface naval forces operated by the Joint Anti-Submarine School to air attacks and to analyse the outcomes. A trend towards the training for and proper evaluation of performance in a multi-threat environment was under way. Some of the early work at Londonderry concentrated upon the description of the analysis and recording facilities that would be required in future naval equipment, the results of which can be seen in today's computerised ship systems.

Financial pressures finally forced the closure of the Joint Anti-Submarine School in 1970 and the transfer of its functions to what became known as the Joint Maritime Operational Training School (JMOTS) based at Turnhouse, Edinburgh Airport, and which drew upon the communications infrastructure at Rosyth. Though much was lost, much remained. There were many TAS Officers who deeply regretted the loss of Londonderry and the opportunities created there to confront the problems of the day in depth and detail but JMOTS proved to be a great success.

In the summer of 1971, an event which had special significance for *Vernon*, brought about a new era in the lives of the lower deck. That summer saw the abolition of the rum ration which had been introduced in 1745 by Admiral Vernon. The event was celebrated in by a discotheque with 'grog' as the theme. It was held inside a very large rum tub erected in the wardroom rose garden. A humorous painting of an old sailor coming into the First Sea Lord's office to complain and addressing the First Sea Lord, Admiral Sir Michael Le Fanu, by his nickname 'Ginger' appeared in a Southampton weekly newspaper. *Vernon* obtained a copy of the original drawing from the editor and it was presented to the red-headed First Sea Lord when he paid a formal visit a few weeks later.

The 1960s came to an end with *Vernon* playing an important administrative role during the multi-national NATO Fleet Review at Spithead. Once again the Fleet Post Office was set up in *Vernon* and all mail to and from the ships at Spithead came through the establishment. First day *Vernon* covers with special stamps were issued. Captain Keppel Edge-Partington, however, was soon reporting the likely effects of a new rationalisation exercise called 'Constrain'. Although the establishment would lose its primary TAS training function it was to be retained by the navy. The Captain was still the co-ordinating authority for the MATCH series of anti-submarine helicopter trials and active sonar command team training continued for the time being; indeed the new £1,000,000 A/S 1079 trainer was proving highly effective. The frigate and submarine trials teams remained very busy, while minesweeping trials moved to join minehunting in *Vernon*.

Vernon's inventiveness continued to appear in many small ways, such as the introduction of mobile vacuum cleaners for scouring the roads and the development of a litter clearance scheme. The run-down of the establishment, however, gathered pace. Although the Second Mine Countermeasures Squadron was based at *Vernon* from 1972 onwards the heart was going out of of the establishment. Sonar training continued but under the control of *Dryad* and when Captain RS Browning handed over command in the summer of 1974, he did so as the last Captain to have full command of what had been for so many years the traditional tasks of the Torpedo and Torpedo Anti-Submarine Branches. The former torpedo display rooms in the establishment were used instead for Seamanship Training and in the late 1970s there was talk of supply training moving to *Vernon*. Nothing came of this latter proposal and the main responsibility of the Captain remained diving, mine countermeasures and mine warfare; for a few more years the old spirit of *Vernon* lingered on.

CHAPTER TWENTY
THE LAST VERNONS

THE LAST OF *VERNON'S* PEOPLE were the Royal Navy's divers. Diving had originally been a Gunnery Branch responsibility but it passed to the torpedomen in October 1944 and *Vernon(D)* had been duly established at Brixham as the Royal Navy's diving centre. With the end of the war *Vernon(D)* was closed and the 'P' Parties set up their office in No 21 Building at *Vernon* in Portsmouth. Their stay was brief as the decision was taken to to integrate the divers more closely with the rest of the mine countermeasures establishment at *Lochinvar* at Port Edgar on the Firth of Forth. The first divers at *Lochinvar* were from the last 'P' Party to return from clearing Dunkirk in March 1946. They were almost all hostilities only personnel so most were soon demobilised. All that was left of Naval Party 2444 were Lieutenant Gutteridge, one Leading Seaman and three Able Seamen. Gutteridge, who had been given a five year short service commission, was joined at Port Edgar by a few additional ratings who had been trained to assist in the early post-war development of mine counter-measures.

Meanwhile *Vernon* became the centre for deep diving. In 1946 the Admiralty Experimental Diving Unit (AEDU) was transferred to *Vernon* from Siebe Gorman's works at Tolworth, where it had been set up the previous year, and Commander WO Shelford, the Superintendent of Diving, took up residence with his team in Building Number 21. The AEDU's immediate concern was oxygen poisoning which had affected the volunteers manning the 'chariots' (manned torpedoes) during long periods at depths of 60-70 feet. Surgeon Lieutenant Commander K Donald and Surgeon Lieutenant WM Davidson, assisted by the diving Gunners E Crouch and P Higgins, produced a document of great importance, 'Oxygen Poisoning in Man', which formed the basis for the physiological design of future underwater breathing equipment.

There was now an unfortunate but clear division between the deep diving team at *Vernon*, the 'Steamers', and the Clearance Divers at *Lochinvar* known as 'Corkheads'. One of the first tasks for Shelford was to go to Germany to find a replacement under the terms of reparations for the old coal burning deep diving vessel *Tedworth*. He found the German torpedo trials ship *Walter Holtzapel* which was turned over to the Royal Navy. She was a great improvement on *Tedworth*, being 217 feet in length and 1500 tons displacement with a speed of 17 knots. *Tedworth's* compression chamber and other diving equipment was installed and she was commissioned as *Deepwater* in March 1946. She berthed alongside the Whitehead Jetty north of *Vernon* Creek and was commanded by the Superintendant of Diving. Another German ship, *Lumme*, was taken over as *Clearwater* to provide additional training capacity.

Many of the deep divers in 1946 had been recalled at the beginning of the war and were now due for demobilisation. The only officers remaining with deep diving experience were WB Filer and P Higgins who were immediately employed training officers and ratings. Very soon these trainees were diving at 200 feet on a wreck 15 miles south of Worthing. The SS *Alaska* had sunk with a valuable cargo of copper ingots, and salvaging these provided valuable experience for the divers and in handling the diving ship over a wreck in strong tides. In this, and other similar operations, *Vernon*'s divers began to develop the system known as 'surface decompression' in which a submersible compression chamber was used which the diver entered at depth. The chamber was then sealed and it was hoisted to the surface under pressure to transfer the diver to a compression chamber on the surface.

While these facilities were being developed, Shelford investigated a report that the Germans had an atmospheric diving suit made from steel, with articulated leg and arm joints, the latter terminating in pincers. It was known as Neufeldt and Khunke's 'Panzer Taucherat' (Iron Man). This grotesque suit underwent trials in the mining tank at *Vernon* where, by delicate manipulation of the suit's trimming tanks, the diver could tie knots and pick up a small coin. Alas, in sea trials such mobility was lost in even the slightest tide, or in muddy conditions. At 200 feet the joints seized up and the suit was reduced to an over elaborate observation chamber with unacceptable maintenance problems.

Of far greater importance were the trials using oxygen and helium mixtures to replace air to support the diver at depths where nitrogen narcosis imposed severe limitations, causing divers to hallucinate. The replacement of air by an oxygen/helium mixture made breathing far easier and did not jeopardise the diver's mental agility. This meant that the maximum diving depth for Royal Naval divers could, in theory, be increased from 300 to 360 feet. The problem of oxygen poisoning at maximum depth was overcome by the adjustment of the mixture of oxygen and helium.

In spite of these successes, the Royal Navy still had a very small diving capability. Higgins had retired, leaving Filer to train a new generation of deep diving officers. Commissioned Boatswains WD Barrington and H Wardle were qualified, together with twelve ratings. By this time it had become apparent that *Deepwater* had many limitations as a deep diving tender and an order was placed by the Admiralty for a ship designed for the task. This new ship, *Reclaim*, entered service in June 1948. *Deepwater* remained alongside at *Vernon* as the Diving School. Within two months of *Reclaim*'s commissioning one of her divers, Petty Officer W Bollard, claimed the world deep diving record at 535 feet.

With Commander FC Goodenough in command and Filer as First Lieutenant and Chief Diving Officer, *Reclaim* sailed for the Mediterranean for a series of trials to increase the limit for Royal Navy diving to 360 feet. Helium was expensive, which severely limited the extent of the trials. It was decided to conduct the trials on whichever side of Malta gave the best lee and thus the most stable position over the diving datum. In achieving this stability *Reclaim* used the mizzen sail with which she had been fitted. This avoided the ship's tendency to yaw in deep moor. The mizzen was also found to improve the speed and fuel economy of the ship when on passage.

It was during this period that a familiar figure re-appeared. Lionel Crabb joined *Reclaim* to take part in a trial which Filer considered to be highly dangerous. He had been working, with Lieutenant J Hodges, at the Admiralty Research Labortatory, Teddington on the development of an encapsulated camera for underwater use. The trial in the spring of 1949 was to photograph a cruiser's propellers at various speeds to ascertain the extent and effect of cavitation. A lane was laid down between danbuoys, through which *Amphion* steamed at increasing speeds. Crabb, in shallow water diving dress, took up his position on one of the danbuoy mooring wires at a depth which he considered favourable to achieve the required result. In spite of Filer's misgivings, the project was completed without incident.

After *Reclaim's* return to home waters, two submarine disasters called for the assistance of *Vernon's* divers. In 1950, when *Truculent* failed to surface in the Thames Estuary. *Reclaim* was refitting but her divers, who were sent to the scene, arrived too late. On 15 April 1951, when *Reclaim* was giving seasonal leave, *Affray* was reported overdue for surfacing. *Reclaim* was ordered to raise steam and to recall the ship's company from leave. She soon joined in the hunt for *Affray* being conducted by the Sixth Frigate Squadron under Captain RS Foster-Brown. It was known aboard *Reclaim* that Sub Lieutenant RG Howard-Johnston, son of the Captain of *Vernon* was in *Affray*; he was one of a training class of thirteen Sub Lieutenants on a day trip in the submarine, and this added an extra sense of urgency and poignancy to the search. Much help was given by Lt Cdr EW (Bill) Ridley whose considerable A/S experience was instrumental in devising a successful search pattern to find the stricken boat.

Starting at a datum point 10 miles south of the Nab Tower, *Reclaim's* divers investigated twelve possible contacts before finally confirming the location of *Affray* on the edge of the Hurd Deep at a depth of 287 feet. It had been an arduous search, taking up six weeks of rigorous diving, day and night, as tides permitted. The diving ship had to moor in the open Channel accurately enough for the divers to descend in safety to the contacts, many at 200 feet or more. Most were old wrecks which had disintegrated into heaps of broken masts, rigging, davits and plating, seriously hazarding the divers' air hoses and communication lines. Eventually Filer, diving to investigate the latest contact, was able to confirm that it was *Affray* and that the 'snort' mast was fractured and hanging over the side. His report supported the theory that *Affray* had been hit by some vessel whilst 'snorting'. Filer's first report was verified by Able Seaman Middleton, a former submarine rating, who was lowered in an observation chamber to the position of the submarine. He stated that no other damage was apparent and that the cause of the disaster seemed to be a damaged 'snort'.

It was now important to discover whether the 'snort' induction valve was open or closed. This was very difficult to establish since it was physically impossible for a diver wearing deep diving equipment to squeeze through the conning tower hatch. Filer and his colleagues devised an adaptation of a gas mask which could be worn by the diver and supplied with air from a panel in the Submersible Compression Chamber (SCC). This would allow the SCC to be lowered over the conning tower hatch, allowing the diver to operate unencumbered by air canisters. This was an audacious and unauthorised scheme but one which the divers were confident they could carry out successfully; it was considered by the Commander-in-Chief Portsmouth's staff to be too risky and permission was refused. *Reclaim's* divers resented this decision. Filer later remarked:

To us in the field it was just another decision taken by those ashore with little or no background of diving, but nonetheless understandable because they did not want to lose any of us as they knew that we could no longer save life. Nevertheless, we had the experience and sense of responsibility to assure the safety of our divers.

A television camera under development at Teddington was sent to Portsmouth in the care of Crabb, in the hope that it would hasten the classification of contacts. The camera initially caused serious problems for the divers but eventually proved to be a valuable aid in the search. After Filer had identified *Affray*, he was able to return to the surface and to position the ship, by adjusting moorings, so that the submarine's name plate appeared on the television's monitor screen in the Captain's cabin. This was the first time that underwater television had been used to identify a wreck. The image on the monitor screen was photographed and made much use of by the press.

The cause of the accident still remained to be established. Using the underwater television camera it was confirmed that the 'snort' mast was broken and lying over the side of the submarine. With the assistance of the divers it was recovered and sent to HM Dockyard Laboratory at Portsmouth for investigation, where metal fatigue was diagnosed. The question of the position of the 'snort' induction valve still remained, and to solve this problem the Underwater Countermeasures and Weapons Establishment (UCWE) was consulted. It had been examining a method of 'radiographing' mines, using a cobalt 60 source. The intention was to place the cobalt 60 source on one side of the 'snort' induction valve and a photographic film on the other side, which when exposed would give an image of the position of the valve. Unfortunately, this radiographing device was only in its intial stages of development. It was lowered to *Affray* but the source was contained in an extemporised casing and in the course of manoeuvring it into position it fell out. It was too dangerous to recover and it still lies in close proximity to *Affray*, thus providing a hazard to anyone venturing too near it for many generations to come. At least it ensures that HM Submarine *Affray* will be left in peace at.

The *Affray* tragedy resulted in three important firsts in diving developments: deep diving with divers operating in the swimming mode, the use of underwater television, and the development of radiographing techniques which have been used extensively for underwater surveys on pipe lines and oil rig constructions. The outstanding performance of the divers in this extended operation was recognised by awards to seven officers and twenty four ratings.

While the deep divers operated from *Reclaim*, Gutteridge and *Lochinvar's* clearance divers were obtaining practical experience in dealing with the World War II mines which continued to be reported. Some caught in fishermen's nets at depths of 60 feet or more were proving to be most hazardous. It had been expected that these mines would die of old age but this was not the case. German mine batteries were of high quality and concealed safely inside a mine were stored in ideal conditions. UCWE scientists estimated correctly that they would continue to operate satisfactorily for approximately ten years.

To transport Gutteridge's team to the sites of these lethal mines the Fleet Air Arm provided an elderly Dominie biplane. The ancient aeroplane took them to mine incidents as far apart as the Orkneys, Islay, Northern Ireland and Alderney. The young pilot showed as much skill as the divers in his part of the operations, landing them on the beach at low tide on Islay and on the main road south of Aberdeen, where he pulled into a garage and asked for 'fifteen gallons on tick'.

Much work had gone on at *Lochinvar* in the late 1940s to improve clearance diving equipment. The 'Universal Breathing Apparatus' (UBA) was developed with help from the Dunlop Rubber Company. The unpopular belly entry 'Clammy Death' Sladen suit used by World War II 'P' Parties was replaced by a high quality, well fitting neck entry 'dry suit', the first prototype being produced by Dunlop as a private venture. Experiments were carried out with the UBA and the new suit complete with experimental Dunlop swim fins. Safe routine diving with the UBA to 120 feet and with the Mine Recovery Suit to 180 feet using oxygen and hydrogen mixtures was established. Problems were posed when divers inexplicably lost consciousness but *Lochinvar*'s Senior Medical officer, Surgeon Commander 'Mac' McClintock, kept a prudent and watchful eye on proceedings. Loss of consciousness was diagnosed as being caused by poor design and careless filling of carbon dioxide absorbtion canisters and/or oxygen poisoning which affected various individuals at different depths. With the help of AEDU, these experiments resulted in naval divers being able, for the first time, to operate at medium depths independent of surface air supply and life lines.

By 1949, minehunting had progressed sufficiently for the system to be tested in exercise 'Curlew'. Supervised by Commander R Parkinson, the four available mine location vessels operated around all the major U.K. ports testing and developing the 'search and destroy' technique that is the foundation of modern minehunting. That year the Clearance Diving Branch was founded at *Lochinvar* and a Home Station Clearance Diving Team was set up in 1950. Commonwealth personnel were also being trained in the United Kingdom, and exchange visits were taking place with the United States Navy Explosive Ordnance Disposal School and other American diving organisations. The Canada/UK/US defence liaison which was being built up throughout the underwater warfare branches of the three navies was thus extended to the field of explosive ordnance disposal.

Clearance diving training moved from *Lochinvar* to *Vernon* in 1951 and a new Clearance Diving School was established there under Lieutenant JL Crawford. Gutteridge moved to UCWE at Havant, together with the Experimental Diving Trials Team to concentrate on the scientific study of clearance diving problems but they continued to work in close liaison with the Superintendent of Diving at *Vernon*. The appointment to this post of Commander RF Harland from *Lochinvar* confirmed the beginning of a new era in which scientists, engineers, medical specialists and divers began to work in harmony. As Gutteridge put it, 'Old hostilities wore away, new blood was introduced and only healthy competition remained'. The Clearance Diving School took on the new task of training ships' divers, ensuring that every ship had a properly equipped diving capability under its own Diving Officer. This rationalisation of diving training was accompanied by the development of a coherent policy for equipment development, experimental trials and user acceptance trials.

The UBA, which went into full production in 1952, was adapted for oxygen breathing for Shallow Water Divers. Shallow water diving was required so that ships had an underwater search capability to combat sabotage attack but in the early 1950s no suitable compressed air breathing apparatus was available from naval stores. But in the Mediterranean in 1952 the Fleet Clearance Officer, Lieutenant P White, was frequently called upon to organise underwater fishing and swimming trips for the new Commander-in-Chief, Admiral Lord Louis Mountbatten and the Governor of Malta, using Cousteau/Gagnon aqualungs purchased out of fleet funds. Mountbatten persuaded the Admiralty to produce a Staff Requirement for a Ship's Diver's breathing apparatus based upon the Cousteau aqualung. AEDU obliged and the Royal Navy's first official aqualung - Swimmer's Air Breathing Apparatus (SABA) - was ready for acceptance trials in 1957, thanks to Commander Harland's enthusiasm and determination. It was superior to any aqualung available at that time, but it was expensive and was later replaced by the commercially available Aquarius. Most divers, including Gutteridge and Filer, considered that this was a penny pinching mistake and that the Royal Navy had abandoned a very much superior piece of shallow water diving equipment.

Gutteridge at UCWE was assisted by the legendary Commander Ouvry who was recalled to write a new manual on rendering mines safe, a task he accomplished with what Gutteridge calls his 'expected diligence'. Problems were created, however, when Crabb was recalled to service and promoted over Gutteridge's head to command the Experimental Clearance Diving Team. This was intended to allow Gutteridge to concentrate on research development work but it had unfortunate effects as Crabb, in Gutteridge's words 'distrusted scientists and avoided all things scientific'. Despite these problems, however, UCWE was able to develop a cohesive programme of development of mine investigation and render safe techniques and equipment. Scientists were fully integrated into the Naval Mine Investigation Team.

The loss of the cobalt 60 source on the *Affray* did not prevent the development of this technique for X-raying mines in situ. It was aided by the availability of high energy long life radioactive sources from the Atomic Energy Establishment at Harwell. The equipment for stereoscopic X-ray examination of mine units and for a full automatic underwater mine X-ray unit was successfully produced.

One of the most intractable problems of World War II was the sweeping of magnetic/acoustic/pressure combination mines buried in tidal mudflats. These mines were very likely to explode if the head of water above them was reduced so that digging down to them was hazardous. An attempt had been made with a ten foot cylindrical concrete block shaft and a water pressure operated digging ejector which, in theory, would dig, line and empty a hole of spoil whilst maintaining a safe hydrostatic head of water in the shaft. UCWE and Messrs. Wimpey evolved the idea of a sectional aluminium 'earthworm'. A five foot prototype was successfully developed. This equipment, known as an 'Ejector', was able to dig itself in and extract itself by remote control.

Now that the diver was no longer tethered to the surface it was

A member of the Diving Clearance Team displaying his waterproof Rolex watch

important that he should be provided with a watch of sufficient accuracy for him to control his own time under water. Such a watch had to be non-magnetic, self winding, capable of surviving its being dropped 8 feet on to concrete, waterproof at 300 feet and able to function in the neighbourhead of a powerful magnetic clock stopper used to stop mines from 'ticking'. Most important was the need for a face designed to avoid mis-reading by the user operating in low visibility and in adverse tidal conditions. The Rolex Watch Company successfully met the challenge using a formally registered design of watch face by Gutteridge. This was the 'Rolex Perpetual Oyster' which became a standard issue to Royal Naval divers, the first watch to reach the top of Mount Everest and the first to go into space.

A fully automatic mine-recovery lifting bag was developed so that mines could be lifted remotely to avoid risks to divers should they explode when being brought to the surface. This was designed at UCWE and patented in the joint names of Gutteridge and the Admiralty. Attention also turned to the development of shaped explosive charges to destroy the mines remotely, or to separate their actuating mechanisms from their explosive charge without detonating them. A simple tool for making up shaped charges on site to fit any circumference of mine was developed . This rather violent means of rendering mines safe, both on the surface and underwater provided a high probability of success, as demonstrated in later operations. To assist the clearance diver to deal with mines underwater communications were improved by introducing throat microphones, voice actuation and diver's float c/w radio. To assist in locating mines, the diver was provided with a hand held portable sonar which would detect a mine proud of the sea bed at ranges of up to 200 feet. The United States Navy produced a comparable device which, whilst more cumbersome, had audio presentation which was preferred by many divers to the visual display on the UCWE unit. Thus expertly equipped the Royal Navy's clearance divers were ready to face the many calls upon their services both within the Service and elsewhere.

In 1954 Crabb was retired although he had one final and notorious contribution to make to the story of *Vernon*. He and was replaced by Lieutenant Mark Terrell. Gutteridge found Terrell to be 'a very tough, able, ex-submarine officer with much technical talent and great imagination'. He soon developed a new inflatable dinghy with modern American outboard motors. As Gutteridge put it, 'almost overnight the limitations of launching diving boats in heavy weather vanished, clearance divers could operate in any weather, anywhere, with nothing more cumbersome than very large suitcases to transport'.

A pleasant diversion in 1954 was the renting of a clearance diving team by the Duke of Argyll to search for the wreck of the *San Juan Baptiste*, reputedly the ship of the Armada's Paymaster, and said to be wrecked in Tobermory Bay. Using ejectors and probes, the ship was located in two pieces under about 15 feet of silt and efforts were made to extract treasure and artefacts. After three weeks of fruitless effort one of the divers, determined to enliven the proceedings, injected a totally spurious medallion, well covered in verdigris, into the ejector pipe. Its arrival in the diving tender caused great excitement and a picture appeared in the press the following day. The incident was in danger of getting out of hand, so it was arranged for the diver concerned to be accidentally knocked overboard so that the 'treasure' could be lost from his pocket!

UCWE now worked closely with AEDU. The latter had become involved in 1951 in the development of a Damage Control Breathing Apparatus (DCBA). A spin off from the DCBA Staff Requirement was the development by Commander Harland, as a replacement for the old helmeted standard diving equipment, of the Surface Demand Diving Equipment (SDDE). Similar components to the DCBA and SABA were used in SDDE, but air was supplied through an umbilical hose from a surface control panel fed with compressed air from 150 cubic feet aluminium cylinders. SDDE was not introduced into service until 1960, its development having been helped by AEDU'S receiving a similar Australian 'Hookah' device in 1958.

As divers were to operate close to influence mines, it was necessary to ensure that their diving suits and breathing equipment were as non-magnetic and silent as possible. Therefore, beginning in 1952, a new mine recovery outfit was developed to replace the equipment developed by the Australians Mould and Goldsworthy in *Vernon* during the war. The Mine Recovery Outfit (MRO), which completed its acceptance trials in 1954, was another successful design but it was expensive and production was limited to fourteen, which were placed in war reserve. It was during the development of the MRO, in 1953, that AEDU moved from 43 Building at *Vernon* to the former Pay Office alongside the football pitch.

In 1954 Gutteridge and Filer received an invitation from the United States Navy to a diving symposium followed by visits to their diving and ordnance disposal establishments. On arrival in the USA, Gutteridge and Filer demonstrated the mine recovery outfit, shaped charge render safe techniques, non-magmnetic tools, the diving watch, underwater radiography and mine dismantling techniques about which the Americans seemed to know very little. In return they inspected new and experimental diving equipment. They were most impressed by the 'Wet and Dry Chamber' for conducting diving experiments down to 500 feet under controlled conditions. Some eight years later this equipment was introduced into the Royal Navy.

While in the United States, Gutteridge and Filer also visited the Mine Countermeasures Base at Charleston, where they 'flew' the Aerojet Corporation's Minisub, which was a free flooding diver's aid to mobility. It had two speeds, 3½ and 7 knots. It looked and behaved like a single seater fighter aircraft and was fully aquabatic. However, in the muddy Charleston River it could not be tested to the limits of its capabilities. A minor crisis occurred during Filer's test runs when the Minisub's marker float disappeared, initiating a miniature 'Subsmash' operation. After the visit to the United States, Gutteridge obtained a similar Minisub for UCWE which underwent trials at Horsea Island and Falmouth. The trials were disappointing and the Royal Navy decided to concentrate instead upon the towed diver search system, which had also been observed during the American visit. In clear water a diver was towed behind a boat at approximately 3 knots while he held onto an aquaplane, 3 feet long, which he could manipulate to the best depth and angle to scan the bottom for mines.

In 1954 AEDU supplied a new Submarine Escape Breathing Apparatus (SEBA) to replace the obsolete Davis Submarine Escape Apparatus (DSEA). Its introduction was followed by a visit by Rear Admiral JH Ruck Keene, Chairman of the Submarine Escape Committee, to the United States to assess the 100 foot escape training facility. On his return approval was given by the Admiralty to build a similar training tank at the Submarine Headquarters at *Dolphin*, but completion was delayed by two fatalities in the US Navy's tank caused by having no provision for recompression at the top of the tank. For a moment it seemed that this useful training facility upon which a great deal of money had been spent would become a political embarrassment but the AEDU had designed a compression chamber for use in minesweepers, and the first of these was fitted at the top of *Dolphin's* escape training tank in time for Filer to make the first ascent.

The AEDU's responsibility for the safety of submariners did not end at the tank. A McCann submarine rescue bell was obtained from the United States Navy. It had been used operationally as early as 1933 to rescue the crew of the USN submarine *Squalus*. Filer had the task of preparing the chamber for sea trials. A dummy submarine escape hatch was manufactured at Portsmouth and placed in a dock ready for the trials. Filer was informed that the Flag Officer Submarines, Rear Admiral SM Raw, would be present to witness the trial, but when he arrived he informed Filer that he wished to accompany him on the first descent. The trials were successful and were repeated in 1955 with the rescue bell embarked first in *Reclaim* and then in *Kingfisher*. The bell was used successfully, at depths of over 240 feet in 4½ knot tides, with the target submarine *Seraph* listing at 37½ degrees. In spite of these successful trials the rescue bell was not accepted for service in the Royal Navy. The Admiralty decided that as it was impossible to keep more than one bell in operational readiness it was better to concentrate on free ascent techniques.

In 1954, Filer was appointed Officer-in-Charge of the Acceptance Trials Team at *Vernon*, deciding on the Captain's behalf whether ot not AEDU designed equipment was acceptable for service. At about this time White, still the Fleet Clearance Diving Officer in the Mediterranean designed a 'sled' upon which a diver could lie while being towed while searching for mines. Filer was anxious to compare this development with the American aquaplane and flew out to Malta to carry out a series of trials. He later wrote that the 'sled' 'gave me some exciting rides over an underwater mountainous-type seabed at approximately five knots'.

The 'sled', although comfortable for the diver, was big and cumbersome and had to be towed too fast for the diver properly to scan the swept path. Some other method had to be found and at Horsea Island Filer took part in the development of the 'shot and toggle' method of towing a diver by his 'shot rope'. Attached to it was the usual half hundred weight sinker and a tail, secured to the lower end, with two short lengths of broom stick rove through it. The diver sat astride one of the toggles while holding on to the other. The shot was lowered to a position close to the bottom and when the diver had taken up his position he signalled that he was ready for the towing boat to get under way. The diver was also able to make the appropriate signals for him to be raised or lowered to the required height above the bottom. On sighting a mine, the diver made a 'bailing out' signal, whereupon the boat's crew released the shot with a buoy attached whilst the diver swam to the mine and attached his signal line. This system proved to be a complete success and was adopted by the Royal Navy. Modern methods have superseded the towed diver system except for use in very shallow waters where mine coutermeasures vessels cannot manoeuvre.

1956 saw, perhaps, the most notorious diving incident involving *Vernon* - the disappearance in Portsmouth Harbour of Crabb, who had retired in 1954, and as far as can be ascertained had carried out no diving until his appearance at Portsmouth on 17 April. According to Gutteridge:

He remained ..., a diver of enormous experience with a singular ability to endure discomfort, but not given to long, hard slogs under water. His lack of fear was unquestioned but his assessment of experimental equipment and techniques bordered on the bizarre. By now his personality, behaviour and dress were set in stone; the quintessential, curmudgeonly but kindly bantam cock, complete with swordstick with a gold engraved crab on the knob. Certainly he was, with his friends, a most pleasant and lively personality.

Lionel Crabb, in cloth cap, with colleagues from the RN Physiological Laboratory and Experimental Diving Team

The first that John Grant, the Captain of *Vernon*, knew of the incident was on 19 April:

when my senior Clearance Diving Officer came and reported to me that he had been asked by Crabb to help him to dress for an important dive he had to make and to take him by car to the waterside in the dockyard somewhere near the Russian cruisers. This he had done, without reference to anyone else, as requested by Crabb, and having seen him into the water waited for his return. My senior Clearance Diving Officer then continued that, owing to the time which elapsed since he last saw Crabb there was cause for alarm. As I myself had received no information whatsoever on this operation which apparently involved a member of my VERNON *staff I was, somewhat naturally, extremely annoyed. Accordingly, I took the officer with me in a car forthwith to see the Chief of Staff to the Commander-in-Chief Portsmouth and asked him to report the matter to the C-in-C as a matter of great urgency. As was to be expected, the C-in-C went through the roof and the wires to the Admiralty must have nearly fused!! There then followed a visit by the Director of Naval Intelligence and then, in my opinion, a stupid statement to the press by the Admiralty to the effect that Crabb had been lost in Stokes Bay. As that was the* VERNON *Exercise Area I was, consequently, bothered by pressmen for a considerable time after. However, they only got 'No comment' out of me.*

Crabb had travelled from London by car on 17 April with a young and relatively junior member of the Secret Intelligence Service. On arrival at Portsmouth, they booked in their own names into the modest but conveniently sited Sally Port Hotel in Old Portsmouth. Later that day, they met the Chief Constable, Mr. AC West who detailed Superintendent Jack Lamport, an officer with experience of security work as his liaison officer. That evening and on 18 April Crabb visited *Vernon* to borrow a car from a steward and also to have tea in the wardroom with the Executive Officer, Commander Emmerson. He also made contact with several Clearance Diving Officers one of whom, Lieutenant GA Franklin, he persuaded to 'dress and attend him' on his proposed dive.

On 18 April, after being delayed by fog, the Soviet cruiser *Ordzhonikidze*, accompanied by the destroyers *Sovershenny* and *Smotryaschy* berthed alongside the railway jetty, in time for Crabb to make a dive at high water. He entered the water at 1730 but soon became caught in the pilings of the jetty and aborted. The cruiser was carrying the Soviet leaders Bulganin and Khruschev who had to come ashore by launch to catch their special train to London to meet the Prime Minister. Early the next morning, the 19th, Crabb and his SIS 'minder' headed for the King's Stairs in Portsmouth Dockyard, four flights of stone steps leading into the water about 80 yards from the Russian warships. It seems probable that Crabb wore his favourite Pirelli dry suit beneath his ordinary street clothes. How they passed through the dockyard gate at a time of high security alert is open to question, but pass through they must have done. It seems likely they were accompanied by Superintendent Lamport or one of his CID officers and that Franklin, who was to dress Crabb, joined them at this point. Under these circumstances Crabb and his SIS companion would have had no difficulty in entering the dockyard. By 0700, when the early morning light was beginning to reveal the shapes of the Russian warships, Crabb had been dressed and was ready to enter the water. Only twenty minutes later he returned to King's Stairs having difficulty with his equipment. After a while he returned to the water and was never seen alive again, except briefly on the surface at 0735 between the destroyers by one of their crew.

When Crabb had not returned by 0830, the SIS officer gathered up Crabb's 'shore side clothing' and went to the Chief Constable's office. The Security Services and SIS were informed of the situation by Lamport who was in turn instructed to ensure that the presence of the intelligence officer was not revealed. After the latter had spoken to the SIS from the police station he went to the Sally Port Hotel, collected his and Crabb's baggage, paid the bill, checked out and returned by train to London. A few days later, Lamport went to the Sally Port and removed pages from the hotel register, including the pages containing the names and signatures of Crabb and his companion. He signed the register by way of receipt and suggested to the proprietor that he keep his mouth shut. Now blunder was heaped upon blunder. The removal of the pages of the register was bound to be noticed. Crabb was not renowned for discretion and he had been drinking with naval diving friends the previous day. The fact that a competent journalist was nearing completion of Crabb's biography meant that there was heightened press interest in his activities. It was not long before news of his disappearance had reached the press and they soon backtracked his movements to the Sally Port Hotel where they saw the hotel register, both before and after the pages were removed.

By now news of the incident had reached the Soviet leaders and at a dinner party Kuruschev made bantering reference to *Ordzhonikidze* and her equipment. Eden was puzzled by this reference as he was unaware of what had happened and was not told until the following day, almost certainly by the Head of SIS. Eden is reported to have taken this matter as a personal affront, most particularly as he had issued specific instructions prior to their visit that the Russians were not, under any circumstances, to be subjected to surveillance. The effect of this blunder by the SIS was very far reaching. In contrast, the Russians handed in only a mildly worded note of protest to the Foreign Office.

There the matter could have rested. Eden made an honest explanation in Parliament that he was unaware of what was going on and this seemed to have been accepted. However, the press, not having been informed officially of the disappearance of Crabb, were still trying to contact him. On 26 April, Marshall Pugh, his biographer, obtained from a naval spokesman the first clear intimation that Crabb was missing, but no details were offered and no explanation given. Three days later, besieged by the press, the Admiralty issued a formal statement that Commander Crabb 'is presumed to be dead as a result of trials with certain underwater apparatus. The location was in Stokes Bay and it is nine days since the accident'. This was so patently untrue that the press immediately began to suspect that Crabb's disappearance was connected with the visit of the Russian leaders. Why, they asked, if Crabb had lost his life in Stokes Bay (several miles from Portsmouth Dockyard) there had been no effort to find the body? The answer was, of course, that in the tides and currents existing in Portsmouth Harbour and Spithead there was no hope of finding a body in Stokes Bay or anywhere else for that matter. In any case, so great had been the confusion after Crabb had disappeared that it is likely the Admiralty was quite unaware of the need to look for a body until long after it had got lost.

On 27 April, amidst the muddle and confusion, a naval captain visited the former Mrs. Crabb at her home in Dover to offer condolences and to suggest that she might be discreet about someone from whom she had been divorced for several years. The panic announcement by the Admiralty of Crabb's death and the hurried visit to his ex-wife whom he had not seen for several years, seemed to indicate a confused over-reaction when it would have been better to have left the perpetrators to make their own excuses and to bear the brunt of responsibility. However, with the Admiralty statement of 29 April the fat was in the fire. The inescapable assumption was that Crabb had been diving under the cruiser *Ordzhonikidze* and every conceivable theory began to appear in the popular press except, of course, the truth that Crabb had bungled his mission, that he had drowned in the attempt and that his body was dragging along the bottom somewhere in Portsmouth Harbour or

Spithead or even out in the English Channel.

On the morning of 9 June 1957, some fourteen months after Crabb's disappearance two fishermen, John Randall and Ted Galbey, were fishing from their boat off Pilsey Island in Chichester Harbour, some ten miles from Portsmouth. There they found a headless and handless corpse, dressed in a Pirelli frogman's suit, floating in the sea. The fishermen, who had been acquaintances of Crabb, recovered the body and took it ashore where they telephoned the Royal Air Force at Thorney Island. They noted that the suit was faded to a dirty grey, was covered with seaweed, had rust marks around the legs and showed deep indentations clean of marine growth where a breathing set would have been strapped for a very long period. It contained the body of a small man which was bent almost double with the head, hands and chest missing.

When the Royal Air Force learned of the discovery they sent a launch for the body but when they found that it was not that of a crashed airman they refused to accept it. The Navy sent a helicopter to the scene but the body was eventually transported by land to Chichester mortuary where a doctor examined it. An experienced diver and acquaintance of Crabb, Lieutenant WY McLanachan, was sent from *Vernon* on 11 June to see whether he could identify the body. He was joined by Crabb's ex-wife at the request of the West Sussex CID, but the body was in far too advanced a stage of decomposition for either to make a positive identification. McLanachan was a surprising choice for this unpleasant task. A far more suitable person would have been Gutteridge, who lived in Chichester and was still serving at UCWE and who probably knew Crabb better than anyone in the Service. Later that same day the inquest was opened; it lasted for one minute and was adjourned for two weeks. On 26 June, at the resumed inquest, which lasted for less than an hour, it was accepted that the body, estimated to have been 5 feet 4 inches to 5 feet 6 inches in height, was of a size similar to that of Commander Crabb. It had straight muscular legs, similar to Crabb's, it was clad in maroon bathing trunks, blue socks and two pairs of foot to neck service issue combinations (one blue, one khaki) as were usually worn by Crabb when he was diving. Finally, the Pirelli dry suit was identical to one of three suits manufactured and sold by Messrs Heinke of Bermondsey (Mr. Eric Blake) to Crabb in October 1955. In his concluding address the Coroner said:

We have all been warned from time to time in the legal profession about a chain being as strong as its weakest link, but there is also such a thing as a number of incidents which are minor indications building up to a conclusion, which I do not think can be resisted. I think it will be beyond all our ideas of possible coincidence if all these different things, the size of the feet, the scar, the colour of the hair, the supply of an identical suit, if all these things were to be put down to sheer coincidence. Looking at the evidence in this case I am quite satisfied that the remains which were found in Chichester harbour on June 9th were those of Commander Crabb.

After forty years the Crabb incident is still being exploited for profit and it has remained an embarrassment to successive governments. However, sufficient evidence can be deduced by experts in underwater affairs to provide a final judgement on this unhappy affair. There seems little doubt that the operation was mounted by the SIS. It is probable that they wished Crabb to measure the propellers of *Ordzhonikidze* to provide information which might be of value in identifying targets located in the newly established bottom arrays of the Sound Surveillance System (SOSUS).

When searching for the truth in this affair it must be remembered that Crabb was a courageous and very professional diver but was a man of action rather than a thinker. He could be counted upon to carry out his instructions to the letter as far as he was physically capable. Under these circumstances the following facts have been clearly established:

(a) He had an abortive dive on 18 April.
(b) He had early problems with his breathing set on the 19th.
(c) He returned to King's Stairs to 'clear' it.
(d) He was seen on the surface by a Russian at a time which fits in with all other evidence.
(e) He was diving at the limit of depth of safety for a fit diver using oxygen, but he was unfit.
(f) The carbon dioxide absorbent in his equipment was known to be inefficient unless it was very carefully packed.
(g) He was involved in a degree of exertion, under conditions of stealth and stress that reduce safety limitations.

Crabb was experienced and would recognise the symptoms of oxygen poisoning, which are mild and persist for only a brief period before the onset of unconsciousness. This would account for his surfacing part way through his dive. However, the importance of being able to proceed with the mission unobserved forced him to submerge without respite so that oxygen poisoning, quickly followed by unconsciousness, could be expected to take place, probably compounded by carbon dioxide poisoning as a result of poor carbon dioxide absorbent and, even more likely, built up by the shallow panting of an unfit man. With Crabb unconscious, and his mouthpiece probably lost, his breathing set would fill with water and he would lose the buoyancy of his breathing bag. This would prevent him from surfacing. He would drown, but what happened to his body? With a negative weight of only a few pounds it would certainly drift out of the harbour. By the afternoon of that day it would most probably be carried by the flood tide into Langstone Harbour, some six miles away, which was cluttered with three old wrecks. It is reasonable to deduce that Crabb's breathing set and his harness became snagged in this wreckage, where the body remained until 8 June 1957 when the breathing set harness finally chafed or rotted through, allowing the suited body to drift clear. In the course of the night it drifted out of Langstone on the ebb tide and as the tide turned it drifted eastward to be found off Pilsey Island on 9 June. The rust marks and deep indentation of the breathing set harness, the condition of the body, taken with the tidal conditions, do not allow of any other plausible explanation.

Sustained public interest and the arousal of largely fanciful speculation demand that these events are put into some sort of perspective. Perhaps, sadly for the speculators and romantics, the explanation is really rather simple, ordinary and not a very important. It is in truth the story about a gallant, middle aged gentleman who made a dive too many. Let his friend Gordon Gutteridge have the last word:

It is, I'm afraid, the story of an ill conceived Intelligence project, most unlikely to have a useful end product, which was sloppily executed using inadequate resources. The pity is that our rabidly anti-communist, down at heel and blinkered monarchist has been denied, in his advancing years, the regard of his peers and the enjoyment of Scotch and beer chasers with his diving chums. But then, it was as much his fault as anyone and he never would come in from the cold!

In January 1957, the UCWE divers were called to a serious situation in London when a Port of London Authority diver discovered a German 'G' Mine in the West India Docks, buried in mud and rubbish. The discovery had been made late on a Friday afternoon and by noon the following day UCWE's combined naval and scientific mine investigation team had arrived. The

German G Type magnetic/acoustic mine recovered from East India Docks January 1957

Lieutenant Comander Gordon Gutteridge taking a rest after the recovery of the East India Docks mine

divers had no idea as to the condition of the mine which was buried in mud, ooze, garbage and was later described by Gutteridge as 'quietly malevolent'. It could not be brought to the surface since its hydrostatic switch would almost certainly have caused it to explode. As a precautionary measure in case the mine exploded while being rendered safe on the bottom it was decided to evacuate the surrounding four hundred households. The mine could not be brought to the surface safely in this densely built up area, nor lifted clear of the bottom and towed through the 20 miles of the dock system and down the Thames for demolition. It seemed to be undamaged and most likely to have an acoustic/magnetic unit, hydrostatic firing and at least one anti-render safe device. For eight cold and miserable hours, the officers and ratings of the experimental trials team took turns to make safe, dismantle and recover the mine and its components. Two experienced UCWE scientists were available throughout the operation to advise and to examine each component as it was recovered. The value of scientists as members of a mine recovery team was demonstrated. They provided minute by minute advice upon which lives and a great deal of property might depend. Lieutenant Commander Gutteridge was awarded the OBE, Terrell and Lieutenant C Heatley MBEs and Petty Officer P Cobby, Leading Seaman P Alderton and Able Seaman E Harris British Empire Medals.

Throughout the 1950s the deep divers also came to the public eye as they continued to explore methods of carrying out practical diving at ever increasing depths. Petty Officer Bollard's record deep dive at 535 feet was exceeded by Lieutenant GA Wookey, the Chief Diving Officer of *Reclaim*, when he set a new record of 600 feet in Sor Fjord, Norway. At 1930 on 12 October 1956, Wookey was lowered to 40 feet in a Submersible Decompression Chamber. He then continued the dive in a specially adapted diving suit, having changed from breathing air to an oxygen/helium mixture. After a brief stop at 540 feet, he continued to the bottom which was reached at 600 feet, seven minutes after leaving the surface. He remained on the bottom for five minutes before embarking upon the long ascent. After nearly twelve hours, and with diver's bends in both shoulders, he was hoisted back on board and transferred to the decompression chamber where he was treated until 0730 next day. He suffered no ill effects.

World records were not the main objective of deep diving trials, which were not concerned with hitting the bottom and immediately making for the surface. It was necessary to carry out at least fifteen minutes of useful work before a deep dive could be classified as successful. In 1959, with Commander JR Carr as Superintendent of Diving, diving techniques were continuing to progress rapidly and the morale of the deep divers was never higher when a shattering blow was delivered by the Admiralty. At a meeting convened to discuss SABA's development and conducted by the Director of Under Surface Warfare, Captain TN Masterson, the divers were given the news that as an economy measure it had been decided to discontinue deep diving in the Royal Navy and concentrate on shallow water clearance diving for mine countermeasures. The specialised deep diving equipment in *Reclaim* was sold to Argentina and the ship went to *Lochinvar* for use in the mine countermeasures role as 'Mine Countermeasures Support and Diving trials Ship'. The last course for deep divers took place in 1960 although clearance diving training and its tender *Miner III* remained at *Vernon*.

Almost immediately after this two valuable research torpedoes were lost in Scottish lochs at depths of over 450 feet. *Vernon* was asked to recover them, but the Superintendent of Diving was obliged to reply that they no longer had the necessary resources to carry out diving at that depth. Carr was, however, determined not to allow the Royal Navy to be deprived completely of deep diving capability and took advantage of *Reclaim*'s subsidiary role to grab her during a gap in her MCM programme. The deep diving was carried out in Norwegian waters testing techniques using a submarine compression chamber. Every effort possible was also being made to keep a nucleus of deep divers. Then, in 1963, Hans Keller, the Swiss mathematician, achieved a deep diving record of 725 feet. This stimulated the Superintendent of the Royal Naval Physiological Laboratory to request a meeting with Commander EC Hannen, the new Superintendent of Diving and Filer his deputy. They met at AEDU to prepare a submission to the Admiralty. As a result of Eric Hannen's well argued submission a Deep Diving Trials Unit was established in the Royal Naval Physical Laboratory at Alverstoke in 1963. *Reclaim* began to concentrate on deep diving once more and in 1965, at Toulon, she demonstrated a capacity to keep divers down at 600 feet for a whole hour.

The following year *Reclaim* faced another challenge. A Buccaneer aircraft from *Hermes* crashed on take-off and was lying almost intact in 370 feet of water 10 miles south of the Lizard. *Vernon* was approached to see whether the aircraft could be salvaged, and it was agreed to send *Reclaim* to the site. While minehunters sailed to locate the aircraft with their sonars, the divers continued to carry out an intensive work up period under Filer's supervision. As soon as the aircraft had been located, *Reclaim* laid her moorings around it and the operation began using the Submersible Compression Chamber (SCC) and an oxygen/helium breathing mixture. Two underwater television cameras were used. One was slung on the outside of the SCC to view the seabed and the second was fitted to the inside of the chamber, positioned so that the divers and the relevant gauges could be observed. In *Reclaim* the television cameras were used to identify the aircraft and to monitor the activities of the divers both inside the SCC and at work on the aircraft. The first dive went well. A good reconnaissance was carried out and from this the plan was made for the recovery.

First, the four flush cover plates over the lifting positions on the aircraft had to be removed. Each plate was secured by countersunk screws. The SDC was prepared for the dive by securing heavy lifting slings on the outside of the chamber and by attaching 20 feet of lifting wire. The chamber was then hoisted over the side of *Reclaim* and lowered, manned by the divers Mike Grubb and 'Mona' Lott. When the SCC reached 350 feet the divers emerged and proceeded to the aircraft. Those in *Reclaim* were unable to see the divers at work; the only evidence of activity were the hollow sounds of metal striking metal. Then came the first report in the high pitched unnatural squeak caused by helium breathing at great depths: 'Aircraft secured!'. There followed a discussion between the divers, who still had to cut the strop securing the coil of wire on the outside of the chamber. Once again the divers disappeared together but a few minutes later the observers in *Reclaim* witnessed a nightmare. Grubb's face appeared on the television screen just above the water level at the bottom of the SCC minus his breathing apparatus. He was barely conscious. His eyes rolled around, he was gasping and crying out so that the sound, influenced by the helium, was like that of an infant in distress. It seemed to the *Reclaim* team that they would have to stand by without being able to help as the diver died before their eyes. Grubb's body blocked the entrance to the chamber preventing Lott from entering and placing him in a less perilous situation. Occasionally Grubb's head would roll up and he would get a breath of air, and it was on one of these occasions that he came to sufficiently to make the rest of the way into the SCC. Lott followed him and was able to clear an air pipe which was fouling the lower hatch. With it safely closed, the divers gave the signal for the chamber to be brought to the surface, where they were transferred to a compression chamber and recompressed for 'a long soak'. The Buccaneer aircraft was successfully recovered but it had proved to be a far more hazardous operation than had been expected.

In 1966, Commander Phil White replaced Eric Hannen as Superintendent of Diving. Diving was now more integrated into the fleet than ever before. Previously Ship's Divers and Ship's Diving Officers had been introduced. Now the combined Mine Warfare and Clearance Diving Branch was formed on 25 February 1966. Those officers who were previously qualified as both CD and TAS automatically became MCD Officers while those qualified CD only were trained in mine warfare. *Laleston*, *Vernon*'s training tender had her sweep gear removed and replaced by a compression chamber, diving store and other equipment.

The MCD rating structure remained unchanged until the formation of the Operations Branch in 1975 when MCD Officers were also supported by the Diver and Mine Warfare sub branches of the Operations Branch. Continuity had been preserved and expertise in mining, mine countermeasures, diving and the disposal of all forms of live unexploded ordnance, including sabotage devices ashore and afloat, was now concentrated within one branch. By 1974, *Vernon* was well prepared for Mine Warfare and Diving to remain there for many years and the MCD Branch had become well institutionalised, overseeing, for example, the training of all non-career Ship's Divers as well as providing personnel for development work, anti-sabotage training for ships, Command Clearance Diving and Explosive Ordnance Disposal Teams, and complement billets in minehunters. In 1981, the MCD Branch assumed responsibility for demolition training.

Since World War II naval divers had been involved in a number of mine clearance operations in wartime minefields. Throughout May 1968 a NATO task force of sixty vessels worked to ensure that a planned traffic separation route between the Texel and Heligoland was safe for shipping. The eastern segment was assigned to British units which included the new exercise minelayer *Abdiel*, ordered to replace *Reclaim* in her MCM duties. She carried Captain MCM and was mother ship to *Laymoor* and nineteen 'Tons'; three of the latter were hunters and the rest sweepers; ten of them manned by the RNR. Almost 35,000 hours on task revealed no mines and the area was declared safe.

In 1975, Operation Rheostat was mounted to clear the Suez Canal of debris. *Abdiel*, *Wilton*, *Bossington* and *Maxton*, with the Fleet Clearance Diving Team embarked, took part in the first phase of this operation. *Wilton* was a unique vessel combining the machinery of the scrapped *Derriton* with a glass reinforced plastic hull; commissioned in 1973 she was a member of *Vernon*'s Second MCM Squadron. Between April and October 1974 a vast amount of ordnance was recovered and destroyed, including 209 tons of TNT, bombs of various sizes, some 800 anti-tank and anti-personnel mines, 6,000 rounds of ammunition and 70 various missiles. The second phase involved *Abdiel*, *Hubberston* and *Sheraton* and took the form of a final check which yielded 142 objects ranging from a main battle tank to a lavatory seat. No explosive items were found and the Canal was reopened on 5 June 1975. The operations in the canal helped confirm the high standards of the Royal Navy's MCD personnel.

Operation Hemicarp saw Royal Navy divers co-operating with Americans at Tarawa and Tuvalu in the Gilbert and Ellis Islands between March and August 1977. Naval divers also became involved with UNESCO in moving important Egyptian monuments submerged by the Aswan Dam to a site replicating Philaeon Agilkia Island. Thirty five naval divers worked with eighteen Egyptian divers from October 1977 to April 1978, shifting 16,000 tons of mud and 320 blocks of stone.

Various equipment improvements took place about this time. The Type 193M solid state sonar entered service with the advantages of reduced weight and volume and greater reliability. Range and beam pattern were also improved. As an alternative to human divers the PAP (Poisson Auto-Propulse) was purchased from France to provide remote examination and counter mining capability. *Laleston* was lost to the Ulster Division of the RNR in 1978 and *Reclaim* took over her training duties. A new class of GRP minehunters also began to enter service with the commissioning of *Brecon* in 1979.

Just as British MCM capabilities remained second to none British divers continued to be at the forefront of diving techniques. Of particular importance was the Royal Navy's entry into the field of 'Saturation Diving'. This involves the use of a compression chamber as a working base. The diver is 'lowered' to a working pressure and kept there for days, or even weeks, thereby 'saturating' his physiological system. When he is required to work in the water he is transferred to a submersible chamber and is transported to a dive site. This allows long periods of work at depths up to 150 feet, and communications with the mobile diving chamber are very much better than directly with a diver. Work began at the DTU in 1968 and continued at the new Admiralty Experimental Diving Unit opened at *Vernon* in 1969. The trials produced 'stop tables' describing the depths and dwell times necessary to recover a diver from saturation without physical damage. Appropriate tables, protective clothing and breathing apparatus were developed and the Royal Navy started general training in these techniques which thereafter became commercially commonplace in offshore oil exploration and production.

The contribution of *Vernon* trained divers to the development of the British off-shore industry was enormous. By the early 1970s accidents had become so frequent that the Government came under pressure to produce safety legislation and the means of enforcing it. At the end of 1973 Lieutenant Commander J Warner, a former Royal Navy clearance diver, was appointed to the Department of Energy as the first government professional diving inspector (later to become the Chief Inspector of Diving). Warner's task involved the drafting of diving safety legislation with particular emphasis on the requirements of the off-shore oil industry and to build an inspectorate to enforce the legislation. A study clearly demonstrated the need for a diving training programme and one that could be quickly implemented. The choice lay between asking the Navy to train civilian divers in naval establishments or the setting up of either an on-site apprentices scheme or a new government diving school. It was considered impractical to ask the Navy to train civilians who would not be under naval discipline and who would be in a salary bracket well beyond anything that a naval diver could earn. No facilities were available for apprenticeship training, and so the only practical option was to set up a civilian diving training school at which all the new techniques could be taught with scope to deal with the rapidly developing field of off-shore diving technology. The oil companies readily accepted the responsibility, and with the assistance of *Vernon*, training standards were drawn up and a suitable site for the school found at Fort William. The appointment of a manager presented a problem since any diver who was in the off-shore industry was too busy earning large sums of money to consider accepting a training position at less pay. *Vernon* was again able to provide the answer; Lieutenant Cobby was allowed to retire from the Royal Navy so that he could take up this important post.

Without divers there would have been no off-shore oil and gas but in the early 1970s there was a world shortage of divers. Once again *Vernon* provided a helping hand: Royal Navy divers queued up to buy themselves out of the Service and there is little doubt that the fleet was reduced to a worrying situation by the shortage of divers. However, the presence of former Royal Navy divers in the North Sea provided a service that was essential and many of them have progressed into top management in the industry. Throughout the world *Vernon* divers can still be found wherever off-shore oilfields exist.

Vernon was not concerned only with the provision of divers, but provided an independent examination authority for accident investigation. Any diving equipment involved in a diving accident was sent to *Vernon* for testing as part of the investigation. Another little known service provided by *Vernon* was the adaption of the *Vernon* mining tank for helicopter rescue and survival training, a facility which was used increasingly by the off-shore oil industry. The contribution made to the establishment of the North Sea oilfields, so vital to Britain's continued economic health, is one of *Vernon*'s major achievements.

It was only fitting that in 1978 the North Sea support vessel *Seaforth Clansman* should be commissioned in the Royal Navy to operate out of Aberdeen as a modern diving support vessel with Diving Party 1007. The divers also succeded that year in obtaining authorisation for a fully fledged 'Seabed Operations Vessel' to replace the venerable *Reclaim*; construction of the new ship began began at an estimated cost of £80 million. She was launched as *Challenger* in 1980 and in March of that year Captain Sutherland surveyed the scene from *Vernon* in an optimistic light. There were plans for a major redevelopment of the establishment, bringing all accommodation up to standard and improving training services. It was hoped that the waterfront could support MCM vessels well into the nineties. The aim was to make *Vernon* the small ship centre for the Royal Navy with enhanced responsibility for training, improved base support facilities, and parental status for all who did business in small ships (not just MCMVs). *Brecon* had been accepted into service at *Vernon* and this pratice was followed with the next vessels of the class, *Brocklesby*, *Cattistock* and *Ledbury*.

Sadly, however these hopes were soon to turn to ashes. The 1981 Defence Review, although it emphasised the construction of MCM vessels, spelled the end of plans to rehabilitate *Vernon*. The establishment began to run down and was formally closed on 31 March 1986. *Challenger* suffered delays due to poor construction and had to be both re-wired and fitted with a new saturation diving system. She proved a black hole for scarce naval funds costing over £100 million more than the original estimated sum ; she was was an early candidate for decommissioning when times proved hard (as they did in 1990) , despite the effect on naval deep diving capabilities. The charter of *Seaforth Clansman* had been been extended but she was paid off by the late 1980s.

The clearance divers however went from strength to strength. In 1984 Operation Harling began in the Gulf of Suez. Some twenty Soviet ground mines had been laid in shipping routes by a merchant ship believed to be under the control of Libya with the aim of causing disruption among the Arab states. Nearly all of these mines did in fact explode in the vicinity of merchant ships, causing varying amounts of comparatively minor damage, probably due to the depth of water and the sensitivity settings used. In response to requests from the Egyptian Government, mine countermeasures vessels from the British, French, Italian, American and Soviet navies were deployed to assigned areas along the major routes. The Royal Navy was allocated the most operationally significant areas which were cleared in eight weeks by the Second MCM Squadron, *Kirkliston, Gavinton, Bossington, Brinton* and *Wilton*, supported by an oilfield support ship taken up from trade named *Oil Endeavour*. Only one mine was discovered, and this by the British. It was recovered and courageously rendered safe by Warrant Officer Diver Terry Settle and Petty Officer Diver Raymond Rowlands. Harling was conducted with great professionalism in unpleasant climatic conditions and clearly vindicated British mine warfare techniques. It was, however, a practical example of the time it takes to clear a substantial area by minehunting.

The same contingency plan which supported Operation Harling was again required in 1987 - the year after *Vernon*'s closure - in the Persian Gulf. The United States flagged Kuwaiti tanker *Bridgeton* was mined near Farsi Island on 22 July and this new dimension to the long running Iran-Iraq War prompted the decision on 11 August to institute Operation Cimnel. The MCM support vessel *Abdiel* and four *Hunt* class MCMVs, *Brecon, Bicester, Brocklesby* and *Hurworth*, sailed from Rosyth after a period of intense activity to store, prepare and enhance the ships. The Iranians were using North Korean M-08 moored contact mines of pre-First World War Russian design. Using intelligence information, this countermeasures force had considerable success in sweeping moored mines as well as detecting and disposing of several that had failed to disengage from their sinkers and were reposing on the seabed. These included those laid in mid-Gulf by the Iranian ship *Iran Ajr* which was caught in the act by American forces and subsequently captured. In 1991 in the same waters during Operation Granby British MCMVs and clearance divers again took the lead in dealing with the serious mining threat created by the Iraqis in defence of conquered Kuwait.

Despite the question marks over the Royal Navy's deep diving capability caused by the premature end of *Challenger* there is no doubt at the beginning of the 1990s that British MCM and MCD capabilities, albeit based at the Navy's chosen small ship centre at Rosyth rather than Portsmouth, are second to none.

'In September 1983 we were dismantling the Weapons Trials operation in *Vernon*; no small task, we had been in commission for 113 years and had accumulated a great deal of moss, lichen, barnacles and corns. The earliest of our records contained details of the issue of Quill Pens and I was being assisted in the demolition task by computer print-outs - that's a fair old hop, skip and jump for mankind. It began to dawn on me that the management did not intend to mark our passing at all; I'd heard of 'And some there be who have no memorial ...' but this was not merely ridiculous. it was outrageous.

Captain Weapons Trials *Vernon* finished trading on 14th October 1983. I stayed on, tidying up, until 28th October when I locked up 17A Building, returned the keys and walked out of the gate. I have known people discharged 'Service no longer required' with more warmth and certainly more enthusiasm.

I did go back once, on the evening of 31st March 1986, it seemed a good idea to see the Ensign come down for the last time. For some reason I had expected quite a crowd but, in the event, apart from the Colour Party (one Sub Lieutenant, one CPO (Caterer) and three young divers) there was a group of three of us, Ramsey Pearson, Trevor Lynn and me. A doctor, a priest and a knocking-on-a-bit torpedoman old enough to know better, quite a selection of pall-bearers, don't you think?'

Thus wrote Lieutenant Commander RSC Robinson MBE Royal Navy, who, having qualified as a Torpedo Gunner's Mate in HMS *Marlborough* in 1943, can fairly claim to the 'Last Torpedoman'.

There is something almost majestic in the way that the Royal Navy, an institution that maintains and celebrates tradition as an article of faith, can sometimes deny itself its history and heritage. This book is a small step towards preserving and codifying the *Vernon* tradition. Other manifestations continue to thrive: the Portobello Association, which is open to all Torpedo Anti-Submarine Warfare Officers, serving and retired, dines annually at the School of Maritime Operations at HMS *Dryad* whilst the Anti-Submarine Warfare Instructors' Association provides the same focus for all Torpedo and Anti-Submarine Rating Instructors. Similarly, Mine Warfare and Clearance Diving Officers have an annual reunion under the auspices of the Royal Naval Barracks, Portsmouth.

Above all else, the tradition of a systematic, thinking and a thoroughly professional approach to the business of underwater warfare that was *Vernon*'s contribution to the Royal Navy has been preserved. The School of Maritime Operations, the Maritime Tactical School, the operational record and the ever closer relationship between the Seaman and Weapon Engineering Branches all bear witness to this.

We deal here with the final years of the history of *Vernon* as well as the technological, operational and organisational trends that have coloured the years between about 1970 and 1986. It was a period of substantial change in naval warfare and in the methods by which the Royal Navy chose to respond. It was also a period of decline for the United Kingdom economy and thus for the resources available for defence, which in turn forced the series of contractions and rationalisations which led eventually to the closure of *Vernon*. It will be recalled that the decision to withdraw from East of Suez had been taken as recently as 1968 and that Rear Admiral JAR Troup, the last Commander Far East Fleet, hauled down his flag on 31 October 1971, the last day of the validity of the Anglo-Malaysian Defence Agreement. This was shortly followed by the broad pendant of Commodore Sir Peter Anson, the last Senior Naval Officer, Persian Gulf. The subsequent creation of a single Royal Navy fleet command under Admiral Sir Edward Ashmore, designated Commander-in-Chief Fleet, was a result not only of economic pressure but of strategic necessity. No longer a post-colonial force, and having made substantial savings on overseas basing costs, a greatly reinforced fleet was deployed in home waters to face a first class superpower opponent. Its role was fully supportive of a North Atlantic Treaty Organisation maritime strategy within which control of the Norwegian Sea and North Atlantic was seen as essential to the security of Europe. The nature of the Soviet Navy, with its formidable, submarine-orientated order of battle, placed emphasis upon anti-submarine warfare. It is worth noting in passing that this era, with its well-managed doctrinal shifts, was another clear example of the efficacy of the Naval Staff whose hard advocacy and subtle bureaucratic in-fighting from the end of World War II thoroughly denies its somewhat chequered reputation. A characteristic of naval operations, of which there have been many since 1945, is that the Royal Navy, with some rare deficiencies such as a lack of adequate carrier-borne aircraft in the Korean War, or airborne early warning and sufficient close range anti-aircraft gunnery in the Falklands conflict, has always been in the right place at the right time and with the right equipment to achieve the desired political objectives. These things do not happen by accident.

1970 itself was a watershed as it saw the initiation of an ambitious plan to concentrate and rationalise naval shore training. Entitled 'Constrain', it would take ten years to implement fully and would result in the foundation of a School of Maritime Operations (SMOPS) and a Tactical School. All aspects of naval warfare training would be carried out under the aegis of SMOPS. Other aspects of 'Constrain' dealt with the rationalisation of weapons engineering training at *Collingwood* and marine engineering training at *Sultan*, and new entry training at *Raleigh*, at Torpoint near Plymouth. This process was to continue throughout the next fifteen years, notably as a result of the 1981 Defence Review described in the celebrated Government White Paper, Command 8288.

Further contractions resulted in, among others, the closure of the Artificer Apprentice Schools *Fisgard* and *Caledonia*; the further reordering of responsibilites within SMOPS such as *Mercury*, the Communications School, also undertaking navigation training; the concentration of the Supply School at *Raleigh* from Chatham; the closure of the firing range on the foreshore at Eastney; the closure of the communications centre at Devonport and the gradual removal of functions from *Vernon*. Very useful manpower savings resulted which were critical to the preservation of an adequate front line strength in the mid to late 1980s. It was Admiralty Board policy to improve the Royal Navy's teeth-to-tail ratio and to achieve the best value for money possible under circumstances of severe financial pressure. Equipment costs were rising faster than inflation throughout this period. There was much debate about the objectivity of training, about how much could effectively be carried out at sea, about the cost effectiveness of simulators and about the balance of investment between equipment, manpower and training.

In 1970, the trials sections at *Vernon*, *Excellent*. *Mercury* and the Admiralty Compass Laboratory at Slough were brought under the central control of Captain Weapons Trials based in Whale Island, the long time home of the Gunnery Branch. At this point we would observe that *Vernon*'s parent and rival, *Excellent*, did not escape the winds that were blowing through the naval estate. It ceased to be the Navy's Gunnery School with all its proud tradition and gradually became host for a wide variety of lodger units; Captain Weapons Trials, the Divisional School, the Regulating School, the Command Sailing Centre, the Engineering Staff of C-in-C Fleet, barrack accommodation and a number of other functions. It finally ceased to carry the name *Excellent* in 1986 and became an adjunct of the Royal Naval Barracks, Portsmouth, entitled *Nelson(Excellent* site). Sic transit gloria mundi.

1972 saw the last annual Long TAS Course and the start of Principal Warfare Officer Training. In sociological terms the end of the old specialisations was a serious upheaval with a number of potentially damaging consequences. At both officer and rating levels much loyalty to the specialisation and to its alma mater, whether it were *Excellent*, *Vernon*, *Mercury* or *Dryad*, had been established over the years, together with a healthy rivalry between them. This was apparently to be reduced in favour of greater efficiency. There was a realistic possibility that the scope of knowledge required by the PWO would be too great and that the depth of expertise held by the individual specialisations, particularly in the area of equipment knowledge, would be irretrievably lost. It was also feared by some Seaman Officers that either a gap would open up between themselves and the Weapons Engineering Branch in the absence of a common technical language, or that much of the operational terrain, the business of the seaman, would fall to weapons engineers.

In a parallel process the Electrical Branch evolved towards the Weapons Engineering Branch. Weapons engineers are now operators; for example, most of the positions in the Sea Dart anti-aircraft missile system are now manned by weapons engineer ratings. Seaman rating structures were also intended to evolve under the same pressures; firstly the link between the 'left and right arm' was codified such that a man's rate also defined his duties in the ship's fighting organisation. Advancement depended not only upon time served and personal qualities but also upon passing the requisite professional courses and examinations. Secondly, all sub-specialisations were grouped under the heading of an Operations Branch, including communicators: the roles of weapon operator, weapon controller or supervisor, and weapons director were tied to the 'substantive' able, leading and petty officer rates for all the individual specialisations of missile, sonar, radar and communications. This structure took effect early in 1975.

The problem of course design for the Principal Warfare Officer proved a thorny one. It was established that the length of the course should not be longer than thirty six weeks, which ill compares with the year that had been generally the case for most single specialisation Long Courses. The curriculum drew upon the syllabi of the specialist schools, but with emphasis placed heavily upon warfare training at the expense of equipment knowledge. The first two PWO courses graduated and went to sea in 1973.

An integral part of the plan envisaged a selected number of PWOs returning to school at SMOPS to undertake further sub specialist training upon completion of their first tour at sea. The intention here was to fill a need for a deeper level of expertise at the levels of Squadron, Flotilla, Fleet and Ministry of Defence staffs; thus Advanced Warfare Officer (AWO) training started in 1975, producung AWO(A), AWO(U) and AWO(C) officers, respectively anti-air warfare, anti-submarine warfare and communication specialists, for those posts.

In 1981, after some eight years of experience, during which the earlier sub specialist officers had been entirely replaced by PWOs and AWOs, it was found to be more flexible, economic and operationally effective to 'stream' the PWOs into 'A', 'U' and 'C' sub specialisations during their initial course. The Navigation Specialist has survived in the shape of the PWO(N) who is capable of carrying out the normal warfare duties in a ship's Operations Room but is also trained in navigation to the level required for large ships or a staff post.

These steps, combined with the institution of a short Technical Course at the Royal Engineering College at Plymouth, and a second 'common training module' dealing with Intelligence and team training matters, increased the total length of the PWO course to forty four weeks, not far off the length of the old 'tribal' specialist course. Indeed, diehards might have said that little had changed and that experience had driven the organisation of officers' training back towards what was evidently a sound system. The fact remains, however, that the development of computerised and highly integrated information display and weapon control systems as well as the multi-threat nature of modern naval warfare demands a broader base of common training than heretofore and much knowledge of all facets of military activity at sea to be resident in each warfare officer. The success of the training system is measured by the outstanding professionalism of today's warfare officers, tested in war and a credit to the Royal Navy internationally in peacetime. Authoratative judgements make a point that the Royal Navy's contemporary escort force is even more efficient in the 1990s and 1980s than it was in the 1960s and 1970s.

Another reason for this was the success of the new Joint Maritime Operational Tactical School (JMOTS). By the late late 1980s this was capable of setting up advanced training of a sophistication undreamed of in the 1960s, with multi-threat enviroments, integration of carrier air groups into fleet air defence, more participation by NATO navies, co-operation with RAF Sector Operation Centres and the UK Air Defence Ground Environment System, shore based air defence and attack aircraft, data link operations with NATO E3A Airborne and Early Warning aircraft and the tactical integration of nuclear submarines and towed arrays. The important progression from basic training at establishments like *Vernon* and SMOPS, through whole-ship work-ups under the aegis of the Flag Officer Sea Training at Portland to advanced training under the aegis of JMOTS had been preserved.

The Operational Evaluation Group, relocated to Northwood , broadened its activities to include all aspects of naval warfare and by reason of its access to fleet planners, was rather more readily able to obtain the resources for individual evaluations. Northwood, besides being the Headquarters of the Commander-in-Chief Fleet (NATO'S Commander-in-Chief Channel and Eastern Atlantic), also houses the person and staff of the Air Officer Commanding 18 Group RAF, the Group responsible for both national and NATO maritime air operations. Never since 1918 has land based air been more fully integrated with the rest of maritime warfare

Within *Vernon* 1974 saw a particularly decisive adjustment to the new reality. Captain SMOPS became responsible to the Commander-in-Chief Naval Home Command for training in anti-submarine warfare, above water warfare, communications and navigation. The Captain, *Vernon*, who was at this time RS Browning, retained responsibility for seamanship training. Sonar training would remain at *Vernon* but under the direction of SMOPS, using the new range of Universal Anti-Submarine Attack Teachers, comparatively complex and realistic simulators, until a home could be found for them at *Dryad*,. Browning was thus the last Captain of *Vernon* to have full command of its traditional tasks.

In 1974-5, thanks to the organisational shake up of 1972 and the General Electric organised 'get well' programme the Mk 24 torpedo finally entered service but it was only able to attack submarine targets, and plans to withdraw the 21-inch Mk VIII** from service had to be shelved. It was hardly surprising that a serious look was taken at the US Mk 48 development, and on two occasions proposals were made to abandon the UK 21-inch torpedo programme. In 1980, and again in 1984, the project underwent two further 'get well' programmes; there were Parliamentary questions and changes of contractor. Finally, in 1984 Marconi Underwater Systems were given full responsibility for the development of the fully dual purpose Mk 24 Mod 2 'Tigerfish'. this was two years after they had been awarded the prime contract for the full development and initial production of the replacement 21-inch torpedo 'Spearfish'. The Tigerfish programme was, however, fully successful and in 1985 Flag Officer Submarines, Rear Admiral RG Heaslip, at last pronounced himself satisfied with a weapon which was quiet, reliable and effective. The last trusty 21-inch Mk 8 weapon was finally disembarked in 1988, fifty years after the first had entered service.

There is no doubt that this agonising experience coloured the United Kingdom's whole weapon acquisition process. Against a background of cost overruns and cancellation scandals a general trend was established towards relinquishing in-house development in favour of the armaments companies. There were several painful episodes of internal Ministry of Defence organisational self-examination. Lessons were learnt, prominent among which were the aerospace techniques of quality control and reliability. It was discovered that investment in ranges, recording equipment and analysis facilities had to be applied up-front and early to sophisticated underwater guided weapons programmes. The benefits were seen in Marconi's Spearfish programme, which completed development in 1988. It might also be argued that a modern armaments organisation with its combination of electrical, electronic and mechanical expertise, not to mention close relationships with the user, is more like the *Vernon* structure of old than the various competitive estabishments with their scientist/operator bureaucratic rivalries.

Marconi also brought to fruition the lightweight torpedo project, Naval Staff Target 7511, begun in the mid 1960s by AUWE. In 1977 Marconi Underwater Systems Ltd. was awarded a contract for full development and initial production of the world's first software controlled programmable torpedo. 'Stingray', with its diving depth to match the Alfa class Soviet nuclear submarine, a speed of 45 knots, a shaped charge to counter Soviet double hulled submarines and such features as dual FM/CW transmissions, the adoption of pulse compression and correlation techniques, and selective software control, is an impressive weapon indeed. The 1000th weapon was delivered in 1989, and all RN ships and RAF squadrons are fully equipped. After many years in the doldrums, the UK torpedo development and manufacture had at last recaptured the pride and competence shown in the thirties.

These developments were made more urgent not only because of the increasing capability of the Soviet submarine fleet, which contained an ever higher proportion of nuclear submarines, but because in response to this, and in the better range capability of lower frequency medium-range sonars, the Mortar Mk 10 'Limbo' depth bomb throwing system, was becoming outmoded by its short (1,000 yard) range and its long unguided time of flight, despite the later incorporation of a proximity fuse to overcome a depth setting inadequacy. The solution was the removal of the Limbo from *Rothesay* and *Leander* class frigates, and the introduction of the Ship Torpedo Weapon System (STWS). These are two triple torpedo tube mountings fitted to most frigates and destroyers, and capable of firing on sonar information either the US Mk 46 or the Stingray torpedoes in a 'Fore-run' or aimed mode. Engagements at longer ranges are dealt with either by the escort's own organic helicopter or by aircraft under radar and computer control to a sonar-generated dropping point. Removing the mortars also allowed lengthening the flight deck in frigates so allowing the operation of the Lynx helicopter. This new aircraft helped expand the MATCH role to guided missile surface attack, electronic warfare and jamming, radar search, radio relay, over the horizon targetting and other fields. The Westland Wasp was finally withdrawn from service in 1988.

A general characteristic of the development of underwater weapons is apparent. They have progressed from equipments like depth charges, Hedgehog, Squid and Mortar Mk 10, which were comparatively 'agricultural' and which required labour-intensive drill, teamwork and simple maintenance procedures readily achievable on board ship, to delicate, expensive, 'no test' weapons supplied as 'bullets' with little or no requirement for on board maintenance. Such support as is required has been appropriately allocated to the Weapons Engineering Branch, including, from the mid 1980s, responsibility for magazines, armament stores accountancy and conformity to explosives regulations. Here are further trends which have done away with functions classically undertaken by *Vernon*.

Increased sonar and ASW performance in general had to be matched to a better understanding of the environment. For many years the temperature profile of the sea had been obtained from a crude bathythermograph device streamed on a wire astern of the ship within which a stylus marked a smoked glass slide for depth and temperature. Many TAS officers will remember with mixed feelings the labours of love involved in streaming and recovering, the preservation, varnishing, recording, storing and forwarding to some name-less authority thousands upon thousands of little finger marked glass slides from the depths of the oceans of the world. But a data base for sonar prediction was essential and the advent of the expendable bathythermograph in 1969 filled a need in terms of depth capability, user friendly read out and freedom in ship manoeuvre that was sorely needed. The new device was a weighted plastic bullet with a thermister in the nose which fell through the depths at a known speed, unreeling a fine wire and transmitting temperature changes to a recorder situated in the ship's Operation Room. The depth capability would be of vital importance, as we shall see, in the era of towed array.

In 1969, *Vernon* was taking a lead in systematising oceanographic knowledge by producing a Sonar Prediction Handbook and setting up instructional courses. The business of plotting sonar ray traces by hand was now commonlace and this technique produced a competent theoretical answer for the surface ship. In 1971, an electronic Acoustic Ray Trace Indicator was produced and trained for at *Vernon* thus enabling much quicker analysis and rapid testing of variables. High power scanning sonars also provoked a need for study of other aspects of propagation besides the thermostructure; problems of mutual interference, ship self noise, primary and secondary reverberation and seabed reflectivity. In 1972, *Vernon* spon-sored much work to evaluate the truth of predictive processes.

An operational limitation of all active sonars to date was the high premium placed upon the alertness of the watch keeping operator, as some of the work at Londonderry in the mid 1960s revealed. The Royal Navy's first computerised sonar, Type 2016, went a long way towards ameliorating this problem by advanced signal processing and software orientated techniques. The use of computerised memory and visual displays which apply math-ematical weighting to all contacts as time elapses serves effectively to direct the attention of the operators to the most promising contacts. The sonar also displays a ping-to-ping analysis of echoes, thus providing a powerful target classification instrument. This sonar was tested on board *Matapan*, the Sonar trials ship in the early 1970s, and entered service with the Type 22 frigate *Broadsword* in 1978. It was later fitted to modernised *Leanders* and the Type 42 destroyers. While not as advanced as the more expensive American equiivalents, 2016 proved exceptionally effective and pushed active sonar detection out to virtually the limits imposed by near-field acoustic propaga-tion conditions; it also has some convergence zone capability. Its design also allows full recording and analysis of performance, enabling reconstruction of events down to the level of each individual 'ping'. More 2000 series of sonars were developed for submarines, the 2007 passive flank array that entered service in 1971 and the 2020 sonar, the submarine version of 2016 developed to replace 2001 in nuclear powered submarines. It was first tested in 1981-2 and was fitted in the *Trafalgar* class submarines beginning with *Tireless* which was commissioned in 1985.

It had long been recognised that an array of hydrophones arranged appropriately to provide beam forming and backed by electronic circuitry of adequate frequency stability and sophistication would be able to detect the noises emitted by submarine over long ranges, even when the amplitude of these noises was below the ambient threshold, provided that they had recognisable characteristics. In the early 1970s, the Directorate of Naval Operational Requirements had defined the characteristics of a surface ship towed array and had made some decisions about its acoustic aperture, its necessary robustness and handling qualities. Towed arrays were first used in the Royal Navy in Polaris ballistic missile submarines, using the American BQR-15 based 2023. This had to be clipped onto the submarine as she left harbour as did the 2024 developed for attack boats, both nuclear and conventional; 2024 entered service in 1975.

Four years later the prototype surface ship towed array sonar, Type 2031, went to sea for trials in *Matapan* and then in the frigate *Lowestoft*. The equipment comprised a 12 ton winch upon which was reeled a towing cable and acoustic element totalling a length of some one and a quarter miles. It was necessary to place this sensitive array as far away from the frigate's radiated noise as possible. 2016 was an immediate success, despite under-investment in peripheral data handling arrangements. In exercises in 1982 *Lowestoft* performed as well as the most advanced US Navy prototype towed array and better than the other variants that they already had in service. In parallel, four other frigates were fitted with a Sonar 2031(I) variant incorporating a Marconi Avionics processor. The conversions were carried out in Devonport Dockyard between 1981-1984 on *Cleopatra*, *Phoebe*, *Sirius* and *Argonaut* and after completion of sea trials, these four ships made an immediate impact both on operational capability and upon Anglo-American co-operation in this new field of passive anti-submarine detection. A more compact and cheaper processor incorporating advanced architectural principles was selected for quantity production and the resultant 2031(Z) was tested in *Arethusa* one of the Ikara *Leanders* and fitted to the later Type 22 frigates. Parallel measures were taken in submarines, resulting in a common 'family' of processors; the first Type 2046 set was delivered in 1987 to replace 2024.

The Falklands War caused some delays in the conversion of the four 2031(I) *Leanders* so that by the time that they were ready for sea there was a substantial number of officers and ratings trained in the principles of towed array operations and 'narrow-band analysis' (the science of detection and classification). Pent up enthusiasm, coupled to the considerable volume of experience held by the submarine service and by those submariners seconded to frigates, promoted a sharp rise in operational expertise as soon as the first towed array *Leanders* got to sea. The inherent advantage of a surface ship towed array system lies in the ability to mount a large winch and thus achieve array dimensions, tow lengths and water depths impossible in submarines; this gives superior acoustic performance in advantageous propagation domains. Within a year, operational results, both in NATO exercises and in surveillance against Soviet submarines, had convinced the sceptics (especially those within the rival submarine, RAF maritime aircraft and Fleet Air Arm helicopter confraternities), that these surface ships were world leaders in this particular anti-submarine art. There was much cross fertilisation of ideas between all passive sonar communities and an almost wholesale importation of submarine Target Motion Analysis techniques into frigates. It will be recognised that to derive a target's position, course and speed using only bearing and bearing rate information requires manoeuvre and mathematical treatment if the target is to be fixed sufficiently accurately to allow localisation and attack by, for example, an anti-submarine aircraft. Ship's companies involved in towed array operations soon cultivated a special pride in mastering the required techniques of quiet, covert passive operations with minimal electronic emissions and attention to 'noise hygiene', the business of keeping a ship acoustically quiet.

Rapid advances were also made in the evolution of tactics and co-operation with other forces, particularly RAF and American maritime patrol aircraft. It was early recognised that in a small navy, with relatively few towed array ships, great attention to the process of capturing, recording and disseminating data would be needed if doctrine was to be firmly and rapidly established. The Meteorological and Oceanographic sub-specialisation among Instructor Officers played a praiseworthy part in furthering the science of acoustic propagation prediction at these new longer target ranges, using both the full depth of the expendable bathythermograph and the ambient noise assessments derivable from the arrays themselves. Reorganisation at Fleet Headquarters combined all these aspects into a peculiarly effective operational capacity on an international basis, the whole earning much credit for the Royal Navy from the Americans. The final accolade wsas the creation in 1984 of a new command within the NATO Striking Fleet organisation, 'Commander ASW Striking Force', ex officio the British Flag Officer Third Flotilla, and the designated officer in charge of the long range ASW protection of the Striking Fleet's carrier battle groups. Flying his flag in one of the smaller Anti-Submarine carriers built to replace the traditional large strike carriers he controls all the Striking Fleet's towed array surface assets, American, Canadian and Dutch as well as British.

With the exception of the surface ship towed array, all the developments in equipment, training and organisation described received the severest possible test in the 1982 Falklands conflict. Operation Corporate concerned the campaign to regain for their people the Falklands Islands after the Argentine invasion on 1 April 1982. Whilst it was essentially a maritime campaign, in which the Navy executed its classical role of launching an army as a projectile to take ground and conclude the business, it was also an all-arms tri-service combined operation of enormous difficulty and complexity. This account will concentrate briefly upon the underwater aspects and their influence upon the campaign as a whole in order to give some idea of the level of expertise of *Vernon* and her people at the time of the establishment's closure.

It was known that the Argentine Navy possessed three diesel electric submarines, one ex-American 'Guppy' built in 1944 and sold to Argentina in 1971, and two smaller German built Type 209 class acquired in 1974. Much experience of small German submarines in work up training at Portland and in major NATO exercises had shown that these were particularly difficult to detect; furthermore it was well known that the South Atlantic was rich in biological life and thus potentially wasteful 'non-submarine' contacts.

The first phase of the British counter-attack was the taking of South Georgia on 25 April. It was known that the ex-American submarine *Santa Fe* was in the area. She was detected on the surface by *Antrim's* Wessex III helicopter radar after landing reinforcements at Grytviken. The Commanding Officer of *Santa Fe* decided not to dive, appreciating correctly his vulnerability to ASW homing torpedoes which have ceiling switches designed to inhibit attack on surface ships. Unfortunately for him the aircraft was carrying Mk 11 depth charges, essentially the same weapon that was in service in 1943. Lieutenant Christopher Parry executed the first British naval attack on a submarine at sea since April 1945, and caused sufficient damage to prevent *Santa Fe* from diving. Her return on the surface to the relative safety of Cumberland Bay was harassed by an expectedly unsuccessful attack with a Mk 46 torpedo by *Brilliant's* Lynx helicopter, as well as multiple hits by AS12 wire guided missiles and machine gun fire from the Wasp helicopters of *Plymouth* and *Endurance*. Two hours after she first came under attack, *Santa Fe* fetched up alongside the pier at Grytviken, listing and apparently on fire.

Of the two Argentine Type 209 submarines, *Salta* was experiencing noise and torpedo firecontrol problems and made no operational patrols, but *San Luis* was at sea for about a month during the early part of the campaign. On 1 May, the day upon which elements of the British Task Force arrived in the vicinity of the Total Exclusion Zone around the Falklands and made the first Sea Harrier attacks against Port Stanley airfield, it was appreciated that she was operating in the area to the north east of East Falkland. Admiral Woodward, the Task Force Commander, detached *Brilliant* and *Yarmouth* together with three Sea King helicopters of 826 Squadron, each of which carried a spare crew. By means of in-flight refuelling from the frigates, these aircraft managed astonishing ten hour sorties during a protracted but inconclusive interdiction sweep, much bedevilled by rocky bottom contacts and shoals of fish. There is no record as to how *San Luis* reacted to this operation, and very little information about her subsequent movements. She did not succeed in making even an unsuccessful attack on either of the aircraft carriers.

Her final brush with the Task Force was on 11 May when *Alacrity* and *Arrow* were returning to the main battle group after nocturnal exploratory excursions up Falkland Sound and around the north coast of West Falkland. These frigates appear to have passed within five thousand yards of *San Luis*, which fired one wire guided SST-4 torpedo on a manually calculated and guided solution as her automatic equipment was unserviceable. There is some inconclusive evidence that this torpedo hit and damaged *Arrow's* torpedo decoy but did not explode. *San Luis* subsequently returned to harbour, did not turn round particularly quickly and was not able to sail for a second patrol before the end of fighting. While the Argentine submarine effort was therefore ineffective, there is no doubt that the threat was a continuous concern to the Task Force, requiring enormous effort by screening helicopters throughout, and much attention by ships to anti-submarine manoeuvres and dispositions.

The sinking of the Argentine cruiser *General Belgrano* on 2 May by *Conqueror* had the effect of neutralising the Argentine surface fleet, which took no part in the campaign. Unemotional and professionally informed assessment of the tactical situation on that day reveals the dire peril confronting the Task Force from not only the powerful *General Belgrano* group but also from the Argentine carrier group, the *24 de Mayo* with her Sea Dart equipped Type 42 destroyer and three Exocet equipped equipped corvette escorts. Uninformed comment has failed to give sufficient weight to speed, time and distance aspects, the lack of British surface weapon systems capable of dealing with an armoured cruiser, the presence of Exocet fitted escorts with the *General Belgrano,* and the very real risk that *Conqueror* could have been shaken off by speed and deceptive manoeuvre over the shallows of the Burdwood Bank, an acoustically difficult area within which the submarine's own speed would have been limited.

The *Belgrano* group had been accompanied since sailing from Ushuaia on 26 April by a noisy oil tanker easily picked up on *Conqueror's* 2024 array. When sighted by *Conqueror* on 1 May, *Belgrano* was fuelling and this oiler was subsequently detached to return to base. A point that has not so far been made is that this was an ominous indicator of future intent; if *General Belgrano's* westerly trend on 2 May up to the time of her sinking denoted a clear intention to retire why was the oiler not retained as a sensible tactical contingency until arrival in Argentina?

The attack was carried out using a spread of three 21-inch Mk 8** torpedoes, expecting one hit. In the event two hits on *General Belgrano* were obtained and there is sound evidence that the third hit the escort *Hipolito Bouchard* but did not explode. Interesting to anti-submariners was the recounted high level of concern in *Conqueror's* control room about the possibility of counter-attack and the radical evasive manoeuvres taken, despite the low level of Argentine ASW expertise. Commander Christopher Wreford-Brown decided to use the ancient 21-inch Mk 8 instead of the modern wire guided 'Tigerfish' torpedoes primarily because of the larger warhead of the older torpedo. If he had attacked the destroyers the Mk 24 Mod 1 would have been his weapon of choice.   It was assessed that the Argentinians were also capable of mounting a mining campaign. To combat this threat, an Assault Mine Sweeping System was rapidly designed and tested at ARE Southwell and shipped south in *Intrepid.* Consisting of a noisemaker and electro-magnets, it could be towed by an assault ship's landing craft, and although not used before the initial landings, it was used to check the approaches at Teal Inlet.

To provide a wire sweeping capability against moored mines, five stern trawlers were taken up from trade, some straight off the fishing grounds, and fitted with WS Mk 9 sweeps; three were also fitted with Acoustic Hammers (AH). To enable them to carry out their own precursor wire sweeping a double Orepesa Sweep System was devised using Mk 9 sweep wires and kites, and minesweeping floats and multiplanes left over from the *Algerine* class. The trawlers were commissioned as HM Ships and sailed from Portland on 27 April, arriving at South Georgia a month later, where they were employed generally on logistic and personnel transfer tasks. Sailing for the Falklands on 4 June, *Cordella, Pict* and *Junella* were involved in special forces operations. *Pict* also distinguished herself in a dangerous precursor minesweeping operation. After the Argentinian surrender on 15 June, all five ships tackled the known moored minefields off Port Stanley, sweeping ten of the suspected twenty one mines that had been laid. Further minehunting operations by two 'Hunt' class MCMVs verified that the field was safe. They also located and surveyed the wrecks of *Ardent* and *Antelope* and re-located the wreck of *Coventry.*

During the conflict four Fleet Clearance Diving Teams (FCDTs) were employed, two on EOD duties and two on ship repair tasks, and a further FCDT had been formed and was on its way south when hostilities ceased. Among other extensive tasks requiring professional skill FCDT1 was responsible for the removal of an unexploded 1000-lb bomb from *Argonaut*, and FCDT3 for the removal of an unexploded bomb from *Sir Galahad*. Following the Argentinian surrender the FCDTs were involved in protracted EOD and ship repair operations, and a new team with saturation diving capability was formed to operate from the Motor Vessel *Stena Seaspread*. Between 13 October 1982 and 2 January 1983 this team removed or destroyed all the sensitive material from *Coventry* at a depth of 95 metres.

Before concluding this long account of the contribution to Britain's naval history made by *Vernon* a number of the major themes that have been exposed by previous chapters bear examination; one is also tempted to make some judgements about future trends. We have seen how the character of naval warfare was fundamentally altered by the advent of underwater weaponry, the submarine, the torpedo and the mine. A political instrument to be used in furtherance of essentially land based objectives, sea power had previously been a relatively simple affair, confined to the tabula rasa of the ocean surface, and in which effectiveness was generally proportional to investment. Technical advances such as armour plate, rifled bores and breech loading might confer brief advantage but were marginal to outcomes. Factors such as tradition, expertise and morale had a part to play, but the yardstick of naval power for many years was the brute number of line of battleships that a nation chose to possess. The decisive fleet engagement was the desired objective, irrespective of peripheral campaigns such as commerce raiding, interdiction of logistic support and the elimination of naval bases. To achieve a fleet engagement was a matter of scouting, concentration of force and, thereafter, close range gunnery, a style that had not changed for centuries.

The *Dreadnought* revolution in long range gunnery, itself brought on by the growing torpedo menace and the First World War that soon followed, suddenly confronted nations and their naval staffs with new and unrehearsed problems. While well understood gunnery battle tactics still played am important part, they became more and more conditioned by the threat of underwater weapons. Both the Commanders-in-Chief at the Battle of Jutland, the big ship apogee, were bedevilled by the threat of the cheap submarine, the cheap torpedo fired by the relatively cheap destroyer and the minefield. The battleships were ceasing to be decisive, although their prestige would not be finally be minimized until the Battle of Leyte Gulf in October 1944, the last use of a tactical battle line that the world will ever see, and the end of an era that opened with the Spanish Armada campaign in 1588. Naval warfare in three dimensions had become complicated; it was forcing organisational and institutional changes no less profound than the technological. It is always easy to criticise with hindsight, but the watershed of the opening months of the First World War provide clear examples of faulty strategy and inept military applications that were directly caused by institutional deficiencies on both sides. The German High Command was illogically organised with unclear responsibility demarcations. The British Admiralty's failure to capitalise fully on its ability to read German wireless traffic, and the tardy introduction of convoy were both direct examples of institutional inadequacy.

It was also unclear in many instances who was the operational commander, the Admiralty or the Grand Fleet Commander-in-Chief. Advances in communications, the telephone, telegraph and wireless, conferred the ability to command and control in real time and at a distance, but also in turn surfaced other institutional inadequacies of a severe sort. Many were the instances of failure to repeat messages to informational addressees with an obvious need to know. The absence of an analytical approach to such things as signal formatting, standardised address lists, and the operational relevance of the signal code book, led to catastrophic ambiguities and confusion.

Likewise, these pages have described the difficulties that were suffered at this time by the Royal Navy in imposing a system for handling technological advances and inventions. There was a lack of proper staff structure and few officers could comprehend how such a structure must be built and managed in order to be able to handle in an orderly, responsive and inter connected way the many new concepts and problems of the age. The erratic genius of men like Fisher and Churchill was, therefore, untamed. This imaginative shortfall was also evident at the tactical level, resulting in a series of disasters of which the sinkings by submarine of *Aboukir*, *Cressy*, *Hogue* and *Formidable* were but examples. It was not exclusively the advent of underwater warfare that provoked intellectual and institutional change in naval affairs. In the later years of the war, the submarine showed itself, unexpectedly to some senior officers and politicians, to be a potentially war winning strategic instrument, a situation that was to repeat itself in the Second World War in both western and eastern hemispheres.

So lessons were learned and applied, and the influence of the operational analyst and the war gaming simulator rose in parallel with an increasing general understanding of how large decision making systems should be organised, whether commercial or military. The theme continues; a self critical and questioning attitude is commonplace among managers and staff officers, and there is not a naval weapon system or tactic that is not subjected to computer-assisted analysis as a matter of course.

We can also see a distinct trend in the management of technical evolution. The early years of *Vernon*'s life were characterised by the fact that all matters connected with the development of torpedoes, mines and their countermeasures were under one roof, whether they were concerned with invention, research, training, engineering, maintenance or tactical employment. Gradually the technological ground became more demanding; no longer was the individual the prime mover for advance, but the team. This book spans the career of the Royal Naval Scientific Service from its institution as a body providing support for naval engineers now no longer humanly capable of mastering all the required disciplines themselves, to its decline as the need for economies and the sheer complexity and scope of naval equipments required decentralisation to, and the harnessing of, commercial armaments companies and research institutes. The Scientific Service has been relegated largely to the role of project management and 'intelligent customer'. Invention has now become the prerogative of integrated organisations with aimed research, massive investment and industrial and scientific collaboration.

But what themes can be discerned at the strategic level? If we disregard peripheral activities such as the Royal Navy's contribution to the American war in the Pacific and both Battles of the Falklands, the central issue of sea control of the Atlantic dominated strategic thought from the onset of the First World War to the victory in the Cold War in 1990. Two World Wars and four decades of Cold War demonstrated that control of this vital waterway, which couples Europe to the industrial might of Northern America, was a condition of victory in the Eurasian heartland. Both Germany and the Soviet Union were disadvantaged by geography in this region in their use of air power and thus also of surface naval forces. Both placed emphasis on submarines. The nuclear submarine did not change the fundamentals of this strategic equation but it did give rise to a major new role, that of strategic nuclear deterrence. The ballistic missile nuclear submarine, by reason of its invulnerability and territorial freedom, provided a heartwarming measure of stability to the nuclear deterrent posture of both sides. It is not possible, and it is safe to predict that it will never be possible, pre-emptively to eliminate this second strike capability. It will always be there to deter; there is no pressure to 'use or lose' as there may be with land based missile silos or nuclear capable aircraft.

During the 1980s NATO and the United States developed a coherent doctrine for dealing with the Soviet submarine menace in both the Atlantic and the Pacific. Forward operations by nuclear powered submarines and carrier and amphibious groups protected by a towed array and helicopter equipped ASW striking force would contain and defeat the Soviet striking forces in and over waters close to the USSR. Such operations would, it was hoped, lower the threat to reinforcement and resupply shipping to levels that might well diminish the need for convoy, a controversial strategy once more, given improvement in surveillance and weapons systems and reduction in escort numbers. Even by the end of that decade, however, the Soviet nuclear submarine quietening programme was undermining many of the premises on which the forward strategy was based. The end of the Cold war and the new emphasis on global operations emphasising strike and amphibious options, as demonstrated in Operation Granby in 1991, also drives ASW back towards the local defeat of local threats.

Anti-submarine measures are being driven back towards active sonar, many years of research having failed to find a solution among non-acoustic methods. In general, active sonar detection carries a significant tactical disadvantage as, evidently, the transmissions can be detected and analysed at far greater ranges than those at which they could be expected to yield a returning target echo. Presence, movement, range and even nationality and warship class can be derived by the enemy. Conversely, passive systems do not alert the target and also impose permanent restraints upon his operations. But if ASW measures are again to be forced down the active road, then detection systems will need to have as wide a surveillance capability as possible with special, and probably separate, acoustic pulse generators at considerable water depths. The latter will probably exploit high powered and complex pulse characteristics and use towed or fixed arrays as receivers. Consideration of the speed of sound in water, discontinuities in the water mass, bottom geography and the prevalence of false targets could also call for a very large information processing capacity, probably sited ashore, and thus also needing satellite borne communication and positioning systems. At a time of falling defence budgets such expeditures seem unlikely. Perhaps they are also unecessary to counter a small number of submarines as possibly possessed by the likely targets of Western or United Nations power projection.

Iraq had no submarines in 1991. The Coalition navies would have had many more problems if she had possessed even one or two and this lesson will not be lost on other smaller nations. Even more, however, the war of 1991 was another demonstration of the inhibiting capacity of the mine. The future of mine countermeasures and explosive ordnance disposal trades would seem to be assured in a world where the developed will maintain order among the less developed and where irregular operations remain more likely than all-out warfare. For many years yet *Vernon* people and *Vernon* skills will be at the forefront of those required by an active Royal Navy.

What remains to be said about *Vernon*? It was always a friendly and cheerful place in which officers and men could acquire their skills. The vast majority were, of course, ratings. Over the years the relationship between officers and men had always been good even if, at one time, the class structure of the nation had made it more remote than it should have been. With the advent of technology the essential bond between officers and men became increasingly stronger until, in World War II, it was exemplified by team work. At sea, in all weathers, ratings worked long hours, much of it below decks keeping essential services running smoothly. Officers, highly skilled themselves, relied upon them to provide loyal and dependable service, they were very rarely disappointed. However, for obvious reasons the 'shop-window' of *Vernon* was, the officers' wardroom. Like the ratings' messes it was a cheerful place, matching the variety and informality of those who were involved in the underwater business, particularly the divers who have always had a social reputation all their own. John Canty managed it for over thirty years, may his name live for ever. Annual celebrity dinners took pride in fitting in everybody who was qualified and wanted to come, irrespective of numbers, leading to some unusual and ad-hoc accommodation arrangements. Portraits of great men hung upon the walls, the less historically well informed objecting to the hideous visage of Jackie Fisher, a Gunnery Officer. Lighthearted contests celebrated this rivalry between *Excellent* and *Vernon*: there were Olympiads featuring unusual indoor and outdoor sports and adjuncts such as circus elephants and cycle powered dinosaurs. With its many exterior affiliations and interior sporting and social activities, its charitable work, its annual Tattoos, its pageant of idiosyncratic personalities, *Vernon* occupies a warm place in the hearts of those who served there.

Curiousness and certain non-conformity have always been *Vernon* attributes and these have been at a premium in an age of maritime endeavour which has placed unusual premiums upon the thoughtful exploitation of new scientific principles, upon practical equipment development and upon imaginative tactical application. The two naval establishments which have most exemplified the Royal Navy for over a century are indeed *Excellent* and its lively child, *Vernon*. That there should have been such healthy rivalry between the two was entirely natural because it sprang from an essential difference in the natures of surface and underwater warfare. Above water, the comparative homogeneity of the atmosphere and its properties in permitting the transmis-

sion of target information visually or by radar at relativistic velocities bred men and weapon systems which placed emphasis on drill, precision, split second teamwork - and thus spit and polish, conformity, and the loud word of command. Underwater, the medium is fickle and strange, whether one is considering acoustic propagation, barytrauma in the diver, or hydrodynamic effects on towed or self propelled structures. The target data rate is limited by the velocity of sound in seawater, five thousand feet per second. This breeds a more reflective person, patient, enquiring, individualistic and with a propensity to keep down the noise level. The strength of *Excellent* was founded in a long tradition of naval gunnery which has persisted into the missile age, while that of *Vernon* was founded in this modern era of rapid technological development. It is remarkable that these fine tribal traditions have been fused so happily as the microchip has overtaken naval warfare in all its facets. The courage and professionalism of the officers and ratings who worked and trained in those two great establishments can never be in doubt.
VERNON SEMPER VIRET

The last torpedo leaves Vernon 1986

TORPEDO LONG COURSES – 1872 - 1986

1872 - 1876
 GS Parker
LA Beaumont
 BW Walker
JW Osborne
EJP Gallwey
GR Maltby
CG Robinson

1876 - 1877
SM Eardley- Wilmot
WH May
RWS Rogers

 1878
AW Chisholm-Batten
TC Fenton
CJ Norcock
FH Rogers

1879
GM Brooke
WPL Heyland
RW White
G Le C Egerton

1880
HR Adams

HS Lake
CJ Conybeare

1881
AE Bethell
CG Dicken

1882
EBDO Aplin
PW Bush
GL King-Harman
CE Gladstone

1883
AH Anson
DA Gamble
FT Hamilton
TFW Ingram
HB Jackson
R de Lisle
WHH Monthresor
EA White
JP White

1884
FL Cambell
HP Hely-Hutchinson
GL Ottley
WRicketts
FCD Sturdee

1885
A Barry
FJ Foley
EJW Slade
L de L Wells
AW Torlesse
L Bayley

1886
EBB Levett
AWJ Portal
WC Slater
CJ Briggs
B Currey

1887
W Carey
CE Madden
AL Duff
RLH Armstrong
A Dodgson
EC Carr
J de C Hamilton
RHS Bacon
HL Heath

1888
RK Arbuthnot
HAS Flyer
WL Grant
WCM Nicholson
DR de Chair

1889
CEE Carey
H Jones
S Nicholson
R Hudleston
SA Gough-Calthorpe

1890
WO Boothby
H Orpen
RBF Charlton
RS Phipps-Hornby

EA Salwey

1891
CW Plenderleath
CF Sowerby
CL Vaughan-Lee
TDW Napier

1892
E Lees
FCA Ogilvy
GW Smith
PH Colomb
Sir ES Fitzherbert
1893
TL Barnardiston
LC Lister
RF Scott
C Greatorex
GC Fraser
CC Fowler

1894
RW Johnson
CH Borrett
AB Dawson
FC Wentworth
TH Foster

1895
AR Hulbert
GL Sclater
PW Dumas
CW Bellairs
HL D'E Skipworth

1896
F Brandt
SS Hall
HW Richmond
ML'E Silver
FG Loring
AW Heneage

1897
TB Bonham
AE Phillips
CWG Crauford
CR Acklom
FL Field
RF Parker

1898
HG Vereker
F St G Brooker
HE Browne
MF Sueter
AK Waistell
HFP Sinclair
HG Glennie

1899
OH Davies

JS Dumaresq
FHM Jackson
FS Litchfield
H Strickland
RH Walters
VHS Haggard
CR Payne
FL Attenborough
WJB Law

1900
P Harvey
CM Trousdale
TJ Croker
RA Newton
A de KL May
FD Arnold-Foster

1900
WE Woodward
AP Addison
JD Allen
RF Hartland-Mahon
HN Garnett
EJ Prendergast

1901
EO Ballantyne
WT Elder
THM Maurice
OW Ormsby
ADPR Pound
MD Evans
WR Napier
CT Hardy
P Withers
AHC Candy
FN Fargus
SL Willis
JB Stevenson
CL Lambe

1902
AT Darley
AC Fellowes
L Hutchings
AE Silvertop
AH Quicke
AU Moore
O Swann
JE Slee
ADM Cherry
Hon A Forbes-Semphill
HS Currey
K Kiddle
LLP Willan
LAB Donaldson

1903
TE Harrison
AH de Kantzow
JH Woodbridge
GGC Wood-Martin

AM Yeates-Browm
NA Sulivan
CR Nichol
GCW Crispin
MK Grant

1903
WR Kettlewell
GO Stephenson
AR Palmer
W Tomkinson
QCA Crauford
WG Rigg
HK Kitson

1904
JF Cole
GH Davey
GF Grayson
RM Groves
RH Waring
RL Way
TC Williams
BM Mansell
PE Parker
BM Money
GL Massey
Wde M Egerton
WHS Ball
MHS Macdonald
JCS Paterson
J Casement
EM Bennett
R Fitzmaurice
CS Forbes
A Lambert
WH Bourne
RJ Howard
JK Imthurn
EAD Masterman
Hon R A Plunkett-Ernle-
    Erle-Drax
GB Riley
RG Hervey
CSt C Cameron
TJ Goldie

1905
NE Archdale
RW Bromley
K Brounger
CD Burke
JL Cather
WL Dodgson
RC Fane
H Greenwood

1905
RC Hamilton
HC Hitchens
NA Marshall
JM Maxwell-Scott
JR Middleton

GR Nixon
TRG O'Connor
RF Pitcairn
DW Roe
WB Rowbotham
AH Walker
FV Williamson

1906
RR Cooke
D Errington
AL Gwynne
GB Harrison
GNE Head
EW Isaacson
GF Montague
A Rice
NF Usborne
JF White
R Howard
HG Thursfield
CAM Sarel
AT Muir
CB Dickson
LP Vavasour
HRG Moore
BE Reinold
EL Wharton
CE Aglionby
FLM Boothby
AB Watts
RS Sneyd
G Hamilton
EG Robinson
JSC Salmond
ET Marshall
R St John
S Boyd-Richardson

1907
EC Burney
CA Carey
LCM Roxby
BC Walker
JS Wilson

1907
MD Bridges
FE Schreiber
TR Fforde
GD Fanshawe
RS Macfarlan
CE Kennedy-Purvis
CS Inglis
SD Tillard
AHD Field
LEH Royle
AA Lovett-Cameron
RM Bellairs
JW Howard
GC Candy
JH Young
RL Nicholson

AD Warrington-Morris
WN Lapage
GFE Mulock

1908
RL Clayton
AE Godsal
HIR Trischler
HB Taylor
WB Mackenzie
GW Hallifax
CE Turle
JF Somerville
CB Palmes
HNM Hardy
R Lane-Poole
GL Coleridge

1909
ET Favell
F Giffard
B Egerton
HL Hitchins
EW Mackichan
EC Watson
LAD Sturdee

1910
JA Lees
WM Robinson
WP Gandell
HR Sawbridge
AH Taylor
R Leatham

1910
EC Ward
KV Orlebar
RC Hamilton

1911
LHB Bevan
Hon HCR Fielding
AC Horsley
DWP Ireland
FH Sandford
GR Bald
WK Conlon
FHT Ree
RBT Miles
AJ Murray
W Mark-Wardlaw
GC Wilkinson
JV Wotton
FD Mowatt
FJ Allen
FR Barry
RB Lane
WF Wake-Walker
K Mackenzie

1912
RL Faulkner

EG Hallewell
LA Montgomery
LF Potter
JE Bashford
WHW Ridley
A Maitland-Dougall
GC Boles
CO Alexander
HH Harwood
ET Wickham
JG Crace
DGW Curry
Ede F Renouf
HP Cotton
RH De'ath
GW Dorling
EW Sinclair

1913
ETD Finch
DH Hyde-Thomsom
HN Lesley
OH Stoehr

1913
THS Tatham
EG Morris
J Barrett
AF Cochrane
JUP Fitzgerald
FN Attwood
AU Willis
PG Turner
BL Johnston
JFB Carslake
RHF de Salis
RA Jackson
CJ Forlong
CS Sandford
HFB Maxse

1914
VJ Bowden-Smith
RI Collier
DF Jones
AC Montague
PEU Townshend
PD Crofton
CH Godwin
CE Tooth
QH Paterson
GB Smith
DA Budgen
CNE Currey
JP Burton
GFL Marx
HR Bennett
HG Grierson
HC Phillips
ED Panter
EP Thomas
GRG Allen

1915
NE Archer
JM McC Crosbie
JF Williams
FT Hewson
HB Rawlings
DW Boyd
HG Gorton
GD Owen
HF Howse
GC Banister

1916
RH Allen
RH Fitzherbert
-Brockholes
RAS Bethell
GA Barratt
R Handcock
CR McCrum
WE Parry
GW Wadham

1917
KFA Wallis
HD Dunbar-Rivers
LH Bell
WP Stocker
CG Lang
HW Skrine
EVJeffreys

1918 (1st Long Course)
AE de BJennings
HE Morse
WS King-Hall
W St G Abbott
RR McGrigor
FH Vaughan
FG Hunter
GB Middleton
FN Stephenson

1918 (2nd Long Course)
AJ Mitchell
A Richard
JW Waller
AB Ritchie
LF Foley
KP Stewart
HL Vaughan-Williams
REF McQ Mackenzie
FHP Maurice
OW Cornwallis
RC Clavell
EG Coore

1919
NV Crace
EC Bindloss
GE Creasy
AG Talbot
WRP Eyre

1919
HF Elderton
HHJ Hodgson
PS Cooper
TH Back
GD Latham

1920
HD Nichols
WH Graves
ELB Damant
TC Greenway
SF Gaisford St Lawrence
DP Cather
QD Graham
FH Austin
HJ Welman
HC Woolrych
AG Mack
JA Brickford-Smith
AC Powell
AC Madden
R Portal
C Farquhar-Smith RAN

1921
A De Salis
W Morley
EG Abbott
JC Maclean
PH Haig-Ferguson
RF Fegen
AAD Grey
GC Adams
JEW Oland RCN

1922
AP Dewing
AAL Miller
W Haynes
HH Rogers
RW James
DG Reid
FW Growse
GEL Veale
HM Huntington-Whitely
NM Bird
AEH Cameron
AR Alston
GMD Maltby
HD Johnston

1922
GM Hibbard RCN

1923
V A L Bradyll-Johnson
GA Bateman
JGD Ouvry
CJ Carr
JS Cowie
CAL Mansergh
JFW Mudford

AS Donovan
WP Carne
PHF Colomb
RA Macdonald
WG Andrewes
SL Bateson
GAC Williams
RBM Long RAN

1924
R Oliver-Bellasis
SH Paton
CP Clarke
RC Wield
NK Calder RAN
RJ Berry
F Schunck
ES Oatley
CL Robertson

1925
HHC Ainslie
JF Bradburne
AV De Labalmonbiere
WB Creery RCN
Hon ALCWG Napier
AH Spurgeon RAN
FCH Bolt RAN
CSD Noakes
JCS Chamberlain
RES Bidwell RCN

1926
PW Dimsdale
HG St J Bury
AM Bingeman
S Brown
WW Davis
PC Voelcker
NP Morgan RAN

1927
SR Ascherson
KHS Cohen
CE Lambe
WA Dallymeyer
ERWilson
J Hughes-Hallett
DH Hall-Thompson

1928
R Heathcote
GV Gladstone
RH Balfour
EO Obbard
P Skelton
LF Durnford-Slater
BJ Fisher
CRL Parry
RC Boyle
JH Allison
RC St VMillington
HC Stock

EFV Dechaineux RCN

1929
TW Botley
KHT Peard
WJC Robertson
ABR Sands
SA Cooper
FS Walford
GW Harper
GB Sayer
TA Godsell RAN
LHT Hollebone
CWC Turner
RJH Ryan
HT Powell
RN Churchill
CJ Smith
ER Collins
JF Shepherd
TFS Wilson
RD Watson
L Gowland
MFB Ward

1930
PW Brock
J Hext-Lewes
AP Gibson

1930
W Smith
GC Blundell
CT Jellicoe
AH Wallis
H Norman
A Gray
EJS James
WA Lindsay-Watson
QP Whitford
KR Buckley
A Pares
GT Smith
RW Griffith
HN Lay RCN
WTA Moran RAN
GIC Hutchison
PE Heseltine
PM Stephens

1931
VD'A Donaldson
WO Bradbury
TAK Maunsell

1932
P Bethell
ED Webb
RS Wellby
RHR Moodie
NA Copeman
GHC Dickens
AL Taylor

ABM Fairbairn
DG Clark

1933
AH Browne
DH Leigh
FR Main
RM Freer
RF Harland
RCM Duckworth
JH Gretton
AL Hobson
GR Murray
GAF Norfolk
CM Donner
E Hale
JC Cole
GHFP Gipps

1933
RE Portlock

1934
PGO Langley
HG Craig
J Spencer
LH Stileman
RBC Hutchinson
EA Blundell
RA Villiers
RC Lewis
AWR McNicoll RAN

1935
DH Fuller
NW Fisher
PMB Chavasse
DA Lawford
RC PEllis
AB Cole
ESW Maclure
AJ Dent
J Plunkett-Cole RAN

1936
LE Moncaster
CD Clarke
RRS Pennefather
CRL Argles
CCB Meckenzie
GR Carver
CRG Wilkinson
J Denny RAN
HS Rayner RCN

1937
DGF Bird
JR Carr
GV Corbett
JGS Cunningham
DV Garde
PPM Green
J Hopkinson

GP Kilroy
TJG Marchant
TK Morrison RAN

1938
RCB Buckley
EG Ducat-Hamersley

1938
EO Daniel
FC Goodenough
GR Heppel
ES Lipscombe
EE Mayo RAN
WDFB Muspratt
SJA Nix
AAW Pollard
SE Post
RGBO'N Roe
RE Topp

1939
RJ Cooper
PC Hopkins
GEP Milburn
RH Royds
TC Seddon
CJ Bennett
SW Hesslegrave
RGM Collins
JEM Glenny
CHS Wise
JC Stodart
DV Whinney
MC Giles
CC Hawkins
RL Clode

1940(1)
WH Wheeler
GAJ Goodhart
F Fletcher
C StC Cameron
IK Rodwell
ALS Hogg
E Ingram
RF Stubbs
NTB Tibbits

1940(2)
RH Fanshawe
A Healey
CE Pollock
RH Rowlandson
GVB Russell
AH Swann
HR Webber
HEP Wilkin

1940(2)
J Beauchamp
RT Coulton

JC Cherry
JF Firth
TH Kershaw

1941(1)
H Burgin
GE Buckle
JPG Brooks
RS Bryden
FB Caldwell
OJE Fountaine
GR Grocock
CWP Lee
DJ Long
OHM St J Steiner
HR Wykeham-Martin
GF Medlam
J GJacjson
JA Lamond
JJ Hurley
VG Earl
TB Penfold

1941(2)
AJR Foster
DD Macfarlan
AS Walker
SE Pritchard
RD Hamilton-Bate
JA Holmes
JF Bayliss
HL Euler
JS Raven
RV Moore
IM Milsted
AG Patterson
F Potts
WF Riddell
LHG Smith
FC Stevens
D Thursfield
DE Youatt
JM Baldock

1941 - (T)611
AV Webb
EA Stubbs
RA Reid
AD Fry
F Mildred
EC McDougall

1942(1)
MJ Head
RFG Elsworth
CL Round-Turner
ECF Coxwell
JH Stucley
E Palmer
THP Wilson
GP Fulcher
CWS Dreyer

IR Johnston
RJ Basset
WST McCully
JR McMurray
MD Rahilly
GA Hodges
WRL Kent
JR Phipps
JG Belsey
SW Francis
WI Nixon
AR Rye
JP Heins
J Johnson
EJ Gillit
JA Dow
JMc C Findlay
FG King
OR Moore
ETA Webb

1942(2)
WDS White
KS Main
JT Mannooch
CE Emerson
DW Horne
LJ Pearson
JM O'Keefe
KR McReath
L Godson
F Bruen
HM Choudri

1942(2)
BA Samson
JB Drake
DR Gales
GP Hutchison
TB Logan
HS Taylor
P Calderara
RP White
JF Dawson
JAMc Avity
TH Pannell
GH Peters
JT Baker

1942 - DEFIANCE
HE Ruddock
RG Bell
PJ Thomas
JA Bryant
J Alderton

1942 - (T)611
FL Millns
CE Doughty
DA Copperwheat
AJ Macmillan
EK Hartwell

1943(1)
CJ Collingwood
RH Hobart
HL Lloyd
EN Poland
GHG Crane
DMH Stobie
DC Wood
PLK Needham
HF Fewins
KM Watling
JH Adams
AGW Bellars
FC Isaac
JAW Gill
WFN Lamacroft
R Gunton
HGB Morgan
TM McCammont
DT Dunlop
BJ Dickinson
AD Armour

1943(1)
D Angus
RMO Simpson
LCW Turner

1943(2)
N Dixon
PJ Durell
JP Cornish
JKH Freeman
DL Binnington
JM Clark-Campbell
WMC Martin
SG Bloomer
RGC Macnab
KF Busbridge
PSW Roberts
TH Pettersen
GS Kapoor
RR Colls
EHH Maskell
GAG Williams
PGE Farwell
EV Hanning
AA Chapman
FG Harris
GN Pink
G Esson
JK Wicks
AN Laight
CF Locke
JF Fennell
CMcD Sullivan
SS Neville
RM Dundas
FA O'Dea

1943 - (T)611
FD Edwards
FA Booth

AE Chiverton
FHWT Foord

1943 - DEFIANCE
RJ Willsmer
SF Morris
J Stevens
SE Groves
AVH Dalzell
AFW Berryman
R Newstead

1943 - DEFIANCE
DM Maclennan
ML Evans

1944(1)
CF Alington
PB Ayling
JR Blake
BE Bulbeck
TA Collier
PLAB Colombi
WM Howard
WD Moseley
RH Sach
SG Moore
RD Green
H Ashworth
JEJ Bell
TLB Cooper
SG Davies
RE Davis
WJE Marryat
CU Fisher
ES Johnson
WHP Johnson
WM Lane
WJG Emery
EPJ Lunch
AW Lymbery
J Marryat
WFI Stephenson
PA Watson
DB Waugh
MT Beardmore
BT McCormack
JE Wiley
KS Upton

1944 - (T)611
PJ Williams

1944(2)
JA Crace
GMH Drummond
RP Fletcher
JLM Joly
JR Marigold
D Scott
JG Stedman
JM Stewart-Moore

TV Stopford

1944(2)
PH Bayley
NFV Satow
B Thomson
MF Payne

1944 -MARLBOROUGH(1)
JW Norman
C Fox
EW Latham
RF Morgan
WW Almond
CS Sandeman
KF Huggons
AW Lewer
LC Eaton
CG Martin

1944 -MARLBOROUGH(2)
WJ Apted
PA Berthon
ES Cotswell
WAD Ford
HH Hughes
RS Miller
JB Robertson

1945(1)
MW Antrobus
JB Butchard
CB Fetherston-Dilke
PR Fletcher
BHC Hearn
HAJ Hollings
MJA Keyworth
TL Martin
BCB Portman
CDS Smith
ED Symes
EP Keatinge
H de Jonge Van Ellemeet
GW Bendien
JL Bommezijn
M Graneek
EG Wakeling
WW Mackereth

1945 -MARLBOROUGH(1)
RCE Hudson
BT Tippets
GG Cooke

1945 - MARLBOROUGH(1)
DW Blair

1945 - MARLBOROUGH(2)
OA Aslaksrud
PW Reid
AV Atkins
AF Dakin
JH Dresler

H Fourie
RS Gilchrist
EC Hannen
WS Palmer
GS Stevens
JE Taylor

1946
W Burns
FLW Hunter
CAJ Nicoll
CH Read
C Sandeman
AH Young
WM Kidd
WC Spicer
W Szuster
M Fahim
BJ Jacobs
WJ McMullen

TAS Long COURSES
1946 - 1972

1946
MP Chapman
MJL Duff
RKN Emden
LA Forbes
SA Hammick
WJ Mann
AJR Whitehead
TR Coulter
H Brekke
CO Herdofsen
UH Gad
HB Gundersen
MT Coyne

1947
HJ Bartlett
JMR Lutley
RA Seaburne-May
WS Crawford
CH Fothergill
JE Lewis
N Rutherford
J Monroe
TMB Firth
RLW Lancaster
MH Cooke
FPR Saunders
MJ Gregory
KM Nanavati
LE Lunel

1948
JDL Repard
SMW Farquharson
-Roberts
JL Crawford
LCP Pritchard
RS Browning

J Brooks
DA Woods
PRM Hughes-Hallett
JWM Pertwee
DN Hoare
PR Barry

1948
RI Pearse
M Ross
RJE Craven
RC Thurber
DR Saxon
WS Blandy
PH Wilson
DR Mugg

1949
MB Edwards
GA Franklin
EBG Aston
ML Stacey
AR Gilmour
RB Moore
JS Glendinning
MF Bright
WEB Godsal
MBH Kersey
JG Wemyss
MW Paynter
ML Molony
TH Cayley
EV Sunderland
GR Macfarlane

1950
WE Bilson
GA Cavendish
Pk Collier
JG Colpoys
WFB Faulkner
CE Fiddian-Green
DDE Gay
DT Heap
RGH Hutchison
PCE Richardson
EMR Skene
HJ Startin
HT Wilson
JH Wheeler
NA Boase
AG Kilpatrick

1950
WE Clayards
DH Davies
JF Mckenzie

1951
JA Barrett
BL Cleary
PH Dunn
CHH Harwood

HH Hawkins
JCK Harley
VG Keeran
NCD Lawton
PJ Mylchreest
DA Ross
PRW Seymour
MO Taylor
JN Underhill
OK Watts
AG Woolley
AG Worsley

1952
WNW Atkin
RM French
MWG Fawcett
FE Dick
JS Carter
JG Davies
JW Bailey
JH St Aubyn-Sayer
BP Selby
PCD Campbell
LJH Povey
A Blease
PR Buckley
HJ Wade
FG Henshaw
GB Wither
WA Hughes
MA Martin

1953
KD Vicary
EJ Sebborn
DCR Waymouth
GY Temple
NS Phillips
PAC Neate
AL Jacks

1953
AFC Wemyss
RJ Davies
BR Longworth
JAP Coates
AJ Dale
IM Hutson
DG Sherrard
DCR Bruce
JD Stevens
JN Crosthwaite
RCK Peers
RC Brown
GT Hodgson
WG Brown
JCT Belcher
JWHF Dickie
WD Hogg

1954
FW Burgess

GHR Morrish
MR Wilson
R Greenshields
DW Brown
J Dickinson
JH Beattie
EMS O'Kelly
DJ Hallifax
TER Kitson
RKS Bethell
RS McCrum
AG Maciver
BH Foster
JJ Streatfield-James
RW Burnett
GMDe Rosenroll
SC Cowen
RL McLean
J Goudy
DA McDonald

1955
FK Steel
LJB Reynolds
GW Greet
GV Philbedge
RF Chalmers
WB Tower
CR Stansbury
CFP Simpson

1955
OTP Carne
WF Charter
N Bearne
GD Trist
RH Gaskin
EMT Segar
GJH Woolrych
IK Wilson
RS Impey
JM Steel
KW Blackburn
H Rusk
JF Watson
AS Morris
JM Reid
DB Reaper

1956
JRA Taylor
MRD Hooke
JA Fawsett
K Barclay-Brown
JN Green
JL Varley
JT Tomlinson
KB Barton
DI Aldrich
RR Richards
ATB Rooke
NW Parker
GK Barr

JPH Morton
DN Mainguy
JHR Laroche
RC Allen
RW Lang
JPD Hall
DC Smith

1957
MH Taylor
WR Harris
JM Tait
AJ Dunn
CB Filmer
GM Craig-McFeely
JF Hall
M Parry
IW Powe
W Norman

1957
AR Barnden
JWT Lewes
JP Tilley
DJW Sheppard
R Percy
IW Knox
RM Titcombe
RH Kirby
RDC Sweeney
SW Riddell
A Bajkov
DR Donaldson
AC Mandy

1958
GC Crisp
KIH Clarke
PHF Hudson
MCS Apps
JB Powell
LT Hickson
VM Howard
HG De Courcy-Ireland
RAB Gowlland
DG Eliot
DG Edwards
JP Colquhoun
CJ Templeton
JRH McIlwraith
HC Davies
DW Falconer
PGN Kennedy
FWP Townend
TM Bevan

1959
CJ Caughey
BG Cooper
GKA Feilder
RH Fox
D Gerrish
EBG Gibson

RE Hoskin
EDL Llewellyn
MC Powys-Maurice
DH Morse
BE Nicolls
JM Phillips
WJ Rogers-Coltman
JF Stewart
RU Todd
DF Watts
J Andrewartha
AL Beaumont
PH James

1960
DPR Lemitte
CB Schofield
NRD King
AD Bax
DK Holder
AJW Wilson
RIT Hogg
JW Perry
DHT Glynn
GF Liardet
MC Bridgman
PRSt Quintin
P Perry
RHC Heptinstall
DJ Partridge
GG Neilson
PV Blackman
BM Commons
DC Rose
JJDe Beer
KE Langford

1961
JP Jameson
AAH Evans
RBE Bell
G Kemp
BH Cain
JHJ Bass
AM Norman
MF Booth
DB Nolan
RSDe Chair
CWB Jones
J Grattan
SE Emberton
DNB Mortimer
PGV Dingemans
RM Carpendale
MD Griffiths
AH Dowling
ET Keane
AP Putter

1962
GJ Dowling
JB Crick
LMcA Jay

RMS delaP Hutchinson
J Harvey-Samuel
RP Burdett
PJ Erskine
DB Davis
JA Hepworth
SC Fraser
DB Mansergh
ANG Smith
GA Hales
DHM Price
JD Foster
JN King
GR Lamperd
NJ Stoker
JAB Lewis
ILSB Bradley
RFC Poole
JJ Parry

1963
RH Woods
PCH Sneath
T Bain-Smith
PDElburn
AP McKenzie-Hill
GJA Shaw
DJ Burton
KG Lees
NL Turner
PG Stephens
CA Fremantle
RT Newman
HL Foxworthy
JMC Sandison
CT Shaw
HFF Thurstan
RC Harper
KH Meads
D Burgess
GL Ramsay
JG Longden
CH Bennett
LAW Urquhart
ES Eide

1964
TR Cattermole
PR Cretney
JR Dennison
P Grace
RDT Lampen
NL Merrick
PA Parker
TJ Sims-Williams
JS Harrison
G Broome
HJ Donohue
DT Read
DT Owens
IA Hunter
RL Shelver

1965
DWW Burnside
P Midgley
CJ Peebles
TJ Smy
PR Stevens
GL Upton
DJ Hillman
R Spindloe
JF Coward
TFN Donald
RGP Memzies
RC Meyrick
JFTG Salt
DF Soppit
AD King
PR Lloyd
AE Rudman

1966
MD Adams
GA Eades
DCW Elliott
KA Gristy
GS Smith
C Walk
TW Plumb
A Blackhurst
CP Bengtsson
RS Forsyth
RM Gee
AR Godfrey
TJK Sloane
RJ Cocking
PA Knife
PA Ross
MR Pate
PG Odendaal

1967
RF Ryan
G Rhys-Jones
RH Chapman
MC Gordon-Lennox
WDS Kay-Smith
DJ Newsom
ER Ruscombe-King
JAJV Stodart
JHS Yorke
LR Hewett
DG Odell
AW Summers
MGT Harris
TM Honnor
DM Jeffreys
MJM Plumridge
AWP Reive
R Trussell
GV Sloper
KG Smith
AK Wait
PDN Rogers

1968
MS Pringle
RN Drummond
J Gilbert
C May
HDM Pound
BJ Stevens
RA Walker
MH White
MA Whitley
JH Collier
E Estyn-Jones
TJ Norman-Walker
HAE Powlett
J Calam
TJ Heppell
CF Bolton
RA Howland
GW Spence
WE Hartz

1969
GR Bartlett
DRM Gregory
MJ Fisher
C Jarvis
AJ Malcolm
J McGrigor
RD Nicholas
DL Ashton
HPM Balloqui
JM Lynas
MC Boyce
DE Ranger
CJH Richards
RH Woolrych
WJH Criddle
KF Wilson

1970(A)
PS Blomeley
DJ Cunningham
LJ Glasson
RD Guilleret
RD Harding
RJ Sandford
PRP Madge
EC Atkinson
RTN Best
P Higgins
RN Lambert
EJ Phillips
J Plunkett-Cole
DN Peterson
GE Cole

1970(B)
PAF Grant
PRS Gibbon
J Perryman
T Jocelyn
AJ Bannister
GS Davison

AR Peters
CR Chandler
T D Elliott
CH Struthers
P Branscombe
AFG Murkin
RA Self
CE Middlemiss

1971(A)
JM Collard
EJ Brown
CM Sloane
PA Marks
JS Chestnutt
MDJ Chase
DLP Evans
DR Russell
MJ Sime
DFW Sarson
JJ Game

1971(B)
JJ Curtis
WG Organ
SR Braidwood
RS Wraith
EI Taylor
HR Granlund
RG Chappell
RD Copsey
TP Picton-Phillips
JJ Howard
PR Newman
PC Morton
DW Jenkins

1972(A)
AJ Millar
RJ Fisher
CH Buckle
RMcM Gay
EH Pockley
BR Liddell
JR Turner
JW Graham
NH West
CH Donnithorne
DL Howells
DR Higham

1972(B)
RN Harm
JF Retief
RB Gardner
HJ Brimbeek

OFFICERS QUALIFIED AS
AWO(U)
1975 - 1982
1975
PJ Bendall

WJ Gardner
RW Lovegrove
RJ Quinlan

1976
Sde Halpert
K Flindell
JW Hewitt
GJ McGeown

1977
PJ Cantelo
JE Dixon
JB McLellan
PJ Melson
DMcL Sandford

JB Crawford
JG Devine
RJ Higham
BC Petley
WJ Savage

1978
RJ Cameron
WK Howat
GR Hoyle
RF Raphael
LA Willocks

MJ Clapp
TH Cox
PR Duffy
P Jordan
SE Saunders
RJ Turner

E Fitzgerald
OJ Hanley
JA Rimington
CA Ritchie

1979
BE Eddes
JG Hurlbatt
SV Mackay
SM Burrell
JD McClimont
GA Manning
JE Sharwood
DE Templeman
CMS Codner
PM Jeffrey
MP Lansdown
AB MacKinnon
DJ Richardson
PC West

1980
TD Barton
T Bell
PD Manning
AB Rowe

AGC Black
Pde Graaff
AC Gordon-Lennox
JPMcM Moodie
DA Phillips

CJ Durnford
RJ Potez
WR Philp
DR Seward

1981
PCM Baker
A MacAulay
JF Rodley
MJ Wardlam

AJ Brawn
W Johnson
JB Richardson

1981
GW Frazer
RJ Lewcock
RE Shalders
D Weller
GA Wellham

1982
SR Aiken
PM Fyfe
NR Owen
W Rathburn
RS Saxby

THV Clark
H Cullen-Jones
D Ewing
MC Smith

OFFICERS QUALIFIED AS
PWO(U)
1974 - 1986

1974
PJ Gage

1978
C Hunt

1979
RJ Bishop

1980
D Walton
G Woodbridge
1981
JW Beavis
JR Fanshawe
JD Oakey
KJ Parris
DK Fraser
ND Williams

J Welch

1982
PM Archdale
M Fewtell
N Overington
SJ Scorer

1982
CR Stone

1983
BN Basterfield
JP Bearne
RW Bell-Davis
AJ Cameron
JW Cook
NM Chambers
HN Gale
DR Goodwin
DB Habershon
MC Hill
RJ Ibbotson
AS Lawrence
RA Marshall
AR Masters
PR Nuth
RH Skelding
RJ Toms
AM Wallington-Smith
FS Ward
MR Williams
MF Bonser
HG Furness
JL McAree
JW Wells

1984
CA Armstrong
K Carter
R Foulkes
CJ Frost
SH Hambrook
TJ Laurence
DJ Lister
DL MacDonald
CP Montgomery
BJ Moxley
GG Paulus
M Rowledge
RJ Sandover
T Sharman
IC Shepherd
GM Spalton
CM Waters
NJ Youseman
K Baddams
GA Dunk
J Goldrick
M Hancock
K Johnson
R Moffitt
N Perry

M Rutherford
B McLennan

1985
MJ Allen
SJ Brown
NA Butler
SA Chandler
TC Churchill
DM Cooke
TR Harris
PJ Jennings
PR Lewis
EA McNair
MA Pilley
M J Washer
NS Westwood
SJ Cullen
DM Stevens
GC Collier

1986
PA Barber
KI Creates
RA Finnemore
NJ Hudson
JA Humphrys
NR Little
IS McKellar
MJ Pamphilon
AJ Rix
EF Seatheron
MV Sloan
G Smith
CA Snow
G Stamp
DM Swain
BH Warren
WS Westwood
W Sullivan

APPENDIX B

CAPTAINS OF *HMS VERNON*
1872-1986

J Fisher	19.9.1872	SD Tillard	1.11.1930
W Arthur	26.4.1876	AH Taylor	8.8.1932
WE Gordon	1.6.1879	RB Miles	8.8.1934
AH Markham	15.2.1883	AU Willis	6.9.1935
S Long	28.5.1886	DW Boyd	21.4.1938
AK Wilson	1.1.1889	B Egerton	30.11.1939
WH Hall	9.2.1892	HE Morse	4.6.1943
Sir BWWalker	1.11.1893	NV Grace	21.9.1944
J Durnford	12.11.1895	J Hughes-Hallett	20.6.1946
CG Robinson	2.10.1899	WJ Robertson	16.5.1948
G Le C Egerton	19.2.1902	CD Howard-Johnson	14.8.1950
HB Jackson	15.9.1904	NA Copeman	7.10.1952
CJ Briggs	24.12.1904	EA Blundell	28.12.1956
DA Gamble	10.5.1907	MC Giles	6.3.1959
RS Phipps-Hornby	16.10.1908	HL Lloyd	4.1.1961
WCM Nicoloson	1.11.1911	DH Stobie	23.4.1963
FL Field	10.9.1914	RE Lloyd	15.6.1965
HL Skipworth	16.9.1915	WP Barber	12.7.1967
FCV Wentworth	10.7.1918	TK Edge-Partington	11.4.1969
AK Waistell	14.3.1919	SMWFarquharson-Roberts	
CR Payne	6.4.1920		16.10.1970
JD Allen	6.4.1922	RS Browning	30.11.1972
WR Napier	6.7.1924	GD Trist	8.7.1974
HK Kitson	1.11.1924	EM O'Kelly	13.7.1976
NE Archdale	1.11.1926	SK Sutherland	9.8.1978
HD Bridges	1.11.1928	G Oxley	9.12.1980
		JD Husband	22.3.1983

BIBLIOGRAPHY

Note – Audiotapes, letters, memos, jottings and critiques collected during research have been lodged with the Royal Naval Museum, Portsmouth, except as indicated.

MDL - Ministry of Defence Library
SL - Submarine Museum
CCCA - Churchill College Cambridge Archives
PRO - Public Record Office
ARTS - Annual Report of the Torpedo Schools

The Early Years

The Wardroom Mess Committee of *Vernon* in 1930 entrusted to Lieutenant Commander GB Sayer (later Vice Admiral Sir Guy Sayer) the task of producing a short history of *Vernon*, from which we have based the account of the career of the frigate *Vernon*, including the declaration of her officers on paying off in March 1837. In compiling these details we have been guided by David Lyon at the National Maritime Museum.

Vernon's parent establishment was the Gunnery School, *HMS Excellent*. We have made good use of Captain J.G.Wells' 'Whaley - The Story of *HMS Excellent* 1830-1980'. For the early history of the development of underwater weapons see the many volumes on the subject in the library of the Naval Historical Department and its successor, the Ministry of Defence Library. Among the books and documents studied were:

C Martin and G Parker - The Spanish Armada
CD Colden - Life of Fulton
WS Hutcheon - Robert Fulton: Pioneer of Undersea Warfare

For other details of Fulton's career in England we referred to ADM1/580 at the PRO and to his 1810 paper 'Torpedo war, or submarine explosions' MDL.

C.Sleeman's 'Torpedoes and Torpedo Warfare' gives an excellent account of contemporary attitudes towards these weapons in the 1880s. For their use in the American Civil war we found a great deal of useful information in 'The Confederate States Navy' at the MOD Library.

For the life of J A Fisher we had access to the relevant papers held at Churchill College, Cambridge and the MOD Library. RF Mackay's 'Fisher of Kilverstone' is a very full and accurate account of Fisher's life. Marder's 'From Dreadnought to Scapa Flow' and R Higham's 'A Guide to the Sources of British Naval History' were also useful. A contemporary opinion of torpedo development in the latter part of the 19th century is in in GE Armstrong's 'Torpedoes and Torpedo Vessels (1896)' and for Robert Whitehead's early career a useful study is in E Gray's 'The Devil's Device'. The description of the trials of the first Whitehead torpedo is based on the 'Report of the Committee on Whitehead's Torpedo' dated 28 October 1870, copy in the Ministry of Defence Library. Other papers referred to were:

Fisher's - A Short Treatise on Electricity and the Management of Electric Torpedoes and the Addenda thereto. MDL ADM 116/158 163 164

The account of the rejection of the Hertz Horn is based upon ADM 1/6314 6315 and ADM 116/163. Admiral Elliot's report of the separation of *Vernon* from *Excellent* is supported by ADM1/6336.

1880 - 1914

Ministry of Defence Library - Naval Section contain many autobiographies and biographies of naval officers who served during the last part of the nineteenth and early twentieth centuries. These are an important source of information and the following were particularly valuable:

Peter Kemp - The British Sailor
Henry Baynham - Men From The Dreadnought
Eardley-Wilmot - An Admiral's Memoirs
Lewis Bailey - Memoirs
TT Jeans - Reminiscences of a Naval Surgeon
Bradford - Life of Arthur Knyvet Wilson
GHA Willis - Royal Navy as I Saw It
RGB Dewar - The Navy From Within
GE Armstrong - Torpedoes and Torpedo Vessels
The Life and Letters of Admiral Sir George Bedford
C Sleeman - Torpedoes and Torpedo Warfare
EJ March - British Destroyers
P Scott - A Cruise Round the World
R Bacon - A Naval Scrapbook From 1900 Onward
Tweedie - The Story of a Naval Life
R Tupper - Reminiscences
Bloch - The Future of War
C Ross - The Russo-Japanese War 1904-1905
D Walker - The Short Victorian War

    With the help of Ernest Bennetts we were able to analyze and cross check the information contained in these volumes before we turned to other contemporary sources among which were:

The Deck Log of HMS*Vernon* PRO
Report - Our Present Position as Regards Electric Lights for Search and Internal Lighting in HM Ships ADM.116/237
Torpedo Manuals for HM Fleet MDL
Annual Reports of the Torpedo Schools MDL
Portsmouth General Memoranda NS 4408/14430 10th November 1903
and C in C No,550 MDL

    Newspapers and magazines were another important source:

The Times
Portsmouth Evening News
The Navy and Army Illustrated
Illustrated London News

    The dramatic technological advances caused great changes in the shape and size of navies and consequently in strategy and tactics. The following books and documents are among those studied:

R Bacon - Notes on the Causes of Accidents to
Submarine Boats and Their Salvage
The Battleship of the Future
Our Effete Parliament MDL
R Keyes - Naval Memoirs
WS Chalmers - Life and Letters of David Beatty
The Gun, Ram and Torpedo - Naval Prize Essays 1874
P Bethell - The Development of the Torpedo
JA Fisher - Invasion and Submarines CCCA
H M Williamson - Note on the Use of Submarines CCCA

    Captain WDS (Knocker) White's analysis of Marder's From the Dreadnought to Scapa Flow and many other references has been invaluable. Of the more modern publications Vice Admiral Sir Arthur Hezlet's The Electron and Sea Power, Gray's Devil's Device and Conway's All the World's Fighting Ships 1860-1905, are no less invaluable. Most notable of the private contributions have been the copious notes on living conditions supplied by Chief Petty Officer Joe Davies, and Captain Gde Courcy Ireland's account of the activities of his grandfather, Captain Harry Jones, when a Lieutenant commanding Torpedo Boat 58 during the Annual Manoeuvres 1888.

The Great War - 1914-1918

The Annual Reports of the Torpedo Schools for the years 1913-1919 are the main source of information about the activities of the Torpedo Branch during World War I. A great deal has been written about the campaigns and battles of the war, but here it has been considered from the specialist's perspective of the Torpedo Branch. Among the published sources of information were:

Jellicoe - The Grand Fleet 1914-1916
The crisis of the Naval War
WS Chalmers - The Life and Letters of David Beatty
AB Cunningham - A Sailor's Odyssey
HW Fawcett & GWW Hooper - The Fighting at Jutland
L Thomas - Raiders of the Deep
RF Mackay - Fisher of Kilverstone
W Hackmann - Seek and Strike
R Keyes - Naval Memoirs
A Marder - Dreadnought to Scapa Flow
JS Cowie - Mines, Minelayers and Mine Laying
R Bacon - From 1900 Onwards

The Ministry of Defence Library and the Churchill College, Cambridge Archives hold many documents associated with the rapid development of the Naval Staff structure during the war:

Naval Staff Monograph (Historical)   MDL
Admiralty Office Memo 563 dated 16th December 1916 (duties of Anti-Submarine Division)   MDL
OU 5031 - Notes on Staff Work at Naval Bases September 1918   MDL

Developments in torpedoes and torpedo control are very fully covered in the ARTS, which include a complete analysis of torpedo firing at Jutland. The following documents have also been used:-

GJ Kirby - A History of the Torpedo
P Bethell - The development of the Torpedo
R Corlett - British Torpedo development: past present and future MDL
Drax - Memo on Torpedo Control in Light Cruisers 27 Aug 1915 CCCA
Drax - *Vernon* Whitehead Dept (Commander.M.Bellairs) Correspondence re-Long Range Torpedoes 18 July 1916 CCCA

Similarly the progress in mine warfare outlined in ARTS is supplemented by a wide range of documents, all available at the Ministry of Defence Library:

AL Gwynne - The Submarine Mine
Lockhart-Leith - The History of British Minefields
Vicker's Ltd - The Protection of Merchant Ships against Moored Mines
Burney Paravanes (handbook) 1917
OU 6292/37 - Handbook of Minelaying Equipment and Mining Accessories
OU 6333 - Mining Operations of German Submarines Around British Isles 1915-1918
AM Low - Mine and Countermine 1940
A Patterson - A Brief History of Mine Warfare
Jb 06 - Paravanes, submarine and minesweeps etc (a bound collection 1914-1918 official handbooks)
CB 1550 - Report of Dardenelles Committee 1919

Rear Admiral Alan Poland provided an oral account of the minelaying activities of the E Class submarines.

Details concerning anti-submarine developments were obtained from the following documents:

Anti-Submarine Division Naval Staff - Technical History of the Navy Dec 1916 - Dec 1918 (TH7)MDL

Anti-Submarine Development and Experiments Prior to Dec 1916 (TH40) MDL

Drax - Menace of Enemy Submarines No.329/BCF 013 25th June 1915 CCCA

Summary of Anti-Submarine Trials with a Kite Balloon 15th October 1915 CCCA

Counter Attack against Enemy Submarines

Prize Essays BCF No 013 10th May 1915 CCCA

Summary of Essays June 1915 CCCA

Memo on Anti-Submarine Nets 3rd Nov 1914 CCCA

Action Required to Deal Effectively with the Submarine Menace 4th December 1914 CCCA

Beatty to Jellicoe re Submarines BCF 013 20th Nov 1916 CCCA

Fisher - Memo on Airships and Zeppelins 1st May 1916 CCCA

H Jackson to A Limpus - Correspondence on submarine threat in Mediterranean CCCA

Southern Patrol Force - Flotilla Hydrophone Office 29.8.18 Instructions for putting fish outboard and taking same inboard

Southern Patrol Force - Memo No.3 Care and Maintenance of Fish Hydrophones

Southern Patrol Force - Memo No.5 Instructions for Hydrophone Officers

Lieut Commander Ross Turner - Submarine experiences SM

The raid on Zeebrugge is well documented in the Keyes Memoirs but a new insight is provided by experiences of James Nathaniel Short, Gunner (T), who died at the great age of 96, in a letter from his son Peter N.Short.

The Cocktail Years

ARTS continue to be the main source of information. Histories of *Vernon* leave the impression that little of importance occurred during this period but it was a time during which some of the senior officers of World War II were obtaining experience as Torpedo Officers ashore and afloat, while their subordinates were still at school. Memories of that era have influenced the writing of this volume especially in considering the battleship mentality which predominated at sea and in the training establishments whenever tactics and strategy were being discussed; this is well described by M.Williams in his biography of Captain Gilbert Roberts.

Conditions in the old hulks which formed *Vernon* in 1919-1923, their disposal and details of the move to the Gunwharf are the subjects of a number of interviews and written notes:

West, Petty Officer Steward - Audiotaped interview

DD MacFarlan, Lieut Commander - *Vernon* as I saw it

D Parry, Mrs - Memories of *Vernon* afloat

G Sayer, Lieut Commander - A History of HMS*Vernon*

JL Rowsell, Mr - Letter dated 6th Nov 1986. Details of career of HJ Rowsell, Petty Officer Torpedo Instructor 1883 - 1919

AA Sewell, Ldg Seaman LTO - Letters headed *Vernon* Semper Viret Sept 1984

A Wheeler, Mr - Letter re-loss of grandfather Fred Wheeler in *Marlborough* Essex Chronicle dated 5th Dec 1924 - Loss of *Marlborough*

J Davis, Chief Petty Officer - Memoirs

The activities of the *Vernon* Flotilla are taken from ships' logs and the account of the career of Rear Admiral OWPhillips (Imperial War Museum). Torpedo developments are reported in detail in ARTS. Further commentary is available in the works of Bethell, Kirby and Corlett. An Atlantic Fleet Report N0.887/AH 44 of 26 September 1919, entitled 'Torpedo Attack by Aeroplanes on HM Ships at Portland', is an important archive. Notes by Captain RC Lewis have also been helpful. Similarly ARTS coverage of mines and minesweeping is comprehensive and this era is also commented upon by Captain JS Cowie in his 'Mines, Minelayers and Minelaying'. In like fashion ARTS reports on the developments in Anti-Submarine Warfare have been augmented by a very full account of his activities by Lieut DM Frost, who also gives a description of the living conditions at the Gun Wharf in the years 1918 to 1923. For 1926 General Strike see Army, Navy and Air Force Gazette Emergency Issue Saturday, May 15, 1926.

From Peace to War 1931 - 39

From 1930 to 1950, Webb's History of *Vernon* becomes an important source and supplements ARTS. In this period what occurred remained strongly in the memories of many of those concerned with the preperation of the book. In many instances the opinions and anecdotes were related directly. This applies to the account of the part played by torpedomen at the Invergordon Mutiny in 1930, a subject recorded in writing and on audiotape by Captain RC Lewis.

In several letters and on audiotape Captain RGBO'N Roe provided an important and fresh perspective on electrical developments during this period. Much assistance was given by the technical library at HMS*Collingwood* and upon Maber's 'Electrical Supply in Warships'is singularly useful. Information about the practical aspect of the working torpedoman came from Captains J Hext Lewes and Captain RC Lewis in their audiotaped interviews.

Details of the daily routine at *Vernon* and of the Silver Jubilee and Coronation Review proceedings are recorded very fully by Webb and in a letter from WG Burbage who served as an Able Seaman in *Vernon* in 1932 and 1933. The despatch of indicator loops and harbour defence asdics to Alexandria during the Abyssinia War is recorded in ARTS and by Webb, as are details of the arrival of MTBs at *Vernon*. Captain HL ('Harpy') Lloyd served in one of these craft and was able to provide information. The part played by Rear Admiral OW Phillips is taken from the account of his career in the Imperial War Museum, where there are also records of service of Admiral Sir William Andrewes.

Webb, Cowie and ARTS were the main sources of information regarding mines and minesweeping. Torpedo developments are based upon the Hext Lewes audiotape, ARTS, Bethell, Kirby, Corlett and the memoirs of J Davis.

Events during the Munich Crisis of 1938 and mobilisation in 1939 are well documented by Webb and recounted in the Hext Lewes audiotape. He also refers to the formation of the *Vernon* Auxiliary Company, but for this subject I was supplied with a very full account provided by JF Glanville. Lieutenant Commander DD MacFarlan and Lieutenant Commander RSC Robinson provided important information and guidance. Useful information on anti-submarine developments up to 1938 is contained in *Vernon* Pamphlet No.123 dated 30 January 1942.

The Second World War 1939 - 1945

Recording the Second World war as seen from the perspective of members of the Torpedo Branch involved studying of a very large number of published works, and the examinination of the personal experiences and opinions of officers, scientists and ratings recorded on audiotapes, in letters, memos, jottings, accounts and critiques. Also studied were official documents, unpublished manuscripts and press and magazine articles. As usual in this project, ARTS were a major source, as were Bethell, Kirby, and Corlett. Among the most important sources were:
Books –
R Baker - The Terror of Tobermory

R Baxter - Stand by to Surface
C Bekker - Hitler's Navy
RS Blue - United and Undaunted The Naval Historical Society of Australia
BJ Bryant - One Man Band
J Campbell - Naval Weapons of World War Two
J Carey - The Faber Book of Reportage
W Churchill - The Second World War
R Compton-Hall - Submarine Boats - The Underwater War 1939-1945
GG Connell - Mediterranean Maelstrom
B Cooper - The Battle of the Torpedo Boats
J Costello & T Hughes - The Battle of the Atlantic
JS Cowie - Mines, Minelayers and Minelaying
J Crane - Submarine
AB Cunningham - A Sailor's Odyssey
Karl Doenitz - Admiral Doenitz Memoirs
PGretton - Maritime Strategy - Convoy Escort Commander
WHackmann - Seek and Strike
JR Hill - Anti-Submarine Warfare
G Jones - Submarines versus U-boats
J Keegan - The Second World War
L Kennedy - Sub-Lieutenant
FW Lipscombe - The British Submarine
P Lund & H Ludlaw - Out Sweeps
D Macintyre - The Naval War Against Hitler - The Battle of the Atlantic
Official Account - The Battle of the Atlantic
J Rohwer - The Critical Convoy Battles - Axis Submarine Successes 1939-1945
SW Roskill - The War at Sea
B Schofield - The Russian Convoys - The Attack on Taranto
J Toland - Adolf Hitler
JF Turner - Service Most Silent
T Waldron & J Gleeson - The Frogmen
CET Warren & J Benson - Above Us the Waves
DEG Wemyss - Relentless Pursuit
M Williams - Captain Gilbert Roberts RN
J Winton - Sink the *Haguro*
Audiotapes –
P Bathhurst, Lieut: RNVR - Edinburgh PO Box 10 and Falmouth Pressure Mine Range
JR Blake, Commander - *Vernon* 1940 and 1944.
WA Dallmeyer, Captain - *Vernon* 1939-40. Destroyer *Harvester*. Boyd. A/S Weapons.
Electrical Responsibilities
TF Gaskell, Doctor - Bullard & Acoustic Sweep. Ahead Thrown Weapons. Edinburgh
PO Box 10. Foxer. Egg Crate. Homing Torpedoes. Influence & Beach Mines. Mining
River Estuaries.
Goodeve Glen, Sir Alexander - The Mining of the Danube
G Hodges, Lieut Commander RNVR - Rendering Mines Safe
SC Kaye, Chief Petty Officer - Submarine Experiences
JH Lewes, Captain - *Vernon* Auxiliary Company. Boyd. Degaussing and related
developments. Bullard. South Africa. Ceylon. Carrier *Ameer*. DTASW
RC Lewis, Captain - Mine Warfare, Torpedoes, Mediterranean and Boyd.
HL Lloyd, Captain - Boyd and MTBs.
Anne Lytle, Mrs - Admiral Boyd's daughter, for unpublished biography.
MC Morgan-Giles, Rear Admiral Sir - Cruisers *Emerald* & *Arethusa*. Mine Warfare

including R Mines and Wellington Bomber Minesweepers at Suez. *Hipper* Attacks Convoy. Operation Lucid. Italian Frogmen at Alexandria. Raid on Bari. Coastal Forces in Adriatic. Bernard Rawlings

JGD Ouvry, Commander - Mine Warfare particularly Rendering Mines Safe and Investigation

RGBO'N Roe, Captain - Shipborne Electrical Systems

P Ward, Senior Principal Scientific Officer - Anti-Submarine Weapons.

Letters, Sketches, Anecdotes –

ML Aspinall, Mr - Letter 11.4.85 Anti-Submarine Training and Sinking of *U135*

P Bathurst, Lieut: RNVR - Letter 30.9.88. Note by White. Edinburgh PO Box 10. Falmouth. Audio tape

JR Blake, Commander - Note by White. Audiotape

DD Bourdice, Electrical Artificer - Letter 9.9.84.*Vernon* 1942

G Britton, Mr - Signalman in submarines, experiences

P Buckley, Mrs - Letter 25.3.86. WRNS *Vernon*. Lieut Commander R Buckley's wife

PD Budge, Rear Admiral RCN - Letters 29.9.85, 22.11.85 Career 'The Royal Navy Years'.

RGM Collins,Commander - Letter 12.11.85. *Vernon* Mine Sweeping. Edinburgh PO Box 10

WA Dallmeyer, Captain - Note by White. Audiotape

J Davies, Chief Petty Officer - Letters and Memoirs 14.9.84

JPT Dawson, Captain RCN - Letter 20.12.84 *Vernon*(R)

SN Devlin, Lieut: Commander - Submarine Experiences

J Dickson, Lieut: RNVR - Letter 15.4.85. *Vernon* Auxiliary Company

RC Didham, Lieut: Commander - *Vernon* Whitehead Department and Torpedo Tubes

V Donaldson, Rear Admiral - Letters 29.12.86, 27.4.87 22.4.88, 28.4.88. Career. *Bismarck*

DB Ellison, Author - Letters 21.10.86. 1.11.86. 19.8.87. Ellison's Editions

WB Filer, Lieut: Commander - Letter 7.11.88. Career as Diver. Frogmen Gibraltar Alexandria

E France, Mr - Letters 7.5.88, 8.5.88, 12,11,85. Career in submarines *Trident* and *Trident*

TF Gaskell, Doctor - Letter and Notes 25.9.88. Acoustic Sweep. Edinburgh PO Box 10. Channel Tunnel. Audiotape.

JF Glanville, Lieut: RNVR - Letter and Details of *Vernon* Auxiliary Company

F Goldsworthy, Lieut: RNVR - Letters 1.6.90, 10.6.90 17.8.90. Mine disposal and harbour clearance.

GAJ Goodhart, Lieut: Commander - *Vernon* Random Comments

EW Goodman, Captain - Notes on Degaussing. Divisional Course. Dunkirk 27.5.85

AS Gower, Mr - Experiences as Torpedoman in 'S' Class Submarines

GR Grocock, Commander - Letters and comments 21.9.84, 4.12.84. Anti-Submarine Weapons. Service with the 'Terror of Tobermory'.

G Gutteridge, Commander - Letter 2.4.89. Harbour N.Africa. 'P' Parties.

GA Hodges, Lieut Commander RNVR - Draft autobiography and other papers on Rendering Mines Safe Audiotape

JLM Joly, Lieut: Commander - Letter 1.2.86 Edinburgh PO Box 10

G Jones, Lieut Commander RNR - Letter and Experiences as a Degaussing Officer

I Jones, Lieut: Commander RCN - Letter and Account of 'Blitz' at *Vernon*

SC Kaye, Chief Petty Officer - Note by White 15.5.88 and letter 4.5.88. Audiotape

EGPB Knapton, Commander - Letters 9.2.86. 19.8.83. Short History of *Defiance*

B Legg, Lieut: Commander - *Collingwood* Details of CCR Pistol

JH Lewes, Captain - Letters 24.5.84. 13.8.84 and Notes on Degaussing. Audiotape
RC Lewis, Captain - See Special File of Memos and Experiences. Note by White 20.8.84.
Audiotape
EW Linton, Commander RAN - Letter 18.5.86 and 'Diving in the Royal Australian Navy.
HL Lloyd, Captain - See Special File of Memos, Letters and Experiences
EPJ Lunch, Lieut: Commander RNR - Letter 7.5.88. Some Memoirs of a Torpedo Officer
M McAloon, Mr - Letter 18.9.87. Advice on Gnat Torpedo
DD MacFarlan, Lieut:Commander - Special File of Memos, Letters and Experiences
IL M.McGeoch, Vice Admiral Sir - Letters 1.5.89,12.5.89 16.12.89, 28.3.90. 9.4.90. Advice on Submarine Warfare
WY McLanachan, Commander - Letter 8.10.84 and Memoirs
KS Main, Commander - Letters 1.10.84. 19.3.85. 19.9.88 Edinburgh PO Box 10
TJG Marchant, Commander - Letter 21.2.90. Note by White and 'Battle of Barents Sea'
MC Morgan-Giles, Rear Admiral Sir - Special File of Letters, Memos and Experiences
CF Mortimer, Mr - Obituary. Ship Equipment Division Portsmouth Dockyard
AFG Murkin, Lieut: Commander - Letter 7.11.84. WRNS at *Vernon(R)*
H Murray, Mr - Letter 24.4.85. "P"Party Techniques.
Press Cuttings. NP1571 Listed
PLK Needham, Commander - Letter 29.11.89. Scuttling of *Courbet*. Demolition at Penang
HM Newcomb, Captain RAN - Australian Anti-Submarine Warfare
JGD Ouvry, Commander - Letters 31.5.84. 16.9.84. Rendering Mines Safe Listed. Audiotape
EJ Palfreyman, Mr - Letter 26.9.84. Rendering Mines Safe. List of seven names
D Parry, Mrs - Letter 22.8.84. *Vernon* Afloat Parties
Postcard of hulks –
S Paton, Captain Sir - Obituary. Captain *Vernon* 1940
JP Perkins, Lieut: RNVR - Letters 13.11.89. 1.12.89. Controlled Mining. MTBs
CTM Pizey, Admiral Sir - Notes on interview by White
DB Reaper, Captain SAN - SAN-*Vernon* Connection
LC Reynolds, Lieut: RNVR - Letter 31.10.89. Note on MTBs in the Mediterranean
RGBO'N Roe, Captain - Letters 15.11.86. 26.11.86. 9.1.87. Electrics. Audiotape
J Rohwer, Doctor - Letter 29.6.87. German Mine Warfare
JL Rowsell, Mr - Letter 6.11.86. Career of grandfather. Torpedoman, survivor from *Barham*
D Spinney, Mr - Letter 9.10.84. Tibbets at St Nazaire
DMH Stobie, Captain - 1939-1945 War Experiences
KS Sutherland, Mr - Letter 10.7.86. Australian Anti-Submarine Warfare
H Walker, Lieut: Commander - Letter 15.10.84. Demolitions Antwerp 1940 and other War Experiences.
D Wallace, Doctor (Lieut:RNVR) - Letters 2.3.85. 14.4.85. *Vernon(D)*. MFV 1034. Chariots
P A Watson, Vice Admiral Sir - Letters 7.8.89. 20.12.89 19.3.90. Need for Electrical Branch
TS Weston, Commander - Letters 19.12.89. 15.1.90. Advice on Submarine Warfare
WDS White, Captain - Special file of Memos, letters, and Experiences.
AJW Wilson, Commander - Special file of Memos and Letters
R Wilson, Captain RAN - Letter 14.8.86. Australian Anti-Submarine Warfare
Miscellaneous Documents –

Vernon Reports - Weapons and Sensors
- German Sea-Mining During Second World War
- HMS*Vernon*'s Mine Recovery Drifters at Dunkirk 28May-1 June 1940 Signed RS Armitage Lieut: Commander
- General Instructions on the Handling and Testing of the CCR Pistol *Vernon*(M)No.X.30(2)/8/55 of 2.6.55 History of the Mining Department 1939-1945 *Vernon* Pamphlet No.202 - 1953 The Airblast Gyroscope for Mark 8** and Mark 9** Torpedoes
Admiralty - Anti-Submarine Reports 1939-1945 - MDL
- Naval Staff History of World War II - MDL
- AFO 228/49 THe Passage of the *Scharnhorst,Gneisenau* and *Prinz Eugen* through the English Channel 12th February 1942 - MDL
- Technical History of Anti-Submarine Weapons - MDL
- Chief of Naval Information's 'Charge of the Old Brigade'. The Destroyer Attack on German Heavy Ships 12.2.42
- Battle Summary No11, 1948. *Scharnhorst,Gneisenau* and *Prinz Eugen*, Passage Through English Channel, 11-12 February 1942
RUSI Journal 1943 - Captain MH Eveleigh, Lecture on Mine Warfare 2.12.42 - MDL
P Harrison,Mrs - Reminiscences of a Torpedo Wren 1942-44 - SM
GE Hunt, Captain - Report of Submarine Operations in the Mediterranean - SM
M Todd, Lieut: Commander - Account of Submarine Torpedo Accidents in Submarines - SM
Naval Message 0030A/14/2/42 C in C Nore to D21 Channel Dash of German Heavy Ships
F Goldsworthy, Author - Draft Manuscript 'They Swam Against a Fleet'
RGBO'N Roe, Captain - HMS*Vernon* Electrical Department
IL M.McGeoch, Vice Admiral Sir - 'The Offensive Value of the Modern Submarine' by 'Salvo'
WDS White, Captain - The Torpedo in World War Two
1946-1970
The end of electrical responsibilities for the Torpedo Branch and the establishment of the Torpedo Anti-Submarine Branch are well within the memory of officers and ratings living while this project proceeded and are therefore well documented. Especially important were Captain GC Blundell's extensive notes and anecdotes describing his time as Captain Hughes-Hallett's Commander, Commander PD Sturdee as the only Anti-Submarine specialist on the staff at *Vernon*, and Webb's 'HMS*Vernon* 1930-1955'. Several very senior members of the lower deck contributed their attitude towards the amalgamation of the Torpedo and Anti-Submarine Branches, particularly Chief Petty Officers J Davies, PR Fair, R Feasey, C Hayman, RV Jackson and S McCombe. Their contributions have been filed with the Project papers.
        The tortuous story of torpedo development between 1945 and 1970 has been described by Kirby, Corlett and in articles in defence journals listed at the Ministry of Defence Library. Of great interest have been the opinions of Captains RC Lewis, EA Blundell and GO Symonds who were in charge of the Torpedo Experimental Establishment at Greenock.
        Of all the TAS responsibilities, mine warfare has been the most extensively reported and leading experts in mine hunting, mine clearance and diving have made important contributions, among them were Commanders G Gutteridge and PA Balink White and Lieutenant Commanders SA Warner, WB Filer, GA Franklin, M Terrell and J Rea. The long statements by Gordon Gutteridge and Bill Filer are important contributions. All these officers included coverage of the 'Crabb Affair'

as did Mr R Hartley who served as a UW rating in the Mining Trials section at *Vernon*. The Ministry of Defence Library has supplied a large number of articles on mine warfare taken from defence journals. Commander P Needham was consulted on mine defence in the Persian Gulf and Commander SA Warner advised on the use of *Vernon*'s divers in the exploration of the North Sea. The Naval Historical Society of Australia's 'United and Undaunted' was of considerable interest and Lieutenant DM Frost provided valuable information about his time as a member of the Royal Naval Scientific Service in minesweeping trials 1953-1965.

Arguably, after 1945, anti-submarine warfare became the most important responsibility of the TAS Branch. With the advent of the true submarine, it began to dominate tactical and strategic considerations in the 'Cold War'. Nearly all the members of the *Vernon* History Project team were TAS specialists and much that has been written is an expression of their experiences and opinions. To this must be added the vast amount of advice and guidance given by several Captains of *Vernon* and other TAS Specialists. Peter Ward provided extensive coverage of the development of Ikara (audiotape). The author's participation in submarine and helicopter asdic (sonar) trials and the development of sonobuoys was particularly fotunate. Captain RS Browning's part as trials officer and air crew in the Dipping Asdic trials meant unique coverage of this significant advance in anti-submarine warfare. W.Hackmann's 'Seek and Strike' was also a valuable source of information. *Anecdotal, political and domestic matters are based upon statements by the following:*
JE Adams - Career from Ordinary Seaman to Fleet Chief Petty Officer
JR Blake - Commander *Vernon* 1960-1963
EA Blundell - Captain *Vernon* 1956-1959
RS Browning - Captain *Vernon* 1972-1974
HJ Clapson - Commander, Engineer Officer *Vernon* 1961
J Davies - Chief Petty Officer Post War Memoirs
RJ Davies - Commander *Vernon* 1970-1972
TK Edge-Partington - Captain *Vernon* 1969-1970
CE Emerson - Commander *Vernon* 1954-1956
WEB Godsal - Captain *Vernon* 1966-1968
GAJ Goodhart - Lieut:Commander First Lieutenant*Vernon* 1948-1950
J Grant - Rear Admiral Commander *Vernon* 1948-1950 Captain *Vernon* 1954-1956
HL Lloyd - Captain *Vernon* 1961-1963
R Macdonald - Vice Admiral Sir Roderick Opinion on officer specialist branches
DD MacFarlan - Lieut:Commander Officers' Records and *Vernon* History
RW Mayo - Rear Admiral Captain OSPREY 1956-1958 Commander Training/Trials *Vernon* 1952-1953 'Way Ahead Committee'
GJ McGeown - Lieut:Commander Naval Staff Author (ASW) *Dryad*
MC Morgan-Giles - Rear Admiral Sir Captain *Vernon* 1958-1960
DG Sherrard - Lieut:Commander *Vernon* Flotilla 1953
DMH Stobie - Captain *Vernon* 1963-1965
PD Sturdee - Anti-Submarine specialist at *Vernon*
1970-1986
The last sixteen years of the life of *Vernon* saw a quantum leap in technology, the end of the TAS Branch, rationalisation and the centralisation of naval training at *Dryad*. It was considered that this final part of the book should be entrusted to a senior serving officer able to obtain the backing of the Navy Department and *Dryad*, and we were fortunate to be able to persuade Rear Admiral GF Liardet, Commandant of the Joint Service Defence College, to undertake this difficult task. His 'Envoi' is a masterpiece which stands as an important archive.

INDEX

Baird, Vice Admiral JKE 46
Baker, Lieutenant S 179
Baldwin, Chief Petty Officer CE 137 138 151 152
  128 133 134
Bangor class 182 192
Barratt, Captain 130 131
Barrington, Commissioned Boatswain W D 342
Basilisk 248
Bateman, Rear Admiral S L 290
Bathurst, Lieutenant Peter 184 191 196
Battenburg, Prince Louis 45
Batterham, Lieutenant M RANVR 208
Bayern 81
Beachampton 333
Beagle class 50 65
Beatty, Admiral of the Fleet Viscount 68 80 81 86
Beaufort, aircraft 221
Beitzen 237
Belfast 130 241 275 278 280 283
Bellerophon 51
Bennett Commander H R 171
Bennett, Lieutenant O P J 267
Berlin 70
Bernhard, Prince 117
Berwick 103
Best, Chief Petty Officer 173
Bethell, Commander Peter 78
Biarritz 75 77
Biber one man submarine 202
Bicester 363
Bickford, Commander 216
Bingley, Admiral Sir Alexander 331 336
Bismarck 236 237
Biter 232
Blacburn aircraft, company 314
Blake, Commander JR 324
Blake, of Ratsey and Lapthorne sail-makers 123
Blanche 129
Blanco Encalada 41
Bligh, Lieutenant Commander T 245
Bliss, company 58
Blundell, Captain GC 293 295 297 298 299 301 304
  307
Blundell, Captain EA 334
Bodenham 329
Bollard, Petty Officer W 342 357
Bolzano 211
Bonnell, Lieutenant CE RCN 244
Boobier, Able Seaman 128
Booms 50 51
Borde 143 144 223
Bose, Professor Jagadis Chunder 52
Bossington 313 333 360 363
Bouvet 73
Bowden, Lieutenant 186
Bowles, Commander 131 132
Boyd, Admiral Sir Denis 115 122-124 129 138 139
  236 249
Boys, Captain Henry 21 25
Bradley, Mr 159
Bramble 237 239
Brandreth, Captain Thomas 25
Brecon 360 362 363

Brenchley 312 313
Breslau 79
Bridge, Lieutenant J 201
Bridgeton 363
Briggs Motor Bodies, company 236
Brigham 329
Brilliant 373
Brinkley 312 313
Brinton 363
Bristol 322
Britannia 45
British Crown 30
British Power Boat, company 113 114 244
Broadsword 370
Brocklesby 320 325 362 363
Brotherhood, radial engines 40
Brown, Chief Petty Officer 'Seaweed' 306
Brown, ED 13
Brown, John ship builders 238
Browning, Captain RS 324 340 368
Buccaneer, aircraft 358 359
Buckley, Lieutenant Commander R 233
Budge, Rear Admiral Patrick RCN 95
Bulganin, Mr 352
Bull Captain JA 119
Bull, Lieutenant JRH 263
Bullard, Professor Sir Edward 139 140 141 178 180
  186
Bullin, JV 124
Buller General Sir Redress 32
Bullivant, company 49
Burfield, Lieutenant John 234
Burgess, Commander FW 324
Buriton, HMS*Mirtle* 157 158 179
Burnett, Vice Admiral Sir RL 237 239
Burney, Lieutenant Denis 70
Burns, Dr 313 314
Bushnell, David 10
Butlin, Sir Billy 140
BYMS 312
Bystander 166 167

Cachalot 217
Caio Duilio 236
Cairo 12
Calcutta 11 22
Caldwell, Lieutenant Commander FB 173 174
Caledonia 365
Callieu, Lieutenant Commander 194
Calypso 47
Cambridge 12 38
Cameron, Lieutenant Commander C 303
Cameron, Lieutenant Commander John (later
  Lord Cameron) 127 128 129 146
Cammell Laird, ship builders 105 106
Campbell 246
Campbeltown 187
Campeador V 156
Camperdown 32 47
Canberra 103
Canty, Lieutenant Commander John 165 307 308
  378
Cape Spartel 129

Magnetic Mk I-II 115 128 142
Electric AA 146 147
Double L (LL Sweep) 147 148 149 183 188
192 209
Skid 142
Acoustic 180 181 188 192 209
WS MK 9 374
Magnetic loop 312
WIP 189
The Flying Wedding Ring 145 183
Drachen 190
Cyrus/Cybele 191 192
Egg-crate 191 192
Pressure waves 192
Borde and Corburn 143 144 223
Mine hunting 155 156 193 194 310 311 312
Mines - German
A104 190
AD104(APMkI) 193
A105 (firing mechanism) 198
Carbonit 73
Classification by *Vernon* 182-183
EMC(GY) and EMD(GX) 128
EMD antenna (X) 161
LMA and LMB 178 179
Oyster (Pressure) 192 193
TMB(S) 154
Types C-G 155 156 160-163 180 190 207 356
UMA(G2) 128
Mine-Russian M-08 363
Mirtle 157
Miscellaneous Weapon Development 252
Mitre, operation 242
MMS(1) and(2) 311
MMS51 114
Modeste 304 329
Monarch 45
Monkton 333
Montcalm 329
Montclare 318
Morgan-Giles, Rear Admiral Sir Morgan 184 202
234
Morris, Lieutenant 156
Morse, Captain HE 232
Mosquito, aircraft 224
Motor Amti-Submarine Boat 114
Motor Gunboats 244 246
Motor Torpedo Boats 112 113 146 165 170 193 226
228 230 243 245
Mould, Lieutenant Commander JS RANVR 199
200 349
Mountbatten, Admiral of the Fleet Lord 346
Mounts Bay 323
Muir, Surgeon Rear Admiral JR 156
Mulberry harbour 212
Musketeer, operation 313
Musketeer 241

Naiad 60 75
Napier Committee 98
Napier, Rear Admiral WR 98
Nasmith, Commander Martin Dunbar 68
Nautilus 320

Navigator 84
Needham, Commander PLR 210-212
Nelson 102 103 108 144 228 280
Nelson (Excellent) 365
Neptune 47
Neptunia 264 265
Nets, anti-torpedo 49 50 84 85
Nightingale 329 330
Norfolk 241
Nusret 73

Obbard, Commander EO 152 162 163
Obdurate 237 238
Obedient 237 239
Oberon class 319
Oberon 17 18
Obry, Ludwig 42
Ocean Gem 237
Ocean 21 73 74
Oceania 264 265
Odell, Leading Seaman J 324
Oil Endeavour 363
Oil, North Sea 362 363
Oliver-Bellasis, Commander R 142 176 182
Olympic 70
Onslaught 82
Onslow 237-241
Opportune 241
Ordzhonikidze 352 353 355
Oribi 237 240
Orvieto 75 77
Orwell 237 238
Osprey 98 100 180 248 252 299 301 305 323 324 331
Ottley Committee 59 60 61
Ottley, Captain Charles 59
Ouvry, Commander John 89 127 128 131-136 139
143 150 152 154 155 157 158 163 178 346
Overlord, operation 226

P parties, 203-209 212 341
P34 submarine 267
Pacific Pioneer 208
Packard engines 244
Paget, Vice Admiral Lord Clarence 13
Pallas 27
Pandora 105
Panzer Taucherat 342
Paravanes, trials 70
Paris 75
Park, Commander RF 315
Parker, Lieutenant GJ 21
Parkinson, Commander R 242 345
Parkinson, Professor 336
Parry, Lieutenant C 373
Pascoe, Captain H 92
Paton, Captain SH 164 172
Payne, Sub Lieutenant 141
Peard, Commander KHT 175
Pearson, Ramsay 364
Pelican 281
Pembroke 75
Penelope 210
Perdita 77

410

Samsonia 192
San Luis 373
San Juan Baptiste 348
Sandfly 44 78
Sandford, Lieutenant Francis 73 76
Santa Fe 372
Sapphire 74
Sarepta 83 98
Saumarez 241 242 243
Savage, Chief Petty Officer 186
Savage 241
Sayer, Lady 113
Sayer, Vice Admiral Sir Guy 113 127 128 137 146 316
Scharnhorst 222 241 245
Schwartzkopff torpedo 40
Schwartzkopff, Louis 40
Scorpion 241 320
Scotia 169
Scott, Lieutenant Commander Sir Peter 245
Scott-Paine, Hubert 112
Scourge 38
Scout 43
Scythia 281
Sea Harrier, aircraft 373
Sea King, helicopter 373
Seaforth Clansman 362
Seahorse 44
Seal 216 217
Sealion 253
Searchlights 37 96 258
Seawolf 269
Seraph 350
Servitor 149
Settle, Warrant Officer, Terry 363
Severn 263
Sewell, Leading Seaman AA 93 94
Shackleton, aircraft 316
Shah 28 29 33
Shandon, Admiralty Experimental Establishment 98
Shark, torpedo bomber 119
Sharpshooter 47
Shaw, Captain TWB 324
Shaw, Mr 137
Sheffield 236 237 241
Shelford, Commander WO 199 341
Shepperton 214
Sheraton 313 329 332 360
Sherbrooke, Captain R St V 237 238 239 241
Sherrard, Lieutenant Commander DG 333
Shikari 138
Short 31 seaplane 86
Short, Lieutenant Commander JN 84
Shoulton 313
Sickle 267
Sidon 314
Siebe Gorman, company 199 341
Signals Branch, formation 62 69 97
Sikh 237
Sikorsky S-55, helicopter 324
Silley, Mrs 207
Silver Dawn 166 169

Simmons, F 92
Simpson, Captain RMO 29688
Simpson, Rear Admiral GWG 256 264 315
Singer, Captain Morgan 17 22
Sir Sydney 155
Sir Echo 194
Sir Galahad 375
Sivius 371
Skua, aircraft 248
Skylark 116
Sladen, Commander Geoffrey 199
Slater, gunner (T) RCN 174 175
Sleeman, naval commentator 243
Slessor, Air Chief Marshall Sir John 225
Smeeton, Vice Admiral Sir Richard 323
Smith, BS scientist 321
Smith, Sir Charles 201
Smotryaschy 352
Smuts, Field Marshall JC 213
Snepp, Lieutenant Commander HE 105
Sonar:-
    AQS4 324
    Type 177 321 322
    184 319 321 332
    192 325
    194 322
    199   325
    2001 319 370
    2007 370
    2016 370
    2020 370
    2023 371
    2024 371
    2031 371
    2031(I) 371
    2031(Z) 371
    2046 371
    Towed array 371
Southampton 101 278
Southern Prince 218
Sovershenny 352
Spartan 289
Speedy 48
Spends, Mr 232
Sperrbrechers 223
Spider 44 47
Spiers, Lieutenant Commander DW 160 161 162 163
Squalus 350
St Vincent, Admiral Lord 11 46
St Nazaire, raid 187-188
St Vincent 165 292
Stalker 338
Stanning, Captain GH 233
Starfish 66
Steam Gunboats 193
Stebbings, Cecil 92
Stebbings, James 92
Steiner, Rear Admiral OHM ST J 332
Stena Seaspread 375
Step aside manoeuvre 197
Stephenson, Vice Admiral Sir Gilbert 256 257
Stobie, Captain DMH 242